American Government and Politics Today

2014–2015 Brief Edition

Steffen W. Schmidt
Iowa State University

Mack C. Shelley II
Iowa State University

Barbara A. Bardes
University of Cincinnati

CENGAGE
Learning®

Australia • Brazil • Japan • Mexico • Singapore • United Kingdom • United States

CENGAGE
Learning·

American Government and Politics Today
2014–2015 Brief Edition

Steffen W. Schmidt
Mack C. Shelley II
Barbara A. Bardes

Product Director: Suzanne Jeans

Product Team Manager: Carolyn Merrill

Associate Product Manager: Scott Greenan

Content Developer: Rebecca Green

Content Coordinator: Jessica Wang

Product Assistant: Abigail Hess

Market Development Manager:
Courtney Wolstoncroft

Marketing Manager: Valerie Hartman

Senior Media Developer: Laura Hildebrand

Senior Content Production Manager:
Ann Borman

Manufacturing Coordinator: Fola Orekoya

Copy Editor: Jeanne Yost

Proofreader: Judy Kiviat

Indexer: Terry Casey

Senior Art Director: Linda May

Interior Design: RHDG

Cover Design: Lisa Kuhn

Compositor: Parkwood Composition Service

For product information and technology assistance, contact us at
Cengage Learning Customer & Sales Support
1-800-354-9706

For permission to use material from this text or product,
submit all requests online at
www.cengage.com/permissions.

Further permissions questions can be e-mailed to
permissionrequest@cengage.com.

Library of Congress Control Number: 2013952135

ISBN-13: 978-1-285-43638-8

Cengage Learning
200 First Stamford Place, 4th Floor
Stamford, CT 06902
USA

Cengage Learning is a leading provider of customized learning solutions with office locations around the globe, including Singapore, the United Kingdom, Australia, Mexico, Brazil, and Japan. Locate your local office at: **www.cengage.com/global.**

Cengage Learning products are represented in Canada by Nelson Education, Ltd.

To learn more about Cengage Learning, visit **www.cengage.com.**

Purchase any of our products at your local college store or at our preferred online store **www.cengagebrain.com.**

Notice to the Reader
Publisher does not warrant or guarantee any of the products described herein or perform any independent analysis in connection with any of the product information contained herein. Publisher does not assume, and expressly disclaims, any obligation to obtain and include information other than that provided to it by the manufacturer. The reader is expressly warned to consider and adopt all safety precautions that might be indicated by the activities described herein and to avoid all potential hazards. By following the instructions contained herein, the reader willingly assumes all risks in connection with such instructions. The publisher makes no representations or warranties of any kind, including but not limited to, the warranties of fitness for particular purpose or merchantability, nor are any such representations implied with respect to the material set forth herein, and the publisher takes no responsibility with respect to such material. The publisher shall not be liable for any special, consequential, or exemplary damages resulting, in whole or part, from the readers' use of, or reliance upon, this material.

Unless otherwise noted, all content © 2015 Cengage Learning.

Printed in the United States of America
1 2 3 4 5 6 7 17 16 15 14 13

ContentsinBrief

Part I: The American System

CHAPTER 1:   The Democratic Republic 1

CHAPTER 2:   Forging a New Government:
              The Constitution 20

CHAPTER 3:   Federalism 45

CHAPTER 4:   Civil Liberties 66

CHAPTER 5:   Civil Rights 92

Part II: The Politics of American Democracy

CHAPTER 6:   Public Opinion, Political Socialization,
              and the Media 116

CHAPTER 7:   Interest Groups and Political Parties 143

CHAPTER 8:   Campaigns and Elections 171

Part III: Institutions of American Government

CHAPTER 9:   The Congress 196

CHAPTER 10:   The Presidency 224

CHAPTER 11:   The Bureaucracy 247

CHAPTER 12:   The Judiciary 271

Part IV: Policymaking

CHAPTER 13:   Domestic and Economic Policy 297

CHAPTER 14:   Foreign Policy 320

Appendix A   The Declaration of Independence 345
Appendix B   The Constitution of the United States 347
Appendix C   Federalist Papers No. 10 and No. 51 363

Glossary 371
Index 383

Contents

PART I: THE AMERICAN SYSTEM

CHAPTER 1
The Democratic Republic 1

Politics and Government 2
  Why Is Government Necessary? 2
  Limiting Government Power 2
  Authority and Legitimacy 3

Democracy and Other Forms of Government 4
  Types of Government 4
  Direct Democracy as a Model 4
  The Dangers of Direct Democracy 5
  A Democratic Republic 5

What Kind of Democracy Do We Have? 6
  Democracy for Everyone 7
  Democracy for the Few 7
  Democracy for Groups 8

Fundamental Values 8
  Liberty versus Order 8
  Liberty versus Equality 9
  The Proper Size of Government 11

Political Ideologies 13
  Conservatism 13
  Liberalism 14
  The Traditional Political Spectrum 15
  Problems with the Traditional Political Spectrum 15
  A Four-Cornered Ideological Grid 16

Key Terms • Chapter Summary • Test Yourself • CourseMate

Scott Olson/Getty Images/AFP

Chapter 1 Features

at issue: Does Entitlement Spending Corrupt Us? 12

making a difference: Seeing Democracy in Action 17

CHAPTER 2 Forging a New Government: The Constitution 20

The Colonial Background 21
  Separatists, the *Mayflower*, and the Compact 21
  More Colonies, More Government 22
  British Restrictions and Colonial Grievances 23
  The First Continental Congress 23
  The Second Continental Congress 24

An Independent Confederation 26
  The Resolution for Independence 26
  July 4, 1776—The Declaration of Independence 26
  The Rise of Republicanism 27
  The Articles of Confederation: Our First Form of Government 28

The Constitutional Convention 30
  Factions among the Delegates 30
  Politicking and Compromises 31
  Working toward Final Agreement 33
  The Final Document 35

The Difficult Road to Ratification 36
  The Federalists Push for Ratification 36
  The March to the Finish 37
  The Bill of Rights 37

Altering the Constitution 38
  The Formal Amendment Process 38
  Informal Methods of Constitutional Change 39

Key Terms • Chapter Summary • Test Yourself • CourseMate

Chapter 2 Features

at issue: Just How Christian Were the Founders? 24
making a difference: How Can You Affect the U.S. Constitution? 42

CHAPTER 3 Federalism 45

Federalism and Its Alternatives 46
  A Unitary System 46
  A Confederal System 46
  A Federal System 47
  Why Federalism? 47
  Other Arguments for Federalism 48
  Arguments against Federalism 49

Chapter 3 Features

at issue: Should the Federal Government Recognize Same-Sex Marriages Performed by the State? 52
making a difference: Writing Letters to the Editor 63

The Constitutional Basis for American Federalism 49

Powers of the National Government 49

Powers of the State Governments 50

Prohibited Powers 51

Concurrent Powers 51

The Supremacy Clause 51

Interstate Relations 53

Defining Constitutional Powers—The Early Years 53

McCulloch v. Maryland (1819) 54

Gibbons v. Ogden (1824) 54

States' Rights and the Resort to Civil War 55

The Continuing Dispute over the Division of Power 56

Dual Federalism 57

The New Deal and Cooperative Federalism 57

The Politics of Federalism 58

Methods of Implementing Cooperative Federalism 59

Federalism and Today's Supreme Court 61

A Trend toward States' Rights? 61

Recent Decisions 62

Key Terms • Chapter Summary • Test Yourself • CourseMate

CHAPTER 4 Civil Liberties 66

The Bill of Rights 67

Extending the Bill of Rights to State Governments 67

Incorporation of the Fourteenth Amendment 68

Freedom of Religion 69

The Separation of Church and State—
The Establishment Clause 69

The Free Exercise Clause 73

Freedom of Expression 73

No Prior Restraint 73

The Protection of Symbolic Speech 74

The Protection of Commercial Speech 75

Attempts to Ban Subversive or Advocacy Speech 75

Unprotected Speech: Obscenity 76

Unprotected Speech: Slander 77

Chapter 4 Features

at issue: Should We Ban Assault-Type Weapons? 70

making a difference: Your Civil Liberties: Searches and Seizures 89

Student Speech 78
Freedom of the Press 79

The Right to Privacy 81
Privacy Rights and Abortion 81
Privacy Rights and the "Right to Die" 83

The Great Balancing Act: The Rights of the Accused versus the Rights of Society 84
Rights of the Accused 84
Extending the Rights of the Accused 85
The Exclusionary Rule 85
Civil Liberties versus Security Issues 86
National Security and the Civil Liberties of Immigrants 87

Key Terms • Chapter Summary • Test Yourself • CourseMate

Yuri Gripas/AFP/Getty Images

CHAPTER 5 Civil Rights 92

The African American Experience and the Civil Rights Movement 93
Ending Servitude 93
The Ineffectiveness of the Early Civil Rights Laws 94
The End of the Separate-but-Equal Doctrine 96
De Jure and *De Facto* Segregation 97
The Civil Rights Movement 97
Modern Civil Rights Legislation 98

Women's Struggle for Equal Rights 100
Early Women's Political Movements 100
The Modern Women's Movement 101
Women in Politics Today 102
Gender-Based Discrimination in the Workplace 103

Experiences of Other Minority Groups 104
Immigration, Latinos, and Civil Rights 104
The Agony of the American Indian 105

Civil Rights: Extending Equal Protection 107
Affirmative Action 108
The *Bakke* Case 108
Additional Limits on Affirmative Action 108
The End of Affirmative Action? 109

Chapter 5 Features

at issue: Should Unauthorized Immigrants be Granted Citizenship? 106

making a difference: Dealing with Discrimination 113

The Rights and Status of Gay Males and Lesbians 110
Growth in the Gay Male and Lesbian Rights Movement 110
State and Local Laws Targeting Gay Men and Lesbians 110
"Don't Ask, Don't Tell" 111
Same-Sex Marriage 111

Key Terms • Chapter Summary • Test Yourself • CourseMate

PART II: THE POLITICS OF AMERICAN DEMOCRACY

CHAPTER 6 Public Opinion, Political Socialization, and the Media 116

Public Opinion and Political Socialization 117
Consensus and Divided Opinion 117
Forming Public Opinion: Political Socialization 117
The Media and Public Opinion 119
Political Events and Public Opinion 120

The Influence of Demographic Factors 121
Educational Achievement 121
Economic Status 121
Religious Denomination 123
Religious Commitment and Beliefs 123
Race and Ethnicity 123
The Hispanic Vote 124
The Gender Gap 125
Geographic Region 125

Measuring Public Opinion 125
The History of Opinion Polls 125
Sampling Techniques 126
The Difficulty of Obtaining Accurate Results 127
Additional Problems with Polls 128

Public Opinion and the Political Process 129
Political Culture and Public Opinion 129
The Most Important Problems 130
Public Opinion and Policymaking 130

The Roles of the Media 131
The Roles of the Media 131
Television versus the New Media 134

Chapter 6 Features
making a difference:
Being a Critical Consumer of the News 138

The Media and Political Campaigns 135

  Political Advertising 135

  Management of News Coverage 137

  Going for the Knockout Punch—Presidential Debates 137

  Political Campaigns and the Internet 138

  Bias in the Media 138

Key Terms • Chapter Summary • Test Yourself • CourseMate

CHAPTER 7 Interest Groups and Political Parties 143

A Nation of Joiners 144

  Interest Groups and Social Movements 145

  Reasons to Join—or Not Join 145

Types of Interest Groups 146

  Economic Interest Groups 146

  Environmental Groups 149

  Public-Interest Groups 149

  Additional Types of Interest Groups 150

  Foreign Interest Groups 151

Interest Group Strategies 151

  Direct Techniques 151

  Indirect Techniques 152

  Regulating Lobbyists 153

Political Parties in the United States 154

  Functions of Political
    Parties in the United States 154

  Party Organization 155

A History of Political Parties in the United States 157

  The Formative Years:
    Federalists and Anti-Federalists 157

  Democrats and Whigs 158

  The Civil War Crisis 158

  The Post–Civil War Period 159

  The Progressive Interlude 159

  The New Deal Era 160

  An Era of Divided Government 160

  The Parties Today 161

AP Photo/*Atlanta Journal-Constitution*/Jason Getz

Chapter 7 Features

politics and economics:
Right-To-Work Laws 148

making a difference:
You Can Be a Convention
Delegate 168

Why Has the Two-Party System Endured? 162
The Historical Foundations of the Two-Party System 162
Political Socialization and Practical Considerations 163
The Winner-Take-All Electoral System 164
State and Federal Laws Favoring the Two Parties 164
The Role of Minor Parties in U.S. Politics 165
The Rise of the Independents 166

Key Terms • Chapter Summary • Test Yourself • CourseMate

CHAPTER 8 Campaigns and Elections 171

The Twenty-First-Century Campaign 172
Who Is Eligible? 172
Who Runs? 172
Managing the Campaign 173

Financing the Campaign 175
The Evolution of the Campaign Finance System 176
The Current Campaign Finance Environment 177

Running for President:
The Longest Campaign 180
Reforming the Primaries 181
Primaries and Caucuses 181
Front-Loading the Primaries 183
On to the National Convention 184
The Electoral College 185

How Are Elections Conducted? 186
Office-Block and Party-Column Ballots 186
Voting by Mail 186
Voting Fraud and Voter ID Laws 186
Turning Out to Vote 188
Legal Restrictions on Voting 190

How Do Voters Decide? 191
Party Identification 191
Other Political Factors 191
Demographic Characteristics 192

Key Terms • Chapter Summary • Test Yourself • CourseMate

Chapter 8 Features

politics and economics:
The Curious Ineffectiveness
of the Super PACs 179

making a difference:
Registering and Voting 193

PART III: INSTITUTIONS OF AMERICAN GOVERNMENT

CHAPTER 9 The Congress 196

The Nature and Functions of Congress 197
  Bicameralism 197
  The Lawmaking Function 197
  The Representation Function 198
  Service to Constituents 199
  The Oversight Function 199
  The Public-Education Function 199
  The Conflict-Resolution Function 199
  The Powers of Congress 200

House-Senate Differences and Congressional Perks 201
  Size and Rules 201
  Debate and Filibustering 201
  Congresspersons and
    the Citizenry: A Comparison 202
  Perks and Privileges 202

Congressional Elections and Apportionment 204
  Candidates for Congressional Elections 205
  Apportionment of the House 205
  Gerrymandering 206
  "Minority-Majority" Districts 208

How Congress is Organized 209
  The Power of Committees 210
  Types of Congressional Committees 210
  The Selection of Committee Members 212
  Leadership in the House 212
  Leadership in the Senate 214

Lawmaking and Budgeting 215
  How Much Will the Government Spend? 215
  Preparing the Budget 217
  Congress Faces the Budget 218
  Budget Resolutions and Crises 218

Chapter 9 Features

at issue: Is It Time to Get Rid of the Filibuster? 203

making a difference: Learning about Your Representatives 220

Office of Kelly Ayotte

Key Terms • Chapter Summary • Test Yourself • CourseMate

CHAPTER 10 The Presidency 224

Who Can Become President? 225
A "Natural Born Citizen" 225
The Process of Becoming President 225

The Many Roles of the President 226
Head of State 226
Chief Executive 227
Commander in Chief 228
Chief Diplomat 229
Chief Legislator 230
Party Chief and Politician 232

Presidential Powers 235
Emergency Powers 235
Executive Orders 236
Executive Privilege 236
Signing Statements 237
Abuses of Executive Power and Impeachment 237

The Executive Organization 238
The Cabinet 238
The Executive Office of the President 239

The Vice Presidency 241
The Vice President's Job 241
Presidential Succession 242

Key Terms • Chapter Summary • Test Yourself • CourseMate

Chapter 10 Features

politics and economics:
The Economy and the Race
for President 234

making a difference:
Communicating with
the White House 244

George Skadding/Time Life
Pictures/Getty Images

CHAPTER 11 The Bureaucracy 247

The Nature and Scope of the Federal Bureaucracy 248
Public and Private Bureaucracies 248
The Size of the Bureaucracy 249
The Federal Budget 250

The Organization of the Federal Bureaucracy 250
Cabinet Departments 251
Independent Executive Agencies 251
Independent Regulatory Agencies 253
Government Corporations 256

Staffing the Bureaucracy 258
  Political Appointees 258
  History of the Federal Civil Service 259

Modern Attempts at Bureaucratic Reform 261
  Sunshine Laws before and after 9/11 261
  Sunset Laws 261
  Privatization, or Contracting Out 262
  Incentives for Efficiency and Productivity 262
  Helping Out the Whistleblowers 263

Bureaucrats as Politicians and Policymakers 264
  The Rulemaking Environment 264
  Negotiated Rulemaking 265
  Bureaucrats as Policymakers 265
  Congressional Control of the Bureaucracy 267

Key Terms • Chapter Summary • Test Yourself • CourseMate

Chapter 11 Features

at issue: Do We Still Have to Worry About the Federal Deficit? 253

making a difference
What the Government Knows about You 268

CHAPTER 12 The Judiciary 271

Sources of American Law 272
  The Common Law Tradition 272
  Constitutions 273
  Statutes and Administrative Regulations 273
  Case Law 273

The Federal Court System 273
  Basic Judicial Requirements 274
  Parties to Lawsuits 274
  Procedural Rules 275
  Types of Federal Courts 275
  Federal Courts and the War on Terrorism 277

The Supreme Court at Work 279
  Which Cases Reach the Supreme Court? 280
  Court Procedures 280
  Decisions and Opinions 281

The Selection of Federal Judges 281
  Judicial Appointments 282
  Partisanship and Judicial Appointments 284
  The Senate's Role 285

Chapter 12 Features

at issue:
Should State Judges
Be Elected? 283

politics and economics:
Getting Ahead With and
Without Affirmative Action 290

making a difference:
Changing the
Legal System 294

Policymaking and the Courts 286
  Judicial Review 286
  Judicial Activism and Judicial Restraint 286
  Ideology and the Rehnquist Court 287
  The Roberts Court 288
  What Checks Our Courts? 289

Key Terms • Chapter Summary • Test Yourself • CourseMate

PART IV: POLICYMAKING

CHAPTER 13 Domestic and Economic Policy 297

The Policymaking Process:
    Health Care as an Example 298
  Health Care: Agenda Building 298
  Health Care: Policy Formulation 300
  Health Care: Policy Adoption 300
  Health Care: Policy Implementation 302
  Health Care: Policy Evaluation 303

Immigration 303
  The Issue of Unauthorized Immigration 303
  Immigration Legislation 304

Energy and the Environment 305
  Energy Independence—A Strategic Issue 305
  Global Warming 307

The Politics of Economic Decision Making 308
  Good Times, Bad Times 308
  Fiscal Policy 309
  Deficit Spending and the Public Debt 310
  Monetary Policy 312

The Politics of Taxation 314
  Federal Income Tax Rates 314
  Loopholes and Lowered Taxes 315

Key Terms • Chapter Summary • Test Yourself • CourseMate

Chapter 13 Features

at issue: Should the Rich Pay Even More in Taxes? 316

making a difference: Learning about Entitlement Reform 317

CHAPTER 14 Foreign Policy 320

Facing the World: Foreign and Defense Policy 321
National Security and Defense Policies 321
Diplomacy 321
Idealism versus Realism in Foreign Policy 322

Terrorism and Warfare 323
The Emergence of Terrorism 323
The War on Terrorism 324
Wars in Iraq 325
Afghanistan 326

U.S. DIPLOMATIC EFFORTS 327
Nuclear Weapons 327
The New Power: China 328
Israel and the Palestinians 331
The Economic Crisis in Europe 332

Who Makes Foreign Policy? 333
Constitutional Powers of the President 333
The Executive Branch and Foreign Policymaking 334
Congress Balances the Presidency 336

The Major Foreign Policy Themes 337
The Formative Years: Avoiding Entanglements 337
The Era of Internationalism 338
Superpower Relations 339

Key Terms • Chapter Summary • Test Yourself • CourseMate

Chapter 14 Features

at issue: Should American—or Israel—Attack Iran's Nuclear Sites? 329

making a difference: Working for Human Rights 342

Jacquelyn Martin/AFP/Getty Images

Appendix A
The Declaration of Independence 345
Appendix B
The Constitution of the United States 347
Appendix C
Federalist Papers No. 10 and No. 51 363

Glossary 371

Index 383

PREFACE

In 2012, Democratic president Barack Obama was reelected over Republican candidate Mitt Romney by a margin of almost 4 percentage points. The Democrats gained seats in the U.S. Senate. They did not gain nearly enough seats in the House of Representatives to endanger the Republican control of that chamber, however. Did these results mean two more years of political polarization and governmental gridlock? Would confrontation threaten the very workings of the federal government? Or could the parties find the will to adopt new policies on immigration and other major issues? Throughout this Brief Edition of *American Government and Politics Today,* you will read about how our government has responded to past issues and how these responses have shaped American government and politics.

This edition is basically a condensed and updated version of the larger editions of *American Government and Politics Today.* It has been created specifically for those of you who want a text that presents the fundamental components of the American political system while retaining the quality and readability of the larger editions. You will find that this edition is up to date in every respect. The text, figures, tables, and all pedagogical features reflect the latest available data. We have also included coverage of all recently issued laws, regulations, and court decisions that have—or will have—a significant impact on American society and our political system.

Like the larger editions, this volume places a major emphasis on political participation and involvement. This brief, fourteen-chapter text has been heralded by reviewers as the best essentials text for its affordability, conciseness, clarity, and readability.

- Getting straight to the point, this text helps pare down a wealth of material, focusing on the essential events, concepts, and topics of an American government course.
- Strong themes of informed and active participation, along with a critical-thinking approach, spark student interest in wanting to get involved and know more.
- *Learning Outcomes* now open each chapter and are correlated to each major section, providing a roadmap to key concepts. A *Test Yourself* quiz assesses students' mastery of these Learning Outcomes.
- *At Issue* feature boxes focus on a controversial topic to provoke discussion and conclude with a *For Critical Analysis* question to ignite critical thinking.
- *Making a Difference* boxes at the end of each chapter promote student participation by answering the questions "Why Should You Care?" and "What Can You Do?" and offer practical ways for students to get involved in politics by using online resources.

NEW TO THIS EDITION

This new edition has been thoroughly updated and revised to reflect the significant events and explosive changes that have occurred in the last two years.

- The text describes the 2012 elections and their consequences, plus the section on campaign finance is completely revised. We have extended the discussion of conservatism and liberalism. New material makes gerrymandering easier to understand.
- New sections cover American Indians, television versus the new media, and voting restrictions. The section on public opinion polls is heavily reworked to incorporate the latest insights. We now provide a detailed breakdown of the federal budget.
- We cover all the latest United States Supreme Court rulings and provide up-to-date material on same-sex marriage. The politics of the current Court are analyzed.

- The discussion of immigration is current, and the section on energy and the environment describes fracking and the growth of domestic energy production. The foreign policy chapter has the latest on the Arab Spring—including Syria—and also on Iran, North Korea, and cyberattacks. We cover the economic crisis in Europe and its implications for us.

COURSEMATE: INTERACTIVE LEARNING, STUDY, & EXAM PREP TOOLS

For the first time, the Brief Edition of *American Government and Politics Today* comes with CourseMate access as the main text package. CourseMate gives students everything they need to succeed in one place. Read the eBook, take notes, watch videos, study with flashcards, simulations, and timelines, take practice quizzes, and more, all online with CourseMate. Students will also have access to American Government NewsWatch—a real-time news and information resource updated daily—and KnowNow!—the go-to blog about current events in American government. The stand-alone text is also available, with optional CourseMate access available through **www.cengagebrain.com**.

HIGH-INTEREST FEATURES

In this edition, we have included special features designed to pique your interest. These features are interspersed throughout the text.

Topical Features

Each *At Issue* feature focuses on a controversial topic and concludes with a *For Critical Analysis* question to invite critical thinking. *Politics and Economics* features address current economic developments. Almost all features are new for this edition. They discuss the following topics:

At Issue **Features:**

- Does Entitlement Spending Corrupt Us? (Chapter 1)
- Just How Christian Were the Founders? (Chapter 2)
- Should the Federal Government Recognize Same-Sex Marriages Performed by the States? (Chapter 3)
- Should We Ban Assault-Type Weapons? (Chapter 4)
- Should Unauthorized Immigrants Be Granted Citizenship? (Chapter 5)
- Is It Time to Get Rid of the Filibuster? (Chapter 9)
- Do We Still Have to Worry about the Federal Deficit? (Chapter 11)
- Should State Judges Be Elected? (Chapter 12)
- Should the Rich Pay Even More in Taxes? (Chapter 13)
- Should America—or Israel—Attack Iran's Nuclear Sites? (Chapter 14)

Politics and Economics **Features:**
- Right-to-Work Laws (Chapter 7)
- The Curious Ineffectiveness of the Super PACs (Chapter 8)
- The Economy and the Race for President (Chapter 10)
- Getting Ahead with and without Affirmative Action (Chapter 12)

Making a Difference Features

At the end of every chapter, a feature entitled *Making a Difference* enhances our emphasis on participation. These features provide you with useful information for active citizenship. We give you tips on how to find information on issues, how to learn about your elected representatives, how to join and participate in advocacy organizations, how to protect your civil rights and liberties, and more.

OTHER SPECIAL PEDAGOGICAL AIDS

The 2014–2015 Brief Edition of *American Government and Politics Today* retains many of the pedagogical aids and features of the larger editions, including the following:

- **Learning Outcomes**—These focus on crucial questions the students should learn to address, section by section.
- **Key Terms**—Important terms that are boldfaced and defined in the text when they are first used. These terms are defined in the text margins, listed at the end of the chapter with the page numbers on which they appear, and included in the Glossary at the back of the book.
- **Helpful Web Sites** and **Social Media in Politics**—These new margin boxes direct students to a variety of online resources.
- **Chapter Summary**—A point-by-point summary of the chapter text.
- **Test Yourself**—A quiz and essay question at the very end of each chapter.

APPENDICES

The Brief Edition of *American Government and Politics Today* includes, as appendices, both the Declaration of Independence (Appendix A) and the U.S. Constitution (Appendix B). The text of the Constitution has been annotated to help you understand the meaning and significance of the various provisions in this important document. Also, Appendix C presents Federalist Papers No. 10 and No. 51. These selections are also annotated to help you grasp their importance in understanding the American philosophy of government.

SUPPLEMENTS

Online PowerLecture with Cognero® for Schmidt/Shelley/Bardes *Cengage Advantage Books: American Government and Politics Today, 2014–2015 Brief Edition*

ISBN-13: 9781285775708

- This PowerLecture is an all-in-one multimedia online resource for class preparation, presentation, and testing. Accessible through Cengage.com/login with your faculty account, you will find available for download: book-specific Microsoft® PowerPoint® presentations; a Test Bank in both Microsoft® Word® and Cognero® formats; an Instructor Manual; Microsoft® PowerPoint® Image Slides; and a JPEG Image Library.
- The Test Bank, offered in Microsoft® Word® and Cognero® formats, contains Learning Objective–specific multiple-choice and essay questions for each chapter. Cognero® is a flexible, online system that allows you to author, edit, and manage test bank content. Create multiple test versions instantly and deliver through your LMS from your class-room, or wherever you may be, with no special installs or downloads required.

- The Instructor's Manual contains chapter-specific learning objectives, an outline, key terms with definitions, and a chapter summary. Additionally, the Instructor's Manual features a critical-thinking question, a lecture-launching suggestion, and an in-class activity for each learning objective. Both the Test Bank and the Instructor's Manual are authored by Professor Mark Hoffman of Wayne County Community College.
- The Microsoft® PowerPoint® presentations are ready-to-use, visual outlines of each chapter. These presentations are easily customized for your lectures and offered along with chapter-specific Microsoft® PowerPoint® Image Slides and JPEG Image Libraries.
- Instructors can access the Online PowerLecture at **www.cengage.com/login**.

Free Companion Site for Schmidt/Shelley/Bardes *Cengage Advantage Books: American Government and Politics Today, 2014–2015 Brief Edition*

ISBN-13: 9781285438436

- This free companion Web site is accessible through **cengagebrain.com** and gives students access to chapter-specific interactive learning tools, including flashcards, quizzes, glossaries, and more.

Political Science CourseMate with eBook for Schmidt/Shelley/Bardes *Cengage Advantage Books: American Government and Politics Today, 2014-2015 Brief Edition*

Printed Access Code ISBN-13: 9781285454740
Instant Access Code ISBN-13: 9781285464282

- Cengage Learning's American Government CourseMate brings course concepts to life with interactive learning, study tools, and exam preparation tools that support the printed textbook. Instructors can use Engagement Tracker to assess student preparation and engagement in the course and watch student comprehension soar as their class works with the textbook-specific Web site. A MindTap Reader eBook allows students to take notes, highlight, and search. Other resources include video activities, flashcards, animated learning modules, simulations, interactive quizzes, and timelines. American Government NewsWatch is a real-time news and information resource, updated daily, that includes interactive maps, videos, podcasts, and hundreds of articles from leading journals, magazines, and newspapers. Also included is the KnowNow! American Government Blog, which highlights three current events stories per week and consists of a succinct analysis of the story, multimedia, and discussion-starter questions. Access your course via **www.cengage.com/login**. CourseMate for students can come packaged with the text or optionally purchased through **www.cengagebrain.com**.

CourseReader 0-30: American Government

Printed Access Code ISBN: 9781111479954
Instant Access Code ISBN: 9781111479978

- CourseReader: American Government allows instructors to create a customized reader in just minutes. This affordable, fully customizable online reader provides access to thousands of permissions-cleared readings, articles, primary sources, and audio and video selections from the regularly updated Gale research library database. Each selection opens with a descriptive introduction to provide context, and concludes with critical-thinking and multiple-choice questions to reinforce key points. CourseReader is loaded with convenient tools such as highlighting, printing, note-taking, and downloadable PDFs and MP3 audio files for each reading. It can be bundled with your current textbook, sold alone, or integrated into your learning management system. CourseReader 0-30 allows access to up to thirty selections in the reader. Please contact your Cengage sales representative for details.

ACKNOWLEDGMENTS

In preparing *American Government and Politics Today,* 2014–2015 Brief Edition, we were the beneficiaries of the expert guidance of a skilled and dedicated team of publishers and editors. We have benefited greatly from the supervision and encouragement given by our associate product manager, Scott Greenan, and product team manager, Carolyn Merrill.

We are grateful to our content project manager, Ann Borman, for her ability to make this project as smooth-running and as perfect as is humanly possible. We are indebted to the staff at Parkwood Composition. Their ability to generate the pages for this text quickly and accurately made it possible for us to meet our ambitious printing schedule. We also thank Rebecca Green, our content developer, for her work on the book's revision plan and project coordination. In addition, our gratitude goes to all of those who worked on the various supplements offered with this text, especially Mark Hoffman of Wayne County Community College, who revised the Test Bank and Instructor's Manual, Eireann Aspell, content coordinator, and Laura Hildebrand, media developer. We would also like to thank Courtney Wolstoncroft, market development manager, for her tremendous efforts in marketing the text.

Many other people helped during the research and editorial stages of this edition as well. Gregory Scott coordinated the authors' efforts and provided editorial and research assistance. Jeanne Yost's copyediting abilities contributed greatly to the book. We also thank Roxie Lee for her assistance, and Sue Jasin of K&M Consulting for her contributions to the smooth running of the project. Finally, we are grateful for the proofreading services provided by Judy Kiviat and Sue Bradley.

Any errors, of course, remain our own. We welcome comments from instructors and students alike. Suggestions that we have received on previous editions have helped us to improve this text and to adapt it to the changing needs of instructors and students.

S.W.S.
M.C.S.
B.A.B.

ABOUT THE AUTHORS

STEFFEN W. SCHMIDT

Steffen W. Schmidt is professor of political science at Iowa State University. He grew up in Colombia, South America, and studied in Colombia, Switzerland, and France. He obtained his Ph.D. in public law and government from Columbia University in New York.

Schmidt has published 12 books and more than 120 journal articles. He is also the recipient of numerous prestigious teaching prizes, including the Amoco Award for Lifetime Career Achievement in Teaching and the Teacher of the Year award. He is a pioneer in the use of Web-based and real-time video courses, as well as a member of the American Political Science Association's section on computers and multimedia. He is on the editorial board of the *Political Science Educator* and is the technology and teaching editor of the *Journal of Political Science Education.*

Schmidt has a political talk show on WOI radio, where he is known as Dr. Politics. The show has been broadcast live from various U.S. and international venues. He is a frequent political commentator for *CNN en Español* and the British Broadcasting Corporation. He is the co-founder of the new Internet magazine Insiderlowa.com.

Schmidt likes to snow ski, ride hunter jumper horses, race sailboats, and scuba dive.

MACK C. SHELLEY II

Mack C. Shelley II is professor of political science and statistics at Iowa State University. After receiving his bachelor's degree from American University in Washington, D.C., he completed graduate studies at the University of Wisconsin at Madison, where he received a master's degree in economics and a Ph.D. in political science. He taught for two years at Mississippi State University before arriving at Iowa State in 1979.

Shelley has published numerous articles, books, and monographs on public policy. From 1993 to 2002, he served as elected coeditor of the *Policy Studies Journal.* His published books include *The Permanent Majority: The Conservative Coalition in the United States Congress; Biotechnology and the Research Enterprise* (with William F. Woodman and Brian J. Reichel); *American Public Policy: The Contemporary Agenda* (with Steven G. Koven and Bert E. Swanson); *Redefining Family Policy: Implications for the 21st Century* (with Joyce M. Mercier and Steven Garasky); and *Quality Research in Literacy and Science Education: International Perspectives and Gold Standards* (with Larry Yore and Brian Hand).

His leisure time includes traveling, working with students, and playing with the family dog and cats.

BARBARA A. BARDES

Barbara A. Bardes is professor emerita of political science and former dean of Raymond Walters College at the University of Cincinnati. She received her B.A. and M.A. from Kent State University. After completing her Ph.D. at the University of Cincinnati, she held faculty positions at Mississippi State University and Loyola University in Chicago. She returned to Cincinnati, her hometown, as a college administrator. She has also worked as a political consultant and directed polling for a research center.

Bardes has written articles on public opinion and foreign policy, and on women and politics. She has authored *Thinking about Public Policy; Declarations of Independence: Women and Political Power in Nineteenth-Century American Fiction;* and *Public Opinion: Measuring the American Mind* (with Robert W. Oldendick).

Bardes's home is located in a very small hamlet in Kentucky called Rabbit Hash, famous for its 150-year-old general store. Her hobbies include traveling, gardening, needlework, and antique collecting.

These children, age six to eighteen, are taking the oath of allegiance at a citizenship ceremony in Chicago. Many of them gained U.S. citizenship when their parents were naturalized. (Scott Olson/Getty Images/AFP)

The Democratic Republic

LEARNING OUTCOMES

The five **Learning Outcomes (LOs)** below are designed to help improve your understanding of this chapter. After reading this chapter, you should be able to:

■ **LO1** Define the terms *politics, government, order, liberty, authority,* and *legitimacy.*

■ **LO2** Distinguish the major features of direct democracy and representative democracy.

■ **LO3** Describe majoritarianism, elite theory, and pluralism as theories of how democratic systems work.

■ **LO4** Summarize the conflicts that can occur between the principles of liberty and order, and between those of liberty and equality.

■ **LO5** Discuss conservatism, liberalism, and other popular American ideological positions.

Check your understanding of the material with the Test Yourself section at the end of the chapter.

Politics, for many people, is the "great game," and it is played for high stakes. After all, the game involves vast sums and the very security of the nation. In the last few years, the stakes have grown higher still. In 2012, the Republicans promised that if they won control of the U.S. Senate and the presidency, they would make dramatic changes to the nation's tax system, health-care policies, and other domestic programs. In the end, however, Democratic president Barack Obama was reelected over Republican Mitt Romney. The Democrats kept control of the U.S. Senate, adding two seats for a total of fifty-five out of one hundred. Democratic gains in the U.S. House, however, were not even close to the number necessary to take that chamber back from the Republicans. The result of the elections was a nation divided down the middle in its politics.

POLITICS AND GOVERNMENT

What is politics? **Politics** can be understood as the process of resolving conflicts and deciding, as political scientist Harold Lasswell put it in his classic definition, "who gets what, when, and how."[1] More specifically, politics is the struggle over power or influence within organizations or informal groups that can grant benefits or privileges.

We can identify many such groups and organizations. In families, all members may meet to decide on values, priorities, and actions. In every community that makes decisions through formal or informal rules, politics exists. For example, when a church decides to construct a new building or hire a new minister, the decision is made politically. Politics can be found in schools, social groups, and any other organized collection of individuals. Of all the organizations that are controlled by political activity, however, the most important is the government.

What is the government? Certainly, it is an **institution**—that is, an ongoing organization that performs certain functions for society and that has a life separate from the lives of the individuals who are part of it at any given moment in time. The **government** can be defined as an institution within which decisions are made that resolve conflicts and allocate benefits and privileges. The government is also the preeminent institution within society because it has the ultimate authority for making these decisions.

Why Is Government Necessary?

Perhaps the best way to assess the need for government is to examine circumstances in which government, as we normally understand it, does not exist. What happens when multiple groups compete with one another for power within a society? There are places around the world where such circumstances exist. A current example is the African nation of Somalia. Since 1991, Somalia has not had a central government capable of controlling the country. The regions of the country are divided among various warlords and factions, each controlling a block of territory. When Somali warlords compete for control of a particular locality, the result is war, generalized devastation, and famine. Normally, multiple armed forces compete by fighting, and the absence of a unified government is equivalent to ongoing civil war.

As the example of Somalia shows, one of the original purposes of government is the maintenance of security, or **order.** By keeping the peace, a government protects its people from violence at the hands of private or foreign armies. It dispenses justice and protects the people from the violence of criminals. If order is not present, it is not possible for the government to provide any of the other benefits that people expect from it. Order is a value to which we will return later in this chapter.

Limiting Government Power

A complete collapse of order and security, as seen in Somalia, actually is an uncommon event. Much more common is the reverse—too much government control. In January 2013, the human rights organization Freedom House judged that forty-seven of the world's countries were "not free." These nations contained 34 percent of the world's population. Such countries may be controlled by individual dictators. Syria's Bashar al-Assad and North Korea's Kim Jong-un are obvious examples. Alternatively, a political

Politics
The struggle over power or influence within organizations or informal groups that can grant or withhold benefits or privileges.

Institution
An ongoing organization that performs certain functions for society.

Government
The preeminent institution within a society. Government has the ultimate authority to decide how conflicts will be resolved and how benefits and privileges will be allocated.

Order
A state of peace and security. Maintaining order by protecting members of society from violence and criminal activity is the oldest purpose of government.

1. Harold Lasswell, *Politics: Who Gets What, When, and How* (Gloucester, Mass.: Peter Smith Publisher, 1990). Originally published in 1936.

party, such as the Communist Party of China, may monopolize all the levels of power. The military may rule, as in Burma (also called Myanmar) until 2011.

In all of these examples, the individual or group running the country cannot be removed by legal means. Freedom of speech and the right to a fair trial are typically absent. Dictatorial governments often torture or execute their opponents. Such regimes may also suppress freedom of religion. Revolution, whether violent or non-violent, is often the only way to change the government.

In short, protection from the violence of domestic criminals or foreign armies is not enough. Citizens also need protection from abuses of power by their own government. To protect the liberties of the people, it is necessary to limit the powers of the government. Liberty—the greatest freedom of the individual consistent with the freedom of other individuals—is a second major political value, along with order. We discuss this value in more detail later in this chapter.

This rebel fighter, a member of the Martyrs of Truth brigade, is engaged in combat against the Syrian army. Why would he have taken up arms? (Benoit De Freine/Photonews via Getty Images)

Authority and Legitimacy

Every government must have **authority**—that is, the right and power to enforce its decisions. Ultimately, the government's authority rests on its control of the armed forces and the police. Few people in the United States, however, base their day-to-day activities on fear of the government's enforcement powers. Most people, most of the time, obey the law because this is what they have always done. Also, if they did not obey the law, they would face the disapproval of friends and family. Consider an example: Do you avoid injuring your friends or stealing their possessions because you are afraid of the police—or because if you undertook these actions, you no longer would have friends?

Under normal circumstances, the government's authority has broad popular support. People accept the government's right to establish rules and laws. When authority is broadly accepted, we say that it has **legitimacy.** Authority without legitimacy is a recipe for trouble.

Events in several Arab nations in 2011 and 2012 can serve as an example. The dictators who ruled Egypt, Libya, and Tunisia had been in power for decades. All three dictators had some popular support when they first gained power. None of these nations had a tradition of democracy, and so it was possible for undemocratic rulers to enjoy a degree of legitimacy. After years of oppressive behavior, however, these regimes slowly lost that legitimacy. The rulers survived only because they were willing to employ violence against any opposition. In Egypt and Tunisia, the end came when soldiers refused to use force against massive demonstrations. Having lost all legitimacy, the rulers of these two countries then lost their authority as well. (Unfortunately, the downfall and death of Muammar Qaddafi in Libya came only after a seven-month civil war.)

Liberty
The greatest freedom of the individual that is consistent with the freedom of other individuals in the society.

Authority
The right and power of a government or other entity to enforce its decisions and compel obedience.

Legitimacy
Popular acceptance of the right and power of a government or other entity to exercise authority.

Totalitarian Regime
A form of government that controls all aspects of the political, social, and economic life of a nation.

Authoritarianism
A type of regime in which only the government itself is fully controlled by the ruler. Social and economic institutions exist that are not under the government's control.

Democracy
A system of government in which political authority is vested in the people.

Direct Democracy
A system of government in which political decisions are made by the people directly, rather than by their elected representatives.

Legislature
A governmental body primarily responsible for the making of laws.

Initiative
A procedure by which voters can propose a law or a constitutional amendment.

Referendum
An electoral device whereby legislative or constitutional measures are referred by the legislature to the voters for approval or disapproval.

Recall
A procedure allowing the people to vote to dismiss an elected official from office before his or her term has expired.

LO2: Distinguish the major features of direct democracy and representative democracy.

DEMOCRACY AND OTHER FORMS OF GOVERNMENT

The different types of government can be classified according to which person or group of people controls society through the government.

Types of Government

At one extreme is a society governed by a **totalitarian regime.** In such a political system, a small group of leaders or a single individual—a dictator—makes all decisions for the society. Every aspect of political, social, and economic life is controlled by the government. The power of the ruler is total (thus, the term *totalitarianism*). A second type of system is authoritarian government. **Authoritarianism** differs from totalitarianism in that only the government itself is fully controlled by the ruler. Social and economic institutions, such as churches, businesses, and labor unions, exist that are not under the government's control.

Many of our terms for describing the distribution of political power are derived from the ancient Greeks, who were the first Western people to study politics systematically. One form of rule was known as *aristocracy,* literally meaning "rule by the best." In practice, this meant rule by wealthy members of ancient families. Another term from the Greeks is *theocracy,* which literally means "rule by God" (or the gods). In practice, theocracy means rule by self-appointed religious leaders. Iran is a rare example of a country in which supreme power is in the hands of a religious leader, the Grand Ayatollah Ali Khamenei. One of the most straightforward Greek terms is *oligarchy,* which simply means "rule by a few."

The Greek term for rule by the people was **democracy.** Within the limits of their culture, some of the Greek city-states operated as democracies. Today, in much of the world, the people will not grant legitimacy to a government unless it is based on democracy.

Direct Democracy as a Model

The Athenian system of government in ancient Greece is usually considered the purest model for **direct democracy** because the citizens of that community debated and voted directly on all laws, even those put forward by the ruling council of the city. The most important feature of Athenian democracy was that the **legislature** was composed of all of the citizens. (Women, resident foreigners, and slaves, however, were excluded because they were not citizens.) This form of government required a high level of participation from every citizen. That participation was seen as benefiting the individual and the city-state. The Athenians believed that although a high level of participation might lead to instability in government, citizens, if informed about the issues, could be trusted to make wise decisions.

Direct democracy also has been practiced at the local level in Switzerland and, in the United States, in New England town meetings. At these town meetings, which may include all of the voters who live in the town, important decisions—such as levying taxes, hiring city officials, and deciding local ordinances—are made by majority vote. Some states provide a modern adaptation of direct democracy for their citizens. In these states, representative democracy is supplemented by the **initiative** or the **referendum.** Both processes enable the people to vote directly on laws or constitutional amendments. The **recall** process, which is available in many states, allows the people to vote to remove an official from state office before his or her term has expired.

The Dangers of Direct Democracy

Although they were aware of the Athenian model, the framers of the U.S. Constitution were opposed to such a system. Democracy was considered to be dangerous and a source of instability. But in the 1700s and 1800s, the idea of government based on the *consent of the people* gained increasing popularity. Such a government was the main aspiration of the American Revolution in 1775, the French Revolution in 1789, and many subsequent revolutions. At the time of the American Revolution, however, the masses were still considered to be too uneducated to govern themselves, too prone to the influence of demagogues (political leaders who manipulate popular prejudices), and too likely to subordinate minority rights to the tyranny of the majority.

James Madison, while defending the new scheme of government set forth in the U.S. Constitution, warned of the problems inherent in a "pure democracy":

These Woodbury, Vermont, residents cast their ballots after a town meeting to vote on the school budget and sales taxes. What type of political system does the town meeting best represent? (AP Photo/Toby Talbot)

> *A common passion or interest will, in almost every case, be felt by a majority of the whole . . . and there is nothing to check the inducements to sacrifice the weaker party or an obnoxious individual. Hence it is that such democracies have ever been spectacles of turbulence and contention, and have ever been found incompatible with personal security or the rights of property; and have in general been as short in their lives as they have been violent in their deaths.[2]*

Republic
A form of government in which sovereign power rests with the people, rather than with a king or a monarch.

Popular Sovereignty
The concept that ultimate political authority is based on the will of the people.

Like other politicians of his time, Madison feared that pure, or direct, democracy would deteriorate into mob rule. What would keep the majority of the people, if given direct decision-making power, from abusing the rights of those in the minority?

A Democratic Republic

The framers of the U.S. Constitution chose to craft a **republic,** meaning a government in which sovereign power rests with the people, rather than with a king or a monarch. A republic is based on **popular sovereignty.** To Americans of the 1700s, the idea of a republic also meant a government based on common beliefs and virtues that would be fostered within small communities. The rulers were to be amateurs—good citizens who would take turns representing their fellow citizens.

---

2. James Madison, in Alexander Hamilton, James Madison, and John Jay, *The Federalist Papers,* No. 10 (New York: Mentor Books, 1964), p. 81. See Appendix C of this book.

Democratic Republic
A republic in which representatives elected by the people make and enforce laws and policies.

Representative Democracy
A form of government in which representatives elected by the people make and enforce laws and policies, but in which the monarchy may be retained in a ceremonial role.

Universal Suffrage
The right of all adults to vote for their representatives.

Majority Rule
A basic principle of democracy asserting that the greatest number of citizens in any political unit should select officials and determine policies.

Limited Government
A government with powers that are limited either through a written document or through widely shared beliefs.

The U.S. Constitution created a form of republican government that we now call a **democratic republic.** The people hold the ultimate power over the government through the election process, but all national policy decisions are made by elected officials. For the founders, even this distance between the people and the government was not sufficient. The Constitution made sure that the Senate and the president would not be elected by a direct vote of the people, although later changes to the Constitution allowed the voters to elect members of the Senate directly.

Despite these limits, the new American system was unique in the amount of power it granted to the ordinary citizen. Over the course of the following two centuries, democratic values became more and more popular, at first in Western nations and then throughout the rest of the world. The spread of democratic principles gave rise to another name for our system of government—**representative democracy.** The term *representative democracy* has almost the same meaning as *democratic republic*, with one exception. Recall that in a republic, not only are the people sovereign, but there is no king. What if a nation develops into a democracy but preserves the monarchy as a largely ceremonial institution? That is exactly what happened in Britain. Not surprisingly, the British found the term *democratic republic* to be unacceptable, and they described their system as a representative democracy instead.

Principles of Democratic Government. All representative democracies rest on the rule of the people as expressed through the election of government officials. In the 1790s in the United States, only free white males were able to vote, and in some states they had to be property owners as well. Women in many states did not receive the right to vote in national elections until 1920, and the right to vote was not secured in all states by African Americans until the 1960s. Today, **universal suffrage** is the rule.

Because everyone's vote counts equally, the only way to make fair decisions is by some form of majority will. But to ensure that **majority rule** does not become oppressive, modern democracies also provide guarantees of minority rights. If political minorities were not protected, the majority might violate the fundamental rights of members of certain groups—especially groups that are unpopular or dissimilar to the majority population, such as racial minorities.

To guarantee the continued existence of a representative democracy, there must be free, competitive elections. Thus, the opposition always has the opportunity to win elective office. For such elections to be totally open, freedom of the press and of speech must be preserved so that opposition candidates can present their criticisms of the government to the people.

Constitutional Democracy. Another key feature of Western representative democracy is that it is based on the principle of **limited government.** Not only is the government dependent on popular sovereignty, but the powers of the government are also clearly limited, either through a written document or through widely shared beliefs. The U.S. Constitution sets down the fundamental structure of the government and the limits to its activities. Such limits are intended to prevent political decisions based on the whims or ambitions of individuals in government rather than on constitutional principles.

WHAT KIND OF DEMOCRACY DO WE HAVE?

LO3: Describe majoritarianism, elite theory, and pluralism as theories of how democratic systems work.

Political scientists have developed a number of theories about American democracy, including *majoritarianism, elite theory,* and *pluralism.* Advocates of these theories use them to describe American democracy either as it actually is or as they believe it should be.

Some scholars argue that none of these three theories, which we discuss next, fully describes the workings of American democracy. These experts say that each theory captures a part of the true reality but that we need all three theories to gain a full understanding of American politics.

Democracy for Everyone

Many people believe that in a democracy, the government ought to do what the majority of the people want. This simple proposition is the heart of majoritarian theory. As a theory of what democracy should be like, **majoritarianism** is popular among both political scientists and ordinary citizens. Many scholars, however, consider majoritarianism to provide a surprisingly poor description of how U.S. democracy actually works. They point to the low level of turnout for elections. Polling data have shown that many Americans are neither particularly interested in politics nor well informed. Few are able to name the persons running for Congress in their districts, and even fewer can discuss the candidates' positions.

Majoritarianism
A political theory holding that in a democracy, the government ought to do what the majority of the people want.

Elite Theory
The argument that society is ruled by a small number of people who exercise power to further their self-interests.

Democracy for the Few

If ordinary citizens are not really making policy decisions with their votes, who is? One theory suggests that elites really govern the United States. **Elite theory** holds that society is ruled by a small number of people who exercise power to further their self-interests. American democracy, in other words, is a sham democracy. Few people today believe it is a good idea for the country to be run by a privileged minority. In the past, however, many people believed that it was appropriate for the country to be governed by an elite. Consider the words of Alexander Hamilton, one of the framers of the Constitution:

> *All communities divide themselves into the few and the many. The first are the rich and the wellborn, the other the mass of the people. . . . The people are turbulent and changing; they seldom judge or determine right. Give therefore to the first class a distinct, permanent share in the government. They will check the unsteadiness of the second, and as they cannot receive any advantage by a change, they therefore will ever maintain good government.*[3]

Some versions of elite theory assume that there is a small, cohesive elite class that makes almost all the important decisions for the nation,[4] whereas others suggest that voters choose among competing elites. Popular movements, such as the Tea Party movement and Occupy Wall Street, often advocate simple versions of elite theory. Members of the Occupy movement believe that the top 1 percent of income earners—especially those who work in the finance industry—have too much power. For Tea Party supporters, the elite is the federal government itself.

This college student is registering to vote for the first time. Why is this action so important for democracy? (AP Photo/Chuck Burton)

---

3. Alexander Hamilton, "Speech in the Constitutional Convention on a Plan of Government," in Joanne B. Freeman, ed., *Writings* (New York: Library of America, 2001).
4. Michael Parenti, *Democracy for the Few,* 9th ed. (Belmont, Calif.: Wadsworth Publishing, 2011).

Pluralism
A theory that views politics as a conflict among interest groups. Political decision making is characterized by bargaining and compromise.

Political Culture
The patterned set of ideas, values, and ways of thinking about government and politics that characterizes a people.

Political Socialization
The process by which people acquire political beliefs and values.

Civil Liberties
Those personal freedoms, including freedom of religion and of speech, that are protected for all individuals in a society.

Democracy for Groups

A different school of thought holds that our form of democracy is based on group interests. Even if the average citizen cannot keep up with political issues or cast a deciding vote in any election, the individual's interests will be protected by groups that represent her or him.

Theorists who subscribe to pluralism see politics as a struggle among groups to gain benefits for their members. Given the structure of the American political system, group conflicts tend to be settled by compromise and accommodation. Because there are a multitude of interests, no one group can dominate the political process. Furthermore, because most individuals have more than one interest, conflict among groups need not divide the nation into hostile camps.

Many political scientists believe that pluralism works very well as a descriptive theory. As a theory of how democracy *should* function, however, pluralism has problems. Poor citizens are rarely represented by interest groups. At the same time, rich citizens may be overrepresented. There are also serious doubts as to whether group decision making always reflects the best interests of the nation.

Indeed, critics see a danger that groups may grow so powerful that all policies become compromises crafted to satisfy the interests of the largest groups. The interests of the public as a whole, then, are not considered. Critics of pluralism have suggested that a democratic system can be almost paralyzed by the struggle among interest groups. We will discuss interest groups at greater length in Chapter 7.

FUNDAMENTAL VALUES

The writers of the U.S. Constitution believed that the structures they had created would provide for both popular sovereignty and a stable political system. They also believed that the nation would be sustained by its **political culture**—the patterned set of ideas, values, and ways of thinking about government and politics that characterized its people. Even today, there is considerable consensus among American citizens about certain concepts—including the rights to liberty, equality, and property—that are deemed to be basic to the U.S. political system. Given that the vast majority of Americans are descendants of immigrants having diverse cultural and political backgrounds, how can we account for this consensus? Primarily, it is the result of **political socialization**—the process by which political beliefs and values are transmitted to new immigrants and to our children. The two most important sources of political socialization are the family and the educational system. (See Chapter 6 for a more detailed discussion of the political socialization process.)

The most fundamental concepts of the American political culture are those of the dominant culture. The term *dominant culture* refers to the values, customs, and language established by the groups that traditionally have controlled politics and government in a society. The dominant culture in the United States has its roots in Western European civilization. From that civilization, American politics inherited a bias toward individualism, private property, and Judeo-Christian ethics.

Liberty versus Order

LO4: Summarize the conflicts that can occur between the principles of liberty and order, and between those of liberty and equality.

In the United States, our **civil liberties** include religious freedom—both the right to practice whatever religion we choose and the right to be free from any state-imposed religion. Our civil liberties also include freedom of speech—the right to express our opinions freely on all matters, including government actions. Freedom of speech is perhaps one of our most prized liberties, because a democracy could not endure without it. These and many other basic guarantees of liberty are found in the **Bill of Rights,** the first ten amendments to the Constitution.

Liberty, however, is not the only value widely held by Americans. A substantial portion of the American electorate believes that certain kinds of liberty threaten the traditional social order. The right to privacy is a particularly controversial liberty. The United States Supreme Court has held that the right to privacy can be derived from other rights that are explicitly stated in the Bill of Rights. The Supreme Court has also held that under the right to privacy, the government cannot ban either abortion[5] or private homosexual behavior by consenting adults.[6] Some Americans believe that such rights threaten the sanctity of the family and the general cultural commitment to moral behavior. Of course, others disagree with this point of view.

Security is another issue that follows from the principle of order. When Americans have felt particularly fearful or vulnerable, the government has emphasized national security over civil liberties. Such was the case after the Japanese attack on Pearl Harbor in 1941, which led to the U.S. entry into World War II. Thousands of Japanese Americans were held in internment camps, based on the assumption that their loyalty to this country was in question. More recently, the terrorist attacks on the Pentagon and the World Trade Center on September 11, 2001, renewed calls for greater security at the expense of some civil liberties.

Liberty versus Equality

The Declaration of Independence states, "All men are created equal." The proper meaning of *equality,* however, has been disputed by Americans since the Revolution. Much of American history—and indeed, world history—is the story of how the value of **equality,** the idea that all people are of equal worth, has been extended and elaborated.

One of the most fundamental rights Americans have is the right to vote. Here, African Americans in Mississippi are registering to vote for the first time after passage of the 1965 Voting Rights Act. Does voting affect political socialization? (Bettmann/Corbis)

First, the right to vote was granted to all adult white males, regardless of whether they owned property. The Civil War resulted in the end of slavery and established that, in principle at least, all citizens were equal before the law. The civil rights movement of the 1950s and 1960s sought to make that promise of equality a reality for African Americans. Other movements have sought equality for additional racial and ethnic groups, for women, for persons with disabilities, and for gay men and lesbians.

Bill of Rights
The first ten amendments to the U.S. Constitution.

Equality
As a political value, the idea that all people are of equal worth.

---

5. *Roe v. Wade,* 410 U.S. 113 (1973).
6. *Lawrence v. Texas,* 539 U.S. 558 (2003).

Barack Obama and Hillary Rodham Clinton, the two leading contenders for the Democratic presidential nomination in 2008, were of historic importance. Why was this so? (Jim Watson/AFP/Getty Images)

Although many people believe that we have a way to go yet in obtaining full equality for all of these groups, we clearly have come a long way already. No American in the nineteenth century could have imagined that the 2008 Democratic presidential primary elections would be closely fought contests between an African American man (Illinois senator Barack Obama) and a white woman (New York senator Hillary Rodham Clinton). The idea that same-sex marriage could even be open to debate would have been mind-boggling as well.

Promoting equality often requires limiting the right to treat people unequally. In this sense, equality and liberty are conflicting values. Today, the right to deny equal treatment to the members of a particular race has very few defenders. Yet as recently as fifty years ago, this right was a cultural norm.

Economic Equality. Equal treatment regardless of race, religion, gender, or other characteristics is a popular value today. Equal opportunity for individuals to develop their talents and skills is also a value with substantial support. Equality of economic status, however, is a controversial value.

For much of history, the idea that the government could do anything about the division of society between rich and poor was not something about which people even thought. Most people assumed that such an effort was either impossible or undesirable. This assumption began to lose its force in the 1800s. As a result of the growing wealth of the Western world and a visible increase in the ability of government to take on large projects, some people began to advocate the value of universal equality, or *egalitarianism.* Some radicals dreamed of a revolutionary transformation of society that would establish an egalitarian system—that is, a system in which wealth and power were redistributed more equally.

Many others rejected this vision but still came to endorse the values of eliminating poverty and at least reducing the degree of economic inequality in society. Antipoverty advocates believed then and believe now that such a program could prevent much suffering. In addition, they believed that reducing economic inequality would promote fairness and enhance the moral tone of society generally.

Property
Anything that is or may be subject to ownership. As conceived by the political philosopher John Locke, the right to property is a natural right superior to human law (laws made by government).

Capitalism
An economic system characterized by the private ownership of wealth-creating assets, free markets, and freedom of contract.

Property Rights and Capitalism. The value of reducing economic inequality is in conflict with the right to **property.** This is because reducing economic inequality typically involves the transfer of property (usually in the form of tax dollars) from some people to others. For many people, liberty and property are closely entwined. Our capitalist system is based on private property rights. Under **capitalism,** property consists not only of personal possessions but also of wealth-creating assets such as farms and factories. Capitalism is also typically characterized by considerable freedom to make binding contracts and by relatively unconstrained markets for goods, services, and investments.

Property—especially wealth-creating property—can be seen as giving its owner political power and the liberty to do whatever he or she wants. At the same time, the ownership of property immediately creates inequality in society. The desire to own property, however, is so widespread among all classes of Americans that radical egalitarian movements have had a difficult time securing a wide following in this country.

The Proper Size of Government

Opposition to "big government" has been a constant theme in American politics. Indeed, the belief that government is overreaching dates back to the years before the American Revolution. Tensions over the size and scope of government have plagued Americans ever since. Citizens often express contradictory opinions on the size of government and the role that it should play in their lives. Those who complain about the amount of taxes that they pay each year may also worry about the lack of funds for more teachers in the local schools. Americans tend to oppose "big government" in principle, even as they endorse its benefits. Indeed, American politics in the twenty-first century can be described largely in terms of ambivalence about big government.

Big Government and War. As of 2000, the Republican and Democratic parties were almost tied in terms of support. Under George W. Bush, the Republicans won the presidency and control of both chambers of Congress in the 2000 elections, but they did so with some of the narrowest victory margins in history.

The terrorist attacks of September 11, 2001, appeared to grant the Republicans an edge because they had a reputation for aggressive foreign policy. In March 2003, U.S. forces occupied the nation of Iraq. Grounds for the attack included the belief, later proved false, that Iraq's government was associated with the 9/11 terrorists. U.S. forces in Iraq soon faced an apparently endless insurrection. In 2006, the Republicans lost control of the U.S. House and Senate to the Democrats. Many saw the war in Iraq as an example of big government gone astray.

Big Government and the Great Recession. In September 2008, a financial meltdown threatened the entire world economy with collapse. Americans demanded government action to save the economy, yet most programs aimed at accomplishing that goal turned out to be unpopular. In the last days of the Bush administration, a $700 billion bailout of banks and other financial institutions angered Republicans and Democrats alike. In November 2008, the voters handed Democrat Barack Obama a solid victory in the presidential elections, and Democrats increased their margins in the House and Senate.

The new administration took major actions in an attempt to combat the recession, including an $800 billion stimulus package in February 2009 and the rescue of the automobile companies General Motors and Chrysler. Conservatives quickly grew alarmed at the new government activism. In March 2010, Congress and President Obama approved a major health-care initiative that had no direct connection to fighting the recession. For many, this act completed the picture of big government out of control. In November 2010, voters swung heavily to the Republicans, granting them control of the House.

Republican Overreach. With government divided between the parties, many observers predicted political deadlock. In fact, in 2011 and 2012 Congress passed less legislation than at any other time in sixty-five years. A symbol of the impasse was the attempt by Republicans in the House to use a periodically scheduled raise in the federal government's debt ceiling to force cuts in spending. House Republicans also called for major tax-rate cuts, tough restrictions on future funding for Medicaid, and the privatization of Medicare for anyone currently under the age of fifty-five. By 2012, for many independents, concern over Democratic affection for big government was now counterbalanced by fears that the Republicans might cut valued social programs. We discuss some of the Republican arguments—and Democratic counterarguments—in the *At Issue* feature on the following page.

at issue

DOES ENTITLEMENT SPENDING CORRUPT US?

The federal government provides benefits to certain individuals and families. Many of these benefits are called *entitlements* because you are entitled to receive them if you meet specific requirements. If you meet certain age requirements, you can receive a monthly Social Security check. If you lose your job, you may be entitled to unemployment benefits for a certain number of weeks. If your family income is below a certain level, you typically qualify for benefits from the Supplemental Nutrition Assistance Program (SNAP, formerly called *food stamps*).

In recent years, federal entitlement spending has ballooned. Indeed, big government has gotten bigger in large part because Americans are receiving more entitlement payments every year. At all levels combined, government spending now has a value equivalent to about 38.5 percent of total national income. Some have argued that large-scale entitlement spending is corrupting us.

THE MORE YOU GIVE PEOPLE, THE LESS THEY'LL WANT TO WORK

Conservatives point out that entitlement transfers—adjusted for rising prices and population growth—are now more than seven times what they were in 1960. (In part, this is because major programs such as Medicare and Medicaid were first created in the 1960s.) Currently, almost half of Americans live in a household that receives at least one government benefit. If you count tax deductions, almost every household receives benefits.

Consider SNAP benefits. In 2007, 26 million Americans received them. By 2013, almost 50 million Americans received them. The same story applies to Social Security disability payments. Three million people received disability checks in 1990. Today, almost 9 million receive them. These are only some of many similar examples.

Fewer people are now in the labor force, and those who are work fewer hours per year. Since 2000, the labor force participation rate has fallen continuously, even during boom times. Many believe that increased entitlement benefits have reduced people's desire to join the labor force. In other words, entitlements corrupt.

ENTITLEMENTS ARE A NECESSARY PART OF THE SOCIAL CONTRACT

While the statistics just presented are accurate, political progressives do not accept the conclusions drawn. They say that with an aging society, we should expect to pay more for Social Security. The same is true for government-financed health care. Health-care expenses are not only driven up by larger numbers of the elderly, but also by increasingly expensive—and effective—medical procedures.

Contrary to what some have argued, Americans are not divided between "makers" and "takers." At various times in our lives, we are all takers and almost all of us are makers. As President Obama said in his second inaugural address, "The commitments we make to each other—through Medicare, and Medicaid, and Social Security—these things do not sap our initiative; they strengthen us. They do not make us a nation of takers; they free us to take the risks that make this country great."

Americans believe in hard work just as much as they always have. The Pew Economic Mobility Project sampled Americans on what is essential for getting ahead. More than 90 percent responded "hard work," and almost 90 percent answered "ambition." That doesn't sound like corruption, does it?

FOR CRITICAL ANALYSIS
Who ultimately pays for entitlement programs?

In the 2012 elections, despite continuing economic troubles, President Obama was reelected and the Democrats posted gains in the U.S. House and Senate. Although Democratic victory margins were not great, some pundits argued that the results were ominous for the Republicans. That party did poorly among growing population groups, such as Latinos and young people. Still, it seemed likely that U.S. national elections would remain close for many years to come.

Speaker of the House John Boehner (R., Ohio) answers reporters' questions at the U.S. Capitol in March 2013. Is Boehner a conservative? (Chip Somodevilla/Getty Images)

POLITICAL IDEOLOGIES

A **political ideology** is a closely linked set of beliefs about politics. The concept of *ideology* is often misunderstood. Many people think that only individuals whose beliefs lie well out on one or the other end of the political spectrum have an ideology—in other words, people with moderate positions are not ideological. Actually, almost everyone who has political opinions can be said to have an ideology. Some people may have difficulty in explaining the principles that underlie their opinions, but the principles are there nonetheless. To give one example: a belief in moderation is itself an ideological principle.

Political ideologies offer people well-organized theories that propose goals for society and the means by which those goals can be achieved. At the core of every political ideology is a set of guiding values. The two ideologies most commonly referred to in discussions of American politics are *conservatism* and *liberalism*.

Conservatism

Traditionally, those who favor the ideology of **conservatism** have sought to conserve traditional practices and institutions. In that sense, conservatism is as old as politics itself. In America, limited government is a key tradition. For much of our history, limited government has included major restrictions on government's ability to interfere with business. In the past, enterprises were largely free to act as they pleased in the marketplace and in managing their employees. Government regulation of business increased greatly in the 1930s, as Democratic president Franklin D. Roosevelt (1933–1945) initiated a series of massive interventions in the economy in an attempt to counter the effects of the Great Depression. Many conservatives consider the Roosevelt administration to be a time when America took a wrong turn.

Political Ideology
A comprehensive set of beliefs about the nature of people and the role of government.

Conservatism
A set of beliefs that includes advocacy of a limited role for the national government in helping individuals, support for traditional values and lifestyles, and a cautious response to change.

Conservative Movement
An American movement launched in the 1950s that provides a comprehensive ideological framework for conservative politics.

Liberalism
A set of beliefs that includes advocacy of positive government action to improve the welfare of individuals, support for civil rights, and tolerance for political and social change.

Social Media in Politics
To find out more about conservative politics in the United States, go to Facebook and search on "national review." You"ll see posts by the staff of *National Review*, a conservative magazine.

Modern Conservatism. It was in the 1950s, however, that American conservatism took its modern shape. The **conservative movement** that arose in that decade provided the age-old conservative impulse with a fully worked-out ideology. The new movement first demonstrated its strength in 1964, when Senator Barry Goldwater of Arizona was nominated as the Republican presidential candidate. Goldwater lost badly to Democrat Lyndon Johnson, but from that time forward *movement conservatives* have occupied a crucial position in the Republican Party.

Conservative Values. American conservatives generally place a high value on the principle of order. This includes support for patriotism and traditional ideals. As a result, conservatives typically oppose such social innovations as same-sex marriage. Conservatives strongly endorse liberty, but they generally define it as freedom from government support of nontraditional ideals such as gay rights or as freedom from government interference in business. Conservatives believe that the private sector probably can outperform the government in almost any activity. Therefore, they usually oppose initiatives that would increase the role of the government in the economy, such as President Obama's health-care reforms. Conservatives place a relatively low value on equality. Believing that individuals and families are primarily responsible for their own well-being, they typically oppose high levels of antipoverty spending and government expenditures to stimulate the economy, favoring tax-rate cuts instead.

Liberalism

The term **liberalism** stems from the word *liberty* and originally meant "free from prejudice in favor of traditional opinions and established institutions." Liberals have always been skeptical of the influence of religion in politics, but in the nineteenth century they were skeptical of government as well. From the time of Democratic presidents Woodrow Wilson (1913–1921) and Franklin D. Roosevelt, however, American liberals increasingly sought to use the power of government for nontraditional ends. Their goals included support for organized labor and for the poor. New programs instituted by the Roosevelt administration included Social Security and unemployment insurance.

Modern Liberalism. American liberalism took its modern form in the 1960s. Liberals rallied to the civil rights movement, which sought to obtain equal rights for African Americans. As the feminist movement grew in importance, liberals supported it as well. Liberals won new federal health-care programs such as Medicare and Medicaid, and the promotion of such programs became a key component of liberal politics. Finally, liberals reacted more negatively to U.S. participation in the Vietnam War (1965–1975) than did other Americans, and for years thereafter liberalism was associated with skepticism about the use of U.S. military forces abroad.

Social Media in Politics
To learn more about liberal politics, go to Twitter and locate "thenation." You'll see tweets by the staff of *The Nation*, a liberal publication.

Liberal Values. Those who favor liberalism place a high value on social and economic equality. As we have seen, liberals champion the rights of minority group members and favor substantial antipoverty spending. In the recent health-care policy debates, liberals strongly endorsed the principle that all citizens should have access to "affordable" insurance. In contrast to conservatives, liberals often support government intervention in the economy. They believe that capitalism works best when the government curbs capitalism's excesses through regulation. Like conservatives, liberals place a high value on liberty, but they tend to view it as the freedom to live one's life according to one's own values. Liberals, therefore, usually support gay rights, often including the right to same-sex marriages.

The Traditional Political Spectrum

A traditional method of comparing political ideologies is to arrange them on a continuum from left to right, based primarily on how much power the government should exercise to promote economic equality. Table 1–1 below shows how ideologies can be arrayed in a traditional political spectrum. In addition to liberalism and conservatism, this example includes the ideologies of socialism and libertarianism.

Socialism falls on the left side of the spectrum. Socialists play a minor role in the American political arena, although socialist parties and movements have been important in other countries around the world. In the past, socialists typically advocated replacing investor ownership of major businesses with either government ownership or ownership by employee cooperatives. Socialists believed that such steps would break the power of the very rich and lead to an egalitarian society. In more recent times, socialists in Western Europe have advocated more limited programs that redistribute income.

On the right side of the spectrum is **libertarianism,** a philosophy of skepticism toward most government activities. Libertarians strongly support property rights and typically oppose regulation of the economy and redistribution of income. Libertarians support *laissez-faire* capitalism. (*Laissez faire* is French for "let it be.") Libertarians also tend to oppose government attempts to regulate personal behavior and promote moral values.

Problems with the Traditional Political Spectrum

Many political scientists believe that the traditional left-to-right spectrum is not sufficiently complete. Take the example of libertarians. In Table 1–1 below, libertarians are placed to the right of conservatives. If the only question is how much power the government should have over the economy, this is where they belong. Libertarians, however, advocate the most complete freedom possible in social matters. They oppose government action to promote traditional moral values, although such action is often favored by other groups on the political right. Their strong support for cultural freedoms seems to align them more closely with modern liberals than with conservatives.

Liberalism is often described as an ideology that supports "big government." If the objective is to promote equality, the description has some validity. In the moral sphere, however, conservatives tend to support more government regulation of social values and moral decisions than do liberals. Thus, conservatives tend to oppose gay rights legislation and propose stronger curbs on pornography. Liberals usually show greater tolerance for alternative life choices and oppose government attempts to regulate personal behavior and morals.

Socialism
A political ideology based on strong support for economic and social equality. Socialists traditionally envisioned a society in which major businesses were taken over by the government or by employee cooperatives.

Libertarianism
A political ideology based on skepticism or opposition toward most government activities.

TABLE 1–1: The Traditional Political Spectrum

	Socialism	Liberalism	Conservatism	Libertarianism
How much power should the government have over the economy?	Active government control of major economic sectors.	Positive government action in the economy.	Positive government action to support capitalism.	Almost no regulation of the economy.
What should the government promote?	Economic equality, community.	Economic security, equal opportunity, social liberty.	Economic liberty, morality, social order.	Total economic and social liberty.

A Four-Cornered Ideological Grid

For a more sophisticated breakdown of recent American popular ideologies, many scholars use a four-cornered grid, as shown in Figure 1–1 below. The grid includes four possible ideologies. Each quadrant contains a substantial portion of the American electorate. Individual voters may fall anywhere on the grid, depending on the strength of their beliefs about economic and cultural issues.

Economic Liberals, Cultural Conservatives. Note that there is no generally accepted term for persons in the lower-left position, which we have labeled "economic liberals, cultural conservatives." Some scholars have used terms such as *populist* to describe this point of view, but these terms can be misleading. *Populism* more accurately refers to a hostility toward political, economic, or cultural elites, and it can be combined with a variety of political positions.

Individuals who are economic liberals and cultural conservatives tend to support government action both to promote the values of economic equality and fairness and to defend traditional values, such as the family and marriage. These individuals may describe themselves as conservative or moderate. They may vote for a Republican candidate based on their conservative values. More often, they may be Democrats due to their support for economic liberalism. Many of these Democrats are African Americans or members of other minority groups.

FIGURE 1–1: A Four-Cornered Ideological Grid

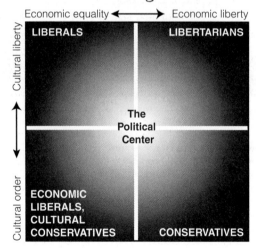

Economic equality ←——→ Economic liberty

Cultural liberty

LIBERALS

LIBERTARIANS

The Political Center

Cultural order

ECONOMIC LIBERALS, CULTURAL CONSERVATIVES

CONSERVATIVES

Libertarians. As a position on the four-cornered grid, *libertarian* does not refer to the small Libertarian Party, which has only a minor role in the American political arena. Rather, libertarians more typically support the Republican Party. Economically successful individuals are more likely than members of other groups to hold libertarian opinions.

The Liberal Label. Even though all four ideologies are popular, the various labels we have used in the four-cornered grid are not equally favored. Voters are much more likely to describe themselves as conservative than as liberal. There are a variety of reasons for this, but one is that *liberal* has come to imply "radical" to many people, whereas *conservative* often implies "moderate." Because most Americans value moderation, the conservative label has an advantage. Indeed, few politicians today willingly describe themselves as liberal, and many liberals prefer to describe themselves as progressive instead. Public opinion polls suggest that *progressive* is a relatively popular label.

making a **difference**

SEEING DEMOCRACY IN ACTION

Betsy Price, right, Republican mayor of Fort Worth, Texas, gives her cowboy hat to the ambassador from the United Arab Emirates. Emirates airline had just introduced the first commercial nonstop flights from Dallas–Fort Worth to the Middle East. (AP Photo/*The Fort Worth Star-Telegram,* Max Faulkner)

One way to begin to understand the American political system is to observe a legislative body in action. By "legislative body," we don't mean only the U.S. Congress and the various state legislatures—there are thousands of elected legislatures in the United States at all levels of government. You might choose to visit a city council, a school board, or a township board of trustees.

Why Should You Care? Local legislative bodies can have a direct impact on your life. For example, city councils or county commissions typically oversee the police or the sheriff's department, and the behavior of the police is a matter of interest even if you live on campus. If you live off campus, local authorities are responsible for an even greater number of issues that affect you directly. Are there items that the sanitation department refuses to pick up, for example? You might be able to change its policies by lobbying your councilperson.

Even if there are no local issues that concern you, there are still benefits to be gained from observing a local legislative session. You may discover that local government works rather differently than you expected. You might learn, for example, that the representatives of your political party do not serve your interests as well as you thought—or that the other party is much more sensible than you had presumed.

What Can You Do? To find out when and where local legislative bodies meet, look up the number of the city hall or county building in the telephone directory or on the Internet, and call the clerk of the council. If you live in a state capital such as Baton Rouge, Louisiana, or Santa Fe, New Mexico, you can view a meeting of the state legislature instead. In many communities, city council meetings and county board meetings can be seen on public-access TV channels. Many cities and almost all state governments have Internet Web sites.

Before attending a business session of the legislature, try to find out how the members are elected. Are the members chosen by the "at-large" method of election, so that each member represents the whole community, or are they chosen by specific geographic districts or wards? Is there a chairperson or official leader who controls the meetings? What are the responsibilities of this body?

When you visit, keep in mind the theory of representative democracy. The commissioners or council members are elected to represent their constituents (those who voted them into office). Observe how often the members refer to their constituents or to the special needs of their community or electoral district. Listen for sources of conflict within a community. If there is a debate, for example, over a zoning proposal that involves an issue of land use, try to figure out why some members oppose the proposal.

If you want to follow up on your visit, try to get a brief interview with one of the members of the council or board. In general, legislators are very willing to talk to students, particularly students who also are voters. Ask the member how he or she sees the job of representative. How can the wishes of the constituents be identified? How does the representative balance the needs of the particular ward or district that she or he represents with the good of the entire community? You can write to many legislators through e-mail. You might ask how much e-mail they receive and who actually answers it.

keyterms

authoritarianism 4	direct democracy 4	liberty 3	popular sovereignty 5
authority 3	elite theory 7	limited government 6	property 10
Bill of Rights 9	equality 9	majoritarianism 7	recall 4
capitalism 10	government 2	majority rule 6	referendum 4
civil liberties 8	initiative 4	order 2	representative
conservatism 13	institution 2	pluralism 8	democracy 6
conservative	legislature 4	political culture 8	republic 5
movement 14	legitimacy 3	political ideology 13	socialism 15
democracy 4	liberalism 14	political socialization 8	totalitarian regime 4
democratic republic 6	libertarianism 15	politics 2	universal suffrage 6

chaptersummary

1 Politics is the process by which people decide which members of society receive certain benefits or privileges and which members do not. It is the struggle over power or influence within institutions or organizations that can grant benefits or privileges. Government is an institution within which decisions are made that resolve conflicts and allocate benefits and privileges. It is the predominant institution within society because it has the ultimate decision-making authority.

2 Two fundamental political values are order, which includes security against violence, and liberty, the greatest freedom of the individual consistent with the freedom of other individuals. To be effective, government authority must be backed by legitimacy.

3 Many of our terms for describing forms of government came from the ancient Greeks. In a direct democracy, such as that of ancient Athens, the people themselves make the important political decisions. The United States is a democratic republic—also called a representative democracy—in which the people elect representatives to make the decisions.

4 Theories of American democracy include majoritarianism, in which the government does what the majority wants; elite theory, in which the real power lies with one or more elites; and pluralism, in which organized interest groups contend for power.

5 Fundamental American values include liberty, order, equality, and property. Not all of these values are fully compatible. The value of order often competes with civil liberties, and economic equality competes with property rights.

6 Popular political ideologies can be arranged on a continuum from left (liberal) to right (conservative). We can also analyze economic liberalism and conservatism separately from cultural liberalism and conservatism.

test**yourself**

LO1 *Define the terms* politics, government, order, liberty, authority, *and* legitimacy.

When citizens of a nation do not enjoy liberty, the government frequently will:
    a. abolish the right to a fair trial.
    b. provide government funds to churches.
    c. hold regular elections.

LO2 *Distinguish the major features of direct democracy and representative democracy.*

A democratic republic is based on all of the following principles except:
    a. popular sovereignty.
    b. majority rule.
    c. unlimited government.

LO3 *Describe majoritarianism, elite theory, and pluralism as theories of how democratic systems work.*

A word or phrase used to describe our democratic system in terms of competition among groups is:
    a. majoritarianism.
    b. elite theory.
    c. pluralism.

LO4 *Summarize the conflicts that can occur between the principles of liberty and order, and between those of liberty and equality.*

A major theme of American politics during the twenty-first century has been:
    a. arguments over whether all citizens should have the right to vote.
    b. controversies over the proper size of government.
    c. disputes as to whether the government should assume the ownership of major banks.

LO5 *Discuss conservatism, liberalism, and other popular American ideological positions.*

Popular American ideologies include:
    a. conservatism, liberalism, and libertarianism.
    b. conservatism, liberalism, and socialism.
    c. communism, liberalism, and libertarianism.

Essay Question:

In Australia and Belgium, citizens are legally required to vote in elections. Would such a requirement be a good idea in the United States? What changes might take place if such a rule were in effect?

Answers to multiple-choice questions: 1. a, 2. c, 3. c, 4. b, 5. a.

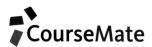

CourseMate

Access CourseMate at www.cengagebrain.com for additional study tools: practice quizzes, key term flashcards and crossword puzzles, audio chapter summaries, simulations, animated learning modules, interactive timelines, videos, and American Government NewsWatch.

2

We the People

of the United States, in Order to form a more perfect Union, lish Justice, insure domestic Tranquility, provide for the common defence, promote the general Welfare, and secure the Blessings of Liberty o ourselv   Posterity, do ordain and establish this Constitution

for the United States of Ame

Two women walk past a painting at the National Constitution Center in Philadelphia, Pennsylvania. The Center is a museum dedicated to honoring and explaining the U.S. Constitution. (William Thomas Cain/Getty Images)

Forging a New Government:
The Constitution

LEARNING OUTCOMES

The five **Learning Outcomes (LOs)** below are designed to help improve your understanding of this chapter. After reading this chapter, you should be able to:

■ **LO1** Explain how the colonial experience prepared Americans for independence, the restrictions that Britain placed on the colonies, and the American response to those restrictions.

■ **LO2** Describe the significance of the Declaration of Independence and the Articles of Confederation, as well as the weaknesses of the Articles.

■ **LO3** Discuss the most important compromises reached at the Constitutional Convention and the basic structure of the resulting government.

■ **LO4** Summarize the arguments in favor of and the arguments against adopting the Constitution, and explain why the Bill of Rights was adopted.

■ **LO5** Describe the process of amending the Constitution and the informal ways in which constitutional interpretation has changed over time.

Check your understanding of the material with the Test Yourself section at the end of the chapter.

We the People *of the United States, in Order to form a more perfect Union, establish Justice, insure domestic Tranquility, provide for the common defence, promote the general Welfare, and secure the Blessings of Liberty to ourselves and our Posterity, do ordain and establish this Constitution for the United States of America.*

Every schoolchild in America has at one time or another been exposed to these famous words from the Preamble to the U.S. Constitution. The document itself is remarkable. The U.S. Constitution, compared with others in the fifty states and in the world, is relatively short. Because amending it is difficult, it also has relatively few amendments. The Constitution has remained largely intact for more than two hundred years. To a great extent, this is because the principles set forth in the Constitution are sufficiently broad that they can be adapted to meet the needs of a changing society.

How and why the U.S. Constitution was created is a story that has been told and retold. It is worth repeating, because knowing the historical and political context in which this country's governmental machinery was formed is essential to understanding American government and politics today. The Constitution did not result just from creative thinking. Many of its provisions were grounded in the political philosophy of the time.

The delegates to the Constitutional Convention in 1787 brought with them two important sets of influences: their political culture and their political experience. In the years between the first settlements in the New World and the writing of the Constitution, Americans had developed a political philosophy about how people should be governed and had tried out several forms of government. These experiences gave the founders the tools with which they constructed the Constitution.

THE COLONIAL BACKGROUND

In 1607, a company chartered by the English government sent a group of settlers to establish a trading post, Jamestown, in what is now Virginia. Jamestown was the first permanent English colony in the Americas. The king of England gave the backers of this colony a charter granting them "full power and authority" to make laws "for the good and welfare" of the settlement. The colonists at Jamestown instituted a **representative assembly,** a legislature composed of individuals who represented the population, thus setting a precedent in government that was to be observed in later colonial adventures.

LO 1: Explain how the colonial experience prepared Americans for independence, the restrictions that Britain placed on the colonies, and the American response to those restrictions.

Separatists, the *Mayflower,* and the Compact

The first New England colony was established in 1620. A group made up in large part of extreme Separatists, who wished to break with the Church of England, came over on the ship *Mayflower* to the New World, landing at Plymouth (Massachusetts). Before going onshore, the adult males—women were not considered to have any political status—drew up the Mayflower Compact, which was signed by forty-one of the forty-four men aboard the ship on November 21, 1620.

The reason for the compact was obvious. This group was outside the jurisdiction of the Virginia Company of London, which had chartered its settlement. The Separatist leaders feared that some of the *Mayflower* passengers might conclude that they were no longer under any obligations of civil obedience. Therefore, some form of public authority was imperative. As William Bradford (one of the Separatist leaders) recalled in his accounts, there were "discontented and mutinous speeches that some of the strangers [non-Separatists] amongst them had let fall from them in the ship; That when they came ashore they would use their owne libertie; for none had power to command them."[1]

The Significance of the Compact. The compact was not a constitution. It was a political statement in which the signers agreed to create and submit to the authority of a government, pending the receipt of a royal charter. The Mayflower Compact's historical and political significance is twofold: it depended on the consent of the affected individuals, and it served as a prototype for similar compacts in American history.

Representative Assembly
A legislature composed of individuals who represent the population.

---

1. John Camp, *Out of the Wilderness: The Emergence of an American Identity in Colonial New England* (Middleton, Conn.: Wesleyan University Press, 1990).

The Mayflower Compact was signed on board the *Mayflower*, off the coast of Massachusetts, in 1620. Was it a constitution? Why or why not? (MPI/Getty Images)

By the time of the American Revolution, the compact was well on its way toward achieving mythic status. In 1802, John Quincy Adams, son of the second American president, spoke these words at a founders' day celebration in Plymouth: "This is perhaps the only instance in human history of that positive, original social compact, which speculative philosophers have imagined as the only legitimate source of government."[2]

Pilgrim Beliefs. Although the Plymouth settlers—later called the Pilgrims—committed themselves to self-government, in other ways their political ideas were not those that are prevalent today. The new community was a religious colony. Separation of church and state and most of our modern civil liberties were alien to the settlers' thinking. By the time the U.S. Constitution was written, the nation's leaders had a very different vision of the relationship between religion and government. We look at some of the founders' beliefs in this chapter's *At Issue* feature on page 24.

More Colonies, More Government

Another outpost in New England was set up by the Massachusetts Bay Colony in 1630. Then followed Rhode Island, Connecticut, New Hampshire, and others. By 1732, the last of the thirteen colonies, Georgia, was established. During the colonial period, Americans developed a concept of limited government, which followed from the establishment of

2. Nathaniel Philbrick, *Mayflower: A Story of Courage, Community, and War* (New York: Penguin, 2007), p. 352.

the first colonies under Crown charters. Theoretically, London governed the colonies. In practice, owing partly to the colonies' distance from London, the colonists exercised a large measure of self-government.

The colonists were able to make their own laws, as in the Fundamental Orders of Connecticut in 1639. The Massachusetts Body of Liberties in 1641 supported the protection of individual rights. In 1682, the Frame of Government of Pennsylvania was passed. Along with the Pennsylvania Charter of Privileges of 1701, it foreshadowed our modern Constitution and Bill of Rights. All of this legislation enabled the colonists to acquire crucial political experience. After independence was declared in 1776, the states quickly set up their own new constitutions.

British Restrictions and Colonial Grievances

The conflict between Britain and the American colonies, which ultimately led to the Revolutionary War, began in the 1760s when the British government decided to raise revenues by imposing taxes on the American colonies. Policy advisers to Britain's King George III, who ascended the throne in 1760, decided that it was only logical to require the American colonists to help pay the costs of Britain's defending them during the French and Indian War (1754–1763). The colonists, who had grown accustomed to a large degree of self-government and independence from the British Crown, viewed the matter differently.

In 1764, the British Parliament passed the Sugar Act, which imposed a tax that many colonists were unwilling to pay. Further regulatory legislation was to come. In 1765, Parliament passed the Stamp Act, providing for internal taxation of legal documents and even newspapers—or, as the colonists' Stamp Act Congress, assembled in 1765, called it, "taxation without representation." The colonists boycotted the purchase of English commodities in return.

The success of the boycott (the Stamp Act was repealed a year later) generated a feeling of unity within the colonies. The British, however, continued to try to raise revenues in the colonies. When Parliament passed duties on glass, lead, paint, and other items in 1767, the colonists again boycotted British goods. The colonists' fury over taxation climaxed in the Boston Tea Party: colonists dressed as Mohawk Indians dumped almost 350 chests of British tea into Boston Harbor as a gesture of tax protest. In retaliation, Parliament passed the Coercive Acts (the "Intolerable Acts") in 1774, which closed Boston Harbor and placed the government of Massachusetts under direct British control. The colonists were outraged—and they responded.

The First Continental Congress

New York, Pennsylvania, and Rhode Island proposed the convening of a colonial gathering, or congress. The Massachusetts House of Representatives requested that all colonies hold conventions to select delegates to be sent to Philadelphia for such a congress.

The First Continental Congress was held in Philadelphia at Carpenter's Hall on September 5, 1774. It was a gathering of delegates from twelve of the thirteen colonies (delegates from Georgia did not attend until 1775). At that meeting, there was little talk of independence. The congress passed a resolution requesting that the colonies send a petition to King George III expressing their grievances. Resolutions were also passed requiring that the colonies raise their own troops and boycott British trade. The British government condemned the congress's actions, treating them as open acts of rebellion.

at issue

JUST HOW CHRISTIAN WERE THE FOUNDERS?

Christianity utterly permeated the world of the first English settlers in America. The oldest colonial documents are filled with endorsements of Christianity. Regular church attendance was often mandatory. Nine of the colonies had churches that were established by law.

The Declaration of Independence, however, makes no reference to Christ. The word *God* does not appear in the Constitution. By 1790, officially established churches were found only in Connecticut and Massachusetts, and the Congregational Church in Massachusetts had drifted so far from its Puritan origins that many of its members no longer accepted the divinity of Jesus. That is, they belonged to *Unitarian* congregations. One result of this development was that in the national elections of 1796 and 1800, neither major party fielded a presidential candidate who was, by modern definition, a Christian. John Adams, Unitarian, squared off against Thomas Jefferson, freethinker.

These facts raise the question: Just how Christian were the founders? More to the point, did the founders intend the United States to be a "Christian nation"? Scholars and school boards often differ on these issues.

BY AND LARGE, THE FOUNDERS WERE DEVOUT CHRISTIANS . . .

Christian conservatives point out that numerous American leaders throughout history have characterized the country as a Christian nation, beginning with John Jay, the first chief justice of the United States Supreme Court. The revolutionaries of 1776 often viewed the struggle in religious terms. Quite a few believed that God had a special plan for America to serve as an example to the world. The overwhelming majority of the colonists considered themselves Christians. Today, 78 percent of Americans identify

themselves as such. If the term *Christian nation* merely identifies the beliefs of the majority, it is undeniably an accurate label.

To Christian conservatives who would like to change what is taught in the schools, however, the term means much more. They contend that American law is based on the laws of Moses as set down in the Bible. They also believe that America's divine mission is not just an opinion held by many people—it should be taught as literal truth. Finally, according to this group, the separation of church and state is a liberal myth. The language of the First Amendment means only that the national government should not prefer one Protestant denomination over the others.

WHO OPPOSED MIXING CHURCH AND STATE

Mainstream scholars disagree with the previous arguments, often vehemently. For example, Steven K. Green, a professor at Willamette University in Oregon, has searched for American court cases that reference the laws of Moses. He found none.

Ultimately, opponents say, to argue that the founders were not serious about the separation of church and state is to ignore the plain language of the Constitution. True, most of the founders were Christians, but they were also steeped in Enlightenment rationalism that rejected "enthusiasm" in religion. *Enthusiasm* meant the spirit that allowed Protestant and Catholic Europeans to kill one another in the name of God over a period of two centuries. For the founders, mixing church and government was a recipe for trouble.

FOR CRITICAL ANALYSIS

Today, candidates for president clearly benefit when they use religious language and when they are comfortable discussing their faith. Is this at all troubling? Why or why not?

The Second Continental Congress

By the time the Second Continental Congress met in May 1775 (all of the colonies were represented this time), fighting had already broken out between the British and the colonists. One of the main actions of the Second Continental Congress was to establish an army. It did this by declaring the militia that had gathered around Boston an army and naming George Washington as commander in chief. Congressional participants still

The minutemen were members of a colonial militia that was ready to fight the British at a moment's notice. Why did the Continental Congress later turn the militia into an army? (MPI/Getty Images)

attempted to reach a peaceful settlement with the British Parliament. One declaration of the congress stated explicitly that "we have not raised armies with ambitious designs of separating from Great Britain, and establishing independent states." But by the beginning of 1776, military encounters had become increasingly frequent.

Public debate was acrimonious. Then Thomas Paine's *Common Sense* appeared in Philadelphia bookstores. The pamphlet was a colonial best seller. (To do relatively as well today, a book would have to sell between 9 million and 11 million copies in its first year of publication.) Many agreed that Paine did make common sense when he argued that

> *a government of our own is our natural right: and when a man seriously reflects on the precariousness* [instability, unpredictability] *of human affairs, he will become convinced, that it is infinitely wiser and safer, to form a constitution of our own in a cool and deliberate manner, while we have it in our power, than to trust such an interesting event to time and chance.*[3]

Paine further argued that "nothing can settle our affairs so expeditiously as an open and determined declaration for Independence."[4]

Students of Paine's pamphlet point out that his arguments were not new—they were common in tavern debates throughout the land. Rather, it was the near poetry of his words—which were at the same time as plain as the alphabet—that struck his readers.

---

3. *The Political Writings of Thomas Paine,* Vol. 1 (Boston: J. P. Mendum Investigator Office, 1870), p. 46.
4. *Ibid.,* p. 54.

AN INDEPENDENT CONFEDERATION

On April 6, 1776, the Second Continental Congress voted for free trade at all American ports with all countries except Britain. This act could be interpreted as an implicit declaration of independence. The next month, the congress suggested that each of the colonies establish a state government unconnected to Britain. Finally, in July, the colonists declared their independence from Britain.

The Resolution for Independence

On July 2, the Resolution for Independence was adopted by the Second Continental Congress:

> RESOLVED, That these United Colonies are, and of right ought to be free and independent States, that they are absolved from allegiance to the British Crown, and that all political connection between them and the state of Great Britain is, and ought to be, totally dissolved.

In June 1776, Thomas Jefferson was already writing drafts of the Declaration of Independence. When the Resolution for Independence was adopted on July 2, Jefferson argued that a declaration clearly putting forth the causes that compelled the colonies to separate from Britain was necessary. The Second Continental Congress assigned the task to him.

July 4, 1776—The Declaration of Independence

LO2: Describe the significance of the Declaration of Independence and the Articles of Confederation, as well as the weaknesses of the Articles.

Jefferson's version of the Declaration was amended to gain unanimous acceptance (for example, his condemnation of the slave trade was eliminated to satisfy Georgia and North Carolina), but the bulk of it was passed intact on July 4, 1776. On July 19, the modified draft became "the unanimous declaration of the thirteen United States of America." On August 2, it was signed by the members of the Second Continental Congress.

Universal Truths. The Declaration of Independence has become one of the world's most renowned and significant documents. The words opening the second paragraph of the Declaration indicate why this is so:

> We hold these Truths to be self-evident, that all Men are created equal, that they are endowed by their Creator with certain unalienable Rights, that among these are Life, Liberty, and the Pursuit of Happiness—That to secure these Rights, Governments are instituted among Men, deriving their just Powers from the Consent of the Governed, that whenever any Form of Government becomes destructive of these Ends, it is the Right of the People to alter or abolish it, and to institute new Government.

Natural Rights
Rights held to be inherent in natural law, not dependent on governments. John Locke stated that natural law, being superior to human law, specifies certain rights of "life, liberty, and property." These rights, altered to become "life, liberty, and the pursuit of happiness," are asserted in the Declaration of Independence.

Natural Rights and Social Contracts. The statement that "all Men are created equal" and have **natural rights** ("unalienable Rights"), including the rights to "Life, Liberty, and the Pursuit of Happiness," was revolutionary at that time. Its use by Jefferson reveals the influence of the English philosopher John Locke (1632–1704), whose writings were familiar to educated American colonists, including Jefferson. In his *Two Treatises of Government*, published in 1690, Locke had argued that all people possess certain natural rights, including the rights to life, liberty, and property. This claim is not inconsistent with English legal traditions.

Locke went on to argue, however, that the primary purpose of government was to protect these rights. Furthermore, government was established by the people through a **social contract**—an agreement among the people to form a government and abide by its rules. As you read earlier, such contracts, or compacts, were not new to Americans. The Mayflower Compact was the first of several documents that established governments or governing rules based on the consent of the governed.

After setting forth these basic principles of government, the Declaration of Independence goes on to justify the colonists' revolt against Britain. Much of the remainder of the document is a list of what "He" (King George III) had done to deprive the colonists of their rights. (See Appendix A at the end of this book for the complete text of the Declaration of Independence.)

The Significance of the Declaration. The concepts of equality, natural rights, and government established through a social contract were to have a lasting impact on American life. The Declaration of Independence set forth ideals that have since become a fundamental part of our national identity. The Declaration also became a model for use by other nations around the world.

Certainly, most Americans are familiar with the beginning words of the Declaration. Yet, as Harvard historian David Armitage noted in his study of the Declaration of Independence in the international context,[5] few Americans ponder the obvious question: What did these assertions in the Declaration have to do with independence? Clearly, independence could have been declared without these words. Even as late as 1857, Abraham Lincoln admitted, "The assertion that 'all men are created equal' was of no practical use in effecting our separation from Great Britain; and it was placed in the Declaration, not for that, but for future use."[6]

Essentially, the immediate significance of the Declaration of Independence, in 1776, was that it established the legitimacy of the new nation in the eyes of foreign governments, as well as in the eyes of the colonists themselves. What the new nation needed most were supplies for its armies and a commitment of foreign military aid. Unless the United States appeared to the world as a political entity separate and independent from Britain, no foreign government would enter into an agreement with its leaders.

Benjamin Franklin, John Adams, and Thomas Jefferson work on the Declaration of Independence. Why was that document so important? (Archive Images/Alamy)

The Rise of Republicanism

Although the colonists had formally declared independence from Britain, the fight to gain actual independence continued for five more years, until British general Charles Cornwallis surrendered at Yorktown in 1781. In 1783, after Britain formally recognized the

Social Contract
A voluntary agreement among individuals to secure their rights and welfare by creating a government and abiding by its rules.

---

5. David Armitage, *The Declaration of Independence: A Global History* (Cambridge, Mass.: Harvard University Press, 2007).
6. As cited in Armitage, *The Declaration of Independence,* p. 26.

Unicameral Legislature
A legislature with only one legislative chamber, as opposed to a bicameral (two-chamber) legislature, such as the U.S. Congress. Today, Nebraska is the only state in the Union with a unicameral legislature.

Confederation
A political system in which states or regional governments retain ultimate authority except for those powers they expressly delegate to a central government.

State
A group of people occupying a specific area and organized under one government. It may be either a nation or a subunit of a nation.

independence of the United States in the Treaty of Paris, George Washington disbanded the army. During these years of military struggles, the states faced the additional challenge of creating a system of self-government for an independent United States.

Some colonists in the middle and lower South had demanded that independence be preceded by the formation of a strong central government. But the anti-Royalists in New England and Virginia, who called themselves Republicans (not to be confused with today's Republican Party), were against a strong central government. They opposed monarchy, executive authority, and virtually any form of restraint on the power of local groups. These Republicans were a major political force from 1776 to 1780. Indeed, they almost prevented victory over the British by their unwillingness to cooperate with any central authority.

During this time, all of the states adopted written constitutions. Eleven of the constitutions were completely new. Two of them—those of Connecticut and Rhode Island—were old royal charters with minor modifications. Republican sentiment led to increased power for the state legislatures. In Georgia and Pennsylvania, **unicameral** (one-body) **legislatures** were unchecked by executive or judicial authority. In almost all states, the legislature was predominant.

The Articles of Confederation: Our First Form of Government

The fear of a powerful central government led to the passage of the Articles of Confederation, which created a weak central government. The term **confederation** is important. It means a voluntary association of independent **states,** in which the member states agree to only limited restraints on their freedom of action. As a result, confederations seldom have an effective executive authority.

In June 1776, the Second Continental Congress began the process of composing what would become the Articles of Confederation and Perpetual Union, more commonly known as the Articles of Confederation. The final draft was completed by November 15, 1777, but not until March 1, 1781, did the last state, Maryland, agree to ratify the Articles. Well before the final ratification, however, many of the articles were implemented—the Continental Congress and the thirteen states conducted American military, economic, and political affairs according to the standards and the form specified by the Articles.[7]

The Articles Establish a Government. Under the Articles, the thirteen original colonies, now states, established on March 1, 1781, a government of the states—the Congress of the Confederation. The congress was a unicameral assembly of so-called ambassadors from each state, with every state possessing a single vote. Each year, the congress would choose one of its members as its president of the congress, but the Articles did not provide for a president of the United States.

The congress was authorized in Article X to appoint an executive committee of the states "to execute in the recess of Congress, such of the powers of Congress as the United States, in Congress assembled, by the consent of nine [of the thirteen] states, shall from time to time think expedient to vest with them." The congress was also allowed to appoint other committees and civil officers necessary for managing the general affairs of the United States. In addition, the congress could regulate foreign affairs and establish

www
Helpful Web Sites
Several universities offer collections of documents relevant to the Constitution, plus commentary. For example, you might try entering "us constitution emory" or "us constitutional cornell" into your favorite search engine.

---

7. Keith L. Dougherty, *Collective Action under the Articles of Confederation* (New York: Cambridge University Press, 2006).

coinage and weights and measures. But it lacked an independent source of revenue and the necessary executive machinery to enforce its decisions throughout the land. Article II of the Articles of Confederation guaranteed that each state would retain its sovereignty. Table 2–1 below summarizes the powers—and the lack of powers—of Congress under the Articles of Confederation.

Accomplishments under the Articles. The new government had some accomplishments during its eight years of existence under the Articles of Confederation. Certain states' claims to western lands were settled. Maryland had objected to the claims of the Carolinas, Connecticut, Georgia, Massachusetts, New York, and Virginia. It was only after these states consented to give up their land claims to the United States as a whole that Maryland signed the Articles of Confederation. Another accomplishment under the Articles was the passage of the Northwest Ordinance of 1787, which established a basic pattern of government for new territories north of the Ohio River. All in all, the Articles represented the first real pooling of resources by the American states.

Weaknesses of the Articles. In spite of these accomplishments, the Articles of Confederation had many defects. Although Congress had the legal right to declare war and to conduct foreign policy, it did not have the right to demand revenues from the states. It could only ask for them. Additionally, the actions of Congress required the consent of nine states. Any amendments to the Articles required the unanimous consent of the congress and confirmation by every state legislature. Furthermore, the Articles did not create a national system of courts.

Basically, the functioning of the government under the Articles depended on the goodwill of the states. Article III simply established a "league of friendship" among the states—no national government was intended.

Probably the most fundamental weakness of the Articles, and the most basic cause of their eventual replacement by the Constitution, was the lack of power to raise funds for the militia. The Articles contained no language giving Congress coercive power to raise revenue (by levying taxes) to provide adequate support for the military forces controlled by

TABLE 2–1: Powers of the Congress of the Confederation

Congress Had Power to	Congress Lacked Power to
■ Declare war and make peace.	■ Provide for effective treaties and control foreign relations. It could not compel states to respect treaties.
■ Enter into treaties and alliances.	
■ Establish and control armed forces.	
■ Requisition men and funds from states.	■ Compel states to meet military quotas. It could not draft soldiers.
■ Regulate coinage.	
■ Borrow funds and issue bills of credit.	■ Regulate interstate and foreign commerce. It left each state free to tax imports from other states.
■ Fix uniform standards of weight and measurement.	
■ Create admiralty courts.	■ Collect taxes directly from the people. It had to rely on states to collect and forward taxes.
■ Create a postal system.	
■ Regulate Indian affairs.	■ Compel states to pay their share of government costs.
■ Guarantee citizens of each state the rights and privileges of citizens in the several states when in another state.	■ Provide and maintain a sound monetary system or issue paper money. This was left up to the states, and paper currencies in circulation differed tremendously in purchasing power.
■ Adjudicate disputes between states on state petition.	

Congress. Due to a lack of resources, the Continental Congress was forced to disband the army after the Revolutionary War, even in the face of serious Spanish and British military threats.

Shays' Rebellion and the Need to Revise the Articles. Because of the weaknesses of the Articles of Confederation, the central government could do little to maintain peace and order in the new nation. The states bickered among themselves and increasingly taxed each other's goods. By 1784, the country faced a serious economic depression. Banks were calling in old loans and refusing to make new ones. People who could not pay their debts were often thrown into debtors' prison.

In August 1786, mobs of musket-bearing farmers led by former revolutionary captain Daniel Shays seized county courthouses and disrupted the trials of debtors in Springfield, Massachusetts. Shays and his men then launched an attack on the federal arsenal at Springfield, but they were repulsed. Shays' Rebellion demonstrated that the central government could not protect the citizenry from armed rebellion or provide adequately for the public welfare. The rebellion spurred the nation's political leaders to action.

THE CONSTITUTIONAL CONVENTION

The Virginia legislature called for a meeting of all the states to be held at Annapolis, Maryland, on September 11, 1786—ostensibly to discuss commercial problems only. It was evident to those in attendance (including Alexander Hamilton and James Madison) that the national government had serious weaknesses that had to be addressed if it was to survive. Among the important problems to be solved were the relationship between the states and the central government, the powers of the national legislature, the need for executive leadership, and the establishment of policies for economic stability. The result of this meeting was a petition to the Continental Congress for a general convention to meet in Philadelphia in May 1787 "to consider the exigencies [needs] of the union."

The designated date for the opening of the convention at Philadelphia, now known as the Constitutional Convention, was May 14, 1787. Few of the delegates had actually arrived in Philadelphia by that time, however, so the opening was delayed. The convention formally began in the East Room of the Pennsylvania State House on May 25.[8] Fifty-five of the seventy-four delegates chosen for the convention actually attended. (Of those fifty-five, only about forty played active roles at the convention.) Rhode Island was the only state that refused to send delegates.

Factions among the Delegates

We know much about the proceedings at the convention because James Madison kept a daily, detailed personal journal. A majority of the delegates were strong nationalists—they wanted a central government with real power, unlike the central government under the Articles of Confederation. George Washington and Benjamin Franklin were among those who sought a stronger government.

Among the nationalists, some—including Alexander Hamilton—went as far as to support monarchy. Another important group of nationalists was of a more democratic stripe. Led by James Madison of Virginia and James Wilson of Pennsylvania, these repub-

LO3: Discuss the most important compromises reached at the Constitutional Convention and the basic structure of the resulting government.

---

8. This was the same room in which the Declaration of Independence had been signed eleven years earlier. The State House was later named Independence Hall.

lican nationalists wanted a central government founded on popular support.

Other factions included a group of delegates who were totally against a national authority. Two of the three delegates from New York quit the convention when they saw the nationalist direction of its proceedings.

Politicking and Compromises

The debates at the convention started on the first day. James Madison had spent months reviewing European political theory. When his Virginia delegation arrived ahead of most of the others, it got to work immediately. By the time George Washington opened the convention, Governor Edmund Randolph of Virginia was prepared to present fifteen resolutions proposing fundamental changes in the nation's government. In retrospect, this was a masterful stroke on the part of the

George Washington, who would become the nation's first president, presided over the Constitutional Convention of 1787. It formally opened in the East Room of the Pennsylvania State House (later named Independence Hall) on May 25. Only Rhode Island did not send any delegates. (Picture History/Newscom)

Virginia delegation. It set the agenda for the remainder of the convention—even though, in principle, the delegates had been sent to Philadelphia for the sole purpose of amending the Articles of Confederation.

The Virginia Plan. Randolph's fifteen resolutions proposed an entirely new national government under a constitution. Basically, the plan called for the following:

- A **bicameral** (two-chamber) **legislature,** with the lower chamber chosen by the people and the smaller upper chamber chosen by the lower chamber from nominees selected by state legislatures. The number of representatives would be proportional to a state's population, thus favoring the large states, including Virginia. The legislature could void any state laws.
- The creation of an unspecified national executive, elected by the legislature.
- The creation of a national judiciary, appointed by the legislature.

It did not take long for the smaller states to realize they would fare poorly under the Virginia Plan, which would enable Massachusetts, Pennsylvania, and Virginia to form a majority in the national legislature. The debate on the plan dragged on for a number of weeks. It was time for the small states to come up with their own plan.

The New Jersey Plan. On June 15, William Paterson of New Jersey offered an alternative plan. After all, argued Paterson, under the Articles of Confederation all states had

Bicameral Legislature
A legislature made up of two parts, called chambers. The U.S. Congress, composed of the House of Representatives and the Senate, is a bicameral legislature.

Supremacy Doctrine
A doctrine that asserts the priority of national law over state laws. This principle is stated in Article VI of the Constitution.

Great Compromise
The compromise between the New Jersey and Virginia plans that created one chamber of the Congress based on population and one chamber representing each state equally; also called the Connecticut Compromise.

equality; therefore, the convention had no power to change this arrangement. He proposed the following:

- The fundamental principle of the Articles of Confederation—one state, one vote—would be retained.
- Congress would be able to regulate trade and impose taxes.
- All acts of Congress would be the supreme law of the land.
- Several people would be elected by Congress to form an executive office.
- The executive office would appoint a Supreme Court.

Basically, the New Jersey Plan was simply an amendment of the Articles of Confederation. Its only notable feature was its reference to the **supremacy doctrine,** which was later included in the Constitution.

The "Great Compromise." The delegates were at an impasse. Most wanted a strong national government and were unwilling even to consider the New Jersey Plan. But when the Virginia Plan was brought up again, the small states threatened to leave. It was not until July 16 that a compromise was achieved. Roger Sherman of Connecticut proposed the following:

- A bicameral legislature in which the lower chamber, the House of Representatives, would be apportioned according to the number of free inhabitants in each state, plus three-fifths of the slaves.
- An upper chamber, the Senate, which would have two members from each state elected by the state legislatures.

This plan, known as the **Great Compromise,** broke the deadlock. (The plan is also called the Connecticut Compromise because of the role of the Connecticut delegates in the proposal.) It did exact a political price, however, because it permitted each state to have equal representation in the Senate. Having two senators represent each state diluted the voting power of citizens living in more heavily populated states and gave the smaller states disproportionate political power. But the Connecticut Compromise resolved the controversy between small and large states. In addition, the Senate would act as a check on the House, which many feared would be dominated by the masses and excessively responsive to them.

The Three-Fifths Compromise. The Great Compromise also settled another major issue—how to deal with slaves in the representational scheme. Slavery was still legal in several northern states, but it was concentrated in the South. Many delegates were opposed to slavery and wanted it banned entirely in the United States. Charles Pinckney of South Carolina led strong southern opposition to a ban on slavery. Furthermore, the South wanted slaves to be counted along with free persons in determining representation in Congress. Delegates from the northern states objected. Sherman's three-fifths proposal was a compromise between northerners who did not want the slaves counted at all and southerners who wanted them counted in the same way as free whites. Actually, Sherman's Connecticut plan spoke of three-fifths of "all other persons" (and that is the language of the Constitution itself). It is not hard to figure out, though, who those other persons were. The three-fifths compromise illustrates the power of the southern states at the convention.[9]

9. See Garry Wills, *"Negro President": Jefferson and the Slave Power* (New York: Houghton Mifflin, 2003).

The three-fifths compromise did not completely settle the slavery issue. There was also the question of the slave trade. Eventually, the delegates agreed that Congress could not ban the importation of slaves until after 1808. The compromise meant that the matter of slavery itself was never addressed directly. The South won twenty years of unrestricted slave trade and a requirement that escaped slaves in free states be returned to their owners in slave states.

Clearly, many delegates, including slave owners such as George Washington and James Madison, had serious objections to slavery. Why, then, did they allow slavery to continue? Historians have long maintained that the framers had no choice—that without a slavery compromise, the delegates from the South would have abandoned the convention. Indeed, this was the fear of a number of antislavery delegates to the convention. Madison, for example, said, "Great as the evil is, a dismemberment of the Union would be even worse."[10]

A number of historians have made an additional point. Many American leaders believed that slavery would die out naturally. These leaders assumed that in the long run, slave labor could not compete with the labor of free citizens. This assumption turned out to be incorrect.

Other Issues. The South also worried that the northern majority in Congress would pass legislation unfavorable to its economic interests. Because the South depended on agricultural exports, it feared the imposition of export taxes. In return for acceding to the northern demand that Congress be able to regulate commerce among the states and with other nations, the South obtained a promise that export taxes would not be imposed. As a result, the United States is among the few countries that do not tax their exports.

There were other disagreements. The delegates could not decide whether to establish only a Supreme Court or to create lower courts as well. They deferred the issue by mandating a Supreme Court and allowing Congress to establish lower courts. They also disagreed over whether the president or the Senate would choose the Supreme Court justices. A compromise was reached with the agreement that the president would nominate the justices and the Senate would confirm the nominations.

These compromises, as well as others, resulted from the recognition that if one group of states refused to ratify the Constitution, it was doomed.

Working toward Final Agreement

The Connecticut Compromise was reached by mid-July. The makeup of the executive branch and the judiciary, however, was left unsettled. The remaining work of the convention was turned over to a five-man Committee of Detail, which presented a rough draft

James Madison took detailed notes of the proceedings of the Constitutional Convention. What was Madison's opinion of slavery? (Visions of America/Joe Sohm/Photodisc/Getty Images)

---

10. Speech before the Virginia ratifying convention on June 17, 1788, as cited in Bruno Leone, ed., *The Creation of the Constitution* (San Diego: Greenhaven Press, 1995), p. 159.

Separation of Powers
The principle of dividing governmental powers among different branches of government.

Madisonian Model
A structure of government proposed by James Madison, in which the powers of the government are separated into three branches: executive, legislative, and judicial.

Checks and Balances
A major principle of the American system of government whereby each branch of the government can check the actions of the others.

Electoral College
A group of persons, called electors, that officially elects the president and the vice president of the United States. The electors are selected by the voters in each state and in the District of Columbia.

of the Constitution on August 6. It made the executive and judicial branches subordinate to the legislative branch.

The Madisonian Model—Separation of Powers. The major issue of **separation of powers** had not yet been resolved. The delegates were concerned with structuring the government to prevent the imposition of tyranny, either by the majority or by a minority. It was Madison who proposed a governmental scheme—sometimes called the **Madisonian model**—to achieve this: the executive, legislative, and judicial powers of government were to be separated so that no one branch had enough power to dominate the others. The separation of powers was by function, as well as by personnel, with Congress passing laws, the president enforcing and administering laws, and the courts interpreting laws in individual circumstances.

Each of the three branches of government would be independent of the others, but they would have to cooperate to govern. According to Madison, in *Federalist Paper* No. 51 (see Appendix C), "the great security against a gradual concentration of the several powers in the same department consists in giving to those who administer each department the necessary constitutional means and personal motives to resist encroachments of the others."

The Madisonian Model—Checks and Balances. The "constitutional means" Madison referred to is a system of **checks and balances** through which each branch of the government can check the actions of the others. For example, Congress can enact laws, but the president has veto power over congressional acts. The Supreme Court has the power to declare acts of Congress and of the executive unconstitutional, but the president appoints the justices of the Supreme Court, with the advice and consent of the Senate. (The Supreme Court's power to declare acts unconstitutional was not mentioned in the Constitution, although arguably the framers assumed that the Court would have this power—see the discussion of *judicial review* later in this chapter.) Figure 2–1 on the facing page outlines these checks and balances.

In the years since the Constitution was ratified, the checks and balances built into it have evolved into a sometimes complex give-and-take among the branches of government. Generally, for nearly every check that one branch has over another, the branch that has been checked has found a way of getting around it. For example, suppose that the president checks Congress by vetoing a bill. Congress can override the presidential veto by a two-thirds vote. Additionally, Congress holds the "power of the purse." If it disagrees with a program endorsed by the executive branch, it can simply refuse to appropriate the funds necessary to operate that program. Similarly, the president can impose a counter-check on Congress if the Senate refuses to confirm a presidential appointment, such as a judicial appointment. The president can simply wait until Congress is in recess and then make what is called a "recess appointment," which does not require the Senate's immediate approval.

The Executive. Some delegates favored a plural executive, made up of representatives from the various regions. This idea was abandoned in favor of a single chief executive. Some argued that Congress should choose the executive. To make the presidency completely independent of Congress, however, an **electoral college** was adopted. This group would be made up of electors chosen by the states, and each state would have as many electors as it had members of Congress. The electoral college created a cumbersome presidential election process, but it supported the separation of powers while insulating the presidency from *direct* popular control.

FIGURE 2–1: Checks and Balances

The major checks and balances among the three branches of the U.S. government are illustrated here. The Constitution does not mention some of these checks, such as judicial review—the power of the courts to declare federal or state acts unconstitutional—and the president's ability to refuse to enforce judicial decisions or congressional legislation. Checks and balances can be thought of as a confrontation of powers or responsibilities. Each branch checks the actions of the others; two branches in conflict have powers that can result in balances or stalemates, requiring one branch to give in or both to reach a compromise.

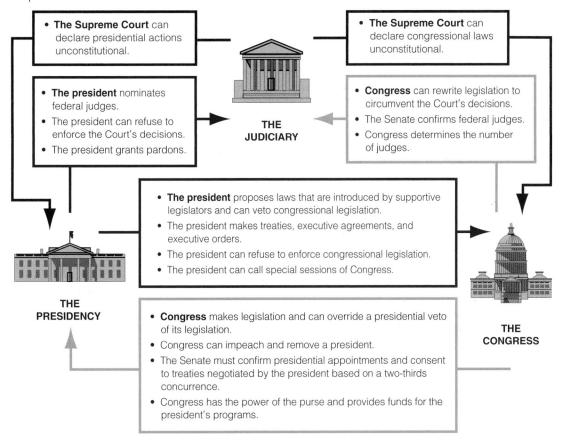

- **The Supreme Court** can declare presidential actions unconstitutional.

- **The Supreme Court** can declare congressional laws unconstitutional.

- **The president** nominates federal judges.
- The president can refuse to enforce the Court's decisions.
- The president grants pardons.

THE JUDICIARY

- **Congress** can rewrite legislation to circumvent the Court's decisions.
- The Senate confirms federal judges.
- Congress determines the number of judges.

- **The president** proposes laws that are introduced by supportive legislators and can veto congressional legislation.
- The president makes treaties, executive agreements, and executive orders.
- The president can refuse to enforce congressional legislation.
- The president can call special sessions of Congress.

THE PRESIDENCY

- **Congress** makes legislation and can override a presidential veto of its legislation.
- Congress can impeach and remove a president.
- The Senate must confirm presidential appointments and consent to treaties negotiated by the president based on a two-thirds concurrence.
- Congress has the power of the purse and provides funds for the president's programs.

THE CONGRESS

The Final Document

On September 17, 1787, the Constitution was approved by thirty-nine delegates. Of the fifty-five who had attended originally, only forty-two remained. Three delegates refused to sign the Constitution. Others disapproved of at least parts of it but signed anyway to begin the **ratification** debate.

The Constitution that was to be ratified established the following fundamental principles:

■ Popular sovereignty, or control by the people.
■ A republican government in which the people choose representatives to make decisions for them.

Ratification
Formal approval.

- Limited government with written laws, in contrast to the powerful British government against which the colonists had rebelled.
- Separation of powers, with checks and balances among branches to prevent any one branch from gaining too much power.
- A federal system that allows for states' rights, because the states feared too much centralized control.

THE DIFFICULT ROAD TO RATIFICATION

LO4: Summarize the arguments in favor of and the arguments against adopting the Constitution, and explain why the Bill of Rights was adopted.

The founders knew that ratification of the Constitution was far from certain. Indeed, because it was almost guaranteed that many state legislatures would not ratify it, the delegates agreed that each state should hold a special convention. Elected delegates to these conventions would discuss and vote on the Constitution. Further departing from the Articles of Confederation, the delegates agreed that as soon as nine states (rather than all thirteen) approved the Constitution, it would take effect, and Congress could begin to organize the new government.

The Federalists Push for Ratification

The two opposing forces in the battle over ratification were the Federalists and the Anti-Federalists. The **Federalists** favored a strong central government and the new Constitution. Their opponents, the **Anti-Federalists,** wanted to prevent the Constitution as drafted from being ratified.[11]

The *Federalist Papers.* In New York, opponents of the Constitution were quick to attack it. Alexander Hamilton answered their attacks under a pseudonym in newspaper columns and secured two collaborators—John Jay and James Madison. In a very short time, those three political figures wrote a series of eighty-five essays in defense of the Constitution and of a republican form of government.

These widely read essays, called the *Federalist Papers,* appeared in New York newspapers from October 1787 to August 1788 and were reprinted in the newspapers of other states. Although we do not know for certain who wrote every one, it is apparent that Hamilton was responsible for about two-thirds of the essays. These included the most important ones interpreting the Constitution, explaining the various powers of the three branches, and presenting a theory of *judicial review*—to be discussed later in this chapter. Madison's *Federalist Paper* No. 10 (see Appendix C), however, is considered a classic in political theory. It deals with the nature of groups—or factions, as he called them. In spite of the rapidity with which the *Federalist Papers* were written, they are considered by many to be perhaps the best example of political theorizing ever produced in the United States.[12]

The Anti-Federalist Response. Many of the Anti-Federalists' attacks on the Constitution were also brilliant. The Anti-Federalists claimed that the Constitution was written by aristocrats and would lead to aristocratic tyranny. More important, the Anti-Federalists believed

Federalist
An individual who was in favor of the adoption of the U.S. Constitution and the creation of a federal union with a strong central government.

Anti-Federalist
An individual who opposed the ratification of the new Constitution in 1787. The Anti-Federalists were opposed to a strong central government.

---

11. There is some irony here. At the Constitutional Convention, those opposed to a strong central government pushed for a federal system because such a system would allow the states to retain some of their sovereign rights. The label *Anti-Federalists* thus contradicted their essential views.
12. Some scholars believe that the *Federalist Papers* played only a minor role in securing ratification of the Constitution. Even if this is true, these writings still have lasting value as an authoritative explanation of the Constitution.

that the Constitution would create an overbearing and overburdening central government hostile to personal liberty. (The Constitution said nothing about freedom of the press, freedom of religion, or any other individual liberty.) They wanted to include a list of guaranteed liberties, or a bill of rights. Finally, the Anti-Federalists decried the weakened power of the states.[13]

The Anti-Federalists cannot be dismissed as unpatriotic extremists. They included such patriots as Patrick Henry and Samuel Adams. They were arguing what had been the most prevalent view in that era. This view derived from the French political philosopher Baron de Montesquieu (1689–1755), an influential political theorist. Montesquieu believed that a republic was possible only in a relatively small society governed

Patrick Henry (1736–1799) addresses the Virginia Assembly. Why were Anti-Federalists such as Henry opposed to the Constitution? (Kean Collection/Getty Images)

by direct democracy or by a large legislature with small districts. The Madisonian view favoring a large republic, particularly as expressed in *Federalist Papers* No. 10 and No. 51 (see Appendix C), was actually an exceptional view in those years. Indeed, some researchers believe it was mainly the bitter experiences with the Articles of Confederation, rather than Madison's arguments, that persuaded the state conventions to ratify the Constitution.

The March to the Finish

The struggle for ratification continued. Strong majorities were procured in Connecticut, Delaware, Georgia, New Jersey, and Pennsylvania. After a bitter struggle in Massachusetts, that state ratified the Constitution by a narrow margin on February 6, 1788. By the spring, Maryland and South Carolina had ratified by sizable majorities. Then on June 21 of that year, New Hampshire became the ninth state to ratify the Constitution. Although the Constitution was formally in effect, this meant little without Virginia and New York. Virginia ratified it a few days later, but New York did not join in for another month.

The Bill of Rights

The U.S. Constitution would not have been ratified in several important states if the Federalists had not assured the states that amendments to the Constitution would be passed to protect individual liberties against incursions by the national government. Many

---

13. Herbert J. Storing edited seven volumes of Anti-Federalist writings and released them in 1981 as *The Complete Anti-Federalist*. Political science professor Murray Dry has prepared a more manageable, one-volume version of this collection: Herbert J. Storing, ed., *The Anti-Federalist: An Abridgment of The Complete Anti-Federalist* (Chicago: University of Chicago Press, 2006).

of the recommendations of the state ratifying conventions included specific rights that were considered later by James Madison as he labored to draft what became the Bill of Rights.

Madison had to cull through more than two hundred state recommendations. It was no small task, and in retrospect he chose remarkably well. One of the rights appropriate for constitutional protection that he left out was equal protection under the laws—but that was not commonly regarded as a basic right at that time. Not until 1868 was the Constitution amended to guarantee that no state shall deny equal protection to any person.

On December 15, 1791, the national Bill of Rights was adopted when Virginia agreed to ratify the ten amendments. On ratification, the Bill of Rights became part of the U.S. Constitution. The basic structure of American government had already been established. Now the fundamental rights and liberties of individuals were protected, at least in theory, at the national level. The proposed amendment that Madison characterized as "the most valuable amendment in the whole lot"—which would have prohibited the states from infringing on the freedoms of conscience, press, and jury trial—had been eliminated by the Senate. Thus, the Bill of Rights as adopted did not limit state power, and individual citizens had to rely on the guarantees contained in a particular state constitution or state bill of rights. The country had to wait until the violence of the Civil War before significant limitations on state power in the form of the Fourteenth Amendment became part of the national Constitution.

Social Media in Politics

The American Civil Liberties Union (ACLU) is the nation's leading civil liberties advocacy group. If you friend "ACLU" on Facebook, you'll get a regular stream of updates on efforts to protect the rights guaranteed by the Constitution.

ALTERING THE CONSTITUTION

LO5: Describe the process of amending the Constitution and the informal ways in which constitutional interpretation has changed over time.

As amended, the U.S. Constitution consists of about seven thousand words. It is shorter than any state constitution except that of Vermont. The federal Constitution is short because the founders intended it to be only a framework for the new government, to be interpreted by succeeding generations. One of the reasons it has remained short is that the formal amending procedure does not allow for changes to be made easily. Article V of the Constitution outlines the ways in which amendments may be proposed and ratified.

The Formal Amendment Process

Two formal methods of proposing an amendment to the Constitution are available: (1) a two-thirds vote in each chamber of Congress or (2) a national convention that is called by Congress at the request of two-thirds of the state legislatures. This second method has never been used.

Ratification can occur by one of two methods: (1) by a positive vote in three-fourths of the legislatures of the various states or (2) by special conventions called in the states and a positive vote in three-fourths of them. The second method has been used only once, to repeal Prohibition (the ban on the production and sale of alcoholic beverages). That situation was exceptional—prohibitionist forces were in control of the legislatures in many states where a majority of the population actually supported repeal.

Congress has considered more than eleven thousand amendments to the Constitution. Only thirty-three amendments have been submitted to the states after having been approved by the required two-thirds vote in each chamber of Congress, and only twenty-seven have been ratified—see Table 2–2 on the facing page. It should be clear that the amendment process is very difficult. Because of competing social and economic interests, the requirement that two-thirds of both the House and the Senate approve the amendments is hard to achieve.

TABLE 2-2: Amendments to the Constitution

Amendment	Subject	Year Adopted	Time Required for Ratification
1st–10th	The Bill of Rights	1791	2 years, 2 months, 20 days
11th	Immunity of states from certain suits	1795	11 months, 3 days
12th	Changes in electoral college procedure	1804	6 months, 3 days
13th	Prohibition of slavery	1865	10 months, 3 days
14th	Citizenship, due process, and equal protection	1868	2 years, 26 days
15th	No denial of vote because of race, color, or previous condition of servitude	1870	11 months, 8 days
16th	Power of Congress to tax income	1913	3 years, 6 months, 22 days
17th	Direct election of U.S. senators	1913	10 months, 26 days
18th	National (liquor) prohibition	1919	1 year, 29 days
19th	Women's right to vote	1920	1 year, 2 months, 14 days
20th	Change of dates for congressional and presidential terms	1933	10 months, 21 days
21st	Repeal of the Eighteenth Amendment	1933	9 months, 15 days
22d	Limit on presidential tenure	1951	3 years, 11 months, 3 days
23d	District of Columbia electoral vote	1961	9 months, 13 days
24th	Prohibition of tax payment as a qualification to vote in federal elections	1964	1 year, 4 months, 9 days
25th	Procedures for determining presidential disability and presidential succession and for filling a vice-presidential vacancy	1967	1 year, 7 months, 4 days
26th	Prohibition of setting the minimum voting age above eighteen in any election	1971	3 months, 7 days
27th	Prohibition of Congress's voting itself a raise or cut in pay that takes effect before the next election	1992	203 years

After an amendment has been approved by Congress, the process becomes even more arduous. Three-fourths of the state legislatures must approve the amendment. Only those amendments that have wide popular support across parties and in all regions of the country are likely to be approved.

Why was the amendment process made so difficult? The framers feared that a simple amendment process could lead to a tyranny of the majority, which could pass amendments to oppress disfavored individuals and groups. The cumbersome amendment process does not seem to stem the number of amendments that are proposed in Congress, however, particularly in recent years.

Informal Methods of Constitutional Change

Looking at the sparse number of formal constitutional amendments gives us an incomplete view of constitutional change. The brevity and ambiguity of the original document have permitted great alterations in the Constitution by way of varying interpretations over time. As the United States grew, both in population and in territory, new social and political realities emerged. Congress, presidents, and the courts found it necessary to interpret the Constitution's provisions in light of these new realities. The Constitution has proved to be a remarkably flexible document, adapting itself time and again to new events and concerns.

Congressional Legislation. The Constitution gives Congress broad powers to carry out its duties as the nation's legislative body. For example, Article I, Section 8, of the

Judicial Review
The power of the Supreme Court or any court to examine and possibly declare unconstitutional federal or state laws and other acts of government.

Constitution gives Congress the power to regulate foreign and interstate commerce. Although there is no clear definition of foreign commerce or interstate commerce in the Constitution, Congress has cited the *commerce clause* as the basis for passing thousands of laws. Similarly, Article III, Section 1, states that the national judiciary shall consist of one supreme court and "such inferior courts, as Congress may from time to time ordain and establish." Through a series of acts, Congress has used this broad provision to establish the federal court system of today.

Presidential Actions. Even though the Constitution does not expressly authorize the president to propose bills or even budgets to Congress,[14] presidents since the time of Woodrow Wilson (1913–1921) have proposed hundreds of bills to Congress each year that are introduced by the president's supporters in Congress. Presidents have also relied on their Article II authority as commander in chief of the nation's armed forces to send American troops abroad into combat, although the Constitution provides that Congress has the power to declare war. Presidents have also conducted foreign affairs by the use of *executive agreements,* which are legally binding understandings reached between the president and a foreign head of state. The Constitution does not mention such agreements.

Judicial Review. Another way that the Constitution adapts to new developments is through judicial review. **Judicial review** refers to the power of U.S. courts to examine the constitutionality of actions undertaken by the legislative and executive branches of government. A state court, for example, may rule that a statute enacted by the state legislature violates the state constitution. Federal courts (and ultimately, the United States Supreme Court) may rule unconstitutional not only acts of Congress and decisions of the national executive branch, but also state statutes, state executive actions, and even provisions of state constitutions.

The Constitution does not specifically mention the power of judicial review. In 1803, the Supreme Court claimed this power for itself in *Marbury v. Madison,*[15] in which the Court ruled that a particular provision of an act of Congress was unconstitutional.

Through the process of judicial review, the Supreme Court adapts the Constitution to modern situations. Electronic technology, for example, did not exist when the Constitution was ratified. Nonetheless, the Supreme Court has used the Fourth Amendment guarantees against unreasonable searches and seizures to place limits on the use of wiretapping and other electronic eavesdropping methods by government officials. Additionally, the Court has changed its interpretation of the Constitution in accordance with changing values. It ruled in 1896 that "separate-but-equal" public facilities for African Americans were constitutional. By 1954, however, the times had changed, and the Supreme Court reversed that decision.[16] Woodrow Wilson summarized the Supreme Court's work when he described it as "a constitutional convention in continuous session." Basically, the law is what the Supreme Court says it is at any point in time.

Interpretation, Custom, and Usage. The Constitution has also been changed through interpretation by both Congress and the president. Originally, the president had a staff

---

14. Note, though, that the Constitution, in Article II, Section 3, does state that the president "shall from time to time . . . recommend to [Congress's] consideration such measures as he shall judge necessary and expedient." Some scholars interpret this phrase to mean that the president has the constitutional authority to propose bills and budgets to Congress for consideration.
15. 5 U.S. 137 (1803).
16. *Brown v. Board of Education of Topeka,* 347 U.S. 483 (1954).

The Supreme Court justices as of 2013. On the top, left to right, are Sonia Sotomayor, Stephen Breyer, Samuel Alito Jr., and Elena Kagan. On the bottom, left to right, are Clarence Thomas, Antonin Scalia, Chief Justice John Roberts, Anthony M. Kennedy, and Ruth Bader Ginsburg. How does the Court exercise judicial review? (Tim Sloan/AFP/Getty Images)

consisting of personal secretaries and a few others. Four small departments reported to President Washington. Today, because Congress delegates specific tasks to the president and to the executive branch, the national executive has grown to include hundreds of departments, agencies, and organizations that employ about 2.7 million civilians.

Changes in ways of doing political business have also led to reinterpretation of the Constitution. The Constitution does not mention political parties, yet these informal, "extraconstitutional" organizations make the nominations for offices, run the campaigns, organize the members of Congress, and in fact change the election system from time to time. In many ways, the Constitution has been adapted from a document serving the needs of a small, rural republic to one that provides a framework of government for an industrial giant with vast geographic, natural, and human resources.

making a difference
HOW CAN YOU AFFECT THE U.S. CONSTITUTION?

The Constitution is an enduring document that has survived more than two hundred years of turbulent history. It is also an evolving document, however. Twenty-seven amendments have been added to the original Constitution. How can you, as an individual, actively help to rewrite the Constitution?

Why Should You Care? The laws of the nation have a direct impact on your life, and none more so than the Constitution—the supreme law of the land. The most important issues in society are often settled by the Constitution. For example, for the first seventy-five years of the republic, the Constitution implicitly protected the institution of slavery. If the Constitution had never been changed through the amendment process, the process of abolishing slavery would have been much different and might have involved revolutionary measures.

Since the passage of the Fourteenth Amendment in 1868, the Constitution has defined who is a citizen and who is entitled to the protections the Constitution provides. Constitutional provisions define our liberties. The First Amendment protects our freedom of speech more thoroughly than do the laws of many other nations. Few other countries have constitutional provisions governing the right to own firearms (the Second Amendment). Disputes involving these rights are among the most fundamental issues we face.

What Can You Do? At the time of this writing, national coalitions of interest groups support or oppose a number of constitutional amendments. One hotly debated proposal would create a constitutional requirement to balance the federal budget. In late 2011, a constitutional amendment to do just that failed in both the U.S. House and the Senate. The measure would have required a three-fifths majority in both chambers of Congress to approve any future deficit spending. If such an amendment sounds like a good idea to you, there are a variety of organizations you might investigate using your favorite search engine, such as Google, Bing, or Yahoo. These organizations include Americans for a Balanced Budget, Americans for a Balanced Budget Amendment, Americans for Prosperity, and the Tea Party Patriots.

A leader of the so-called Coffee Party speaks during a protest in front of the U.S. Supreme Court. The Coffee Party wants the Court to overturn *Citizens United v. Federal Election Commission.* Why does this group object to the Court's decision? (Alex Wong/Getty Images)

Other Americans have different concerns. In 2010, the Supreme Court struck down a wide range of campaign finance laws in *Citizens United v. Federal Election Commission.*[17] One result of this ruling was the "super PACs" that flooded television networks with attack advertisements during the 2012 elections. Often funded by very wealthy individuals, super PACs can spend as much as they want, provided that they do not openly coordinate their activities with a candidate's campaign. A proposed constitutional amendment would overturn the *Citizens United* ruling. If getting the money out of politics is of interest to you, you can examine the activist groups that support this amendment. They include Common Cause, Democracy Is for People, MoveOn.org, and Occupy Wall Street.

---

17. 130 S.Ct. 876 (2010).

key terms

Anti-Federalist 36	Federalist 36	ratification 35	state 28
bicameral legislature 31	Great Compromise 32	representative	supremacy doctrine 32
checks and balances 34	judicial review 40	assembly 22	unicameral
confederation 28	Madisonian model 34	separation of powers 34	legislature 28
electoral college 34	natural rights 26	social contract 27	

chapter summary

1 The first permanent English colonies were established at Jamestown in 1607 and Plymouth in 1620. The Mayflower Compact created the first formal government in New England.

2 In the 1760s, the British began to impose on their increasingly independent-minded colonies a series of taxes and legislative acts. The colonists responded with protests and boycotts of British products. Representatives of the colonies formed the First Continental Congress in 1774. The Second Continental Congress established an army in 1775 to defend colonists against attacks by British soldiers.

3 On July 4, 1776, the Second Continental Congress approved the Declaration of Independence. Perhaps the most revolutionary aspects of the Declaration were its statements that people have natural rights to life, liberty, and the pursuit of happiness; that governments derive their power from the consent of the governed; and that people have a right to overthrow oppressive governments. During the Revolutionary War, the states signed the Articles of Confederation, creating a weak central government with few powers. The Articles proved to be unworkable because the national government had no way to ensure compliance by the states with such measures as securing tax revenues.

4 General dissatisfaction with the Articles of Confederation prompted the call for a convention in Philadelphia in 1787. Delegates focused on creating a constitution for a new form of government. The Virginia Plan, which favored the larger states, and the New Jersey Plan, which favored small ones, did not garner sufficient support. A compromise offered by Connecticut provided for a bicameral legislature and thus resolved the large-state/small-state dispute. The final version of the Constitution provided for the separation of powers, checks and balances, and a federal form of government.

5 Fears of a strong central government prompted the addition of the Bill of Rights to the Constitution. The Bill of Rights, which includes the freedoms of religion, speech, and assembly, was initially applied only to the federal government, but amendments to the Constitution following the Civil War were interpreted to ensure that the Bill of Rights would apply to the states as well.

6 An amendment to the Constitution may be proposed either by a two-thirds vote in each chamber of Congress or by a national convention called by Congress at the request of two-thirds of the state legislatures. Ratification can occur either by the approval of three-fourths of the legislatures of the states or by special conventions called in the states for the purpose of ratifying the amendment and approval by three-fourths of these conventions. Informal methods of constitutional change include reinterpretation through congressional legislation, presidential actions, and judicial review.

test**yourself**

LO1 *Explain how the colonial experience prepared Americans for independence, the restrictions that Britain placed on the colonies, and the American response to those restrictions.*

When the First Continental Congress convened in 1774, the British government:

    a. welcomed the advice offered by the colonists.

    b. agreed to allow the colonies to form a separate government.

    c. treated the meeting as an act of rebellion.

LO2 *Describe the significance of the Declaration of Independence and the Articles of Confederation, as well as the weaknesses of the Articles.*

A major defect in the Articles of Confederation was:

    a. the lack of power to raise funds for military forces.

    b. the lack of treaty-making power.

    c. the inability to easily communicate with citizens.

LO3 *Discuss the most important compromises reached at the Constitutional Convention and the basic structure of the resulting government.*

Which of the following fundamental principles was not established by the Constitution of 1787?

    a. popular sovereignty, or control by the people.

    b. limited government with written laws.

    c. a system in which the central government had complete power over the states.

LO4 *Summarize the arguments in favor of and the arguments against adopting the Constitution, and explain why the Bill of Rights was adopted.*

The major drafter of the Bill of Rights was:

    a. Washington.

    b. Jefferson.

    c. Madison.

LO5 *Describe the process of amending the Constitution and the informal ways in which constitutional interpretation has changed over time.*

The reason the U.S. Constitution has so few amendments is that:

    a. the formal amendment process is exceedingly difficult.

    b. the Constitution was written so well that it hasn't needed to be amended.

    c. Congress doesn't have time to consider new amendments.

Essay Question:

Consider what might have happened if Georgia and the Carolinas had stayed out of the Union because of a desire to protect slavery. What would subsequent American history have been like? Would the eventual freedom of the slaves have been delayed—or advanced?

Answers to multiple-choice questions: 1. c, 2. a, 3. c, 4. c, 5. a.

CourseMate

Access CourseMate at **www.cengagebrain.com** for additional study tools: practice quizzes, key term flashcards and crossword puzzles, audio chapter summaries, simulations, animated learning modules, interactive timelines, videos, and American Government NewsWatch.

A cultivator in Denver, Colorado, harvests marijuana plants. In 2012, citizens of Colorado and Washington voted to legalize and tax the recreational use of marijuana, but the drug remains illegal under federal law. What do you think will happen? (Kathryn Scott Osler/ The *Denver Post* via Getty Images)

Federalism

3

LEARNING OUTCOMES

The five **Learning Outcomes (LOs)** below are designed to help improve your understanding of this chapter. After reading this chapter, you should be able to:

■ **LO1** Explain some of the benefits of the federal system for the United States.

■ **LO2** Describe how the various provisions of the U.S. Constitution provide a framework for federalism.

■ **LO3** Discuss how, in the early years of the republic, the United States Supreme Court confirmed the authority of the national government, and how that authority was ratified by the Civil War.

■ **LO4** Define the terms *dual federalism, cooperative federalism, categorical grants, block grants,* and *fiscal federalism.*

■ **LO5** Detail recent Supreme Court rulings that affect the distribution of power between the national government and the states.

Check your understanding of the material with the Test Yourself section at the end of the chapter.

In the United States, rights and powers are reserved to the

states by the Tenth Amendment. It may appear to some that since Barack Obama became president in 2009, the federal government, sometimes called the national or central government, has predominated. Nevertheless, that might be an exaggerated perception, for there are 89,528 separate governmental units in this nation.

Visitors from France or Spain are often awestruck by the complexity of our system of government. Consider that a criminal action can be defined by state law, by national law, or by both. Thus, a criminal suspect can be prosecuted in the state court system or in the federal court system (or both). Often, economic regulation covering exactly the same issues exists at the local level, the state level, and the national level—generating

45

Unitary System
A centralized governmental system in which ultimate governmental authority rests in the hands of the national, or central, government.

Confederal System
A system consisting of a league of independent states, in which the central government created by the league has only limited powers over the states.

multiple forms to be completed, multiple procedures to be followed, and multiple laws to be obeyed. Many programs are funded by the national government but administered by state and local governments.

Relations between central governments and local units can be structured in various ways. *Federalism* is one of these ways. Understanding federalism and how it differs from other forms of government is important in understanding the American political system. Indeed, many political issues today would not arise if we did not have a federal form of government in which governmental authority is divided between the central government and various subunits.

FEDERALISM AND ITS ALTERNATIVES

There are almost two hundred independent nations in the world today. Each of these nations has its own system of government. Generally, though, we can describe how nations structure relations between central governments and local units in terms of three models: (1) the unitary system, (2) the confederal system, and (3) the federal system. The most popular, both historically and today, is the unitary system.

A Unitary System

A **unitary system** of government is the easiest to define. Unitary systems place ultimate governmental authority in the hands of the national, or central, government. Consider a typical unitary system—France. The regions, departments, communes, and municipalities in France have elected and appointed officials.

So far, the French system appears to be very similar to the U.S. system, but the similarity is only superficial. Under the unitary French system, the decisions of the lower levels of government can be overruled by the national government. The national government also can cut off the funding for many local government activities. Moreover, in a unitary system such as that in France, all questions of education, police, the use of land, and welfare are handled by the national government. Britain, Egypt, Ghana, Israel, Japan, the Philippines, and Sweden—in fact, a majority of all nations—have unitary systems of government.[1]

A Confederal System

You were introduced to the elements of a **confederal system** of government in Chapter 2, when we examined the Articles of Confederation. A confederation is the opposite of a unitary governing system. It is a league of independent states in which a central government or administration handles only those matters of common concern expressly delegated to it by the member states. The central government has no ability to make laws directly applicable to member states unless the members explicitly support such laws. The United States under the Articles of Confederation was a confederal system.

Few, if any, confederations of this kind exist. One possible exception is the European Union (EU), a league of countries that has developed a large body of Europe-wide laws that all members must observe. Many members even share a common currency, the euro. Not all members of the EU use the euro, however, which demonstrates the limits of a confederal system.

---

1. Recent legislation has altered somewhat the unitary character of the French political system. In Britain, the unitary nature of the government has been modified by the creation of the Scottish Parliament.

A Federal System

The federal system lies between the unitary and confederal forms of government. As mentioned in Chapter 2, in a *federal system,* authority is divided, usually by a written constitution, between a central government and regional, or subdivisional, governments (often called *constituent governments*). The central government and the constituent governments both act directly on the people through laws and through the actions of elected and appointed governmental officials. Within each government's sphere of authority, each is supreme, in theory. Thus, a federal system differs sharply from a unitary one, in which the central government is supreme and the constituent governments derive their authority from it. In addition to the United States, Australia, Brazil, Canada, Germany, India, and Mexico are examples of nations with federal systems. See Figure 3–1 below for a comparison of the three systems.

LO1: Explain some of the benefits of the federal system for the United States.

Why Federalism?

Why did the United States develop in a federal direction? Here, we look at that question, as well as at some of the arguments for and against a federal form of government. As you saw in Chapter 2, the historical basis of our federal system was laid down in Philadelphia at the Constitutional Convention, where advocates of a strong national government opposed states' rights advocates. This conflict continued through to the ratifying conventions in the several states. The resulting federal system was a compromise. The supporters of the new Constitution were political pragmatists—they realized that without a federal arrangement, there would be no ratification of the new Constitution. The appeal of federalism was that it retained state traditions and local power while establishing a strong national government capable of handling common problems.

Even if the founders had agreed on the desirability of a unitary system, size and regional isolation would have made such a system difficult operationally. At the time of the Constitutional Convention, the thirteen states taken together were much larger geographically than England or France. Slow travel and communication, combined with

FIGURE 3–1: The Flow of Power in Three Systems of Government

In a unitary system, power flows from the central government to the local and state governments. In a confederal system, power flows in the opposite direction—from the state governments to the central government. In a federal system, the flow of power, in principle, goes both ways.

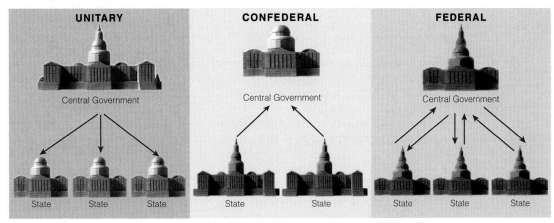

A jackhammer operator from New York's Department of Environmental Protection removes asphalt from a street to fix a water pipe damaged during Hurricane Sandy. In January 2013, Congress voted a $51 billion Hurricane Sandy aid package to be distributed to affected states. Why is disaster relief funding a national responsibility? (Robert Nickelsberg/Getty Images)

geographic spread, contributed to the isolation of many regions within the states. It could take several weeks for all of the states to be informed about a particular political decision.

Other Arguments for Federalism

Even with modern transportation and communications systems, the large area or population of some nations makes it impractical to locate all political authority in one place. Federalism brings government closer to the people. It allows more direct access to, and influence on, government agencies and policies, rather than leaving the population restive and dissatisfied with a remote, faceless, all-powerful central authority.

Benefits for the United States. In the United States, federalism historically has yielded many benefits. State governments have long been a training ground for future national leaders. Many presidents made their political mark as state governors. The states themselves have been testing grounds for new government initiatives. As United States Supreme Court justice Louis Brandeis once observed:

It is one of the happy incidents of the federal system that a single courageous state may, if its citizens choose, serve as a laboratory and try novel social and economic experiments without risk to the rest of the country.[2]

Examples of programs pioneered at the state level include unemployment compensation, which began in Wisconsin, and air-pollution control, which was initiated in California. Today, states are experimenting with policies ranging from educational reforms to homeland security strategies. Since the passage of the 1996 welfare reform legislation—which gave more control over welfare programs to state governments—states have also experimented with different methods of delivering welfare assistance.

Allowance for Many Political Subcultures. The American way of life always has been characterized by a number of political subcultures, which divide along the lines of race and ethnic origin, region, wealth, education, and, more recently, degree of religious commitment and sexual preference. The existence of diverse political subcultures would appear to be incompatible with a political authority concentrated solely in a central government. Had the United States developed into a unitary system, various political subcultures certainly would have been less able to influence government behavior than they have been, and continue to be, in our federal system.

WWW
Helpful Web Sites
This book contains footnotes for court cases, such as *New State Ice Co. v. Liebmann*, 285 U.S. 262 (1932). The mysterious "285 U.S. 262" gives the location of this case in an official publication. Usually, however, you can enter just the name of the case in a search engine to find the ruling and articles that describe it.

2. *New State Ice Co. v. Liebmann,* 285 U.S. 262 (1932).

Arguments against Federalism

Not everyone thinks federalism is such a good idea. Some see it as a way for powerful state and local interests to block progress and impede national plans. Smaller political units are more likely to be dominated by a single political group. (This was essentially the argument that James Madison put forth in *Federalist Paper* No. 10, which you can read in Appendix C of this text.) In fact, the dominant groups in some cities and states have resisted implementing equal rights for minority groups. Some argue, however, that the dominant factions in some states have been more progressive than the national government in many areas, such as environmental protection.

Critics also feel that there is too much inequity among the states, so they call for increased federal oversight of various programs. Others, however, see dangers in the expansion of national powers at the expense of the states. President Ronald Reagan (1981–1989) said, "The Founding Fathers saw the federalist system as constructed something like a masonry wall. The States are the bricks, the national government is the mortar. . . . Unfortunately, over the years, many people have increasingly come to believe that Washington is the whole wall."[3]

Enumerated Powers
Powers specifically granted to the national government by the Constitution. The first seventeen clauses of Article I, Section 8, specify most of the enumerated, or expressed, powers of the national government.

Elastic Clause, or Necessary and Proper Clause
The clause in Article I, Section 8, that grants Congress the power to do whatever is necessary to execute its specifically delegated powers.

THE CONSTITUTIONAL BASIS FOR AMERICAN FEDERALISM

The term *federal system* cannot be found in the U.S. Constitution. Nor is it possible to find a systematic division of governmental authority between the national and state governments in that document. Rather, the Constitution sets out different types of powers. These powers can be classified as (1) the powers of the national government, (2) the powers of the states, and (3) prohibited powers. The Constitution also makes it clear that if a state or local law conflicts with a national law, the national law will prevail.

LO2: Describe how the various provisions of the U.S. Constitution provide a framework for federalism.

Powers of the National Government

The powers delegated to the national government include both expressed and implied powers, as well as the special category of inherent powers. Most of the powers expressly delegated to the national government are found in the first seventeen clauses of Article I, Section 8, of the Constitution. These **enumerated powers,** also called *expressed powers,* include coining money, setting standards for weights and measures, making uniform naturalization laws, admitting new states, establishing post offices and post roads, and declaring war. Another important enumerated power is the power to regulate commerce among the states—a topic we deal with later in this chapter.

The Necessary and Proper Clause. The implied powers of the national government are also based on Article I, Section 8, which states that the Congress shall have the power

> [t]o make all Laws which shall be necessary and proper for carrying into Execution the foregoing Powers, and all other Powers vested by this Constitution in the Government of the United States, or in any Department or Officer thereof.

This clause is sometimes called the **elastic clause,** or the **necessary and proper clause,** because it provides flexibility to our constitutional system. It gives Congress the power to

---

3. As quoted in Edward Millican, *One United People: The Federalist Papers and the National Idea* (Lexington: The University Press of Kentucky, 1990).

While the United States as a whole uses a federal system of government, each individual state has a unitary system. Here, the governor of Michigan announces a state takeover of the city of Detroit in March 2013. What gives a state government the power to make such a move? (Jeff Kowalsky/Bloomberg via Getty Images)

do whatever is necessary to execute its specifically delegated powers. The clause was first used in the Supreme Court decision of *McCulloch v. Maryland*[4] (discussed later in this chapter) to develop the concept of implied powers. Through this concept, the national government has succeeded in strengthening the scope of its authority to meet the many problems that the framers of the Constitution did not, and could not, anticipate.

Inherent Powers. A special category of national powers that is not implied by the necessary and proper clause consists of what have been labeled the *inherent powers* of the national government. These powers derive from the fact that the United States is a sovereign power among nations, and so its national government must be the only government that deals with other nations. Under international law, it is assumed that all nation-states, regardless of their size or power, have an inherent right to ensure their own survival. To do this, each nation must have the ability to act in its own interest among and with the community of nations—by, for instance, making treaties, waging war, seeking trade, and acquiring territory.

Note that no specific clause in the Constitution says anything about the acquisition of additional land. Nonetheless, the federal government's inherent powers allowed it to make the Louisiana Purchase in 1803 and then go on to acquire Florida, Texas, Oregon, Alaska, Hawaii, and other lands. The United States grew from a mere thirteen states to fifty states, plus several territories.

Powers of the State Governments

The Tenth Amendment states that the powers not delegated to the United States by the Constitution, nor prohibited by it to the states, are reserved to the states, or to the people. These are the *reserved powers* that the national government cannot deny to the states. Because these powers are not expressly listed, there is sometimes a question as to whether a certain power is delegated to the national government or reserved to the states.

State powers have been held to include each state's right to regulate commerce within its borders and to provide for a state militia. States also have the reserved power to make laws on all matters not prohibited to the states by the U.S. Constitution or state constitutions and not expressly, or by implication, delegated to the national government. Furthermore, the states have **police power**—the authority to legislate for the protection of the health, morals, safety, and welfare of the people. Their police power enables states to pass laws governing such activities as crimes, marriage, contracts, education, intrastate transportation, and land use.

Police Power
The authority to legislate for the protection of the health, morals, safety, and welfare of the people. In the United States, most police power is reserved to the states.

Given that marriage law has traditionally been left to the states, should the national government always defer to state definitions of marriage—even when some of these marriages are between people of the same sex? We examine that question in the *At Issue* feature on the following page.

The ambiguity of the Tenth Amendment has allowed the reserved powers of the states to be defined differently at different times in our history. When there is widespread

4. 17 U.S. 316 (1819).

support for increased regulation by the national government, the Tenth Amendment tends to recede into the background. When the tide turns the other way (in favor of states' rights), the Tenth Amendment is resurrected to justify arguments supporting the states.

Prohibited Powers

The Constitution prohibits or denies a number of powers to the national government. For example, the national government has expressly been denied the power to impose taxes on goods sold to other countries (exports). Moreover, any power not granted expressly or implicitly to the federal government by the Constitution is prohibited to it. For example, many legal experts believe that the national government could not create a national divorce law system without a constitutional amendment. The states are also denied certain powers. For example, no state is allowed to enter into a treaty on its own with another country.

A same-sex couple participates in a sit-in at the county clerk's office in San Francisco in February 2013. The couple is demanding that the clerk issue them a marriage license. What is the current state of the law on same-sex marriage in California? (Justin Sullivan/Getty Images)

Concurrent Powers

In certain areas, the states share **concurrent powers** with the national government. Most concurrent powers are not specifically listed in the Constitution; they are only implied. An example of a concurrent power is the power to tax. The types of taxation are divided between the levels of government. For example, states may not levy a tariff (a set of taxes on imported goods). Only the national government may do this. Neither government may tax the facilities of the other. If the state governments did not have the power to tax, they would not be able to function other than on a ceremonial basis.

Additional concurrent powers include the power to borrow funds, to establish courts, and to charter banks and corporations. To a limited extent, the national government exercises police power, and to the extent that it does, police power is also a concurrent power. Concurrent powers exercised by the states are normally limited to the geographic area of each state and to those functions not granted by the Constitution exclusively to the national government. Examples of functions exclusive to the national government are the coinage of money and the negotiation of treaties.

The Supremacy Clause

The supremacy of the national constitution over subnational laws and actions is established in the **supremacy clause** of the Constitution. The supremacy clause (Article VI, Clause 2) states the following:

> *This Constitution, and the Laws of the United States which shall be made in Pursuance thereof; and all Treaties made . . . under the Authority of the United States, shall be the supreme Law of the Land; and the Judges in every State shall be bound thereby, any Thing in the Constitution or Laws of any State to the Contrary notwithstanding.*

In other words, states cannot use their reserved or concurrent powers to thwart national policies. All national and state officers, including judges, must be bound by oath to

Concurrent Powers
Powers held jointly by the national and state governments.

Supremacy Clause
The constitutional provision that makes the Constitution and federal laws superior to all conflicting state and local laws.

at issue

SHOULD THE FEDERAL GOVERNMENT RECOGNIZE SAME-SEX MARRIAGES PERFORMED BY THE STATES?

In November 2003, the Massachusetts Supreme Judicial Court ruled that same-sex couples have a right to civil marriage under the state constitution. The California Supreme Court legalized same-sex marriages in May 2008, but California voters overturned the ruling in November of that year by amending the state constitution. Still, as of January 2013, same-sex marriage was legal in eight states and the District of Columbia.

The U.S. Constitution requires that each state give full faith and credit to every other state's public acts. If a man and woman are married under the laws of Nevada, the other forty-nine states must recognize that marriage. But what if one state recognizes same-sex marriages? Does that mean that all other states must recognize such marriages?

In 1996, Congress attempted to prevent such a result through the Defense of Marriage Act, which allows state governments to ignore same-sex marriages performed in other states. It is conceivable that someday in the future, the United States Supreme Court could rule that the Constitution requires all states to recognize same-sex marriages performed in other states. In June 2013, by refusing to decide a case, the Court in effect upheld gay marriage in California, but that refusal had no effect on other states.[a]

Same-sex marriage also raises a second important issue: Should the federal government have to accept all state-defined marriages? If so, same-sex couples would be entitled to substantial federal benefits.

THE FEDERAL GOVERNMENT SHOULD TREAT ALL STATES THE SAME

Should the national government be required to recognize same-sex marriages performed by the states? In June 2013, the Court found that the federal government was in fact required to recognize such marriages.[b] Many opponents of same-sex marriage were appalled by this ruling.

Opponents of same-sex marriage contend that marriage between a man and a woman is the only true basis for creating and defining a family. Major world religions agree in rejecting same-sex marriage. True, federal recognition of same-sex marriages in states such as California and New York won't force Alabama or Utah to recognize these unions. But the people of conservative states will still be forced to subsidize these marriages. When same-sex couples are allowed to pay less income tax, citizens of conservative states will have to help make up the difference. When same-sex partners die, all taxpayers will have to contribute to the resulting Social Security survivors benefits. This is not right.

STATES SHOULD BE ABLE TO DECIDE WHO GETS MARRIAGE BENEFITS

In recent public opinion polls, a majority of Americans now favor same-sex marriage. Why should a couple be denied the many benefits of marriage just because of sexual orientation? Same-sex marriages do not interfere with traditional unions in any way—indeed, gay and lesbian couples strengthen the institution of marriage by their attachment to it. Banning same-sex marriage is unfair discrimination against a minority group.

The argument that citizens of conservative states should not be required to fund benefits for same-sex couples does not hold water. We do not let pacifists avoid paying taxes that support the military. Further, almost all of the states that have legalized same-sex marriages are prosperous ones that pay more into the federal Treasury than they receive in return. Conservative states are more likely to be the net beneficiaries of federal spending. Citizens of these states have no grounds for complaint.

FOR CRITICAL ANALYSIS

If same-sex marriage became common, what impact would this have on American culture generally?

a. *Hollingsworth v. Perry,* 570 U.S. ___ (2013).
b. *United States v. Windsor,* 570 U.S. ___ (2013).

support the Constitution. Hence, any legitimate exercise of national governmental power supersedes any conflicting state action. Of course, deciding whether a conflict actually exists is a judicial matter, as you will soon learn when we discuss the case of *McCulloch v. Maryland.*

The National Guard can serve as an example of how federal power supersedes that of the states. Normally, the National Guard functions as a state militia under the command of the governor. It is frequently called out to assist with recovery efforts after natural disasters such as hurricanes, floods, and earthquakes. The president can assume command of any National Guard unit at any time, however. Presidents George W. Bush and Barack Obama repeatedly "federalized" such units for deployment in Afghanistan and Iraq. In the conflicts in these countries, National Guard members and reservists made up a larger percentage of the forces on combat duty than during any previous war in U.S. history.

National government legislation in a concurrent area is said to preempt (take precedence over) conflicting state or local laws or regulations in that area. One of the ways in which the national government has extended its powers, particularly since 1900, is through the preemption of state and local laws by national legislation. In the first decade of the twentieth century, fewer than twenty national laws preempted laws and regulations issued by state and local governments. By the beginning of the twenty-first century, the number had grown into the hundreds.

Interstate Relations

So far, we have examined only the relationship between central and state governmental units. The states, however, have constant commercial, social, and other dealings among themselves. The national Constitution imposes certain "rules of the road" on interstate relations. These rules have had the effect of preventing any one state from setting itself apart from the other states. The three most important clauses governing interstate relations in the Constitution, all taken from the Articles of Confederation, require each state to do the following:

- Give full faith and credit to every other state's public acts, records, and judicial proceedings (Article IV, Section 1).
- Extend to every other state's citizens the privileges and immunities of its own citizens (Article IV, Section 2).
- Agree to return persons who are fleeing from justice in another state back to their home state when requested to do so (Article IV, Section 2).

States may also enter into agreements with each other, called *interstate compacts,* so long as the compacts do not increase the power of the contracting states relative to other states or to the federal government. An example is the Port Authority of New York and New Jersey, established by an agreement between those states in 1921.

DEFINING CONSTITUTIONAL POWERS—THE EARLY YEARS

Although political bodies at all levels of government play important roles in the process of settling disputes over the nature of our federal system, normally it is the United States Supreme Court that casts the final vote. As might be expected, the character of the referee will have an impact on the ultimate outcome of any dispute. From 1801 to 1835, the Supreme Court was headed by Chief Justice John Marshall, a Federalist who advocated

LO3: Discuss how, in the early years of the republic, the United States Supreme Court confirmed the authority of the national government, and how that authority was ratified by the Civil War.

a strong central government. We look here at two cases decided by the Marshall Court: *McCulloch v. Maryland*[5] and *Gibbons v. Ogden*.[6] Both cases are considered milestones in the movement toward national government supremacy.

McCulloch v. Maryland (1819)

The U.S. Constitution says nothing about establishing a national bank. Nonetheless, at different times Congress chartered two banks—the First and Second Banks of the United States—and provided part of their initial capital. Thus, they were national banks. The government of Maryland imposed a tax on the Second Bank's Baltimore branch in an attempt to put that branch out of business. The branch's cashier, James William McCulloch, refused to pay the Maryland tax. When Maryland took McCulloch to its state court, the state of Maryland won. The national government appealed the case to the Supreme Court.

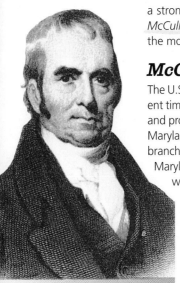

John Marshall
(1755–1835) was the fourth chief justice of the Supreme Court. (Library of Congress)

One of the issues before the Court was whether the national government had the implied power, under the necessary and proper clause, to charter a bank and contribute capital to it. The other important question before the Court was the following: If the bank was constitutional, could a state tax it? In other words, was a state action that conflicted with a national government action invalid under the supremacy clause?

Chief Justice Marshall held that if establishing a national bank aided the national government in the exercise of its designated powers, then the authority to set up such a bank could be implied. Having established this doctrine of implied powers, Marshall then answered the other question before the Court and established the doctrine of national supremacy. Marshall ruled that no state could use its taxing power to tax a part of the national government. If it could, "the declaration that the Constitution . . . shall be the supreme law of the land, is [an] empty and unmeaning [statement]."

Marshall's decision enabled the national government to grow and to meet problems that the Constitution's framers were unable to foresee. Today, practically every expressed power of the national government has been expanded in one way or another by use of the necessary and proper clause.

Gibbons v. Ogden (1824)

One of the most important parts of the Constitution, included in Article I, Section 8, is the **commerce clause,** in which Congress is given the power "[t]o regulate Commerce with foreign Nations, and among the several States, and with the Indian Tribes." The meaning of this clause was at issue in *Gibbons v. Ogden.*

The Background of the Case. Robert Fulton and Robert Livingston secured a monopoly on steam navigation on the waters in New York State from the New York legislature in 1803. They licensed Aaron Ogden to operate steam-powered ferryboats between New York and New Jersey. Thomas Gibbons, who had obtained a license from the U.S. government to operate boats in interstate waters, decided to compete with Ogden, but he did so without New York's permission. Ogden sued Gibbons. New York's state courts prohibited Gibbons from operating in New York waters. Gibbons appealed to the Supreme Court.

Commerce Clause
The section of the Constitution in which Congress is given the power to regulate trade among the states and with foreign countries.

There were actually several issues before the Court in this case. The first issue was how the term *commerce* should be defined. New York's highest court had defined the term narrowly to mean only the shipment of goods, or the interchange of commodities,

5. 17 U.S. 316 (1819).
6. 22 U.S. 1 (1824).

not navigation or the transport of people. The second issue was whether the national government's power to regulate interstate commerce extended to commerce within a state (*intrastate* commerce) or was limited strictly to commerce among the states (*interstate* commerce). The third issue was whether the power to regulate interstate commerce was a concurrent power (as the New York court had concluded) or an exclusive national power.

Marshall's Ruling. Marshall defined *commerce* as *all* commercial interactions—all business dealings—including navigation and the transport of people. Marshall also held that the commerce power of the national government could be exercised in state jurisdictions, even though it could not reach *solely* intrastate commerce. Finally, Marshall emphasized that the power to regulate interstate commerce was an *exclusive* national power. Marshall held that because Gibbons was duly authorized by the national government to navigate in interstate waters, he could not be prohibited from doing so by a state court.

Marshall's expansive interpretation of the commerce clause in *Gibbons v. Ogden* allowed the national government to exercise increasing authority over economic affairs throughout the land. Congress did not immediately exploit this broad grant of power. In the 1930s and subsequent decades, however, the commerce clause became the primary constitutional basis for national government regulation—as you will read later in this chapter.

States' Rights and the Resort to Civil War

The controversy over slavery that led to the Civil War took the form of a dispute over national government supremacy versus the rights of the separate states. Essentially, the Civil War brought to an ultimate and violent climax the ideological debate begun by the Federalist and

John Brown (1800–1859), an advocate of abolishing slavery, led an ill-fated raid on a federal arsenal at Harper's Ferry, Virginia. Brown had hoped to set off a slave uprising. He was executed on charges of treason and murder. Today, we would doubtless call him a terrorist. Why do some people nevertheless consider him a hero? (Photo by Time Life Pictures/Mansell/Time Life Pictures/Getty Images)

Social Media in Politics

The *New York Times* sponsors a series on the United States Civil War that uses contemporary accounts, diaries, and images. To follow it on Twitter, enter "nytcivilwar."

Anti-Federalist parties even before the Constitution was ratified. With the resort to arms, Supreme Court rulings were, for a time, irrelevant.

The Shift Back to States' Rights. As we have seen, while John Marshall was chief justice of the Supreme Court, he did much to increase the power of the national government and to reduce that of the states. During the Jacksonian era (1829–1837), however, a shift back to states' rights began. The question of the regulation of commerce became one of the major issues in federal-state relations. When Congress passed a tariff in 1828, the state of South Carolina unsuccessfully attempted to nullify the tariff (render it void), claiming that in cases of conflict between a state and the national government, the state should have the ultimate authority over its citizens.

During the next three decades, the North and the South became even more sharply divided—especially over the slavery issue. On December 20, 1860, South Carolina formally repealed its ratification of the Constitution and withdrew from the Union. On February 4, 1861, representatives from six southern states met at Montgomery, Alabama, to form a new government called the Confederate States of America.

War and the Growth of the National Government. The ultimate defeat of the South in 1865 permanently ended the idea that a state could successfully claim the right to secede, or withdraw, from the Union. Ironically, the Civil War—brought about in large part because of the South's desire for increased states' rights—resulted in the opposite: an increase in the political power of the national government.

Thousands of new employees were hired to run the Union war effort and to deal with the social and economic problems that had to be handled in the aftermath of the war. A billion-dollar ($1.3 billion, which is about $19 billion in today's dollars) national government budget was passed for the first time in 1865 to cover the increased government expenditures. The first (temporary) income tax was imposed on citizens to help pay for the war.

The Civil War Amendments. The expansion of the national government's authority during the Civil War was also reflected in the passage of the Civil War amendments to the Constitution. Before the war, it was a bedrock constitutional principle that the national government should not interfere with slavery in the states. The Thirteenth Amendment, ratified in 1865, did more than interfere with slavery—it abolished the institution altogether.

The Fourteenth Amendment, ratified in 1868, defined who was a citizen of each state. It sought to guarantee equal rights under state law with this language:

[No] State [shall] deprive any person of life, liberty, or property, without due process of law; nor deny to any person within its jurisdiction the equal protection of the laws.

In time, the courts interpreted these words to mean that the national Bill of Rights applied to state governments, a development that we will examine in Chapter 4. Finally, the Fifteenth Amendment (1870) gave African Americans the right to vote in all elections, including state elections—although a century would pass before that right was enforced in all states.

THE CONTINUING DISPUTE OVER THE DIVISION OF POWER

Although the outcome of the Civil War firmly established the supremacy of the national government and put to rest the idea that a state could secede from the Union, the war by no means ended the debate over the division of powers between the national government and the states.

Dual Federalism

During the decades following the Civil War, the prevailing model of federalism was what political scientists have called **dual federalism**—a doctrine that emphasizes a distinction between national and state spheres of government authority. Various images have been used to describe different configurations of federalism over time. Dual federalism is commonly depicted as a layer cake, because the state governments and the national government are viewed as separate entities, like separate layers of a cake. Under the doctrine of dual federalism, national and state governments are co-equal sovereign powers, and neither level of government should interfere in the other's sphere. The doctrine represented a revival of states' rights following the expansion of national authority during the Civil War. Many people viewed this change as a return to normal—that is, to the conditions that had existed before the war.

The Civil War crisis drastically reduced the influence of the United States Supreme Court, which had supported the institution of slavery in the years leading up to the war. Over time, however, the Court reestablished itself as the legitimate constitutional umpire. For the Court, dual federalism meant that the national government could intervene in state activities through grants and subsidies, but in most cases it was barred from regulating matters that the Court considered to be purely local.

The Court generally limited the exercise of police power to the states. For example, in 1918, the Court ruled that a 1916 national law banning child labor was unconstitutional because it attempted to regulate a local problem.[7] In effect, the Court placed severe limits on the ability of Congress to legislate under the commerce clause of the Constitution.

Dual Federalism
A model of federalism that looks on national and state governments as co-equal sovereign powers. Neither the state government nor the national government should interfere in the other's sphere.

LO4: Define the terms *dual federalism, cooperative federalism, categorical grants, block grants,* and *fiscal federalism.*

The New Deal and Cooperative Federalism

The doctrine of dual federalism receded into the background in the 1930s as the nation attempted to deal with the Great Depression. Franklin D. Roosevelt was inaugurated as president on March 4, 1933. In the previous year, nearly 1,500 banks had failed (and 4,000 more would fail in 1933). Thirty-two thousand businesses had closed down, and almost one-fourth of the labor force was unemployed. The public expected the national government to do something about the disastrous state of the economy. For the first three years of the Great Depression (1930–1932), the national government did very little.

Roosevelt, however, energetically intervened in the economy. Roosevelt's "New Deal" included large-scale emergency antipoverty programs and introduced major new laws regulating economic activity. Initially, the Supreme Court blocked many of Roosevelt's initiatives. Beginning in 1937, however, after a change in membership, the Court ceased to limit the federal government's actions. An expansive interpretation of the commerce clause became dominant.

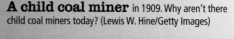
A child coal miner in 1909. Why aren't there child coal miners today? (Lewis W. Hine/Getty Images)

---

7. *Hammer v. Dagenhart,* 247 U.S. 251 (1918). This decision was overruled in *United States v. Darby,* 312 U.S. 100 (1940).

President Franklin D. Roosevelt (1933–1945) chats with two Georgia farmers. Roosevelt's national approach to addressing the effects of the Great Depression was overwhelmingly popular, although many of his specific initiatives were controversial. How did the Great Depression change the political beliefs of many ordinary Americans? (H. William Tetlow/Getty Images)

Some political scientists have described national-state relations since 1937 as **cooperative federalism,** in which the states and the national government cooperate in solving complex common problems. Roosevelt's New Deal programs, for example, often involved joint action between the national government and the states. The pattern of national-state relationships during these years gave rise to a new metaphor for federalism—that of a marble cake. Unlike a layer cake, in a marble cake the two types of cake are intermingled, and any bite contains cake of both flavors.

The 1960s and 1970s were a time of even greater expansion of the national government's role in domestic policy. Today, few activities are beyond the reach of the regulatory arm of the national government.

The Politics of Federalism

In determining the allocation of powers between the state and national governments, conservatives traditionally have favored the states, and liberals have favored the federal government. After all, national authority has been an agent of change throughout U.S. history. The expansion of national authority during the Civil War freed the slaves, and beginning in the 1960s, the federal government was likewise responsible for extending civil rights such as the right to vote to African Americans.

Republicans and Democrats. For much of American history, conservative southern Democrats were the major advocates of states' rights. Then, under Republican presidents Richard Nixon (1969–1974) and Ronald Reagan (1981–1989), **devolution,** or the transfer of power from the national government to state governments, became a major theme for the Republican Party. In recent decades, however, competing theories of federalism often appeared not to divide the two parties in practice. While the Republicans continued to advocate devolution in theory, they did not follow it at all in reality.

Consider that the passage of welfare reform legislation in 1996, which involved transferring significant control over welfare programs to the states, took place under Democratic president Bill Clinton (1993–2001). In contrast, under Republican president George W. Bush (2001–2009), Congress enacted the No Child Left Behind Act of 2001. This act increased federal control over education, which had traditionally been under the purview of state governments. In another example, the Bush administration prevented

Cooperative Federalism
A model of federalism in which the states and the national government cooperate in solving problems.

Devolution
The transfer of powers from a national or central government to a state or local government.

California from implementing its own tough new laws to regulate air pollution. Upon taking office, the Obama administration reversed the Bush policies and allowed California to proceed.

Conservatives Look Again to the States. Beginning in 2009, conservatives began to rediscover states' rights. One reason may be that from January 2009 through January 2011, the Democrats were in control of the presidency, the U.S. House, and the U.S. Senate. Republicans were shut out at the national level, and many conservatives hoped that the states would be a counterweight to the newly active national government.

Methods of Implementing Cooperative Federalism

One means of implementing cooperative federalism is through grants. Even before the Constitution was adopted, the national government gave grants to the states in the form of land to finance education. The national government also provided land grants for canals, railroads, and roads. In the twentieth century, federal grants increased significantly, especially during the Great Depression and again in the 1960s, when the dollar amount of these grants quadrupled. These funds were used for improvements in education, pollution control, recreation, and highways. With this increase in grants, however, came a bewildering number of restrictions and regulations.

Categorical Grants. By the 1980s, **categorical grants** were spread out across four hundred separate programs, but the largest five accounted for more than 50 percent of the revenues spent. These five programs were Medicaid (health care for the poor),

Categorical Grant
A federal grant to a state or local government for a specific program or project.

A teacher high-fives an elementary school student in Miami. This teacher is funded by Teach for America, a non-profit organization that places recent high-achieving college graduates in low-income community schools. The program receives federal grants. (AP Photo/J. Pat Carter)

Block Grant
A federal grant that provides funds to a state or local government for a general functional area, such as criminal justice or mental-health programs.

Fiscal
Having to do with government revenues and expenditures.

Fiscal Federalism
A process by which funds raised through taxation or borrowing by one level of government (usually the national government) are spent by another level (typically, state or local governments).

highway construction, unemployment benefits, housing assistance, and welfare programs to assist mothers with dependent children and people with disabilities. For fiscal year 2013, the national government gave about $636 billion to the states. This sum was actually somewhat less than some recent figures, due to the winding down of President Obama's February 2009 stimulus program. The stimulus had included special funding to counteract some of the devastating effects of the Great Recession on state budgets.

Over the decades, federal grants to the states have increased significantly. One reason is that Congress has decided to offload some programs to the states and provide a major part of the funding for them. Also, Congress continues to use grants to persuade states and cities to operate programs devised by the federal government. Finally, states often are happy to apply for grants because they are relatively "free," requiring only that the state match a small portion of each grant.

Block Grants. Block grants lessen the restrictions on federal grants given to state and local governments by grouping a number of categorical grants under one broad heading. Governors and mayors generally prefer block grants because such grants give state and local governments more flexibility in how the funds are spent. In contrast, Congress generally favors categorical grants because the expenditures can be targeted according to congressional priorities.

One major set of block grants provides aid to state welfare programs. The Personal Responsibility and Work Opportunity Reconciliation Act of 1996 ended the previously existing welfare program and substituted for it a block grant to each state. Each grant has an annual cap. According to some, this is one of the more successful block grant programs.

Fiscal Federalism and State Budgets. In discussions of government policy, you may have heard the word *fiscal.* This word simply means "having to do with government revenues and expenditures." **Fiscal** policy, therefore, is policy concerning taxing or borrowing—and then spending the revenues. When the federal government makes grants to state and local governments, funds raised through taxation or borrowing by one level of government (the national government) are spent by another level (state and local governments). We can speak of this process as **fiscal federalism.** With more than 20 percent of state and local revenues supplied by the federal government, fiscal federalism is clearly important.

The Great Recession had a devastating impact on state budgets, and in response the federal government substantially increased the amount of funding available to the states. From 2011 on, however, these extra funds were no longer available. State governments cut spending and employment substantially—so much so that total government spending as a share of the economy actually fell in 2011 and 2012.

In 2011, new conservative governors in many states argued that excessively generous pension benefits for state workers were a major part of state budget problems. Many of them sponsored new laws to reduce pension benefits. Several governors also campaigned against state employee labor unions, a step that led to controversy in states such as Ohio and Wisconsin.

Feeling the Pressure—The Strings Attached to Federal Grants. No dollars sent to the states are completely free of "strings." All funds come with requirements that must be met by the states. Often, through the use of grants, the national government has been able to exercise substantial control over matters that traditionally have been under the purview of state governments. When the federal government gives federal funds for highway improvements, for example, it may condition the funds on the state's cooperation with a federal policy. This is exactly what the federal government did in the

1980s and 1990s to force the states to raise their minimum alcoholic beverage drinking age to twenty-one.

Federal Mandates. For years, the federal government has passed legislation requiring that states improve environmental conditions or the civil rights of various groups. Since the 1970s, the national government has enacted hundreds of **federal mandates** requiring the states to take some action in areas ranging from voter registration, to ocean-dumping restrictions, to the education of people with disabilities. The Unfunded Mandates Reform Act of 1995 requires the Congressional Budget Office to identify mandates that cost state and local governments more than $50 million to implement. Nonetheless, the federal government routinely continues to pass mandates for state and local governments that cost more than that to put into place.

Federal Mandate
A requirement in federal legislation that forces states and municipalities to comply with certain rules.

FEDERALISM AND TODAY'S SUPREME COURT

The United States Supreme Court, which normally has the final say on constitutional issues, plays a major role in determining where the line is drawn between federal and state powers. Consider the decisions rendered by Chief Justice John Marshall in the cases discussed earlier in this chapter. Since the 1930s, Marshall's broad interpretation of the commerce clause has made it possible for the national government to justify its regulation of almost any activity, even when the activity appears to be completely local in character. In the 1990s and early 2000s, however, the Court evidenced a willingness to impose some limits on the national government's authority under the commerce clause and other constitutional provisions. As a result, it is difficult to predict how today's Court might rule on a particular case involving federalism.

LO5: Detail recent Supreme Court rulings that affect the distribution of power between the national government and the states.

A Trend toward States' Rights?

Since the mid-1990s, the Supreme Court has tended to give greater weight to states' rights than it did during previous decades. In a widely publicized 1995 case, the Supreme Court held that Congress had exceeded its constitutional authority under the commerce clause when it passed the Gun-Free School Zones Act in 1990.[8] The Court stated that the act, which banned the possession of guns within one thousand feet of any school, was unconstitutional because it attempted to regulate an area that had "nothing to do with commerce, or any sort of economic enterprise." This marked the first time in sixty years that the Supreme Court had placed a limit on the national government's authority under the commerce clause.

Although the Court has tended to favor states' rights in some decisions, in other decisions it has backed the federal government's position. For example, in 2005 the Court held that the federal government's power to declare various substances to be illegal drugs superseded California's law legalizing the use of marijuana for medical treatment.[9] Yet less than a year later, the Court favored states' rights when it upheld Oregon's controversial "death with dignity" law, which allows patients with terminal illnesses to choose to end their lives early and thus avoid suffering.[10]

---

8. *United States v. Lopez,* 514 U.S. 549 (1995).
9. *Gonzales v. Raich,* 545 U.S. 1 (2005).
10. *Gonzales v. Oregon,* 546 U.S. 243 (2006).

Arizona governor Jan Brewer was the center of much controversy over a 2010 state law restricting the rights of illegal immigrants. The United States Supreme Court overturned parts of the law in 2012. Is it appropriate for state governments to adopt special state policies on immigration? (Mark Wilson/Getty Images)

Recent Decisions

In recent rulings, the Supreme Court has often shown sympathy for states' rights, while sometimes backing the federal government.

Immigration. In one important opinion, the Court found that Arizona had gone too far in its attempt to subject unauthorized immigration to state authority. Under the ruling, Arizona cannot make it a crime when illegal immigrants fail to carry identification papers or attempt to find work. Arizona police cannot arrest individuals solely on suspicion of illegal status.[11]

Health-Care Reform. It was the Court's opinion on the Affordable Care Act (Obamacare) that was expected to be the most important states' rights ruling in decades. In the end, the Court's 2012 verdict was somewhat anticlimactic. It did not find that the *individual mandate*—a penalty imposed on those who do not buy health-care insurance—violated the police powers of the states. (The Court also found that while the mandate could not be justified under the commerce clause, it was legitimate under the national government's power to tax.) Chief Justice John Roberts's ruling on Medicaid expansion did hearten states' rights advocates, however. By making Medicaid expansion optional for the states, the Court for the first time put limits on the ability of the federal government to coerce states by withholding grants.[12]

Same-Sex Marriage. In 2013, the Court's two rulings on same-sex marriage also tended to enhance the authority of the states. (We described these rulings in the *At Issue* feature in this chapter.) True, by refusing to rule on a California case, the Court in effect prevented the state's voters from banning same-sex marriage. This step, however, allowed all the other states to continue making their own decisions about the issue.[13] Also, the Court's ruling that the federal government must recognize state-approved same-sex marriages was a victory for states' rights, as well as for same-sex couples in the affected states.[14]

The Voting Rights Act. Finally, the Court's ruling on the Voting Rights Act was a striking triumph for states' rights. The 1965 act imposed certain requirements on states and localities—mostly in the South—with a history of violating the voting rights of minority group members. Such areas had to obtain *preclearance* from the federal government to make changes in voting procedures or districts. In June 2013, the Court effectively destroyed the preclearance system, giving all affected governments the right to set their own voting rules without restriction.[15]

---

11. *Arizona v. United States,* 132 S.Ct. 2492 (2012).
12. *National Federation of Independent Business v. Sebelius,* 132 S.Ct. 2566 (2012).
13. *Hollingsworth v. Perry,* 570 U.S. ___ (2013).
14. *United States v. Windsor,* 570 U.S. ___ (2013).
15. *Shelby County v. Holder,* 570 U.S. ___ (2013).

making a difference
WRITING LETTERS TO THE EDITOR

Our federal system encourages debate over whether a particular issue should be a national, state, or local question. Many questions are, in fact, state or local ones, and it is easier for you to make a significant contribution to the discussion on these issues. Even in the largest states, there are many fewer people to persuade than in the nation as a whole. Attempts to influence your fellow citizens can therefore be more effective.

Why Should You Care?
In this chapter, we have mentioned a variety of issues arising from our federal system that may concern you directly. Although the national government provides aid to educational programs, education is still primarily a state and local responsibility. The total amount of money spent on education is determined by state and local governments. Therefore, you can address this issue at the state or local level. Gambling laws are another state responsibility. Do you enjoy gambling—or do you believe that the effects of gambling make it a social disaster? State law—or state negotiations with Native American tribes—determines the availability of gambling.

What Can You Do?
In our modern era, the number of ways in which you can communicate your opinion is vast. You can post a response on any of thousands of blogs. You could develop your own minivideo and post it on YouTube. Politicians use Facebook and Twitter to organize their supporters and often have thousands of online "friends." This can provide you with the opportunity to present your views to someone who might be able to act on them.

If you want to effect policy change at the state or local level, however, the local newspaper, in both its paper and its online formats, continues to be essential. Blogs, YouTube, and other online venues tend to be nationally and even internationally oriented. Still, newspapers are resolutely local and the natural hub for discussions of local issues. Most papers allow responses and comments on their Web sites, and you can make a point by contributing in that fashion. Nothing, however, will win you a wider audience than an old-fashioned letter to the editor. Use the following rules to compose an effective communication:

1. Use a computer, and double-space the lines. Use a spelling checker and grammar checker.
2. Include a lead topic sentence that is short, to the point, and powerful.
3. Keep your thoughts on target—choose only one topic to discuss. Make sure it is newsworthy and timely.
4. Make sure your communication is concise; never let it exceed a page and a half in length (double-spaced).
5. If you know that facts were misstated or left out in current news stories about your topic, supply the facts. The public wants to know.
6. Don't be afraid to express moral judgments. You can go a long way by appealing to the reader's sense of justice.
7. Personalize the communication by bringing in your own experiences, if possible.
8. If you are writing a letter, sign it and give your address (including your e-mail address) and your telephone number. Comments posted to blogs and other communications may have their own rules for identifying yourself. Follow them.
9. If writing a letter, send or e-mail it to the editorial office of the newspaper of your choice. Almost all publications now have e-mail addresses. Their Web sites usually give information on where you can send mail.

Facebook and Twitter are now used by politicians to organize their supporters. (Annette Shaff/Shutterstock.com)

key**terms**

block grant 60

categorical grant 59

commerce clause 54

concurrent powers 51

confederal system 46

cooperative
   federalism 58

devolution 58

dual federalism 57

elastic clause, or
   necessary and proper
   clause 49

enumerated powers 49

federal mandate 61

fiscal 60

fiscal federalism 60

police power 50

supremacy clause 51

unitary system 46

chapter**summary**

1 There are three basic models for ordering relations between central governments and local units: (a) a unitary system (in which ultimate power is held by the national government), (b) a confederal system (in which ultimate power is retained by the states), and (c) a federal system (in which governmental powers are divided between the national government and the states).

2 The Constitution expressly grants certain powers to the national government in Article I, Section 8. In addition to these enumerated powers, the national government has implied and inherent powers. Implied powers are those that are reasonably necessary to carry out the powers expressly given to the national government. Inherent powers are those that the national government holds by virtue of being a sovereign state with the right to preserve itself.

3 The Tenth Amendment to the Constitution states that powers not delegated to the United States by the Constitution, nor prohibited by it to the states, are reserved to the states, or to the people. In certain areas, the Constitution provides for concurrent powers (such as the power to tax), which are powers that are held jointly by the national and state governments. The Constitution also denies certain powers to both the national government and the states.

4 The supremacy clause of the Constitution states that the Constitution, congressional laws, and national treaties are the supreme law of the land. States cannot use their reserved or concurrent powers to override national policies.

5 Chief Justice John Marshall's expansive interpretation of the necessary and proper clause of

the Constitution in *McCulloch v. Maryland* (1819), along with his affirmation of the supremacy clause, enhanced the power of the national government. Marshall's broad interpretation of the commerce clause in *Gibbons v. Ogden* (1824) further extended the powers of the national government.

6 The controversy over slavery that led to the Civil War took the form of a fight over national government supremacy versus the rights of the separate states. Since the Civil War, federalism has evolved through at least two general phases: dual federalism and cooperative federalism. In dual federalism, each of the states and the federal government remain supreme within their own spheres. The era since the Great Depression has sometimes been labeled one of cooperative federalism, in which states and the national government cooperate in solving complex common problems.

7 Categorical grants from the federal government to state governments help finance many projects. By attaching special conditions to federal grants, the national government can effect policy changes in areas typically governed by the states. Block grants usually have fewer strings attached, thus giving state and local governments more flexibility in using the funds. Federal mandates—laws requiring states to implement certain policies—have generated controversy.

8 The United States Supreme Court plays a significant role in determining the line between state and federal powers. Since the mid-1990s, there has been a trend on the part of the Court to support states' rights. Yet the Court has also issued several rulings in support of the federal government.

test**yourself**

LO1 *Explain some of the benefits of the federal system for the United States.*

One reason the founders chose a federal system is that:
   a. there were no supporters of states' rights.
   b. the United States was already large geographically, and it would have been difficult to govern just from the national capital.
   c. the thirteen states were smaller geographically than France, so a federal system was appropriate.

LO2 *Describe how the various provisions of the U.S. Constitution provide a framework for federalism.*

When both the national government and the state governments share certain powers, we call them:
   a. prevailing powers.
   b. concurrent powers.
   c. constitutional powers.

LO3 *Discuss how, in the early years of the republic, the United States Supreme Court confirmed the authority of the national government, and how that authority was ratified by the Civil War.*

In the Supreme Court case of *McCulloch v. Maryland* (1819), the Court clearly established:
   a. that the Constitution is the supreme law of the land.
   b. that state governments can tax the national government.
   c. that the national government can tax the state governments.

LO4 *Define the terms* dual federalism, cooperative federalism, categorical grants, block grants, *and* fiscal federalism.

When the federal (national) government sends dollars to state governments, those funds:
   a. are given without any restrictions.
   b. are to be returned to the federal government at a later date.
   c. come with many "strings" attached.

LO5 *Detail recent Supreme Court rulings that affect the distribution of power between the national government and the states.*

When ruling on the Affordable Care Act (Obamacare) in 2012, the Supreme Court:
   a. found the act to be entirely constitutional.
   b. found the act to be entirely unconstitutional.
   c. found the act to be mostly constitutional.

Essay Question:

Traditionally, conservatives have favored states' rights and liberals have favored national authority. Can you think of modern-day issues in which these long-standing preferences might be reversed, with conservatives favoring national authority and liberals favoring states' rights? Explain.

Answers to multiple-choice questions: 1. b, 2. b, 3. a, 4. c, 5. c.

CourseMate

Access CourseMate at www.cengagebrain.com for additional study tools: practice quizzes, key term flashcards and crossword puzzles, audio chapter summaries, simulations, animated learning modules, interactive timelines, videos, and American Government NewsWatch.

These demonstrators are participating in a March on Washington for Gun Control in January 2013 in response to a shooting that killed twenty-six children and teachers at Sandy Hook Elementary School, Newtown Connecticut. (Yuri Gripas/AFP/Getty Images)

Civil Liberties

LEARNING OUTCOMES

The five **Learning Outcomes (LOs)** below are designed to help improve your understanding of this chapter. After reading this chapter, you should be able to:

■ **LO1** Describe the Bill of Rights and how it came to be applied to state governments as well as the national government.

■ **LO2** Explain how the First Amendment's establishment clause and free exercise clause guarantee our freedom of religion.

■ **LO3** Specify the limited circumstances, including obscenity and slander, in which the national and state governments may override the principles of free speech and freedom of the press.

■ **LO4** Provide the constitutional basis of the right to privacy, and explain how the principle has been applied to the abortion and right-to-die controversies.

■ **LO5** Identify the constitutional rights of those who are accused of a crime, describe the *Miranda* and exclusionary rules, and cite examples of how recent security concerns have affected our civil liberties.

Check your understanding of the material with the Test Yourself section at the end of the chapter.

"The land of the free." When asked what makes the United States distinctive, Americans will commonly say that it is a free country. Americans have long believed that limits on the power of government are an essential part of what makes this country free. Recall from Chapter 1 that restraints on the actions of government against individuals generally are referred to as *civil liberties.* The first ten amendments to the U.S. Constitution—the Bill of Rights—place such restraints on the national government. Of these amendments, none is more famous than the First Amendment, which guarantees freedom of religion, speech, and the press, along with many additional rights.

Most other democratic nations have laws to protect these and other civil liberties, but none of the laws is quite like the First Amendment. Take the issue of "hate speech." What if someone makes statements that stir up hatred toward a particular race or other group of people? In Germany, where memories of Nazi anti-Semitism remain alive, such speech is unquestionably illegal. In the United States, the issue is not so clear. The courts have often extended constitutional protection to this kind of speech.

In this chapter, we describe the civil liberties provided by the Bill of Rights and some of the controversies that surround them. In addition to First Amendment liberties, we look at the right to privacy and the rights of defendants in criminal prosecutions.

THE BILL OF RIGHTS

As you read through this chapter, bear in mind that the Bill of Rights, like the rest of the Constitution, is relatively brief. The framers set forth broad guidelines, leaving it up to the courts to interpret these constitutional mandates and apply them to specific situations. Thus, judicial interpretations shape the true nature of the civil liberties and rights that we possess. Because judicial interpretations change over time, so do our liberties and rights. As you will read in the following pages, there have been many conflicts over the meaning of such simple phrases as *freedom of religion* and *freedom of the press.*

LO1: Describe the Bill of Rights and how it came to be applied to state governments as well as the national government.

To understand what freedoms we actually have, we need to examine how the courts—and particularly the United States Supreme Court—have resolved some of those conflicts. One important conflict was over the issue of whether the Bill of Rights in the federal Constitution limited the powers of the state governments as well as the national government.

Extending the Bill of Rights to State Governments

Social Media in Politics
Two organizations of interest when studying civil liberties issues are the Civil Liberties Defense Center (CLDC), which you can find by searching on "civil liberties" in Facebook, and the National Rifle Association (NRA), which you can locate by entering "nra."

Many citizens do not realize that, as originally intended, the Bill of Rights limited the powers only of the national government. At the time the Bill of Rights was ratified, there was little concern over the potential of state governments to curb civil liberties. For one thing, state governments were closer to home and easier to control. For another, most state constitutions already had bills of rights. Rather, the fear was of the potential tyranny of the national government. The Bill of Rights begins with the words, "Congress shall make no law . . . ." It says nothing about states making laws that might abridge citizens' civil liberties. In 1833, the United States Supreme Court held that the Bill of Rights did not apply to state laws.[1]

We mentioned that most states had bills of rights. These bills of rights were similar to the national one, but there were some differences. Furthermore, each state's judicial system interpreted the rights differently. Citizens in different states, therefore, effectively had different sets of civil liberties. It was not until after the Fourteenth Amendment was ratified in 1868 that civil liberties guaranteed by the national Constitution began to be applied to the states. Section 1 of that amendment provides, in part, as follows:

> *No State shall . . . deprive any person of life, liberty, or property, without due process of law.*

---

1. *Barron v. Baltimore,* 32 U.S. 243 (1833).

Incorporation Theory
The view that most of the protections of the Bill of Rights apply to state governments through the Fourteenth Amendment's due process clause.

Incorporation of the Fourteenth Amendment

There was no question that the Fourteenth Amendment applied to state governments. For decades, however, the courts were reluctant to define the liberties spelled out in the national Bill of Rights as constituting "due process of law," which was protected under the Fourteenth Amendment. Not until 1925, in *Gitlow v. New York,*[2] did the United States Supreme Court hold that the Fourteenth Amendment protected the freedom of speech guaranteed by the First Amendment to the Constitution from state infringement.

Only gradually, and never completely, did the Supreme Court accept the **incorporation theory**—the view that most of the protections of the Bill of Rights are incorporated into the Fourteenth Amendment's protection against state government actions. Table 4–1 below shows the rights that the Court has incorporated into the Fourteenth Amendment and the case in which it first applied each protection. As you can see in the table, in the fifteen years following the *Gitlow* decision, the Supreme Court incorporated into the Fourteenth Amendment the other basic freedoms (of the press, assembly, the right to petition, and religion) guaranteed by the First Amendment.

It took time for the Supreme Court to require the states to accept other liberties. Only in 2010 did the Court rule that the states were obligated to recognize an individual's right

---

2. 268 U.S. 652 (1925).

TABLE 4–1: Incorporating the Bill of Rights into the Fourteenth Amendment

Year	Issue	Amendment Involved	Court Case
1925	Freedom of speech	I	*Gitlow v. New York*, 268 U.S. 652.
1931	Freedom of the press	I	*Near v. Minnesota*, 283 U.S. 697.
1932	Right to a lawyer in capital punishment cases	VI	*Powell v. Alabama*, 287 U.S. 45.
1937	Freedom of assembly and right to petition	I	*De Jonge v. Oregon*, 299 U.S. 353.
1940	Freedom of religion	I	*Cantwell v. Connecticut*, 310 U.S. 296.
1947	Separation of church and state	I	*Everson v. Board of Education*, 330 U.S. 1.
1948	Right to a public trial	VI	*In re Oliver*, 333 U.S. 257.
1949	No unreasonable searches and seizures	IV	*Wolf v. Colorado*, 338 U.S. 25.
1961	Exclusionary rule	IV	*Mapp v. Ohio*, 367 U.S. 643.
1962	No cruel and unusual punishment	VIII	*Robinson v. California*, 370 U.S. 660.
1963	Right to a lawyer in all criminal felony cases	VI	*Gideon v. Wainwright*, 372 U.S. 335.
1964	No compulsory self-incrimination	V	*Malloy v. Hogan*, 378 U.S. 1.
1965	Right to privacy	I, III, IV, V, IX	*Griswold v. Connecticut*, 381 U.S. 479.
1966	Right to an impartial jury	VI	*Parker v. Gladden*, 385 U.S. 363.
1967	Right to a speedy trial	VI	*Klopfer v. North Carolina*, 386 U.S. 213.
1969	No double jeopardy	V	*Benton v. Maryland*, 395 U.S. 784.
2010	Right to bear arms	II	*McDonald v. Chicago*, 561 U.S. 3025.

to bear arms. Even with that ruling, the national and state governments retain the power to regulate the ownership of firearms. We examine a major gun-regulation topic in the *At Issue* feature on the following page.

Establishment Clause
The part of the First Amendment prohibiting the establishment of a church officially supported by the national government.

FREEDOM OF RELIGION

In the United States, freedom of religion consists of two principal rules that are presented in the First Amendment. The first rule guarantees the separation of church and state, and the second guarantees the free exercise of religion.

The Separation of Church and State—The Establishment Clause

The First Amendment to the Constitution states, in part, that "Congress shall make no law respecting an establishment of religion." In the words of Thomas Jefferson, the **establishment clause** was designed to create a "wall of separation of Church and State." As interpreted by the Supreme Court, the establishment clause in the First Amendment means at least the following:

LO2: Explain how the First Amendment's establishment clause and free exercise clause guarantee our freedom of religion.

> *Neither a state nor the federal government can set up a church. Neither can pass laws which aid one religion, aid all religions, or prefer one religion over another. Neither can force nor influence a person to go to or to remain away from church against his will or force him to profess a belief or disbelief in any religion. No person can be punished for entertaining or professing religious beliefs or disbeliefs, for church attendance or nonattendance. No tax in any amount, large or small, can be levied to support any religious activities or institutions, whatever they may be called, or whatever form they may adopt to teach or practice religion. Neither a state nor the federal government can, openly or secretly, participate in the affairs of any religious organizations or groups and vice versa.[3]*

The establishment clause covers all conflicts about such matters as the legality of giving state and local government aid to religious organizations and schools, allowing or requiring school prayers, teaching evolution versus creationist theories that reject evolution, placing religious displays in schools or public places, and discriminating against religious groups in publicly operated institutions.

Aid to Church-Related Schools. In the United States, almost 11 percent of school-age children attend private schools, of which about 80 percent have religious affiliations. The United States Supreme Court has tried to draw a fine line between permissible public aid to students in church-related schools and impermissible public aid to religion. These issues have arisen most often at the elementary and secondary levels.

In 1971, in *Lemon v. Kurtzman,*[4] the Court ruled that direct state aid could not be used to subsidize religious instruction. The Court in the *Lemon* case gave its most general pronouncement on the constitutionality of government aid to religious schools, stating that (1) the aid had to be secular (nonreligious) in aim, (2) it could not have the primary effect of advancing or inhibiting religion, and (3) the government must avoid "an excessive government entanglement with religion." All laws that raise issues under the establishment

---

3. *Everson v. Board of Education,* 330 U.S. 1 (1947).
4. 403 U.S. 602 (1971).

at issue

SHOULD WE BAN ASSAULT-TYPE WEAPONS?

The Second Amendment to the United States Constitution provides a right to keep and bear arms. In 2008, the United States Supreme Court found this to be a right enjoyed by individuals. The national government therefore lacks the power to ban handguns completely. In 2010, the rule was imposed on the states.[a]

In December 2012, a young man in Connecticut stole his mother's semiautomatic Bushmaster XM15 rifle, which had a magazine holding thirty rounds of bullets. He murdered her and then attacked Sandy Hook Elementary School, killing twenty-six students and staff. In July 2012, in Aurora, Colorado, a shooter used a hundred-round drum in a semiautomatic rifle to kill or wound most of his seventy victims before the weapon jammed. They were attending a midnight showing of the Batman film *The Dark Knight Rises*. Such violence has prompted calls to ban the assault-type weapons used in these crimes. Is such a ban desirable? Is it even constitutional?

NOBODY NEEDS THESE WEAPONS FOR HUNTING OR PROTECTION

Those in favor of banning the sale of assault-type weapons argue that such a step does not violate the Second Amendment. After all, who really needs these military-type weapons? Semiautomatic weapons based on military assault rifles are not optimized for hunting. They are second-rate deer rifles and completely useless for waterfowl. These firearms are not ideal for target shooting either—they are not used in international and Olympic competition.

The use of such weapons for self-defense is problematic. A handgun is more portable, and a shotgun is easier to aim. So, why do so many people want such weapons? Some argue that buyers are fulfilling fantasies. The dream is that the guns will be used to protect homes and families after a collapse of civilization, or even to rebel against the government. Let's base gun laws on reality instead. These weapons have no place in America's homes and businesses.

BANNING ASSAULT-TYPE WEAPONS WILL HAVE NO EFFECT

Those who oppose a ban observe that the vast majority of firearm deaths result from weapons that would not be subject to the proposed ban on assault-style weapons. In 1994, Congress passed the Federal Assault Weapons Ban. Two leading researchers concluded that the ban had no detectable impact on murder rates, which have fallen since the ban expired in 2004.

An alternative to a ban on assault-style weapons would be to limit the size of the magazines that hold ammunition. Proponents of such legislation argue that no one needs a thirty- or hundred-round magazine for hunting, target shooting, or self-protection. Still, such a law would not have prevented the disaster at Virginia Tech in 2007. In that instance, the shooter fired 176 rounds from multiple ten- and fifteen-round magazines. If magazines were limited to ten rounds, shooters could just arm themselves with multiple magazines.

FOR CRITICAL ANALYSIS

Does the Second Amendment give all Americans the right to bear arms of any type at all times in any location? Why or why not?

---

a. *District of Columbia v. Heller,* 554 U.S. 570 (2008); and MacDonald v. Chicago, 561 U.S. 3025 (2010).

---

clause are now subject to the three-part *Lemon* test. How the test is applied, however, has varied over the years.

In a number of cases, the Supreme Court has held that state programs helping church-related schools are unconstitutional. In other cases, however, the Supreme Court has allowed states to use tax funds for lunches, textbooks, diagnostic services for speech and hearing problems, standardized tests, and special educational services for disadvantaged students attending religious schools.

School Vouchers. An ongoing controversy concerning the establishment clause has to do with school vouchers. Many people believe that the public schools are failing to educate our children adequately. One proposed solution to the problem has been for state and local governments to issue school vouchers. These vouchers represent state-issued funds that can be used to purchase education at any school, public or private. At issue is whether voucher programs violate the establishment clause.

In 2002, the United States Supreme Court held that a voucher program in Cleveland, Ohio, did not violate the establishment clause. The Court concluded that because the vouchers could be used for public as well as private schools, the program did not unconstitutionally entangle church and state.[5] The Court's 2002 decision was encouraging to those who support school choice, whether it takes the form of school vouchers or tuition tax credits to offset educational expenses in private schools.

Today, a variety of states allow public funds to be used for private school expenses. Some have small-scale voucher or scholarship programs for a limited number of students, frequently special-needs students. A growing number of states provide tax deductions for private school expenses. Interest in such programs became more widespread in 2011, after the 2010 elections gave conservatives control of many state governments. Still, voucher programs have also been eliminated in several jurisdictions. In 2005, the Florida Supreme Court ruled that vouchers violated the Florida state constitution. In 2007, Utah voters rejected a voucher plan that was created earlier that year by the state legislature.

The Issue of School Prayer—*Engel v. Vitale.* Do the states have the right to promote religion in general, without making any attempt to establish a particular religion? That is the question raised by school prayer and was the precise issue presented in 1962 in *Engel v. Vitale,*[6] the so-called Regents' Prayer case in New York. The State Board of Regents of New York had suggested that a prayer be spoken aloud in the public schools at the beginning of each day. The recommended prayer was as follows:

These high school students pray around the school flagpole before classes in Lufkin, Texas. Do their actions violate the separation of church and state? (AP Photo/Joel Andrews/*The Lufkin Daily News*)

> *Almighty God, we acknowledge our dependence upon Thee, And we beg Thy blessings upon us, our parents, our teachers, and our Country.*

Such a prayer was implemented in many New York public schools.

The parents of a number of students challenged the action of the regents, maintaining that it

5. *Zelman v. Simmons-Harris,* 536 U.S. 639 (2002).
6. 370 U.S. 421 (1962).

violated the establishment clause of the First Amendment. At trial, the parents lost. On appeal, however, the Supreme Court ruled that the regents' action was unconstitutional because "the constitutional prohibition against laws respecting an establishment of a religion must mean at least that in this country it is no part of the business of government to compose official prayers for any group of the American people to recite as part of a religious program carried on by any government."

The Debate over School Prayer Continues. Although the Supreme Court has ruled repeatedly against officially sponsored prayer and Bible-reading sessions in public schools, other means for bringing some form of religious expression into public education have been attempted. In 1985, the Supreme Court struck down as unconstitutional an Alabama law authorizing one minute of silence for prayer or meditation in all public schools.[7] The Court concluded that the law violated the establishment clause because it was "an endorsement of religion lacking any clearly secular purpose." Since then, the lower courts have interpreted the Supreme Court's decision to mean that states can require a moment of silence in the schools as long as they make it clear that the purpose of the law is secular, not religious.

Forbidding the Teaching of Evolution. For many decades, certain religious groups have opposed the teaching of evolution in the schools. To these groups, evolutionary theory directly counters their religious belief that human beings did not evolve but were created fully formed, as described in the biblical story of the creation. State and local attempts to forbid the teaching of evolution, however, have not passed constitutional muster in the eyes of the United States Supreme Court. For example, in 1968 the Supreme Court held that an Arkansas law prohibiting the teaching of evolution violated the establishment clause because it imposed religious beliefs on students.[8]

Nonetheless, state and local groups around the country continue their efforts against the teaching of evolution. Some school districts have considered teaching the creationist theory of "intelligent design" as an alternative explanation of the origin of life. Proponents of intelligent design contend that evolutionary theory has "gaps" that can be explained only by the existence of an intelligent creative force (God).

The federal courts took up the issue of intelligent design in 2005. The previous year, the Dover Area Board of Education in Pennsylvania had voted to require the presentation of intelligent design as an explanation of the origin of life. In December 2005, a U.S. district court ruled that the Dover mandate was unconstitutional. Judge John E. Jones III criticized the intelligent design theory in depth.[9] All of the school board members who endorsed intelligent design were voted out of office, and the new school board declined to appeal the decision.

Religious Displays on Public Property. On a regular basis, the courts are asked to determine whether religious symbols placed on public property violate the establishment clause. A frequent source of controversy is the placement of a crèche, or nativity scene, on public property during the Christmas season. The Supreme Court has allowed some displays but prohibited others. In general, a nativity scene is acceptable if it is part of a broader display that contains secular objects such as lights, Christmas trees, Santa Claus

7. *Wallace v. Jaffree,* 472 U.S. 38 (1985).
8. *Epperson v. Arkansas,* 393 U.S. 97 (1968).
9. *Kitzmiller v. Dover Area School District,* 400 F.Supp.2d 707 (M.D.Pa. 2005).

figures, and reindeer. A stand-alone crèche is not acceptable.[10] A related issue is whether the Ten Commandments may be displayed on public property. As with nativity displays, acceptability turns on whether the Ten Commandments exhibit is part of a larger secular display or whether the context is overtly religious.

The Free Exercise Clause

The First Amendment constrains Congress from prohibiting the free exercise of religion. Does this **free exercise clause** mean that no type of religious practice can be prohibited or restricted by government? Certainly, a person can hold any religious belief that he or she wants, or a person can have no religious belief. When, however, religious *practices* work against public policy and the public welfare, the government can act. For example, regardless of a child's or parent's religious beliefs, the government can require vaccinations. Additionally, public school students can be required to study from textbooks chosen by school authorities.

Churches and other religious organizations are tax-exempt bodies, and as a result they are not allowed to endorse candidates for office or make contributions to candidates' campaigns. Churches are allowed to take positions on ballot proposals, however, and may contribute to referendum campaigns. For example, both the Latter-Day Saints (the Mormons) and the Roman Catholic Church were able to fund the campaign for California's 2008 Proposition 8, a measure to ban same-sex marriage.

The Internal Revenue Service (IRS) rarely bothers to threaten the tax-exempt status of a church based on simple candidate endorsements, however. For example, in October 2012, about 1,400 ministers collectively endorsed Republican presidential candidate Mitt Romney in a deliberate challenge to the 1954 law that prohibits such endorsements. The IRS did not respond. In 1995, however, the IRS did revoke the tax-exempt status of Branch Ministries, Inc., and in 2000 a federal district court supported the revocation.[11] Branch Ministries went far beyond simply endorsing a candidate from the pulpit. The church had used tax-exempt income to buy newspaper advertisements denouncing Democratic presidential candidate Bill Clinton.

Free Exercise Clause
The provision of the First Amendment guaranteeing the free exercise of religion.

Prior Restraint
Restraining an activity before it has actually occurred. When expression is involved, this means censorship.

FREEDOM OF EXPRESSION

Perhaps the most frequently invoked freedom that Americans have is the right to free speech and a free press. Each of us has the right to have our say, and all of us have the right to hear what others say. For the most part, Americans can criticize public officials and their actions without fear of reprisal by any branch of our government.

LO3: Specify the limited circumstances, including obscenity and slander, in which the national and state governments may override the principles of free speech and freedom of the press.

No Prior Restraint

Restraining an activity before that activity has actually occurred is called **prior restraint.** When expression is involved, prior restraint means censorship, as opposed to subsequent punishment. Prior restraint of expression would require, for example, that a permit be obtained before a speech could be made, a newspaper published, or a movie or TV show exhibited. Most, if not all, Supreme Court justices have been very critical of any governmental action that imposes prior restraint on expression.

---

10. *Lynch v. Donnelly,* 465 U.S. 668 (1984).
11. *Branch Ministries v. Rossetti,* 211 F.3d 137 (D.C.Cir. 2000).

The national Christmas tree and the national Hanukkah menorah share space on the Ellipse in Washington, D.C. Why is this joint display constitutional? (Tim Sloan/AFP/Getty Images)

Symbolic Speech
Expression made through articles of clothing, gestures, movements, and other forms of nonverbal communication.

One of the most famous cases concerning prior restraint was *New York Times v. United States*[12] (1971), the so-called Pentagon Papers case. The *Times* and the *Washington Post* were about to publish the Pentagon Papers, an elaborate secret history of the U.S. government's involvement in the Vietnam War (1965–1975). The secret documents had been obtained illegally by a disillusioned former Pentagon official. The government wanted a court order to bar publication of the documents, arguing that national security was threatened and that the documents had been stolen. The newspapers argued that the public had a right to know the information contained in the papers and that the press had the right to inform the public. The Supreme Court ruled six to three in favor of the newspapers' right to publish the information. This case affirmed the no-prior-restraint doctrine.

The Protection of Symbolic Speech

Not all expression is in words or in writing. Articles of clothing, gestures, movements, and other forms of nonverbal expressive conduct are considered **symbolic speech.** Such speech is given substantial protection today by our courts. For example, in a landmark decision issued in 1969, *Tinker v. Des Moines School District,*[13] the United States Supreme Court held that the wearing of black armbands by students in protest against the Vietnam War was a form of speech protected by the First Amendment.

Flag Burning. In 1989, the Supreme Court ruled that state laws that prohibited the burning of the American flag as part of a peaceful protest also violated the freedom of expression protected by the First Amendment.[14] Congress responded by passing the Flag Protection Act of 1989, which was ruled unconstitutional by the Supreme Court in 1990. Congress and President George H. W. Bush immediately pledged to work for a constitutional amendment to "protect our flag"—an effort that has yet to be successful.

Cross Burning. In 2003, the Supreme Court concluded in a Virginia case that a state, consistent with the First Amendment, may ban cross burnings carried out with the intent to intimidate. The Court reasoned that historically, cross burning was a sign of impending violence, and a state has the right to ban threats of violence. The Court also ruled, however, that the state must prove intimidation and cannot infer it from the cross burnings themselves. In an impassioned dissent, Justice Clarence Thomas, who is African American and usually one of the Court's most conservative members, argued that cross burnings should be automatic evidence of intent to intimidate.[15]

---

12. 403 U.S. 713 (1971).
13. 393 U.S. 503 (1969).
14. *Texas v. Johnson,* 488 U.S. 884 (1989).
15. *Virginia v. Black,* 538 U.S. 343 (2003).

The Protection of Commercial Speech

Commercial speech usually is defined as advertising statements. Can advertisers use their First Amendment rights to prevent restrictions on the content of commercial advertising? Until the 1970s, the Supreme Court held that such speech was not protected at all by the First Amendment. By the mid-1970s, however, more and more commercial speech had been brought under First Amendment protection. According to Justice Harry A. Blackmun, "Advertising, however tasteless and excessive it sometimes may seem, is nonetheless dissemination of information as to who is producing and selling what product for what reason and at what price."[16] Nevertheless, the Supreme Court will consider a restriction on commercial speech valid as long as it (1) seeks to implement a substantial government interest, (2) directly advances that interest, and (3) goes no further than necessary to accomplish its objective. In particular, a business engaging in commercial speech can be subject to liability for factual inaccuracies in ways that do not apply to noncommercial speech.

Attempts to Ban Subversive or Advocacy Speech

Over the past hundred years, the United States Supreme Court has established, in succession, a number of doctrines regarding language allegedly subversive to the public order.

Clear and Present Danger Test. In 1919, the Supreme Court ruled that when a person's remarks present a clear and present danger to the peace or public order, they can be curtailed constitutionally. Justice Oliver Wendell Holmes used this reasoning when examining the case of a socialist who had been convicted of violating the Espionage Act by distributing a leaflet that opposed the military draft. According to the *clear and present danger test,* expression may be restricted if evidence exists that such expression would cause a dangerous condition, actual or imminent, that Congress has the power to prevent.[17]

The Bad Tendency Rule. Over the course of the twentieth century, the Supreme Court modified the clear and present danger rule, limiting the constitutional protection of free speech in 1925 and 1951, and then broadening it substantially in 1969. In *Gitlow v. New York,*[18] the Court reintroduced an earlier *bad tendency rule,* which placed greater

This ad for cigarettes appeared in 1946. Despite protection of commercial speech, it would be impossible for such an ad to appear today. Why? (Apic/Getty Images)

Commercial Speech
Advertising statements, which increasingly have been given First Amendment protection.

---

16. *Virginia State Board of Pharmacy v. Virginia Citizens Consumer Council, Inc.,* 425 U.S. 748 (1976).
17. *Schenck v. United States,* 249 U.S. 47 (1919).
18. 268 U.S. 652 (1925).

Imminent Lawless Action Test
The current standard established by the Supreme Court for evaluating the legality of advocacy speech. Such speech can be forbidden only when it is "directed to inciting . . . imminent lawless actions."

Obscenity
Sexually offensive material. Obscenity can be illegal if it is found to violate a four-part test established by the United States Supreme Court.

restrictions on speech than Justice Holmes's formulation. According to this rule, speech may be curtailed if there is a possibility that such expression might lead to some "evil."

In the *Gitlow* case, a member of a left-wing group was convicted of violating New York State's criminal anarchy statute when he published and distributed a pamphlet urging the violent overthrow of the U.S. government. In its majority opinion, the Supreme Court held that the First Amendment afforded protection against state incursions on freedom of expression—the first time that the First Amendment was ever invoked against a state government (see the discussion of incorporation theory on pages 68 and 69). Nevertheless, Gitlow could be punished legally because his expression would tend to bring about evils that the state had a right to prevent.

The Imminent Lawless Action Test. Some claim that the United States did not achieve true freedom of political speech until 1969. In that year, in *Brandenburg v. Ohio*,[19] the Supreme Court overturned the conviction of a Ku Klux Klan leader for violating a state statute. The statute prohibited anyone from advocating "the duty, necessity, or propriety of sabotage, violence, or unlawful methods of terrorism as a means of accomplishing industrial or political reform." The Court held that the guarantee of free speech does not permit a state "to forbid or proscribe [disallow] advocacy of the use of force or of law violation except where such advocacy is directed to inciting or producing imminent [immediate] lawless actions and is likely to incite or produce such action." The **imminent lawless action test** enunciated by the Court is a difficult one for prosecutors to meet. As a result, the Court's decision significantly broadened the protection given to advocacy speech.

Unprotected Speech: Obscenity

A large number of state and federal statutes make it a crime to disseminate obscene materials. Generally, the courts have not been willing to extend constitutional protections of free speech to what they consider obscene materials. But what is obscenity? Justice Potter Stewart once stated that even though he could not define *obscenity,* "I know it when I see it."

Definitional Problems. The Supreme Court has grappled from time to time with the difficulty of specifying an operationally effective definition of **obscenity.** In 1973, in *Miller v. California*,[20] Chief Justice Warren Burger created a formal list of requirements that must be met for material to be legally obscene. Material is obscene if (1) the average person finds that it violates contemporary community standards, (2) the work taken as a whole appeals to a prurient interest in sex, (3) the work shows patently offensive sexual conduct, and (4) the work lacks serious redeeming literary, artistic, political, or scientific merit. The problem, of course, is that one person's prurient interest is another person's medical interest or artistic pleasure. The Court went on to state that the definition of *prurient interest* would be determined by the community's standards. The Court avoided presenting a definition of *obscenity,* leaving this determination to local and state authorities. Consequently, the *Miller* case has been applied in a widely inconsistent manner.

Protecting Children. The Supreme Court has upheld state laws making it illegal to sell materials showing sexual performance by minors. In 1990, the Court ruled that states can

---

19. 395 U.S. 444 (1969).
20. 413 U.S. 5 (1973).

outlaw the possession of child pornography in the home.[21] The Court reasoned that the ban on private possession is justified because owning the material perpetuates commercial demand for it and for the exploitation of the children involved. In 2008, the Court upheld the legality of a 2003 federal law that made it a crime to offer child pornography, even if the pornography in question does not actually exist.[22]

(Tom Nulens/iStockphoto)

Pornography on the Internet. A significant problem facing Americans and their lawmakers today is how to spare young children from exposure to pornography that is disseminated through the Internet. In 1996, Congress first attempted to protect minors from pornographic materials on the Internet by passing the Communications Decency Act (CDA). Under the act, it was a crime to make available to minors online any "obscene or indecent" message that "depicts or describes, in terms patently offensive as measured by contemporary community standards, sexual or excretory activities or organs." In 1997, the Supreme Court held that the act imposed unconstitutional restraints on free speech and was therefore invalid.[23] A second attempt to protect children from online obscenity, the Child Online Protection Act (COPA) of 1998, met with a similar fate.[24]

In 2000, Congress enacted the Children's Internet Protection Act (CIPA), which requires public schools and libraries to install filtering software to prevent children from viewing Web sites with "adult" content. The CIPA was also challenged on constitutional grounds, but in 2003 the Supreme Court held that the act did not violate the First Amendment. The Court concluded that because libraries can disable the filters for any patrons who ask, the system does not burden free speech to an unconstitutional extent.[25]

Young people today are not dependent on libraries for Internet access, however. Free Wi-Fi, for use by laptops and tablets, is available almost everywhere. Students also access the Internet using smartphones. Instead of prohibition, parents and teachers may need to rely on information about pornography to help children avoid it and react to it appropriately when they do come across it.

Unprotected Speech: Slander

Can you say anything you want about someone else? Not really. Individuals are protected from **defamation of character,** which is defined as wrongfully hurting a person's good reputation. The law imposes a general duty on all persons to refrain from making false, defamatory statements about others. Breaching this duty orally is the wrongdoing called **slander.** Breaching it in writing is the wrongdoing called *libel,* which we discuss later. The government itself does not bring charges of slander or libel. Rather, the defamed person may bring a civil (as opposed to a criminal) suit for damages.

Legally, slander is the public uttering of a false statement that harms the good reputation of another. "Public uttering" means that the defamatory statement is made to,

WWW
Helpful Web Sites
Two organizations that focus on constitutional issues raised by the Internet are the Center for Democracy and Technology (search on "center democracy technology") and the Electronic Privacy Information Center (search on "electronic privacy").

Defamation of Character
Wrongfully hurting a person's good reputation.

Slander
The public uttering of a false statement that harms the good reputation of another. The statement must be made to, or within the hearing of, someone other than the defamed party.

---

21. *Osborne v. Ohio,* 495 U.S. 103 (1990).
22. *United States v. Williams,* 553 U.S. 285 (2008).
23. *Reno v. American Civil Liberties Union,* 521 U.S. 844 (1997).
24. *American Civil Liberties Union v. Ashcroft,* 542 U.S. 646 (2004).
25. *United States v. American Library Association,* 539 U.S. 194 (2003).

A librarian at a middle school in Durham, North Carolina, holds up *The Lorax* by Dr. Suess. Some people demanded that the book be removed from school libraries because it allegedly portrays the foresting industry in a negative way. Why do some believe that it is appropriate to limit what public school students can read? (AP Photo/ *The Herald-Sun*, Bernard Thomas)

or within the hearing of, a person other than the defamed party. If one person calls another dishonest, manipulative, and incompetent to his or her face when no one else is around, that does not constitute slander. If, however, a third party accidentally overhears defamatory statements, the courts have generally held that this constitutes a public uttering and therefore slander.

Student Speech

In recent years, high school and university students at public institutions have faced a variety of free speech challenges. Court rulings on these issues have varied by the level of school involved. Elementary schools, in particular, have great latitude in determining what kinds of speech are appropriate for their students. High school students have more free speech rights than do elementary students, and college students have the most speech rights of all.

Rights of Public School Students. High schools can impose restrictions on speech that would not be allowed in a college setting or in the general society. For example, high school officials may censor publications such as newspapers and yearbooks produced by the school's students. Courts have argued that a school newspaper is an extension of the school's educational mission, and thus subject to control by the school administration.

One of the most striking rulings to illustrate the power of school officials was handed down by the United States Supreme Court in 2007. An Alaska high school student had displayed a banner reading "Bong Hits 4 Jesus" on private property across from the school as students on the school grounds watched the Winter Olympics torch relay. The school principal crossed the street, seized the banner, and suspended the student from school. The Supreme Court later held that the school had an "important—indeed, perhaps compelling—interest" in combating drug use that allowed it to suppress the banner.[26] The Court's decision was widely criticized.

College Student Activity Fees. Should a college student have to subsidize, through student activity fees, organizations that promote causes that the student finds objectionable? In 2000, this question came before the United States Supreme Court in a case brought by several University of Wisconsin students. The students argued that their man-

---

26. *Morse v. Frederick,* 551 U.S. 393 (2007).

datory student activity fees—which helped to fund liberal causes with which they disagreed, including gay rights—violated their First Amendment rights of free speech, free association, and free exercise of religion.

To the surprise of many, the Supreme Court rejected the students' claim and ruled in favor of the university. The Court stated that "the university may determine that its mission is well served if students have the means to engage in dynamic discussions of philosophical, religious, scientific, social, and political subjects in their extracurricular life. If the university reaches this conclusion, it is entitled to impose a mandatory fee to sustain an open dialogue to these ends."[27]

Campus Speech and Behavior Codes. Another free speech issue is the legitimacy of campus speech and behavior codes at some state universities. These codes prohibit so-called hate speech—abusive speech attacking persons on the basis of their ethnicity, race, or other criteria. For example, a University of Michigan code banned "any behavior, verbal or physical, that stigmatizes or victimizes an individual on the basis of race, ethnicity, religion, sex, sexual orientation, creed, national origin, ancestry, age, marital status, handicap," or Vietnam-veteran status. A federal court found that the code violated students' First Amendment rights.[28] Although the courts generally have held that campus speech codes are unconstitutional restrictions on the right to free speech, such codes continue to exist.

Freedom of the Press

Freedom of the press can be regarded as a special instance of freedom of speech. Of course, at the time of the framing of the Constitution, *the press* meant only newspapers, pamphlets, magazines, and books. As technology has modified the ways in which we disseminate information, the laws touching on freedom of the press have been modified. What can and cannot be printed still occupies an important place in constitutional law, however.

Defamation in Writing. Libel is defamation in writing or in pictures, signs, films, or any other communication. As with slander, libel occurs only if the defamatory statements are observed by a third party. If Jane Smith writes a private letter to John Jones wrongfully accusing him of embezzling funds, that does not constitute libel.

The case of *New York Times Co. v. Sullivan*[29] (1964) explored an important question regarding libelous statements made about public officials. The Supreme Court held that only when a statement against a public official is made with **actual malice**—that is, with either knowledge of its falsity or a reckless disregard for the truth—can damages be obtained.

The standard set by the Court in the *New York Times* case has since been applied to **public figures** generally. Public figures include not only public officials but also any persons, such as movie stars, who are generally in the public limelight. Statements made about public figures usually are related to matters of general public interest. They are made about people who substantially affect all of us. Furthermore, public figures generally have some access to a public medium for answering disparaging falsehoods about themselves, whereas private individuals do not. For these reasons, public figures have a greater burden of proof in defamation cases than do private individuals.

Libel
A written defamation of a person's character, reputation, business, or property rights. The defamatory statement must be observed by a third party.

Actual Malice
Either knowledge of a defamatory statement's falsity or a reckless disregard for the truth.

Public Figure
A public official, movie star, or other person known to the public because of his or her positions or activities.

---

27. *Board of Regents of the University of Wisconsin System v. Southworth,* 529 U.S. 217 (2000).
28. *Doe v. University of Michigan,* 721 F.Supp. 852 (1989).
29. 376 U.S. 254 (1964).

Rush Limbaugh is perhaps one of the most listened to talk radio hosts in America. At times, he has been considered the spokesperson for American conservatives. Should the Federal Communications Commission be able to regulate what he says? (George Gojkovich/Getty Images)

Gag Order
An order issued by a judge restricting the publication of news about a trial or a pretrial hearing to protect the accused's right to a fair trial.

A Free Press versus a Fair Trial: Gag Orders. Another major issue relating to freedom of the press concerns media coverage of criminal trials. The Sixth Amendment to the Constitution guarantees the right of criminal suspects to a fair trial. In other words, the accused have rights. The First Amendment guarantees freedom of the press. What if the two rights appear to be in conflict?

Jurors may be influenced by reading news stories about the trial in which they are participating. In the 1970s, judges increasingly issued **gag orders**—orders that restricted the publication of news about a trial in progress or even a pretrial hearing to protect the accused's right to a fair trial. In a landmark 1976 case, *Nebraska Press Association v. Stuart,*[30] the Supreme Court unanimously ruled that a Nebraska judge's gag order had violated the First Amendment's guarantee of freedom of the press. Despite the *Nebraska Press Association* ruling, the Court has upheld gag orders when it believed that publicity was likely to harm a defendant's right to a fair trial. Given how easy it is for a modern juror to access social media through a smartphone, however, gag orders may have become pointless.

Films, Radio, and TV. As we have noted, in only a few cases has the Supreme Court upheld prior restraint of published materials. The Court's reluctance to accept prior restraint is less evident with respect to motion pictures. In the first half of the twentieth century, films were routinely submitted to local censorship boards. Only in 1952 did the Court find that motion pictures were covered by the First Amendment.[31] In contrast, the Court extended full protection to the Internet almost immediately by striking down provisions of the 1996 Telecommunications Act.[32] Cable TV received broad protection in 2000.[33]

While the Court has held that the First Amendment is relevant to radio and television, it has never extended full protection to these media. The Court has used a number of arguments to justify this stand—initially, the scarcity of broadcast frequencies. The Court later held that the government could restrict "indecent" programming based on the "pervasive" presence of broadcasting in the home.[34] On this basis, the Federal Communications Commission (FCC) has the authority to fine broadcasters for indecency or profanity. The extent of the FCC's authority to penalize broadcasters for such infractions is unclear, however. A Supreme Court ruling in 2012 overturned a specific penalty imposed by the FCC without addressing the fundamental constitutional question.

30. 427 U.S. 539 (1976).
31. *Joseph Burstyn, Inc. v. Wilson,* 343 U.S. 495 (1952).
32. *Reno v. American Civil Liberties Union,* 521 U.S. 844 (1997).
33. *United States v. Playboy Entertainment Group,* 529 U.S. 803 (2000).
34. *FCC v. Pacifica Foundation,* 438 U.S. 726 (1978). In this case, the Court banned seven swear words (famously used by the late comedian George Carlin) during hours when children could hear them.

Radio and television broadcasting has the least First Amendment protection. In 1934, the national government established the Federal Communications Commission (FCC) to regulate electromagnetic wave frequencies. This was done to keep stations from interfering with each other's broadcasts—the number of airwave frequencies is limited. No one has a right to use the airwaves without a license granted by the FCC. The FCC grants licenses for limited periods, and because broadcasts take place under a federal license, it imposes a variety of regulations on broadcasters. For example, the FCC can impose sanctions on radio or TV stations that broadcast "filthy words," even if the words are not legally obscene.

THE RIGHT TO PRIVACY

No explicit reference is made anywhere in the Constitution to a person's right to privacy. Until relatively recently, the courts did not take a very positive approach toward this right. In 1965, however, in *Griswold v. Connecticut*,[35] the Supreme Court overthrew a Connecticut law that effectively prohibited the use of contraceptives, holding that the law violated the right to privacy. Justice William O. Douglas formulated a unique way of reading this right into the Bill of Rights. He claimed that the First, Third, Fourth, Fifth, and Ninth Amendments created "penumbras formed by emanations [shadows, formed by the light], from those guarantees that help give them life and substance," and he went on to describe zones of privacy that are guaranteed by these rights. When we read the Ninth Amendment, we can see the foundation for his reasoning: "The enumeration in the Constitution, of certain rights, shall not be construed to deny or disparage others retained by the people." In other words, the fact that the Constitution, including its amendments, does not specifically talk about the right to privacy does not mean that this right is denied to the people.

LO 4: Provide the constitutional basis of the right to privacy, and explain how the principle has been applied to the abortion and right-to-die controversies.

Privacy Rights and Abortion

Historically, abortion was not a criminal offense before the "quickening" of the fetus (the first movement of the fetus in the uterus, usually between the sixteenth and eighteenth weeks of pregnancy). During the last half of the nineteenth century, however, state laws became more severe. By 1973, performing an abortion at any time during pregnancy was a criminal offense in a majority of the states.

Roe v. Wade. In *Roe v. Wade*[36] (1973), the United States Supreme Court accepted the argument that the laws against abortion violated "Jane Roe's" right to privacy under the Constitution. The Court held that during the first trimester (three months) of pregnancy, abortion was an issue solely between a woman and her physician. The state could not limit abortions except to require that they be performed by licensed physicians. During the second trimester, to protect the health of the mother, the state was allowed to specify the conditions under which an abortion could be performed. During the final trimester, the state could regulate or even outlaw abortions except when they were necessary to preserve the life or health of the mother.

After the *Roe* case, the Supreme Court issued decisions in a number of cases defining and redefining the boundaries of state regulation of abortion. During the 1980s, the

---

35. 381 U.S. 479 (1965).
36. 410 U.S. 113 (1973). Jane Roe was not the real name of the woman in this case. It is a common legal pseudonym used to protect a person's privacy.

This protester stands in front of the Planned Parenthood center in Aurora, Illinois. What limits are placed on anti-abortion protesters? (AP Photo/Stacie Freudenberg)

Court twice struck down laws that required a woman who wished to have an abortion to undergo counseling designed to discourage abortions. In the late 1980s and early 1990s, however, the Court took a more conservative approach. For example, in 1989, the Court upheld a Missouri statute that, among other things, banned the use of public hospitals or other taxpayer-supported facilities for performing abortions.[37] In 1992, the Court upheld a Pennsylvania law that required preabortion counseling, a waiting period of twenty-four hours, and for girls under the age of eighteen, parental or judicial permission.[38] As a result, abortions are more difficult to obtain in some states than in others.

The Controversy Continues. Abortion continues to be a divisive issue. Groups opposed to abortion continue to push for laws restricting abortion, to endorse political candidates who support their views, and to organize protests. Because of several episodes of violence attending protests at abortion clinics, in 1994 Congress passed the Freedom of Access to Clinic Entrances Act. The act prohibits protesters from blocking entrances to such clinics.

In recent years, abortion opponents have concentrated—often unsuccessfully—on state ballot proposals that could lay the groundwork for an eventual challenge to *Roe*. In one 2011 example, in Mississippi voters rejected a measure that would have outlawed all abortions and some forms of birth control. Abortion opponents have been more successful in winning new restrictions on abortion clinics. New state laws became especially common after the 2010 elections, when Republicans took over many state legislative chambers.

---

37. *Webster v. Reproductive Health Services,* 492 U.S. 490 (1989).
38. *Planned Parenthood v. Casey,* 505 U.S. 833 (1992).

"Partial-Birth" Abortion. In 2000, the Supreme Court again addressed the abortion issue directly when it reviewed a Nebraska law banning "partial-birth" abortions. A partial-birth abortion, which physicians call intact dilation and extraction, is a procedure that can be used during the second trimester of pregnancy. Abortion rights advocates claim that in limited circumstances the procedure is the safest way to perform an abortion and that the government should never outlaw specific medical procedures. Opponents argue that the procedure has no medical merit and that it ends the life of a fetus that might be able to live outside the womb. The Supreme Court invalidated the Nebraska law on the ground that the law could be used to ban other abortion procedures and contained no provisions for protecting the health of the pregnant woman.[39]

In 2003, legislation similar to the Nebraska statute was passed by the U.S. Congress and signed into law by President George W. Bush. In 2007, the Supreme Court, with several changes in membership since the 2000 ruling, upheld the federal law in a five-to-four vote, effectively reversing its position on partial-birth abortions.[40]

Privacy Rights and the "Right to Die"

A 1976 case involving Karen Ann Quinlan was one of the first publicized right-to-die cases.[41] The parents of Quinlan, a young woman who had been in a coma for nearly a year and who had been kept alive during that time by a respirator, wanted her respirator removed. The ruling of the New Jersey Supreme Court, *In re Quinlan,* stated that the right to privacy includes the right of a patient to refuse treatment and that patients unable to speak can exercise that right through a family member or guardian. In 1990, the Supreme Court took up the issue. In *Cruzan v. Director, Missouri Department of Health,*[42] the Court stated that a patient's life-sustaining treatment can be withdrawn at the request of a family member only if there is "clear and convincing evidence" that the patient did not want such treatment.

What If There Is No Living Will? Since the 1976 *Quinlan* decision, most states have enacted laws permitting people to designate their wishes concerning life-sustaining procedures in "living wills" or durable health-care powers of attorney. These laws and the Supreme Court's *Cruzan* decision have resolved the right-to-die controversy for cases in which a living will has been drafted. Disputes are still possible if there is no living will.

An example is the case of Terri Schiavo. After the Florida woman had been in a persistent vegetative state for over a decade, her husband sought to have her feeding tube removed on the basis of oral statements that she would not want her life prolonged in such circumstances. Schiavo's parents fought this move in court but lost on the ground that a spouse, not a parent, is the appropriate legal guardian for a married person. Although the Florida legislature passed a law allowing then-governor Jeb Bush to overrule the courts, the state supreme court held that the law violated the state constitution.[43] The federal courts agreed with the Florida state courts and Schiavo died shortly thereafter.

Physician-Assisted Suicide. In the 1990s, another issue surfaced: Do privacy rights include the right of terminally ill people to end their lives through physician-assisted suicide? Until 1996, the courts consistently upheld state laws that prohibited this practice.

---

39. *Stenberg v. Carhart,* 530 U.S. 914 (2000).
40. *Gonzales v. Carhart,* 550 U.S. 124 (2007).
41. 70 N.J. 10 (1976).
42. 497 U.S. 261 (1990).
43. *Bush v. Schiavo,* 885 So.2d 321 (Fla. 2004).

In 1996, after two federal appellate courts ruled that state laws banning assisted suicide were unconstitutional, the issue reached the United States Supreme Court. In 1997, the Court stated that the liberty interest protected by the Constitution does not include a right to commit suicide, with or without assistance.[44] The Court left the decision on whether to permit the practice in the hands of the states. Since then, assisted suicide has been allowed in only three states—Montana, Oregon, and Washington. In 2006, the Supreme Court upheld Oregon's physician-assisted suicide law against a challenge from the George W. Bush administration.[45]

THE GREAT BALANCING ACT: THE RIGHTS OF THE ACCUSED VERSUS THE RIGHTS OF SOCIETY

LO5: Identify the constitutional rights of those who are accused of a crime, describe the *Miranda* and exclusionary rules, and cite examples of how recent security concerns have affected our civil liberties.

The United States has one of the highest murder rates in the industrialized world. It is not surprising, therefore, that many citizens have extremely strong opinions about the rights of those accused of violent crimes. When an accused person, especially one who has confessed to some criminal act, is set free because of an apparent legal "technicality," many people believe that the rights of the accused are being given more weight than the rights of potential or actual victims. Why, then, give criminal suspects rights? The answer is partly to avoid convicting innocent people, but mostly because due process of law and fair treatment benefit everyone who comes into contact with law enforcement or the courts.

The courts and the police must constantly engage in a balancing act of competing rights. The basis of all discussions about the appropriate balance is, of course, the U.S. Bill of Rights. The Fourth, Fifth, Sixth, and Eighth Amendments deal specifically with the rights of criminal defendants.

Rights of the Accused

The basic rights of criminal defendants are outlined below. When appropriate, the specific constitutional provision or amendment on which a right is based is also given.

Writ of Habeas Corpus
Habeas corpus means, literally, "you have the body." A writ of *habeas corpus* is an order that requires jailers to bring a prisoner before a court or judge and explain why the person is being held.

Arraignment
The first act in a criminal proceeding, in which the defendant is brought before a court to hear the charges against him or her and enter a plea of guilty or not guilty.

Limits on the Conduct of Police Officers and Prosecutors
- No unreasonable or unwarranted searches and seizures (Amendment IV).
- No arrest except on probable cause (Amendment IV).
- No coerced confessions or illegal interrogation (Amendment V).
- No entrapment.
- On questioning, following an arrest, a suspect must be informed of her or his rights.

Defendant's Pretrial Rights
- **Writ of *habeas corpus*** (Article I, Section 9).
- Prompt **arraignment** (Amendment VI).
- Legal counsel (Amendment VI).
- Reasonable bail (Amendment VIII).
- To be informed of charges (Amendment VI).
- To remain silent (Amendment V).

44. *Washington v. Glucksberg*, 521 U.S. 702 (1997).
45. *Gonzales v. Oregon*, 546 U.S. 243 (2006).

Trial Rights

- Speedy and public trial before a jury (Amendment VI).
- Impartial jury selected from a cross section of the community (Amendment VI).
- Trial atmosphere free of prejudice, fear, and outside interference.
- No compulsory self-incrimination (Amendment V).
- Adequate counsel (Amendment VI).
- No cruel and unusual punishment (Amendment VIII).
- Appeal of convictions.
- No double jeopardy (Amendment V).

Extending the Rights of the Accused

During the 1960s, the Supreme Court, under Chief Justice Earl Warren, significantly expanded the rights of accused persons. In a case decided in 1963, *Gideon v. Wainwright,*[46] the Court held that if a person is accused of a felony and cannot afford an attorney, an attorney must be made available to the accused person at the government's expense. Although the Sixth Amendment to the Constitution provides for the right to counsel, the Supreme Court had previously held that only criminal defendants in capital cases automatically had a right to free legal counsel.

Miranda v. Arizona. In 1966, the Court issued its decision in *Miranda v. Arizona.*[47] The case involved Ernesto Miranda, who was charged with the kidnapping and rape of a young woman. After questioning, Miranda confessed and was later convicted. Miranda's lawyer appealed his conviction, arguing that the police had never informed Miranda that he had a right to remain silent and a right to be represented by counsel. The Court, in ruling in Miranda's favor, enunciated the now-familiar *Miranda* rights. Today, *Miranda* rights statements typically take the following form:

> *You have the right to remain silent. Anything you say can and will be used against you in a court of law. You have the right to speak to an attorney. If you cannot afford an attorney, one will be appointed for you. Do you understand these rights as they have been read to you?*

Exceptions to the *Miranda* Rule. As part of a continuing attempt to balance the rights of accused persons against the rights of society, the Supreme Court has made a number of exceptions to the *Miranda* rule. As one example, in an important 1991 decision, the Court stated that a suspect's conviction will not be automatically overturned if the suspect was coerced into making a confession. If the other evidence admitted at trial is strong enough to justify the conviction without the confession, then the fact that the confession was obtained illegally can be effectively ignored.[48]

The Exclusionary Rule

At least since 1914, judicial policy has prohibited the admission of illegally seized evidence at trials in federal courts. This is the so-called **exclusionary rule.** Improperly obtained evidence, no matter how telling, cannot be used by prosecutors. This includes evidence obtained by police in violation of a suspect's *Miranda* rights or of the Fourth Amendment.

Exclusionary Rule
A judicial policy prohibiting the admission at trial of illegally seized evidence.

---

46. 372 U.S. 335 (1963).
47. 384 U.S. 436 (1966).
48. *Arizona v. Fulminante,* 499 U.S. 279 (1991).

The Fourth Amendment protects against unreasonable searches and seizures and provides that a judge may issue a search warrant to a police officer only on probable cause (a demonstration of facts that permit a reasonable belief that a crime has been committed). The courts must determine what constitutes an "unreasonable" search and seizure.

The reasoning behind the exclusionary rule is that it forces police officers to gather evidence properly, in which case their due diligence will be rewarded by a conviction. Nevertheless, the exclusionary rule has always had critics who argue that it permits guilty persons to be freed because of innocent procedural errors by the police.

This rule was first extended to state court proceedings in a 1961 United States Supreme Court decision, *Mapp v. Ohio*.[49] In this case, the Court overturned the conviction of Dollree Mapp for the possession of obscene materials. Police found pornographic books in her apartment after searching it without a search warrant and despite her refusal to let them in. Under the Fourth Amendment, search warrants must describe the persons or things to be seized. However, officers are entitled to seize items not mentioned in the search warrant if the materials are in "plain view" and reasonably appear to be contraband or evidence of a crime.[50]

During the past several decades, the Supreme Court has diminished the scope of the exclusionary rule by creating exceptions to its applicability. For example, in 1984 the Court held that illegally obtained evidence could be admitted at trial if law enforcement personnel could prove that they would have obtained the evidence legally anyway.[51] The Court has also created a "good faith" exception to the exclusionary rule. In 2009, for example, the Court found that the good faith exception applies when an officer makes an arrest based on an outstanding warrant in another jurisdiction, even if the warrant in question was based on a clerical error.[52]

Civil Liberties versus Security Issues

As former Supreme Court justice Thurgood Marshall once said, "Grave threats to liberty often come in times of urgency, when constitutional rights seem too extravagant to endure." Not surprisingly, antiterrorist legislation since the attacks on September 11, 2001, has eroded certain basic rights, in particular the Fourth Amendment protections against unreasonable searches and seizures.

The USA Patriot Act. The most significant piece of antiterrorism legislation, the USA Patriot Act, was passed in 2001 and renewed in 2006. Many in government believed that a lack of cooperation among government agencies was a major reason for the failure to anticipate the 9/11 attacks. One goal of the Patriot Act was to lift such barriers to cooperation. Under the Patriot Act, law enforcement officials can also secretly search a suspect's home and monitor a suspect's Internet activities, phone conversations, and financial records. The government can even open a suspect's mail. While many believe that the Patriot Act is a necessary safety measure to prevent future terrorist attacks, others argue that it endangers civil liberties.

"Roving" Wiretaps. One civil liberties issue involves "roving" wiretaps. Previously, only specific telephone numbers, cell phone numbers, or computers could be tapped.

---

49. 367 U.S. 643 (1961).
50. *Texas v. Brown*, 460 U.S. 730 (1983); and *Horton v. California*, 496 U.S. 128 (1990).
51. *Nix v. Williams*, 467 U.S. 431 (1984).
52. *Herring v. United States*, 555 U.S. 135 (2009).

Now a person under suspicion can be monitored electronically regardless of location or the technology in use. Such roving wiretaps appear to be inconsistent with the Fourth Amendment, which requires a judicial warrant to describe the *place* to be searched, not just the person. As an unavoidable side effect, the government has access to the conversations and e-mail of many innocent people.

National Security Agency Surveillance. In 2001, President Bush authorized the National Security Agency (NSA) to conduct secret surveillance without court warrants, even warrants from special security courts. The NSA was to monitor phone calls and other communications between foreign parties and persons within the United States when one of the parties had suspected links to terrorist organizations. When news of the program came out in 2005, it was criticized by civil liberties groups. In 2007 and 2008, however, Congress passed laws to authorize the NSA wiretaps.

Recent Revelations of NSA Activity. In June 2013, leaks provided by an employee of a federal contractor revealed that NSA surveillance was far more extensive than previously assumed. Among the most striking revelations was that the NSA gathers information on *every* domestic phone call made in the United States and other countries. The NSA does not record the contents of the calls, but rather *"metadata,"* which includes time of call, the number of the caller, and the number of the phone that was called.

Under a second program, PRISM, the NSA collects information from the Web sites of corporations, including Apple, Google, Facebook, Microsoft, Skype, and others. A third revelation was of major espionage actions against European countries. These included bugging the offices of the European Union in advance of trade talks between the United States and that organization. The reports resulted in an outcry by U.S. civil libertarians and by European leaders. The Obama administration defended the programs, however, noting—correctly—that they had been authorized by secret courts and that foreign citizens are not protected by the Bill of Rights.

National Security and the Civil Liberties of Immigrants

For many U.S. citizens, immigration—especially unauthorized or illegal immigration—is a national security issue. The terrorist attacks on September 11, 2001, reinforced the belief that the civil liberties of noncitizens should be limited. Among the most obvious characteristics of the terrorists who perpetrated the 9/11 attacks is that they were all foreign citizens. Still, legal immigrants who are not citizens have rights. The Bill of Rights contains no language that limits its protections to citizens.

A Hong Kong protester holds a placard supporting Edward Snowden, a former NSA contractor charged under the U.S. Espionage Act. Snowden fled to Hong Kong after exposing U.S. surveillance programs and is now living in Russia. (Luke Casey/Bloomberg via Getty Images)

The Fourteenth Amendment specifies that all *persons* (as opposed to all *citizens*) shall enjoy "due process of law."

Illegal immigrants are subject to deportation. In 1903, however, the Supreme Court ruled that the government could not deport someone without a hearing that meets constitutional due process standards.[53] Today, most people facing deportation are entitled to a hearing before an immigration judge, to representation by a lawyer, and to the right to see the evidence presented against them. The government must prove that its grounds for deportation are valid.

Limits to the Rights of Deportees: Due Process. Despite the language of the Fourteenth Amendment, the courts have often deferred to government assertions that noncitizens cannot make constitutional claims. The Antiterrorism and Effective Death Penalty Act passed by Congress in 1996 was especially restrictive. The government was given the right to deport noncitizens for alleged terrorism without any court review of the deportation order. Further, the government is now allowed to deport noncitizens based on secret evidence that the deportee is not permitted to see.

Limits to the Rights of Deportees: Freedom of Speech. A case in 1999 involved a group of noncitizens associated with the Popular Front for the Liberation of Palestine (PFLP). The PFLP had carried out terrorist acts in Israel, but there was no evidence of criminal conduct by the group arrested in the United States. In this case, the Supreme Court ruled that aliens have no First Amendment rights to object to deportation, even if the deportation is based on their political associations.[54] This ruling also covers permanent residents—noncitizens with "green cards" that allow them to live and work in the United States on a long-term basis.

Limits to the Rights of Deportees: *Ex Post Facto* Laws. Article I, Section 9, of the Constitution prohibits *ex post facto* laws—laws that inflict punishments for acts that were not illegal when they were committed. This provision may not apply in deportation cases, however. The 1996 law mentioned earlier provided mandatory deportation for noncitizens convicted of an aggravated felony, even if the crime took place before 1996. Under the 1996 law, permanent residents have been deported to nations that they left when they were small children. In some cases, deported persons did not even speak the language of the country to which they were deported.

---

53. *Yamataya v. Fisher,* 189 U.S. 86 (1903).
54. *Reno v. American-Arab Anti-Discrimination Committee,* 525 U.S. 471 (1999).

making a **difference**

YOUR CIVIL LIBERTIES: SEARCHES AND SEIZURES

Our civil liberties include numerous provisions, many of them listed in the Bill of Rights, that protect persons who are suspected of criminal activity. Among these are limits on how the police—as agents of the government—can conduct searches and seizures.

Why Should You Care? You may be the most law-abiding person in the world, but that does not guarantee that you will never be stopped, arrested, or searched by the police. Sooner or later, the great majority of all citizens will have some kind of interaction with the police. People who do not understand their rights or how to behave toward law enforcement officers can find themselves in serious trouble.

What Are Your Rights? How should you behave if you are stopped by police officers? Your civil liberties protect you from having to provide information other than your name and address. Normally, even if you have not been placed under arrest, the officers have the right to frisk you for weapons, and you must let them proceed. The officers cannot, however, check your person or your clothing further if, in their judgment, no weaponlike object is produced.

The officers may search you only if they have a search warrant or probable cause to believe that a search will likely produce incriminating evidence. What if the officers do not have probable cause or a warrant? Physically resisting their attempt to search you can lead to disastrous results. You can simply refuse orally to give permission for the search, if possible in the presence of a witness. Being polite is better than acting out of anger and making the officers irritable.

If you are in your car and are stopped by the police, the same fundamental rules apply. Always be ready to show your driver's license and car registration. You may be asked to get out of the car. The officers may use a flashlight to peer inside if it is too dark to see otherwise. None of this constitutes a search. A true search requires either a warrant or a probable cause. No officer has the legal right to search your car simply to find out if you may have committed a crime.

If you are in your home and a police officer with a search warrant appears, you can ask to examine the warrant before granting entry. A warrant that is correctly made out will state the place or persons to be searched, the object sought, and the date of the warrant (which should be no more than ten days old). It will also bear the signature of a judge or magistrate. If you believe the warrant to be invalid, or if no warrant is produced, you should make it clear orally that you have not consented to the search, if possible in the presence of a witness.

Officers who attempt to enter your home without a search warrant can do so only if they are pursuing a suspected felon into the house. Rarely is it advisable to give permission for a warrantless search. You, as the resident, must be the one to give permission if any evidence obtained is to be considered legal. A landlord, manager, or head of a college dormitory cannot give legal permission. A roommate, however, can give permission for a search of his or her room, which may allow the police to search areas where you have belongings.

If you would like to find out more about your rights and obligations under the laws of searches and seizures, you might want to contact the American Civil Liberties Union. You can find its Web site by entering the initials "aclu" into your favorite search engine.

This man was arrested on suspicion of shooting his estranged wife and his mother-in-law. Can the police legally search him without a warrant? (AP Photo/Sharon Cekada/Post-Crescent)

key**terms**

actual malice 79
arraignment 84
commercial speech 75
defamation of
    character 77
establishment clause 69

exclusionary rule 85
free exercise clause 73
gag order 80
imminent lawless action
    test 76

incorporation theory 68
libel 79
obscenity 76
prior restraint 73
public figure 79

slander 77
symbolic speech 74
writ of *habeas corpus* 84

chapter**summary**

1 Originally, the Bill of Rights limited only the power of the national government, not that of the states. Gradually and selectively, however, the Supreme Court accepted the incorporation theory, under which no state can violate most provisions of the Bill of Rights.

2 The First Amendment protects against government interference with freedom of religion by requiring a separation of church and state (under the establishment clause) and by guaranteeing the free exercise of religion. Controversial issues that arise under the establishment clause include aid to church-related schools, school vouchers, school prayer, the teaching of evolution, and religious displays on public property. The government can interfere with the free exercise of religion only when religious practices work against public policy or the public welfare.

3 The First Amendment protects against government interference with freedom of speech, which includes symbolic speech (expressive conduct). The Supreme Court has been especially critical of government actions that impose prior restraint on expression. Commercial speech (advertising) by businesses has received limited First Amendment protection. Restrictions on expression are permitted when the expression may incite imminent lawless action. Other speech that has not received First Amendment protection includes expression judged to be obscene or slanderous.

4 The First Amendment protects against government interference with the freedom of the press, which can be regarded as a special instance of freedom of speech. Speech by the press that does not receive protection includes libelous statements.

Publication of news about a criminal trial may be restricted by a gag order in some circumstances.

5 Under the Ninth Amendment, people's rights are not limited to those specifically mentioned in the Constitution. Among the unspecified rights protected by the courts is a right to privacy, which has been inferred from the First, Third, Fourth, Fifth, and Ninth Amendments. Whether an individual's privacy rights include a right to an abortion or a "right to die" continues to provoke controversy.

6 The Constitution includes protections for the rights of persons accused of crimes. Under the Fourth Amendment, no one may be subject to an unreasonable search or seizure or be arrested except on probable cause. Under the Fifth Amendment, an accused person has the right to remain silent. Under the Sixth Amendment, an accused person must be informed of the reason for his or her arrest. The accused also has the right to adequate counsel, even if he or she cannot afford an attorney, and the right to a prompt arraignment and a speedy and public trial before an impartial jury selected from a cross section of the community.

7 In *Miranda v. Arizona* (1966), the Supreme Court held that criminal suspects, before interrogation by law enforcement personnel, must be informed of the right to remain silent and the right to counsel. The exclusionary rule forbids the admission in court of illegally obtained evidence. There is a "good faith" exception to the exclusionary rule: evidence need not be thrown out due to, for example, a clerical error in a database.

8 Another major challenge concerns the extent to which we must forfeit civil liberties to control terrorism.

test**yourself**

LO1 *Describe the Bill of Rights and how it came to be applied to state governments as well as the national government.*

As originally intended, the Bill of Rights limited the powers of:

    a. only the state governments.

    b. both the national government and the state governments.

    c. only the national government.

LO2 *Explain how the First Amendment's establishment clause and free exercise clause guarantee our freedom of religion.*

The Supreme Court has held that any law prohibiting the teaching of evolution:

    a. violates the establishment clause because it imposes religious beliefs on students.

    b. violates the free exercise clause of the First Amendment because it bars the beliefs of atheists.

    c. violates both the establishment clause and the free exercise clause.

LO3 *Specify the limited circumstances, including obscenity and slander, in which the national and state governments may override the principles of free speech and freedom of the press.*

If you utter a false statement that harms the good reputation of another, it is called slander and such expression is:

    a. always protected under the First Amendment.

    b. unprotected speech and a potential basis for a lawsuit.

    c. prosecuted as a felony in most states.

LO4 *Provide the constitutional basis of the right to privacy, and explain how the principle has been applied to the abortion and right-to-die controversies.*

The right to privacy:

    a. is explicitly guaranteed by the original text of the Constitution.

    b. is explicitly guaranteed by the Fifth Amendment to the Constitution.

    c. has been inferred from other rights by the Supreme Court.

LO5 *Identify the constitutional rights of those who are accused of a crime, describe the Miranda and exclusionary rules, and cite examples of how recent security concerns have affected our civil liberties.*

Illegally seized evidence is not admissible at trial because of the:

    a. exclusionary rule.

    b. *Miranda* rule.

    c. writ of *habeas corpus*.

Essay Question:

The courts have never held that the provision of military chaplains by the armed forces is unconstitutional, despite the fact that chaplains are religious leaders who are employed by and under the authority of the U.S. government. What arguments might the courts use to defend the military chaplain system?

Answers to multiple-choice questions: 1. c, 2. a, 3. b, 4. c, 5. a.

CourseMate

Access CourseMate at **www.cengagebrain.com** for additional study tools: practice quizzes, key term flashcards and crossword puzzles, audio chapter summaries, simulations, animated learning modules, interactive timelines, videos, and American Government NewsWatch.

5

Alabama citizens stand outside the United States Supreme Court in February 2013. The Court was hearing arguments in a legal challenge to provisions of the Voting Rights Act of 1965. Does the federal government still need to intervene to protect the voting rights of African Americans? (Chip Somodevilla/Getty Images)

Civil Rights

LEARNING OUTCOMES

The five **Learning Outcomes (LOs)** below are designed to help improve your understanding of this chapter. After reading this chapter, you should be able to:

■ **LO1** Summarize the historical experience of African Americans, state how the separate-but-equal doctrine was abolished, and describe the consequences of the civil rights movement.

■ **LO2** Contrast the goals of the women's suffrage movement with the goals of modern feminism.

■ **LO3** Explain the demographic impacts of immigration and of the interactions between European settlers and American Indians.

■ **LO4** Define *affirmative action*, and provide some of the arguments against it.

■ **LO5** Summarize the recent revolution in the rights enjoyed by gay men and lesbians.

Check your understanding of the material with the Test Yourself section at the end of the chapter.

Civil Rights
Generally, all rights rooted in the Fourteenth Amendment's guarantee of equal protection under the law.

Equality is at the heart of the concept of civil rights.

Generally, the term **civil rights** refers to the rights of all Americans to equal protection under the law, as provided for by the Fourteenth Amendment to the Constitution. Although the terms *civil rights* and *civil liberties* are sometimes used interchangeably, scholars make a distinction between the two. As discussed in Chapter 4, civil liberties are basically *limitations* on government. They specify what the government *cannot* do. Civil rights, in contrast, specify what the government *must* do to ensure equal protection and freedom from discrimination.

The history of civil rights in America is the story of the struggle of various groups to be free from discriminatory treatment. In this chapter, we first look at two movements that had significant consequences for civil rights in America: the civil rights movement of the 1950s and 1960s and the women's movement, which began in the mid-1800s and continues today. Each of these movements resulted in legislation that secured important basic rights for all Americans—the right to vote and the right to equal protection under the laws. We then explore a question with serious implications for today's voters and policymakers: What should the government's responsibility be when equal protection under the law is not enough to ensure truly equal opportunities for Americans?

Note that most minorities in this nation have suffered—and some continue to suffer—from discrimination. These include such groups as older Americans and persons with disabilities. The fact that some groups are not singled out for special attention in the following pages should not be construed to mean that their struggle for equality is any less significant than the struggles of those groups that we do discuss.

Social Media in Politics

Twitter contains a large number of hashtags devoted to civil rights. You could check out #civilrights, #womensrights, or #gayrights.

THE AFRICAN AMERICAN EXPERIENCE AND THE CIVIL RIGHTS MOVEMENT

Before 1863, the Constitution protected slavery and made equality impossible in the sense in which we use the word today. The inferior status of African Americans was confirmed just a few years before the outbreak of the Civil War in the infamous *Dred Scott v. Sandford*[1] case of 1857. The Supreme Court held that slaves and their descendants—even if free—were not citizens of the United States, nor were they entitled to the rights and privileges of citizenship. The *Dred Scott* decision had grave consequences. Many historians contend that the ruling contributed to making the Civil War inevitable.

LO1: Summarize the historical experience of African Americans, state how the separate-but-equal doctrine was abolished, and describe the consequences of the civil rights movement.

Ending Servitude

With the emancipation of the slaves by President Lincoln's Emancipation Proclamation in 1863 and the passage of the Thirteenth, Fourteenth, and Fifteenth Amendments during the Reconstruction period (1865–1877) following the Civil War, constitutional inequality was ended.

Constitutional Amendments. The Thirteenth Amendment (1865) states that neither slavery nor involuntary servitude shall exist within the United States. The Fourteenth Amendment (1868) tells us that *all* persons born or naturalized in the United States are citizens of the United States. It states, furthermore, that "[n]o State shall make or enforce any law which shall abridge the privileges or immunities of citizens of the United States; nor shall

An African American soldier in the Union Army during the Civil War, about 1863. What influence might such troops have had on the struggle for African American rights after the Civil War? (Archive Photos/Getty Images)

1. 60 U.S. 393 (1857).

any State deprive any person of life, liberty, or property, without due process of law; nor deny to any person within its jurisdiction the equal protection of the laws." Note the use of the terms *citizen* and *person* in this amendment. *Citizens* have political rights, such as the right to vote and run for political office. Citizens also have certain privileges or immunities (see Chapter 3). All *persons,* however, including noncitizen immigrants, have a right to due process of law and equal protection under the law.

Finally, the Fifteenth Amendment (1870) reads as follows: "The right of citizens of the United States to vote shall not be denied or abridged by the United States or by any State on account of race, color, or previous condition of servitude."

The Civil Rights Acts of 1865 to 1875. From 1865 to 1875, Congress passed a series of civil rights acts to enforce the Thirteenth, Fourteenth, and Fifteenth Amendments. The Civil Rights Act of 1866 implemented the extension of citizenship to anyone born in the United States and gave African Americans full equality before the law. The act further authorized the president to enforce the law with the national armed forces. The Enforcement Act of 1870 set out specific criminal penalties for interfering with the right to vote as protected by the Fifteenth Amendment and by the Civil Rights Act of 1866.

Equally important was the Civil Rights Act of 1872, known as the Anti–Ku Klux Klan Act. This act made it a federal crime for anyone to use law or custom to deprive an individual of rights, privileges, and immunities secured by the Constitution or by any federal law. The Second Civil Rights Act, passed in 1875, declared that everyone is entitled to full and equal enjoyment of public accommodations, theaters, and other places of public amusement, and it imposed penalties on violators.

The Ineffectiveness of the Early Civil Rights Laws

The Reconstruction statutes, or civil rights acts, ultimately did little to secure equality for African Americans. Both the *Civil Rights Cases* and the case of *Plessy v. Ferguson* (discussed next) effectively nullified these acts. Additionally, various barriers were erected that prevented African Americans from exercising their right to vote.

The *Civil Rights Cases*. The United States Supreme Court invalidated the 1875 Second Civil Rights Act when it held, in the *Civil Rights Cases*[2] of 1883, that the enforcement clause of the Fourteenth Amendment (which states that "[n]o State shall make or enforce any law which shall abridge the privileges or immunities of citizens") was limited to correcting *official* actions taken by states. Thus, the discriminatory acts of private citizens were not illegal. ("Individual invasion of individual rights is not the subject matter of the Amendment.") The 1883 Supreme Court decision met with widespread approval by whites throughout most of the United States.

Twenty years after the Civil War, the white majority was all too willing to forget about the Civil War amendments to the U.S. Constitution and the civil rights legislation of the 1860s and 1870s. The other civil rights laws that the Court did not specifically invalidate became dead letters in the statute books, although they were never officially repealed by Congress. At the same time, many former Confederate leaders had regained political power in the southern states.

Plessy v. Ferguson: Separate but Equal. A key decision during this period concerned Homer Plessy, a Louisiana resident who was one-eighth African American. In 1892,

---

2. 109 U.S. 3 (1883).

he boarded a train in New Orleans. The conductor made him leave the car, which was restricted to whites, and directed him to a car for nonwhites. At that time, Louisiana had a statute providing for separate railway cars for whites and African Americans.

Plessy went to court, claiming that such a statute was contrary to the Fourteenth Amendment's equal protection clause. In 1896, the United States Supreme Court rejected Plessy's contention in *Plessy v. Ferguson*.[3] The Court concluded that the Fourteenth Amendment "could not have been intended to abolish distinctions based upon color, or to enforce social . . . equality." The Court stated that segregation alone did not violate the Constitution: "Laws permitting, and even requiring, their separation in places where they are liable to be brought into contact do not necessarily imply the inferiority of either race to the other." So was born the **separate-but-equal doctrine.**

Plessy v. Ferguson became the judicial cornerstone of racial discrimination throughout the United States. Even though Plessy upheld segregated facilities in railway cars only, it was assumed that the Supreme Court was upholding segregation everywhere. The result was a system of racial segregation, particularly in the South, supported by state and local "Jim Crow" laws. (*Jim Crow* was an insulting term for African Americans derived from a song-and-dance-show.) These laws required separate drinking fountains; separate seats in theaters, restaurants, and hotels; separate public toilets; and separate waiting rooms for the two races. "Separate" was indeed the rule, but "equal" was never enforced, nor was it a reality.

Voting Barriers. The brief voting enfranchisement of African Americans ended after 1877, when the federal troops that occupied the South during the Reconstruction era were withdrawn. White supremacist politicians regained control of state governments and, using everything except race as a formal criterion, passed laws that effectively deprived African Americans of the right to vote. By using the ruse that political parties were private entities, the Democratic Party managed to keep black voters from its primaries. The **white primary** was upheld by the Supreme Court until 1944, when the Court ruled it a violation of the Fifteenth Amendment.[4]

Another barrier to African American voting was the **grandfather clause,** which restricted voting to those who could prove that their grandfathers had voted before 1867. **Poll taxes** required the payment of a fee to vote. Thus, poor African Americans—as well as poor whites—who could not afford to pay the tax were excluded from voting. Not until the Twenty-fourth Amendment to the Constitution was ratified in 1964 was the poll tax eliminated as a precondition to voting. **Literacy tests** were also used to deny the vote to African Americans. Such tests asked potential voters to read, recite, or interpret complicated texts, such as a section of the state constitution, to the satisfaction of local registrars—who were, of course, rarely satisfied with the responses of African Americans.

Extralegal Methods of Enforcing White Supremacy. The second-class status of African Americans was also a matter of social custom, especially in the South. In their inter-actions with southern whites, African Americans were expected to observe an informal but detailed code of behavior that confirmed their inferiority. The most serious violation of the informal code was "familiarity" toward a white woman by an African American man. The code was backed up by the common practice of *lynching*—mob action to murder an accused individual, usually by hanging and sometimes accompanied by torture. Of course,

Separate-but-Equal Doctrine
The doctrine holding that separate-but-equal facilities do not violate the equal protection clause of the Fourteenth Amendment to the U.S. Constitution.

White Primary
A state primary election that restricted voting to whites only. Outlawed by the Supreme Court in 1944.

Grandfather Clause
A device used by southern states to disenfranchise African Americans. It restricted voting to those whose grandfathers had voted before 1867.

Poll Tax
A special tax that had to be paid as a qualification for voting. The Twenty-fourth Amendment to the Constitution outlawed the poll tax in national elections, and in 1966, the Supreme Court declared it unconstitutional in state elections as well.

Literacy Test
A test administered as a precondition for voting, often used to prevent African Americans from exercising their right to vote.

---

3. 163 U.S. 537 (1896).
4. *Smith v. Allwright,* 321 U.S. 649 (1944).

lynching was illegal, but southern authorities rarely prosecuted these cases, and white juries would not convict.

The End of the Separate-but-Equal Doctrine

As early as the 1930s, several court rulings began to chip away at the separate-but-equal doctrine. The United States Supreme Court did not explicitly overturn *Plessy v. Ferguson* until 1954, however, when it issued one of the most famous judicial decisions in U.S. history.

In 1951, Oliver Brown decided that his eight-year-old daughter, Linda Carol Brown, should not have to go to an all-nonwhite elementary school twenty-one blocks from her home, when there was a white school only seven blocks away. The National Association for the Advancement of Colored People (NAACP), formed in 1909, decided to support Oliver Brown. The outcome would have a monumental impact on American society.

Brown v. Board of Education of Topeka. The 1954 unanimous decision of the United States Supreme Court in *Brown v. Board of Education of Topeka*[5] established that the segregation of races in the public schools violates the equal protection clause of the Fourteenth Amendment. Chief Justice Earl Warren said that separation implied inferiority, whereas the majority opinion in *Plessy v. Ferguson* had said the opposite.

"With All Deliberate Speed." The following year, in *Brown v. Board of Education*[6] (sometimes called the second *Brown* decision), the Court declared that the lower courts needed to ensure that African Americans would be admitted to schools on a nondiscriminatory basis "with all deliberate speed." The district courts were to consider devices in their desegregation orders that might include "the school transportation system, personnel, [and] revision of school districts and attendance areas into compact units to achieve a system of determining admission to the public schools on a nonracial basis."

When Oliver Brown wanted his daughter Linda (shown here) to attend a white school close to their home, he took his case all the way to the United States Supreme Court. The outcome of that case is considered a landmark decision. Why? (AP Photo)

Reactions to School Integration. The white South did not let the Supreme Court ruling go unchallenged. Governor Orval Faubus of Arkansas used the state's National Guard to block the integration of Central High School in Little Rock in September 1957. A federal court demanded that the troops be withdrawn. Finally, President Dwight Eisenhower had to federalize the Arkansas National Guard and send in the Army's 101st Airborne Division to quell the violence. Central High became integrated.

Universities in the South remained segregated. When James Meredith, an African American student, attempted to enroll at the University of Mississippi in Oxford in 1962, violence flared there, as it had in Little Rock. The white riot at Oxford was so intense that President John Kennedy was forced to send in thirty thousand U.S. combat troops, a larger force than the one then stationed in Korea. There were 375 military and civilian injuries, many from gunfire, and two bystanders were killed. Ultimately, peace was restored, and Meredith began attending classes.[7]

---

5. 347 U.S. 483 (1954).
6. 349 U.S. 294 (1955).
7. William Doyle, *An American Insurrection: James Meredith and the Battle of Oxford, Mississippi, 1962* (New York: Anchor, 2003).

De Jure and *De Facto* Segregation

The kind of segregation faced by Linda Carol Brown and James Meredith is called ***de jure segregation,*** because it is the result of discriminatory laws or government actions. (*De jure* is Latin for "by law.") A second kind of public school segregation was common in many northern communities—***de facto* segregation.** This term refers to segregation that is not due to an explicit law but results from other causes, such as residential patterns. Neighborhoods inhabited almost entirely by African Americans naturally led to *de facto* segregation of the public schools.

Discrimination was still involved, however. In many communities, landlords would only rent to African Americans in specific districts, and realtors would not allow them to view houses for sale outside of these zones. In other words, nongovernmental discrimination confined African Americans to all-black districts, which became known as *ghettos.*[8]

One method used by federal courts in the 1970s and 1980s to address both *de jure* and *de facto* segregation in the public schools was to bus students from black neighborhoods into white ones, and vice versa. Busing proved to be enormously unpopular. In the mid-1970s, about three-fourths of all whites opposed the policy, as did almost half of all African Americans. By the 1990s, federal courts were backing away from the practice. The desegregation of U.S. public schools peaked in 1988, and since then the schools have grown more segregated. Indeed, today, school admissions policies that favor minority applicants in an attempt to reduce *de facto* segregation may end up being challenged on equal protection grounds. (For a further discussion of this issue, see the section on affirmative action later in this chapter.)

The Civil Rights Movement

The *Brown* decisions applied only to public schools. Not much else in the structure of existing segregation was affected. In December 1955, an African American woman, Rosa Parks, boarded a public bus in Montgomery, Alabama. When the bus became crowded, Parks was asked to move to the rear of the bus, the "colored" section. She refused, was arrested, and was fined $10. But that was not the end of the matter. For an entire year, African Americans boycotted the Montgomery bus line. The protest was headed by a twenty-seven-year-old Baptist minister, Dr. Martin Luther King, Jr. In the face of overwhelming odds, the protesters won. In 1956, a federal district court issued an injunction prohibiting the segregation of buses in Montgomery. The era of civil rights protests had begun.

King's Philosophy of Nonviolence. In the following year, 1957, King formed the Southern Christian Leadership Conference (SCLC). King advocated nonviolent **civil disobedience** as a means to achieve racial justice. The SCLC used tactics such as demonstrations and marches, as well as nonviolent, public disobedience of unjust laws. King's followers successfully used these methods to gain wider public acceptance of their cause.

For the next decade, African Americans and sympathetic whites engaged in sit-ins, freedom rides, and freedom marches. In the beginning, such demonstrations were often met with violence, and the contrasting image of nonviolent African Americans and violent, hostile whites created strong public support for the civil rights movement.

***De Facto* Segregation**
Racial segregation that occurs because of patterns of racial residence and similar social conditions.

***De Jure* Segregation**
Racial segregation that occurs because of laws or administrative decisions by public agencies.

Civil Disobedience
A nonviolent, public refusal to obey allegedly unjust laws.

---

8. *Ghetto* was originally the name of a district in Venice, Italy, in which Venetian Jews were required to live.

Martin Luther King, Jr.'s, speech at the Washington Monument in 1963 was watched by millions of Americans on television. What were his most famous words? (AFP/Stringer/Getty Images)

The March on Washington. In August 1963, African American leaders A. Philip Randolph and Bayard Rustin organized the massive March on Washington for Jobs and Freedom. Before nearly a quarter-million white and African American spectators and millions watching on television, Martin Luther King told the world: "I have a dream that my four little children will one day live in a nation where they will not be judged by the color of their skin but by the content of their character."

Modern Civil Rights Legislation

Attacks on demonstrators using police dogs, cattle prods, high-pressure water hoses, beatings, and bombings—plus the March on Washington—all led to an environment in which Congress felt compelled to act on behalf of African Americans. The second era of civil rights acts, sometimes referred to as the second Reconstruction period, was under way.

The Civil Rights Act of 1964. The Civil Rights Act of 1964, the most far-reaching bill on civil rights in modern times, banned discrimination on the basis of race, color, religion, gender, or national origin. The major provisions of the act were as follows:

■ It outlawed arbitrary discrimination in voter registration.
■ It barred discrimination in public accommodations, such as hotels and restaurants, which have operations that affect interstate commerce.
■ It authorized the federal government to sue to desegregate public schools and facilities.
■ It expanded the power of the Civil Rights Commission, which had been created in 1957, and extended its life.

- It provided for the withholding of federal funds from programs administered in a discriminatory manner.
- It established the right to equality of opportunity in employment.

Title VII of the Civil Rights Act of 1964 is the cornerstone of employment-discrimination law. It prohibits discrimination in employment based on race, color, religion, gender, or national origin. Under Title VII, executive orders were issued that banned employment discrimination by firms that received any federal funding. The 1964 Civil Rights Act created the Equal Employment Opportunity Commission (EEOC), to administer Title VII. It was not until 1972, however, that Congress gave the EEOC the right to sue employers, unions, and employment agencies. Litigation then became an important agency activity.

The Voting Rights Act of 1965. As late as 1960, only 29 percent of African Americans of voting age were registered in the southern states, in stark contrast to 61 percent of whites. The Voting Rights Act of 1965 addressed this issue. The act had two major provisions. The first outlawed discriminatory voter-registration tests. The second authorized federal registration of voters and federally administered voting procedures in any political subdivision or state that discriminated electorally against a particular group. The act also provided that certain political subdivisions could not change their voting procedures and election laws without federal approval, a provision revoked by the Supreme Court in 2013.

The act targeted counties, mostly in the South, in which fewer than 50 percent of the eligible population were registered to vote. Federal voter registrars were sent to those areas to register African Americans who had been kept from voting by local registrars. Within one week after the act was passed, forty-five federal examiners were sent to the South. A massive voter-registration drive covered the country.

The Civil Rights Act of 1968 and Other Housing Reform Legislation. The Civil Rights Act of 1968 banned discrimination in most housing and provided penalties for those attempting to interfere with individual civil rights (giving protection to civil rights workers, among others). Subsequent legislation added enforcement provisions to the federal government's rules against discriminatory mortgage-lending practices.

Consequences of Civil Rights Legislation. As a result of the Voting Rights Act of 1965 and its amendments, and the large-scale voter-registration drives in the South, the number of African Americans registered to vote climbed dramatically. By 1980, 55.8 percent of African Americans of voting age in the South were registered. In recent national elections, turnout by African American voters has come very close to the white turnout. In 2008, with an African American on the presidential ballot, African American turnout exceeded that of whites for the first time in history.[9]

Political Participation by African Americans. Today, there are more than ten thousand African American elected officials in the United States. After the 2012 elections, the U. S. Congress included forty-two African Americans. The movement of African American citizens into high elected office has been sure, if exceedingly slow. Notably, recent polling data show that most Americans do not consider race a significant factor in choosing a president. In 1958, when a Gallup poll first asked whether respondents would be

---

9. A widely reported study claimed that African American turnout did not quite match that of whites, but this conclusion was based on an overestimate of the number of African Americans eligible to vote.

South Carolina Republican Tim Scott, formerly a member of the U.S. House, was appointed to fill a vacant U.S. Senate seat in December 2012. African Americans can be found today holding high offices at all levels of government. (Tim Dominick/*The State*/MCT via Getty Images)

willing to vote for an African American as president, only 38 percent of the public said yes. By 2008, this number had reached 94 percent. This high figure may have been attained, at least in part, because of the emergence of African Americans of presidential caliber. Of course, Barack Obama, first elected president in 2008 on the Democratic ticket, is African American. Two Republican African Americans were also mentioned in the past as presidential possibilities: Colin Powell, formerly chair of the Joint Chiefs of Staff and later secretary of state under President George W. Bush, and Condoleezza Rice, who succeeded Powell at the State Department.

Political Participation by Other Minorities. The civil rights movement focused primarily on the rights of African Americans. Yet the legislation resulting from the movement ultimately benefited almost all minority groups. The Civil Rights Act of 1964, for example, prohibits discrimination against any person because of race, color, or national origin. Subsequent amendments to the Voting Rights Act of 1965 extended its protections to other minorities, including Hispanic Americans (or Latinos), Asian Americans, Native Americans, and Native Alaskans.

The political participation of non–African American minority groups has increased in recent years. Hispanics, for example, have gained political power in several states. The Latino vote in national elections has grown, and it was important in Barack Obama's two victories. Hispanics do not vote at the same rate as African Americans, in large part because many Hispanics are immigrants who are not yet citizens. Still, there are now about five thousand Hispanic elected officials in the United States. After the 2012 elections, thirty Latinos had seats in the U.S. House and Senate. Nine members were Asian American.

WOMEN'S STRUGGLE FOR EQUAL RIGHTS

LO2: Contrast the goals of the women's suffrage movement with the goals of modern feminism.

Like African Americans and other minorities, women have had to struggle for equality. During the first phase of this struggle, the primary goal of women was to obtain **suffrage,** or the right to vote.

Early Women's Political Movements

Suffrage
The right to vote. A vote given in favor of a proposed measure, candidate, or the like.

In 1848, Lucretia Mott and Elizabeth Cady Stanton organized the first women's rights convention in Seneca Falls, New York. The three hundred people who attended approved a Declaration of Sentiments: "We hold these truths to be self-evident: that all men *and women* are created equal." In the following twelve years, groups that supported women's rights held seven conventions in different cities in the Midwest and East.

In 1869, after the Civil War, Susan B. Anthony and Stanton formed the National Woman Suffrage Association. In their view, women's suffrage was a means to achieve major improvements in the economic and social situation of women in the United States. In other words, the vote was to be used to seek broader goals. Lucy Stone, however, a key founder of the rival American Woman Suffrage Association, believed that the vote was the only major issue. In 1880, the two organizations joined forces. The resulting National American Woman Suffrage Association had just one goal—the enfranchisement of women—but it made little progress.

Feminism
The movement that supports political, economic, and social equality for women.

The Congressional Union for Woman Suffrage, founded in the early 1900s by Alice Paul, adopted a national strategy of obtaining an amendment to the U.S. Constitution. The Union employed militant tactics. It sponsored large-scale marches and civil disobedience—which resulted in hunger strikes, arrests, and jailings. Finally, in 1920, the Nineteenth Amendment was passed: "The right of citizens of the United States to vote shall not be denied or abridged by the United States or by any State on account of sex." (Today, the word *gender* is typically used instead of *sex*.) Women now had the right to vote in all states.

The Modern Women's Movement

Historian Nancy Cott contends that the word *feminism* first began to be used around 1910. At that time **feminism** meant, as it does today, political, social, and economic equality for women—a radical notion that gained little support then.

After gaining the right to vote in 1920, women engaged in little independent political activity until the 1960s. The civil rights movement of that decade resulted in a growing awareness of rights for all groups, including women. Increased participation in the workforce gave many women greater self-confidence. Additionally, the publication of Betty Friedan's *The Feminine Mystique* in 1963 focused national attention on the unequal status of women in American life.

In 1966, Friedan and others formed the National Organization for Women (NOW). Many observers consider the founding of NOW to be the beginning of the modern women's movement—the feminist movement.

Feminism gained additional impetus from young women who entered politics to support the civil rights movement or to oppose the Vietnam War. In the late 1960s, "women's liberation" organizations began to spring up on college campuses. Women also began organizing independent "consciousness-raising groups," in which they discussed how gender issues affected their lives. The new women's movement experienced explosive growth, and by 1970 it had emerged as a major social force.

The Equal Rights Amendment. The initial focus of the modern women's movement was to eradicate gender inequality through a constitutional amendment. The proposed Equal Rights Amendment (ERA), which was first introduced in Congress in 1923, states as follows: "Equality of rights under the law shall not be denied or abridged by the United States or by any state on account of sex." For years, the amendment was not even given a hearing in Congress, but finally it was approved by both chambers and sent to the state legislatures for ratification in 1972. The necessary thirty-eight states failed to ratify the ERA within the time specified by Congress, however. To date, efforts to reintroduce the amendment have failed.

Challenging Gender Discrimination in the Courts. When ratification of the ERA failed, women's rights organizations began a campaign to win national and state laws that would guarantee the equality of women. This more limited campaign met with much success. Women's rights organizations also challenged discriminatory statutes and policies

This female soldier is a medic assigned to a Medevac helicopter in Afghanistan. Medevac pilots, crew, and medics are ready to fly at a moment's notice, picking up coalition soldiers as well as Afghans who require help. Under a Defense Department ruling, women in the U.S. armed forces can now compete to join units that engage in direct combat. Is this rule a positive development? (John D. McHugh/Getty Images)

in the federal courts, contending that **gender discrimination** violated the Fourteenth Amendment's equal protection clause. Since the 1970s, the United States Supreme Court has tended to scrutinize gender classifications closely and has invalidated many such statutes and policies. For example, in 1977 the Court held that police and firefighting units cannot establish arbitrary rules, such as height and weight requirements, that tend to keep women from participating in those occupations.[10] In 1983, the Court ruled that life insurance companies cannot charge different rates for women and men.[11]

Women in the Military. One of the most controversial issues involving women's rights has been the role of women in the armed forces. Many believe that the ERA failed because of the fear that women might be drafted (forced) into military service. Currently, no draft exists, but to this day young American men must register for it. Women do not face such a requirement.

A recent issue has been whether women should be allowed to serve in military combat units. In the past, women were not allowed to join such units. Due to the fluid nature of modern combat, however, women in support positions have often found themselves in firefights anyway. In January 2013, the Department of Defense lifted the Combat Exclusion Policy, and in the future women will be able to compete for assignment to combat units. Participation in such units is usually a requirement for promotion to top military positions.

Women in Politics Today

The efforts of women's rights advocates have helped to increase the number of women holding political offices at all levels of government. Although a "men's club" atmosphere still prevails in Congress, the number of women holding congressional seats has increased significantly in recent years. Elections during the 1990s brought more women to Congress than either the Senate or the House had seen before.

Gender Discrimination
Any practice, policy, or procedure that denies equality of treatment to an individual or to a group because of gender.

In 2001, for the first time, a woman was elected to a leadership post in Congress—Nancy Pelosi of California became the Democrats' minority whip in the U.S. House of Representatives. In 2002, Pelosi was elected minority leader. In 2006, she became the first woman to be Speaker of the House, although she was forced to drop back to minority

10. *Dothard v. Rawlinson*, 433 U.S. 321 (1977).
11. *Arizona v. Norris*, 463 U.S. 1073 (1983).

leader again in 2010 when the Republicans regained control of the House. The number of women in Congress reached a new high after the 2012 elections, with seventy-eight women in the House and thirty in the Senate.

In 1984, for the first time, a woman, Geraldine Ferraro, became the Democratic nominee for vice president. In 2008, Hillary Clinton mounted a major campaign for the presidency, and Sarah Palin became the Republican nominee for vice president. Recent Gallup polls show that close to 90 percent of Americans said they would vote for a qualified woman for president if she was nominated by their party.

Increasing numbers of women are also being appointed to cabinet posts. President George W. Bush appointed several women to cabinet positions, including Condoleezza Rice as his secretary of state in 2005. President Barack Obama named his former rival Hillary Clinton to be secretary of state and added six other women to his cabinet.

Increasing numbers of women are sitting on federal judicial benches as well. President Ronald Reagan (1981–1989) was credited with an historic first when he appointed Sandra Day O'Connor to the United States Supreme Court in 1981. (O'Connor retired in 2005.) President Bill Clinton also appointed a woman, Ruth Bader Ginsburg, to the Court. In 2009, President Obama named Sonia Sotomayor to the Court, the first Hispanic and third woman to serve. In 2010, Obama appointed Elena Kagan to the Court, bringing the number of women currently serving on the Court to three.

Gender-Based Discrimination in the Workplace

Traditional cultural beliefs concerning the proper role of women in society continue to be evident not only in the political arena but also in the workplace. Since the 1960s, however, women have gained substantial protection against discrimination through laws that require equal employment opportunities and equal pay.

Title VII of the Civil Rights Act of 1964. Title VII of the Civil Rights Act of 1964 prohibits gender discrimination in employment and has been used to strike down employment policies that discriminate against employees on the basis of gender. In 1978, Congress amended Title VII to expand the definition of *gender discrimination* to include discrimination based on pregnancy.

Sexual Harassment. The United States Supreme Court has also held that Title VII's prohibition of gender-based discrimination extends to **sexual harassment** in the workplace. One form of sexual harassment occurs when job opportunities, promotions, salary increases, and other benefits are given in return for sexual favors. Another form of sexual harassment, called *hostile-environment harassment,* occurs when an employee is subjected to sexual conduct or comments that interfere with the employee's job

Meg Whitman, currently the CEO of Hewlett Packard, was formerly the CEO of eBay and the 2010 Republican candidate for governor of California. She is speaking at the George W. Bush Presidential Center in Dallas, Texas. What could be done to make it easier for talented women to rise to the top? (Tom Pennington/ Getty Images)

Sexual Harassment
Unwanted physical or verbal conduct or abuse of a sexual nature that interferes with a recipient's job performance, creates a hostile work environment, or carries with it an implicit or explicit threat of adverse employment consequences.

performance or are so pervasive or severe as to create an intimidating, hostile, or offensive environment.

Wage Discrimination. Although Title VII and other legislation since the 1960s has mandated equal employment opportunities for men and women, women continue to earn less, on average, than men do. The Equal Pay Act, which was enacted in 1963, basically requires employers to provide equal pay for substantially equal work. In other words, males cannot legally be paid more than females who perform essentially the same job.

The Equal Pay Act did not address the fact that certain types of jobs traditionally held by women pay lower wages than the jobs usually held by men. For example, more women than men are salesclerks and nurses, whereas more men than women are construction workers and truck drivers. Even if all clerks performing substantially similar jobs for a company earned the same salaries, they typically would still be earning less than the company's truck drivers.

In 2009, the Lilly Ledbetter Fair Pay Restoration Act extended the period during which women can sue under the Equal Pay Act. It was the first bill signed by President Obama after his inauguration.

EXPERIENCES OF OTHER MINORITY GROUPS

In a brief textbook edition, it is not possible to describe the experiences of all groups of Americans who have had to struggle for civil rights. Still, two groups deserve mention: Hispanic Americans, or Latinos, are now the nation's largest minority group by population. American Indians are notable for their unusual and troubled history, and of course because they were here first.

Immigration, Latinos, and Civil Rights

A century ago, most immigrants to the United States came from Europe. Today, however, most come from Latin America and Asia. The many new immigrants from Spanish-speaking countries have significantly increased the Hispanic proportion of the U.S. population. The number of persons who identify themselves as *multiracial* is also growing due to interracial marriages.

LO3: Explain the demographic impacts of immigration and of the interactions between European settlers and American Indians.

Hispanic versus Latino. To the U.S. Census Bureau, **Hispanics** can be of any race. They can be new immigrants or members of families that have lived in the United States for centuries. Hispanics may come from any of about twenty primarily Spanish-speaking countries and, as a result, are a highly diverse population. The four largest Hispanic groups include Mexican Americans, at 65.5 percent of all Hispanics. Puerto Ricans, all of whom are U.S. citizens, constitute 9.1 percent of the total. Salvadorans make up 3.6 percent, and Cuban Americans, 3.5 percent. The term *Hispanic* itself, although used by the government, is not particularly popular among Hispanic Americans. Many prefer the term **Latino.**

Hispanic
Someone who can claim a heritage from a Spanish-speaking country. Hispanics may be of any race.

Latino
An alternative to the term *Hispanic* that is preferred by many.

The Changing Face of America. As a result of immigration, the ethnic makeup of the United States is changing. Yet immigration is not the only factor contributing to changes in the American ethnic mosaic. Another factor is ethnic differences in the *fertility rate.* The fertility rate measures the average number of children that women in a given group are expected to have over the course of a lifetime. A rate of 2.1 is the "long-term replacement rate." In other words, if a nation or group maintains a fertility rate of 2.1, its population will eventually stabilize. This can take many years, however.

Today, the United States has a below-replacement fertility rate of 1.9 children per woman. Hispanic Americans, however, have a current fertility rate of 2.4. African Americans have a fertility rate of 2.0. Non-Hispanic white Americans have a fertility rate of 1.8. Figure 5–1 below shows the projected changes in U.S. ethnic distribution in future years. These estimates could change if immigration rates continue to be lower than in the past, as they have been since 2008.

The Civil Rights of Immigrants. The law recognizes that Latinos have been subjected to many of the same forms of ill treatment as African Americans, so Latinos are usually grouped with African Americans and Native Americans in laws and programs that seek to protect minorities from discrimination or to address the results of past discrimination. Such programs often cover Asian Americans as well.

Immigrants who are not yet citizens, however, possess fewer civil rights than any other identifiable group in the United States. The rights of unauthorized immigrants (also called illegal aliens or undocumented workers) are fewer still. As you learned in Chapter 4, the terrorist attacks on September 11, 2001, reinforced the belief that the rights of noncitizens should be limited. Should the roughly 11 million unauthorized immigrants currently in this country be granted a route to legal status and even citizenship? We take a look at that question in the *At Issue* feature on the following page.

The Agony of the American Indian

Whether living on rural reservations or in urban neighborhoods, American Indians have long experienced high rates of poverty. There is much history behind this problem. (In recent years, a majority of American Indians have come to prefer this description—or even, simply, Indian—to Native American. Still, both terms are in use.)

FIGURE 5–1: Percentage Changes in U.S. Ethnic Distribution

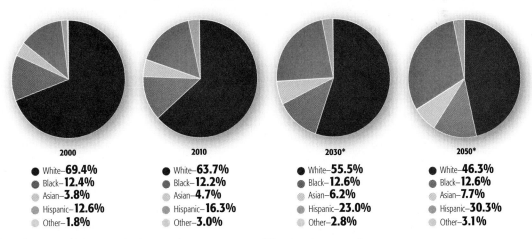

2000
- ● White–**69.4%**
- ● Black–**12.4%**
- ● Asian–**3.8%**
- ● Hispanic–**12.6%**
- ● Other–**1.8%**

2010
- ● White–**63.7%**
- ● Black–**12.2%**
- ● Asian–**4.7%**
- ● Hispanic–**16.3%**
- ● Other–**3.0%**

2030*
- ● White–**55.5%**
- ● Black–**12.6%**
- ● Asian–**6.2%**
- ● Hispanic–**23.0%**
- ● Other–**2.8%**

2050*
- ● White–**46.3%**
- ● Black–**12.6%**
- ● Asian–**7.7%**
- ● Hispanic–**30.3%**
- ● Other–**3.1%**

*Data for 2030 and 2050 are projections. Numbers may not sum to 100 percent due to rounding.
Hispanics may be of any race. The chart categories *White, Black, Asian,* and *Other* are limited to non-Hispanics.
Other consists of the following non-Hispanic groups: *American Indian, Native Alaskan, Native Hawaiian, Other Pacific Islander,* and *Two or more races.*

Source: U.S. Bureau of the Census and authors' calculations.

at issue

SHOULD UNAUTHORIZED IMMIGRANTS BE GRANTED CITIZENSHIP?

It is impossible to know for sure how many unauthorized immigrants are in this country, but experts put the figure at about 11 million. The largest number of these persons came to the United States from Latin American countries—in particular, Mexico.

How to respond to unauthorized immigration has long been a controversial issue in American politics. Some wish to allow illegal immigrants to regularize their status and eventually become citizens. Others oppose this, and some even want to send millions of illegal immigrants back to their countries of origin.

NO AMNESTY FOR ILLEGAL IMMIGRANTS

Those who oppose letting unauthorized immigrants regularize their status call such programs "amnesty." If we grant such individuals the legal right to stay in this country, we are rewarding people who have violated the law. That is unfair. Why should the unauthorized find it easier to stay in the United States than those who play by the rules? Amnesty would only encourage more individuals to enter the United States illegally. That, after all, is what happened in 1986, the last time Congress granted amnesty to a large number of illegal immigrants. After the law was passed, illegal immigration did not slow down at all.

Most illegal immigrants are low-skilled, low-wage workers. They compete against high school dropouts in America and drive down the wages of our poorest citizens. Illegal immigration can result in overcrowded schools and hospital emergency rooms. Conservatives also note that a majority of the immigrants who would benefit from amnesty would vote for Democrats if they became citizens. Even if we let such people stay, let's not support a Democratic Party power grab. These persons should not be allowed to become citizens and vote.

UNAUTHORIZED IMMIGRANTS SHOULD HAVE A PATH TO CITIZENSHIP

Those who favor a path to legitimacy for unauthorized immigrants say that America was built by immigrants, and we should celebrate immigration, not penalize it. Pro-immigrant activists observe that the majority of unauthorized immigrants come to the United States to work. Even at the height of the Great Recession, western farmers found it impossible to recruit enough American citizens to perform such backbreaking labor as picking fruits and vegetables. The simple fact is that we have a large number of illegal immigrants because we rely on their labor. The reason so many of these workers enter the country illegally is that current law makes it too difficult for Mexicans and other Latin Americans to immigrate lawfully.

Illegal immigration, in effect, creates a second-class pool of workers whom employers can exploit with impunity. The solution to this problem is citizenship. Allowing former illegal immigrants to stay and work without ever letting them become citizens is not an acceptable alternative. We would still have a subordinate caste of people with an inferior status. We used to have such a caste—African Americans, first under slavery and then under segregation. The Fourteenth Amendment exists in part to prevent such a social disaster.

FOR CRITICAL ANALYSIS

Given current economic conditions, if the United States unveiled a policy to grant citizenship to unauthorized immigrants, would immigration significantly increase? Why or why not?

The Demographic Collapse. During the years after Columbus arrived in America, native population numbers—both in the future United States and in the Americas generally—experienced one of the most catastrophic collapses in human history. The Europeans brought with them Old World diseases to which Native Americans had no immunity. A person who was able to resist one disease might die from another. By one estimate, 90 percent of the inhabitants of the New World died. For their part, the Europeans had no idea what caused diseases and did not understand what was happening. When the Pilgrims landed at Plymouth in 1620, the coast of New England was lined with empty Indian village sites. The villages had been abandoned because of an epidemic touched off by shipwrecked French sailors in 1616.

American Indians in the Nineteenth and Twentieth Centuries. In the United States, the American Indian population continued to decrease through the nineteenth century—a time when the European American and African American populations were experiencing explosive growth. The decrease was largely due to the concentration of Native Americans into ever-smaller territories. The U.S. Indian population bottomed out at 250,000 at the end of the nineteenth century. Since that time, however, it has recovered substantially. The figure is about 3.2 million today, possibly close to the number living here before Columbus.

American Indians faced additional challenges. A federal policy of "assimilation" adopted in the late 1880s resulted in further loss of territory and the suppression of traditional cultures. Indians did not become U.S. citizens until 1924.

Russell Means, a member of the Oglala Sioux Tribe and a former head of the American Indian Movement, testifies before a Senate committee. Means died in October 2012 at his ranch in South Dakota. He was 72. The struggle for American Indian rights has been popular among other Americans. Why might that be so? (AP Photo/Marcy Nighswander, File)

In the late twentieth century, some native tribes hit upon a new strategy for economic development—gambling casinos on reservation lands. This strategy was possible because the U.S. Constitution grants the responsibility for Indian relations to the national government. As a result, reservations are not subject to the full authority of the states in which they are located.

CIVIL RIGHTS: EXTENDING EQUAL PROTECTION

As noted earlier in this chapter, the Civil Rights Act of 1964 prohibited discrimination against any person on the basis of race, color, national origin, religion, or gender. The act also established the right to equal opportunity in employment. A basic problem remained, however: minority groups and women, because of past discrimination, often lacked the education and skills to compete effectively in the marketplace. In 1965, the federal government attempted to remedy this problem by implementing the concept of affirmative action. **Affirmative action** policies attempt to "level the playing field" by giving special preferences in educational admissions and employment decisions to groups that have been discriminated against in the past. These policies go beyond a strict interpretation of the equal protection clause of the Fourteenth Amendment. So do a number of other laws and programs established by the government during and since the 1960s.

LO4: Define *affirmative action,* and provide some of the arguments against it.

Affirmative Action
A policy in educational admissions or job hiring that gives special attention or compensatory treatment to traditionally disadvantaged groups in an effort to overcome present effects of past discrimination.

Affirmative Action

In 1965, President Lyndon Johnson issued Executive Order 11246, which mandated affirmative action policies to remedy the effects of past discrimination. All government agencies, including those of state and local governments, were required to implement such policies. Additionally, affirmative action requirements were imposed on companies that sell goods or services to the federal government and on institutions that receive federal funds, such as universities. Affirmative action policies were also required whenever an employer had been ordered to develop such a plan by a court or by the Equal Employment Opportunity Commission because of evidence of past discrimination. Finally, labor unions that had been found to discriminate against women or minorities in the past were required to establish and follow affirmative action plans.

Affirmative action programs have been controversial because they allegedly result in discrimination against "majority" groups, such as white males (or discrimination against other minority groups that may not be given preferential treatment under a particular affirmative action program). At issue in the current debate over affirmative action programs is whether such programs, because of their discriminatory nature, violate the equal protection clause of the Fourteenth Amendment to the Constitution.

The *Bakke* Case

The first United States Supreme Court case addressing the constitutionality of affirmative action examined a program implemented by the University of California at Davis. Allan Bakke, a white student who had been turned down for medical school at the Davis campus, discovered that his academic record was better than those of some of the minority applicants who had been admitted to the program. He sued the University of California regents, alleging **reverse discrimination.** The UC Davis Medical School had held sixteen places out of one hundred for educationally "disadvantaged students" each year, and the administrators at that campus admitted to using race as a criterion for admission for these particular slots.

In 1978, the Supreme Court handed down its decision in *Regents of the University of California v. Bakke*.[12] The Court did not rule against affirmative action programs. Rather, it held that Bakke had to be admitted to the UC Davis Medical School because its admissions policy had used race as the sole criterion for the sixteen "minority" positions. Justice Lewis Powell, speaking for the Court, indicated that while race can be considered "as a factor" among others in admissions (and presumably hiring) decisions, race cannot be the sole factor. So affirmative action programs, but not specific quota systems, were upheld as constitutional.

Reverse Discrimination
Discrimination against individuals who are not members of a minority group.

Strict Scrutiny
A judicial standard for assessing the constitutionality of a law or government action when the law or action threatens to interfere with a fundamental right or potentially discriminates on the basis of race.

Additional Limits on Affirmative Action

A number of cases decided during the 1980s and 1990s placed further limits on affirmative action programs. In a landmark decision in 1995, *Adarand Constructors, Inc. v. Peña*,[13] the United States Supreme Court held that any federal, state, or local affirmative action program that uses racial or ethnic classifications as the basis for making decisions is subject to **strict scrutiny** by the courts. Under a strict-scrutiny standard, to be constitutional, a discriminatory law or action must be narrowly tailored to meet a *compelling* government

---

12. 438 U.S. 265 (1978).
13. 515 U.S. 200 (1995).

interest. In effect, the Court's opinion in *Adarand* means that an affirmative action program cannot make use of quotas or preferences for unqualified persons. In addition, once the program has succeeded in achieving the purpose it was tailored to meet, the program must be changed or dropped.

In 2003, in two cases involving the University of Michigan, the Supreme Court indicated that limited affirmative action programs continued to be acceptable and that diversity was a legitimate goal. The Court struck down the affirmative action plan used for undergraduate admissions at the university, which automatically awarded a substantial number of points to applicants based on minority status.[14] At the same time, in *Grutter v. Bollinger,* it approved the admissions plan used by the law school, which took race into consideration as part of a complete examination of each applicant's background.[15]

The End of Affirmative Action?

Despite the position taken by the Supreme Court in *Grutter v. Bollinger,* the University of Michigan Law School case, affirmative action is subject to serious threats. A variety of states have banned all state-sponsored affirmative action programs. These include Michigan, which banned such programs through a ballot initiative in 2006. Others include Arizona, California, Florida, Nebraska, Oklahoma, and Washington. Voters in Colorado rejected such a measure in 2008, however, and in 2011 and 2012 a federal appeals court overturned the Michigan ban.[16]

Additional Restrictions. In 2007, the Supreme Court tightened the guidelines for permissible affirmative action programs. In rejecting school integration plans in Seattle, Washington, and Louisville, Kentucky, the Court found that race could not be used as a "tiebreaker" when granting admission to a school.[17]

Fisher v. University of Texas. In June 2013, the Supreme Court decided the most recent affirmative action case, *Fisher v. University of Texas.* Many observers thought that the Supreme Court would use this case to overturn *Grutter v. Bollinger* and administer a fatal blow to state-sponsored affirmative action. As it turned out, however, the Court sent the case back to the federal appeals court with instructions to decide it under existing law. Affirmative action could be used for purposes of diversity, but only when no alternative way of reaching that goal is available.[18] The ruling did not affect affirmative action programs at privates schools and colleges.

Abigail Fisher is the plaintiff in the key case *Fisher v. University of Texas.* In 2013, the United States Supreme Court was tasked with ruling on whether the university's consideration of race in admissions is constitutional. (Mark Wilson/Getty Images)

---

14. *Gratz v. Bollinger,* 539 U.S. 244 (2003).
15. 539 U.S. 306 (2003).
16. *Coalition to Defend Affirmative Action v. University of Michigan,* 701 F.3d 466 (2012).
17. *Parents Involved in Community Schools v. Seattle School District No. 1,* 551 U.S. 701 (2007).
18. ___ U.S. ___ (2013).

THE RIGHTS AND STATUS OF GAY MALES AND LESBIANS

LO5: Summarize the recent revolution in the rights enjoyed by gay men and lesbians.

On June 27, 1969, patrons of the Stonewall Inn, a New York City bar popular with gay men and lesbians, responded to a police raid by throwing beer cans and bottles because they were angry at what they felt was unrelenting police harassment. In the ensuing riot, which lasted two nights, hundreds of gay men and lesbians fought with police. Before Stonewall, the stigma attached to homosexuality and the resulting fear of exposure had tended to prevent most gay men and lesbians from engaging in activism. In the months immediately after Stonewall, however, "gay power" graffiti began to appear in New York City. The Gay Liberation Front and the Gay Activist Alliance were formed, and similar groups sprang up in other parts of the country.

Growth in the Gay Male and Lesbian Rights Movement

The Stonewall incident marked the beginning of the movement for gay and lesbian rights. Since then, gay men and lesbians have formed thousands of organizations to exert pressure on legislatures, the media, schools, churches, and other organizations to recognize their right to equal treatment.

To a great extent, lesbian and gay groups have succeeded in changing public opinion—and state and local laws that pertain to their status and rights. Nevertheless, they continue to struggle against age-old biases against homosexuality, often rooted in deeply held religious beliefs, and the rights of gay men and lesbians remain an extremely divisive issue in American society.

State and Local Laws Targeting Gay Men and Lesbians

Before the Stonewall incident, forty-nine states had sodomy laws that made various kinds of sexual acts, including homosexual acts, illegal (Illinois, which had repealed its sodomy law in 1962, was the only exception). During the 1970s and 1980s, about half of these laws were either repealed or struck down by the courts.

Lawrence v. Texas. The states—mostly in the South—that resisted the movement to abolish sodomy laws received a boost in 1986 with the Supreme Court's decision in *Bowers v. Hardwick*.[19] In that case, the Court upheld, by a five-to-four vote, a Georgia law that made homosexual conduct between two adults a crime. But in 2003, the Court reversed its earlier position on sodomy with its decision in *Lawrence v. Texas*.[20] In this case, the Court held that laws against sodomy violate the due process clause of the Fourteenth Amendment. The Court stated: "The liberty protected by the Constitution allows homosexual persons the right to choose to enter upon relationships in the confines of their homes and their own private lives and still retain their dignity as free persons." As a result, *Lawrence v. Texas* invalidated the sodomy laws that remained on the books in fourteen states.

State Actions. Today, twenty-five states, the District of Columbia, and more than 180 cities and counties have enacted laws protecting lesbians and gay men from discrimination in employment in at least some workplaces. Many of these laws also ban discrimination in housing, in public accommodation, and in other contexts.

In contrast, Colorado adopted a constitutional amendment in 1992 to invalidate all state and local laws protecting homosexuals from discrimination. Ultimately, however, the

19. 478 U.S. 186 (1986).
20. 539 U.S. 558 (2003).

Supreme Court ruled against the amendment because it violated the equal protection clause of the U.S. Constitution by denying to homosexuals in Colorado—but to no other Colorado residents—"the right to seek specific protection of the law."[21]

"Don't Ask, Don't Tell"

Until recently, the armed forces have viewed homosexuality as incompatible with military service. In 1993, however, President Bill Clinton announced a new policy, described as "don't ask, don't tell." Enlistees would not be asked about their sexual orientation, and gay men and lesbians would be allowed to serve in the military so long as they did not declare that they were gay men or lesbians or commit homosexual acts. The new policy was a compromise—Clinton had promised during his presidential campaign to repeal outright the long-standing ban on gay male and lesbian military service. Despite the new policy, large numbers of gay men and lesbians were expelled from the military in subsequent years.

During his presidential campaign, Barack Obama promised to repeal "don't ask, don't tell" and allow lesbians and gay men to serve openly, but throughout 2010, Congress failed to act on legislation that would repeal the policy gradually. Public opinion was running ahead of the government, however—by December 2010, respondents in a typical public opinion poll supported the right of gay men and lesbians to serve openly by a margin of 77 to 21 percent.

In September 2010, a U.S. district court judge ruled that the ban on open service was unconstitutional and issued an injunction that would prohibit its enforcement.[22] A federal court of appeals then stayed [suspended] the injunction. Faced with the possibility that the courts might force the immediate abolition of "don't ask, don't tell," in December Congress finally passed the gradual repeal legislation that had been tied up for most of 2010. "Don't ask, don't tell" was phased out in mid-2011.

In 2013, the Department of Defense announced that same-sex spouses of service members would, for the first time, be eligible for certain benefits, such as the right to access on-base shops and other facilities. The perks did not include measures that would require additional spending, such as medical care, housing allowances, or death benefits.

Same-Sex Marriage

One of the hottest political issues concerning the rights of gay and lesbian couples has been whether they should be allowed to marry in the same way as heterosexual couples.

The Defense of Marriage Act. Controversy over this issue flared up in 1993 when the Hawaii Supreme Court ruled that denying marriage licenses to gay couples might violate the equal protection clause of the Hawaii constitution.[23] In response, the U.S. Congress passed the Defense of Marriage Act of 1996, which bans federal recognition of lesbian and gay couples and allows state governments to ignore same-sex marriages performed in other states. (Chapter 3's *At Issue* feature discussed the Defense of Marriage Act in greater depth—see page 52.)

The controversy over gay marriage was further fueled by developments in the state of Vermont. In 1999, the Vermont Supreme Court ruled that gay couples are entitled to the same benefits of marriage as opposite-sex couples.[24] Subsequently, in April 2000 the Vermont legislature passed a law permitting gay and lesbian couples to form "civil

---

21. *Romer v. Evans,* 517 U.S. 620 (1996).
22. *Log Cabin Republicans v. United States,* 716 F.Supp.2d 884 (C.D.Cal. 2010).
23. *Baehr v. Lewin,* 852 P.2d 44 (Hawaii 1993).
24. *Baker v. Vermont,* 744 A.2d 864 (Vt. 1999).

This same-sex couple in California was married during a several-month interval in 2008 when such marriages were legal in that state. California continued to recognize these marriages even after a vote in November 2008 that prohibited new same-sex marriages. Why has support for same-sex marriage grown so rapidly in the United States and around the world? (Justin Sullivan/Getty Images)

unions." The law entitled partners forming civil unions to receive some three hundred state benefits available to married couples, including the right to inherit a partner's property and to decide on medical treatment for an incapacitated partner. It did not, however, entitle those partners to receive any benefits allowed to married couples under federal law, such as spousal Social Security benefits. A number of states have now approved some system of rights for same-sex couples. Several other states (and the District of Columbia) fully recognize same-sex marriages.

State Recognition of Same-Sex Marriages. Massachusetts was the first state to recognize gay marriage. In November 2003, the Massachusetts Supreme Judicial Court ruled that same-sex couples have a right to civil marriage under the Massachusetts state constitution.[25] For four years, Massachusetts stood alone in approving such marriages. Beginning in 2008, however, one or more additional states have legalized same-sex marriage with every passing year.

Initially, state courts took the lead. In 2008, for example, the Connecticut Supreme Court granted same-sex couples marriage rights, and the state began issuing licenses the following year. In 2009, state legislatures began authorizing the practice. In 2012, for the first time, voters in three states endorsed same-sex marriage through a referendum or initiative.[26] By mid-2013, same-sex marriage was legal in California, Connecticut, Delaware, the District of Columbia, New Hampshire, Iowa, Maine, Maryland, Massachusetts, Minnesota, New York, Rhode Island, Vermont, and Washington.

The Supreme Court Supports the States. California's route to recognizing same-sex marriages was lengthy and unusual. In June 2008, the state Supreme Court legalized such marriages. In November of that year, however, California voters approved Proposition 8, a state constitutional amendment that overturned the court's ruling. Despite Proposition 8, the state continued to recognize same-sex marriages contracted between June and November. In 2010, a federal judge ruled that Proposition 8 violated the U.S. Constitution because it singled out a particular group to deprive it of a right.

Same-sex marriages did not resume in California until 2013, after the United States Supreme Court refused to rule on the case. The Court thus preserved lower-court rulings that Proposition 8 was unconstitutional. With no ruling, the Court also refused to extend same-sex marriage rights to any other state. While the Court in effect reversed a vote of the California citizenry, every sign was that California was ready to change its mind on gay marriage anyway.[27]

Also in 2013, the Supreme Court found that the provision of the Defense of Marriage Act that banned federal recognition of same-sex marriages performed by the states was unconstitutional.[28] This ruling, while also a victory for states' rights, was of enormous value to same-sex couples in states that permitted them to marry.

---

25. *Goodridge v. Department of Public Health,* 798 N.E.2d 941 (Mass. 2003).
26. The states were Maine, Maryland, and Washington.
27. *Hollingsworth v. Perry,* 547 U.S. ___ (2013).
28. *United States v. Windsor,* 547 U.S. ___ (2013).

making a **difference**
DEALING WITH DISCRIMINATION

Anyone applying for a job may be subjected to a variety of potentially discriminatory practices. There may be tests, some of which could have a discriminatory effect. At both the state and the federal levels, the government continues to examine the fairness and validity of criteria used in job-applicant screening, and as a result, there are ways of addressing the problem of discrimination.

Why Should You Care? Some people may think that discrimination is a problem only for members of racial or ethnic minorities. Actually, almost anyone can be affected. Consider that in some instances, white men have actually experienced "reverse discrimination"—and have obtained redress for it. Also, discrimination against women is common, and women constitute half the population. Even if you are male, you probably have female friends and relatives whose well-being is of interest to you. Therefore, the knowledge of how to proceed when you suspect discrimination is another useful tool to have when living in the modern world.

What Can You Do? If you believe that you have been discriminated against by a potential employer, consider the following steps:

1. Evaluate your own capabilities, and determine if you are truly qualified for the position.
2. Analyze the reasons why you were turned down. Would others agree with you that you have been the object of discrimination, or would they uphold the employer's claim?
3. If you still believe that you have been treated unfairly, you have recourse to several agencies and services.

You should first speak to the personnel director of the company and explain politely that you believe you have not been evaluated adequately. If asked, explain your concerns clearly. If necessary, go into explicit detail, and indicate that you may have been discriminated against.

If a second evaluation is not forthcoming, contact your local state employment agency. If you still do not obtain adequate help, contact one or more of the following state agencies, usually listed in your telephone directory under "State Government."

1. If a government entity is involved, a state ombudsperson or citizen aide may be available to mediate.
2. You can contact the state civil rights commission, which at least should give you advice, even if it does not wish to take up your case.
3. The state attorney general's office normally has a division dealing with discrimination and civil rights.
4. There may be a special commission or department specifically set up to help people in your position, such as a women's status commission or a commission on Hispanics or Asian Americans. If so, contact this commission.

Finally, at the national level, you can contact:

Equal Employment Opportunity Commission
131 M St. N.E.
Washington, DC 20507
202-663-4900
www.eeoc.gov

The American Civil Liberties Union (ACLU) often supports those involved with immigration problems. This young man was held for 15 days at a border immigration center in spite of the fact that he is a U.S. citizen. ACLU lawyers proved to federal authorities that he was a citizen by presenting his birth certificate. (AP Photo/ Reed Saxon)

key**terms**

affirmative action 107

civil disobedience 97

civil rights 92

de facto segregation 97

de jure segregation 97

feminism 101

gender

    discrimination 102

grandfather clause 95

Hispanic 104

Latino 104

literacy test 95

poll tax 95

reverse

    discrimination 108

separate-but-equal

    doctrine 95

sexual harassment 103

strict scrutiny 108

suffrage 100

white primary 95

chapter**summary**

1 Before the Civil War, most African Americans were slaves, and slavery was protected by the Constitution. Constitutional amendments after the Civil War ended slavery, and African Americans gained citizenship, the right to vote, and other rights through legislation. This protection was largely a dead letter by the 1880s, however, and African American inequality continued.

2 Segregation was declared unconstitutional by the Supreme Court in *Brown v. Board of Education of Topeka* (1954), in which the Court stated that separation implied inferiority. In 1955, the modern civil rights movement began with a boycott of segregated public buses in Montgomery, Alabama. The Civil Rights Act of 1964 bans discrimination in employment and public accommodations on the basis of race, color, religion, gender, or national origin.

3 The Voting Rights Act of 1965 outlawed discriminatory voter-registration tests and authorized federal voter registration. The Voting Rights Act and other protective legislation apply not only to African Americans but also to other ethnic groups. Minorities have been increasingly represented in national and state politics.

4 In the early history of the United States, women had no political rights. After the first women's rights convention in 1848, the women's movement gained momentum. Not until 1920, when the Nineteenth Amendment was ratified, did women finally obtain the right to vote in all states. The modern women's movement began in the 1960s in the wake of the civil rights and anti–Vietnam War movements. Efforts to secure the ratification of the Equal Rights Amendment failed, but the women's movement was successful in obtaining new laws, changes in social customs, and increased political representation of women.

5 The number of women in Congress and in other government bodies increased significantly in the 1990s and early 2000s. Federal government efforts to eliminate gender discrimination in the workplace include Title VII of the Civil Rights Act of 1964, which prohibits gender-based discrimination, including sexual harassment on the job. Wage discrimination continues to be a problem for women.

6 Today, most immigrants come from Asia and Latin America, especially Mexico. Many are unauthorized immigrants (also called illegal aliens or undocumented workers). The percentage of Latinos, or Hispanic Americans, in the population is growing rapidly. By 2050, non-Hispanic whites will make up only about half of the nation's residents. While Latinos who are citizens benefit from the same antidiscrimination measures as African Americans, immigrants who are not citizens have few civil rights.

7 Affirmative action programs have been controversial because they may lead to reverse discrimination against majority groups or even other minority groups. Supreme Court decisions have limited affirmative action programs drastically and several states now ban state-sponsored affirmative action.

8 Gay and lesbian rights groups became commonplace after 1969. After 1969, sodomy laws that criminalized specific sexual practices were repealed or struck down by the courts in about half of the states. In 2003, a Supreme Court decision effectively invalidated all remaining sodomy laws nationwide. Many states, cities, and counties now have laws prohibiting at least some types of discrimination based on sexual orientation. The issues of same-sex marriage and whether gays and lesbians can serve openly in the military have fueled extensive controversy.

test**yourself**

LO1 *Summarize the historical experience of African Americans, state how the separate-but-equal doctrine was abolished, and describe the consequences of the civil rights movement.*

The separate-but-equal doctrine was announced by the Supreme Court:
    a. in *Plessy v. Ferguson.*
    b. in *Roe v. Wade.*
    c. nowhere, because the Supreme Court never addressed the issue.

LO2 *Contrast the goals of the women's suffrage movement with the goals of modern feminism.*

The Equal Rights Amendment today requires:
    a. that women be treated equally to men.
    b. that women be treated equally in the labor market.
    c. nothing at all, because the Equal Rights Amendment never passed.

LO3 *Explain the demographic impacts of immigration and of the interaction between European settlers and American Indians.*

Currently, most immigrants come from:
    a. Europe.
    b. Africa.
    c. Latin America (especially Mexico) and Asia.

LO4 *Define* affirmative action, *and provide some of the arguments against it.*

During the years in which they were allowed by law, affirmative action programs assisted groups that had been discriminated against in the past. In educational admissions and employment, these programs:
    a. awarded preferences to minority group members.
    b. relied on numerical quotas to improve outcomes.
    c. involved federal grants to complying institutions.

LO5 *Summarize the recent revolution in the rights enjoyed by gay men and lesbians.*

The Defense of Marriage Act (DOMA) provided for all of the following except:
    a. states were not required to recognize same-sex marriages conducted in other states.
    b. states were not required to recognize divorces obtained in other states.
    c. the federal government was barred from recognizing same-sex marriages when awarding benefits or collecting taxes.

Essay Question:

Not all African Americans agreed with the philosophy of nonviolence espoused by Dr. Martin Luther King, Jr. Advocates of black power called for a more militant approach. Can militancy make a movement more effective (possibly by making a more moderate approach seem like a reasonable compromise), or is it typically counterproductive? Either way, why?

Answers to multiple-choice questions: 1. a, 2. c, 3. c, 4. a, 5. b.

CourseMate

Access CourseMate at www.cengagebrain.com for additional study tools: practice quizzes, key term flashcards and crossword puzzles, audio chapter summaries, simulations, animated learning modules, interactive timelines, videos, and American Government NewsWatch.

6

A volunteer persuades a St. Louis resident to sign a petition calling for an increase in the Missouri state minimum wage. (Sid Hastings/MCT via Getty Images)

Public Opinion, Political Socialization, and
The Media

LEARNING OUTCOMES

The six **Learning Outcomes (LOs)** below are designed to help improve your understanding of this chapter. After reading this chapter, you should be able to:

■ **LO1** Define *public opinion, consensus opinion,* and *divided opinion,* and discuss major sources of political socialization, including the family, schools, the media, and political events.

■ **LO2** Identify the effects of various influences on voting behavior, including education, income, religion, race/ethnicity, gender and geography.

■ **LO3** Describe the characteristics of a scientific opinion poll, and list some of the problems pollsters face in obtaining accurate results.

■ **LO4** Consider the effect that public opinion may have on the political process.

■ **LO5** Describe the different types of media and the changing roles that they play in American society.

■ **LO6** Summarize the impact of the media on political campaigns, and consider the issue of political bias in the media.

Check your understanding of the material with the Test Yourself section at the end of the chapter.

In a democracy, the ability of the people to freely express their opinions is fundamental. Americans can express their opinions in many ways. They can write letters to newspapers. They can share their ideas in online forums. They can organize politically. They can vote. They can respond to opinion polls.

Immediately after the 2012 elections, President Barack Obama and the Republican majority in the U.S. House of Representatives had to respond to the power of public opinion. As a result of earlier political decisions, America faced what became known as the "fiscal cliff." If nothing were done, the nation would experience considerable tax increases and serious cuts in federal expenditures. The impact on the economy was expected to be dire. Obama and the Republicans escaped popular blame for such an outcome with a compromise that raised taxes on those with incomes above $400,000 and made minor cuts to federal spending. Major issues remained unresolved, however. Public opinion was certain to shape the resolution of future tax and spending issues.

There is no doubt that public opinion can be powerful. The extent to which public opinion affects policymaking is not always so clear, however. For example, suppose that public opinion strongly supports a certain policy. If political leaders adopt that position, is it because they are responding to public opinion or because they share the public's beliefs? Also, political leaders themselves can shape public opinion to a degree.

PUBLIC OPINION AND POLITICAL SOCIALIZATION

There is no single public opinion, because there are many different "publics." In a nation of more than 315 million people, there may be innumerable gradations of opinion on an issue. What we do is describe the distribution of opinions about a particular question. Thus, we define **public opinion** as the aggregate of individual attitudes or beliefs shared by some portion of the adult population.

LO1: Define *public opinion,* *consensus opinion,* and *divided opinion,* and discuss major sources of political socialization, including the family, schools, the media, and political events.

Consensus and Divided Opinion

Typically, public opinion is distributed among several different positions, and the distribution of opinion can tell us how divided the public is on an issue and whether compromise is possible. When polls show that a large proportion of the American public appears to express the same view on an issue, we say that a **consensus** exists, at least at the moment the poll was taken. Figure 6–1 on the next page shows a pattern of opinion that might be called consensual. Issues on which the public holds widely differing attitudes result in **divided opinion** (see Figure 6–2 on the following page). Sometimes, a poll shows a distribution of opinion indicating that most Americans either have no information about the issue or do not care enough about the issue to formulate a position.

An interesting question arises as to when *private* opinion becomes *public* opinion. Everyone probably has a private opinion about the competence of the president, as well as private opinions about more personal concerns, such as the state of a neighbor's lawn. We say that private opinion becomes public opinion when the opinion is publicly expressed and concerns public issues. When someone's private opinion becomes so strong that the individual is willing to take action, then the opinion becomes public opinion. Many kinds of action are possible. An individual may go to the polls to vote for or against a candidate or an issue, participate in a demonstration, discuss the issue at work, speak out online, or participate in the political process in any one of a dozen other ways.

Public Opinion
The aggregate of individual attitudes or beliefs shared by some portion of the adult population.

Consensus
General agreement among the citizenry on an issue.

Divided Opinion
Public opinion that is polarized between two quite different positions.

Political Socialization
The process by which people acquire political beliefs and values.

Forming Public Opinion: Political Socialization

Most Americans are willing to express opinions on political issues when asked. How do people acquire these opinions and attitudes? Typically, views that are expressed as political opinions are acquired through the process of **political socialization.** By this, we mean

FIGURE 6–1: Consensual Opinion

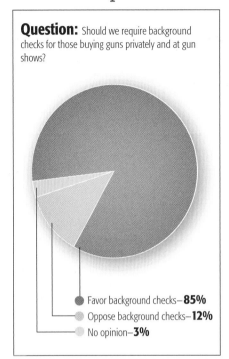

Question: Should we require background checks for those buying guns privately and at gun shows?

- Favor background checks–**85%**
- Oppose background checks–**12%**
- No opinion–**3%**

FIGURE 6–2: Divided Opinion

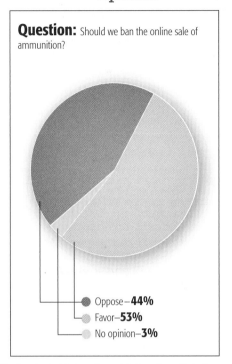

Question: Should we ban the online sale of ammunition?

- Oppose–**44%**
- Favor–**53%**
- No opinion–**3%**

Source: Pew Research Center for the People and the Press, "In Gun Control Debate, Several Options Draw Majority Support," January 14, 2013.

that people acquire their political beliefs and values, often including their party identification, through relationships with their families, friends, and co-workers. The most important early sources of political socialization are the family and the schools. Individuals' basic political orientations are formed in the family if other family members hold strong views. When the adults in a family view politics as relatively unimportant and describe themselves as independent voters or disaffected from the political system, however, children may receive very little political socialization.

In the past few decades, more and more sources of information about politics have become available to all Americans, especially to young people through the Web. Thus, although their basic outlook on the political system still may be formed by early family influences, young people are now exposed to many other sources of information about issues and values. This greater access to information may explain why young Americans are often more liberal than their parents on certain social issues such as gay rights.

The Family. Not only do our parents' political beliefs, values, and actions affect our opinions, but the family also links us to other factors that affect opinion, such as race, social class, educational environment, and religious beliefs. How do parents transmit their political values to their offspring?

Studies suggest that the influence of parents is due to two factors: communication and receptivity. Parents communicate their feelings and preferences to their children constantly. Because children have such a strong need for parental approval, they are very receptive to their parents' views.

Children are less likely to influence their parents, because parents expect deference from their children.[1] Nevertheless, other studies show that if children are exposed to political ideas at school and in the media, they will share these ideas with their parents, giving the parents what some scholars call a "second chance" at political socialization.

Education as a Source of Political Socialization. From the early days of the republic, schools were perceived to be important transmitters of political information and attitudes. Children in the primary grades learn about their country mostly in patriotic ways. They learn about the Pilgrims, the flag, and some of the nation's presidents. In the middle grades, children learn additional historical facts and come to understand the structure of government and the functions of the president, judges, and Congress. By high school, students have a more complex understanding of the political system, may identify with a political party, and may take positions on issues.

Generally, the more education a person receives, the more likely it is that the person will be interested in politics, be confident in his or her ability to understand political issues, and be an active participant in the political process.

Peers and Peer Group Influence. Once a child enters school, the child's friends become an important influence on behavior and attitudes. For children and for adults, friendships and associations in **peer groups** affect political attitudes. We must, however, separate the effects of peer group pressure on attitudes in general from the effects of peer group pressure on political opinions. For the most part, associations among peers are nonpolitical. Political attitudes are more likely to be shaped by peer groups when those groups are involved directly in political activities. For example, individuals who join an interest group based on ethnic identity, may find a common political bond through working for the group's civil liberties and rights.

Opinion Leaders' Influence. We are all influenced by those with whom we are closely associated or whom we hold in high regard—friends at school, family members and other relatives, and teachers. In a sense, these people are **opinion leaders,** but on an *informal* level. That is, their influence on our political views is not necessarily intentional or deliberate. We are also influenced by *formal* opinion leaders, such as presidents, lobbyists, congresspersons, news commentators, and religious leaders, who have as part of their jobs the task of swaying people's views.

The Media and Public Opinion

Clearly, the **media**—newspapers, television, radio, and Internet sources—strongly influence public opinion. This is because the media inform the public about the issues and events of our times and thus have an **agenda-setting** effect. To borrow from Bernard Cohen's classic statement about the media and public opinion, the media may not be successful in telling people what to think, but they are "stunningly successful in telling their audience what to think about."[2]

The Popularity of the Media. Today, many contend that the media's influence on public opinion has grown to equal that of the family. For example, in her analysis of the role

Peer Group
A group consisting of members who share common social characteristics. Such groups play an important part in the socialization process, helping to shape attitudes and beliefs.

Opinion Leader
One who is able to influence the opinions of others because of position, expertise, or personality.

Media
The channels of mass communication.

Agenda Setting
Determining which public-policy questions will be debated or considered.

1. Barbara A. Bardes and Robert W. Oldendick, *Public Opinion: Measuring the American Mind,* 4th ed. (Lanham, Md.: Rowman & Littlefield Publishers, 2012).
2. Bernard C. Cohen, *The Press and Foreign Policy* (Princeton, N.J.: Princeton University Press, 1963), p. 81.

Pastor Rick Warren, author of *The Purpose Driven Life,* speaks to a conference on AIDS in Washington, D.C. Is Warren an opinion leader? (Michael Kovac/Getty Images for the Elton John AIDS Foundation)

played by the media in American politics,[3] media scholar Doris A. Graber points out that high school students, when asked where they obtain the information on which they base their views, mention the mass media far more than they mention their families, friends, and teachers. This trend may significantly alter the nature of the media's influence on public debate in the future.

The Impact of the New Media. The extent to which new forms of media have supplanted older ones—such as newspapers and the major broadcast networks—has been a major topic of discussion for several years. New forms include not only the Web but also talk radio and cable television. Talk radio would seem to be a very dated medium, given that radio first became important early in the twentieth century. Between 1949 and 1987, however, the Federal Communications Commission (FCC) enforced the *Fairness Doctrine,* which required radio and television to present controversial issues in a manner that was (in the FCC's view) honest, equitable, and balanced. Modern conservative talk radio took off only after the Fairness Doctrine was abolished.

The impact of the various forms of new media appears to vary considerably. Talk radio and cable networks such as Fox News have given conservatives new methods for promoting their views and socializing their audiences. It is probable, however, that such media mostly strengthen the beliefs of those who are already conservative, rather than recruiting new members to the political right. Indeed, cable news and talk radio are widely blamed for the increased polarization that has characterized American politics in recent years. A similar observation is often made about political blogs on the Internet, although in this medium liberals are at least as well represented as conservatives.

The impact of social networking sites such as Facebook is more ambiguous. Facebook does have strongly political "pages" that, in effect, are political blogs. Many interactions on Facebook, however, are between members of peer groups, such as students who attend a particular school or individuals who work in the same profession. Such groups are more likely to contain a variety of views than groups explicitly organized around a political viewpoint. Facebook, in other words, may enhance peer group influence. The media's influence will be discussed in more detail later in the chapter.

Social Media in Politics

U.S. Politics on Facebook has almost 250,000 "likes" and is a major gateway to dozens of other sites. You can search for it by name, using Facebook or any search engine.

Political Events and Public Opinion

Generally, older Americans tend to be somewhat more conservative than younger Americans—particularly on social issues but also, to some extent, on economic issues. This effect probably occurs because older adults are likely to retain the social values that they learned at a younger age. The experience of marriage and raising a family also has a measurable conservatizing effect. Young people, especially today, are more liberal than their grandparents on social issues, such as on the rights of gay men and lesbians and on

3. Doris A. Graber, *On Media: Making Sense of Politics* (Boulder, Colo.: Paradigm Publishers, 2011).

racial and gender equality. Nevertheless, a more important factor than a person's age is the impact of momentous political events that shape the political attitudes of an entire generation. When events produce such a long-lasting result, we refer to it as a **generational effect** (also called the *cohort effect*).

Generational Effect
A long-lasting effect of the events of a particular time on the political opinions of those who came of political age at that time.

Working class voters who grew up in the 1930s during the Great Depression were likely to form lifelong attachments to the Democratic Party, the party of Franklin D. Roosevelt. In the 1960s and 1970s, the war in Vietnam, the Watergate break-in, and the subsequent presidential cover-up fostered widespread cynicism toward government. (The Watergate break-in was the 1972 illegal entry into Democratic National Committee offices by members of President Richard Nixon's reelection organization.) There is evidence that the years of economic prosperity under President Ronald Reagan during the 1980s led many young people to identify with the Republican Party. The very high levels of support that younger voters have given to Barack Obama during his presidential campaigns may be good news for the Democratic Party in future years.

THE INFLUENCE OF DEMOGRAPHIC FACTORS

Demographic characteristics, such as education, income, religion, race/ethnicity, gender, and geographic location, are strongly correlated with political party preferences and political ideologies. Table 6–1 on the following page illustrates the impact of some of these variables on voting behavior.

LO2: Identify the effects of various influences on voting behavior, including education, income, religion, race/ethnicity, gender and geography.

Educational Achievement

In the past, having a college education tended to be associated with voting for Republicans. In recent years, however, this correlation has become weaker. In particular, individuals with a postgraduate education—more than a bachelor's degree—have become predominantly Democratic. Many people with postgraduate degrees are professionals, such as physicians, attorneys, and college instructors. Also, a higher percentage of voters with only a high school education voted Republican in the last four presidential elections, compared with the pattern in previous elections, in which that group of voters tended to favor Democrats more strongly.

Economic Status

Family income is a strong predictor of economic liberalism or conservatism. Those with low incomes tend to favor government action to benefit the poor or to promote economic equality. Those with high incomes tend to oppose government intervention in the economy or to support it only when it benefits business. The rich often tend toward the right and the poor often lean toward the left.

If we examine cultural as well as economic issues, however, the four-cornered ideological grid discussed in Chapter 1 becomes important. It happens that upper class voters are more likely to endorse cultural liberalism, and lower class individuals are more likely to favor cultural conservatism. Support for the right to have an abortion, for example, rises with income. It follows that libertarians—those who oppose government action on both economic and social issues—are concentrated among the wealthier members of the population. (Libertarians constitute the upper-right-hand corner of the grid in Figure 1–1 in Chapter 1.) Those who favor government action both to promote traditional moral values and to promote economic equality—economic liberals, cultural conservatives—are concentrated among groups that are less well off. (This group fills up the lower-left-hand corner of the grid.)

TABLE 6–1: Votes by Groups in Presidential
Elections, 1996–2012 (in Percentages)

	1996		2000		2004		2008		2012	
	Clinton (Dem.)	Dole (Rep.)	Gore (Dem.)	Bush (Rep.)	Kerry (Dem.)	Bush (Rep.)	Obama (Dem.)	McCain (Rep.)	Obama (Dem.)	Romney (Rep.)
Total vote	49	41	48	48	48	51	53	46	51	47
Gender										
Men	43	44	42	53	44	55	49	48	45	52
Women	54	38	54	43	51	48	56	43	55	44
Race or ethnicity										
White	43	46	42	54	41	58	43	55	39	59
Black	84	12	90	8	88	11	95	4	93	6
Hispanic	72	21	67	31	58	40*	67	31	71	27
Educational attainment										
Not a high school graduate	59	28	59	39	50	50	63	35	54	35
High school only	51	35	48	49	47	52	52	46	51	48
College graduate	44	46	45	51	46	52	50	48	47	51
Postgraduate education	52	40	52	44	54	45	58	40	55	42
Religion										
White Protestant	36	53	34	63	32	68	34	65	30	69†
Catholic	53	37	49	47	47	52	54	45	50	48
Jewish	78	16	79	19	75	24	78	21	69	30
White evangelical	NA	NA	NA	NA	21	79	24	74	21	78
Union status										
Union household	59	30	59	37	59	40	59	39	58	40
Family income										
Under $15,000	59	28	57	37	63	37	73	25	NA	NA
$15,000–29,000	53	36	54	41	57	41	60	37	63	35‡
$30,000–49,000	48	40	49	48	50	49	55	43	57	42
Over $50,000	44	48	45	52	43	56	49	49	45	53
Size of place of residence										
Population over 500,000	68	25	71	26	60	40	70	28	69	29
Population 50,000–500,000	50	39	57	40	50	50	59	39	58	40
Population 10,000–50,000	48	41	38	59	48	51	45	53	42	56
Rural	44	46	37	59	39	60	45	53	37	61

NA = Not asked.

*The official figure reported by the National Election Pool was 44. Studies later proved that this figure was impossibly high. NBC News lowered it to 40, but even that figure may be somewhat too high.

†In 2012, Protestant or "other Christian."

‡In 2012, below $30,000.

Sources: *New York Times;* Voter News Service; CBS News; and National Election Pool.

That said, it remains generally true that the higher a person's income, the more likely that person will be to vote Republican. Manual laborers, factory workers, and especially union members are more likely to vote Democratic. Small-business owners, managers, and corporate executives tend to vote Republican. As just noted, however, professionals such as physicians, attorneys, and college instructors now tend to vote Democratic.

Religious Denomination

Traditionally, scholars have examined the impact of religion on political attitudes by dividing the population into such categories as Protestant, Catholic, and Jewish. In recent decades, however, such a breakdown has become less valuable as a means of predicting someone's political preferences. It is true that Jewish voters, as they were in the past, are notably more liberal than members of other groups on both economic and cultural issues. Persons reporting no religion are very liberal on social issues but have mixed economic views. Protestants and Catholics, however, have grown closer to each other politically in recent years. This represents something of a change—in the late 1800s and early 1900s, northern Protestants were distinctly more likely to vote Republican, and northern Catholics were more likely to vote Democratic. Even now, in a few parts of the country, Protestants and Catholics tend to line up against each other when choosing a political party.

Religious Commitment and Beliefs

Today, two factors turn out to be major predictors of political attitudes among members of the various Christian denominations. One factor is the degree of religious commitment, as measured by such actions as regular churchgoing. The other is the degree to which the voter adheres to religious beliefs that (depending on the denomination) can be called conservative, evangelical, or fundamentalist. High scores on either factor are associated with cultural conservatism on political issues—that is, with beliefs that place a high value on social order. (See Chapter 1 for a discussion of the contrasting values of order and liberty.)

In 2012, for example, Protestants who attended church weekly gave 70 percent of their votes to Republican candidate Mitt Romney, compared with 55 percent of those who attended church less often. Among Catholics, there was a similar pattern: 57 percent of Catholics who attended church weekly voted for Romney, while 42 percent of Catholics who were not regular churchgoers voted for him. There is an exception to this trend— African Americans of all religious tendencies have been strongly supportive of Democrats.

Race and Ethnicity

Although African Americans, on average, are somewhat conservative on certain cultural issues, such as same-sex marriage and abortion, they tend to be more liberal than whites on social-welfare matters, civil liberties, and even foreign policy. African Americans voted principally for Republicans until Democrat Franklin D. Roosevelt's New Deal in the 1930s. Since then, they have largely identified with the Democratic Party. Indeed, Democratic presidential candidates have received, on average, more than 80 percent of the African American vote since 1956. Of course, Barack Obama's support among African Americans has been overwhelming.

Most Asian American groups lean toward the Democrats, although Vietnamese Americans are strongly Republican. Most Vietnamese Americans left Vietnam because of the Communist victory in the Vietnam War, and their strong anticommunism translates into conservative politics.

A Latino woman and her eighteen-month-old daughter march to the White House in support of immigration reform. How is the daughter acquiring political values by attending a rally with her mother? (Ryan Rodrick Beiler/Shutterstock.com)

Muslim American immigrants and their descendants make up an interesting category.[4] In 2000, a majority of Muslim Americans of Middle Eastern ancestry voted for Republican George W. Bush because they shared his cultural conservatism. By 2012, the issues of Muslim civil liberties and discrimination against Muslims had turned Islamic voters into one of the nation's most Democratic blocs.

The Hispanic Vote

The diversity among Hispanic Americans has resulted in differing political behavior. The majority of Hispanic Americans vote Democratic. Cuban Americans, however, are often Republican. Most Cuban Americans left Cuba because of Fidel Castro's Communist regime. As in the example of the Vietnamese, anticommunism leads to political conservatism. By 2012, however, increasing numbers of young Cuban Americans were supporting the Democrats.

In 2004, Republican presidential candidate George W. Bush may have received almost 40 percent of the Latino vote. Since his days as Texas governor, Bush had envisioned creating a stronger long-term Republican coalition by adding Hispanics. Indeed, Latino voters appeared to show considerable sympathy for Bush's campaign appeals based on religious and family values and patriotism.

In 2008, however, Barack Obama won more than two-thirds of the Hispanic vote. Why did Hispanic support for the Republicans fall so sharply? In a word: immigration. Bush favored a comprehensive immigration reform that would have granted unauthorized immigrants (also known as illegal or undocumented immigrants) a path to citizenship. Most Republicans in Congress, however, refused to support Bush on this issue and instead called for a hard line against unauthorized immigration. The harsh rhetoric of some Republicans on this issue convinced many Latinos that the Republicans were hostile to Hispanic interests.

In 2012, according to a Latino poll, Obama's support among Hispanics reached 75 percent, an all-time high. At the same time, Hispanics were a growing share of the voting population—10 percent, up from 9 percent in 2008 and 8 percent in 2004. These trends were widely

---

4. About one-third of U.S. Muslims actually are African Americans whose ancestors have been in this country for a long time. In terms of political preferences, African American Muslims are more likely to resemble other African Americans than Muslim immigrants from the Middle East.

seen as a serious problem for the Republican Party. Following the elections, several leading Republicans began to take a much more positive line toward unauthorized immigrants.

The Gender Gap

Until the 1980s, there was little evidence that men's and women's political attitudes were very different. Following the election of Ronald Reagan in 1980, however, scholars began to detect a **gender gap.** A May 1983 Gallup poll revealed that men were more likely than women to approve of Reagan's job performance. The gender gap reappeared in subsequent elections, with women being more likely than men to support Democratic candidates. In 2012, 55 percent of women voted for Democrat Barack Obama, compared with 45 percent of men.

Women's attitudes also appear to differ from those of their male counterparts on a range of issues other than presidential preferences. They are much more likely than men to oppose capital punishment and the use of force abroad. Studies also have shown that women are more concerned about risks to the environment, more supportive of social welfare, and more in agreement with extending civil rights to gay men and lesbians than are men.

Geographic Region

Finally, where you live can influence your political attitudes. In 2012, many commentators suggested that the white working class was hostile to Obama. This conclusion was not entirely accurate. In a preelection poll by the Public Religion Research Institute, neither Obama nor Romney held a statistically significant lead among white working class voters in the East, Midwest, or West. In the South, however, Romney's margin was 62 percent to 22 percent (16 percent were undecided). Regardless of region, opposition to Obama was strongest among those who saw themselves culturally as Southerners—that is, as persons who identified with the losing side in the American Civil War.

The split between the city and the country is almost as important as the one between the North and the South. In 2012, Obama did far better than Romney in large cities. The northern states that Romney carried were often heavily rural.

MEASURING PUBLIC OPINION

In a democracy, people express their opinions in a variety of ways, as mentioned in this chapter's introduction. One of the most common means of gathering and measuring public opinion on specific issues is through the use of **opinion polls.**

The History of Opinion Polls

During the 1800s, certain American newspapers and magazines spiced up their political coverage by conducting face-to-face polls or mail surveys of their readers' opinions. In the early twentieth century, the magazine *Literary Digest* mailed large numbers of questionnaires to individuals, many of whom were its own subscribers, to determine their political opinions. From 1916 to 1932, more than 70 percent of the magazine's election predictions were accurate.

In 1936, however, the magazine predicted that Republican Alfred Landon would defeat Democrat Franklin D. Roosevelt in the presidential race. Landon won in only two states. A major problem was that in 1936, several years into the Great Depression, the *Digest*'s subscribers were considerably wealthier than the average American. In other words, they did not accurately represent all of the voters in the U.S. population.

Gender Gap
The difference between the percentage of women who vote for a particular candidate and the percentage of men who vote for the candidate.

Opinion Poll
A method of systematically questioning a small, selected sample of respondents who are deemed representative of the total population.

LO3: Describe the characteristics of a scientific opinion poll, and list some of the problems pollsters face in obtaining accurate results.

Several newcomers to the public opinion poll industry accurately predicted Roosevelt's landslide victory. These newcomers are still active in the poll-taking industry today: the Gallup poll of George Gallup and the Roper poll, founded by Elmo Roper. Gallup and Roper, along with Archibald Crossley, developed the modern polling techniques of market research. Using personal interviews with small samples of selected voters (fewer than two thousand), they showed that they could predict with relative accuracy the behavior of the total voting population.

Sampling Techniques

How can interviewing fewer than two thousand voters tell us what tens of millions of voters will do? Clearly, it is necessary that the sample of individuals be representative of all voters in the population.

The most important principle in sampling, or poll taking, is randomness. Every person should have a known chance, and especially an *equal chance*, of being sampled. If sampling follows this principle, then a small sample should be representative of the whole group, both in demographic characteristics (age, religion, race, region, and the like) and in opinions. The ideal way to sample the voting population of the United States would be to put all voter names into a jar—or a computer file—and randomly sample, say, two thousand of them. Because this is too costly and inefficient, pollsters have developed other ways to obtain good samples. One technique is simply to choose a random selection of telephone numbers and interview the respective households. This technique used to produce a relatively accurate sample at a low cost.

To ensure that the random samples include respondents from relevant segments of the population—rural, urban, northeastern, southern, and the like—most survey organizations randomly choose, say, urban areas that they will consider as representative of all urban areas. Then they randomly select their respondents within those areas.

The Statistical Nature of Polling. Universally, when the results of an opinion poll are announced, the findings are reported as specific numbers. A poll might find, for example, that 10 percent of those surveyed approve of the job performance of Congress. Such precise figures can mislead you as to the essential nature of polling. In reality, it makes more sense to consider the results of a particular survey question as a range of numbers, not a single integer. That would mean that the question about Congress's job performance yielded an answer that fell somewhere between 7 percent and 13 percent. The figure of 10 percent is only the midpoint of the possible spread—the most probable result. If we had been able to question all members of the public, the chances that they would give Congress exactly a 10 percent rating are not high. Even if the pollster in this case employed

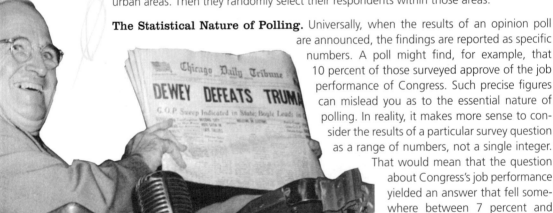

Harry Truman won the presidential election in 1948 despite the prediction of most opinion polls that he would lose. Would a newspaper today make such an inaccurate prediction and put it on newsstands? (AP Photo/Byron Rollins)

the best possible practices, the odds are better than 50-50 that the true answer is not 10 percent, but some other number in the 7–13 percent range.

Sampling Error. Reputable polling firms report the margin of error associated with their results. The results of a carefully conducted poll that surveys a large number of respondents—say, two thousand people—might have a 95 percent chance of falling within a 3 percent margin of error. The 95 percent figure is an industry standard. What this means, however, is that the pollster believes that any given poll result has a 5 percent chance of landing four or more percentage points away from the true answer, which we would get if we really could interview everyone. In the example of the question about Congress, there is a 5 percent chance—one chance in twenty—that the approval rating is actually below 7 percent or above 13 percent.

These variations are called **sampling error.** They follow from the fact that the poll taker is examining a sample and not the entire population. Sampling error is one reason that knowledgeable poll watchers disregard small variations in poll results. Gallup, for example, polls the public on its approval of the president's job performance every day. Such continuous polls are known as **tracking polls.** Suppose that on Monday, the tracking poll shows that the president has a 45 percent approval rating. On Tuesday, it is 47 percent; on Wednesday, 46 percent; and on Thursday, 43 percent. Was the president really more popular on Tuesday and Wednesday? Almost certainly not. These variations are simply so much "statistical noise."

The Difficulty of Obtaining Accurate Results

Reputable polling organizations devote substantial effort to ensuring that their samples are truly random. If they succeed, then the accuracy of their results should be limited only by sampling error. Unfortunately, obtaining a completely random sample of the population is difficult. Women are more likely to answer the telephone than men. Some kinds of people, such as students and low-income individuals, are relatively hard to contact.

Many poll takers now rely on automated scripts—"robocalls"—rather than live interviewers. Under the law, however, robocallers are not allowed to dial cell phones. As a result, automated surveys are less accurate than traditional ones. Pollsters currently have no way at all to reach people who rely on Skype or similar systems for telephone service. Finally, more than 85 percent of households contacted by typical polls refuse to be interviewed. Despite their best efforts, pollsters may be unable to gather a pool of respondents that precisely mirrors the general public.

Weighting the Sample. Polling firms address this problem of obtaining a true random sample by weighting their samples. That is, they correct for differences between the sample and the public by adding extra "weight" to the responses of underrepresented groups. For example, 20 percent of the respondents in a survey might state that they are evangelical Christians. Based on other sources of information, the poll taker believes that the true share of evangelicals in the target population is 25 percent. Therefore, the responses of the evangelical respondents receive extra weight so that they make up 25 percent of the reported result.

It is relatively easy to correct a sample for well known demographic characteristics such as education, gender, race/ethnicity, religion, and geography. It is much harder—and more dangerous—to adjust for political ideology, partisan preference, or likelihood of voting. The formulas that firms use to weight their responses are typically trade secrets and are never disclosed to the public.

Sampling Error
The difference between a sample result and the true result if the entire population had been interviewed.

Tracking Poll
A poll that is taken continuously—sometimes every day—to determine how support for an issue or candidate changes over time.

House Effects. One consequence of the use of secret in-house weighting schemes is that the results reported by one polling firm may differ from those reported by another systematically. Pollster A might consistently rate the chances of Republican candidates as 2 percentage points higher than does pollster B. A consistent difference in polling results between firms is known as a **house effect.** (*House* here means the organization or firm, as when referring to casinos.) House effects are measured by comparing a firm's results with the average results of all other poll takers. A house effect does not mean that a firm's results are in error. It could be noticing something important that its rivals have missed.

How Accurate Are the Results? Despite all of the practical difficulties involved in poll taking, the major polling organizations have usually enjoyed a good record in predicting the outcome of presidential contests. Most major firms predicted the outcome of the 2012 presidential elections—and most of the U.S. Senate races—with considerable accuracy. Two major poll takers, however, reported results that were embarrassingly inaccurate. Gallup seriously overestimated voter turnout among Republicans and underestimated Democratic turnout. Rasmussen overweighted Republican respondents. Both pollsters predicted that Romney would win a substantially larger share of the votes than he actually did.

Additional Problems with Polls

Public opinion polls are snapshots of the opinions and preferences of the people at a specific moment in time and as expressed in response to a specific question. Given that definition, it is fairly easy to understand situations in which the polls are wrong. For example, opinion polls leading up to the 1980 presidential elections showed President Jimmy Carter defeating challenger Ronald Reagan. Only a few analysts noted the large number of "undecided" respondents a week before the election. Those voters shifted massively to Reagan at the last minute, and Reagan won the election. The famous photo of Harry Truman showing the front page that declared his defeat in the 1948 presidential elections is another tribute to the weakness of polling. Again, the poll that predicted his defeat was taken more than a week before Election Day.

Poll Questions. It makes sense to expect that the results of a poll will reflect the questions that are asked. Depending on what question is asked, voters could be said either to support a particular proposal or to oppose it. One of the problems with many polls is the yes/no answer format. For example, suppose that a poll question asks, "Do you favor arming the rebels in Syria?" A respondent who has a complicated view of these events, as many people do, has no way of indicating this view because "yes" and "no" are the only possible answers.

How a question is phrased can change the polling outcome dramatically. The Roper polling organization once asked a double-negative question that many people found hard to understand: "Does it seem possible or does it seem impossible to you that the Nazi extermination of the Jews never happened?" The survey results showed that 20 percent of Americans seemed to doubt that the Holocaust ever occurred. When the Roper organization rephrased the question more clearly, the percentage of doubters dropped to less than 1 percent.

Respondents' answers are also influenced by the order in which questions are asked and, in some cases, by their interactions with the interviewer. To a certain extent, people try to please the interviewer.

Unscientific and Fraudulent Polls. A perennial issue is the promotion of surveys that are unscientific or even fraudulent. All too often, a magazine or Web site asks its readers to respond to a question—and then publishes the answers as if they were based on a scientifically chosen random sample. Other news media may then publicize the survey as if it were a poll taken by such reliable teams as Gallup, CBS and the *New York Times,* or the *Wall Street Journal* and NBC. Critical consumers should watch out for surveys with self-selected respondents and other types of skewed samples. These so-called polls may be used to deliberately mislead the public.

PUBLIC OPINION AND THE POLITICAL PROCESS

Public opinion affects the political process in many ways. Politicians, whether in office or in the midst of a campaign, see public opinion as important to their careers. The president, members of Congress, governors, and other elected officials realize that strong support by the public as expressed in opinion polls is a source of power in dealing with other politicians. It is more difficult for a senator to say no to the president if the president is immensely popular and if polls show approval of the president's policies. Public opinion also helps political candidates identify voters' most important concerns and may help them shape their campaigns successfully.

LO4: Consider the effect that public opinion may have on the political process.

Political Culture and Public Opinion

Americans are divided into a multitude of ethnic, religious, regional, and political subgroups. Given the diversity of American society and the wide range of opinions contained within it, how is it that the political process continues to function without being stalemated by conflict and dissension?

One explanation is rooted in the concept of the American political culture, which can be described as a set of attitudes and ideas about the nation and the government. As discussed in Chapter 1, our political culture is widely shared by Americans of many different backgrounds. To some extent, it consists of symbols, such as the American flag, the Liberty Bell, and the Statue of Liberty. The elements of our political culture also include certain shared beliefs about the most important values in the American political system, including liberty, equality, and property.

The political culture provides a general environment of support for the political system. If the people share certain beliefs about the system and a reservoir of good feeling exists toward the institutions of government, the nation will be better able to weather periods of crisis.

Political Trust. The political culture also helps Americans

Mick Stevens/www.cartoonbank.com

"Never mind what the voters are saying. What are the pollsters saying?"

Political Trust
The degree to which individuals express trust in the government and political institutions, usually measured through a specific series of survey questions.

evaluate their government's performance. **Political trust,** the degree to which individuals express trust in political institutions, has been measured by a variety of polling questions. One of these is whether the respondent is satisfied with "the way things are going in the United States." As you can see in Figure 6–3 below, during the successful presidency of Republican Ronald Reagan (1981–1989), satisfaction levels rose from a fairly dismal 20 percent range to around 50 percent. Republican George H. W. Bush (1989–1993) enjoyed high levels of satisfaction until 1992, when rates fell back to the 20 percent range. This fall reflected the economic problems and other difficulties that handed the presidency to Democrat Bill Clinton (1993–2001).

Clinton's two terms appear to have been mostly a success, as satisfaction levels rose as high as 70 percent. Under Republican George W. Bush (2001–2009), however, satisfaction levels slowly fell. In October 2008, at the peak of the crisis in the financial industry, satisfaction bottomed out at an unprecedented 7 percent. Thereafter, the rate fluctuated between 11 and 36 percent, reflecting continued economic difficulties and a variety of political crises.

The Most Important Problems

Although people may not always have much confidence in government, they nonetheless turn to it to solve what they perceive to be the major problems facing the country. Table 6–2 on the following page, which is based on various polls conducted from 1990 to 2013, shows that the most important problems have changed over time. The public tends to emphasize problems that are immediate. It is not at all unusual to see fairly sudden, and even apparently contradictory, shifts in public perceptions of what government should do. In recent years, the economic crisis and unemployment have reached the top of the problems list.

Public Opinion and Policymaking

Policymakers cannot always be guided by opinion polls. In the end, politicians must make their own choices, and those choices necessarily involve trade-offs. If politicians vote for increased spending to improve education, for example, by necessity fewer resources are available for other worthy projects. Individuals who are polled do not have to make such trade-offs when they respond to questions. Indeed, survey respondents usually are not

FIGURE 6–3: Political Satisfaction Trend

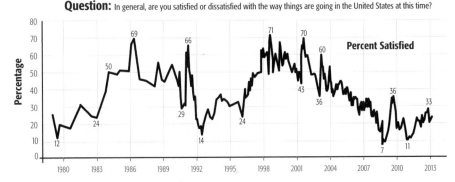

Question: In general, are you satisfied or dissatisfied with the way things are going in the United States at this time?

Sources: Gallup polls, 1979 through 2013.

TABLE 6–2: Most Important Problem Trend, 1990 to Present

Each year, one or two major issues are most on people's minds. Here you can see that some issues recur years later.			
1990	War in Middle East	2002	Terrorism, economy
1991	Economy	2003	Terrorism, economy
1992	Unemployment, budget deficit	2004	War in Iraq, economy
1993	Health care, budget deficit	2005	War in Iraq
1994	Crime, violence, health care	2006	War in Iraq, terrorism
1995	Crime, violence	2007	War in Iraq, health care
1996	Budget deficit	2008	Economy, war in Iraq
1997	Crime, violence	2009	Economy
1998	Crime, violence	2010	Economy, unemployment
1999	Crime, violence	2011	Unemployment, economy
2000	Morals, family decline	2012	Economy, unemployment
2001	Economy, education	2013	Economy, unemployment

Sources: *New York Times*/CBS News poll, January 1996; Gallup polls, 1997 through 2013.

even given a choice of trade-offs in their policy opinions. Moreover, to make an informed policy choice requires an understanding not only of the policy area but also of the consequences of any given choice. Public opinion polls rarely ensure that those polled have such information.

Finally, government decisions cannot be made simply by adding up individual desires. Politicians engage in "horse trading" with each other. Politicians also know that they cannot satisfy every desire of every constituent. Therefore, each politician attempts to maximize the net benefits to his or her constituents, while keeping within the limits of whatever the politician believes the government can afford.

THE ROLES OF THE MEDIA

The study of people and politics must take into account the role played by the media. Historically, the print media played the most important role in informing public debate. The print media developed, for the most part, our understanding of how news is to be reported. Today, however, 69 percent of Americans use television news as their primary source of information.

LO5: Describe the different types of media and the changing roles that they play in American society.

In addition, the Internet has become a major source for news, political communication, and fund-raising. The Internet is now the second most widely used source of information—34 percent of all persons consider it their primary source of news. Only 22 percent of the public now relies on newspapers as a primary news source. The system of gathering and sharing news and information is changing from one in which the media have a primary role to one in which the individual citizen may play a greater part.

The Roles of the Media

The mass media perform a number of different functions in any country. In the United States, we can list at least six media functions. Almost all of them can have political implications, and some are essential to the democratic process. These functions are as follows: (1) entertainment, (2) reporting the news, (3) identifying public problems, (4) socializing new generations, (5) providing a political forum, and (6) making profits.

Many young people get much of their television news from Stephen Colbert and Jon Stewart on the Comedy Central cable/satellite channel. (Scott Gries/PictureGroup. via AP Images)

Entertainment. By far the greatest number of radio and television hours are dedicated to entertaining the public. The battle for prime-time ratings indicates how important successful entertainment is to the survival of networks and individual stations. A number of network shows have a highly political content. Many younger people report that they get much of their political information from two programs on the Comedy Central network, hosted by Jon Stewart and Stephen Colbert. Both are liberal, although as part of his routine, Colbert pretends to be a conservative.

For many Americans, especially younger ones, the Internet is replacing television as a source of entertainment. While much time on the Internet may be spent chatting with friends on Skype or even watching television programs online, politics is often a topic. YouTube, in particular, offers a large number of politically oriented videos, many of which are satirical. Talk radio and television shows that feature personalities are another form of politically oriented entertainment—one that is dominated by the political right.

Reporting the News. A primary function of the mass media in all their forms is the reporting of news. The media provide words and pictures about events, facts, personalities, and ideas. The protections of the First Amendment are intended to keep the flow of news as free as possible, because it is an essential part of the democratic process. If citizens cannot obtain unbiased information about the state of their communities and their leaders' actions, how can they make voting decisions? One of the more incisive comments about the importance of the media was made by James Madison, who said, "A people who mean to be their own governors must arm themselves with the power knowledge gives. A popular government without popular information or the means of acquiring it, is but a prologue to a farce or a tragedy or perhaps both."[5]

Public Agenda
Issues that are perceived by the political community as meriting public attention and governmental action.

Identifying Public Problems. The power of the media is important not only in revealing what the government is doing but also in determining what the government ought to do—in other words, in setting the **public agenda.** As we noted earlier in this chapter, the mass media identify public issues. An example is the release of convicted sex offenders to residential neighborhoods after the end of their prison terms.

5. James Madison, "Letter to W. T. Barry" (August 4, 1822), in Gaillard P. Hunt, ed., *The Writings of James Madison*, Vol. 9 (1910), p. 103.

The media have influenced the passage of legislation, such as "Megan's Law," which requires police to notify neighbors about the release and/or resettlement of certain sex offenders. American journalists also work in a long tradition of uncovering public wrongdoing, corruption, and bribery, and of bringing such wrongdoing to the public's attention.

Closely related to this investigative function is that of presenting policy alternatives. Public policy is often complex and difficult to make entertaining, but programs devoted to public policy are frequently scheduled for prime-time television, especially on cable networks. For its part, the Web offers an enormous collection of political sites, with policy proposals representing every point of view.

Socializing New Generations. As mentioned earlier in this chapter, the media strongly influence the beliefs and opinions of Americans. Because of this influence, the media play a significant role in the political socialization of the younger generation and of immigrants to this country. Through the transmission of historical information (sometimes fictionalized), the presentation of American culture, and the portrayal of the diverse regions and groups in the United States, the media teach young people and immigrants about what it means to be an American. Many children's television shows are designed not only to entertain young viewers but also to instruct them in the moral values of American society. On the Internet, young Americans participate in political forums, obtain information for writing assignments, and, in general, acquire much of their political socialization.

Providing a Political Forum. As part of their news function, the media also provide a political forum for leaders and the public. Candidates for office use news reporting to sustain interest in their campaigns, while officeholders use the media to gain support for their policies or to present an image of leadership. Presidential trips abroad are one way for the chief executive to get colorful, positive, and exciting news coverage that makes the president look "presidential." The media also offer ways for citizens to participate in public debate through letters to the editor, blog posts, Twitter posts, and other channels.

Making Profits. Most of the news media in the United States are private, for-profit corporate enterprises. One of their goals is to make profits for expansion and for dividends to the stockholders who own the companies. In general, profits are made as a result of charging for advertising. Advertising revenues usually are related directly to circulation or to listener/viewer ratings.

Several well-known media outlets, in contrast, are publicly owned—public television stations in many communities and National Public Radio. These outlets operate without extensive commercials, are locally supported, and are often subsidized by the government and corporations.

For the most part, however, the media depend on advertisers for their revenues. Consequently, reporters may feel pressure from media owners and from advertisers. Media owners may take their cues from what advertisers want. If an important advertiser does not like the political bent of a particular newspaper reporter, for example, the reporter could be asked to alter his or her "style" of writing. According to the Pew Research Center's Project for Excellence in Journalism, 38 percent of local print and broadcast journalists know of instances in which their newsrooms were encouraged to do a story because it related to an owner, advertiser, or sponsor.[6]

---

6. Pew Research Center for the People & the Press and the Project for Excellence in Journalism, *The State of the News Media 2007: An Annual Report on American Journalism.*

The Financial Crisis of the Press. Lately, newspapers have found it increasingly difficult to make a profit. Newspaper revenues have fallen because online services have taken over a greater share of classified advertising. The recent economic crisis, which depressed all forms of advertising spending, pushed many large daily newspapers over the edge. Newspapers in Chicago, Denver, and Seattle went out of business. Even some of the most famous papers, such as the *New York Times,* the *Chicago Tribune,* and the *Boston Globe,* were in serious financial trouble.

Although all major newspapers are now online, they have found it difficult to turn a profit on their Web editions. News sites typically cannot sell enough advertising to meet their costs. One problem is that most online advertising revenue is collected by sites that provide search and aggregation services but do not create original content. Google, for example, collects a full 41 percent of all online ad revenue but provides almost no original material. In response to this problem, major newspapers have begun charging for online access, a process dubbed *retreating behind a paywall.* Access charges, however, reduce the number of users who are willing to view a site.

Television versus the New Media

As we explained earlier, new forms of media are displacing older ones as sources of information on politics and society in general. Although it is only recently that newspapers have experienced severe economic difficulties, they were losing ground to television as early as the 1950s. Today, the Internet has begun to displace television.

New Patterns of Media Consumption. Not everyone, however, migrates to new media at the same rate. Among Americans older than sixty-five years of age, only 11 percent obtain information about political campaigns by going online, up from 5 percent in 2000. In this older generation, 31 percent still rely on a daily newspaper, although that is down from 58 percent in 2000.[7]

The media consumption patterns of "early adapters" of new technology are different. Some older high-income persons are among the early adapters, but the new media are most popular among youth. Indeed, many younger people have abandoned e-mail, relying on Facebook, texting, and other systems for messages. Some have moved on from Facebook to newer, more innovative social networking platforms. Television becomes something to watch only if you cannot find the program you want to see online.

Young early adapters may find much of the older media irrelevant to their lives. It does not matter whether national television news shows are willing to pay personalities, such as Diane Sawyer, and Matt Lauer millions of dollars if few people ever watch these shows. Yet television news, cable networks, talk radio, and other older forms of media are not irrelevant to American politics. Older voters outnumber younger ones by a

Political blogger Ezra Klein of the *Washington Post* has become well known as a guest host on the Rachel Maddow television show. Are political blogs influential? (Photo by Dimitrios Kambouris/Getty Images for *The New Yorker*)

7. Pew Research Center for the People & the Press, "Cable Leads the Pack as Campaign News Source," February 7, 2012.

wide margin. As of the 2010 census, about 99 million Americans were age fifty or older. U.S. residents ages eighteen through twenty-nine numbered about 52 million. Older voters are more likely to make it to the polls—and many early adapters of new media technology are too young to vote. It follows that television remains essential to American politics.

Sound Bite
A brief, memorable comment that can easily be fit into news broadcasts.

The Continuing Influence of Television. Television's continuing influence on the political process is recognized by all who engage in that process. Television news is often criticized for being superficial, particularly compared with the detailed coverage available in newspapers and magazines. In fact, television news is constrained by its technical characteristics, the most important being the limitations of time—stories must be reported in only a few minutes.

The most interesting aspect of television—and of online videos—is the fact that it relies on pictures rather than words to attract the viewer's attention. Therefore, video that is chosen for a particular political story has exaggerated importance. Viewers do not know what other photos may have been taken or what other events may have been recorded— they see only those appearing on their screens. Video clips, whether they appear on network news or YouTube, can also use well-constructed stories to exploit the potential for drama. Some critics suggest that there is pressure to produce television news that has a "story line," like a novel or movie. The story should be short, with exciting pictures and a clear plot. In extreme cases, the news media are satisfied with a **sound bite,** a several-second comment selected or crafted for its immediate impact on the viewer.

It has been suggested that these formatting characteristics of video increases its influence on political events. As you are aware, real life is usually not dramatic, nor do all events have a plot that is neat or easily understood. Political campaigns are continuing events, lasting perhaps as long as two years. The significance of their daily turns and twists is only apparent later. The "drama" of Congress, with its 535 players and dozens of important committees and meetings, is also difficult for the media to present. Television requires, instead, dozens of daily three-minute stories.

THE MEDIA AND POLITICAL CAMPAIGNS

All forms of the media—television, newspapers, radio, magazines, and online services— have a significant political impact on American society. Although younger voters get a relatively small share of their news from television, it remains the primary news source for older voters. Therefore, candidates and their consultants spend much of their time devising strategies that use television to their benefit. Three types of TV coverage are generally employed in campaigns for the presidency and other offices: advertising, including negative ads; management of news coverage; and campaign debates.

LO6: Summarize the impact of the media on political campaigns, and consider the issue of political bias in the media.

Political Advertising

Political advertising has become increasingly important for the profitability of television station owners. Hearst Television, for example, obtains well over 10 percent of its revenues from political ads during an election year. During the 2012 presidential elections, total spending exceeded $7 billion. Among other expenses, candidates purchased more than 3 million campaign advertisements.

Perhaps one of the most effective political ads of all time was a thirty-second spot created by President Lyndon Johnson's media adviser in 1964. Johnson's opponent in the campaign was Barry Goldwater, a conservative Republican candidate known for his expansive views on the role of the U.S. military. In the ad, a little girl stood in a field of

VOTE FOR PRESIDENT JOHNSON
ON NOVEMBER 3.

President Lyndon Johnson's "Daisy Girl" ad contrasted the innocence of childhood with the horror of an atomic attack. Would such a campaign ad be effective today? (Doyle, Dane, Bernbach)

daisies. As she held a daisy, she pulled the petals off and quietly counted to herself. Suddenly, when she reached number ten, a deep bass voice cut in and began a countdown: "10, 9, 8, 7, 6 . . . ." When the voice intoned "zero," the mushroom cloud of an atomic bomb began to fill the screen. Then President Johnson's voice was heard: "These are the stakes. To make a world in which all of God's children can live, or to go into the dark. We must either love each other or we must die." At the end of the commercial, the message read, "Vote for President Johnson on November 3."

Since the "Daisy Girl" advertisement, negative advertising has come into its own. In recent elections, an ever-increasing share of political ads have been negative in nature. The public claims not to like negative advertising, but as one consultant put it, "Negative advertising works." Negative ads can backfire, though, when there are three or more candidates in the race, a typical state of affairs in the early presidential primaries. If one candidate attacks another, the attacker as well as the candidate who is attacked may come to be viewed negatively by the public. A candidate who "goes negative" may thus unintentionally boost the chances of a third candidate who is not part of the exchange.

Management of News Coverage

Using political advertising to get a message across to the public is a very expensive tactic. Coverage by the news media, however, is free. The campaign simply needs to ensure that coverage takes place. In recent years, campaign managers have shown increasing sophistication in creating newsworthy events for journalists to cover.

The campaign staff uses several methods to try to influence the quantity and type of coverage the campaign receives. First, the staff understands the technical aspects of media coverage—camera angles, necessary equipment, timing, and deadlines—and plans political events to accommodate the press. Second, the campaign organization is aware that political reporters and their sponsors—networks, newspapers, or blogs—are in competition for the best stories and can be manipulated through the granting of favors, such as a personal interview with the candidate. Third, the scheduler in the campaign has the important task of planning events that will be photogenic and interesting enough for the evening news.

A related goal, although one that is more difficult to attain, is to convince reporters that a particular interpretation of an event is true. Today, the art of putting the appropriate **spin** on a story or event is highly developed. Press advisers, often referred to as **spin doctors,** try to convince journalists that the advisers' interpretations of political events are correct.

For example, the Obama administration and the Republicans engaged in a major spinning duel over the so-called budget sequester in March 2013. Under the sequester, if Congress could not reach agreement on a plan to reduce the federal budget deficit, automatic cuts would go into effect worth $1.2 trillion over a ten-year period. Half of the cuts would come out of national defense spending, and the rest out of discretionary domestic spending (entitlements are largely spared). Obama and his representatives blamed the Republicans for the failure to reach an agreement, and Republicans blamed the administration.

Going for the Knockout Punch—Presidential Debates

In presidential elections, perhaps just as important as political advertisements and general news coverage is the performance of the candidates in televised presidential debates. After the first such debate in 1960, in which John Kennedy, the young senator from Massachusetts, took on the vice president of the United States, Richard Nixon, candidates became aware of the great potential of television for changing the momentum of a campaign. In general, challengers have much more to gain from debating than do incumbents. Challengers hope that the incumbent will make a mistake in the debate and undermine the "presidential" image. Incumbent presidents are loath to debate their challengers, because it puts their opponents on an equal footing with them, but the debates have become so widely anticipated that it is difficult for an incumbent to refuse to participate.

The 2011–2012 Republican Primary Debates. Presidential candidates have often debated during primary election campaigns. Traditionally, such debates have not attracted much interest, but the Republican presidential primary race in 2011 and 2012 was a dramatic exception. The Republicans held twenty-seven televised debates that were widely viewed. The political context was the belief of many strong conservatives that Mitt Romney, the front-runner, was not really one of them. Romney, therefore, was challenged by a series of anti-Romney candidates. Texas governor Rick Perry, African

Spin
An interpretation of political events that is favorable to a candidate or officeholder.

Spin Doctor
A political adviser who tries to convince journalists of the truth of a particular interpretation of events.

Bias
An inclination or a preference that interferes with impartial judgment.

American businessman Herman Cain, former U.S. House Speaker Newt Gingrich, and former Pennsylvania senator Rick Santorum each had their day in the sun. All of these candidacies proved to be flawed in one way or another, however, and in the end Romney prevailed without great difficulty.

Obama versus Romney. The 2012 general election debates in October were also important. During 2012, Obama's team tried to present Romney as a rich financier who cared only for the interests of other wealthy Americans. Through September, this characterization appeared to be damaging Romney's campaign. In the first of three debates, however, Romney was successful in presenting himself as compassionate, reasonable, and, above all, moderate. Obama, meanwhile, seemed to be half asleep. Obama did much better in the next two debates. Romney's performance in the first debate tightened up the elections for a time, but by Election Day the effects had largely worn off.

Political Campaigns and the Internet

Today, the campaign staff of almost every candidate running for a significant political office includes an Internet campaign strategist—a professional hired to create and maintain the campaign Web site, social media accounts, blogs, and podcasts. The work of this strategist includes designing a user-friendly and attractive Web site for the candidate and tracking campaign contributions made through the site. The strategist also manages the candidate's e-mail, Twitter, and Facebook communications. Finally, this staffer hires bloggers to promote the candidate's agenda on the Web and monitors Web sites for favorable or unfavorable comments or video clips about the candidate.

Additionally, major interest groups in the United States use the Internet to promote their causes. Prior to elections, various groups engage in issue advocacy from their Web sites. At little or no cost, they can promote positions taken by favored candidates and solicit contributions.

Bias in the Media

For decades, the contention that the mainstream media have a liberal **bias** has been repeated time and again. A number of studies appear to back up this claim. For example, research at the University of Connecticut has shown that journalists consider themselves Democrats three times as often as they identify with the Republicans. A recent Gallup poll reports that 47 percent of the public thinks that the news media are too liberal, while 13 percent see the media as too conservative. These views are strongly associated with the politics of the respondent: 75 percent of Republicans believe the media are too liberal, while only 20 percent of Democrats think that is true.

Alternative Forms of Bias. Some writers have argued that the mainstream media are really biased in favor of stories that involve conflict and drama—the better to attract viewers. Still others contend the media are biased against "losers," and when a candidate falls behind in a race, his or her press quickly becomes negative. The Republican primary campaigns in 2011 and 2012 provided many opportunities for candidates to complain about such bias, as one candidate after another shot up in the polls, only to be rejected by opinion poll respondents a month or two later.

Bias and Professionalism. While many journalists may be Democrats at heart, most operate under a code of professional ethics that dictates "objectivity" and a commitment to the truth. Journalists may not always succeed in living up to such a code, but it helps that it exists.

To be sure, many media outlets have an explicit political point of view. This is especially common in the blogosphere, but it is true of some cable news channels as well. Fox News, for example, takes pride in avoiding what it sees as the liberal bias of the mainstream media.

Some progressives, however, have accused Fox and other conservative outlets of allowing politics to interfere with their objectivity. They argue that conservatives find liberal bias even in reporting that is scrupulously accurate. In the words of humorist Stephen Colbert, "Reality has a well-known liberal bias." An example was the widespread refusal of conservative media to believe opinion polls that showed Barack Obama leading in the 2012 presidential race.

Other observers contend that the issue of media bias is declining in importance due to the rise of the Internet. Today's technologically savvy media consumers can easily find information from a wide variety of sources, mainstream and alternative, liberal and conservative. The best answer to bias may be a willingness to consult a wide range of sources.

Commentator Bill O'Reilly is one of the stars of Fox News. Fox is known for its conservative slant on the news, and it is also more popular than its competitors. Why might this be? (Slevan Vlasic/Getty Images)

making a difference

BEING A CRITICAL CONSUMER OF THE NEWS

Television, print media, and the Internet provide a wide range of choices for Americans who want to stay informed. Still, critics of the media argue that a substantial amount of what you read and see is colored either by the subjectivity of editors and bloggers or by the demands of profit making. Few Americans take the time to become critical consumers of the news.

Why Should You Care?
Even if you do not plan to engage in political activism, you have a stake in ensuring that your beliefs are truly your own and that they represent your values and interests. To guarantee this result, you need to obtain accurate information from the media and avoid being swayed by subliminal appeals, loaded terms, or outright bias. If you do not take care, you could find yourself voting for a candidate who is opposed to what you believe in or voting against measures that are in your interest.

Even when journalists themselves are relatively successful at remaining objective, they will of necessity give publicity to politicians and interest group representatives who are far from impartial. You need the ability to determine what motivates the players in the political game and how much they are "shading" the news or even propagating outright lies. You also need to determine which news outlets are reliable.

What Can You Do?
To become a critical news consumer, you must develop a critical eye and ear. Ask yourself what stories are given prominence at the top of a newspaper's Web site. For a contrast to most daily papers, visit the sites of publications with explicit points of view, such as the *National Review* (search on "national review") or the *New Republic* (search on "tnr"). Take note of how they handle stories.

Sources such as blogs often have strong political preferences, and you should try to determine what these are. Does a blog merely give opinions, or does it back up its arguments with data? It is possible to select anecdotes to support almost any argument—does an anecdote represent typical circumstances, or is it a rare occurrence highlighted to make a point?

Watching the evening news can be far more rewarding if you look at how much the news depends on video effects. You will note that stories on the evening news tend to be no more than three minutes long, that stories with excellent video footage get more attention, and that considerable time is taken up with "happy talk" or human-interest stories.

Another way to critically evaluate news coverage is to compare how the news is covered by different outlets. For example, you might compare the coverage of events on Fox News with the presentation on MSNBC, or compare the radio commentary of Rush Limbaugh with that of National Public Radio's *All Things Considered.* When does a show cross the line between news and opinion?

A variety of organizations try to monitor news sources for accuracy and bias. Consider visiting the following sites:

- The *American Journalism Review* covers a wide variety of journalistic issues, including the migration from print media to online sources. Find its site by entering "ajr" in a search engine.

- The Committee of Concerned Journalists is a professional organization concerned with journalistic ethics. Search on "concerned journalists."

- Fairness & Accuracy in Reporting is a media watchdog with a strong liberal viewpoint. Locate its Web site by entering "fair reporting."

- Accuracy in Media takes a combative conservative position on media issues. Find its site by entering "accuracy in media."

The *National Review Online.*
(http:www.nationalreview.com)

key**terms**

agenda setting 119	house effect 128	political	sampling error 127
bias 138	media 119	socialization 117	sound bite 135
consensus 117	opinion leader 119	political trust 130	spin 137
divided opinion 117	opinion poll 125	public agenda 132	spin doctor 137
gender gap 125	peer group 119	public opinion 117	tracking poll 127
generational effect 121			

chapter**summary**

1 Public opinion is the aggregate of individual attitudes or beliefs shared by some portion of the adult population. A consensus exists when a large proportion of the public appears to express the same view on an issue. Divided opinion exists when the public holds widely different attitudes on an issue.

2 People's opinions are formed through the political socialization process. Important factors in this process are the family, educational experiences, peer groups, opinion leaders, the media, and political events. The influence of the media as a socialization factor may be growing relative to that of the family. Voting behavior is also influenced by demographic factors such as education, economic status, religion, race and ethnicity, gender, and geographic region.

3 Most descriptions of public opinion are based on the results of opinion polls. The accuracy of polls depends on the sampling techniques used. An accurate poll includes a representative sample of the population being surveyed and ensures randomness in the selection of respondents.

4 Problems with polls include the difficulty of persuading people to participate, badly weighted samples, questions that are poorly worded or do not allow a sufficient range of responses, and sometimes the respondents' interactions with the interviewer. "Polls" that rely on self-selected respondents are inherently inaccurate and should be discounted.

5 The political culture provides a general environment of support for the political system, allowing the nation to weather periods of crisis. The political culture also helps Americans to evaluate their government's performance. At times, the level of trust in government has been relatively high; at

other times, the level of trust has declined steeply. Generally, though, Americans turn to government to solve what they perceive to be the major problems facing the country.

6 Public opinion also plays an important role in policymaking. Politicians cannot always be guided by opinion polls, however. This is because respondents often do not understand the costs and consequences of policy decisions or the trade-offs involved in making such decisions.

7 The media are enormously important in American politics today. They perform a number of functions, including (a) entertainment, (b) news reporting, (c) identifying public problems, (d) socializing new generations, (e) providing a political forum, and (f) making profits. Television remains the most important medium, in particular among older voters, who are the most likely to make it to the polls. Younger Americans are turning to the Internet as a source of information.

8 The political influence of the media is most obvious during political campaigns. Today's campaigns use advertising and expert management of news coverage. For presidential candidates, how they appear in campaign debates is of major importance. Internet blogs and podcasts, as well as sites such as YouTube and Facebook, are transforming today's political campaigns.

9 Frequently, the mainstream media have been accused of liberal bias, although some observers contend that these accusations result from true stories that offend conservatives. Other possible media biases include a bias against political "losers" and in favor of drama.

test**yourself**

LO1 *Define public opinion, consensus opinion, and divided opinion, and discuss major sources of political socialization, including the family, schools, the media, and political events.*

We can best define *public opinion* as:
   a.   beliefs held by moderate voters.
   b.   beliefs shared by both Democrats and Republicans.
   c.   the aggregate of individual beliefs shared by some portion of adults.

LO2 *Identify the effects of various influences on voting behavior, including education, income, religion, race/ethnicity, gender, and geography.*

The gender gap refers to:
   a.   the difference in college attendance rates for males and females.
   b.   the tendency for women to be more likely to vote for a particular candidate than men.
   c.   the tendency for men to dominate the political process.

LO3 *Describe the characteristics of a scientific opinion poll, and list some of the problems pollsters face in obtaining accurate results.*

One way to compensate for underrepresented groups in a polling sample is to:
   a.   eliminate all answers from those who are part of the underrepresented group.
   b.   reduce the weight given to the underrepresented group so that it does not count excessively.
   c.   add extra weight to correct for the underrepresented group.

LO4 *Consider the effect that public opinion may have on the political process.*

The trend in political satisfaction in this country has:

   a.   always been very high.
   b.   fallen since around 2001.
   c.   risen since around 2001.

LO5 *Describe the different types of media and the changing roles that they play in American society.*

Television remains a key medium in American politics because:
   a.   it is the number-one source of information for older voters, who dominate the electorate.
   b.   young people are avoiding the Internet as a source of information.
   c.   television advertisements are not that expensive to buy.

LO6 *Summarize the impact of the media on political campaigns, and consider the issue of political bias in the media.*

Critics of the mainstream media have often accused it of exhibiting which of the following forms of bias:
   a.   bias against conservatives, bias against losers, and bias in favor of conflict and drama.
   b.   bias against Democrats, bias in favor of religion, and bias in favor of whoever is president.
   c.   bias against science, bias against entertainment figures, and bias in favor of minority group members.

Essay Question:

Years ago, people with postgraduate degrees were more likely to vote for Republican than Democratic candidates, but in recent years, highly educated voters have been trending Democratic. Why might physicians and lawyers be more likely to vote Democratic than in the past? For what reasons might college professors lean Democratic?

Answers to multiple-choice questions: 1. c, 2. b, 3. c, 4. b, 5. a, 6. a.

CourseMate

Access CourseMate at **www.cengagebrain.com** for additional study tools: practice quizzes, key term flashcards and crossword puzzles, audio chapter summaries, simulations, animated learning modules, interactive timelines, videos, and American Government NewsWatch.

Members of the Allied Pilots Association picket American Airlines at O'Hare International Airport in Chicago. This labor dispute caused the airline's on-time performance to tumble to 54 percent. (Tim Boyle/Bloomberg via Getty Images)

Interest Groups and Political Parties

LEARNING OUTCOMES

The six **Learning Outcomes (LOs)** below are designed to help improve your understanding of this chapter. After reading this chapter, you should be able to:

■ **LO1** Describe the basic characteristics of interest groups, and explain why Americans join them.

■ **LO2** List the major types of interest groups, especially those with economic motivations.

■ **LO3** Discuss direct and indirect interest group techniques, and describe the main ways in which lobbyists are regulated.

■ **LO4** Cite some of the major activities of U.S. political parties, and discuss how they are organized.

■ **LO5** Explain how the history of U.S. political parties has led to the two major parties that exist today.

■ **LO6** Give reasons why the two-party system has endured in America, and evaluate the impact of third parties and independents on U.S. politics.

Check your understanding of the material with the Test Yourself section at the end of the chapter.

The structure of American government invites the participation of **interest groups** at various stages of the policymaking process. Americans can form groups in their neighborhoods or cities and lobby the city council or their state government. They can join statewide groups or national groups and try to influence government policy through Congress or through one of the executive agencies or cabinet departments. Representatives of large corporations may seek to influence the president personally at social events or fund-raisers. When attempts to influence government through the

Interest Group
An organized group of individuals sharing common objectives who actively attempt to influence policymakers.

These women are leaders of a new lobbying firm called Chamber Hill Strategies. Do lobbyists spend their time supporting political candidates? Why or why not? (Tom Williams/CQ Roll Call/Getty Images)

executive and legislative branches fail, interest groups can turn to the courts, filing suits in state or federal courts to achieve their political objectives.

The large number of "pressure points" in American government helps to explain why there are so many—more than one hundred thousand—interest groups at work in our society. Another reason for the multitude of interest groups is that the right to join a group is protected by the First Amendment to the U.S. Constitution (see Chapter 4). Not only are all people guaranteed the right "peaceably to assemble," but they are also guaranteed the right "to petition the Government for a redress of grievances." This constitutional provision encourages Americans to form groups and to express their opinions to the government or to their elected representatives as group members.

Political Party
A group of political activists who organize to win elections, operate the government, and determine public policy.

Lobbyist
An organization or individual who attempts to influence the passage, defeat, or content of legislation and the government's administrative decisions.

Another way to influence policymaking is to become an active member of a political party and participate in the selection of political candidates, who, if elected, will hold government positions. A **political party** might be formally defined as a group of political activists who organize to win elections, operate the government, and determine public policy. This definition explains the difference between an interest group and a political party. Interest groups do not want to operate the government, and they do not put forth political candidates—even though they support candidates who will promote their interests if elected or reelected.

In this chapter, we define interest groups, describe how they try to affect the government, and summarize the legal restrictions on **lobbyists,** people or groups who try to affect legislation and government administrative decisions. We also describe the major political parties, their history, and their organization. Finally, we explain why the two-party system has prevailed in the United States.

A NATION OF JOINERS

LO1: Describe the basic characteristics of interest groups, and explain why Americans join them.

Alexis de Tocqueville observed in the early 1830s that "in no country of the world has the principle of association been more successfully used or applied to a greater multitude of objectives than in America."[1] The French traveler was amazed at the degree to which Americans formed groups to solve civic problems, establish social relationships, and speak for their economic or political interests. Perhaps James Madison, when he wrote *Federalist Paper* No. 10 (see Appendix C), had already judged the character of his country's citizens similarly. He supported the creation of a large republic with many states to encourage the formation of multiple interests. The multitude of interests, in

---

1. Alexis de Tocqueville, *Democracy in America,* Vol. 1 [1835], ed. Phillips Bradley (New York: Knopf, 1980), p. 191.

Madison's view, would work to discourage the formation of an oppressive majority interest.

Poll data show that more than two-thirds of all Americans belong to at least one group or association. Although the majority of these affiliations could not be classified as "interest groups" in the political sense, Americans certainly understand the principles of working in groups.

Today, interest groups range from the elementary school parent-teacher association and the local "Stop the Sewer Plant Association" to the statewide association of insurance agents. They include small groups such as local environmental organizations and national groups such as the American Civil Liberties Union, the National Education Association, and the American League of Lobbyists.

Interest Groups and Social Movements

Interest groups are often spawned by mass **social movements.** Such movements represent demands by a large segment of the population for change in the political, economic, or social system. A social movement is often the first expression of latent discontent with the existing system. It may be the authentic voice of weaker or oppressed groups in society that do not have the means or standing to organize as interest groups.

The civil rights movement of the 1950s and 1960s was clearly a social movement. To be sure, several formal organizations worked to support the movement—including the Southern Christian Leadership Conference, the National Association for the Advancement of Colored People, and the Urban League—but only a social movement could generate the kinds of civil disobedience that took place in hundreds of towns and cities across the country.

Social movements may generate interest groups with specific goals. In the example of the women's movement of the 1960s, the National Organization for Women was formed in part out of a demand to end gender-segregated job advertising in newspapers.

Reasons to Join—or Not Join

Individuals may join interest groups for a variety of reasons. We can identify three types of incentives for joining.

Three Reasons to Join. People may join an interest group for companionship and the pleasure of associating with others who share their enjoyments. We can call these benefits of association *solidary incentives.*

Some interest groups offer *material incentives.* For example, people may join the American Automobile Association (AAA) for emergency roadside assistance and trip planning. Members may not realize that the AAA is also an interest group seeking to shape laws that affect drivers.

Finally, members may join interest groups precisely because they want to pursue political or economic goals through joint action. Such *purposive incentives* are important when individuals feel strongly about issues.

Those Who Do Not Join. It can be rational for someone *not* to join an interest group even when that person stands to benefit from the group's activities. A dairy farmer, for example, will benefit from the lobbying of the American Dairy Association whether he or she joins the organization or not. The difficulty that interest groups face in recruiting members when benefits can be obtained without joining is referred to as the **free-rider problem.** This problem is especially acute for labor unions, as we explain in the *Politics and Economics* feature later in this chapter.

Social Movement
A movement that represents the demands of a large segment of the public for political, economic, or social change.

Free-Rider Problem
The difficulty that interest groups face in recruiting members when the benefits they achieve can be gained without joining the group.

TYPES OF INTEREST GROUPS

Thousands of groups exist to influence government. Among the major types of interest groups are those that represent the main sectors of the economy. In addition, a number of environmental groups and public-interest organizations have been formed to protect the environment and represent the needs of the general citizenry. Other types of groups include single-issue groups, ideological groups, and groups based on race, sex, or sexual orientation. The interests of foreign governments and foreign businesses are represented in the American political arena as well.

Economic Interest Groups

LO2: List the major types of interest groups, especially those with economic motivations.

More interest groups are formed to represent economic interests than any other set of interests. The variety of economic interest groups mirrors the complexity of the American economy. Major sectors that seek influence in Washington, D.C., include business, agriculture, labor unions, government workers, and professionals.

Business Interest Groups. Thousands of business groups and trade associations work to influence government policies that affect their respective industries. "Umbrella groups" represent collections of businesses or other entities. For example, the National Association of Manufacturers is an umbrella group that represents manufacturing concerns. Some business groups are decidedly more powerful than others. Consider the U.S. Chamber of Commerce, which represents about 3 million member companies. It can bring constituent influence to bear on every member of Congress.

Social Media in Politics

Entering the name or initials of most interest groups into a Facebook search box is likely to bring up a page with recent posts by the group's supporters. For labor, try "afl-cio." The U.S. Chamber of Commerce page at "uschamber" is very active.

Agricultural Interest Groups. American farmers and their employees represent less than 1 percent of the U.S. population. In spite of this, farmers' influence on legislation beneficial to their interests has been significant. Farmers have succeeded in their aims because they have very strong interest groups. For example, the American Farm Bureau Federation, or Farm Bureau, established in 1919, represents more than 5.5 million families (a majority of whom are not actually farm families) and is usually seen as conservative.

Agricultural interest groups have probably been more successful than any other groups in obtaining subsidies from American taxpayers. U.S. farm subsidies cost taxpayers about $16 billion a year. Republicans and Democrats alike have supported agricultural subsidies. Farmers may not be as successful in today's budget-cutting environment, however. The most recent "farm bill" expired in 2012, and the next one may prove to be less generous.

Labor Movement

The economic and political expression of working class interests.

Service Sector

The sector of the economy that provides services—such as health care, banking, and education—in contrast to the sector that produces goods.

Labor Interest Groups. Interest groups representing the **labor movement** date back to at least 1886, when the American Federation of Labor (AFL) was formed. In 1955, the AFL joined forces with the Congress of Industrial Organizations (CIO). The AFL-CIO experienced discord within its ranks during 2005, however, as four key unions left the federation and formed the Change to Win Coalition. Today, Change to Win has a membership of about 6 million workers, while the AFL-CIO's membership is about 10 million. Many labor advocates fear that the split will reduce organized labor's influence.

Even before the split, the role of unions in American society had been waning, as witnessed by a decline in union membership (see Figure 7–1 on the facing page). This decline has reduced labor's political influence. In the age of automation and with the rise of the **service sector,** blue-collar workers in basic industries (auto, steel, and the like) represent a smaller and smaller percentage of the total working population. Because of this decline in the industrial sector of the economy, national unions are looking to nontraditional areas for their membership, including migrant farmworkers, service workers, and, especially, public employees.

FIGURE 7–1: Decline in Union Membership, 1948 to Present

The percentage of the total workforce that consists of labor union members has declined precipitously over the past forty years. The percentage of government workers who are union members, however, increased significantly in the 1960s and 1970s and has remained stable since then.

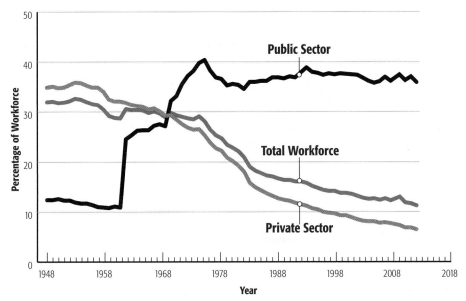

Source: Bureau of Labor Statistics.

Public Employee Unions. The degree of unionization in the private sector has declined over the past fifty years, but this has been partially offset by growth in the unionization of public employees. With a total membership of almost 8 million, public sector unions are a powerful force.

In recent years, conservatives have taken a strong stand against public employee unions, in particular teachers' unions such as the National Education Association and the American Federation of Teachers. In some states, mostly in the South, bargaining with public sector unions is prohibited. In 2011, Republican governors in several midwestern states—notably Ohio and Wisconsin—attempted to restrict or abolish the bargaining rights of public employees.

The Political Environment Faced by Labor. The success or failure of attempts to form unions depends greatly on popular attitudes. Many business-oriented conservatives have never accepted unions as legitimate institutions. In states where this position is widely held, local laws and practices can make it hard for labor to organize. One example is "right-to-work" laws, which we discuss in the *Politics and Economics* feature on the following page.

Interest Groups of Professionals. Many professional organizations exist, including the American Bar Association, the Association of General Contractors of America, the Institute of Electrical and Electronic Engineers, and others. Some professional groups, such as those representing physicians, are more influential than others because of their ability to restrict entry into their professions. Lawyers have a unique advantage—a large number

politics and **economics**

RIGHT-TO-WORK LAWS

The share of private sector workers represented by labor unions has declined steadily for decades. In about half of the states, unions face "right-to-work" laws. Under such legislation, contracts between unions and employers that require workers to pay dues or fees to the union as a condition of employment are banned. Nonunion workers cannot be required to pay fees to support collective bargaining, the filing of grievances, and other services. Most right-to-work states are in the South and the West, although Michigan and Indiana became right-to-work states in 2012.

OPPOSITION TO RIGHT-TO-WORK LAWS

Unions and other opponents of right-to-work laws argue that such laws create a *free-rider problem*. Federal law requires unions to represent everyone in a given workplace, whether they are members or not. Employees who do not pay dues or a representation fee still benefit from any services that the union can supply. If union representatives negotiate better wages and working conditions, nonunion workers obtain these benefits as well. Unions must also represent nonpaying workers who file grievances. Not surprisingly, opponents of right-to-work laws call them "right-to-freeload" laws.

THE EFFECT OF RIGHT-TO-WORK LAWS

Not surprisingly, right-to-work states have lower rates of unionization than states that lack such legislation. For example, Georgia and North Carolina, both right-to-work states, have unionization rates of about 5 percent. In contrast, without right-to-work laws, California and New York have unionization rates of almost 20 percent and 27 percent, respectively. Data also suggest that employees in right-to-work states earn wages about three percentage points lower than wages for comparable jobs elsewhere. Employer-sponsored health-insurance plans are almost three percentage points—and pensions about five percentage points—less common in right-to-work states.

WHAT IS THE IMPACT ON EMPLOYMENT?

Other studies report numbers that can be used to support right-to-work laws. The Mackinac Center for Public Policy contends that from 1980 to 2012, employment growth in right-to-work states exceeded 70 percent, compared to about 30 percent in non-right-to-work states. Another study compared Ohio (with no right-to-work law) with Texas (a right-to-work state) from 1998 to 2008. Employment in Ohio remained about the same, while Texas added more than 1.5 million jobs. Opponents of right-to-work laws argue that such figures merely show that states with such laws have an unfair advantage.

THE CONSTITUTIONAL ARGUMENTS

Supporters of right-to-work laws argue that the First Amendment to the Constitution guarantees *freedom of association*. Accordingly, workers should have the right both to join a union and to *not* join a union. The right to avoid forced unionization should include freedom from paying any fees. Others, however, argue that right-to-work laws violate *freedom of contract*. If an employer and a union chosen by the majority of all employees agree that all employees should either join the union or pay a representation fee, they should have the right to make such a contract.

FOR CRITICAL ANALYSIS

Rates of unionization are falling all over the world. Some argue that the real problem for unions isn't unfriendly legislation but the disappearance of traditionally unionized manufacturing jobs. Do you agree? Why or why not?

---

of members of Congress share their profession. In terms of funds spent on lobbying, however, one professional organization stands head and shoulders above the rest—the American Medical Association. Founded in 1847, it is affiliated with more than 1,000 local and state medical societies and has a total membership of about 216,000.

The Unorganized Poor. Some have argued that the system of interest group politics leaves out poor Americans. If they are members of the working poor, they may hold two or more jobs just to survive, leaving them no time to participate in interest groups.

Consequently, some scholars suggest that interest groups and lobbyists are the privilege of upper-middle-class Americans and those who belong to unions or other special groups.

Others, however, observe that the poor do obtain benefits from government. Without federal tax and spending programs aimed at low-income persons, as many as 25 percent of U.S. families would have incomes below the official poverty line. If you take into account all benefits that low-income families obtain, that number drops to about 10 percent. True, the poor cannot represent themselves. But for decades, liberal groups and, especially, religious groups have lobbied on behalf of those suffering from poverty. These interest groups have done for the poor what the poor cannot do for themselves.

Environmental Groups

Environmental interest groups are not new. The National Audubon Society was founded in 1905 to protect the snowy egret from the commercial demand for hat decorations. The patron of the Sierra Club, John Muir, worked for the creation of national parks more than a century ago. But the blossoming of national environmental groups with mass memberships did not occur until the 1970s.

Today's Environmental Groups. Since the first Earth Day, organized in 1972, many interest groups have sprung up to protect the environment in general or unique ecological niches. The groups range from the National Wildlife Federation, with a membership of more than 4 million and an emphasis on education, to the more elite Environmental Defense Fund, with a membership of five hundred thousand and a focus on influencing federal policy.

Global Warming. The topic of global warming has become a major focus for environmental groups in recent years. This issue has pitted environmentalists against other interest groups—for example, interests representing industries that release "greenhouse" gases into the atmosphere. Indeed, the reaction against environmentalism has been strong enough in such coal-producing states as West Virginia to transform them politically. Once a Democratic bastion, West Virginia now usually supports Republicans in presidential contests.

Public-Interest Groups

Public interest is a difficult term to define because, as we noted in Chapter 6, there are many publics in our nation of more than 315 million. It is almost impossible for one particular public policy to benefit everybody, which in turn makes it practically impossible to define the public interest. Nonetheless, over the past few decades, a variety of lobbying organizations have been formed "in the public interest."

The Consumer Movement. As an organized movement, consumerism began in 1936 with the founding of the Consumers Union, which continues to publish the popular magazine *Consumer Reports.* Consumerism took off during the 1960s. Ralph Nader, who gained notice by exposing allegedly unsafe automobiles, was a key figure in the new movement and a major sponsor of new organizations. These included Public Interest Research Groups (PIRGs)—campus organizations that emerged in the early 1970s and continue to provide students with platforms for civic engagement. Partly in response to the PIRG organizations and other groups, several conservative public-interest legal foundations have sprung up that are often pitted against liberal groups in court.

Other Public-Interest Groups. One of the largest public-interest groups is Common Cause, founded in 1968. Its goal is to reorder national priorities toward "the public" and

Public Interest
The best interests of the overall community; the national good, rather than the narrow interests of a particular group.

to make governmental institutions more responsive to the needs of the public. Another public-interest group is the League of Women Voters, founded in 1920. Although officially nonpartisan, it has lobbied for the Equal Rights Amendment and for government reform.

Additional Types of Interest Groups

A number of interest groups focus on just one issue. Single-interest groups, being narrowly focused, may be able to call attention to their causes because they have simple and straightforward goals and because their members tend to care intensely about the issues. Thus, such groups can easily motivate their members to contact legislators or to organize demonstrations in support of their policy goals.

The abortion debate has created groups opposed to abortion (such as the National Right to Life Committee) and groups in favor of abortion rights (such as NARAL Pro-Choice America). Further examples of single-issue groups are the National Rifle Association and the American Israel Public Affairs Committee (a pro-Israel group).

Ideological Groups. Among the most important interest groups are those that unite citizens around a common ideological viewpoint. Americans for Democratic Action, for example, was founded in 1947 to represent liberals who were explicitly anti-Communist. On the political right, Americans for Tax Reform, organized by Grover Norquist, has been successful in persuading almost all leading Republicans to sign a pledge promising never to vote to raise taxes. The various organizations making up the Tea Party movement are widely seen as ideological interest groups.

Identity Groups. Still other groups represent Americans who share a common identity, such as membership in a particular race or ethnic group. The NAACP, founded in

1909 as the National Association for the Advancement of Colored People, represents African Americans. The National Organization for Women (NOW) has championed women's rights since 1966.

Elderly Americans can be considered to have a common identity. AARP (formerly the American Association of Retired Persons) is one of the most powerful interest groups in Washington, D.C., and, according to some, the strongest lobbying group in the United States. It is certainly the nation's largest interest group, with a membership of about 40 million. AARP has accomplished much for its members over the years. It played a significant role in the creation of Medicare and Medicaid, as well as in obtaining annual cost-of-living increases in Social Security payments. (Medicare pays for medical expenses incurred by those who are

During the last presidential campaign, Barack Obama showed his support for the American Israel Public Affairs Committee. (Alex Wong/Getty Images)

at least sixty-five years of age. Medicaid provides health-care support for the poor.) In 2009 and 2010, AARP strongly supported the Democratic health-care reform bills and argued against those who feared that the new legislation might harm the Medicare program.

Foreign Interest Groups

Homegrown interest groups are not the only players in the game. Washington, D.C., is also the center for lobbying by foreign governments, as well as private foreign interests. The governments of the largest U.S. trading partners, such as Japan, South Korea, Canada, and the European Union (EU) countries, maintain substantial research and lobbying staffs. Even smaller nations, such as those in the Caribbean, engage lobbyists when vital legislation affecting their trade interests is considered.

Direct Technique
An interest group technique that uses direct interaction with government officials to further the group's goals.

Indirect Technique
An interest group technique that uses third parties to influence government officials.

INTEREST GROUP STRATEGIES

Interest groups employ a wide range of techniques and strategies to promote their policy goals. Although few groups are successful at persuading Congress and the president to endorse their programs completely, many are able to block—or at least weaken—legislation injurious to their members. The key to success for interest groups is access to government officials. To gain such access, interest groups and their representatives try to cultivate long-term relationships with legislators and government officials. The best of these relationships are based on mutual respect and cooperation. The interest group provides the official with sources of information and assistance, and the official in turn gives the group opportunities to express its views.

LO3: Discuss direct and indirect interest group techniques, and describe the main ways in which lobbyists are regulated.

The techniques used by interest groups can be divided into direct and indirect techniques. With **direct techniques,** the interest group and its lobbyists approach officials personally to present their case. With **indirect techniques,** in contrast, the interest group uses the general public or individual constituents to influence the government on behalf of the interest group.

Direct Techniques

Lobbying, publicizing ratings of legislative behavior, and providing campaign assistance are three main direct techniques used by interest groups.

Lobbying Techniques. As you might have guessed, the term *lobbying* comes from the activities of private citizens regularly congregating in the lobbies of legislative chambers to petition legislators. In the latter part of the 1800s, railroad and industrial groups openly bribed state legislators to pass legislation beneficial to their interests, giving lobbying a well-deserved bad name.

Georgia governor Nathan Deal (on the left) meets with a lobbyist during a session of the state's legislature. Why would he willingly be photographed with lobbyists? (AP Photo/*Atlanta Journal-Constitution*/Jason Getz)

Most lobbyists today are professionals. They are either consultants to a company or interest group or members of one of the Washington, D.C., law firms that specialize in providing lobbying services. Such firms employ hundreds of former members of Congress and former government officials. Lobbyists are valued for their network of contacts in Washington.

Lobbyists engage in an array of activities to influence legislation and government policy. These include the following:

- Meeting privately with public officials to make known the interests of the lobbyists' clients. Although they are acting on behalf of their clients, lobbyists often furnish needed information to senators and representatives (and government agency appointees) that these officials could not easily obtain on their own. It is to the lobbyists' advantage to provide useful information so that policymakers will rely on them in the future.
- Testifying before congressional committees for or against proposed legislation.
- Testifying before executive rulemaking agencies—such as the Federal Trade Commission or the Consumer Product Safety Commission—for or against proposed rules.
- Assisting legislators or bureaucrats in drafting legislation or regulations. Often, lobbyists furnish advice on the specific details of legislation.
- Inviting legislators to social occasions, such as cocktail parties, boating expeditions, and other events, including conferences at exotic locations. Most lobbyists believe that meeting legislators in a social setting is effective.
- Providing political information to legislators and other government officials. Sometimes, lobbyists have better information than the party leadership about how other legislators are going to vote. When this is so, the political information they furnish may be a key to legislative success.
- Suggesting nominations for federal appointments to the executive branch.

The Ratings Game. Many interest groups attempt to influence the overall behavior of legislators through their rating systems. Each year, these interest groups identify the legislation that they consider most important to their goals and then monitor how legislators vote on it. Legislators receive scores based on their votes. The usual ratings scheme ranges from 0 to 100 percent. In the scheme of the liberal Americans for Democratic Action, for example, a rating of 100 means that a member of Congress voted with the group on every issue and is, by that measure, very liberal.

Campaign Assistance. Interest groups have additional strategies to use in their attempts to influence government policies. Groups recognize that the greatest concern of legislators is to be reelected, so they focus on the legislators' campaign needs. Associations with large memberships, such as labor unions, are able to provide workers for political campaigns, including precinct workers to get out the vote, volunteers to put up posters and pass out literature, and people to staff telephone banks at campaign headquarters.

Candidates vie for the groups' endorsements in a campaign. Gaining those endorsements may be automatic, or it may require that the candidates participate in debates or interviews with the interest groups. An interest group usually publicizes its choices in its membership publication, and the candidate can use the endorsement in her or his campaign literature.

Indirect Techniques

Interest groups can also try to influence government policy by working through others, who may be constituents or the general public. Indirect techniques mask an interest group's own activities and make the effort appear to be spontaneous. Furthermore, legislators and government officials are often more impressed by contacts from constituents than from an interest group's lobbyist.

Generating Public Pressure. In some instances, interest groups try to produce a "groundswell" of public pressure to influence the government. Such efforts may include advertisements in national magazines and newspapers, mass mailings, television publicity, and demonstrations. The Internet and satellite links make communication efforts even more effective. Interest groups may commission polls to find out what the public's sentiments are and then publicize the results. The intent of this activity is to convince policymakers that public opinion supports the group's position.

Using Constituents as Lobbyists. An interest group may also use constituents of elected officials to lobby for the group's goals. In the "shotgun" approach, the interest group tries to mobilize large numbers of constituents to write, phone, or send e-mails and tweets to their legislators or to the president. Often, the group provides postcards or form letters for constituents to fill out and mail. These efforts are effective on Capitol Hill only when the number of responses is very large, however, because legislators know that the voters did not initiate the communications on their own. Artificially manufactured grassroots activity has been aptly labeled *astroturf lobbying.*

A more powerful variation of this technique uses only important constituents. With this approach, known as the "rifle" technique or the "Utah plant manager theory," the interest group might, for example, ask the manager of a local plant in Utah to contact the senator from Utah. Because the constituent is seen as responsible for many jobs or other resources, the legislator is more likely to listen carefully to the constituent's concerns about legislation than to a paid lobbyist.

Regulating Lobbyists

Congress made its first attempt to control lobbyists and lobbying activities through Title III of the Legislative Reorganization Act of 1946, otherwise known as the Federal Regulation of Lobbying Act. The law actually provided for public disclosure more than for regulation, and it neglected to specify which agency would enforce its provisions. The 1946 legislation defined a *lobbyist* as any person or organization that received funds to be used principally to influence legislation before Congress. Such persons and organizations were supposed to "register" their clients and the purposes of their efforts, and to report quarterly on their activities. The act proved to be ineffective, however.

The Lobbying Disclosure Act. The reform-minded Congress of 1995–1996 overhauled the lobbying legislation, fundamentally changing the ground rules for those who seek to influence the federal government. The Lobbying Disclosure Act passed in 1995 included the following provisions:

- A *lobbyist* is defined as anyone who spends at least 20 percent of his or her time lobbying members of Congress, their staffs, or executive-branch officials.
- Lobbyists must register with the clerk of the House and the secretary of the Senate.
- Semiannual reports must disclose the general nature of the lobbying effort.

"Please understand, I don't sell access to the government. I merely sell access to the guys who do sell access to the government."

Independent
A voter or candidate who does not identify with a political party.

Also in 1995, both the House and the Senate adopted new rules on gifts and travel expenses provided by lobbyists. The House adopted a flat ban on gifts, while the Senate established limits: senators were prohibited from accepting any gift with a value of more than $50 and from accepting gifts worth more than $100 from a single source in a given year. These gift rules stopped the broad practice of taking members of Congress to lunch or dinner at high-priced restaurants, but the various exemptions and exceptions have allowed much gift giving to continue.

Recent Legislation. The regulation of lobbying resurfaced as an issue in 2005 after a number of scandals. When the Democrats took control of Congress in January 2007, one of their initial undertakings was ethics and lobbying reform. In the first one hundred hours of the session, the House tightened its rules on gifts and on travel funded by lobbyists. The Senate followed shortly thereafter.

In September 2007, President George W. Bush signed the Honest Leadership and Open Government Act. Under the new law, lobbyists must report quarterly, and the registration threshold is $10,000 in spending per quarter. Organizations must report coalition activities if they contribute more than $5,000 to a coalition. The House and the Senate must now post lobbying information in a searchable file on the Internet. In a significant alteration to legislative practices, "earmarked" expenditures, commonly called "pork," must now be identified and made public. This last change has not always had its intended effect of reducing earmarks, however, because it turns out that many legislators are actually proud of their "pork" and are happy to tell the folks back home all about it.

POLITICAL PARTIES IN THE UNITED STATES

Every two years, usually starting in early fall, the media concentrate on the state of the political parties. Prior to an election, a typical poll usually asks the following question: "Do you consider yourself to be a Republican, a Democrat, or an independent?" For many years, Americans were divided fairly evenly among these three choices. Today, about 40 percent of all voters call themselves **independents,** although in fact three-quarters or more of all independents lean toward either the Republicans or the Democrats.

LO4: Cite some of the major activities of U.S. political parties, and discuss how they are organized.

In the United States, being a member of a political party does not require paying dues, passing an examination, or swearing an oath of allegiance. If nothing is really required to be a member of a political party, what, then, is a political party? As discussed earlier in this chapter, a political party is a group that seeks to win elections, operate the government, and determine public policy. Political parties are thus quite different from interest groups, which, as mentioned, seek to influence, not run, the government.

Functions of Political Parties in the United States

Political parties in the United States engage in a wide variety of activities, many of which are discussed in this chapter. Through these activities, parties perform a number of functions for the political system. These functions include the following:

1. *Recruiting candidates for public office.* Because it is the goal of parties to gain control of government, they must work to recruit candidates for all elective offices.
2. *Organizing and running elections.* Although elections are a government activity, political parties actually organize voter-registration drives, recruit volunteers to work at the

polls, provide much of the campaign activity to stimulate interest in the election, and work to increase voter participation.

3. *Presenting alternative policies to the electorate.*

4. *Accepting responsibility for operating the government.* When a party elects the president or governor—or a majority of the members of a legislative body—it accepts responsibility for running the government. This includes developing linkages among elected officials in the various branches of government to gain support for policies and their implementation.

5. *Acting as the organized opposition to the party in power.* The "out" party, or the one that does not control the government, is expected to articulate its own policies and oppose the winning party when appropriate.

The major functions of American political parties are carried out by a small, relatively loose-knit nucleus of party activists. This arrangement is quite different from the more highly structured, mass-membership organization typical of many European parties. American parties concentrate on winning elections rather than on signing up large numbers of deeply committed, dues-paying members who believe passionately in the party's program.

Party Organization

Each of the American political parties is often seen as having a pyramid-shaped organization, with the national chairperson and committee at the top and the local precinct chairperson on the bottom. This structure, however, does not accurately reflect the relative power of the individual components of the **party organization.** If it did, the national chairperson of the Democratic Party or the Republican Party, along with the national committee, could simply dictate how the organization was to be run, just as if it were ExxonMobil or Apple. In reality, the political parties have a confederal structure, in which each unit has significant autonomy and is linked only loosely to the other units.

The National Party Organization. Each party has a national organization, the most conspicuous part of which is the **national convention,** held every four years. The convention is used to officially nominate the presidential and vice-presidential candidates. In addition, the **party platform** is developed at the national convention. The platform sets forth the party's position on the issues and makes promises to initiate certain policies if the party wins the presidency.

After the convention, the platform sometimes is neglected or ignored when party candidates disagree with it. Because candidates are trying to win votes from a wide spectrum of voters, it can be counterproductive to emphasize the fairly narrow and sometimes controversial goals set forth in the platform. Still, once elected, the parties do try to carry out platform promises, and many of the promises eventually become law. Of course, some general goals, such as economic prosperity, are included in the platforms of both parties.

Convention Delegates. The party convention provides the most striking illustration of the difference between the ordinary members of a party, or party identifiers, and party activists. As a series of studies by the *New York Times* shows, delegates to the national party conventions are different from ordinary party identifiers. Delegates to the Democratic National Convention are far more liberal than ordinary Democratic voters. Typically, delegates to the Republican National Convention are far more conservative than ordinary Republicans. Why does this happen? In part, it is because a person, to become a delegate, must be appointed by party leaders or gather votes in a primary election from

Party Organization
The formal structure and leadership of a political party, including election committees; local, state, and national executives; and paid professional staff.

National Convention
The meeting held every four years by each major party to select presidential and vice-presidential candidates, write a platform, choose a national committee, and conduct party business.

Party Platform
A document drawn up at each national convention, outlining the policies, positions, and principles of the party.

National Committee
A standing committee of a national political party established to direct and coordinate party activities between national party conventions.

State Central Committee
The principal organized structure of each political party within each state. This committee is responsible for carrying out policy decisions of the party's state convention.

Patronage
The practice of rewarding faithful party workers and followers with government employment and contracts.

party members who care enough to vote in a primary. In addition, the primaries generally pit presidential candidates against one another on intraparty issues. Competition within each party tends to pull candidates away from the center, and delegates even more so.

The National Committee. At the national convention, each of the parties formally chooses a national standing committee, elected by the individual state parties. This **national committee** directs and coordinates party activities during the following four years. One of the jobs of the national committee is to ratify the presidential nominee's choice of a national chairperson, who in principle acts as the spokesperson for the party. The national chairperson and the national committee plan the next campaign and the next convention, obtain financial contributions, and publicize the national party.

The State Party Organization. Because every state party is unique, it is impossible to describe what an "average" state political party is like. Nonetheless, state parties have several organizational features in common. Each state party has a chairperson, a committee, and a number of local organizations. In theory, the role of the **state central committee**—the principal organized structure of each political party within each state—is similar in the various states. The committee has responsibility for carrying out the policy decisions of the party's state convention. The committee also has control over the use of party campaign funds during political campaigns. Usually, the state central committee has little, if any, influence on party candidates once they are elected.

Local Party Machinery: The Grassroots. The lowest layer of party machinery is the local organization, supported by district leaders, precinct or ward captains, and party workers. In the 1800s, the institution of **patronage**—rewarding the party faithful with government jobs or contracts—held the local organization together. For immigrants and the poor, the political machine often furnished important services and protections.

The last big-city local political machine to exercise substantial power was run by Chicago mayor Richard J. Daley (1955–1976), who was also an important figure in national Democratic politics. City machines are now dead, mostly because their function of providing social services (and reaping the reward of votes) has been taken over by state and national agencies.

Local political organizations still provide the foot soldiers of politics—individuals who pass out literature and get out the vote on Election Day, which can be crucial in local elections. In many regions, local Democratic and Republican organizations still exercise some patronage, such as awarding courthouse jobs, contracts for street repair, and other lucrative construction contracts. The constitutionality of awarding—or not awarding—contracts on the basis of political affiliation has been subject to challenge, however. The Supreme Court has ruled that failing to hire or firing individuals because of their political affiliation is an infringement of these individuals' First Amendment rights to free expression.[2] Local party organizations are also the most important vehicles for recruiting young adults into political work, because political involvement at the local level offers activists many opportunities to gain experience.

The Party-in-Government. After the election is over and the winners are announced, the focus of party activity shifts from getting out the vote to organizing and controlling the government. As you will see in Chapter 9, party membership plays an important role in the day-to-day operations of Congress, with partisanship determining everything from office space to committee assignments and power on Capitol Hill. For the president, the

2. *Rutan v. Republican Party of Illinois,* 497 U.S. 62 (1990).

political party furnishes a pool of qualified applicants for political appointments to run the government. Presidents can, and occasionally do, appoint executive personnel, such as cabinet members, from the opposition party, but it is uncommon to do so. (One recent example was President Obama's first secretary of defense—Robert Gates, a Republican.) Judicial appointments also offer a great opportunity to the winning party. For the most part, presidents are likely to appoint federal judges from their own party.

All of these party appointments suggest that the winning political party, whether at the national, state, or local level, has a great deal of control in the American system. Because of the checks and balances and the relative lack of cohesion in American parties, however, such control is the exception rather than the rule. One reason is that Americans have often seemed to prefer a **divided government,** with the executive and legislative branches controlled by different parties. The prevalence of **ticket splitting**—splitting votes between the president and members of Congress—may indicate a lack of trust in government or the relative weakness of party identification among many voters.

A HISTORY OF POLITICAL PARTIES IN THE UNITED STATES

The United States has a **two-party system,** and that system has been around since before 1800. The function and character of the political parties, as well as the emergence of the two-party system itself, have much to do with the unique historical forces operating from this country's beginning as an independent nation. Indeed, James Madison linked the emergence of political parties to the form of government created by our Constitution.

Generally, we can divide the evolution of our nation's political parties into seven periods:

1. The formation of parties, from 1789 to 1816.
2. The era of one-party rule, from 1816 to 1828.
3. The period from Andrew Jackson's presidency to the eve of the Civil War, from 1828 to 1856.
4. The Civil War and post–Civil War period, from 1856 to 1896.
5. The Republican ascendancy and the progressive period, from 1896 to 1932.
6. The New Deal period, from 1932 to about 1968.
7. The modern period, from approximately 1968 to the present.

The Formative Years: Federalists and Anti-Federalists

The first partisan political division in the United States occurred before the adoption of the Constitution. As you will recall from Chapter 2, the Federalists were those who pushed for the adoption of the Constitution, whereas the Anti-Federalists were against ratification.

In September 1796, George Washington, who had served as president for two terms, decided not to run again. In his farewell address, he made a somber assessment of the nation's future. Washington felt that the country might be destroyed by the "baneful [harmful] effects of the spirit of party." He viewed parties as a threat to both national unity and the concept of popular government. Nevertheless, in the years after the ratification of the Constitution, Americans came to realize that something more permanent than a faction would be necessary to identify candidates for office and represent political differences among the people. The result was two political parties.

LO5: Explain how the history of U.S. political parties has led to the two major parties that exist today.

Divided Government
A situation in which one major political party controls the presidency and the other controls Congress or in which one party controls a state governorship and the other controls the state legislature.

Ticket Splitting
Voting for candidates of two or more parties for different offices. For example, a voter splits her ticket if she votes for a Republican presidential candidate and for a Democratic congressional candidate.

Two-Party System
A political system in which only two parties have a reasonable chance of winning.

Thomas Jefferson, founder of the first Republican Party. His election to the presidency in 1800 was one of the world's first peaceful transfers of power from one party to another through a free election. (Library of Congress)

Democratic Party
One of the two major American political parties evolving out of the Republican Party of Thomas Jefferson.

Whig Party
A major party in the United States during the first half of the nineteenth century, formally established in 1836. The Whig Party was anti-Jackson and advocated spending on infrastructure.

Republican Party
One of the two major American political parties. It emerged in the 1850s as an antislavery party and consisted of former northern Whigs and antislavery Democrats.

Federalists and Republicans. One party was the Federalists, which included John Adams, the second president (1797–1801). The Federalists represented commercial interests such as merchants and large planters. They supported a strong national government.

Thomas Jefferson led the other party, which came to be called the Republicans. These Republicans should not be confused with the later Republican Party of Abraham Lincoln. (To avoid confusion, some scholars refer to Jefferson's party as the Democratic Republicans, but this name was never used during the time that the party existed.) Jefferson's Republicans represented artisans and farmers. They strongly supported states' rights. In 1800, when Jefferson defeated Adams in the presidential contest, one of the world's first peaceful transfers of power from one party to another was achieved.

The One-Party Interlude. From 1800 to 1820, a majority of U.S. voters regularly elected Jeffersonian Republicans to the presidency and to Congress. By 1816, the Federalist Party had nearly collapsed, and two-party competition did not really exist at the national level. Because there was no real political opposition to the Jeffersonian Republicans and thus little political debate, the administration of James Monroe (1817–1825) came to be known as the era of good feelings.

Democrats and Whigs

Organized two-party politics returned after 1824. Following the election of John Quincy Adams as president, the Republican Party split in two. The supporters of Adams called themselves National Republicans. The supporters of Andrew Jackson, who defeated Adams in 1828, formed the **Democratic Party.** Later, the National Republicans took the name **Whig Party,** which had been a traditional name for British liberals. The Whigs stood for, among other things, federal spending on "internal improvements," such as roads. The Democrats opposed this policy. The Democrats, who were the stronger of the two parties, favored personal liberty and opportunity for the "common man." It was understood implicitly that the "common man" was a white man—hostility toward African Americans was an important force holding the disparate Democratic groups together.[3]

The Civil War Crisis

In the 1850s, hostility between the North and the South over the issue of slavery divided both parties. The Whigs were the first to split in two. The Whigs had been the party of an active federal government, but Southerners had come to believe that "a government strong enough to build roads is a government strong enough to free your slaves." The southern Whigs therefore ceased to exist as an organized party. In 1854, the northern Whigs united with antislavery Democrats and members of the radical antislavery Free Soil Party to found the modern **Republican Party.**

---

3. Edward Pessen, *Jacksonian America: Society, Personality, and Politics* (Homewood, Ill.: Dorsey Press, 1969). See especially pages 246–247. The small number of free blacks who could vote were overwhelmingly Whig.

The Post–Civil War Period

After the Civil War, the Democratic Party was able to heal its divisions. Southern resentment of the Republicans' role in defeating the South and fears that the federal government would intervene on behalf of African Americans ensured that the Democrats would dominate the white South for the next century. It was in this period that the Republicans adopted the nickname **GOP,** which stands for "grand old party."

Cultural Politics. Northern Democrats feared a strong government for other reasons. The Republicans thought that the government should promote business and economic growth, but many Republicans also wanted to use the power of government to impose evangelical Protestant moral values on society. Democrats opposed what they saw as culturally coercive measures. Many Republicans wanted to limit or even prohibit the sale of alcohol. They favored the establishment of public schools—with a Protestant curriculum. As a result, Catholics were strongly Democratic. In this period, the parties were very evenly matched in strength.

The Triumph of the Republicans. In the 1890s, however, the Republicans gained a decisive edge. In that decade, the populist movement emerged in the West and South to champion the interests of small farmers, who were often greatly in debt. Populists supported inflation, which benefited debtors by reducing the real value of outstanding debts. In 1896, when William Jennings Bryan became the Democratic candidate for president, the Democrats embraced populism.

As it turned out, the few western farmers who were drawn to the Democrats by this step were greatly outnumbered by urban working class voters who believed that inflation would reduce the purchasing power of their paychecks and who therefore became Republicans. Political scientists use the term **realignment** to refer to this kind of large-scale change in support for the two major parties. From 1896 until 1932, the GOP was successful in presenting itself as the party that knew how to manage the economy.

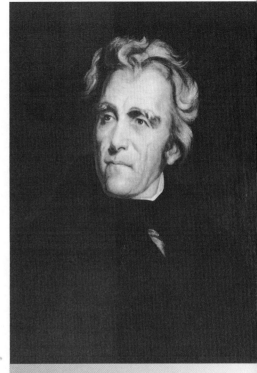

Andrew Jackson earned the name "Old Hickory" for exploits during the War of 1812. In 1828, Jackson was elected president as the candidate of the new Democratic Party. (Corbis/Bettmann)

The Progressive Interlude

In the early 1900s, a spirit of political reform arose in both major parties. Called *progressivism,* this spirit was compounded of a fear of the growing power of large corporations and a belief that honest, impartial government could regulate the economy effectively. In 1912, the Republican Party temporarily split as former Republican president Theodore Roosevelt campaigned for the presidency on a third-party Progressive ticket. The Republican split permitted the election of Woodrow Wilson, the Democratic candidate, along with a Democratic Congress.

Like Roosevelt, Wilson considered himself a progressive, although he and Roosevelt did not agree on how progressivism ought to be implemented. Wilson's progressivism marked the beginning of a radical change in Democratic policies. Dating back to its very foundation, the Democratic Party had been the party of limited government. Under Wilson, the Democrats became for the first time at least as receptive as the Republicans

GOP
A nickname for the Republican Party, which stands for "grand old party."

Realignment
A large-scale, lasting change in the types of voters who support each of the major political parties.

U.S. senator Kirsten Gillibrand (D., N.Y.) attends Lifetime Television's 2012 "Every Woman Counts" campaign at Hofstra University. Why are an ever-greater number of women serving in Congress? (Joe Corrigan/Getty Images for A&E)

to government action in the economy. (Wilson's progressivism did not extend to race relations—for African Americans, the Wilson administration was something of a disaster.)

The New Deal Era

The Republican ascendancy resumed after Wilson left office. It ended with the election of 1932, in the depths of the Great Depression. Republican Herbert Hoover was president when the Depression began in 1929. While Hoover took some measures to fight the Depression, they fell far short of what the public demanded. Significantly, Hoover opposed federal relief for the unemployed and the destitute. In 1932, Democrat Franklin D. Roosevelt was elected president by an overwhelming margin. As with the election of 1896, the vote in 1932 constituted a major political realignment.

The Great Depression shattered the working class belief in Republican economic competence. Under Roosevelt, the Democrats began to make major interventions in the economy in an attempt to combat the Depression and to relieve the suffering of the unemployed. Roosevelt's New Deal relief programs were open to all citizens, both black and white. As a result, African Americans began to support the Democratic Party in large numbers—a development that would have stunned any American politician of the 1800s.

Roosevelt's political coalition was broad enough to establish the Democrats as the new majority party, in place of the GOP. In the 1950s, Republican Dwight D. Eisenhower, the leading U.S. general during World War II, won two terms as president. Otherwise, with minor interruptions, the Democratic ascendancy lasted until about 1968.

An Era of Divided Government

The New Deal coalition managed the unlikely feat of including both African Americans and whites who were hostile to African American advancement. This balancing act came to an end in the 1960s, a decade that was marked by the civil rights movement, by several years of "race riots" in major cities, and by increasingly heated protests against the Vietnam War (1965–1975). For many economically moderate, socially conservative voters, especially in the South, social issues had become more important than economic ones, and these individuals left the Democratic Party. These voters outnumbered the new voters who joined the Democrats—newly enfranchised African Americans and former liberal Republicans in New England and the upper Midwest.

The Parties in Balance. The result, after 1968, was a slow-motion realignment that left the nation almost evenly divided in politics. In presidential elections, the Republicans had more success than the Democrats. Until the 1990s, Congress remained Democratic, but official party labels can be misleading. Some of the Democrats were southern conservatives who normally voted with the Republicans on issues. As these conservative Democrats retired, they were largely replaced by Republicans. In 1994, Republicans were able to take control of both the House and the Senate for the first time in many years.

Red State, Blue State. Nothing demonstrated the nation's close political divisions more clearly than the 2000 presidential elections. Democratic presidential candidate Al Gore won the popular vote, but lost the Electoral College by a narrow margin to Republican George W. Bush. The closeness of the vote in the Electoral College led the press to repeatedly publish maps showing state-by-state results. Commentators discussed at length the supposed differences between the Republican "red states" and the Democratic "blue states."

An interesting characteristic of the red state–blue state division is that it is an almost exact reversal of the results of the presidential elections of 1896, which established the Republican ascendancy that lasted until the Great Depression. Except for the state of Washington, every state that supported Democrat William Jennings Bryan in 1896 supported Republican George W. Bush in 2000 and 2004. This reversal parallels the transformation of the Democrats from an anti–civil rights to a pro–civil rights party and from a party that supported limited government to a party that favors positive government action.

The Parties Today

Not only was the presidential election of 2000 very close, but the partisan balance in the U.S. Congress was also very close in the opening years of the twenty-first century. It is true that from 1995 until the elections of 2006, the Republicans generally controlled Congress. Their margins of control, however, were very narrow.

From time to time, voters demonstrate that they are relatively dissatisfied with the performance of one or another of the major parties. This dissatisfaction can produce a "wave" of support for the other party. Unlike realignments, the effects of *wave elections* are temporary. The first decade of the twenty-first century was marked by a series of wave elections, in which the voters punished first one party and then the other.

Wave Elections Sweep out the Republicans. By 2006, an ever-larger number of voters came to believe that U.S. intervention in Iraq had been a mistake. In the 2006 midterm elections, the Democrats took control of the U.S. House and Senate in a wave election. In September 2008, a worldwide financial panic turned what had been a modest recession into the greatest economic downturn since the Great Depression of the 1930s. The political consequences were inevitable. In November, Democratic presidential candidate Barack Obama was elected with one of the largest margins in recent years.

Democrats in Trouble. By 2010, the Democrats had lost popularity. In the midterm elections of 2010, the Republicans benefited from one of the strongest wave elections in decades and took control of the House. The Democrats retained control of the Senate.

It is likely that some voters now blamed the Democrats for the state of the economy. Many observers, however, argued that independents turned away from the Democrats in the belief that the party was expanding the scope of the federal government to an unacceptable degree. In particular, the Democratic health-care reform package was crucial in fostering the perception of the party as being committed to "big government."

Governor Susana Martinez (R., N.M.) addresses the Republican National Convention in 2012. Why do political parties often choose governors as presidential candidates? (Tom Williams/CQ Roll Call/Getty Images)

Republican Overreach. The Republican House elected in 2010 included a large contingent loyal to the Tea Party movement. These legislators were pledged to oppose any compromise with the Democrats—even though the Democratic Party still controlled the Senate and the presidency.

The uncompromising spirit of the Republicans received its greatest test in June and July of 2011, when House Republicans refused to lift the nation's debt ceiling unless the Democrats accepted large cuts in spending. President Obama and Republican House Speaker John Boehner reached a compromise at the end of July, but the threat to the nation's ability to meet its obligations damaged the popularity of everyone concerned.

The 2012 Elections. In 2012, Obama was reelected by a clear margin—four percentage points in the popular vote. We show the state-by-state results in Figure 7–2 on the following page. While the voters favored the Democrats, the results were hardly a crushing blow to the Republicans. Mitt Romney, the Republican candidate, had done well. The Republicans lost seats in Congress but remained in control of the House.

Still, exit polls showed that Hispanics now cast 10 percent of the vote, a new high, and Obama won 71 percent of that vote. Some political observers argued that the Republicans should modify their immigration policies in an attempt to court Latinos. Others pointed to a deeper problem. Government programs are widely popular among most Hispanics, and also among the growing population of Asian Americans. Republicans were simply not doing well with groups that were growing in numbers—an ominous portent for the future.

WHY HAS THE TWO-PARTY SYSTEM ENDURED?

LO6: Give reasons why the two-party system has endured in America, and evaluate the impact of third parties and independents on U.S. politics.

There are several reasons why two major parties have dominated the political landscape in the United States for almost two centuries. These reasons have to do with (1) the historical foundations of the system, (2) political socialization and practical considerations, (3) the winner-take-all electoral system, and (4) state and federal laws favoring the two-party system.

The Historical Foundations of the Two-Party System

As we have seen, at many times in American history one preeminent issue or dispute has divided the nation politically. In the beginning, Americans were at odds over ratifying the Constitution. After the Constitution went into effect, the power of the federal government became the major national issue. Thereafter, the dispute over slavery divided the nation,

FIGURE 7–2: The 2012 Presidential Election Results by State

In the 2012 presidential elections, Democrat Barack Obama received a majority of the Electoral College votes, defeating Republican Mitt Romney. Obama carried two fewer states than in 2008—he lost Indiana and North Carolina. Despite the relatively good showing by the Democrats, regional political preferences in this election were similar to those in recent elections.

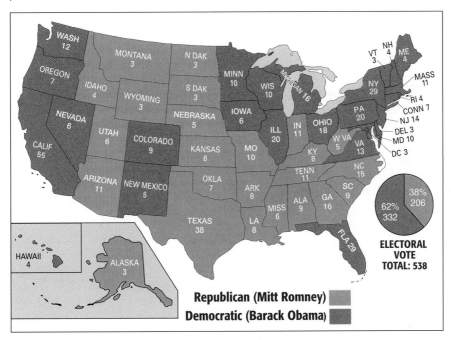

North versus South. At times—for example, in the North after the Civil War—cultural differences have been important, with advocates of government-sponsored morality (such as banning alcoholic beverages) pitted against advocates of personal liberty. During much of the twentieth century, economic differences were preeminent. In the New Deal period, the Democrats became known as the party of the working class, while the Republicans became known as the party of the middle and upper classes and commercial interests.

In situations like these, when politics is based on an argument between two opposing points of view, advocates of each viewpoint can mobilize most effectively by forming a single, unified party. The result is a two-party system. When such a system has been in existence for almost two centuries, it becomes difficult to imagine an alternative.

Political Socialization and Practical Considerations

Given that the majority of Americans identify with one of the two major political parties, it is not surprising that most children learn at a fairly young age to think of themselves as either Democrats or Republicans. This generates a built-in mechanism to perpetuate a two-party system. Also, most politically oriented people who aspire to work for change consider that the only realistic way to capture political power in this country is to be either a Republican or a Democrat.

Plurality
A number of votes cast for a candidate that is greater than the number of votes for any other candidate but not necessarily a majority.

Electoral College
A group of persons, called electors, who are selected by the voters in each state. This group officially elects the president and the vice president of the United States.

Unit Rule
A rule by which all of a state's electoral votes are cast for the presidential candidate who receives a plurality of the votes in that state.

The Winner-Take-All Electoral System

At almost every level of government in the United States, the outcome of elections is based on the **plurality,** winner-take-all principle. In a plurality system, the winner is the person who obtains the most votes, even if that person does not receive a majority (more than 50 percent) of the votes. Whoever gets the most votes gets everything. Most legislators in the United States are elected from single-member districts in which only one person represents the constituency, and the candidate who finishes second in such an election receives nothing for the effort.

Presidential Voting. The winner-take-all system also operates in the election of the U.S. president. Recall that the voters in each state do not vote for a president directly but vote for **Electoral College** delegates who are committed to the various presidential candidates. These delegates are called *electors*.

In all but two states (Maine and Nebraska), if a presidential candidate wins a plurality in the state, then *all* of the state's electoral votes go to that candidate. This is known as the **unit rule.** For example, suppose that the electors pledged to a particular presidential candidate receive a plurality of 40 percent of the votes in a state. That presidential candidate will receive all of the state's votes in the Electoral College. Minor parties have a difficult time competing under such a system. Because voters know that minor parties cannot win any electoral votes, they often will not vote for minor-party candidates, even if the candidates are in tune with them ideologically.

Popular Election of the Governors and the President. In most of Europe, the chief executive (usually called the prime minister) is elected by the legislature, or parliament. If the parliament contains three or more parties, as is usually the situation, two or more of the parties can join together in a coalition to choose the prime minister and the other leaders of the government. In the United States, however, the people elect the president and the governors of all fifty states. There is no opportunity for two or more parties to negotiate a coalition. Here, too, the winner-take-all principle discriminates powerfully against any third party.

Proportional Representation. Many other nations use a system of proportional representation with multimember districts. If, during the national election, party X obtains 12 percent of the vote, party Y gets 43 percent of the vote, and party Z gets the remaining 45 percent of the vote, then party X gets 12 percent of the seats in the legislature, party Y gets 43 percent of the seats, and party Z gets 45 percent of the seats. Because even a minor party may still obtain at least a few seats in the legislature, smaller parties have a greater incentive to organize under such electoral systems than they do in the United States.

State and Federal Laws Favoring the Two Parties

Many state and federal election laws offer a clear advantage to the two major parties. In some states, the established major parties need to gather fewer signatures to place their candidates on the ballot than minor parties or independent candidates do. The criterion for determining how many signatures will be required is often based on the total party vote in the last general election, thus penalizing a new political party that did not compete in that election.

At the national level, minor parties face different obstacles. All of the rules and procedures of both chambers of Congress divide committee seats, staff members, and other privileges on the basis of party membership. A legislator who is elected on a minor-party ticket, such as the Conservative Party of New York, must choose to be counted with one of the major parties to obtain a committee assignment. The Federal Election Commission (FEC) rules for campaign financing also place restrictions on minor-party candidates. Such candidates are not eligible for federal matching funds in either the primary or the general election. In the 1980 elections, John Anderson, running for president as an independent, sued the FEC for campaign funds. The commission finally agreed to repay part of his campaign costs after the election in proportion to the votes he received. Giving funds to a candidate when the campaign is over is, of course, much less helpful than providing funds while the campaign is still under way.

The Role of Minor Parties in U.S. Politics

Gary Johnson, a former Republican governor of New Mexico, ran as the Libertarian Party presidential candidate in 2012. How much support do minor parties usually receive? (Scott Olson/Getty Images)

For the reasons just discussed, minor parties have a difficult, if not impossible, time competing within the American two-party political system. Still, minor parties have played an important role in our political life. Parties other than the Republicans or Democrats are usually called **third parties.** (Technically, of course, there could be fourth, fifth, or sixth parties as well, but we use the term *third* party because it has endured.) Third parties can come into existence in a number of ways. They may be founded from scratch by individuals or groups who are committed to a particular interest, issue, or ideology. They can split off from one of the major parties when a group becomes dissatisfied with the major party's policies. Finally, they can be organized around a particular charismatic leader and serve as that person's vehicle for contesting elections.

Frequently, third parties have acted as barometers of change in the political mood, forcing the major parties to recognize new issues or trends in the thinking of Americans. Political scientists also believe that third parties have acted as safety valves for dissident groups, preventing major confrontations and political unrest.

Ideological Third Parties. The longest-lived third parties have been those with strong ideological foundations that are typically at odds with the majority mind-set. Ideology has at least two functions in such parties. First, the members of the party regard themselves as outsiders and look to one another for support—ideology provides great psychological cohesiveness. Second, because the rewards of ideological commitment are partly psychological, these parties do not think in terms of immediate electoral success. A poor showing at the polls therefore does not dissuade either the leadership or the grassroots participants from continuing their quest for change in American government (and, ultimately, American society).

Third Party
A political party other than the two major political parties (Republican and Democratic).

Splinter Party
A new party formed by a dissident faction within a major political party. Often, splinter parties have emerged when a particular personality was at odds with the major party.

Party Identification
Linking oneself to a particular political party.

Straight-Ticket Voting
Voting exclusively for the candidates of one party.

www

Helpful Web Sites
The two leading third parties are the Libertarian Party and the Green Party. Find their Web sites by searching on "libertarians" and "green party," respectively.

Today's active ideological parties include the Libertarian Party and the Green Party. As you learned in Chapter 1, the Libertarian Party supports a *laissez-faire* ("let it be") capitalist economic program, together with a hands-off policy on regulating matters of moral conduct. The Green Party began as a grassroots environmentalist organization with affiliated political parties across North America and Western Europe. It was established in the United States as a national party in 1996 and nominated Ralph Nader to run for president in 2000. Nader campaigned against what he called "corporate greed," advocated universal health insurance, and promoted environmental concerns. He ran again for president as an independent in 2004 and 2008.

Splinter Parties. Some of the most successful minor parties have been those that split from major parties. The impetus for these **splinter parties**, or factions, has usually been a situation in which a particular personality was at odds with the major party. The most successful of these splinter parties was the "Bull Moose" Progressive Party, formed in 1912 to support Theodore Roosevelt for president. The Republican national convention of that year denied Roosevelt the nomination, despite the fact that he had won most of the primaries. He therefore left the GOP and ran against Republican "regular" William Howard Taft in the general election. Although Roosevelt did not win the election, he did split the Republican vote so that Democrat Woodrow Wilson became president.

Third parties have also been formed to back individual candidates who were not rebelling against a particular party. H. Ross Perot, for example, who challenged Republican George H. W. Bush and Democrat Bill Clinton for the presidency in 1992, had not previously been active in a major party. Perot's supporters probably would have split their votes between Bush and Clinton had Perot not been in the race. In theory, Perot ran in 1992 as a nonparty independent. In practice, he had to create a campaign organization. By 1996, Perot's organization was formalized as the Reform Party.

The Impact of Minor Parties. Third parties have rarely been able to affect American politics by actually winning elections. (One exception is that third-party and independent candidates have occasionally won races for state governorships—for example, Jesse Ventura was elected governor of Minnesota on the Reform Party ticket in 1998.) Instead, the impact of third parties has taken two forms. First, third parties can influence one of the major parties to take up one or more issues. Second, third parties can determine the outcome of a particular election by pulling votes from one of the major-party candidates in what is called the "spoiler effect."

The presidential elections of 2000 were one instance in which a minor party may have altered the outcome. Green candidate Ralph Nader received almost one hundred thousand votes in Florida, a majority of which would probably have gone to Democrat Al Gore if Nader had not been in the race. The real question, however, is not whether the Nader vote had an effect—clearly, it did—but whether the effect was important. The problem is that in elections as close as the presidential elections of 2000, *any* factor with an impact on the outcome can be said to have determined the results.

The Rise of the Independents

Polls that track **party identification** show increasing numbers of voters who identify themselves as independents. (See Figure 7–3 on the facing page.) Not only has the number of independents grown over the last half century, but voters are also less willing to vote a straight ticket—that is, to vote for all the candidates of one party. In the early twentieth century, **straight-ticket voting** was nearly universal. By midcentury, 12 percent of voters engaged in split-ticket voting. By the 1970s and 1980s, 25 to 30 percent of all ballots cast

FIGURE 7–3: Party Identification from 1944 to the Present

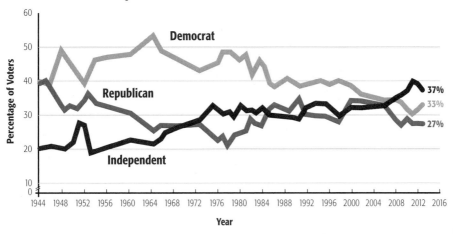

Sources: *Gallup Report,* August 1995; *New York Times*/CBS poll, June 1996; *Gallup Report,* February 1998; Pew Research Center for the People and the Press, November 2003; Gallup polls, 2004 through 2013.

in presidential election years were split-ticket. A major reason was that many voters, especially in the South, were pairing a Republican for president with a conservative Democrat for Congress. In recent years, conservative Democrats have become scarce, and the incidence of split-ticket voting has ranged only from 17 to 19 percent.

While the number of voters who identify as independents has never been greater, many voters who call themselves independents actually lean toward one or the other of the two major parties. In a poll taken in March 2013, for example, 48 percent of all voters reported either that they were Democrats or that they were independents who leaned toward the Democratic Party. The corresponding figure for the Republicans was 41 percent. Leaving aside respondents who were unable to answer the question, true independents were less than 10 percent of the polling sample.

A third of voters self-report being independents. Why might the true percentage be less? (Jeffrey Coolidge)

making a difference
YOU CAN BE A CONVENTION DELEGATE

The most exciting political party event, staged every four years, is the national convention. State conventions also take place on a regular basis. Surprising as it might seem, there are opportunities for the individual voter to become involved in nominating delegates to a state or national convention, or even to become a delegate.

Why Should You Care? How would you like to exercise a small amount of real political power yourself—power that goes beyond simply voting in an election? You might be able to become a delegate to a county, district, or even state party convention. Many of these conventions nominate candidates for various offices. For example, in Michigan, the state party conventions nominate the candidates for the Board of Regents of the state's top three public universities. The regents set university policies, so these are nominations in which students have an obvious interest. In Michigan, if you are elected as a party precinct delegate, you can attend your party's state convention.

In much of the country, there are more openings for party precinct delegates than there are people willing to serve. In such circumstances, almost anyone can become a delegate by collecting a handful of signatures on a nominating petition or by mounting a small-scale write-in campaign. You are then eligible to take part in one of the most educational political experiences available to an ordinary citizen. You will get a firsthand look at how political persuasion takes place, how resolutions are written and passed, and how candidates seek support from their fellow party members.

What Can You Do? When the parties choose delegates for the national convention, the process begins at the local level—either the congressional district or the state legislative district. District delegates may be elected in party primary elections or chosen in neighborhood or precinct caucuses. If the delegates are elected in a primary, persons who want to run for these positions must file petitions with the board of elections. If you are interested in committing yourself to a particular presidential candidate and running for the delegate position, check with the local county committee or with the party's national committee about the rules you must follow.

These delegates to the 2012 Democratic National Convention in Charlotte, North Carolina, cheer as Barack Obama accepts the Democratic nomination for president. (Tom Pennington/Getty Images)

It is even easier to get involved in the grassroots politics of presidential caucuses. In some states—Iowa being the earliest and most famous one—delegates are first nominated at the local precinct caucus. These caucuses, in addition to being the focus of national media attention in January or February, select delegates to the county conventions who are pledged to specific presidential candidates. This is the first step toward the national convention. At both the county caucus and the convention levels, both parties often try to find younger members to fill some of the seats.

For further information about these opportunities (some states hold caucuses and state conventions in every election year), contact the state party office or your local state legislator. You can also contact the national committees for information on how to become a delegate. Use your favorite search engine to locate the Republican National Committee by entering "rnc" or the Democratic National Committee by typing in "dnc."

key**terms**

Democratic Party 158
direct technique 151
divided government 157
Electoral College 164
free-rider problem 145
GOP 159
independent 154
indirect technique 151
interest group 143

labor movement 146
lobbyist 144
national committee 156
national convention 155
party identification 166
party organization 155
party platform 155
patronage 156
plurality 164

political party 144
public interest 149
realignment 159
Republican Party 158
service sector 146
social movement 145
splinter party 166
state central
   committee 156

straight-ticket
   voting 166
third party 165
ticket splitting 157
two-party system 157
unit rule 164
Whig Party 158

chapter**summary**

1 An interest group is an organization whose members share common objectives and actively attempt to influence government policy. Interest groups proliferate in the United States because they can influence government at many points in the political structure. A political party is a group of political activists who organize to win elections, operate the government, and determine public policy.

2 Major types of interest groups include business, agricultural, labor, professional, and environmental groups. Other important groups include public-interest, ideological, and identity groups.

3 Interest groups use direct and indirect techniques to influence government. Direct techniques include testifying before committees and rulemaking agencies, providing information to legislators, rating legislators' voting records, and aiding in political campaigns. Indirect techniques include conducting campaigns to rally public sentiment and using constituents to lobby for a group's interests.

4 In 1995, the Lobbying Disclosure Act defined lobbyists and their reporting requirements. In 2007, the Honest Leadership and Open Government Act increased the frequency of reports, required reports on coalition activity, and created a searchable Internet file on lobbying activity.

5 Functions of political parties include recruiting candidates for public office, organizing and running elections, presenting alternative policies to voters, assuming responsibility for operating the government, and acting as the opposition to the party in power.

6 A political party consists of the voters who identify with the party, the party organization, and the party-in-government. Each level of the party organization—local, state, and national—has considerable autonomy.

7 The evolution of our nation's political parties can be divided into seven periods: (a) the creation and formation of political parties, from 1789 to 1816; (b) the era of one-party rule from 1816 to 1828; (c) the period from Andrew Jackson's presidency to the eve of the Civil War, from 1828 to 1856; (d) the Civil War and post–Civil War period, from 1856 to 1896; (e) the Republican ascendancy and progressive period, from 1896 to 1932; (f) the New Deal period, from 1932 to about 1968; and (g) the modern period, from approximately 1968 to the present. Throughout most of the modern period, the parties have been closely matched in strength.

8 Two major parties have dominated the political landscape in the United States for almost two centuries. The reasons for this include (a) the historical foundations of the system, (b) political socialization and practical considerations, (c) the winner-take-all electoral system, and (d) state and federal laws favoring the two-party system. For these reasons, minor parties have found it extremely difficult to win elections. Still, minor, or third, parties have emerged from time to time. Third parties can affect the political process (even if they do not win) if major parties adopt their issues or if they determine which major party wins an election.

9 From the 1940s to the present, independent voters have formed an increasing proportion of the electorate, with a consequent decline in Democratic and Republican party identification. Nevertheless, many independent voters lean toward one major party or the other.

test**yourself**

LO1 *Describe the basic characteristics of interest groups, and explain why Americans join them.*

When individuals benefit by the actions of an interest group but do not support that group, they are:
   a. free riders.
   b. freeloaders.
   c. usually just waiting to join the group.

LO2 *List the major types of interest groups, especially those with economic motivations.*

Union membership in the United States has:
   a. been growing, especially since 2000.
   b. stayed about the same since the Great Depression.
   c. been declining in recent years, except in the public sector.

LO3 *Discuss direct and indirect interest group techniques, and describe the main ways in which lobbyists are regulated.*

There are many direct techniques that interest groups can use to affect legislation. They include:
   a. sending out large numbers of direct-mail advertising pieces.
   b. attempts at weakening other interest groups.
   c. hiring lobbyists to argue their positions in Congress.

LO4 *Cite some of the major activities of U.S. political parties, and discuss how they are organized.*

The three faces of a political party include:
   a. the party-in-the-electorate, the party organization, and the members of the party.

   b. the party organization, the party-in-government, and the party-in-the-electorate.
   c. the party-in-government, the party-in-the-electorate, and the lobbyists for that party.

LO5 *Explain how the history of U.S. political parties has led to the two major parties that exist today.*

The New Deal era under Democratic President Franklin D. Roosevelt occurred:
   a. at the beginning of the twentieth century.
   b. during the 1960s.
   c. during the Great Depression of the 1930s.

LO6 *Give reasons why the two-party system has endured in America, and evaluate the impact of third parties and independents on U.S. politics.*

At almost every level of government in this country, the outcome of elections is based on the plurality voting system, which means that:
   a. the candidate with the largest number of votes wins, even if the winner does not receive 50 percent or more of the votes.
   b. when no one receives 50 percent of the vote, a runoff election is held.
   c. there is no need for everyone to vote in each election.

Essay Question:
About half of the paid lobbyists in Washington, D.C., are former government staff members or former members of Congress. Why would interest groups employ such people? Why might some reformers want to limit the ability of interest groups to employ them? On what basis might an interest group argue that such limits are unconstitutional?

Answers to multiple-choice questions: 1. a, 2. c, 3. c, 4. b, 5. c, 6. a.

CourseMate

Access CourseMate at www.cengagebrain.com for additional study tools: practice quizzes, key term flashcards and crossword puzzles, audio chapter summaries, simulations, animated learning modules, interactive timelines, videos, and American Government NewsWatch.

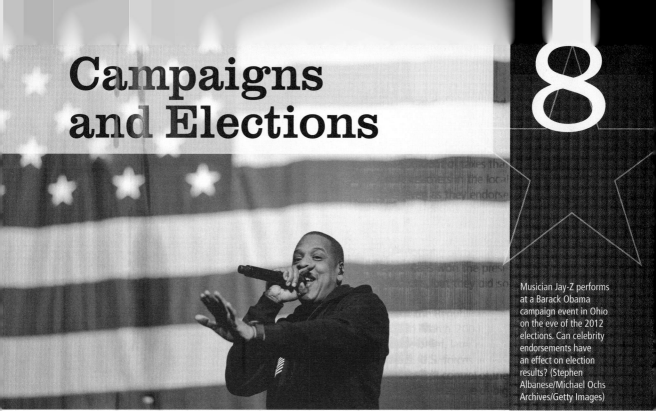

Campaigns and Elections

8

Musician Jay-Z performs at a Barack Obama campaign event in Ohio on the eve of the 2012 elections. Can celebrity endorsements have an effect on election results? (Stephen Albanese/Michael Ochs Archives/Getty Images)

LEARNING OUTCOMES

The five **Learning Outcomes (LOs)** below are designed to help improve your understanding of this chapter. After reading this chapter, you should be able to:

■ **LO1** Discuss who runs for office and how campaigns are managed.

■ **LO2** Describe the current system of campaign finance.

■ **LO3** Summarize the process of choosing a president of the United States.

■ **LO4** Explain the mechanisms through which voting takes place on Election Day, and discuss voter turnout in the United States.

■ **LO5** Provide some of the reasons why people vote in particular ways.

Check your understanding of the material with the Test Yourself section at the end of the chapter.

Free elections are the cornerstone of the American political system. By casting ballots in local, state, and federal elections, voters choose one candidate over another to hold political office. There are thousands of elective offices in the United States—and consequently, thousands of elections. Although the major political parties strive to provide a slate of candidates for every election, recruiting candidates is easier for some offices than for others. Political parties may have difficulty finding candidates for the board of the local water control district, for example, but they generally find a sufficient number of candidates for county commissioner or sheriff. The higher the office and the more prestige attached to it, the more candidates are likely to want to run. In many areas of the country, however, one major party may be considerably stronger than the other is. In those situations, the minority party may have difficulty finding nominees for elections in which victory is unlikely.

THE TWENTY-FIRST-CENTURY CAMPAIGN

The presidential campaign provides the most colorful and exciting look at candidates and how they prepare to compete for office—in this instance, the highest office in the land. The men and women who wanted to be the Republican candidate in the 2012 presidential campaign faced a long and obstacle-filled path. First, they needed to raise sufficient funds to tour the nation—particularly the states with early **presidential primaries**—to see if they had enough local supporters. They needed funds to create an organization and to win primary votes. Finally, when nominated as the party's candidate, the winner required funds to finance a successful campaign for president. Always, at every turn, there was the question of whether there were enough funds to effectively compete against their opponents, and eventually against President Barack Obama.

Who Is Eligible?

There are few constitutional restrictions on who can be elected to national office in the United States. As detailed in the Constitution, the formal requirements are as follows:

1. *President.* Must be a natural-born citizen, have attained the age of thirty-five years, and be a resident of the country for fourteen years by the time of inauguration.
2. *Vice president.* Must meet the same requirements as the president and also not be a resident of the same state as the president.[1]
3. *Senator.* Must be a citizen for at least nine years, have attained the age of thirty by the time of taking office, and be a resident of the state from which elected.
4. *Representative.* Must be a citizen for at least seven years, have attained the age of twenty-five by the time of taking office, and be a resident of the state from which elected.

The qualifications for state legislators are set by state constitutions and likewise include age, place of residence, and citizenship. (Usually, the requirements for the upper chamber of a legislature are somewhat higher than those for the lower chamber.) The legal qualifications for serving as governor or in other state offices are similar.

Who Runs?

LO1: Discuss who runs for office and how campaigns are managed.

In spite of these minimal legal qualifications for office at both the national and the state levels, a quick look at the slate of candidates in any election—or at the current members of Congress—will reveal that not all segments of the population enjoy these opportunities equally. Holders of political office in the United States have been predominantly white and male. Until the twentieth century, presidential candidates were exclusively of northern European origin and of Protestant heritage.[2] Laws that effectively denied voting rights made it impossible to elect African American public officials in many areas in which African Americans constituted a significant portion of the population. As a result of the passage of major civil rights legislation in the 1960s, however, the number of African American public officials has increased throughout the United States, and in a groundbreaking vote, the nation elected an African American president in 2008.

Presidential Primary
A statewide primary election of delegates to a political party's national convention, held to determine a party's presidential nominee.

---

1. Technically, a presidential and a vice-presidential candidate can be from the same state, but if they are, one of the two must forfeit the electoral votes of their home state.
2. A number of early presidents were Unitarian. The Unitarian Church is not Protestant, but it is historically rooted in the Protestant tradition.

Women as Candidates. Until recently, women generally were considered to be appropriate candidates only for lower-level offices, such as state legislator or school board member. The past twenty years have seen a tremendous increase in the number of women who run for office, not only at the state level but for the U.S. Congress as well. In 2012, 184 women ran for Congress on major-party tickets, and 97 were elected. Today, a majority of Americans say they would vote for a qualified woman for president of the United States. Indeed, Hillary Clinton came close to winning the Democratic presidential nomination in 2008, a year in which the eventual Democratic nominee was favored to win the general election.

Professional Status. Political campaigning and officeholding are simply easier for some occupational groups than for others, and political involvement can make a valuable contribution to certain careers. Lawyers, for example, have more flexible schedules than do many other professionals, can take time off for campaigning, and can leave their jobs to hold public office full time. Furthermore, holding political office is good publicity for their professional practice. Perhaps most important, many jobs that lawyers aspire to—federal or state judgeships, state's attorney offices, or work in a federal agency—can be attained by political appointment.

Managing the Campaign

After the candidates have been nominated, typically through a **primary election,** the most exhausting and expensive part of the election process begins—the **general election** campaign, which actually fills the offices at stake. Political campaigns are becoming more

Primary Election
An election in which political parties choose their candidates for the general election.

General Election
An election, normally held on the first Tuesday in November, that determines who will fill various elected positions.

Democratic presidential candidate Barack Obama and Republican candidate Mitt Romney speak to their supporters during the 2012 campaigns. As it turned out, Obama's campaign was the more effective of the two. (left: Chip Somodevilla/Getty Images; right: Spencer Platt/Getty Images)

Political Consultant
A paid professional hired to devise a campaign strategy and manage a campaign.

complex and more sophisticated with every election. Even with the most appealing of candidates, today's campaigns require a strong organization with (1) expertise in political polling and marketing, (2) professional assistance in fund-raising and accounting, (3) financial management, and (4) technological capabilities in every aspect of the campaign.

The Changing Campaign. The goal is the same for all campaigns—to convince voters to choose a candidate or a slate of candidates for office. In recent decades, the typical campaign for high office has no longer been centered on the party but on the candidate. The candidate-centered campaign emerged in response to changes in the electoral system, the increased importance of television in campaigns, technological innovations such as computers, and the increased cost of campaigning.

To run a successful and persuasive campaign, the candidate's organization must be able to raise funds for the effort, produce and pay for political commercials and advertising, and obtain coverage from the media. In addition, the organization needs to schedule the candidate's time effectively, convey the candidate's position on the issues to the voters, and conduct research on the opposing candidate. Finally, the campaign must get the voters to go to the polls. When party identification was greater among voters and before the advent of television campaigning, a strong party organization at the local, state, or national level could furnish most of the services and expertise that the candidate needed. Parties used their precinct organizations to distribute literature, register voters, and get out the vote on Election Day. Less effort was spent on advertising each candidate's positions and character, because the party label presumably communicated that information to many voters.

One of the reasons that campaigns no longer depend on parties is that fewer people identify with them, as is evident from the increased number of political independents. In 1954, fewer than 20 percent of adults identified themselves as independents, whereas today that share is about 40 percent.

Two of the best-known political consultants are Mary Matalin for the Republicans and James Carville for the Democrats. They happen to be married to each other. What functions do they perform? (Heather Wines/CBS via Getty Images)

The Professional Campaign. Whether the candidate is running for the state legislature, for the governor's office, for the U.S. Congress, or for the presidency, every campaign has some fundamental tasks to accomplish. Today, in national elections, most of these tasks are handled by paid professionals rather than volunteers or amateur politicians.

The most sought-after and possibly the most criticized campaign expert is the **political consultant,** who, for a large fee, takes charge of the candidate's campaign. Paid political consultants began to displace volunteer campaign managers in the 1960s, about the same time that television became a force in campaigns. The paid consultant devises a campaign strategy and theme, oversees campaign advertising, and plans media appearances. Consultants and the firms they represent are not politically neutral. Most will work only for candidates from one party.

The Strategy of Winning. In the United States, unlike some European countries, there are no rewards for a candidate who comes in second. The winner takes all. Candidates seek to capture all the votes of their party's supporters, to convince a majority of independent voters to vote for them, and to gain some votes from supporters of the other party. To accomplish these goals, candidates must consider their visibility, their message, and their campaign strategy.

One of the more important concerns is how well known the candidate is. If she or he is a highly visible incumbent, there may be little need for campaigning except to remind voters of the officeholder's good deeds. If, however, the candidate is an unknown challenger or a largely unfamiliar character who is opposing a well-known public figure, the campaign requires a strategy to get the candidate before the public.

Opinion Polls and Focus Groups. One of the major sources of information for both the media and the candidates is opinion polls. Poll taking is widespread during the primaries. Presidential hopefuls have private polls taken to make sure that there is at least some chance they could be nominated and, if nominated, elected. During the presidential campaign itself, polling is even more frequent. Polls are taken not only by the regular pollsters—Gallup, Mason-Dixon, Opinion Research, and others—but also privately by each candidate's campaign organization. These private polls are for the exclusive and confidential use of the candidate and his or her campaign organization. As the election approaches, many candidates use *tracking polls,* which are polls taken almost every day, to find out how well they are competing for votes. Tracking polls enable consultants to fine-tune advertising and the candidate's speeches in the last days of the campaign.

Another tactic used by campaign organizations to gain insights into public perceptions of the candidate is the **focus group.** The ten to fifteen ordinary citizens who comprise the group discuss the candidate or certain political issues. Professional consultants who conduct the discussion select focus group members from specific target groups in the population—for example, working women, blue-collar men, senior citizens, or young voters. Recent campaigns have tried to reach groups such as "soccer moms," "Walmart shoppers," or "NASCAR dads."[3] The group may discuss personality traits of the candidate, political advertising, and other candidate-related issues. Focus groups can reveal more emotional responses to candidates or the deeper anxieties of voters—feelings that consultants believe often are not tapped by more impersonal telephone surveys. The campaign then can shape its messages to respond to those feelings and perceptions.

FINANCING THE CAMPAIGN

The connection between money and elections is a sensitive issue in American politics. The belief is widespread that large campaign contributions by special interests corrupt the political system. Indeed, spending reached unprecedented heights during the 2011–2012 election cycle. Total spending for the presidential candidates alone exceeded $2.6 million. These funds had to be provided by the candidates and their families, borrowed, or raised by contributions from individuals, organizations, or *political action committees (PACs),* which are set up under federal or state law for the express purpose of making political donations.

3. NASCAR stands for the National Association for Stock Car Auto Racing.

Focus Group
A small group of individuals who are led in discussion by a professional consultant to gather opinions on, and responses to, candidates and issues.

LO2: Describe the current system of campaign finance.

Hatch Act
An act passed in 1939 that restricted the political activities of government employees. It also prohibited a political group from spending more than $3 million in any campaign and limited individual contributions to a campaign committee to $5,000.

Federal Election Commission (FEC)
The federal regulatory agency with the task of enforcing federal campaign laws. As a practical matter, the FEC's role is largely limited to collecting data on campaign contributions.

Political Action Committee (PAC)
A committee set up by and representing a corporation, labor union, or special interest group. PACs raise campaign donations.

The way campaigns are financed has changed dramatically in the past several years. For decades, candidates and political parties had to operate within the constraints imposed by complicated laws regulating campaign financing. Many of these constraints still exist, but recent developments have opened up the process to a striking degree. Today, there are no limits on how much any person or institution can invest in the political process, and only modest limits on how this spending can take place.

The Evolution of the Campaign Finance System

Throughout much of early American history, campaign financing was unregulated. No limits existed on contributions, and no data were collected on campaign funding. During the twentieth century, however, a variety of federal corrupt practices acts were adopted to regulate campaign financing. The first of these acts, initially passed in 1910, contained many loopholes and proved to be ineffective. The **Hatch Act** (Political Activities Act) of 1939 is best known for restricting the political activities of civil servants. The act also made it unlawful for a political group to spend more than $3 million in any campaign and limited individual contributions to a campaign committee to $5,000. Of course, such restrictions were easily circumvented by creating additional political organizations.

The Federal Election Campaign Act. The Federal Election Campaign Act (FECA) of 1971, which became effective in 1972, replaced all previous laws. The act restricted the amount that could be spent on campaign advertising. It also limited the amount that candidates could contribute to their own campaigns and required disclosure of all contributions and expenditures over $100. In principle, the FECA limited the role of labor unions and corporations in political campaigns.

Amendments to the FECA passed in 1974 created the **Federal Election Commission (FEC).** This commission consists of six bipartisan administrators whose duty is to enforce compliance with the requirements of the act. The 1974 amendments also placed limits on the sums that individuals and committees could contribute to candidates.

The principal role of the FEC today is to collect data on campaign contributions. Candidate committees must file periodic reports with the FEC listing who contributed, how much was spent, and for what it was spent. As an enforcement body, however, the FEC is conspicuously ineffective and typically does not determine that a campaign has violated the rules until an election is over, if then.

The original FECA of 1971 limited the amount that each individual could spend on his or her own behalf. The Supreme Court overturned the provision in 1976, in *Buckley v. Valeo*,[4] stating that it was unconstitutional to restrict in any way the amount congressional candidates could spend on their own behalf. The Court later extended this principle to state elections as well.

Political Action Committees. Changes to the FECA in 1974 and 1976 allowed corporations, labor unions, and other interest groups to set up **political action committees (PACs)** to raise funds for candidates. PACs can contribute up to $5,000 to each candidate in each election. Each corporation or each union is limited to one PAC. The number of PACs grew significantly after 1976, as did the amounts that they spent on elections. Since the 1990s, however, the number of traditional PACs has leveled off because interest groups and activists have found alternative mechanisms for funneling resources into campaigns.

---

4. 424 U.S. 1 (1976).

Issue Advocacy Advertising. Business corporations, labor unions, and other interest groups have also developed ways of making independent expenditures that are not coordinated with those of a candidate or political party. A common tactic is **issue advocacy advertising,** which promotes positions on issues rather than candidates. Although promoting issue positions aligns very closely with promoting candidates who support those positions, the courts repeatedly have held that interest groups have a First Amendment right to advocate their positions.

Soft Money. Interest groups and PACs hit upon the additional strategy of generating **soft money**—that is, campaign contributions to political parties that escaped the limits of federal or state election law. No limits existed on contributions to political parties or party committees for activities such as voter education and voter-registration drives. This loophole enabled the parties to raise millions of dollars from corporations and individuals.

The Rise and Fall of the McCain-Feingold Act. The Bipartisan Campaign Reform Act of 2002, also known as the McCain-Feingold Act after its chief sponsors in the Senate, took effect on the day after the midterm elections of 2002. The law sought to regulate the new campaign-finance practices developed since the passage of the FECA. It banned soft money at the federal level, but it did not ban such contributions to state and local parties. It attempted to curb issue advocacy advertising, but also increased the sums that individuals could contribute directly to candidates.

The constitutionality of the 2002 act was immediately challenged. In December 2003, the Supreme Court upheld almost all of the clauses of the act.[5] In 2007, however, the Court eased the act's restrictions on issue advocacy ads when it ruled that only those ads "susceptible of no reasonable interpretation other than as an appeal to vote for or against a specific candidate" could be restricted prior to an election.[6] Finally, in 2010, *Citizens United v. FEC*[7] swept away almost all remaining restrictions on independent expenditures, leading to the system we have today.

Issue Advocacy Advertising
Advertising paid for by interest groups that support or oppose a candidate or a candidate's position on an issue without mentioning the candidate, voting, or elections.

Soft Money
Campaign contributions unregulated by federal or state law, usually given to parties and party committees to help fund general party activities.

Independent Expenditures
Unregulated political expenditures by PACs, organizations, and individuals that are not coordinated with candidate campaigns or political parties.

The Current Campaign Finance Environment

As of 2012, political campaigns are financed in two distinct ways. One of these is spending by the candidate's own committee. Contributions made directly to the candidate's committee are subject to limitations: an individual can donate no more than $2,500 to a candidate in a single election, and contributions by committees are limited as well. In exchange for these limits, candidates have almost complete control over how their own campaign money is spent.

Another way in which campaigns are financed is through **independent expenditures.** These funds may be spent on advertising and other political activities, but in theory the expenditures

Karl Rove, left, former political adviser to President George W. Bush, speaks with senator Orrin Hatch at the 2012 Republican National Convention. That year, Rove headed the Crossroads super PAC, which spent large sums with modest results. (Chip Somodevilla/Getty Images)

5. *McConnell v. FEC,* 540 U.S. 93 (2003).
6. *FEC v. Wisconsin Right to Life,* 551 U.S. 449 (2007).
7. 130 S.Ct. 876 (2010).

Super PAC
A political organization that aggregates unlimited contributions by individuals and organizations to be spent independently of candidate committees.

cannot be coordinated with those of a candidate. No limits exist on how much can be spent in this fashion. This two-part system is the direct result of the 2010 *Citizens United v. FEC* ruling by the United States Supreme Court.

Citizens United v. FEC. In January 2010, the Supreme Court ruled that corporations, unions, and nonprofits may spend funds to support or oppose candidates, so long as the expenditures are made independently and are not coordinated with candidate campaigns. (Political parties may also make independent expenditures on behalf of candidates.) These rulings overturned campaign-finance laws dating back decades. Democrats, plus many journalists and bloggers, accused the Court of granting corporations rights that ought to be exercised only by flesh-and-blood human beings. Republicans and others defended the ruling as protecting freedom of speech. Two months later, a federal court of appeals held that it was not possible to limit contributions to independent-expenditure groups based on the size of the contribution.[8]

Super PACs. These rulings led directly to a new type of political organization: the **super PAC.** Traditional PACs, which continue to exist, are set up to represent a corporation, labor union, or interest group. The super PAC, in contrast, is established to aggregate unlimited contributions by individuals and organizations and then funnel these sums into independent expenditures. By 2011, every major presidential candidate had a super PAC. It soon became clear that the supposed independence of these organizations is a fiction. Presidential super PACs are usually chaired by individuals who are closely associated with the candidate. Frequently, the chair is a former top member of the candidate's campaign.

A variety of other super PACs were established as well. These groups are often oriented toward a party, rather than a candidate. Such super PACs might seek, for example, to support Republican or Democratic candidates for the U.S. Senate, or to intervene within a particular party. The super PAC founded by the Club for Growth, for example, devotes its considerable resources to supporting strong conservatives in Republican primaries and to running negative advertisements against more moderate Republicans.

One interesting development in 2011–2012 was the tendency for super PACs to be supported primarily by very wealthy individuals, rather than by corporations or other organizations. The funding was still provided by business interests but came from individuals who owned corporations, not from the corporations themselves. A striking example of this phenomenon was a $10 million contribution in January 2012 to the super PAC of Republican presidential candidate Newt Gingrich, former Speaker of the U.S. House.

The contribution, supplied by casino magnate Sheldon Adelson and his wife, amounted to almost half of all the funds that Gingrich had raised throughout the entire primary season. Without this contribution, Gingrich would have been forced to end his campaign much earlier than he actually did. How effective were super PACs overall in 2012? We address that question in the *Politics and Economics* feature on the following page.

The 527 Organization. Well before *Citizens United*, interest groups realized that they could set up new organizations outside the parties to encourage voter registration and to run issue ads aimed at energizing supporters. So long as these committees did not endorse candidates, they faced no limits on fund-raising. These tax-exempt groups, called 527 organizations after the section of the tax code that provides for them, first made a major impact during the 2003–2004 election cycle. Since then, they have largely been replaced by super PACs, but a number continue to be active to the present day.

WWW
Helpful Web Sites
To find excellent reports on where campaign money comes from and how it is spent, view the site maintained by the Center for Responsive Politics by typing in "opensecrets."

---

8. *Speechnow v. FEC,* 599 F.3d 686 (D.C.Cir. 2010).

politics and **economics**

THE CURIOUS INEFFECTIVENESS OF THE SUPER PACS

Political action committees (PACs) have been around for a long time, but only recently have we seen the super PACs. These groups became popular after court rulings that the First Amendment prohibited the federal government from restricting *independent political expenditures.* Such expenditures are supposedly not coordinated with candidate campaigns. The result of these court rulings was the super PAC, a committee that is allowed to raise and spend unlimited sums from corporations, unions and other associations, and individuals. Indeed, due to the rise of 501(c)4 organizations (described in the text), some nonprofit groups can contribute to super PACs without disclosing their donors.

AND THE MONEY CAME ROLLING IN

During the 2011–2012 presidential election cycle, more money was available for campaigning than ever before. Some scholars estimate that various committees spent more than $6 billion on all races—for president, for Congress, and for state offices. Of that, an estimated $1.3 billion was spent by outside groups. Most of these funds were used for negative advertising in the "battleground states." Of the $1.3 billion, about 65 percent was spent to boost Republican candidates.

Does money buy elections? Did all of those billions of dollars make a significant difference in election outcomes? When it comes to super PACs, at least, the evidence is in—super PAC dollars do not seem to have made much difference, particularly in the presidential contests.

DONORS GOT A POOR RETURN ON THEIR INVESTMENT

Consider some spectacular super PAC failures. Casino owner Sheldon Adelson and his wife spent more than $53 million in donations to super PACs. Of that, $15 mil-

lion was spent in the hope of winning the Republican presidential nomination for Newt Gingrich (he lost), and $20 million was spent in the general election to make Mitt Romney president (he lost, too).

Consider another super PAC with poor results—American Crossroads, managed by conservative strategist Karl Rove. According to a study by the Sunlight Foundation, only 1.3 percent of the $104 million that American Crossroads spent in the general election helped produce a winner. The group spent $85 million in ads attacking Barack Obama. It used $6.5 million to support Mitt Romney. That was $91.5 million spent with a zero rate of return. Almost all of the Senate candidates supported by American Crossroads lost.

LOOKING TO THE FUTURE

Republicans had an advantage in super PAC spending in 2012, but they lost seats in both the House and the Senate and, of course, they failed to win the presidency. Some conservative strategists concluded that super PACs had made a mistake by concentrating on television ads. These experts advised that in the future, super PACs should focus more on financing get-out-the-vote drives. Despite a poor performance in 2012, most observers believe that super PACs will be back in force in 2014 and 2016.

FOR CRITICAL ANALYSIS

Why might huge sums spent on television advertisements have a limited effect on swaying voters, especially in presidential elections?

The 501(c)4 Organization. In the 2007–2008 election cycle, campaign-finance lawyers began recommending a new type of independent group—the 501(c)4 organization, which, like the 527 organization, is named after the relevant provision of the tax code. A 501(c)4 is ostensibly a "social welfare" group and, unlike a 527, is not required to disclose the identity of its donors or to report spending to the Federal Election Commission (FEC).

Lawyers then began suggesting that 501(c)4 organizations claim a special exemption that would allow the organization to ask people to vote for or against specific candidates as long as a majority of the group's effort was devoted to issues. Only those funds

(Mort Gerberg/The New Yorker Collection/www.cartoonbank.com)

"Dear J.J.: Thank you so much for your lovely present of fourteen million dollars for my campaign. It was sweet of you to remember. I promise to spend it on something nice."

spent directly to support candidates had to be reported to the FEC, and the 501(c)4 could continue to conceal its donors. One result was to make it all but impossible to determine exactly how much was spent by independent groups on the 2008, 2010, and 2012 elections. Critics claimed that 501(c)4s were being used illegally. The FEC has never ruled on their validity, however.

Presidential Candidate Committees. Despite the limits on contributions to candidate committees, these organizations continued to collect large sums. The committees of the major-party presidential nominees, Mitt Romney and Barack Obama, were able to amass more than $1 billion each, often from relatively small contributions.

Candidate committees are much more generously funded than in the past. From 1976 through 2004, most presidential candidates relied on a system of public funding financed by a checkoff on federal income tax forms. This system provided funds to match what a candidate could raise during the primary season. During the general election campaign, the system would pay for a candidate's entire campaign. Publicly funded candidates, however, could not raise funds independently for the general election or exceed the program's overall spending limits.

The system began to break down after 2000, when many candidates rejected public support throughout the primaries in the belief that they could raise larger sums privately. In 2008, Barack Obama became the first candidate since the program was founded to opt out of federal funding for the general elections as well. By 2012, the public financing system was essentially out of business. None of the major candidates in either party was willing to use it. Public funds continued to be available to support the parties' national conventions, but in 2012 Congress revoked funding for conventions in future election years.

RUNNING FOR PRESIDENT: THE LONGEST CAMPAIGN

LO3: Summarize the process of choosing a president of the United States.

The American presidential election is the culmination of two different campaigns: the presidential primary campaign and the general election campaign following the party's national convention. Traditionally, both the primary campaigns and the final campaigns take place during the first ten months of an election year. Increasingly, though, the states are holding their primaries earlier in the year, which has motivated the candidates to begin their campaigns earlier as well. Indeed, candidates in the 2012 presidential races began campaigning in early 2011, thus launching one of the longest presidential campaigns to date.

Primary elections were first organized for state officials in 1904 in Wisconsin. The purpose of the primary was to open the nomination process to ordinary party members and to weaken the influence of party bosses. Until 1968, however, there were fewer than twenty primary elections for the presidency. They were often "beauty contests," in which the candidates competed for popular votes but the results did not control the selection of delegates to the national convention. National conventions were meetings of the party elite—legislators, mayors, county chairpersons, and loyal party workers—who were mostly appointed to their delegations. The leaders of large blocs of delegates could direct their delegates to support a favorite candidate.

Reforming the Primaries

In recent decades, the character of the primary process and the makeup of the national convention have changed dramatically. The public, rather than party elites, now generally controls the nomination process. After the disruptive riots outside the doors of the 1968 Democratic convention in Chicago, many party leaders pushed for serious reforms of the convention system.

The Democratic National Committee appointed a special commission to study the problems of the primary system. During the next several years, the group—called the McGovern-Fraser Commission—formulated new rules for delegate selection that had to be followed by state Democratic parties beginning in 1972.

The reforms instituted by the Democratic Party, which were mostly imitated by the Republicans, revolutionized the nomination process for the presidency. The most important changes require that a majority of the convention delegates be elected by the voters in primary elections, in caucuses held by local parties, or at state conventions. Delegates are normally pledged to a particular candidate, although the pledge is not always formally binding at the convention. The delegation from each state must also include a proportion of women, younger party members, and representatives of the minority groups within the party. At first, almost no special privileges were given to party leaders and elected party officials, such as senators and governors. In 1984, however, many of these individuals returned to the Democratic convention as **superdelegates.**

Primaries and Caucuses

Various types of primaries are used by the states. One notable difference is between proportional and winner-take-all primaries. Another important consideration is whether independent voters can take part in a primary. Some states also use caucuses and conventions to choose candidates for various offices.

Direct and Indirect Primaries. A **direct primary** is one in which voters decide party nominations by voting directly for candidates. In an **indirect primary,** voters instead choose convention delegates, and the delegates determine the party's candidate in the general election. Delegates may be pledged to a particular candidate. Indirect primaries are used almost exclusively in presidential elections. Most candidates in state and local elections are chosen by direct primaries.

Proportional and Winner-Take-All Primaries. Most primaries are winner-take-all. Proportional primaries are used mostly to elect delegates to the national conventions of the two major parties—delegates who are pledged to one or another candidate for president. Under the proportional system, if one candidate for president wins 40 percent of the vote in a primary, that candidate receives about 40 percent of the pledged delegates.

Superdelegate
A party leader or elected official who is given the right to vote at the party's national convention. Superdelegates are not elected at the state level.

Direct Primary
A primary election in which voters decide party nominations by voting directly for candidates.

Indirect Primary
A primary election in which voters choose convention delegates, and the delegates determine the party's candidate in the general election.

Closed Primary
A type of primary in which the voter is limited to choosing candidates of the party of which he or she is a member.

Open Primary
A primary in which any voter can vote in either party primary (but must vote for candidates of only one party).

In recent years, the Democrats have used the proportional system for all of their presidential primaries and caucuses. For the most part, the Republicans have relied on the winner-take-all principle. In 2012, however, the Republican National Committee ruled that any state choosing national convention delegates before April 1 would be required to use the proportional system. States voting later could adopt whatever method they preferred. A number of early-voting states, such as Arizona and Florida, refused to follow the rules and used winner-take-all systems. They were penalized. Still, a majority of the states now allocate Republican National Convention delegates on a proportional basis.

Closed and Open Primaries. A closed primary is one of several types of primaries distinguished by how independent voters are handled. In a **closed primary,** only declared members of a party can vote in that party's primary. In other words, voters must declare their party affiliation, either when they register to vote or at the primary election. In a closed-primary system, voters cannot cross over into the other party's primary in order to nominate the weakest candidate of the opposing party or to affect the ideological direction of that party. In an **open primary,** any voter can vote in either party's primary without declaring a party affiliation. Basically, the voter makes the choice in the privacy of the voting booth. The voter must, however, choose one party's list from which to select candidates.

Blanket Primary. A *blanket primary* is one in which the voter can vote for candidates of more than one party. Until 2000, a few states, including Alaska, California, and Washington, had blanket primaries. In 2000, however, the United States Supreme Court abolished the blanket primary. The Court ruled that the blanket primary violated political parties' First Amendment right of association. Because the nominees represent the party, party members—not the general electorate—should have the right to choose the party's nominee.[9]

Four Republican presidential candidates were still in the running by February 2012. From left to right, they were Texas representative Ron Paul, former Pennsylvania senator Rick Santorum, former Massachusetts governor Mitt Romney, and former Speaker of the House Newt Gingrich. (Don Emmert/AFP/Getty Images).

Run-Off Primary. Some states have a two-primary system. If no candidate receives a majority of the votes in the first primary, the top two candidates must compete in another primary, called a *run-off primary.*

The "Top-Two" Primary. Louisiana has long used a special type of primary for filling some offices. Under the system, all candidates appear on a single ballot. A party cannot prevent a candidate from appearing on the primary ballot—an insurgent Republican, for example, could appear on the ballot alongside the party-supported Republican.

9. *California Democratic Party v. Jones,* 530 U.S. 567 (2000).

The two candidates receiving the most votes, regardless of party, then move on to the general election. Following the abolition of the blanket primary, the state of Washington adopted this system. In 2008, the Court upheld the new plan.[10] In 2010, Californians voted to use the system beginning in 2012.

Conventions and Caucuses. In 2012, sixteen states relied at least in part on the **caucus system** for choosing delegates to the Republican and Democratic national conventions. Strictly speaking, the caucus system is a caucus/convention system. In North Dakota, for example, local citizens gather in party meetings, called caucuses, at the precinct level. They choose delegates to district conventions. The district conventions elect delegates to the state convention, and the state convention actually chooses the delegates to the national convention. The national delegates, however, are pledged to reflect the presidential preferences that voters expressed at the caucus level.

Front-Loading the Primaries

As soon as potential presidential candidates realized that winning as many primary elections as possible guaranteed them the party's nomination for president, their tactics changed dramatically. Candidates concentrated on building organizations in states that held early, important primary elections. By the 1970s, candidates recognized that the winner of an early contest, such as the Iowa caucuses or the New Hampshire primary election (both now held in January), would instantly become seen as the **front-runner,** increasing the candidate's media exposure and escalating the pace of contributions to his or her campaign.

The Rush to Be First. The state political parties began to see that early primaries had a much greater effect on the outcome of the presidential contest than did later ones. Accordingly, in every successive presidential election, more and more states moved their primaries into the first months of the year, a process known as **front-loading** the primaries. One result was a series of "Super Tuesdays," when multiple states held simultaneous primaries. In 2008, twenty-four states held their primaries or caucuses on February 5, making it the largest Super Tuesday ever. So many states were in play on February 5 that it was impossible for the candidates to campaign strongly in all of them. Rather than winning more attention, many Super Tuesday states found that they were ignored. Because the Democratic race was not decided until the very end of the process in June 2008, the later Democratic primaries, such as those in Indiana, North Carolina, Ohio, Pennsylvania, and Texas, were hotly contested.

Front-loading, in short, had become counterproductive. As a result, in 2012 Super Tuesday was held on March 6, a month later than in 2008. Ten states participated instead of twenty-four.

The National Parties Seek to Regain Control. The process of front-loading the primaries alarmed many observers, who feared that a front-runner might wrap up the nomination before voters were able to make a thorough assessment of the candidates. In the many months between the early primaries and the general election, the voters might come to regret their decision.

In response, the national Democratic and Republican parties took steps to regain control of the primary schedule in 2012. Such steps included a requirement that states could not hold primaries or caucuses before a specified date. States would need special

---

Caucus System
A meeting of party members to select candidates and propose policies.

Front-Runner
The presidential candidate who appears to be ahead at a given time in the primary season.

Front-Loading
The practice of moving presidential primary elections to the early part of the campaign to maximize the impact of these primaries on the nomination.

Social Media in Politics
For politics, Facebook, Twitter, and YouTube may be the most important social media sites, but there are many others. *Pinterest* is an online pinboard that is wildly popular with women. *Instagram* lets you share smartphone photos.

---

10. *Washington State Grange v. Washington State Republican Party,* 552 U.S. 442 (2008).

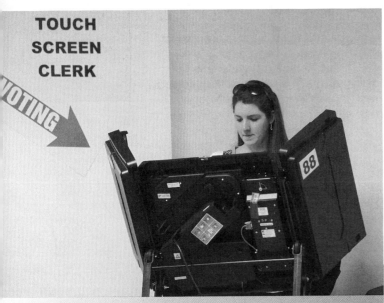

TOUCH SCREEN CLERK

VOTING

A District of Columbia voter casts her ballot in the District's 2012 primary elections. Can D.C. residents choose voting members of the U.S. House and Senate? (Alex Wong/Getty Images)

permission to choose delegates before that date. Traditional lead-off states such as Iowa and New Hampshire were allowed to go first, and a limited number of other states also received such permission.

Not all states were willing to follow the official schedule, however. In principle, the national parties had all the power they needed to enforce the rules—they could cut the number of delegates a state was authorized to send to the national convention, or even refuse to seat a state delegation altogether. The two national committees found it politically difficult to impose tough punishments.

On to the National Convention

Presidential candidates have been nominated by the convention method in every election since 1832. Extra delegates are allowed from states that had voting majorities for the party in the preceding elections. Parties also accept delegates from the District of Columbia, the territories, and U.S. citizens living abroad.

Seating the Delegates. At the convention, each political party uses a **credentials committee** to determine which delegates may participate. Controversy may arise when rival groups claim to be the official party organization. The Mississippi Democratic Party split along racial lines in 1964 at the height of the civil rights movement in the Deep South. Two separate sets of delegates were selected at the state level—one made up of white delegates and the other including both whites and African Americans—and both factions showed up at the national convention. After much debate on party rules, the committee decided to seat the pro–civil rights delegates and exclude those who represented the traditional "white" party.

Credentials Committee
A committee used by political parties at their national conventions to determine which delegates may participate. The committee inspects the claim of each prospective delegate to be seated as a legitimate representative of his or her state.

Convention Activities. Most delegates arrive at the convention committed to a presidential candidate. No convention since 1952 has required more than one ballot to choose a nominee. Conventions normally last four days, but in both 2008 and 2012 the Republican convention was shortened to three days due to hurricanes. On each night, featured speakers seek to rally the party faithful and draw in uncommitted voters who are watching on television. In 2012, about 25 million viewers saw presidential candidate Mitt Romney speak to the Republican convention. At the Democratic convention, almost 36 million Americans tuned in to see President Obama, and 25 million watched the nomination address by former president Bill Clinton.

Public opinion polls following each convention showed a definite "bounce" for the Democrats but not for the Republicans. Some attributed this result to Clinton—his speech was widely considered to be unusually effective.

The Electoral College

Some people who vote for the president and vice president think that they are voting directly for a candidate. In actuality, they are voting for **electors** who will cast their ballots in the electoral college. Article II, Section 1, of the Constitution outlines in detail the method of choosing electors for president and vice president. The framers of the Constitution did not want the president and vice president to be selected by the "excitable masses." Rather, they wished the choice to be made by a few supposedly dispassionate, reasonable men (but not women).

The Choice of Electors. Electors are selected during each presidential election year. The selection is governed by state laws. After the national party convention, the electors are pledged to the candidates chosen. Each state's number of electors equals that state's number of senators (two) plus its number of representatives. The total number of electors today is 538, equal to 100 senators, 435 members of the House, and 3 electors for the District of Columbia. (The Twenty-third Amendment, ratified in 1961, added electors for the District of Columbia.)

The Electors' Commitment. A plurality of voters in a state chooses a slate of electors. Those electors are pledged to cast their ballots on the first Monday after the second Wednesday in December in the state capital for the presidential and vice-presidential candidates of their party.[11] The Constitution does not, however, *require* the electors to cast their ballots for the candidates of their party, and on rare occasions so-called *faithless electors* have voted for a candidate to whom they were not pledged.

The ballots are counted and certified before a joint session of Congress early in January. The candidates who receive a majority (270) of the electoral votes are certified as president-elect and vice president–elect. According to the Constitution, if no candidate receives a majority of the electoral votes, the election of the president is decided in the House of Representatives from among the candidates with the three highest numbers of votes, with each state having one vote (decided by a plurality of each state delegation). The selection of the vice president is determined by the Senate in a choice between the two candidates with the most votes, each senator having one vote. The House was required to choose the president in 1801 (Thomas Jefferson), and again in 1825 (John Quincy Adams).

Problems with the Electoral College System. It is possible for a candidate to become president without obtaining a majority of the popular vote. There have been many "minority" presidents in our history, who did not win a majority of the popular vote, including Abraham Lincoln, Woodrow Wilson, Harry Truman, John F. Kennedy, Richard Nixon (in 1968), and Bill Clinton. Such an event becomes more likely when there are important third-party candidates.

Perhaps more distressing is the possibility of a candidate's being elected when an opposing candidate receives a plurality of the popular vote. This has occurred on four occasions—in the elections of John Quincy Adams in 1824, Rutherford B. Hayes in 1876, Benjamin Harrison in 1888, and George W. Bush in 2000. All of these candidates won elections in which an opponent received more popular votes than they did. Such results have led to calls for replacing the electoral college with a popular-vote system.

Elector
A member of the electoral college, which selects the president and vice president. Each state's electors are chosen in each presidential election year according to state laws.

---

11. In Maine and Nebraska, electoral votes are based in part on congressional districts. Each district chooses one elector. The remaining two electors are chosen by a plurality of all votes cast statewide.

Abolishing the college would require a constitutional amendment, however, and the likelihood of such an amendment is remote. As an alternative, the National Popular Vote movement advocates an interstate compact to bypass the existing system. This proposal would require each participating state to cast all of its electoral votes for the candidate who receives the most popular votes nationwide. The plan will go into effect if the number of participating states grows to the point at which these states can elect a majority of the electoral college. As of mid-2013, eight states and the District of Columbia had joined the compact.

HOW ARE ELECTIONS CONDUCTED?

The United States uses the **Australian ballot**—a secret ballot that is prepared, distributed, and counted by government officials at public expense. Since 1888, all states have used the Australian ballot. Before that, many states used oral voting or differently colored ballots prepared by the parties. Obviously, knowing which way a person was voting made it easy to apply pressure on the person to change his or her vote, and vote buying was common.

Office-Block and Party-Column Ballots

Australian Ballot
A secret ballot prepared, distributed, and tabulated by government officials at public expense. Since 1888, all states have used the Australian ballot rather than an open, public ballot.

Office-Block, or Massachusetts, Ballot
A form of general election ballot in which candidates for elective office are grouped together under the title of each office. It emphasizes voting for the office and the individual candidate, rather than for the party.

Party-Column, or Indiana, Ballot
A form of general election ballot in which all of a party's candidates for elective office are arranged in one column under the party's label and symbol. It emphasizes voting for the party, rather than for the office or individual.

Coattail Effect
The influence of a popular candidate on the electoral success of other candidates on the same party ticket. The effect is increased by the party-column ballot, which encourages straight-ticket voting.

Two types of Australian ballots are used in the United States in general elections. The first, called an **office-block ballot,** or sometimes a **Massachusetts ballot,** groups all the candidates for a particular elective office under the title of that office. Parties dislike the office-block ballot because it places more emphasis on the office than on the party—it discourages straight-ticket voting and encourages split-ticket voting. Most states now use this type of ballot.

A **party-column ballot** is a form of general election ballot in which all of a party's candidates are arranged in one column under the party's label and symbol. It is also called an **Indiana ballot.** In some states, it allows voters to vote for all of a party's candidates for local, state, and national offices by simply marking a single "X" or by pulling a single lever. Because it encourages straight-ticket voting, the two major parties favor this form. When a party has an exceptionally strong presidential or gubernatorial candidate to head the ticket, the use of the party-column ballot increases the **coattail effect** (the influence of a popular candidate on the success of other candidates on the same party ticket).

Voting by Mail

Voting by mail has been accepted for absentee ballots for many decades (for example, for individuals who are doing business away from home or for members of the armed forces). Recently, several states have offered mail ballots to all of their voters. The rationale for using the mail ballot is to make voting easier and increase turnout. Oregon has gone one step further: since 1998, that state has employed postal ballots exclusively, and there are no polling places. (Voters who do not prepare their ballots in time for the U.S. Postal Service to deliver them can drop off their ballots at drop boxes on Election Day.) In addition, most counties in the state of Washington now use mail ballots exclusively. By national standards, voter turnout in those two states has been high, but not exceptionally so.

Voting Fraud and Voter ID Laws

Voting fraud is something regularly suspected but seldom proved. Voting in the 1800s, when secret ballots were rare and people had a cavalier attitude toward the open buying of votes, was probably much more conducive to fraud than modern elections are. Still, some observers claim that the potential for voting fraud is high in many states, particularly through the use of phony voter registrations and absentee ballots. Other observers claim, however, that errors due to fraud are trivial in number and that a few mistakes are inevitable in a system involving millions of voters. These people argue that an excessive concern with voting fraud makes it harder for minorities and poor people to vote.

Voter ID Requirements. In recent years, many states have adopted laws requiring enhanced proof of identity before voters can cast their ballots. Indiana imposed the nation's toughest voter identification (ID) law in 2005. Indiana legislators claimed that they were motivated by a desire to prevent voting fraud, but critics argued that they were really trying to suppress voter turnout among minority group members and the poor—the individuals least likely to possess adequate identification. In 2008, the United States Supreme Court upheld the Indiana voter ID law.[12]

Voting Restrictions during the 2012 Election Cycle. In the wake of the Court's ruling, dozens of states moved to tighten voter ID requirements. Republicans provided almost

12. *Crawford v. Marion County Election Board,* 128 S.Ct. 1610 (2008).

Senator Charles Schumer (D., N.Y.) points to a blowup of a flyer with misleading voting information. Schumer cosponsored a bill to make the distribution of fraudulent election material a federal offense. How likely is it that a voter would be misled by such a flyer? (Alex Wong/Getty Images)

Voter Turnout
The percentage of citizens taking part in the election process; the number of eligible voters who actually "turn out" on Election Day to cast their ballots.

Midterm Elections
National elections in which candidates for president are not on the ballot. In midterm elections, voters choose all members of the U.S. House of Representatives and one-third of the members of the U.S. Senate.

all of the support for the new ID laws. In 2011 and 2012, nineteen states enacted voter ID requirements, and eleven of these states mandated photo IDs. Not all of these laws were actually in effect on Election Day, however. In Wisconsin, a state court held that the new law violated the state constitution. In Maine and Ohio, voters repealed new voting laws before the November elections.

Also, until 2013, most southern states with a history of racial discrimination had to obtain preclearance from the federal government for any significant change to their voting laws and procedures under the 1965 Voting Rights Act. The Department of Justice refused to preclear voter ID laws in South Carolina and Texas on the ground that the laws impose a greater burden on minority voters than on whites. More than 239,000 registered voters in South Carolina lacked the identification needed to vote under that state's proposed law.

The Impact of Restrictive Voting Laws on Voter Turnout. As we explain in the next section, the number of Americans who fail to vote in any election is very large. Any factor that affects voter turnout, therefore, can have a major impact on election results. Heavy voter turnout among conservatives, for example, made 2010 a banner year for the Republicans. In 2012, a belief by minority group members that their voting rights were at risk seems to have increased minority turnout measurably. If the new voting laws really were meant to reduce the Democratic vote, they apparently backfired.

Helpful Web Sites
Professor Michael McDonald of George Mason University hosts a top site for presidential election returns. Search on "us elections project" to get the nation's best analysis of voter turnout. For historical data, try "leip 2012 results" for a page from Dave Leip's Atlas of U.S. Presidential Elections.

Turning Out to Vote

In 2012, the number of Americans eligible to vote was about 221.9 million people. Of that number, about 130.3 million, or 58.7 percent of the eligible population, actually cast a ballot. When voter turnout is this low, it means, among other things, that the winner of a close presidential election may be voted in by less than a third of those eligible to vote.

Figure 8–1 on the facing page shows **voter turnout** for presidential and congressional elections from 1910 to 2012. Each of the peaks in the figure represents voter turnout in a presidential election. Thus, we can also see that turnout for congressional elections is influenced greatly by whether there is a presidential election in the same year. Whereas voter turnout during the presidential elections of 2012 was 58.7 percent, it was only 41.6 percent in the **midterm elections** of 2010.

The same is true at the state level. When there is a race for governor, more voters participate in the elections than when only state legislators are on the ballot. Voter participation rates in gubernatorial elections are also greater in presidential election years. The average turnout in state elections is about 14 percentage points higher when a presidential election is held.

Now consider local elections. In races for mayor, city council, county auditor, and the like, it is fairly common for only 25 percent or less of the electorate to vote. Is something amiss here? It would seem that people should be more likely to vote in elections that directly affect them. At the local level, each person's vote counts more (because there are fewer voters). Furthermore, the issues—crime control, school bonds, sewer bonds, and the like—touch the immediate interests of the voters. In reality, however, potential voters are most interested in national elections, when a presidential choice is involved. Otherwise, voter participation in our representative government is very low (and, as we have seen, it is not overwhelmingly high even in presidential elections).

The Effect of Low Voter Turnout. There are two schools of thought concerning low voter turnout. Some view low voter participation as a threat to our democratic republic. Too few individuals are deciding who wields political power in our society. In addition, low

FIGURE 8–1: Voter Turnout for Presidential and Congressional Elections, 1910–2012

The peaks represent voter turnout in presidential election years. The troughs represent voter turnout in off years with no presidential elections.

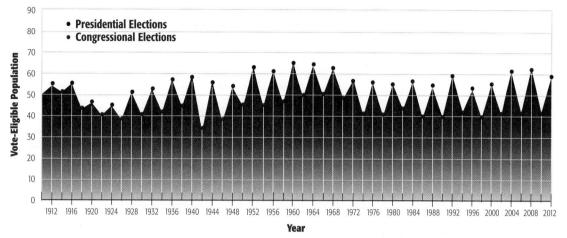

Note: Prior to 1948, the voting-age population is used as a proxy for the population eligible to vote.

Sources: Historical Data Archive, Inter-university Consortium for Political and Social Research; Michael P. McDonald and Samuel L. Popkin, "The Myth of the Vanishing Voter," *American Political Science Review*, Vol. 95, No. 4 (December 2001), p. 966; and the United States Elections Project.

voter participation presumably signals apathy about our political system in general. It also may signal that potential voters simply do not want to take the time to learn about the issues.

Others are less concerned about low voter participation. They contend that low participation simply indicates more satisfaction with the status quo. Also, they believe that representative democracy is a reality even if a very small percentage of eligible voters vote. If everyone who does not vote thinks that the outcome of the election will accord with his or her own desires, then representative democracy is working. The nonvoters are obtaining the type of government—with the type of people running it—that they want to have anyway.

The Voting-Age Population and the Vote-Eligible Population. In the past, the press and even many political scientists calculated voter turnout by taking the number of people who vote as a percentage of the nation's **voting-age population.** Until about 1972, this was a reasonable way to obtain an approximate figure for turnout. In recent decades, however, turnout figures based on the voting-age population have become less and less reliable. The problem is that the voting-age population is not the same as the population of eligible voters, the **vote-eligible population.** The figure for the voting-age population includes felons and ex-felons who have lost the right to vote. Above all, it includes a large number of new immigrants who are not yet citizens. Finally, it does not include Americans living abroad, who can cast absentee ballots.

In 2012, the voting-age population included 3.2 million ineligible felons and ex-felons and an estimated 20.5 million noncitizens. It did not include 4.7 million Americans abroad.

Voting-Age Population
The number of people of voting age living in the country at a given time, regardless of whether they have the right to vote.

Vote-Eligible Population
The number of people who, at a given time, enjoy the right to vote in national elections.

Franchise
The right to vote.

Registration
The entry of a person's name onto the list of registered voters for elections. To register, a person must meet certain legal requirements of age, citizenship, and residency.

The voting-age population in 2012 was 240.9 million people. The number of eligible voters, however, was only 221.9 million. If we calculated 2010 voter turnout based on the larger voting-age population, turnout would appear to be 53.6 percent, not 58.7 percent—a substantial error.

Legal Restrictions on Voting

Legal restrictions on voter registration have existed since the founding of our nation. Most groups in the United States have been concerned with the suffrage (voting) issue at one time or another. In colonial times, only white males who owned property with a certain minimum value were eligible to vote, leaving more Americans ineligible to take part in elections than were eligible.

Property Requirements. Many government functions concern property rights and the distribution of income and wealth, and some of the founders of our nation believed it was appropriate that only people who had an interest in property should vote on these issues.

The writers of the Constitution allowed the states to decide who should vote. Thus, women were allowed to vote in Wyoming in 1870 but not in the entire nation until the Nineteenth Amendment was ratified in 1920. By about 1850, most white adult males in almost all the states could vote without any property qualification.

Further Extensions of the Franchise. Extension of the **franchise** to black males occurred with the passage of the Fifteenth Amendment in 1870. This enfranchisement was short lived, however, as the "redemption" of the South by white supremacists had rolled back those gains by the end of the century. As discussed in Chapter 5, it was not until the 1960s that African Americans, both male and female, were able to participate in the electoral process in all states. Women received full national voting rights with the Nineteenth Amendment in 1920. The most recent extension of the franchise occurred when the voting age was reduced from twenty-one to eighteen by the Twenty-sixth Amendment in 1971. One result of lowering the voting age was to depress voter turnout for several decades beginning in 1972, as you can see in Figure 8–1 earlier in this section. Young people are less likely to vote than older citizens.

Current Eligibility and Registration Requirements. Voting generally requires **registration,** and to register, a person must meet the following voter qualifications, or legal requirements: (1) citizenship, (2) age (eighteen or older), and (3) residency. Since 1972, states cannot impose residency requirements of more than thirty days.

Each state has different laws for voting and registration. In 1993, Congress passed the "motor voter" bill, which requires that states provide voter-registration materials when people receive or renew driver's licenses, that all states allow voters to register by mail, and that voter-registration forms be made available at a wider variety of public places and agencies. In 2004, Arizona challenged the motor voter law with an initiative that placed greater requirements on citizens seeking to register than those in the national legislation. In 2013, however, the Supreme Court overruled the Arizona law.[13]

In general, a person must register well in advance of an election, although voters in the District of Columbia, Idaho, Iowa, Maine, Minnesota, Montana, New Hampshire, North Carolina, Wisconsin, and Wyoming are allowed to register up to, or even on, Election Day. North Dakota has no voter registration at all. Some argue that registration requirements are responsible for much of the nonparticipation in our political process.

---

13. *Arizona v. The Inter Tribal Council of Arizona,* ___ U.S. ___ (2013).

The Voting Rights Act. As we discussed in Chapter 5, the Voting Rights Act was enacted in 1965 to ensure that African Americans had equal access to the polls. Section 5 of the act requires that new voting practices or procedures in jurisdictions with a history of discrimination in voting have to be approved by the national government before being implemented.

Section 5 permits jurisdictions to "bail out" of coverage if they can demonstrate a clean record on discrimination during the previous ten years. By 2009, however, seventeen Virginia counties were the only jurisdictions in the country to successfully bail out. In June 2009, the Supreme Court permitted a Texas utility district to file for a bailout and strongly indicated that relief from the requirements of the act should be granted more freely.[14]

In June 2013, in *Shelby County v. Holder*, the Supreme Court effectively invalidated the requirement that changes to voting procedures in covered states and districts receive preclearance.[15] The Court did not throw out Section 5. Rather, it overturned Section 4, which determined which states and localities should be covered by Section 5. The Court contended that Section 4, which dated back to the 1960s, was obsolete. In principle, Congress could adopt a new set of Section 4 formulas based on more current conditions. The chances of such legislation making its way through a polarized Congress, however, seemed slight.

African American and liberal leaders accused the Court of engaging in one of the most sweeping examples of conservative judicial activism ever. The Voting Rights Act had been reaffirmed by Congress in 2006, with the House supporting it by 390 to 33 and the Senae by 98 to 0.

HOW DO VOTERS DECIDE?

A variety of factors appear to influence political preferences. Party identification is among the most important. Other factors include the perception of the candidates and issue preferences. Various demographic factors influence political preferences as well.

LO5: Provide some of the reasons why people vote in particular ways.

Party Identification

With the possible exception of race, party identification is the most important determinant of voting behavior in national elections. Party affiliation is influenced by family and peer groups, by generational effects, by the media, and by the voter's assessment of candidates and issues.

As we have observed on more than one occasion, the number of independent voters has grown over the years. While party identification may have little effect on the voting behavior of true independents, it remains a crucial determinant for the majority of the voters, who have established party preferences.

Other Political Factors

Factors such as perception of the candidates and issue preferences also affect how people vote. While most people do not change their party identification from year to year, candidates and issues can change greatly, and voting behavior can therefore change as well.

---

14. *Northwest Austin Municipal Utility District No. One v. Holder,* 557 U.S. 193 (2009).
15. ___ U.S. ___ (2013).

College students buy a T-shirt during a Rock the Vote bus tour of the University of North Carolina at Charlotte. Rock the Vote encourages young people to register to vote and to become politically active. Why are young people often less likely to vote? (Ann Hermes/*Christian Science Monitor* via Getty Images)

Perception of the Candidates. The image of the candidate seems to be important in a voter's choice, especially of a president. To some extent, voter attitudes toward candidates are based on emotions (such as trust) rather than on any judgment about experience or policy. In some years, voters have been attracted to a candidate who appeared to share their concerns and worries. In other years, voters have sought a candidate who appeared to have high integrity and honesty.

Issue Preferences. Issues make a difference in presidential and congressional elections. Although personality or image factors may be very persuasive, most voters have some notion of how the candidates differ on basic issues or at least know which candidates want a change in the direction of government policy.

Historically, economic concerns have been among the most powerful influences on public opinion. When the economy is doing well, it is very difficult for a challenger, especially at the presidential level, to defeat the incumbent. In contrast, inflation, unemployment, or high interest rates are likely to work to the disadvantage of the incumbent.

Demographic Characteristics

Demographic characteristics that influence political preferences include race, religion, education, income and **socioeconomic status,** and similar traits. People who share the same religion or any other demographic trait are likely to influence one another and may also have common political concerns that follow from the common characteristic. We examined these factors in depth in Chapter 6, as part of the discussion of political socialization.

Demographic influences reflect an individual's personal background and place in society. Some factors have to do with the family into which a person was born: race and (for most people) religion. Others may be the result in large part of choices made throughout an individual's life: place of residence, educational achievement, and profession.

Socioeconomic Status
The value assigned to a person due to occupation or income. A professional person with a substantial income, for example, has high socioeconomic status.

Many of these factors are interrelated. People who have more education are likely to have higher incomes and to hold professional jobs. Similarly, children born into wealthier families are far more likely to complete college than children from poor families. A number of other interrelationships are not so immediately obvious. For example, many people might not realize that 79 percent of African Americans report that religion is very important in their lives, compared with only 56 percent of the total population.[16]

16. The Pew Forum on Religion and Public Life, "A Religious Portrait of African-Americans," January 30, 2009.

making a **difference**

REGISTERING AND VOTING

Very close elections, such as the 2008 Minnesota Senate race, demonstrate that your vote can make a difference. In local races, elections have sometimes been decided by one or two votes. In nearly every state, before you are allowed to cast a vote in an election, you must first register. Registration laws vary considerably from state to state.

Residency and Age Requirements What do you have to do to register and cast a vote? In general, you must be a citizen of the United States, at least eighteen years old on or before Election Day, and a resident of the state in which you intend to register. A number of states require that you meet a minimum-residency requirement. The minimum-residency requirement is very short in some states—for example, ten days in Wisconsin. No state requires more than thirty days. Thirty states do not have any minimum-residency requirement.

Time Limits Nearly every state also specifies a closing date by which you must be registered before an election. You may not be able to vote if you register too close to the day of the election. The closing date for registration varies from Election Day itself to thirty days before the election. In North Dakota, no registration is necessary.

In most states, your registration can be revoked if you do not vote within a certain number of years or do not report a change of address. Federal regulations place limits on how purges are conducted, but Democrats have frequently accused Republican state officials of violating the rules. The belief is that those who move frequently or who often fail to vote—and who are therefore purged—tend to be Democrats. For their part, Republicans contend that aggressive purges limit voter fraud.

An Example Let us look at voter registration in Texas as an example. If you live in Texas, you may have registered to vote when you obtained your Texas driver's license. If not, you can find a voter registration form online by searching on "texas vrapp." You must mail the application to the voter registrar in your county. (The registrar's address appears on the form after you finish filling it out.) Applications are also available at post offices, libraries, Texas Department of Public Safety offices, and Texas Department of Human Services offices. Your application must be postmarked thirty days before Election Day.

Disputed ballots are always a part of the election process. Did this Minnesota voter mean to vote for Norm Coleman? Coleman supporters argued that he or she did, whereas supporters of Al Franken (the eventual winner) contended that it was an invalid ballot. What do you think? (AP Photo/Dawn Villella)

key**terms**

Australian ballot 186	credentials	Federal Election	franchise 190
caucus system 183	committee 184	Commission (FEC)	front-loading 183
closed primary 182	direct primary 181	176	front-runner 183
coattail effect 186	elector 185	focus group 175	general election 173

Hatch Act 176

independent
expenditures 177

indirect primary 181

issue advocacy
advertising 177

midterm elections 188

office-block, or
Massachusetts,
ballot 186

open primary 182

party-column, or
Indiana, ballot 186

political action
committee (PAC) 176

political consultant 174

presidential primary 172

primary election 173

registration 190

socioeconomic
status 192

soft money 177

superdelegate 181

super PAC 178

vote-eligible
population 189

voter turnout 188

voting-age
population 189

chaptersummary

1 The legal qualifications for holding political office are minimal at both the state and the local levels, but holders of political office still are predominantly white and male and are likely to have professional status.

2 American political campaigns are lengthy and extremely expensive. In recent decades, they have become more candidate centered rather than party centered in response to decreasing party identification. Candidates have begun to rely on paid professional consultants to perform the various tasks necessary to wage a political campaign. The campaign organization devises a campaign strategy to maximize the candidate's chances of winning. Candidates use public opinion polls and focus groups to gauge their popularity and to test strategies.

3 Interest groups are major sources of campaign funds. The contributions are often made through political action committees, or PACs. Other methods of contributing include issue advocacy advertising. The McCain-Feingold Act of 2002 imposed significant restrictions on campaign finance, but in 2010 these restrictions were largely swept away by the Supreme Court in its ruling *Citizens United v. FEC.*

4 Campaign finance today is largely based on two types of committees. Super PACs can raise unlimited funds from any source, but supposedly are not allowed to coordinate with candidate campaigns. Candidate committees face restrictions on contributions but are not limited in how they may spend their funds to support a campaign.

5 After the Democratic convention of 1968, the McGovern-Fraser Commission formulated new rules for primaries, most of which were also adopted

by Republicans. These reforms opened up the nomination process for the presidency to all voters.

6 A presidential primary is a statewide election to help a political party determine its presidential nominee at the national convention. Some states use the caucus system of choosing convention delegates. The primary campaign recently has been shortened to the first few months of the election year.

7 The voter technically does not vote directly for president but chooses between slates of presidential electors. In most states, the slate that wins the most popular votes throughout the state gets to cast all the electoral votes for the state. The candidate receiving a majority (270) of the electoral votes wins the election. Both the mechanics and the politics of the electoral college have been criticized sharply.

8 The United States uses the Australian ballot, a secret ballot that is prepared, distributed, and counted by government officials. The office-block ballot groups candidates according to office. The party-column ballot groups candidates according to their party labels and symbols.

9 Voter participation in the United States is often considered to be low, especially in elections that do not feature a presidential contest. Turnout is lower when measured as a percentage of the voting-age population than it is when measured as a percentage of the population actually eligible to vote.

10 In colonial times, only white males who owned property were eligible to vote. The suffrage issue has concerned, at one time or another, most groups in the United States. Today, to be eligible to vote, a person must satisfy registration, citizenship, age, and residency requirements. Each state has different qualifications.

test**yourself**

LO1 *Discuss who runs for office and how campaigns are managed.*

To be eligible to serve as president of the United States, you must be:

    a. a natural-born citizen, a resident of the country for twenty-five years, and at least forty-two years old.

    b. a naturalized citizen, a resident of the country for twenty-five years, and at least thirty-five years old.

    c. at least thirty-five years old, a natural-born citizen, and a resident of the country for fourteen years.

LO2 *Describe the current system of campaign finance.*

Today, presidential candidates do not accept matching public funds because:

    a. candidates can raise far more outside of the public system than they would receive if they participated in it.

    b. once candidates accept public funds for the primaries, they must match public funds in a ratio of two to one for the general elections.

    c. public funds are no longer available.

LO3 *Summarize the process of choosing a president of the United States.*

In an indirect primary:

    a. voters decide party nominations by voting directly for candidates.

    b. voters make no decisions directly about convention delegates.

    c. voters choose convention delegates, and those delegates determine the party's candidate in the general election.

LO4 *Explain the mechanisms through which voting takes place on Election Day, and discuss voter turnout in the United States.*

In the United States today, all states use secret ballots that are prepared, distributed, and counted by government officials at public expense. This system is called:

    a. the Australian ballot.

    b. the Massachusetts ballot.

    c. the office-block ballot.

LO5 *Provide some of the reasons why people vote in particular ways.*

Perhaps the two most important factors in determining how voters cast their ballots are:

    a. perception of the candidates and issue preferences.

    b. party identification and race.

    c. level of education and gender.

Essay Question:

Some have argued that limits on campaign spending violate First Amendment guarantees of freedom of speech. How strong is this argument? Can such spending be seen as a form of protected expression? Under what circumstances can contributions be seen instead as a method of bribing elected officials?

Answers to multiple-choice questions: 1. c, 2. a, 3. c, 4. a, 5. b.

CourseMate

Access CourseMate at www.cengagebrain.com for additional study tools: practice quizzes, key term flashcards and crossword puzzles, audio chapter summaries, simulations, animated learning modules, interactive timelines, videos, and American Government NewsWatch.

9

MR. SHULMAN

MS. LERNER

MR.

The Congress

LEARNING OUTCOMES

The five **Learning Outcomes (LOs)** below are designed to help improve your understanding of this chapter. After reading this chapter, you should be able to:

■ **LO1** Describe the various roles played by Congress and the constitutional basis of its powers.

■ **LO2** Explain some of the differences between the House and the Senate, and some of the privileges enjoyed by members of Congress.

■ **LO3** Examine the implications of apportioning House seats.

■ **LO4** Describe the committee structure of the House and the Senate, and specify the key leadership positions in each chamber.

■ **LO5** Discuss the process by which a bill becomes law and how the federal government establishes its budget.

Check your understanding of the material with the Test Yourself section at the end of the chapter.

Most Americans view Congress in a less-than-flattering light. In recent years, Congress has appeared to be deeply split, highly partisan in its conduct, and not very responsive to public needs. Polls show that, recently, as few as 9 percent of the public have had a favorable opinion about Congress as a whole. In one poll, respondents rated traffic jams, root canal operations, and cockroaches more favorably than Congress. (Congress did beat Fidel Castro, meth labs, and the Ebola virus.) Yet individual members of Congress often receive much higher approval ratings from the voters in their districts. This is one of the paradoxes of the relationship between the people and Congress. Members of the public hold the institution in relatively low regard compared with the satisfaction they express with their individual representatives.

Part of the explanation for these seemingly contradictory appraisals is that members of Congress spend considerable time and effort serving their **constituents.** If the federal bureaucracy makes a mistake, the office of the constituent's senator or representative tries to resolve the issue. On a personal level, what most Americans see, therefore, is the work of these local representatives in their home states. Congress, however, was created to work not just for local constituents but also for the nation as a whole. Understanding the nature of the institution and the process of lawmaking is an important part of understanding how the policies that shape our lives are made.

In this chapter, we describe the functions of Congress, including constituent service, representation, lawmaking, and oversight of the government. We review how the members of Congress are elected and how Congress organizes itself when it meets. We also examine how bills pass through the legislative process and how the federal budget is established.

Constituent
One of the persons represented by a legislator or other elected or appointed official.

Bicameralism
The division of a legislature into two separate assemblies.

Lawmaking
The process of establishing the legal rules that govern society.

THE NATURE AND FUNCTIONS OF CONGRESS

The founders of the American republic believed that the bulk of the power that would be exercised by a national government should be in the hands of the legislature. The leading role envisioned for Congress in the new government is apparent from its primacy in the Constitution. Article I deals with the structure, the powers, and the operation of Congress.

LO1: Describe the various roles played by Congress and the constitutional basis of its powers.

Bicameralism

The **bicameralism** of Congress—its division into two legislative houses—was in part the result of the Connecticut Compromise, which tried to balance the large-state population advantage, reflected in the House, and the small-state demand for equality in policy-making, which was satisfied in the Senate. Beyond that, the two chambers of Congress also reflected the social class biases of the founders. They wished to balance the interests and the numerical superiority of the common citizens with the property interests of the less numerous landowners, bankers, and merchants. They achieved this goal by providing that members of the House of Representatives should be elected directly by "the People," whereas members of the Senate were to be chosen by the elected representatives sitting in state legislatures, who were more likely to be members of the elite. (The latter provision was changed in 1913 by the passage of the Seventeenth Amendment, which provides that senators are also to be elected directly by the people.)

The logic of the bicameral Congress was reinforced by differences in length of tenure. Members of the House are required to face the electorate every two years, whereas senators can serve for a much more secure term of six years—even longer than the four-year term provided for the president. Furthermore, the senators' terms are staggered so that only one-third of the senators face the electorate every two years, along with all of the House members.

The bicameral Congress was designed to perform certain functions for the political system. These functions include lawmaking, representation, service to constituents, oversight (regulatory supervision), public education, and conflict resolution. Of these, the two most important and the ones that most often interfere with each other are lawmaking and representation.

The Lawmaking Function

The principal and most obvious function of any legislature is **lawmaking.** Congress is the highest elected body in the country, charged with making binding rules for all Americans. This does not mean, however, that Congress initiates most of the ideas for legislation

Earmarks
Special provisions in legislation to set aside funds for projects that have not passed an impartial evaluation by agencies of the executive branch. Also known as *pork*.

Representation
The function of members of Congress as elected officials representing the views of their constituents as well as larger national interests.

Trustee
A legislator who acts according to her or his conscience and the broad interests of the entire society.

Instructed Delegate
A legislator who is an agent of the voters who elected him or her and who votes according to the views of constituents, regardless of personal beliefs.

that it eventually considers. A majority of the bills that Congress acts on originate in the executive branch, and many other bills are traceable to interest groups and political party organizations. Through the processes of compromise and *logrolling* (offering to support a fellow member's bill in exchange for that member's promise to support your bill in the future), as well as debate and discussion, backers of legislation attempt to fashion a winning majority coalition.

Traditionally, logrolling often involved agreements to support another member's legislative **earmarks,** also known as *pork*. Earmarks are special provisions in legislation to set aside funds for projects that have not passed an impartial evaluation by agencies of the executive branch. (Normal spending projects pass through such evaluations.) Recent attempts to ban pork have not eliminated the process altogether but have substantially reduced its frequency.

The Representation Function

Representation includes both representing the desires and demands of the constituents in the member's home district or state and representing larger national interests, such as the nation's security or the environment. Because the interests of constituents in a specific district may be at odds with the demands of national policy, the representation function is often a source of conflict for individual lawmakers—and sometimes for Congress as a whole. For example, although it may be in the interest of the nation to reduce defense spending by closing military bases, such closures are not in the interest of the states and districts that will lose jobs and local spending. Every legislator faces votes that set local representational issues against lawmaking realities.

How should the legislators fulfill the representation function? There are several views on how this task should be accomplished.

The Trustee View of Representation. One approach to the question of how representation should be achieved is that legislators should act as **trustees** of the broad interests of the entire society. They should vote against the narrow interests of their constituents if their conscience and their perception of national needs so dictate. For example, in 2011 Congress approved trade agreements with Colombia, Panama, and South Korea, despite the widely held belief that such agreements cost Americans jobs.

The Instructed-Delegate View of Representation. Directly opposed to the trustee view of representation is the notion that members of Congress should behave as **instructed delegates**—that is, they should mirror the views of the majority of the constituents who elected them. For this approach to work, however, we must assume that constituents actually have well-formed views on the issues that are decided in Congress and, further, that they have clear-cut preferences about these issues. Neither condition is likely to be satisfied very often.

Generally, most legislators hold neither a pure trustee view nor a pure instructed-delegate view. Typically, they combine both perspectives in a pragmatic mix.

Senator Kelly Ayotte (R., N.H.) receives an award from the Women's Democracy Network (WDN). The network is a project of the International Republican Institute, which in turn is sponsored by the Republican Party. The WDN is active in sixty-one nations. Why might U.S. political parties sponsor nonprofit organizations to work around the world? (Office of Kelly Ayotte)

Service to Constituents

Individual members of Congress are expected by their constituents to act as brokers between private citizens and the imposing, often faceless federal government. This function of providing service to constituents usually takes the form of **casework.** The legislator and her or his staff spend a considerable portion of their time in casework activities, such as tracking down a missing Social Security check, explaining the meaning of particular bills to people who may be affected by them, promoting a local business interest, or interceding with a regulatory agency on behalf of constituents who disagree with proposed agency regulations.

Legislators and many analysts of congressional behavior regard this **ombudsperson** role as an activity that strongly benefits the members of Congress. A government characterized by a large, confusing bureaucracy and complex public programs offers innumerable opportunities for legislators to come to the assistance of (usually) grateful constituents.

The Oversight Function

Oversight of the bureaucracy is essential if the decisions made by Congress are to have any force. **Oversight** is the process by which Congress follows up on the laws it has enacted to ensure that they are being enforced and administered in the way Congress intended. This is done by holding committee hearings and investigations, changing the size of an agency's budget, and cross-examining high-level presidential nominees to head major agencies.

Senators and representatives traditionally have seen their oversight function as a critically important part of their legislative activities. In part, oversight is related to the concept of constituency service, particularly when Congress investigates alleged arbitrariness or wrongdoing by bureaucratic agencies.

A problem with oversight is that it has become entangled in partisan politics. During the past two decades, members of Congress have tended to ease up on oversight whenever the president is of their political party. In contrast, oversight can become intense, and even excessive, when the president faces a chamber of Congress that is controlled by the other party.

The Public-Education Function

Educating the public is a function that Congress performs whenever it holds public hearings, exercises oversight of the bureaucracy, or engages in committee and floor debate on such major issues and topics as immigration, firearms, and the concerns of small businesses. In so doing, Congress presents a range of viewpoints on pressing national questions. Congress also decides what issues will come up for discussion and decision. This **agenda setting** is a major facet of its public-education function.

The Conflict-Resolution Function

Congress is commonly seen as an institution for resolving conflicts within American society. Organized interest groups and spokespersons for different racial, religious, economic, and ideological interests look on Congress as an access point for airing their grievances and seeking help. This puts Congress in the position of trying to resolve the differences among competing points of view by passing laws to accommodate as many interested parties as possible. To the extent that Congress meets pluralist expectations in accommodating competing interests, it tends to build support for the entire political process. Its failure to do so, however, tends to bring the political process into disrepute.

Social Media in Politics
Two Facebook pages worth investigating if you are interested in Congress are sponsored by Politico, a political news website, and *Roll Call,* a newspaper covering Congress. You can also follow these organizations on Twitter.

WWW

Helpful Web Sites
The Hill, a newspaper that investigates various activities of Congress, can be found at "thehill."

Casework
Personal work for constituents by members of Congress.

Ombudsperson
A person who hears and investigates complaints by private individuals against public officials or agencies (from the Swedish word *ombudsman,* meaning "representative").

Oversight
The process by which Congress follows up on laws it has enacted to ensure that they are being enforced and administered in the way Congress intended.

Agenda Setting
Determining which public-policy questions will be debated or considered.

Enumerated Powers
Powers specifically granted to the national government by the Constitution. The first seventeen clauses of Article I, Section 8, specify most of the enumerated powers of Congress.

The Powers of Congress

The Constitution is both highly specific and extremely vague about the powers that Congress may exercise. The first seventeen clauses of Article I, Section 8, specify most of the **enumerated powers** of Congress—that is, powers expressly given to that body.

Enumerated Powers. The enumerated, or expressed, powers of Congress include the right to:

- Impose a variety of taxes, including tariffs on imports.
- Borrow funds.
- Regulate interstate commerce and international trade.
- Establish procedures for naturalizing citizens.
- Make laws regulating bankruptcies.
- Coin (and print) currency, and regulate its value.
- Establish standards of weights and measures.
- Punish counterfeiters.
- Establish post offices and post roads.
- Regulate copyrights and patents.
- Establish the federal court system.
- Punish illegal acts on the high seas.
- Declare war.
- Raise and regulate an army and a navy.
- Call up and regulate the state militias to enforce laws, to suppress insurrections, and to repel invasions.
- Govern the District of Columbia.

Senator Elizabeth Warren (D., Mass.) is a well known critic of the banking industry. Why might such a record help a senator get elected? (United States Senate)

The most important of the domestic powers of Congress, listed in Article I, Section 8, are the rights to impose taxes, to spend, and to regulate commerce. The most important foreign policy power is the power to declare war. Other sections of the Constitution allow Congress to establish rules for its own members, to regulate the electoral college, and to override a presidential veto. Congress may also regulate the extent of the Supreme Court's authority to review cases decided by the lower courts, regulate relations among states, and propose amendments to the Constitution.

Powers of the Senate. Some functions are restricted to one chamber. The Senate must advise on, and consent to, the ratification of treaties and must accept or reject presidential nominations of ambassadors, Supreme Court justices, other federal judges, and "all other Officers of the United States." But the Senate may delegate to the president or lesser officials the power to make lower-level appointments.

Constitutional Amendments. Amendments to the Constitution provide for other congressional powers. Congress must certify the election of a president and a vice president or itself choose those officers if no candidate has a majority of the electoral vote (Twelfth Amendment). It may levy an income tax (Sixteenth Amendment) and determine who will be acting president in case of the death or incapacity of the president or vice president (Twentieth Amendment and Twenty-fifth Amendment).

The Necessary and Proper Clause. Beyond these numerous specific powers, Congress enjoys the right under clause 18 of Article I, Section 8 (the elastic, or "necessary and proper," clause), "to make all Laws which shall be necessary and proper for carrying into Execution the foregoing Powers [of Article I], and all other Powers vested by this Constitution in the Government of the United States, or in any Department or Officer thereof." As discussed in Chapter 3, this vague statement of congressional responsibilities has provided, over time, the basis for a greatly expanded national government. It has also constituted, at least in theory, a check on the expansion of presidential powers.

Rules Committee
A standing committee of the House of Representatives that provides special rules under which specific bills can be debated, amended, and considered by the House.

Filibuster
The use of the Senate's tradition of unlimited debate as a delaying tactic to block a bill.

HOUSE-SENATE DIFFERENCES AND CONGRESSIONAL PERKS

Congress is composed of two markedly different—but co-equal—chambers. Although the Senate and the House of Representatives exist within the same legislative institution, each has developed certain distinctive features that clearly distinguish one from the other.

Size and Rules

The central difference between the House and the Senate is simply that the House is much larger than the Senate. The House has 435 voting representatives, plus delegates from the District of Columbia, Puerto Rico, Guam, American Samoa, and the Virgin Islands, compared with just 100 senators. This size difference means that a greater number of formal rules are needed to govern activity in the House, whereas correspondingly looser procedures can be followed in the less crowded Senate. This difference is most obvious in the rules governing debate on the floors of the two chambers.

LO2: Explain some of the differences between the House and the Senate, and some of the privileges enjoyed by members of Congress.

The Senate usually permits extended debate on all issues that arise before it. In contrast, the House generally operates with an elaborate system in which its **Rules Committee** proposes time limitations on debate for any bill, and a majority of the entire body accepts or modifies those suggested time limits. As a consequence of its stricter time limits on debate, the House, despite its greater size, often is able to act on legislation more quickly than the Senate.

Debate and Filibustering

The Senate tradition of the **filibuster,** or the use of unlimited debate as a blocking tactic, dates back to 1790.[1] In that year, a proposal to move the U.S. capital from New York to Philadelphia was stalled by such time-wasting maneuvers. This unlimited-debate tradition—which also existed in the House until 1811—is not absolute, however.

Cloture. Under Senate Rule 22, debate may be ended by invoking *cloture.* Cloture shuts off discussion on a bill. Amended in 1975 and 1979, Rule 22 states that debate may be closed off on a bill if sixteen senators sign a petition requesting it and if, after two days have elapsed, three-fifths of the entire membership (sixty votes, assuming no vacancies) vote for cloture. After cloture is invoked, each senator may speak on a bill for a maximum of one hour before a vote is taken.

---

1. *Filibuster* comes from a Spanish word for pirate, which in turn came from the Dutch term *vrijbuiter,* or freebooter. The word was first used in 1851 to accuse senators of pirating or hijacking debate.

Patrick Leahy (D., Vt.) is the Democrat with the longest continuous term of service in the U.S. Senate. For that reason, he serves as the president pro tempore of the Senate. What powers, if any, does Leahy gain by holding this position? (Senate Judiciary Committee)

Reconciliation
A special rule that can be applied to budget bills sent from the House of Representatives to the Senate. Reconciliation measures cannot be filibustered.

Franking
A policy that enables members of Congress to send material through the mail by substituting their facsimile signature (frank) for postage.

Increased Use of the Filibuster. Traditionally, filibusters were rare, and the tactic was employed only on issues of principle. Filibustering senators spoke for many hours, sometimes reading names from a telephone book. By the twenty-first century, however, filibusters could be invoked without such speeches, and senators were threatening to filibuster almost every significant piece of legislation to come before the body. The threats were sufficient to create a new, ad hoc rule that important legislation needed the support of sixty senators, not fifty. As a result of the increased use of the filibuster, some senators have called for its abolition. We discuss that topic in this chapter's *At Issue* feature on the following page.

Reconciliation. An additional way of bypassing the filibuster is known as **reconciliation.** Budget bills sent from the House of Representatives to the Senate can be handled under special reconciliation rules that do not permit filibusters. Under the rules, reconciliation can be used *only* to handle budgetary matters. Also, in principle, the procedure is to be invoked only for measures that would have the net effect of reducing the federal deficit. This last restriction, however, has frequently been avoided by the use of misleading bookkeeping.

One of the most striking examples of reconciliation took place in March 2010, when the Democrats used the procedure to make a series of amendments to the just-passed Patient Protection and Affordable Care Act, also known as Obamacare. Reconciliation was necessary because at the end of January, the Republicans won a special U.S. Senate election, thus reducing the number of Democratic senators to fifty-nine.

Congresspersons and the Citizenry: A Comparison

Members of the Senate and the House of Representatives are not typical American citizens. Members of Congress are older than most Americans, partly because of constitutional age requirements and partly because a good deal of political experience normally is an advantage in running for national office. Members of Congress are also disproportionately white, male, and trained in high-status occupations. Lawyers are by far the largest occupational group among congresspersons, although the proportion of lawyers in the House is lower now than it was in the past. Compared with the average American citizen, members of Congress are well paid. Annual congressional salaries are now $174,000. Increasingly, members of Congress are also much wealthier than the average citizen. Whereas about 3 percent of Americans have assets exceeding $1 million (not including their homes), more than half of the members of Congress are millionaires. Table 9–1 on page 204 summarizes selected characteristics of the members of Congress.

Perks and Privileges

Legislators have many benefits that are not available to most people. For example, members of Congress are granted generous **franking** privileges that permit them to mail newsletters and other correspondence to their constituents for free.[2] The annual cost of

---

2. The word *franking* derives from the Latin *francus,* which means "free."

at issue

IS IT TIME TO GET RID OF THE FILIBUSTER?

It is not in the Constitution, but it is an important institution. It is the filibuster, and it follows from Senate Rule 22, which allows for unlimited debate. Throughout American history, senators could tie up the Senate's business by talking indefinitely. In 1975, Rule 22 was revised. Since that year, a vote by sixty senators is required to stop floor debate (instead of the previous sixty-seven). A second significant change in Senate practice developed, however—today, senators don't actually have to *talk* to hold a filibuster. All they have to do to maintain a filibuster is to announce that a filibuster exists. The practical effect has been to create a new rule that all important legislation requires sixty votes in the Senate. Some want the filibuster abolished. Others do not agree.

THE FILIBUSTER IS NOT EVEN CONSTITUTIONAL

Critics of the filibuster argue that it has no constitutional basis and implicitly violates many actual provisions of the Constitution. After all, the Constitution requires a *supermajority*—more than a simple majority—only for special situations such as ratifying treaties, proposing constitutional amendments, overriding presidential vetoes, and convicting impeached officials.

Consider this statement by Alexander Hamilton in *Federalist Paper* No. 75: "All provisions which require more than a majority of any [legislative] body to its resolutions have a direct tendency to embarrass the operations of the government and an indirect one to subject the sense of the majority to that of the minority." Hamilton was writing about a proposal to require that more than half of a chamber's members be present to convene a session, but his argument certainly applies to whether a body should need more than a majority of its members to take a vote.

THE FILIBUSTER AS DAMAGE CONTROL

True, filibusters today are not as colorful as they were before 1975, when senators were forced to read out of a telephone book or even wear diapers to keep a filibuster going. Yet the current filibuster system continues to provide an important protection for minority rights. Why shouldn't Congress be forced to obtain broad support for important legislation? It would be dangerous to allow major taxation and spending measures to be decided by a bare majority vote. Public opinion polling has shown that the filibuster is quite popular among the public at large. Clearly, Americans see the importance of slowing down legislation created by only a single party in Congress. The filibuster still serves a useful purpose, so let's keep it.

FOR CRITICAL ANALYSIS

What would be likely to happen if the filibuster were abolished?

---

congressional mail is now about $10 million to $15 million a year. The cost of franking has dropped since 1990 due to the growth of Internet home pages, e-mail, blogs, Facebook, and Twitter. Typically, the costs for these mailings rise substantially during election years.

Permanent Professional Staffs. More than thirty thousand people are employed in the Capitol Hill bureaucracy. About half of them are personal and committee staff members. The personal staff includes office clerks and assistants; professionals who deal with media relations, draft legislation, and satisfy constituency requests for service; and staffers who maintain local offices in the member's home district or state.

The average Senate office on Capitol Hill employs about thirty staff members, and twice that number work on the personal staffs of senators from the most populous states. House office staffs typically are about half as large as those of the Senate. The number of staff members in both chambers has increased dramatically since 1960.

Privileges and Immunities under the Law. Members of Congress also benefit from a number of special constitutional protections. Under Article I, Section 6, of the Constitution,

TABLE 9–1: Characteristics of the 113th Congress, 2013–2015

Characteristic	U.S. Population	House	Senate
Age (median)	36.8	56.2	61.5
Percentage minority	34.9	18.2	5
Religion			
Percentage church or synagogue members	66.4	84.8	90
Percentage Roman Catholic	23.9	30.3	28
Percentage Protestant	51.3	50.1	51
Percentage Jewish	1.7	5.1	10
Percentage female	50.7	18.2	17
Percentage with advanced degrees (persons age 25 or above only)	10.1	64.6	75
Occupation			
Percentage lawyers of those employed	0.8	36.8	56
Family income			
Percentage of families earning more than $50,000 annually	44.9	100.0	100
Personal wealth*			
Percentage with assets over $1 million	4.7	53.3	80

Data applies to members immediately after the 2012 elections. Thereafter, congressional membership changes slowly due to resignation, death, and other factors.
*112th Congress.

Sources: *CIA Factbook*, 2010; Census Bureau; and authors' updates.

for example, "for any Speech or Debate in either House, they shall not be questioned in any other Place." The "speech or debate" clause means that a member may make any allegations or other statements he or she wishes in connection with official duties and normally not be sued for defamation (libel or slander) or otherwise be subject to legal action.

CONGRESSIONAL ELECTIONS AND APPORTIONMENT

LO3: Examine the implications of apportioning House seats.

The process of electing members of Congress is decentralized. Congressional elections are conducted by the individual state governments. The states, however, must conform to the rules established by the U.S. Constitution and federal statutes. The Constitution states that representatives are to be elected every second year by popular ballot, and the number of seats awarded to each state is to be determined every ten years by the results of the census. Each state has at least one representative, with most congressional districts having about 725,000 residents. Senators are elected by popular vote (since the passage of the Seventeenth Amendment) every six years. Approximately one-third of the seats are chosen every two years. Each state has two senators. Under Article I, Section 4, of the Constitution, state legislatures are given control over "[t]he Times, Places and Manner of holding Elections for Senators and Representatives," although "the Congress may at any time by Law make or alter such Regulations."

Candidates for Congressional Elections

Congressional campaigns have changed considerably in the past two decades. Like all other campaigns, they are much more expensive, with the average cost of a winning Senate campaign now $9 million and a winning House campaign more than $1.5 million. In addition, large sums are spent on congressional campaigns by independent committees, as explained in Chapter 8. Once in office, legislators spend time almost every day raising funds for their next campaign.

Most candidates for Congress must win the nomination through a direct primary, in which those who identify with a particular party vote for the candidate who will be on the party ticket in the general election. To win the primary, candidates may take more liberal or more conservative positions to get the votes of "party identifiers." In the general election, they may moderate their views to attract the votes of independents and voters from the other party.

Presidential Effects. Congressional candidates are always hopeful that a strong presidential candidate on their ticket will have "coattails" that will sweep in senators and representatives of the same party. (In fact, in some recent presidential elections coattail effects have not materialized at all.) One way to measure the coattail effect is to look at the subsequent midterm elections, held in the even-numbered years following the presidential contests. In these years, voter turnout falls sharply. The party controlling the White House frequently loses seats in Congress in the midterm elections, in part because the coattail effect ceases to apply. Table 9–2 on the right shows the pattern for midterm elections since 1946.

The Power of Incumbency. The power of incumbency in the outcome of congressional elections cannot be overemphasized. Table 9–3 on the following page shows that a sizable majority of representatives and a slightly smaller proportion of senators who decide to run for reelection are successful. This conclusion holds for both presidential-year and midterm elections. Even in 2010, when the Republicans made very large gains, most incumbents were safe.

TABLE 9–2: Midterm Gains and Losses by the Party of the President, 1946–2010

Seats Gained or Lost by the Party of the President in the House of Representatives		
Year	President's Party	Outcome
1946	D.	−55
1950	D.	−29
1954	R.	−18
1958	R.	−47
1962	D.	−4
1966	D.	−47
1970	R.	−12
1974	R.	−48
1978	D.	−15
1982	R.	−26
1986	R.	−5
1990	R.	−8
1994	D.	−52
1998	D.	+5
2002	R.	+5
2006	R.	−30
2010	D.	−63

Apportionment of the House

Two of the more complicated aspects of congressional elections are apportionment issues—**reapportionment** (the allocation of seats in the House to each state after a census) and **redistricting** (the redrawing of the boundaries of the districts within each state). In a landmark six-to-two vote in 1962, the United States Supreme Court made the redistricting of state legislative seats a *justiciable* (that is, a reviewable) *question*.[3] The Court did so by invoking the Fourteenth Amendment principle that no state can deny to any person "the equal protection of the laws." In 1964, the Court held that both chambers of a state legislature must be designed so that all districts are equal in population.[4] Later that year, the Court applied this "one person, one vote" principle to U.S. congressional districts on

Reapportionment
The allocation of seats in the House of Representatives to each state after a census.

Redistricting
The redrawing of the boundaries of the congressional districts within each state.

---

3. *Baker v. Carr,* 369 U.S. 186 (1962). The term *justiciable* is pronounced juhs-*tish*-a-buhl.
4. *Reynolds v. Sims,* 377 U.S. 533 (1964).

TABLE 9–3: The Power of Incumbency

	Election Year													
	1986	1988	1990	1992	1994	1996	1998	2000	2002	2004	2006	2008	2010	2012
House														
Number of incumbent candidates	394	409	406	368	387	384	402	403	393	404	405	404	397	390
Reelected	385	402	390	325	349	361	395	394	383	397	382	381	338	351
Percentage of total	97.7	98.3	96.0	88.3	90.2	94.0	98.3	97.8	97.5	98.3	94.3	94.3	85.1	80.7
Defeated	9	7	16	43	38	23	7	9	10	7	23	23	59	39
In primary	3	1	1	19	4	2	1	3	3	1	2	5	4	14
In general election	6	6	15	24	34	21	6	6	7	6	21	18	55	25
Senate														
Number of incumbent candidates	28	27	32	28	26	21	29	29	28	26	29	30	24	23
Reelected	21	23	31	23	24	19	26	23	24	25	23	26	20	21
Percentage of total	75.0	85.2	96.9	82.1	92.3	90.5	89.7	79.3	85.7	96.2	79.3	86.7	83.3	91.3
Defeated	7	4	1	5	2	2	3	6	4	1	6	4	4	2
In primary	0	0	0	1	0	1	0	0	1	0	1*	0	3*	1
In general election	7	4	1	4	2	1	3	6	3	1	6	3	2	1

*In 2006, Joe Lieberman of Connecticut lost the Democratic primary but won the general election as an independent. He then caucused with the Democrats. In 2010, Alaska's Lisa Murkowski lost the Republican primary but won the general election as a write-in candidate. She continued to caucus with the Republicans.

Sources: Norman Ornstein, Thomas E. Mann, and Michael J. Malbin, *Vital Statistics on Congress, 2008* (Washington, D.C.: The Brookings Institution Press; Rev. edition, 2008); and authors' updates.

the basis of Article I, Section 2, of the Constitution, which requires that members of the House be chosen "by the People of the several States."[5]

As a result of severe malapportionment of congressional districts before 1964, some districts contained two or three times the population of other districts in the same state, thereby diluting the effect of a vote cast in the more populous districts. This system generally benefited the conservative residents of rural areas and small towns and harmed the interests of the more heavily populated and liberal cities.

Gerrymandering

Gerrymandering
The drawing of legislative district boundary lines for the purpose of obtaining partisan advantage. A district is said to be gerrymandered when its shape is altered substantially to determine which party will win it.

Although the general issue of apportionment has been dealt with fairly successfully by the one person, one vote principle, the **gerrymandering** issue has not yet been resolved. This term refers to the tactics that were used under Elbridge Gerry, the governor of Massachusetts, in the 1812 elections to draw legislative boundaries (see Figure 9–1 on the facing page). A district is said to have been gerrymandered when its shape is altered substantially to determine which party will win it.

In 1986, the Supreme Court heard a case that challenged gerrymandered congressional districts in Indiana. The Court ruled for the first time that redistricting for the political benefit of one group could be challenged on constitutional grounds. In this specific case, *Davis v. Bandemer,*[6] however, the Court did not agree that the districts had been drawn

---

5. *Wesberry v. Sanders,* 376 U.S. 1 (1964).
6. 478 U.S. 109 (1986).

FIGURE 9–1: The Original Gerrymander

The practice of gerrymandering—manipulating the shape of a legislative district to benefit a certain incumbent or party—is probably as old as the republic, but the name originated in 1812. In that year, the Massachusetts legislature carved out a misshapen district in Essex County. The resulting cartoon likening the district to a mythical salamander was probably drawn by Elkanah Tisdale, a Boston painter and engraver. Editor Nathan Hale is widely credited with naming the creature a "gerrymander" (after Elbridge Gerry, then governor of Massachusetts).

Source: Boston *Centinel*, 1812.

unfairly, because it could not be proved that a group of voters would consistently be deprived of influence at the polls as a result of the new districts.

How Gerrymandering Works. Congressional and state legislative redistricting decisions are often made by a small group of political leaders within a state legislature. Typically, their goal is to shape voting districts in such a way as to maximize their party's chances of winning state legislative seats, as well as seats in Congress. Two of the techniques in use are called *packing* and *cracking*. By employing powerful computers and software, voters supporting the opposing party are "packed" into as few districts as possible or the opposing party's supporters are "cracked" into different districts.

Figure 9–2 on the following page illustrates the redistricting process. In these three examples, sixty-four individuals must be distributed among four districts, each of which has a population of sixteen. Two political parties are involved: the O Party and the X Party.

In Example 1, supporters of the two parties are sorted so that each district contains only one kind of voter. Such a pattern sometimes appears when the members of a state legislature are most interested in preserving the seats of incumbents, regardless of party. In this example, it would be almost impossible to dislodge a sitting member in a general election. Example 2 is the reverse case. Every district is divided evenly between the parties, and even a very slight swing toward one of the parties could give that party all four seats.

Example 3 is a classic partisan gerrymander benefiting the X Party. The district in the lower right is an example of packing—the maximum possible number of supporters of the O Party are packed into that district. The other three districts are examples of cracking. The O Party supporters are cracked so that they do not have a majority in any of the three districts. In these districts, the X Party has majorities of eleven to five, ten to six, and eleven to five.

FIGURE 9–2: Examples of Districting

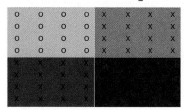 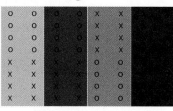 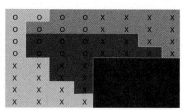

Example 1. A bipartisan gerrymander, aimed at protecting incumbents in both the O Party and the X Party.

Example 2. An unstable system. All districts have the same number of supporters in each party.

Example 3. A classic partisan gerrymander. The X Party is almost guaranteed to carry three districts.

Redistricting after the 2012 Census. As we have observed repeatedly, 2010 was a very good year for the Republican Party—and 2010 was also a census year. Republicans, therefore, controlled an unusually large number of the state legislatures responsible for redistricting. As you might expect, gerrymandering in 2012 favored the Republicans. Consider Pennsylvania. In 2012, Democratic candidates for the U.S. House of Representatives in that state received a total of 2.72 million votes. Republican candidates did slightly less well with 2.65 million votes. With these votes, Pennsylvania elected five Democrats and thirteen Republicans. True, some states, such as Illinois, were gerrymandered for the Democrats. Nationally, however, the Republicans retained control of the U.S. House after the 2012 elections, even though they received fewer votes overall than the Democrats. Such a result is unusual.

"Minority-Majority" Districts

Under the mandate of the Voting Rights Act of 1965, the Justice Department issued directives to states after the 1990 census instructing them to create congressional districts that would maximize the voting power of minority groups—that is, create districts in which minority group voters were the majority. The result was a number of creatively drawn congressional districts—see, for example, the depiction of Illinois's Fourth Congressional District in Figure 9–3 on the facing page, which is commonly described as "a pair of earmuffs."

Many of these "minority-majority" districts were challenged in court by citizens who claimed that creating districts based on race or ethnicity alone violates the equal protection clause of the Constitution. In 2001, for example, the Supreme Court reviewed, for a second time, a case involving North Carolina's Twelfth District. The district was 165 miles long, following Interstate 85 for the most part. According to a local joke, the district was so narrow that a car traveling down the interstate highway with both doors open would kill most of the voters in the district. In 1996, the Supreme Court had held that the district was unconstitutional because race had been the dominant factor in drawing the district's boundaries. Shortly thereafter, the boundaries were redrawn, but the district was again challenged as a racial gerrymander. In 2001, however, the Supreme Court held that there was insufficient evidence that race had been the dominant factor when the boundaries were redrawn.[7] The Twelfth District's boundaries remained in place.

7. *Easley v. Cromartie,* 532 U.S. 234 (2001).

FIGURE 9–3: The Fourth Congressional District of Illinois

This district, which is mostly within Chicago's city limits, was drawn to connect two Hispanic neighborhoods separated by an African American majority district.

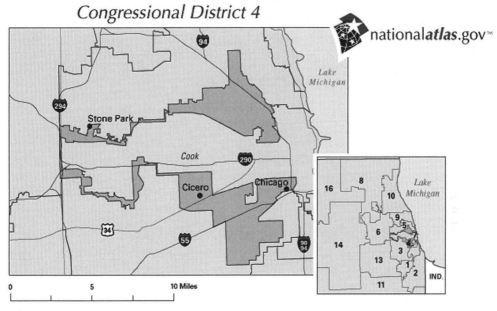

Source: *National Atlas of the United States,* U.S. Department of the Interior.

HOW CONGRESS IS ORGANIZED

The limited amount of centralized power that exists in Congress is exercised through party-based mechanisms. Congress is organized by party. When the Democratic Party, for example, wins a majority of seats in either the House or the Senate, Democrats control the official positions of power in that chamber, and every important committee has a Democratic chairperson and a majority of Democratic members. The same process holds when Republicans are in the majority.

In each chamber of Congress, members of the two major political parties elect leaders to coordinate party action and to negotiate with the other chamber and with the president. Still, much of the actual work of legislating is performed by the committees and subcommittees within Congress. Thousands of bills are introduced in every session of Congress, and no single member can possibly be adequately informed on all the issues that arise. The committee system is a way to provide for specialization, or a division of the legislative labor. Members of a committee can concentrate on just one area or topic—such as taxation or energy—and develop sufficient expertise to draft appropriate legislation when needed. The flow of legislation through both the House and the Senate is determined largely by the speed with which the members of these committees act on bills and resolutions.

LO4: Describe the committee structure of the House and the Senate, and specify the key leadership positions in each chamber.

Discharge Petition
A procedure by which a bill in the House of Representatives may be forced (discharged) out of a committee that has refused to report it for consideration by the House.

Standing Committee
A permanent committee in the House or Senate that considers bills within a certain subject area.

The Power of Committees

Sometimes called "little legislatures," committees usually have the final say on pieces of legislation.[8] Committee actions may be overturned on the floor by the House or Senate, but this rarely happens. Legislators normally defer to the expertise of the chairperson and other members of the committee who speak on the floor in defense of a committee decision. Chairpersons of committees exercise control over the scheduling of hearings and formal actions on bills. They also decide which subcommittee will act on legislation falling within their committee's jurisdiction. Committees normally have the power to kill proposed legislation by refusing to act on it—that is, by never sending it to the entire chamber for a vote.

Committees only very rarely are deprived of control over bills—although this kind of action is provided for in the rules of each chamber. In the House, if a bill has been considered by a standing committee for thirty days, the signatures of a majority (218) of the House membership on a **discharge petition** can pry a bill out of an uncooperative committee's hands. From 1909 to 2012, however, although over nine hundred such petitions were initiated, only slightly more than two dozen resulted in successful discharge efforts. Of those, twenty resulted in bills that passed the House.[9]

Types of Congressional Committees

Over the past two centuries, Congress has created several types of committees, each of which serves particular needs of the institution.

Standing Committees. By far, the most important committees in Congress are the **standing committees**—permanent bodies that are established by the rules of each chamber and that continue from session to session. A list of the standing committees of the 113th Congress is presented in Table 9–4 on the facing page. In addition, most of the standing committees have created subcommittees to carry out their work. For example, the 113th Congress has 73 subcommittees in the Senate and 104 in the House. Each standing committee is given a specific area of legislative policy jurisdiction, and almost all legislative measures are considered by the appropriate standing committees.

Because of the importance of their work and the traditional influence of their members in Congress, certain committees are considered to be more prestigious than others. Seats on standing committees that handle spending

In 2013, President Obama named Chuck Hagel to be Secretary of Defense. Even though Hagel was a former Republican senator from Nebraska, he received an intense grilling from the Senate Armed Services Committee. He was eventually confirmed, but forty-one Republicans voted against him. What kinds of questions might senators have asked him? (Department of Defense)

8. The term *little legislatures* is from Woodrow Wilson, *Congressional Government* (New York: Meridian Books, 1956 [first published in 1885]).
9. *Congressional Quarterly's Guide to Congress,* 6th ed. (Washington, D.C.: Congressional Quarterly Press, 2007); and authors' update.

TABLE 9–4: Standing Committees of the 113th Congress, 2013–2015

House Committees	Senate Committees
Agriculture	Agriculture, Nutrition, and Forestry
Appropriations	Appropriations
Armed Services	Armed Services
Budget	Banking, Housing, and Urban Affairs
Education and the Workforce	Budget
Energy and Commerce	Commerce, Science, and Transportation
Financial Services	Energy and Natural Resources
Foreign Affairs	Environment and Public Works
Homeland Security	Finance
House Administration	Foreign Relations
Judiciary	Health, Education, Labor, and Pensions
Natural Resources	Homeland Security and Governmental Affairs
Oversight and Government Reform	Judiciary
Rules	Rules and Administration
Science and Technology	Small Business and Entrepreneurship
Small Business	Veterans' Affairs
Standards of Official Conduct	
Transportation and Infrastructure	
Veterans' Affairs	
Ways and Means	

issues are especially sought after because members can use these positions to benefit their constituents. Committees that control spending include the Appropriations Committee in either chamber and the Ways and Means Committee in the House. Members also normally seek seats on committees that handle matters of special interest to their constituents. A member of the House from an agricultural district, for example, will have an interest in joining the House Agriculture Committee.

Select Committees. In principle, a **select committee** is created for a limited time and for a specific legislative purpose. For example, a select committee may be formed to investigate a public problem, such as child nutrition or aging. In practice, a select committee, such as the Select Committee on Intelligence in each chamber, may continue indefinitely. Select committees rarely create original legislation.

Joint Committees. A **joint committee** is formed by the concurrent action of both chambers of Congress and consists of members from each chamber. Joint committees, which may be permanent or temporary, have dealt with the economy, taxation, and the Library of Congress.

Conference Committees. Special joint committees—**conference committees**—are formed for the purpose of achieving agreement between the House and the Senate on the exact wording of legislative acts when the two chambers pass legislative proposals in different forms. No bill can be sent to the White House to be signed into law unless it first

Select Committee
A temporary legislative committee established for a limited time period and for a special purpose.

Joint Committee
A legislative committee composed of members from both chambers of Congress.

Conference Committee
A special joint committee appointed to reconcile differences when bills pass the two chambers of Congress in different forms.

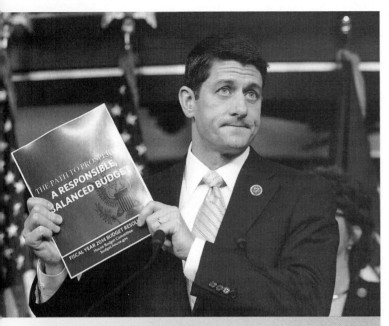

Representative Paul Ryan (R., Wisconsin) chairs the House Budget Committee. He holds in his hands a program to cut federal government spending. Why does his position as chair give Ryan significant powers? (Win McNamee/Getty Images)

passes both chambers in identical form. Conference committees are in a position to make significant alterations to legislation and frequently become the focal point of policy debates.

The House Rules Committee. Due to its special "gatekeeping" power over the terms on which legislation will reach the floor of the House of Representatives, the House Rules Committee holds a uniquely powerful position. A special committee rule sets the time limit on debate and determines whether and how a bill may be amended. The Rules Committee has the unusual power to convene while the House is meeting as a whole, to have its resolutions considered immediately on the floor, and to initiate legislation on its own.

The Selection of Committee Members

In both chambers, members are appointed to standing committees by the steering committee of their party. The majority-party member with the longest term of continuous service on a standing committee is given preference when the committee selects its chairperson. The most senior member of the minority party is called the *ranking committee member* for that party. This **seniority system** is not required by law but is an informal, traditional process, and it applies to other significant posts in Congress as well. The system, although it deliberately treats members unequally, provides a predictable means of assigning positions of power within Congress.

The general pattern until the 1970s was that members of the House or Senate who represented safe seats would be reelected continually and eventually could accumulate enough years of continuous committee service to enable them to become the chairpersons of their committees. In the 1970s, reforms in the chairperson selection process somewhat modified the seniority system in the House. The reforms introduced the use of a secret ballot in electing House committee chairpersons and allowed for the possibility of choosing a chairperson on a basis other than seniority. The Democrats immediately replaced three senior chairpersons who were out of step with the rest of their party. In 1995, under Speaker Newt Gingrich, the Republicans chose relatively junior House members as chairpersons of several key committees, thus ensuring conservative control of the committees. The Republicans also passed a rule limiting the term of a chairperson to six years.

Leadership in the House

The House leadership is made up of the Speaker, the majority and minority leaders, and the party whips.

Seniority System
A custom followed in both chambers of Congress specifying that the member of the majority party with the longest term of continuous service will be given preference when a committee chairperson (or a holder of some other significant post) is selected.

The Speaker. The foremost power holder in the House of Representatives is the **Speaker of the House.** The Speaker's position is technically a nonpartisan one, but in fact, for the better part of two centuries, the Speaker has been the official leader of the majority party in the House. When a new Congress convenes in January of odd-numbered years, each party nominates a candidate for Speaker. All Republican members of the House are expected to vote for their party's nominee, and all Democrats are expected to support their candidate. The vote to organize the House is the one vote in which representatives *must* vote with their party. In a sense, this vote defines a member's partisan status.

The major formal powers of the Speaker include the following:

- Presiding over meetings of the House.
- Appointing members of joint committees and conference committees.
- Scheduling legislation for floor action.
- Deciding points of order and interpreting the rules with the advice of the House parliamentarian.
- Referring bills and resolutions to the appropriate standing committees of the House.

A Speaker may take part in floor debate and vote, as can any other member of Congress, but recent Speakers usually have voted only to break a tie.

The Majority Leader. The **majority leader of the House** is elected by a caucus of the majority party to foster cohesion among party members and to act as a spokesperson for the party. The majority leader influences the scheduling of debate and acts as the chief supporter of the Speaker. The majority leader cooperates with the Speaker and other party leaders, both inside and outside Congress, to formulate the party's legislative program and to guide that program through the legislative process in the House. The parties have often recruited future Speakers from those who hold the position of majority leader.

The Minority Leader. The **minority leader of the House** is the candidate nominated for Speaker by a caucus of the minority party. Like the majority leader, the leader of the minority party has as her or his primary responsibility the maintaining of cohesion within the party's ranks. The minority leader works for cooperation among the party's members and speaks on behalf of the president if the minority party controls the White House. In

Speaker of the House
The presiding officer in the House of Representatives. The Speaker is chosen by the majority party and is the most powerful and influential member of the House.

Majority Leader of the House
Elected by members of the majority party to foster cohesion and to act as a spokesperson for the majority party.

Minority Leader of the House
The party leader elected by members of the minority party in the House.

Former House minority leader

John Boehner (R., Ohio) became Speaker of the House in January 2011 after the Republicans won control of the House in the 2010 elections. The former Speaker, Nancy Pelosi (D., Calif.), had to step down. She then became the minority leader. Does the Speaker normally participate in floor debate? (Photos Courtesy of the U.S. Congress)

After the Democrats took control of the U.S. Senate in the 2006 elections, Republican senator Mitch McConnell of Kentucky, right, was elected Senate minority leader. Democratic senator Harry Reid of Nevada, left, became the Senate majority leader. Both were reelected to their leadership positions after the 2012 elections. It is very rare for a congressional leader to become president. How might a congressional leadership position interfere with presidential aspirations? (Photos Courtesy of Senator Reid and Senator McConnell)

relations with the majority party, the minority leader consults with both the Speaker and the majority leader on recognizing members who wish to speak on the floor, on House rules and procedures, and on the scheduling of legislation. Minority leaders have no actual power in these areas, however.

Whips. The leadership of each party includes assistants to the majority and minority leaders known as **whips.**[10] The whips are members of Congress who assist the party leaders by passing information down from the leadership to party members and by ensuring that members show up for floor debate and cast their votes on important issues. Whips conduct polls among party members about the members' views on legislation, inform the leaders about whose vote is doubtful and whose is certain, and may exert pressure on members to support the leaders' positions.

Leadership in the Senate

The Senate is less than one-fourth the size of the House. This fact alone probably explains why a formal, complex, and centralized leadership structure is not as necessary in the Senate as it is in the House.

Whip
A member of Congress who aids the majority or minority leader of the House or the Senate.

President Pro Tempore
The senator who presides over the Senate in the absence of the vice president.

The two highest-ranking formal leadership positions in the Senate are essentially ceremonial in nature. Under the Constitution, the vice president of the United States is the president (that is, the presiding officer) of the Senate and may vote to break a tie. The vice president, however, is only rarely present for a meeting of the Senate. The Senate elects instead a **president pro tempore** ("pro tem") to preside over the Senate in the vice president's absence. Ordinarily, the president pro tem is the member of the majority party with the longest continuous term of service in the Senate. As mentioned, the president pro tem is mostly a ceremonial position. More junior senators take turns actually presiding over the sessions of the Senate.

---

10. *Whip* comes from "whipper-in," a fox-hunting term for someone who keeps the hunting dogs from straying.

The real leadership power in the Senate rests in the hands of the **Senate majority leader,** the **Senate minority leader,** and their respective whips. The Senate majority and minority leaders have the right to be recognized first in debate on the floor and generally exercise the same powers available to the House majority and minority leaders. They control the scheduling of debate on the floor in conjunction with the majority party's policy committee, influence the allocation of committee assignments for new members or for senators attempting to transfer to a new committee, influence the selection of other party officials, and participate in selecting members of conference committees. The leaders are expected to mobilize support for partisan legislative or presidential initiatives. They act as liaisons with the White House when the president is of their party, try to obtain the cooperation of committee chairpersons, and seek to facilitate the smooth functioning of the Senate through the senators' unanimous consent to various procedural motions. The majority and minority leaders are elected by their respective party caucuses.

Senate party whips, like their House counterparts, maintain communication within the party on platform positions and try to ensure that party colleagues are present for floor debate and important votes. The Senate whip system is far less elaborate than its counterpart in the House, because there are fewer members to track and senators have a greater tradition of independence.

Senate Majority Leader
The chief spokesperson of the majority party in the Senate, who directs the legislative program and party strategy.

Senate Minority Leader
The party officer in the Senate who commands the minority party's opposition to the policies of the majority party and directs the legislative program and strategy of his or her party.

Executive Budget
The budget prepared and submitted by the president to Congress.

LAWMAKING AND BUDGETING

Each year, Congress and the president propose and approve many laws. Some are budget and appropriation laws that require extensive bargaining but must be passed for the government to continue to function. Other laws are relatively free of controversy and are passed with little dissension. Still other proposed legislation is extremely controversial and reaches to the roots of differences between Republicans and Democrats.

Figure 9–4 on the following page shows that each law begins as a bill, which must be introduced in either the House or the Senate. Often, similar bills are introduced in both chambers. A "budget bill," however, must start in the House. In each chamber, the bill follows similar steps. It is referred to a committee and its subcommittees for study, discussion, hearings, and markup (rewriting). When the bill is reported out to the full chamber, it must be scheduled for debate (by the Rules Committee in the House and by the leadership in the Senate). After the bill has been passed in each chamber, if it contains different provisions, a conference committee is formed to write a compromise bill, which must be approved by both chambers before it is sent to the president to sign or veto.

LO5: Discuss the process by which a bill becomes law and how the federal government establishes its budget.

How Much Will the Government Spend?

The Constitution is very clear about where the power of the purse lies in the national government: all taxing or spending bills must originate in the House of Representatives. Today, much of the business of Congress is concerned with approving government expenditures through the budget process and with raising the revenues to pay for government programs.

From 1922, when Congress required the president to prepare and present to the legislature an **executive budget,** until 1974, the congressional budget process was so disjointed that it was difficult to visualize the total picture of government finances. The president presented the executive budget to Congress in January. It was broken down into thirteen or more appropriations bills. Some time later, after all of the bills had been debated, amended, and passed, it was more or less possible to estimate total government spending for the next year.

FIGURE 9–4: How a Bill Becomes Law

This illustration shows the most typical way in which proposed legislation is enacted into law. Most legislation begins as similar bills introduced into the House and the Senate. The process is illustrated here with two hypothetical bills, House Bill No. 100 (HR 100) and Senate Bill No. 200 (S 200). The path of HR 100 is shown on the left, and that of S 200, on the right.

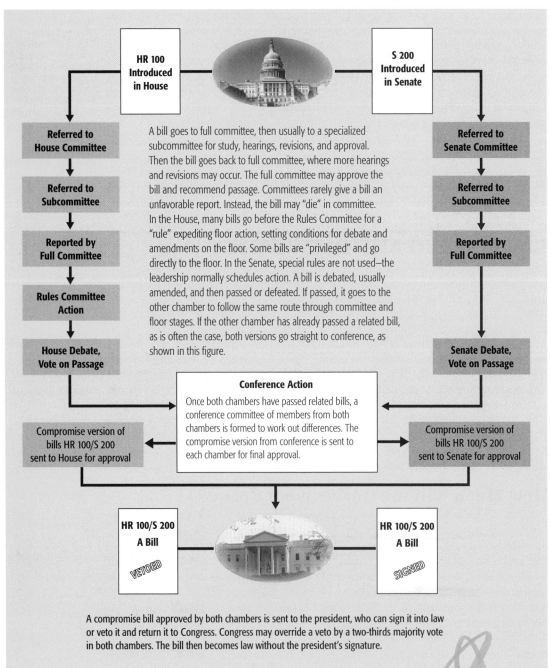

HR 100 Introduced in House

S 200 Introduced in Senate

Referred to House Committee

Referred to Subcommittee

Reported by Full Committee

Rules Committee Action

House Debate, Vote on Passage

Referred to Senate Committee

Referred to Subcommittee

Reported by Full Committee

Senate Debate, Vote on Passage

A bill goes to full committee, then usually to a specialized subcommittee for study, hearings, revisions, and approval. Then the bill goes back to full committee, where more hearings and revisions may occur. The full committee may approve the bill and recommend passage. Committees rarely give a bill an unfavorable report. Instead, the bill may "die" in committee. In the House, many bills go before the Rules Committee for a "rule" expediting floor action, setting conditions for debate and amendments on the floor. Some bills are "privileged" and go directly to the floor. In the Senate, special rules are not used—the leadership normally schedules action. A bill is debated, usually amended, and then passed or defeated. If passed, it goes to the other chamber to follow the same route through committee and floor stages. If the other chamber has already passed a related bill, as is often the case, both versions go straight to conference, as shown in this figure.

Conference Action

Once both chambers have passed related bills, a conference committee of members from both chambers is formed to work out differences. The compromise version from conference is sent to each chamber for final approval.

Compromise version of bills HR 100/S 200 sent to House for approval

Compromise version of bills HR 100/S 200 sent to Senate for approval

HR 100/S 200 A Bill VETOED

HR 100/S 200 A Bill SIGNED

A compromise bill approved by both chambers is sent to the president, who can sign it into law or veto it and return it to Congress. Congress may override a veto by a two-thirds majority vote in both chambers. The bill then becomes law without the president's signature.

Frustrated by the president's ability to impound, or withhold, funds and dissatisfied with the entire budget process, Congress passed the Budget and Impoundment Control Act of 1974 to regain some control over the nation's spending. The act required the president to spend the funds that Congress had appropriated, ending the president's ability to kill programs by withholding funds. The other major result of the act was to force Congress to examine total national taxing and spending at least twice in each budget cycle. (See Figure 9–5 below for a graphic illustration of the budget cycle.)

Preparing the Budget

The federal government operates on a **fiscal year (FY)** cycle. The fiscal year runs from October through September, so that fiscal 2015, or FY15, runs from October 1, 2014, through September 30, 2015. Eighteen months before a fiscal year starts, the executive branch begins preparing the budget. The Office of Management and Budget (OMB) receives advice from the Council of Economic Advisers and the Treasury Department. The OMB outlines the budget and then sends it to the various departments and agencies. Bargaining follows, in which—to use only two of many examples—the Department of Health and Human Services argues for more antipoverty spending, and the armed forces argue for more defense spending.

The OMB Reviews the Budget. Even though the OMB has fewer than 550 employees, it is one of the most powerful agencies in Washington. It assembles the budget documents and monitors federal agencies throughout each year. Every year, it begins the budget process with a **spring review,** in which it requires all of the agencies to review their programs, activities, and goals. At the beginning of each summer, the OMB sends out a letter instructing agencies to submit their requests for funding for the next fiscal year. By the end of the summer, each agency must submit a formal request to the OMB.

In actuality, the "budget season" begins with the **fall review.** At this time, the OMB looks at budget requests and, in almost all cases, routinely cuts them back. Although the

Fiscal Year (FY)
A twelve-month period that is used for bookkeeping, or accounting, purposes. Usually, the fiscal year does not coincide with the calendar year. For example, the federal government's fiscal year runs from October 1 through September 30.

Spring Review
The annual process in which the Office of Management and Budget (OMB) requires federal agencies to review their programs, activities, and goals, and submit their requests for funding for the next fiscal year.

Fall Review
The annual process in which the OMB, after receiving formal federal agency requests for funding for the next fiscal year, reviews the requests, makes changes, and submits its recommendations to the president.

FIGURE 9–5: The Budget Cycle

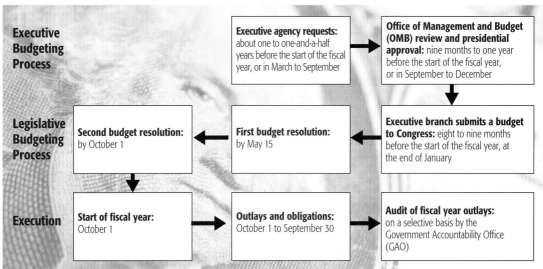

Executive Budgeting Process		**Executive agency requests:** about one to one-and-a-half years before the start of the fiscal year, or in March to September	**Office of Management and Budget (OMB) review and presidential approval:** nine months to one year before the start of the fiscal year, or in September to December
Legislative Budgeting Process	**Second budget resolution:** by October 1	**First budget resolution:** by May 15	**Executive branch submits a budget to Congress:** eight to nine months before the start of the fiscal year, at the end of January
Execution	**Start of fiscal year:** October 1	**Outlays and obligations:** October 1 to September 30	**Audit of fiscal year outlays:** on a selective basis by the Government Accountability Office (GAO)

Authorization
A formal declaration by a legislative committee that a certain amount of funding may be available to an agency. Some authorizations terminate in a year; others are renewable automatically without further congressional action.

Appropriation
The passage, by Congress, of a spending bill specifying the amount of authorized funds that actually will be allocated for an agency's use.

First Budget Resolution
A resolution passed by Congress in May that sets overall revenue goals and spending targets for the following fiscal year.

Second Budget Resolution
A resolution passed by Congress in September that sets binding limits on taxes and spending for the following fiscal year.

OMB works within guidelines established by the president, specific decisions often are left to the OMB director and the director's associates. By the beginning of November, the director's review begins. The director meets with cabinet secretaries and budget officers. Time becomes crucial. The budget must be completed by January so that it can be included in the *Economic Report of the President.*

The Election-Year Budget. The schedule just described cannot apply to a year in which the voters elect a new president or to a year in which a new president is inaugurated. In 2008, George W. Bush did not engage in a fall review of the FY 2010 budget, because he would no longer be in office when the budget went into effect in October 2009. Barack Obama could hardly have undertaken the fall review either, given that he was still campaigning for the presidency. Following the election of a new president, the budget process is compressed into the first months of the new administration.

Congress Faces the Budget

In January, nine months before the fiscal year starts, the president takes the OMB's proposed budget, approves it, and submits it to Congress. Then the congressional budgeting process takes over. The budgeting process involves two steps: authorization and appropriation.

The Authorization Process. First, Congress must authorize funds to be spent. The **authorization** is a formal declaration by the appropriate congressional committee that a certain amount of funding may be available to an agency. Congressional committees and subcommittees look at the proposals from the executive branch and the Congressional Budget Office in making the decision to authorize funds.

The Appropriation Process. After the funds have been authorized, they must be appropriated by Congress. The appropriations committees of both the House and the Senate forward spending bills to their respective bodies. The **appropriation** of funds occurs when the final bill is passed. In this process, large sums are in play. Representatives and senators, especially those who chair key committees, have traditionally found it easy to slip earmarks, or pork, into a variety of bills. These proposals may have nothing to do with the explicitly stated purpose of the bill.

Evading the Ban on Earmarks. In March 2010, the Republican-controlled House implemented rules designed to eliminate earmarks. The new rules have substantially reduced the amount of pork inserted into appropriations bills, but lawmakers have been creative in attempting to circumvent the ban. In some instances, legislators have simply denied that a particular funding request is actually an earmark. More commonly, members have lobbied the various executive agencies to include projects that benefit their districts. According to the OMB definition, spending requested by executive agencies is not pork. Further, the White House itself frequently inserts special requests into the executive budget, thus making the president the biggest "porkmeister" of all.

Budget Resolutions and Crises

The **first budget resolution** by Congress is due in May. It sets overall revenue goals and spending targets. Spending and tax laws that are drawn up over the summer are supposed to be guided by the first budget resolution. By September, Congress is scheduled to pass its **second budget resolution,** one that will set binding limits on taxes and spending for the fiscal year beginning October 1.

The Continuing Resolution. In actuality, Congress has finished the budget on time in only three years since 1977. The budget is usually broken into a series of appropriations bills. If Congress has not passed one of these bills by October 1, it normally passes a **continuing resolution** that allows the affected agencies to keep on doing whatever they were doing the previous year with the same amount of funding. By the 1980s, continuing resolutions had ballooned into massive measures.

Budget delays reached a climax in 1995 and 1996, when, in a spending dispute with Democratic president Bill Clinton, the Republican Congress refused to pass any continuing resolutions. As a result, some nonessential functions of the federal government were shut down for twenty-seven days. Since then, Congress has generally managed to limit continuing resolutions to their original purpose. This forbearance remained in effect even during the successive budget crises that began in 2011.

The Federal Debt Ceiling. After gaining control of the U.S. House in 2011, Republicans sought to use their control of the House to force cuts in federal spending. The result was a series of confrontations between the Republican House and the Democratic president and Senate. The most serious of these was the debt ceiling crisis of mid-2011.

If the federal government runs a budget deficit—if it spends more than it takes in—it must issue new debt. The government has, in fact, run a deficit in most recent years. (The exception was the four fiscal years from 1998 to 2001, when the budget had a surplus.) Under current law, the national government is limited in the amount of debt it can issue, and if the federal debt approaches the legal ceiling, Congress must raise the limit to allow additional debt.

Raising the debt ceiling is entirely independent of the tax and spending decisions reached by Congress—the ceiling must be raised to allow the government to fund activities that are already established by law. Many people mistakenly believe that raising the ceiling is a prerequisite for new, future spending, but that is not the case. If the debt ceiling is not raised as needed, the government might be forced to default on its existing obligations.

Traditionally, members of Congress often "grandstanded" by voting against the debt ceiling hike, even though passage was never in doubt. In 2011, however, House Republicans, for the first time, sought to use the ceiling as a tool to force Democrats to accept spending cuts. At the last minute, House Republicans and the Democrats under President Obama reached a deal: if Congress could not agree on a spending-cut plan, a series of across-the-board cuts known as the *sequester* would go into effect on January 1, 2013. Social Security, Medicare benefits, and Medicaid would be exempt from cuts, half of which would come from the defense budget. Congress then failed to agree on an alternative plan.

The Fiscal Cliff and the Sequester. Tax rate cuts adopted in 2003 under the George W. Bush administration were set to expire on January 1, 2013, at the same time that the sequester was to go into effect. Other tax increases and spending cuts were scheduled for January 1 as well. This series of deadlines, known as the *fiscal cliff*, put the Republicans at a disadvantage. If Congress did nothing, the nation would experience large tax increases, something the Republicans were sworn to oppose. In the end, Republicans agreed to a tax rate hike on persons with incomes of more than $400,000 per year in exchange for no increases for other taxpayers. The sequester was put off until March 1.

By March, most Republicans had concluded that large cuts to defense spending would not be the disaster that they initially feared, and the sequester went into effect on schedule. The budget conflicts were not over, however. House Speaker John Boehner promised a confrontation over the next debt ceiling increase, scheduled for mid-2013.

Continuing Resolution
A temporary funding law that Congress passes when an appropriations bill has not been passed by the beginning of the new fiscal year on October 1.

making a difference

LEARNING ABOUT YOUR REPRESENTATIVES

Do you know the names of your senators and your representative in Congress? A surprising number of Americans do not. Even if you know the names and parties of your elected delegates, there is still much more you could learn about them that would be useful.

Why Should You Care?
The legislation that Congress passes can directly affect your life. Consider, for example, the Patient Protection and Affordable Care Act, commonly known as Obamacare. In recent years, many Americans have had mixed reactions to the new law, largely because it does not go into effect fully until January 1, 2014. By that time, however, you may have to make some decisions. Say that you no longer receive health insurance through your parents, do not receive it through employment, and are not eligible for Medicaid. You may then need to buy an insurance plan through a state insurance exchange—or pay a penalty on your income taxes.

You can make a difference in our democracy simply by going to the polls on Election Day and voting for the candidates you would like to represent you in Congress. It goes without saying, though, that to cast an informed vote, you need to know how your congressional representatives stand on the issues and, if they are incumbents, how they have voted on bills that are important to you.

What Can You Do?
To contact a member of Congress, start by going to the Web sites of the U.S. House of Representatives (search on "ushouse") and the U.S. Senate ("senate").

Although you can communicate easily with your representatives by e-mail, using e-mail has some drawbacks. Representatives and senators are now receiving large volumes of e-mail from constituents, which they rarely read themselves. They have staff members who read and respond to e-mail instead. Many interest groups argue that U.S. mail, or even express mail or a phone call, is more likely

to capture the attention of a representative than e-mail. You can contact your representatives and senators by using one of the following addresses or phone numbers:

United States House of Representatives
Washington, DC 20515
202-224-3121

United States Senate
Washington, DC 20510
202-224-3121

Performance Evaluations
Interest groups also track the voting records of members of Congress and rate the members on the issues. Project Vote Smart tracks the performance of thousands of political leaders, including their campaign finances, issue positions, and voting records. You can locate the Web site of Project Vote Smart by entering "votesmart" into a search engine.

In addition, if you want to know how your representatives funded their campaigns, try the Center for Responsive Politics (CRP), a research group that tracks money in politics, campaign fund-raising, and similar issues. You can see the CRP site by typing in "opensecrets."

OpenSecrets.org provides facts about how politicians obtain their campaign funds. (www.opensecrets.org)

key**terms**

agenda setting 199

appropriation 218

authorization 218

bicameralism 197

casework 199

conference
    committee 211

constituent 197

continuing
    resolution 219

discharge petition 210

earmarks 198

enumerated powers 200

executive budget 215

fall review 217

filibuster 201

first budget
    resolution 218

fiscal year (FY) 217

franking 202

gerrymandering 206

instructed delegate 198

joint committee 211

lawmaking 197

majority leader of the
    House 213

minority leader of the
    House 213

ombudsperson 199

oversight 199

president pro
    tempore 214

reapportionment 205

reconciliation 202

redistricting 205

representation 198

Rules Committee 201

second budget
    resolution 218

select committee 211

Senate majority
    leader 215

Senate minority
    leader 215

seniority system 212

Speaker of the
    House 213

spring review 217

standing committee 210

trustee 198

whip 214

chapter**summary**

1 The authors of the U.S. Constitution believed that the bulk of national power should be in the legislature. The Connecticut Compromise established a balanced legislature, with the membership in the House of Representatives based on population and the membership in the Senate based on the equality of states.

2 The functions of Congress include (a) lawmaking, (b) representation, (c) service to constituents, (d) oversight, (e) public education, and (f) conflict resolution.

3 The Constitution specifies the enumerated, or expressed, powers of Congress, including the rights to impose taxes, to borrow funds, to regulate commerce, and to declare war. In addition, Congress enjoys the right, under the elastic, or "necessary and proper," clause, "to make all Laws which shall be necessary and proper for carrying into Execution the foregoing Powers, and all other Powers vested by this Constitution in the Government of the United States, or in any Department or Officer thereof."

4 There are 435 members in the House of Representatives and 100 members in the Senate. Owing to its larger size, the House has a greater number of formal rules. The Senate tradition of unlimited debate dates back to 1790 and has been used over the years to frustrate the passage of bills.

5 Members of Congress are not typical American citizens. They are older and wealthier than most Americans, disproportionately white and male, and more likely to be lawyers.

6 Most candidates for Congress win nomination through a direct primary. Most incumbent representatives and senators who run for reelection are successful. Apportionment is the allocation of legislative seats to constituencies. The Supreme Court's "one person, one vote" rule means that the populations of congressional and state legislative districts must be effectively equal. Still, district boundaries are frequently drawn to benefit one or another of the parties through the process of gerrymandering.

7 Most of the work of legislating is performed by committees and subcommittees within Congress. Legislation introduced into the House or Senate is assigned to standing committees for review. Joint committees are formed by the action of both chambers and consist of members from each. Conference committees are joint committees set up to achieve agreement between the House and the Senate on the exact wording of legislative acts that were passed by the chambers in different forms. The seniority rule, which is usually followed, specifies that the longest-serving member of the majority party will be the chairperson of a committee.

8 The foremost power holder in the House of Representatives is the Speaker of the House. Other leaders are the House majority leader, the House minority leader, and the majority and minority whips. Formally, the vice president is the presiding officer of the Senate. Actual leadership in the Senate rests with the majority leader, the minority leader, and their whips.

9 A bill becomes law by progressing through both chambers of Congress and their appropriate standing and joint committees before submission to the president.

10 The budget process for a fiscal year begins with the preparation of an executive budget by the president. This is reviewed by the Office of Management and Budget and then sent to Congress, which is supposed to pass a final budget by the end of September. Since 1977, Congress generally has not followed its own time rules.

test**yourself**

LO1 *Describe the various roles played by Congress and the constitutional basis of its powers.*

The bicameralism of Congress means that:
    a. every district has two members.
    b. every state has two senators.
    c. Congress is divided into two legislative bodies.

LO2 *Explain some of the differences between the House and the Senate, and some of the privileges enjoyed by members of Congress.*

The central difference between the House and the Senate is that:
    a. the House is much larger than the Senate.
    b. the Senate is much larger than the House.
    c. the Senate meets only occasionally, but the House meets all of the time.

LO3 *Examine the implications of apportioning House seats.*

Congressional redistricting often involves gerrymandering, which means that the redistricting:
    a. results in an equal number of Democratic and Republican districts.
    b. results in strange-shaped districts designed to favor one party.
    c. results in districts that have almost no representation.

LO4 *Describe the committee structure of the House and the Senate, and specify the key leadership positions in each chamber.*

There are several types of committees in Congress. They include:
    a. standing committees, sitting committees, and joint committees.
    b. sitting committees, joint committees, and select committees.
    c. standing committees, select committees, and joint committees.

LO5 *Discuss the process by which a bill becomes law and how the federal government establishes its budget.*

When an appropriations bill has not been passed by the beginning of the new fiscal year, Congress may pass a temporary funding law called:
    a. a continuing resolution.
    b. a second budget resolution.
    c. a temporary authorization.

Essay Question:

The District of Columbia is not represented in the Senate and has a single, nonvoting delegate to the House. Should the District of Columbia be represented in Congress by voting legislators? Why or why not? If it should be represented, how? Would it make sense to admit it as a state? To give it back to Maryland? Explain your reasoning.

Answers to multiple-choice questions: 1. c, 2. a, 3. b, 4. c, 5. a.

CourseMate

Access CourseMate at www.cengagebrain.com for additional study tools: practice quizzes, key term flashcards and crossword puzzles, audio chapter summaries, simulations, animated learning modules, interactive timelines, videos, and American Government NewsWatch.

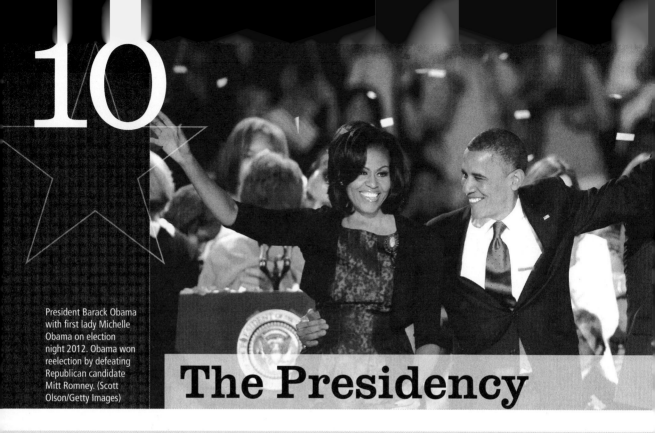

10

President Barack Obama with first lady Michelle Obama on election night 2012. Obama won reelection by defeating Republican candidate Mitt Romney. (Scott Olson/Getty Images)

The Presidency

LEARNING OUTCOMES

The five **Learning Outcomes (LOs)** below are designed to help improve your understanding of this chapter. After reading this chapter, you should be able to:

■ **LO1** Identify the types of people who typically undertake serious campaigns for the presidency.

■ **LO2** Distinguish some of the major roles of the president, including head of state, chief executive, commander in chief, chief diplomat, chief legislator, party chief, and politician.

■ **LO3** Describe some of the special powers of the president, and tell how a president can be removed from office.

■ **LO4** Explain the organization of the executive branch and, in particular, the executive office of the president.

■ **LO5** Evaluate the role of the vice president, and describe what happens if the presidency becomes vacant.

Check your understanding of the material with the Test Yourself section at the end of the chapter.

The writers of the Constitution had no models to follow when they created the presidency of the United States. Nowhere else in the world was there an elected head of state. What the founders did not want was a king. The two initial plans considered by the founders—the Virginia and New Jersey plans—both called for a relatively weak executive elected by Congress. Other delegates, especially those who had witnessed the need for a strong leader in the Revolutionary Army, believed a powerful executive would be necessary for the new republic. The delegates, after much debate, created a chief executive who had enough powers granted in the Constitution to balance those of Congress. In this chapter, after looking at who can become president and at the process involved, we examine closely the nature and extent of the constitutional powers held by the president.

WHO CAN BECOME PRESIDENT?

The president receives a salary of $400,000, plus $169,000 for expenses and a vast array of free services, beginning with residence in the White House. The requirements for becoming president, as outlined in Article II, Section 1, of the Constitution, are not overwhelmingly stringent:

> *No person except a natural born Citizen, or a Citizen of the United States, at the time of the Adoption of this Constitution, shall be eligible to the Office of President; neither shall any Person be eligible to that Office who shall not have attained to the Age of thirty-five Years, and been fourteen Years a Resident within the United States.*

LO1: Identify the types of people who typically undertake serious campaigns for the presidency.

A "Natural Born Citizen"

The only question that arises about these qualifications relates to the term *natural born Citizen*. Does that mean only citizens born in the United States and its territories? What about a child born to a U.S. citizen visiting or living in another country? Although the question has not been dealt with directly by the United States Supreme Court, it is reasonable to expect that someone would be eligible if her or his parents were Americans.

Birth Controversies. These questions were debated when George Romney, who was born in Chihuahua, Mexico, made a serious bid for the Republican presidential nomination in the 1960s.[1] The issue came up again when opponents of President Barack Obama claimed that Obama was not a natural born citizen. In reality, Obama was born in Honolulu, Hawaii, in 1961. Those who disputed Obama's birth claimed that the short-form birth certificate released by the Obama campaign was a forgery—even though Obama's birth was also recorded by two Honolulu newspapers. The White House later released Obama's long-form birth certificate, which was endorsed as valid by every relevant Hawaiian official, Republican and Democrat.

The Age of the President. Although the Constitution states that the minimum-age requirement for the presidency is thirty-five years, most presidents have been much older than that when they assumed office. John F. Kennedy, at the age of forty-three, was the youngest elected president, and the oldest was Ronald Reagan, at age sixty-nine. The average age at inauguration has been fifty-four. There has clearly been a demographic bias in the selection of presidents. All have been male, white, and from the Protestant tradition, except for John F. Kennedy, a Roman Catholic, and Barack Obama, an African American.

The Process of Becoming President

Major and minor political parties nominate candidates for president and vice president at national conventions every four years. The nation's voters do not elect a president and vice president directly but rather cast ballots for presidential electors, who then vote for president and vice president in the Electoral College.

In 1960, John F. Kennedy became the youngest person elected president of the United States. (AP Photo)

1. George Romney, father of Republican presidential candidate Mitt Romney, was governor of Michigan from 1963 to 1969. Romney was not nominated, and the issue remains unresolved.

Because victory goes to the candidate with a majority in the Electoral College, it is conceivable that someone could be elected to the office of the presidency without having a plurality of the popular vote cast. Indeed, on four occasions candidates won elections even though their major opponents received more popular votes. One of those elections occurred in 2000, when George W. Bush won the Electoral College vote and became president even though his opponent, Al Gore, won the popular vote. In elections in which more than two candidates were running for office, many presidential candidates have won with less than 50 percent of the total popular votes cast for all candidates—including Abraham Lincoln, Woodrow Wilson, Harry Truman, John F. Kennedy, Richard Nixon, and in 1992, Bill Clinton.

Thus far, on two occasions the Electoral College has failed to give any candidate a majority. At that point, the House of Representatives takes over, and the president is then chosen from among the three candidates having the most Electoral College votes, as noted in Chapter 8. In 1800, Thomas Jefferson and Aaron Burr tied in the Electoral College. This happened because the Constitution had not been explicit in indicating which of the two electoral votes was for president and which was for vice president. In 1804, the **Twelfth Amendment** clarified the matter by requiring that the president and the vice president be chosen separately. In 1824, the House again had to make a choice, this time among William H. Crawford, Andrew Jackson, and John Quincy Adams. It chose Adams, even though Jackson had more electoral and popular votes.

THE MANY ROLES OF THE PRESIDENT

The Constitution speaks briefly about the duties and obligations of the president. Based on this brief list of powers and on the precedents of history, the presidency has grown into a very complicated job that requires balancing at least five constitutional roles. These are (1) head of state, (2) chief executive, (3) commander in chief of the armed forces, (4) chief diplomat, and (5) chief legislator of the United States. In addition to these constitutional roles, the president serves as the leader of his or her political party. Of course, the president is also the nation's most prominent and successful politician. Here we examine each of these significant presidential functions, or roles. It is worth noting that one person plays all these roles simultaneously and that the needs of the roles may at times come into conflict.

Head of State

Every nation has at least one person who is the ceremonial head of state. In most democratic nations, the role of **head of state** is given to someone other than the chief executive, who leads the executive branch of government. In Britain, for example, the head of state is the queen. In much of Europe, the head of state is a relatively powerless president, and the prime minister is the chief executive. But in the United States, the president is both chief executive and head of state. According to William Howard Taft, as head of state the president symbolizes the "dignity and majesty" of the American people.

Some observers of the American political system believe that having the president serve as both the chief executive and the head of state drastically limits the time available to do "real" work. Not all presidents have agreed with this conclusion, however—particularly those presidents who have skillfully blended these two roles with their role as politician. Being head of state gives the president tremendous public exposure, which can be an important asset in a campaign for reelection. When that exposure is positive, it helps

LO2: Distinguish some of the major roles of the president, including head of state, chief executive, commander in chief, chief diplomat, chief legislator, party chief, and politician.

Twelfth Amendment
An amendment to the Constitution, adopted in 1804, that specifies the separate election of the president and the vice president by the Electoral College.

Head of State
The role of the president as ceremonial head of the government.

the president deal with Congress over proposed legislation and increases the chances of being reelected—or getting the candidates of the president's party elected.

Chief Executive

According to the Constitution, "The executive Power shall be vested in a President of the United States of America. . . . [H]e may require the Opinion, in writing, of the principal Officer in each of the executive Departments, upon any Subject relating to the Duties of their respective Offices . . . and he shall nominate, and by and with the Advice and Consent of the Senate, shall appoint . . . Officers of the United States. . . . [H]e shall take Care that the Laws be faithfully executed."

As **chief executive,** the president is constitutionally bound to enforce the acts of Congress, the judgments of federal courts, and treaties signed by the United States. The duty to "faithfully execute" the laws has been a source of constitutional power for presidents.

The Powers of Appointment and Removal. To assist in the various tasks of the chief executive, the president has a federal bureaucracy, which currently consists of 2.1 million federal civilian employees, not counting the U.S. Postal Service (522,000 employees). You might think that the president, as head of the largest bureaucracy in the United States, wields enormous power. The president, however, only nominally runs the executive bureaucracy. Most government positions are filled by **civil service** employees, who generally gain government employment through a merit system rather than presidential appointment.[2] Therefore, even though the president has important **appointment power,** it is limited to cabinet and subcabinet jobs, federal judgeships, agency heads, and several thousand lesser jobs—about eight thousand positions in total. This means that most of the 2.6 million employees of the executive branch owe no political allegiance to the president. They are more likely to owe loyalty to congressional committees or to interest groups representing the sector of society that they serve.

The president's power to remove from office those officials who are not doing a good job or who do not agree with the president is not explicitly granted by the Constitution and has been limited. In 1926, however, a Supreme Court decision prevented Congress from interfering with the president's ability to fire those executive-branch officials whom the president had appointed with Senate approval.[3]

Harry Truman spoke candidly of the difficulties a president faces in trying to control the executive bureaucracy. On leaving office, he referred to the problems that Dwight Eisenhower, as a former general of the army, was going to have: "He'll sit here and he'll say do this! do that! and nothing will happen. Poor Ike—it won't be a bit like the Army. He'll find it very frustrating."[4]

The Power to Grant Reprieves and Pardons. Section 2 of Article II of the Constitution gives the president the power to grant **reprieves** and **pardons** for offenses against the United States except in cases of impeachment. All pardons are administered by the Office of the Pardon Attorney in the Department of Justice.

Chief Executive
The role of the president as head of the executive branch of the government.

Civil Service
A collective term for the body of employees working for the government. Generally, civil service is understood to apply to all those who gain government employment through a merit system.

Appointment Power
The authority vested in the president to fill a government office or position.

Reprieve
A formal postponement of the execution of a sentence imposed by a court of law.

Pardon
A release from the punishment for, or legal consequences of, a crime. A pardon can be granted by the president before or after a conviction.

---

2. See Chapter 11 for a discussion of the Civil Service Reform Act.
3. *Meyers v. United States,* 272 U.S. 52 (1926).
4. Quoted in Richard E. Neustadt, *Presidential Power: The Politics of Leadership* (New York: Wiley, 1960), p. 9. Truman may not have considered the amount of politics involved in decision making in the upper reaches of the army.

Commander in Chief
The role of the president as supreme commander of the military forces of the United States and of the state National Guard units when they are called into federal service.

War Powers Resolution
A law passed in 1973 spelling out the conditions under which the president can commit troops without congressional approval.

The Supreme Court upheld the president's power to grant reprieves and pardons in a 1925 case concerning a pardon granted by the president to an individual convicted of contempt of court. A federal circuit court had contended that only judges had the authority to convict individuals for contempt of court when court orders were violated and that the courts should be free from interference by the executive branch. The Supreme Court simply stated that the president could grant reprieves or pardons for all offenses "either before trial, during trial, or after trial, by individuals, or by classes, conditionally or absolutely, and this without modification or regulation by Congress."[5]

Commander in Chief

The president, according to the Constitution, "shall be Commander in Chief of the Army and Navy of the United States, and of the Militia of the several States, when called into the actual Service of the United States." In other words, the armed forces are under civilian, rather than military, control.

Wartime Powers. Those who wrote the Constitution had George Washington in mind when they made the president the **commander in chief.** Although we do not expect our president to lead the troops into battle, presidents as commanders in chief have wielded dramatic power. Harry Truman made the extraordinary decision to drop atomic bombs on Hiroshima and Nagasaki in 1945 to force Japan to surrender and thus bring World War II to an end. Lyndon Johnson ordered bombing missions against North Vietnam in the 1960s, and he personally selected some of the targets. Richard Nixon decided to invade Cambodia in 1970. Ronald Reagan sent troops to Lebanon and Grenada in 1983 and ordered U.S. fighter planes to attack Libya in 1986. George H. W. Bush sent troops to Panama in 1989 and to the Middle East in 1990. Bill Clinton sent troops to Haiti in 1994 and to Bosnia in 1995, ordered missile attacks on alleged terrorist bases in 1998, and sent American planes to bomb Serbia in 1999. George W. Bush ordered the invasion of Afghanistan in 2002 and of Iraq in 2003, and most recently, Barack Obama ordered more troops into Afghanistan in 2009 and authorized air strikes in Libya in 2011.

The president is the ultimate decision maker in military matters. Everywhere the president goes, so too goes the "football"—a briefcase filled with all of the codes necessary to order a nuclear attack. Only the president has the power to order the use of nuclear force.

As commander in chief, the president exercises more authority than in any other role. Constitutionally, Congress has the sole power to declare war, but the president can send the armed forces into situations that are certainly the equivalent of war. Harry Truman dispatched troops to Korea in 1950. Kennedy, Johnson, and Nixon waged an undeclared war in Southeast Asia, where more than 58,000 Americans were killed and 300,000 were wounded. In neither of these situations had Congress declared war.

The War Powers Resolution. In an attempt to gain more control over such military activities, in 1973 Congress passed the **War Powers Resolution**—over President Nixon's veto—

President Harry Truman (1945–1953, at right), stands with General Dwight Eisenhower in 1951. A year later, Eisenhower successfully ran for president. (George Skadding/Time Life Pictures/Getty Images)

---

5. *Ex parte Grossman,* 267 U.S. 87 (1925).

requiring that the president consult with Congress when sending American forces into action. Once they are sent, the president must report to Congress within forty-eight hours. Unless Congress approves the use of troops within sixty days or extends the sixty-day time limit, the forces must be withdrawn.

In spite of the War Powers Resolution, the powers of the president as commander in chief are more extensive today than they were in the past. These powers are linked closely to the president's powers as chief diplomat, or chief crafter of foreign policy.

Chief Diplomat

The Constitution gives the president the power to recognize foreign governments, to make treaties with the **advice and consent** of the Senate, and to make special agreements with other heads of state that do not require congressional approval. In addition, the president nominates U.S. ambassadors to other countries. As **chief diplomat,** the president dominates American foreign policy, a role that has been supported many times by the Supreme Court.

Diplomatic Recognition. An important power of the president as chief diplomat is that of **diplomatic recognition,** or the power to recognize—or refuse to recognize—foreign governments as legitimate. In the role of ceremonial head of state, the president has always received foreign diplomats. In modern times, the simple act of receiving a foreign diplomat has been equivalent to accrediting the diplomat and officially recognizing his or her government. Such recognition of the legitimacy of another country's government is a prerequisite to diplomatic relations or treaties between that country and the United States.

Deciding when to recognize a foreign power is not always simple. The United States, for example, did not recognize the Soviet Union until 1933—sixteen years after the Russian Revolution of 1917. It was only after all attempts to reverse the effects of that revolution—including military invasion of Russia and diplomatic isolation—had proved futile that Franklin D. Roosevelt extended recognition to the Soviet government. In December 1978, long after the Communist victory in China in 1949, President Jimmy Carter (1977–1981) granted official recognition to the People's Republic of China.[6]

Proposal and Ratification of Treaties. The president has the sole power to negotiate treaties with other nations. These treaties must be presented to the Senate. A two-thirds vote in the Senate is required for approval, or ratification. After ratification, the president can approve the treaty as adopted by the Senate. Approval poses a problem when the Senate has added substantive amendments or reservations to a treaty, particularly when such changes may require reopening negotiations

---

6. The Nixon administration first encouraged new relations with the People's Republic of China by allowing a cultural exchange of table tennis teams. Nixon subsequently traveled to China.

Advice and Consent
Terms in the Constitution describing the U.S. Senate's power to review and approve treaties and presidential appointments.

Chief Diplomat
The role of the president in recognizing foreign governments, making treaties, and effecting executive agreements.

Diplomatic Recognition
The formal acknowledgment of a foreign government as legitimate.

Social Media in Politics
In no field is the president more powerful, relative to the rest of the government, than in foreign policy. If you have an interest in that topic, consider following *Foreign Policy* magazine on Facebook. Simply search on "foreign policy."

President Obama speaks at the Pentagon in January 2012. He is flanked, left to right, by the Army's top general, the chairman of the Joint Chiefs of Staff, and the commandant of the Marine Corps. Obama announced new priorities that will cut the Pentagon budget by hundreds of billions of dollars over the next decade. How are top members of the military likely to react to budget cuts? (Mark Wilson/Getty Images)

Executive Agreement
An international agreement made by the president, without senatorial ratification, with the head of a foreign state.

Chief Legislator
The role of the president in influencing the making of laws.

with the other signatory governments. Sometimes, a president may decide to withdraw a treaty if the senatorial changes are too extensive—as Woodrow Wilson did with the Versailles Treaty in 1919 that concluded World War I. Wilson believed that the senatorial reservations would weaken the treaty so much that it would be ineffective.

Recent Treaty Efforts. Before September 11, 2001, President George W. Bush indicated his intention to steer the United States in a unilateral direction on foreign policy. After the terrorist attacks of 9/11, however, Bush sought cooperation from other nations in the war on terror. Nonetheless, his attempts to gain international support for a war against Iraq to overthrow that country's government were not as successful as he had hoped.

In April 2010, President Obama and the then Russian president Dmitry Medvedev signed the New START Treaty, a follow-up to earlier arms-control treaties. The ten-year pact will cut the number of nuclear warheads allowed to each party by 30 percent, to 1,550 warheads. The number of permitted missile launchers will be cut in half. The treaty includes a verification process. In December 2010, the U.S. Senate approved the treaty.

Executive Agreements. Presidential power in foreign affairs is enhanced greatly by the use of **executive agreements** made between the president and other heads of state. Such agreements do not require Senate approval, although the House and Senate may refuse to appropriate the funds necessary to implement them. Whereas treaties are binding on all succeeding administrations, executive agreements require each new president's consent to remain in effect.

Among the advantages of executive agreements are speed and secrecy. The former is essential during a crisis. The latter is important when the administration fears that open senatorial debate may be detrimental to the best interests of the United States or to the interests of the president.[7] There have been far more executive agreements (about nine thousand) than treaties (about thirteen hundred). Many executive agreements contain secret provisions calling for American military assistance or other support.

President George H. W. Bush (1989–1993) meets with the foreign minister of Saudi Arabia in 1990. George H. W. Bush is the father of George W. Bush, making the Bush family a true political dynasty. It is not uncommon for the children of elected officials to go into politics. (AP Photo/Barry Thumma)

Chief Legislator

Constitutionally, presidents must recommend to Congress legislation that they judge necessary and expedient. Not all presidents have wielded their power as **chief legislator** in the same manner. Some

---

7. The Case Act of 1972 requires that all executive agreements be transmitted to Congress within sixty days after taking effect. Secret agreements are transmitted to the foreign relations committees as classified information.

presidents have been almost completely unsuccessful in getting their legislative programs implemented by Congress. Presidents Franklin D. Roosevelt and Lyndon Johnson, however, saw much of their proposed legislation put into effect.

Creating the Congressional Agenda. In modern times, the president has played a dominant role in creating the congressional agenda. In the president's annual **State of the Union message,** which is required by the Constitution (Article II, Section 3) and is usually given in late January shortly after Congress reconvenes, the president presents a legislative program. The message gives a broad, comprehensive view of what the president wishes the legislature to accomplish during its session. It is as much a message to the American people and to the world as it is to Congress. Its impact on public opinion can determine the way in which Congress responds to the president's agenda.

Since 1913, the president has delivered the State of the Union message in a formal address to Congress. Today, this address is one of the great ceremonies of American governance, and many customs have grown up around it. For example, one cabinet member, the "designated survivor," stays away to ensure that the country will always have a president even if someone manages to blow up the Capitol building. Everyone gives the president an initial standing ovation out of respect for the office, but this applause does not necessarily represent support for the individual who holds the office. During the speech, senators and House members either applaud or remain silent to indicate their opinion of the policies that the president announces.

Getting Legislation Passed. The president can propose legislation, but Congress is not required to pass—or even introduce—any of the administration's bills. How, then, does the president get those proposals made into law? One way is by exercising the power of persuasion. The president writes to, telephones, and meets with various congressional leaders. He or she makes public announcements to influence public opinion. Finally, as head of his or her party, the president exercises leadership over the party's members in Congress. A president whose party holds a majority in both chambers of Congress usually has an easier time getting legislation passed than does a president who faces a hostile Congress.

Saying No to Legislation. The president has the power to say no to legislation through use of the veto,[8] by which the White House returns a bill unsigned to Congress with a **veto message** attached. Because the Constitution requires that every bill passed by the House and the Senate be sent to the president before it becomes law, the president must act on each bill:

1. If the bill is signed, it becomes law.
2. If the bill is not sent back to Congress after ten congressional working days, it becomes law without the president's signature.
3. The president can reject the bill and send it back to Congress with a veto message setting forth objections. Congress then can change the bill, hoping to secure presidential approval, and repass it. Or Congress can simply reject the president's objections by overriding the veto with a two-thirds roll-call vote of the members present in both the House and the Senate.
4. If the president refuses to sign the bill and Congress adjourns within ten working days after the bill has been submitted to the president, the bill is killed for that session of

State of the Union Message
An annual message to Congress in which the president proposes a legislative program. The message is addressed not only to Congress but also to the American people and to the world.

Veto Message
The president's formal explanation of a veto, which accompanies the vetoed legislation when it is returned to Congress.

---

8. *Veto* in Latin means "I forbid."

Pocket Veto
A special veto exercised by the chief executive after a legislative body has adjourned. Bills not signed by the chief executive die after a specified period of time.

Line-Item Veto
The power of an executive to veto individual lines or items within a piece of legislation without vetoing the entire bill.

Patronage
The practice of rewarding faithful party workers and followers with government employment and contracts.

Congress. This is called a **pocket veto.** If Congress wishes the bill to be reconsidered, the bill must be reintroduced during the following session.

Presidents employed the veto power infrequently until after the Civil War, but it has been used with increasing vigor since then. Presidents George W. Bush and Barack Obama, however, made little or no use of the veto during the periods when their parties controlled Congress.

The Line-Item Veto. Ronald Reagan lobbied strenuously for Congress to give another tool to the president—the **line-item veto,** which would allow the president to veto specific spending provisions of legislation that was passed by Congress. Reagan saw the line-item veto as the only way that he could control overall congressional spending. In 1996, Congress passed the Line Item Veto Act, which provided for the line-item veto. President Clinton used the line-item veto on several occasions, but the act was challenged in court. In 1998, by a six-to-three vote, the United States Supreme Court agreed with the veto's opponents and overturned the act. The Court stated that "there is no provision in the Constitution that authorizes the president to enact, to amend, or to repeal statutes."[9]

Congress's Power to Override Presidential Vetoes. A veto is a clear-cut indication of the president's dissatisfaction with congressional legislation. Congress, however, can override a presidential veto, although it rarely exercises this power. Consider that two-thirds of the members of each chamber who are present must vote to override the president's veto in a roll-call vote. This means that if only one-third plus one of the members voting in one of the chambers of Congress do not agree to override the veto, the veto holds. In American history, only about 7 percent of all vetoes have been overridden.

Party Chief and Politician

Presidents are by no means above political partisanship, and one of their many roles is that of chief of party. Although the Constitution says nothing about the function of the president within a political party (the mere concept of political parties was abhorrent to most of the authors of the Constitution), today presidents are the actual leaders of their parties.

As party leader, the president chooses the national committee chairperson and can try to discipline party members who fail to support presidential policies. One way of exerting political power within the party is through **patronage**—appointing individuals to government or public jobs. This power was more extensive in the past, before the establishment of the civil service in 1883, but the president still retains important patronage power. As we noted earlier, the president can appoint several thousand individuals to jobs in the cabinet, the White House, and the federal regulatory agencies.

Perhaps the most important partisan role that the president has played in the late 1900s and early 2000s has been that of fund-raiser. The president is able to raise large sums for the party through appearances at dinners, speaking engagements, and other social occasions. President Clinton may have

---

9. *Clinton v. City of New York,* 524 U.S. 417 (1998).

President Ronald Reagan (1981–1989) fought hard for the line-item veto. Why did the Supreme Court overturn the Line Item Veto Act? (AP Photo)

raised more than half a billion dollars for the Democratic Party during his two terms. President Bush was even more successful than Clinton. Barack Obama's spectacular success in raising funds for his presidential campaign (particularly via the Internet) indicates that he is carrying on this fund-raising tradition.

Presidents have a number of other ways of exerting influence as party chief. The president may make it known that a particular congressperson's choice for federal judge will not be appointed unless that member of Congress is more supportive of the president's legislative program.[10] The president may agree to campaign for a particular program or for a particular candidate. Presidents also reward loyal members of Congress with support for the funding of local projects, tax breaks for regional industries, and other forms of "pork."

Presidential Constituencies. Presidents have many constituencies. In principle, they are beholden to the entire electorate—the public of the United States—even those who did not vote. Presidents are certainly beholden to their party, because its members helped to put them in office. The president's constituencies also include members of the opposing party whose cooperation the president needs. Finally, the president must take into consideration a constituency that has come to be called the *Washington community,* also known as those "inside the beltway."[11] This community consists of individuals who—whether in or out of political office—are intimately familiar with the workings of government, thrive on gossip, and measure on a daily basis the political power of the president.

Public Approval. All of these constituencies are impressed by presidents who maintain a high level of public approval, partly because doing so is very difficult to accomplish. Presidential popularity, as measured by national polls, gives the president an extra political resource to use in persuading legislators or bureaucrats to pass legislation.

Recent Presidents and the Public Opinion Polls. The impact of popular approval on a president's prospects was placed in sharp relief by the experiences of President George W. Bush. Immediately after 9/11, Bush had the highest job approval ratings ever recorded. By the time he left office, only 25 percent of the public approved of his performance as president. As a result of his declining popularity, Bush accomplished very little in his second term.

Obama's initial popularity figures were also very high, but they were bound to fall. Most of the erosion took place during 2009, a period of intense governmental activity and bad economic news. Obama then endured a period of sub-50-percent job approval ratings that lasted almost until the 2012 presidential elections. (One exception was a spike in approval in May 2011, after U.S. Navy SEALS killed Osama bin Laden.) By October 2012, however, Obama's approval ratings were back above 50 percent, and they remained at those levels into 2013.

Perhaps more important than the job approval ratings were the polls that reported how citizens intended to vote. Obama held a modest but unvarying lead over Republican presidential candidate Mitt Romney throughout the 2012 presidential campaign. What is the effect of economic conditions on a president's reelection prospects? We look at that question in the *Politics and Economics* feature on the following page.

---

10. "Senatorial courtesy" (see Chapter 12) often puts the judicial appointment in the hands of the Senate, however.

11. Here, the *beltway* refers to I-495, the interstate highway that completely encircles the District of Columbia as well as many close-in Washington suburbs.

politics and economics

THE ECONOMY AND THE RACE FOR PRESIDENT

A presidential campaign adviser once coined a memorable saying: "It's the economy, stupid." He meant that the state of the economy would determine the outcome of the election. Since then, political scientists have constantly argued over how much of an effect the economy has on presidential elections.

OBAMA'S PROSPECTS IN 2012

The recovery from the Great Recession of 2008 and 2009 was painfully slow. The unemployment rate, which peaked at 10 percent in 2009, remained above 8 percent through most of 2012 and was still well above 7 percent on Election Day. Many observers, especially Republicans, concluded that such rates spelled doom for President Obama's prospects. One pundit observed, "No president since Franklin Roosevelt has won reelection with unemployment over 7.5 percent."

This statement, while true, is trivial. Since Roosevelt's time, Jimmy Carter was the only elected president ever to run for reelection with unemployment that high. Indeed, much of the problem in developing an economic model to predict election results is that we have so few cases. Only eight elected presidents have sought reelection since 1944.

THE DIFFICULTY IN MAKING ACCURATE PREDICTIONS

Clearly, voters do judge incumbent presidents in part based on the current state of employment. Surprisingly, the unemployment rate itself has no predictive power. It doesn't matter whether unemployment is high or low, but whether it is getting better or worse. Ronald Reagan won reelection in 1984 with an unemployment rate of 7.3 percent because the economy was visibly improving.

Several years ago, political scientist Douglas Hibbs developed a model to predict presidential elections using growth in per-person income and the number of military deaths. The model seemed to explain almost 90 percent of the variation in presidential election results from 1952 through 1988. Yet Nate Silver, statistics guru at the *New York Times,* noted that the Hibbs model has performed badly in recent years and it is almost worthless in explaining election results before 1952.

In early 2012, Silver publicized his own simple gauge of Obama's reelection chances. If the economy created an average of 150,000 net new jobs per month, Obama should win. Silver also admitted, however, that historically, such economic variables only explained about 40 percent of an incumbent's vote.

In the end, the economy created an average of 157,000 jobs in the nine months leading up to the election. That figure would appear to predict a narrow Obama victory. In fact, Obama's margin over Republican Mitt Romney was almost 4 percentage points of the popular vote. That margin suggests that Obama had other advantages working for him. Some observers concluded that Republican budget proposals had alarmed many independent voters.

FOR CRITICAL ANALYSIS

Why should the economy be so important in determining how people vote?

"Going Public." Since the early 1900s, presidents have spoken more to the public and less to Congress. In the 1800s, only 7 percent of presidential speeches were addressed to the public. Since 1900, 50 percent have been addressed to the public. Presidents frequently go over the heads of Congress and the political elites, taking their cases directly to the people. This strategy, dubbed "going public," gives the president additional power through the ability to persuade and manipulate public opinion. By identifying their own positions so clearly, presidents can weaken the legislators' positions. In times when the major political parties are highly polarized, however, the possibility of compromise with the opposition party may actually be reduced if the president openly "nails his colors to the mast."

PRESIDENTIAL POWERS

Presidents have at their disposal a variety of special powers and privileges not available in the other branches of the U.S. government. Most of the powers of the president discussed earlier in this chapter in the section on the roles of the president are called **constitutional powers,** because their basis lies in the Constitution. In addition, Congress has established by law, or statute, numerous other presidential powers—such as the ability to declare national emergencies. These are called **statutory powers.** Both constitutional and statutory powers have been labeled the **expressed powers** of the president, because they are expressly written into the Constitution or into law.

Presidents also have what have come to be known as **inherent powers.** These depend on the statements in the Constitution that "the executive Power shall be vested in a President" and that the president should "take Care that the Laws be faithfully executed." The most common example of inherent powers are those emergency powers invoked by the president during wartime. Franklin D. Roosevelt, for example, used his inherent powers to move the Japanese and Japanese Americans living in the United States into internment camps for the duration of World War II. President George W. Bush often justified expanding the powers of the presidency by saying that such powers were necessary to fight the war on terrorism.

Emergency Powers

If you were to read the Constitution, you would find no mention of the additional powers that the executive office may exercise during national emergencies. Indeed, the Supreme Court has stated that an "emergency does not create power."[12] But it is clear that presidents have made strong use of their inherent powers during times of emergency, particularly in the realm of foreign affairs. The **emergency powers** of the president were first enunciated in the Supreme Court's decision in *United States v. Curtiss-Wright Export Corp.*[13] In that case, President Franklin D. Roosevelt, without authorization by Congress, ordered an embargo on the shipment of weapons to two warring South American countries. The Court recognized that the president may exercise inherent powers in foreign affairs and that the national government has primacy in these affairs.

Examples of emergency powers are abundant, coinciding with crises in domestic and foreign affairs. Abraham Lincoln suspended civil liberties at the beginning of the Civil War (1861–1865) and called the state militias into national service. These actions and his subsequent governance of conquered areas—and even of areas of northern states— were justified by claims that they were essential to preserve the Union. Franklin Roosevelt declared an "unlimited national emergency" following the fall of France in World War II (1939–1945) and mobilized the federal budget and the economy for war.

President Harry Truman authorized the federal seizure of steel plants and their operation by the national government in 1952 during the Korean War. Truman claimed that he was using his inherent emergency power as chief executive and commander in chief to safeguard the nation's security, as an ongoing steel mill strike threatened the supply of weapons to the armed forces. The Supreme Court did not agree, holding that the president had no authority under the Constitution to seize private property or to legislate such

Constitutional Power
A power vested in the president by Article II of the Constitution.

Statutory Power
A power created for the president through laws enacted by Congress.

Expressed Power
A power of the president that is expressly written into the Constitution or into statutory law.

Inherent Power
A power of the president derived from the statements in the Constitution that "the executive Power shall be vested in a President" and that the president should "take Care that the Laws be faithfully executed."

Emergency Power
An inherent power exercised by the president during a period of national crisis.

LO3: Describe some of the special powers of the president, and tell how a president can be removed from office.

---

12. *Home Building and Loan Association v. Blaisdell,* 290 U.S. 398 (1934).
13. 299 U.S. 304 (1936).

President George W. Bush gives a State of the Union address while Vice President Dick Cheney listens. Where is that address given? (AP Photo/ Charles Dharapak)

action.[14] According to legal scholars, this was the first time a limit had been placed on the exercise of the president's emergency powers.

Executive Orders

Congress allows the president (as well as administrative agencies) to issue **executive orders** that have the force of law. These executive orders can do the following: (1) enforce legislative statutes, (2) enforce the Constitution or treaties with foreign nations, and (3) establish or modify rules and practices of executive administrative agencies.

An executive order, then, represents the president's legislative power. The only apparent requirement is that under the Administrative Procedure Act of 1946, all executive orders must be published in the *Federal Register,* a daily publication of the U.S. government. Executive orders have been used to implement national affirmative action regulations; to restructure the White House bureaucracy; and under emergency conditions, to ration consumer goods and administer wage and price controls. They have also been used to classify government information as secret, to regulate the export of restricted items, and to establish military tribunals for suspected terrorists.

Executive Privilege

Another inherent executive power that has been claimed by presidents concerns the right of the president and the president's executive officials to withhold information from, or refuse to appear before, Congress or the courts. This is called **executive privilege,** and it relies on the constitutional separation of powers for its basis.

Invoking Executive Privilege. Presidents have frequently invoked executive privilege to avoid having to disclose information to Congress about actions of the executive branch. Executive privilege rests on the assumption that a certain degree of secrecy is essential to national security. Critics of executive privilege believe that it can be used to shield from public scrutiny actions of the executive branch that should be open to Congress and to the American citizenry.

Limiting Executive Privilege. Limits to executive privilege went untested until the Watergate affair in the early 1970s. Five men had broken into the headquarters of the Democratic National Committee and were caught searching for documents that might damage the candidacy of the Democratic nominee, George McGovern. Later investigation showed that the break-in had been planned by members of Richard Nixon's campaign committee and that Nixon and his closest advisers had devised a strategy for impeding the investigation of the crime. After it became known that all conversations held in the Oval

Executive Order
A rule or regulation issued by the president that has the effect of law.

Federal Register
A publication of the U.S. government that prints executive orders, rules, and regulations.

Executive Privilege
The right of executive officials to withhold information from, or to refuse to appear before, a legislative committee or a court.

14. *Youngstown Sheet and Tube Co. v. Sawyer,* 343 U.S. 579 (1952).

Office had been recorded on a secret system, Nixon was ordered to turn over the tapes to the special prosecutor in charge of the investigation.

Nixon refused to do so, claiming executive privilege. He argued that "no president could function if the private papers of his office, prepared by his personal staff, were open to public scrutiny." In 1974, in one of the Supreme Court's most famous cases, *United States v. Nixon*,[15] the justices unanimously ruled that Nixon had to hand over the tapes. The Court held that executive privilege could not be used to prevent evidence from being heard in criminal proceedings.

Signing Statements

Is the president allowed to refuse to enforce certain parts of legislation if he or she believes that they are unconstitutional? This question came to the forefront in recent years because of President George W. Bush's extensive use of signing statements. A **signing statement** is a written declaration that a president may make when signing a bill into law regarding the law's enforcement. Presidents have been using such statements for decades, but President Bush used 161 statements to invalidate more than one thousand provisions of federal law. No previous president used signing statements to make such sweeping claims on behalf of presidential power. Earlier presidents often employed statements to serve notice that parts of bills might be unconstitutional, but they were just as likely to issue statements that were purely rhetorical. Statements might praise Congress and the measure it had just passed—or denounce the opposition party. During his first presidential campaign, Barack Obama criticized Bush's use of signing statements. As president, Obama's statements have been more in line with tradition. About half of his statements have been entirely rhetorical.

Abuses of Executive Power and Impeachment

Presidents normally leave office either because their first term has expired and they have not sought (or won) reelection or because, having served two full terms, they are not allowed to be elected for a third term (owing to the Twenty-second Amendment, passed in 1951). Eight presidents have died in office. But there is still another way for a president to leave office—by **impeachment** and conviction. Articles I and II of the Constitution authorize the House and Senate to remove the president, the vice president, or other civil officers of the United States for committing "Treason, Bribery, or other high Crimes and Misdemeanors." According to the Constitution, the impeachment process begins in the House, which impeaches (accuses) the federal officer involved. If the House votes to impeach the officer, it draws up articles of impeachment and submits them to the Senate, which conducts the actual trial.

Presidents Andrew Johnson and Richard Nixon. In the history of the United States, no president has ever actually been impeached and also convicted—and thus removed from office—by means of this process. President Andrew Johnson (1865–1869), who succeeded to the office after the assassination of Abraham Lincoln, was impeached by the House but acquitted by the Senate. More than a century later, the House Judiciary Committee approved articles of impeachment against President Richard Nixon for his involvement in the cover-up of the Watergate break-in of 1972. Informed by members of his own party that he had no hope of surviving the trial in the Senate, Nixon resigned

Signing Statement
A written declaration that the president may make when signing a bill into law. It may contain instructions to the bureaucracy on how to administer the law or point to sections of the law that the president considers unconstitutional or contrary to national security interests.

Impeachment
An action by the House of Representatives to accuse the president, vice president, or other civil officers of the United States of committing "Treason, Bribery, or other high Crimes and Misdemeanors."

---

15. 318 U.S. 683 (1974).

on August 9, 1974, before the full House voted on the articles. Nixon is the only president to have resigned from office.

President Bill Clinton. The second president to be impeached by the House but not convicted by the Senate was President Bill Clinton. In 1998, the House approved two charges against Clinton: lying to a grand jury about his affair with White House intern Monica Lewinsky and obstruction of justice. The articles of impeachment were then sent to the Senate, which acquitted Clinton. The attempt to remove Clinton was very unpopular, although the allegations against him did damage his popularity as well. Part of the problem for Clinton's Republican opponents was that the charges against the president essentially boiled down to his lying about sex. As one pundit put it, "Everyone lies about sex." Of course, not everyone lies about sex when under oath.

President Bill Clinton speaks to Democratic members of Congress after receiving news of his impeachment in 1998. Standing next to him is Vice President Al Gore. What has to happen after an impeachment for a president to be removed from office? (AP Photo/Doug Mills)

THE EXECUTIVE ORGANIZATION

Gone are the days when presidents answered their own mail, as George Washington did. It was not until 1857 that Congress authorized a private secretary for the president, to be paid by the federal government. Woodrow Wilson typed most of his correspondence, even though he did have several secretaries. At the beginning of Franklin D. Roosevelt's long tenure in the White House, the entire staff consisted of thirty-seven employees. With the New Deal and World War II, however, the presidential staff became a sizable organization.

The Cabinet

LO4: Explain the organization of the executive branch and, in particular, the executive office of the president.

Although the Constitution does not include the word *cabinet,* it does state that the president "may require the Opinion, in writing, of the principal Officer in each of the executive Departments." Since the time of George Washington, these officers have formed an advisory group, or **cabinet,** to which the president turns for counsel.

Members of the Cabinet. Originally, the cabinet consisted of only four officials—the secretaries of State, Treasury, and War and the attorney general. Today, the cabinet numbers fourteen department secretaries and the attorney general. The cabinet may include others as well. The president at his or her discretion can, for example, ascribe cabinet rank to the vice president, the head of the Office of Management and Budget, the national security adviser, or additional officials. Under President Barack Obama, the additional members of the cabinet are the following:

Cabinet
An advisory group selected by the president to aid in making decisions. The cabinet includes the heads of fifteen executive departments and others named by the president.

- The vice president
- The White House chief of staff
- The administrator of the Environmental Protection Agency
- The director of the Office of Management and Budget
- The U.S. trade representative
- The U.S. ambassador to the United Nations

- The chair of the Council of Economic Advisers
- The administrator of the Small Business Administration

Often, a president will use a **kitchen cabinet** to replace the formal cabinet as a major source of advice. The term *kitchen cabinet* originated during the presidency of Andrew Jackson, who relied on the counsel of close friends who allegedly met with him in the kitchen of the White House. A kitchen cabinet is a very informal group of advisers. Usually, they are friends with whom the president worked before being elected.

Presidential Use of Cabinets. Because neither the Constitution nor statutory law requires the president to consult with the cabinet, its use is purely discretionary. Some presidents have relied on the counsel of their cabinets more than others. Dwight Eisenhower was used to the team approach to solving problems from his experience as supreme allied commander during World War II, and therefore he frequently turned to his cabinet for advice on a wide range of issues. More often, presidents have solicited the opinions of their cabinets and then have done what they wanted to do. Lincoln supposedly said—after a cabinet meeting in which a vote was seven nays against his one aye—"Seven nays and one aye; the ayes have it." In general, few presidents have relied heavily on the advice of their cabinet members.

It is not surprising that presidents tend to disregard their cabinet members' advice. Often, the departmental heads are more responsive to the wishes of their own staffs or to their own political ambitions than they are to the president. They may be more concerned with obtaining resources for their departments than with achieving the president's goals. So there is often a strong conflict of interest between presidents and their cabinet members.

The Executive Office of the President

When President Franklin D. Roosevelt appointed a special committee on administrative management, he knew that the committee would conclude that the president needed help. Indeed, the committee proposed a major reorganization of the executive branch. Congress did not approve the entire reorganization, but it did create the **Executive Office of the President (EOP)** to provide staff assistance for the chief executive and to help coordinate the executive bureaucracy. Since that time, a number of agencies have been created within the EOP to supply the president with advice and staff help. Presidents reorganize the EOP and the White House Office constantly, and any table of organization is therefore temporary. As of 2013, however, the EOP agencies under Barack Obama were the following:

- Council of Economic Advisers
- Council on Environmental Quality
- National Security Staff
- Office of Administration
- Office of Management and Budget
- Office of National Drug Control Policy
- Office of Science and Technology Policy
- Office of the United States Trade Representative
- Office of the Vice President
- White House Office

Many staff members within the EOP are assigned to specific policy areas, and the number of such individuals grew noticeably during Obama's first term. Popularly referred to as "czars," they have included a cyber security czar, an urban affairs czar, and even an Asian carp czar, who coordinates efforts to keep Asian carp out of the Great Lakes. Unlike cabinet officers and many other top executive officials, czars are not subject to confirmation by the U.S. Senate. This exemption has been a source of controversy.

Kitchen Cabinet
The informal advisers to the president.

Executive Office of the President (EOP)
An organization established by President Franklin D. Roosevelt to assist the president in carrying out major duties.

White House Office
The personal office of the president, which tends to presidential political needs and manages the media.

Chief of Staff
The person who is named to direct the White House Office and advise the president.

Several of the offices within the EOP are especially important, including the White House Office and the Office of Management and Budget.

The White House Office. The **White House Office** includes most of the key personal and political advisers to the president. Among the jobs held by these aides are those of secretary, press secretary, appointments secretary, and legal counsel to the president. Often, the individuals who hold these positions are recruited from the president's campaign staff. Their duties—mainly protecting the president's political interests—are similar to campaign functions. In 2013, the White House Office was made up of the following units:

- Domestic Policy Council
- National Economic Council
- National Security Adviser
- Office of Cabinet Affairs
- Office of the Chief of Staff
- Office of Communications
- Office of Digital Strategy
- Office of the First Lady
- Office of Legislative Affairs

- Office of Management and Administration
- Oval Office Operations
- Office of Presidential Personnel
- Office of Public Engagement and Intergovernmental Affairs
- Office of Scheduling and Advance
- Office of the Staff Secretary
- Office of the White House Counsel

Key White House Staff. In all recent administrations, one member of the White House Office has been named **chief of staff.** This person, who is responsible for coordinating the office, is also one of the president's chief advisers. In addition to civilian advisers, the president is supported by a large number of military personnel, who are organized under the White House Military Office. These members of the military provide communications, transportation, medical care, and food services to the president and the White House staff.

Members of the national security team receive an update on the mission against Osama bin Laden in the Situation Room of the White House on May 1, 2011. Those present included Vice President Joe Biden (left), President Barack Obama (second left), then Secretary of State Hillary Clinton (second right), and then Secretary of Defense Robert Gates (right). (Pete Souza/EPA/Landov)

White House staff members are closest to the president and may have considerable influence over the administration's decisions. Often, when presidents are under fire for their decisions, the staff is accused of keeping the chief executive too isolated from criticism or help. Presidents insist that they will not allow the staff to become too powerful, but given the difficulty of the office, each president eventually turns to staff members for loyal assistance and protection.

The Office of Management and Budget. The **Office of Management and Budget (OMB)** was originally the Bureau of the Budget, which was created in 1921 within the Department of the Treasury. Recognizing the importance of this agency, Franklin D. Roosevelt moved it into the White House Office in 1939. Richard Nixon reorganized the Bureau of the Budget in 1970 and changed its name to reflect its new managerial function. It is headed by a director, who drafts the annual federal budget that the president presents to Congress each January for approval. In principle, the director of the OMB has broad fiscal powers in planning and estimating various parts of the federal budget, because all agencies must submit their proposed budget to the OMB for approval. In reality, it is not so clear that the OMB truly can affect the greater scope of the federal budget. The OMB may be more important as a clearinghouse for legislative proposals initiated in the executive agencies.

The National Security Council. The **National Security Council (NSC)** is a link between the president's key foreign and military advisers and the president. Its members consist of the president, the vice president, and the secretaries of State and Defense, plus other informal members. The NSC is managed by the president's assistant for national security affairs, also known as the national security adviser.

Office of Management and Budget (OMB)
A division of the Executive Office of the President. The OMB assists the president in preparing the annual budget, clearing and coordinating departmental agency budgets, and supervising the administration of the federal budget.

National Security Council (NSC)
An agency in the Executive Office of the President that advises the president on national security.

THE VICE PRESIDENCY

The Constitution does not give much power to the vice president. The only formal duty is to preside over the Senate—which is rarely necessary. This obligation is fulfilled when the Senate organizes and adopts its rules and also when the vice president is needed to decide a tie vote. In all other cases, the president pro tem manages parliamentary procedures in the Senate. The vice president is expected to participate only informally in senatorial deliberations, if at all.

LO5: Evaluate the role of the vice president, and describe what happens if the presidency becomes vacant.

The Vice President's Job

Vice presidents have traditionally been chosen by presidential nominees to balance the ticket by attracting groups of voters or appeasing party factions. If a presidential nominee is from the North, it is not a bad idea to have a vice-presidential nominee who is from the South. If the presidential nominee is from a rural state, perhaps someone with an urban background would be most suitable as a running mate. Presidential nominees who are strongly conservative or strongly liberal would do well to have vice-presidential nominees whose views lie more in the middle of the political road.

In recent presidential elections, however, vice-presidential candidates have often been selected for other reasons. Barack Obama picked Joe Biden to be his running mate in 2008 to add gravitas (seriousness) and foreign policy experience to the ticket. Republican presidential candidate John McCain's choice of Alaska governor Sarah Palin balanced the ticket not only by gender, but also politically. Social conservatives, many of whom were suspicious of McCain, gave enthusiastic support to Palin. In 2012, Republican presidential candidate Mitt Romney chose Representative Paul Ryan of Wisconsin as his running mate. Ryan, the author of conservative House budget proposals, was greeted with enthusiasm by Republicans who were skeptical of Romney's conservative credentials.

Traditionally, the job of the vice president has not been very demanding. In recent years, however, presidents have granted their running mates increased responsibilities and power. President Jimmy Carter was the first modern president to rely on his vice president—Walter Mondale—as a major adviser. Under President George W. Bush, Dick Cheney became the most powerful vice president in history. Cheney was able to place his supporters throughout the bureaucracy and exert influence on a wide range of issues. He could exercise this degree of power, however, only because he had the support of the president. In contrast, Vice President Biden's relationship to President Obama has been more conventional.

Presidential Succession

Eight vice presidents have become president because of the death of the president. John Tyler, the first to do so, took over William Henry Harrison's position in 1841 after only one month. No one knew whether Tyler should simply be a care-taker until a new president could be elected three and a half years later or whether he actually should be president. Tyler assumed that he was supposed to be the chief execu-tive, and he acted as such—although he was commonly referred to as "His Accidency." Since then, vice presidents taking over the position of the presidency because of the incumbent's death have assumed the presidential powers.

But what should a vice president do if a president becomes incapable of carrying out necessary duties while in office? When James Garfield was shot in 1881, he remained alive for two and a half months. What was Vice President Chester Arthur's role?

This question was not addressed in the original Constitution. Article II, Section 1, says only that "[i]n Case of the Removal of the President from Office, or of his Death, Resignation, or Inability to discharge the Powers and Duties of the said Office, the same shall devolve on [the same powers shall be exercised by] the Vice President." There have been many instances of presidential disability. When Dwight Eisenhower became ill for a second time in 1958, he entered into a pact with Richard Nixon specifying that the vice president could determine whether the president was inca-pable of carrying out his duties if the president could not communicate. John F. Kennedy and Lyndon Johnson entered into similar agreements with their vice presidents. Finally, in 1967, the **Twenty-fifth Amendment** was passed, establishing procedures in the event of presidential incapacity, death, or resignation.

Twenty-fifth Amendment
A 1967 amendment to the Constitution that establishes procedures for filling presidential and vice-presidential vacancies and makes provisions for presidential incapacity.

When the President Becomes Incapacitated. According to the Twenty-fifth Amendment, when a president believes that he or she is incapable of performing the duties of office, the president must inform Congress in writing. Then the vice president serves as acting president until the president can resume normal duties. When the presi-dent is unable to communicate, a majority of the cabinet, including the vice president, can declare that fact to Congress. Then the vice president serves as acting president until the

U.S. Vice President Joseph Biden speaks at a conference at the White House. What is the vice president's formal role in our government? (Chris Kleponis/AFP/Getty Images)

president resumes normal duties. If a dispute arises over the return of the president's ability, a two-thirds vote of Congress is required to allow the vice president to remain acting president. Otherwise, the president resumes normal duties.

When the Vice Presidency Becomes Vacant. The Twenty-fifth Amendment also addresses the issue of how the president should fill a vacant vice presidency. Section 2 of the amendment simply states, "Whenever there is a vacancy in the office of the Vice President, the President shall nominate a Vice President who shall take office upon confirmation by a majority vote of both Houses of Congress."

The question of who shall be president if both the president and the vice president die is answered by the Presidential Succession Act of 1947. If the president and vice president die, resign, or are disabled, the Speaker of the House will become president, after resigning from Congress. Next in line is the president pro tem of the Senate, followed by the cabinet officers in the order of the creation of their departments (see Table 10–1 below).

TABLE 10–1: Line of Succession to the Presidency of the United States

1. Vice president
2. Speaker of the House of Representatives
3. Senate president pro tempore
4. Secretary of State
5. Secretary of the Treasury
6. Secretary of Defense
7. Attorney general (head of the Justice Department)
8. Secretary of Interior
9. Secretary of Agriculture
10. Secretary of Commerce
11. Secretary of Labor
12. Secretary of Health and Human Services
13. Secretary of Housing and Urban Development
14. Secretary of Transportation
15. Secretary of Energy
16. Secretary of Education
17. Secretary of Veterans Affairs
18. Secretary of Homeland Security

making a difference

COMMUNICATING WITH THE WHITE HOUSE

When it comes to caring about the presidency, most people do not need much encouragement. The president is our most important official. The president serves as the public face of the government and, indeed, of the nation as a whole. Many people, however, believe the president is such a remote figure that nothing they can do will affect what he or she does. That is not always true. On many issues, your voice—combined, of course, with the voices of many others—can have an impact. Writing to the president is a traditional way for citizens to express their opinions. Every day, the White House receives several thousand letters and other communications.

Why Should You Care? The president makes many decisions that directly influence your life. For example, in 2012 and 2013 many voices began to raise the question of reforming the nation's immigration policies. If any changes to immigration policies were to succeed, they would need strong support from the president. Immigration might be a subject on which you have firm opinions.

What Can You Do? The most traditional way to communicate with the White House is by letter. Letters to the president should be addressed to:

The President of the United States
The White House
1600 Pennsylvania Avenue N.W.
Washington, DC 20500

Letters may be sent to the First Lady at the same address. Will you get an answer? Almost certainly. The White House mail room is staffed by volunteers and paid employees who sort the mail for the president and tally the public's concerns. You may receive a standard response to your comments or a more personal, detailed response.

You can also call the White House on the telephone and leave a message for the president or First Lady. The White House has a round-the-clock comment line, which you can reach at 202-456-1111. When you call that number, an operator will take down your comments and forward them to the president's office.

To find the home page for the White House, type "white house" into any major search engine. The site is designed to be entertaining and to convey information about the president. You can also send your comments and ideas to the White House using e-mail. Send comments to the president at:

comments@whitehouse.gov

Address e-mail to the vice president at:

vice_president@whitehouse.gov

The White House has an active Web presence. Here, you see its home page. You can find information on just about all aspects of the federal government through this particular portal. Additionally, you can go to the "contact" section to e-mail your comments to the president and to the vice president. Even though both of those top officials are unlikely to personally read your e-mails, why is it still important to communicate with them? (www.whitehouse.gov)

key**terms**

advice and consent 229
appointment power 227
cabinet 238
chief diplomat 229
chief executive 227
chief legislator 230
chief of staff 240
civil service 227
commander in chief 228
constitutional
   power 235
diplomatic
   recognition 229

emergency power 235
executive
   agreement 230
Executive Office of the
   President (EOP) 239
executive order 236
executive privilege 236
expressed power 235
Federal Register 236
head of state 226
impeachment 237
inherent power 235
kitchen cabinet 239

line-item veto 232
National Security
   Council (NSC) 241
Office of Management
   and Budget
   (OMB) 241
pardon 227
patronage 232
pocket veto 232
reprieve 227
signing statement 237
State of the Union
   message 231

statutory power 235
Twelfth Amendment 226
Twenty-fifth
   Amendment 242
veto message 231
War Powers
   Resolution 228
White House Office 240

chapter**summary**

1 The office of the presidency in the United States, combining as it does the functions of chief of state and chief executive into a single elected official, was unique at the time of its creation. The framers of the Constitution were divided over whether the president should be a weak or a strong executive.

2 The requirements for the office of the presidency are outlined in Article II, Section 1, of the Constitution. The president's roles include both formal and informal duties. The roles of the president include head of state, chief executive, commander in chief, chief diplomat, chief legislator, party chief, and politician.

3 As head of state, the president is ceremonial leader of the government. As chief executive, the president is bound to enforce the acts of Congress, the judgments of the federal courts, and treaties. The chief executive has the power of appointment and the power to grant reprieves and pardons.

4 As commander in chief, the president is the ultimate decision maker in military matters. As chief diplomat, the president recognizes foreign governments, negotiates treaties, signs agreements, and nominates and receives ambassadors.

5 The role of chief legislator includes recommending legislation to Congress, lobbying for the legislation, approving laws, and exercising the veto power. Presidents are also leaders of their political parties and politicians. Presidents rely on their personal popularity to help them fulfill these functions.

6 In addition to constitutional and inherent powers, the president has statutory powers written into law by Congress. Presidents also have a variety of special powers not available to other branches of the government. These include emergency powers and the power to issue executive orders, to invoke executive privilege, and to issue signing statements.

7 Abuses of executive power are dealt with by Articles I and II of the Constitution, which authorize the House and Senate to impeach and remove the president, vice president, or other officers of the federal government for committing "Treason, Bribery, or other high Crimes and Misdemeanors."

8 The president receives assistance from the cabinet and from the Executive Office of the President (including the White House Office).

9 The vice president is the constitutional officer assigned to preside over the Senate and to assume the presidency in case of the death, resignation, removal, or disability of the president. The Twenty-fifth Amendment, passed in 1967, established procedures to be followed in case of presidential incapacity, death, or resignation, and when filling a vacant vice presidency.

test**yourself**

LO1 *Identify the types of people who typically undertake serious campaigns for the presidency.*

Anyone can become president of the United States, as long as she or he:

    a. is at least 35 years old.

    b. is at least 35 years old and a natural born citizen.

    c. is at least 40 years old and a natural born citizen.

LO2 *Distinguish some of the major roles of the president, including head of state, chief executive, commander in chief, chief diplomat, chief legislator, party chief, and politician.*

Our president is both head of state and chief executive, which means that the president:

    a. engages in ceremonial activities both at home and abroad, as well as faithfully ensures that the acts of Congress are enforced.

    b. designates the vice president to represent the United States in public ceremonies abroad.

    c. makes sure that treaties are upheld but delegates other actions to the cabinet.

LO3 *Describe some of the special powers of the president, and tell how a president can be removed from office.*

Upon impeachment by the House of Representatives, the president:

    a. must leave office immediately.

    b. cannot run for reelection.

    c. is tried by the Senate.

LO4 *Explain the organization of the executive branch and, in particular, the executive office of the president.*

The White House chief of staff, the ambassador to the United Nations, and the head of the Environmental Protection Agency:

    a. have at different times been named members of the president's cabinet.

    b. are all part of the Executive Office of the President.

    c. are not subject to presidential appointment.

LO5 *Evaluate the role of the vice president, and describe what happens if the presidency becomes vacant.*

If the president dies, the vice president takes over. If the vice president is also unavailable, then the following officer becomes president:

    a. the president pro tempore of the Senate.

    b. the Speaker of the House.

    c. the secretary of State.

Essay Question:

What characteristics do you think voters look for when choosing a president? Might these characteristics change as a result of changes in the political environment and the specific problems facing the nation? If you believe voters almost always look for the same characteristics when selecting a president, why is this? If voters seek somewhat different people as president depending on circumstances, which circumstances favor which kinds of leaders?

Answers to multiple-choice questions: 1. b, 2. a, 3. c, 4. a, 5. b.

CourseMate

Access CourseMate at www.cengagebrain.com for additional study tools: practice quizzes, key term flashcards and crossword puzzles, audio chapter summaries, simulations, animated learning modules, interactive timelines, videos, and American Government NewsWatch.

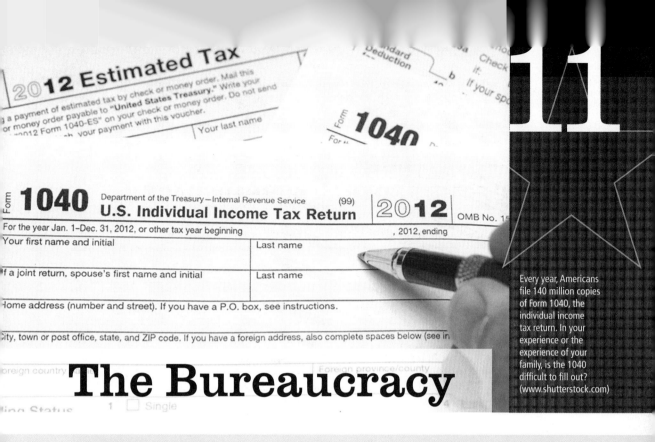

The Bureaucracy

LEARNING OUTCOMES

The five **Learning Outcomes (LOs)** below are designed to help improve your understanding of this chapter. After reading this chapter, you should be able to:

■ **LO1** Discuss the nature of the federal bureaucracy, and identify the largest federal spending programs.

■ **LO2** Describe the various types of agencies and organizations that make up the federal executive branch.

■ **LO3** Explain how government employees are hired and how they are administered.

■ **LO4** Evaluate different methods that have been put into place to reform bureaucracies and make them more efficient.

■ **LO5** Discuss how federal agencies make rules and what the role of Congress is in this process.

Check your understanding of the material with the Test Yourself section at the end of the chapter.

Faceless bureaucrats—this image provokes a negative reaction from many, if not most, Americans. Polls consistently report that the majority of Americans support "less government." The same polls, however, report that the majority of Americans support almost every specific program that the government undertakes. The conflict between the desire for small government and the desire for the benefits that only a large government can provide has been a constant feature of American politics. For example, the goal of preserving endangered species has widespread support. At the same time, many people believe that restrictions imposed under the Endangered Species Act violate the rights of landowners. Helping the elderly pay their medical bills is a popular objective, but hardly anyone enjoys paying the Medicare tax that supports this effort.

Bureaucracy
A large organization that is structured hierarchically to carry out specific functions.

In this chapter, we describe the size, organization, and staffing of the federal bureaucracy. We review modern attempts at bureaucratic reform and the process by which Congress exerts ultimate control over the bureaucracy. We also discuss the bureaucracy's role in making rules and setting policy.

THE NATURE AND SCOPE OF THE FEDERAL BUREAUCRACY

Bureaucracy is the name given to an organization that is structured hierarchically to carry out specific functions. Generally, bureaucracies are characterized by an organization chart. The units of the organization are divided according to the specialization and expertise of the employees.

LO1: Discuss the nature of the federal bureaucracy, and identify the largest federal spending programs.

Public and Private Bureaucracies

We should not think of bureaucracy as unique to government. Any large corporation or university can be considered a bureaucratic organization. The fact is that the handling of complex problems requires a division of labor. Individuals must concentrate their skills on specific, well-defined aspects of a problem and depend on others to solve the rest of it.

Public or government bureaucracies differ from private organizations in some important ways, however. A private corporation has a single leader—its chief executive officer (CEO). Public bureaucracies do not have a single leader. Although the president is the chief administrator of the federal system, all agencies are subject to the dictates of Congress for their funding, staffing, and, indeed, their continued existence. Public bureaucracies supposedly serve all citizens, while private ones serve private interests.

One other important difference between private corporations and government bureaucracies is that government bureaucracies are not organized to make a profit. Rather, they are supposed to perform their functions as efficiently as possible to conserve taxpayers' dollars. Perhaps it is this ideal that makes citizens hostile toward government bureaucracy when they experience inefficiency and red tape.

Every modern president, at one time or another, has proclaimed that his administration was going to "fix government." All modern presidents also have put forth plans to end government waste and inefficiency (see Table 11–1 below). Their success has been, in

TABLE 11–1: Selected Presidential Plans to End Government Inefficiency

President	Plan
Lyndon Johnson (1963–1969)	Programming, planning, and budgeting systems
Richard Nixon (1969–1974)	Management by Objectives
Jimmy Carter (1977–1981)	Zero-Based Budgeting
Ronald Reagan (1981–1989)	President's Private Sector Survey on Cost Control (the Grace Commission)
George H. W. Bush (1989–1993)	Right-Sizing Government
Bill Clinton (1993–2001)	Reinventing Government
George W. Bush (2001–2009)	Performance-Based Budgeting
Barack Obama (2009–)	Appointment of a chief performance officer

a word, underwhelming. Presidents generally have been powerless to affect significantly the structure and operation of the federal bureaucracy.

The Size of the Bureaucracy

In 1789, the new government's bureaucracy was tiny. There were three departments—State (with nine employees), War (with two employees), and Treasury (with thirty-nine employees)—and the Office of the Attorney General (which later became the Department of Justice). The bureaucracy was still small in 1798. At that time, the secretary of state had seven clerks and spent a total of $500 (about $10,000 in 2014 dollars) on stationery and printing. In that same year, an appropriations act allocated $1.4 million, or $28 million in 2014 dollars, to the War Department.

Government Employment Today. Times have changed. Excluding 1.4 million military service members, but including employees of Congress, the courts, and the U.S. Postal Service, the federal bureaucracy includes approximately 2.7 million employees. That number has remained relatively stable for the past several decades. It is somewhat deceiving, however, because many other individuals work directly or indirectly for the federal government as subcontractors or consultants and in other capacities.

Figure 11–1 below shows the combined growth in government employment at the federal, state, and local levels. Since 1952, this growth has been mainly at the state and local levels. If all government employees are included, about 16 percent of all civilian employment is accounted for by government.

The Impact of Ronald Reagan. Notice in Figure 11–1 that government employment as a share of the total U.S. population grew rapidly from the mid-1950s until 1980. In that year, Republican Ronald Reagan was elected president. Under Reagan, government

FIGURE 11–1: Government Employees

Total local, state, and federal employees, as a percentage of the total U.S. population (1952–2013)

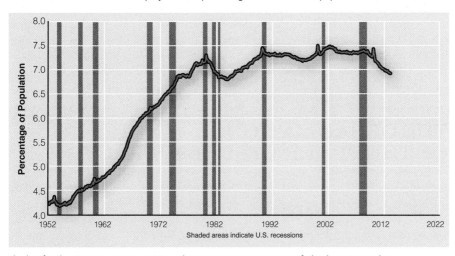

The brief spikes in 1980, 1990, 2000, and 2010 represent temporary federal census workers.

Source: The Federal Reserve Economic Data (FRED) service of the St. Louis Federal Reserve.

employment actually fell, in large part because of the elimination of revenue sharing, a program through which the federal government transferred large sums to state and local governments. While government employment picked up later in Reagan's administration, it never resumed the constant upward course characteristic of the 1960s and 1970s. In short, Reagan's "conservative revolution" had a genuine impact on the trajectory of government.

The Federal Budget

In 1929, spending by all levels of government was equivalent to only about 11 percent of the nation's gross domestic product. For fiscal year 2013, it was about 38 percent. One factor driving the rate of government spending recently has been the Great Recession that began in December 2007. Increased spending enacted in an attempt to combat the recession—plus a fall in federal revenues—dramatically increased the size of the federal budget deficit. How much of a problem is the deficit? We examine that topic in the *At Issue* feature on page 253.

Social Spending. Studies repeatedly show that most Americans have a very inaccurate idea of how the federal budget is spent. Figure 11–2 on the facing page can help. This pie chart demonstrates that more than a third of all federal spending goes to two programs that benefit older Americans—Social Security and Medicare. Additional social programs, many aimed at low-income individuals and families, push the total amount of social spending past the 50 percent mark. In effect, the federal government spends much more on the poor than many people realize. Medicaid, a joint federal-state program that provides health-care services, is the largest of these programs. (CHIP is the Children's Health Insurance Program, and SNAP is the Supplementary Nutrition Assistance Program, previously known as food stamps.) In contrast, traditional cash welfare—Temporary Assistance for Needy Families (TANF)—accounts for only 0.5 percent of the budget ($17 billion) and is buried in the "Miscellaneous low-income and disability support" slice.

Defense and All the Rest. Military defense and veterans' benefits are nearly a quarter of the whole. Interest payments on the national debt are 6 percent. Education, transportation, law enforcement, and other functions amount to only 17 percent of the budget. Foreign aid, which is included in the "Everything else" slice, is 1.5 percent, or $57 billion. This is a substantial sum, but it is much smaller than many people imagine.

THE ORGANIZATION OF THE FEDERAL BUREAUCRACY

LO2: Describe the various types of agencies and organizations that make up the federal executive branch.

Within the federal bureaucracy are a number of different types of government agencies and organizations. Figure 11–3 on page 252 outlines the several bodies within the executive branch, as well as the separate organizations that provide services to Congress, to the courts, and directly to the president. The executive branch, which employs most of the government's staff, has four major types of structures. They are (1) cabinet departments, (2) independent executive agencies, (3) independent regulatory agencies, and (4) government corporations. Each has a distinctive relationship to the president, and some have unusual internal structures, overall goals, and grants of power.

FIGURE 11-2: Federal Government Spending, Fiscal Year 2013

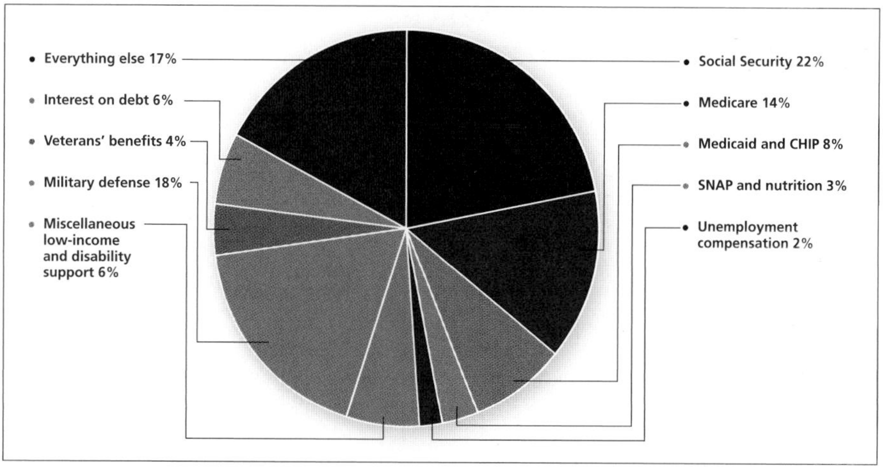

- Everything else 17%
- Interest on debt 6%
- Veterans' benefits 4%
- Military defense 18%
- Miscellaneous low-income and disability support 6%

- Social Security 22%
- Medicare 14%
- Medicaid and CHIP 8%
- SNAP and nutrition 3%
- Unemployment compensation 2%

Source: usgovernmentspending.com.

Cabinet Departments

The fifteen **cabinet departments** are the major service organizations of the federal government. They can also be described in management terms as **line organizations.** This means that they are directly accountable to the president and are responsible for performing government functions, such as printing money and training troops. These departments were created by Congress when the need for each department arose. The first department to be created was State, and the most recent one was Homeland Security, established in 2003. A president might ask that a new department be created or an old one abolished, but the president has no power to do so without legislative approval from Congress.

Each department is headed by a secretary (except for the Justice Department, which is headed by the attorney general). Each department also has several levels of under-secretaries, assistant secretaries, and other personnel.

Presidents theoretically have considerable control over the cabinet departments, because presidents are able to appoint or fire all of the top officials. Even cabinet departments do not always respond to the president's wishes, though. One reason why presidents are frequently unhappy with their departments is that the entire bureaucratic structure below the top political levels is staffed by permanent employees. Many of these employees are committed to established programs or procedures and resist change. Table 11-2 on pages 254-255 shows that each cabinet (executive) department employs thousands of individuals, only a handful of whom are under the direct control of the president. The table also describes some of the functions of each of the departments.

Independent Executive Agencies

Independent executive agencies are bureaucratic organizations that are not located within a department but report directly to the president, who appoints their chief officials. When a new federal agency is created—the Environmental Protection Agency, for

Social Media in Politics
Most federal agencies now have a social media presence, and the Centers for Disease Control offers one of the best. For up-to-the-minute health advice, follow CDCgov on Twitter. For hilarious advice on what to do in a natural disaster, search on "cdc zombie apocalypse" on Twitter.

Cabinet Department
One of the fifteen major departments of the executive branch.

Line Organization
In the federal government, an administrative unit that is directly accountable to the president.

Independent Executive Agency
A federal agency that is not part of a cabinet department but reports directly to the president.

FIGURE 11–3: Organization Chart of the Federal Government, 2013

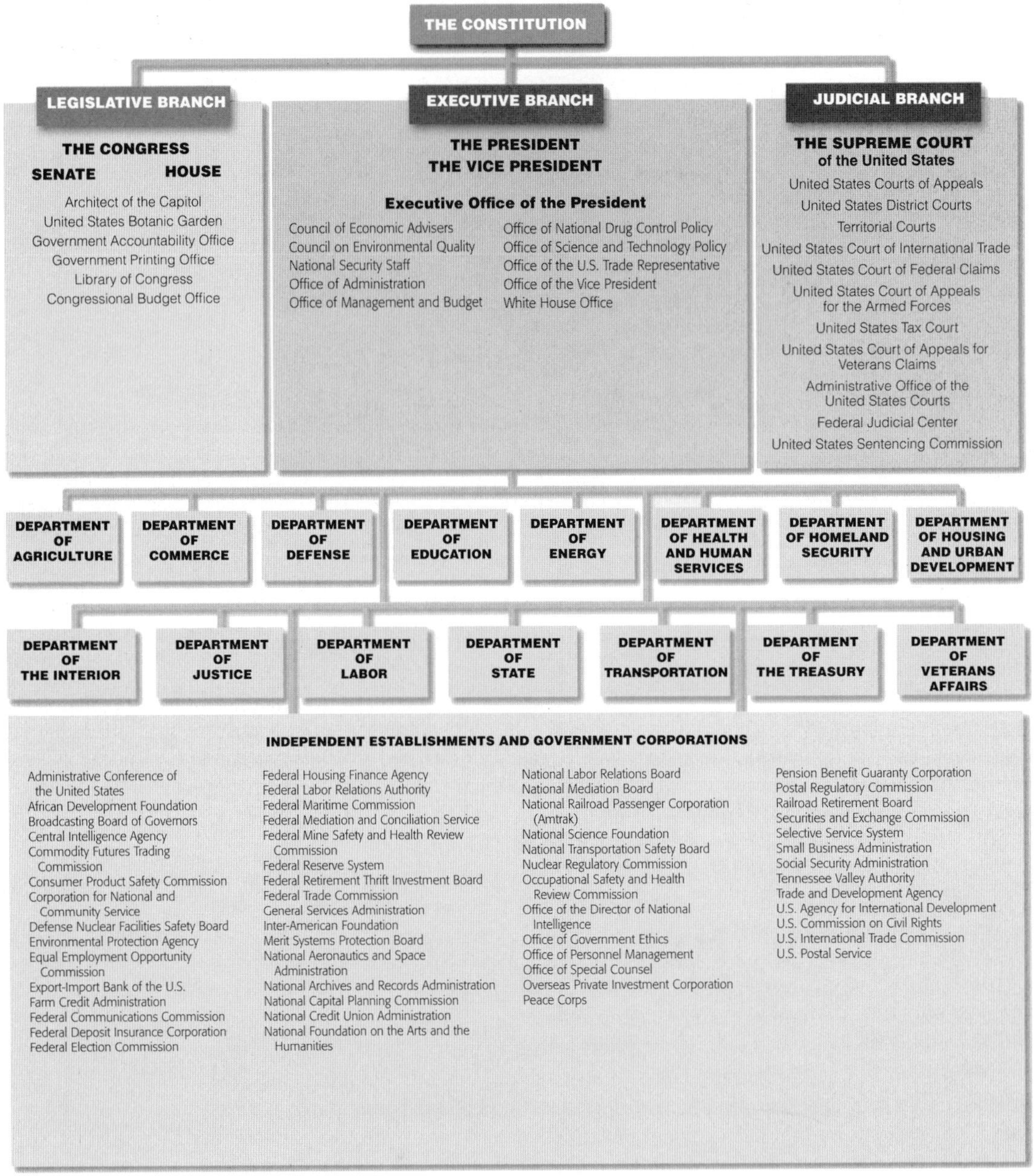

THE CONSTITUTION

LEGISLATIVE BRANCH

THE CONGRESS

SENATE **HOUSE**

Architect of the Capitol
United States Botanic Garden
Government Accountability Office
Government Printing Office
Library of Congress
Congressional Budget Office

EXECUTIVE BRANCH

THE PRESIDENT
THE VICE PRESIDENT

Executive Office of the President

Council of Economic Advisers
Council on Environmental Quality
National Security Staff
Office of Administration
Office of Management and Budget

Office of National Drug Control Policy
Office of Science and Technology Policy
Office of the U.S. Trade Representative
Office of the Vice President
White House Office

JUDICIAL BRANCH

THE SUPREME COURT
of the United States

United States Courts of Appeals
United States District Courts
Territorial Courts
United States Court of International Trade
United States Court of Federal Claims
United States Court of Appeals
for the Armed Forces
United States Tax Court
United States Court of Appeals for
Veterans Claims
Administrative Office of the
United States Courts
Federal Judicial Center
United States Sentencing Commission

DEPARTMENT OF AGRICULTURE

DEPARTMENT OF COMMERCE

DEPARTMENT OF DEFENSE

DEPARTMENT OF EDUCATION

DEPARTMENT OF ENERGY

DEPARTMENT OF HEALTH AND HUMAN SERVICES

DEPARTMENT OF HOMELAND SECURITY

DEPARTMENT OF HOUSING AND URBAN DEVELOPMENT

DEPARTMENT OF THE INTERIOR

DEPARTMENT OF JUSTICE

DEPARTMENT OF LABOR

DEPARTMENT OF STATE

DEPARTMENT OF TRANSPORTATION

DEPARTMENT OF THE TREASURY

DEPARTMENT OF VETERANS AFFAIRS

INDEPENDENT ESTABLISHMENTS AND GOVERNMENT CORPORATIONS

Administrative Conference of
the United States
African Development Foundation
Broadcasting Board of Governors
Central Intelligence Agency
Commodity Futures Trading
Commission
Consumer Product Safety Commission
Corporation for National and
Community Service
Defense Nuclear Facilities Safety Board
Environmental Protection Agency
Equal Employment Opportunity
Commission
Export-Import Bank of the U.S.
Farm Credit Administration
Federal Communications Commission
Federal Deposit Insurance Corporation
Federal Election Commission

Federal Housing Finance Agency
Federal Labor Relations Authority
Federal Maritime Commission
Federal Mediation and Conciliation Service
Federal Mine Safety and Health Review
Commission
Federal Reserve System
Federal Retirement Thrift Investment Board
Federal Trade Commission
General Services Administration
Inter-American Foundation
Merit Systems Protection Board
National Aeronautics and Space
Administration
National Archives and Records Administration
National Capital Planning Commission
National Credit Union Administration
National Foundation on the Arts and the
Humanities

National Labor Relations Board
National Mediation Board
National Railroad Passenger Corporation
(Amtrak)
National Science Foundation
National Transportation Safety Board
Nuclear Regulatory Commission
Occupational Safety and Health
Review Commission
Office of the Director of National
Intelligence
Office of Government Ethics
Office of Personnel Management
Office of Special Counsel
Overseas Private Investment Corporation
Peace Corps

Pension Benefit Guaranty Corporation
Postal Regulatory Commission
Railroad Retirement Board
Securities and Exchange Commission
Selective Service System
Small Business Administration
Social Security Administration
Tennessee Valley Authority
Trade and Development Agency
U.S. Agency for International Development
U.S. Commission on Civil Rights
U.S. International Trade Commission
U.S. Postal Service

Sources: *United States Government Manual,* December 2012 edition (Washington, D.C.: U.S. Government Printing Office, 2012), and authors' updates.

example—Congress decides where it will be located in the bureaucracy. In recent decades, presidents often have asked that a new organization be kept separate or independent rather than added to an existing department, particularly if a department may be hostile to the agency's creation.

at issue

DO WE STILL HAVE TO WORRY ABOUT THE FEDERAL DEFICIT?

The federal spending budget is large relative to the size of the economy. Each year, if spending exceeds revenues, the federal government runs a deficit. That deficit is added to the national debt. Every year for almost half a century, the government has run a deficit—large or small—except for four years that began during the Clinton administration (1993–2001).

The absolute amount of the federal deficit and debt may not matter that much, however. What is important is their size relative to the size of the economy (typically measured as gross domestic product, or GDP). If GDP grows faster than the national debt, which has happened, the government's fiscal position gets better, not worse. If GDP falls or fails to rise, however, there may be trouble. In 2007, just before the Great Recession, the federal deficit was 1.15 percent of GDP and net national debt was about 36 percent of GDP. By 2013, after four years of trillion-dollar-plus deficits, the net debt stood at 65 percent of GDP. Should we be worried—or even panicked—about continuing federal deficits and the resulting increases in the national debt?

THINGS ARE LOOKING UP

Recently, a number of liberal economists, such as Nobel Prize winner Paul Krugman, have argued that the deficit problem is mostly solved. Congress passed budget cuts in 2011. In December 2012, due to the "fiscal cliff" crisis, tax rates on wealthier Americans went up, raising more revenue. In March 2013, the so-called sequester imposed additional budget cuts. The Congressional Budget Office (CBO) predicts that if current laws remain in effect, the deficit as a percentage of GDP will fall sharply until 2015, after which it will rise slowly. It would take only a small amount of extra budget cutting after 2015 to stabilize the national debt over the next decade.

Thereafter, every model predicts budget trouble due to increased health-care costs. Liberal economists argue that our main task should be controlling health-care costs by eliminating inefficiencies. That is certainly doable—there is some evidence that attempts to curb costs may already be having an effect. We should focus our political energies there, instead of worrying about the supposed imminent bankruptcy of the U.S. government.

WE MUST CUT—NOT JUST STABILIZE—THE NATIONAL DEBT

Those who believe that we still have a serious debt and deficit problem say that it is not enough to merely stabilize the debt at a high level. High levels of debt can be trouble all by themselves. Economists Carmen Reinhart and Kenneth Rogoff have argued that at levels only slightly higher than what the CBO predicts, national debt interferes with economic growth. Their paper has been widely cited by conservatives and establishment institutions such as the *Washington Post* editorial page, though other economists have criticized it harshly.

Whether Reinhart and Rogoff are right or wrong, high levels of debt are dangerous for another reason. During the Great Recession, the national debt as a percentage of GDP almost doubled. If the debt doesn't come down again, what happens if there is another recession? Sooner or later, we will have one, even if it is not as bad as the last one was. Can we afford to ramp up the debt *again*? An additional serious problem—what if interest rates go back up? If that were to happen, the costs of sustaining a large national debt could become painful indeed.

FOR CRITICAL ANALYSIS

If we do have a long-term need to reduce the national debt, is it important that we start right away—or should we wait until the economy is booming again? Either way, why?

Independent Regulatory Agencies

Typically, an **independent regulatory agency** is responsible for a specific type of public policy. Its function is to make and implement rules and regulations in a particular sphere of action to protect the public interest. The earliest such agency was the Interstate Commerce Commission (ICC), which was established in 1887 when Americans began to seek some

Independent Regulatory Agency
An agency outside the major executive departments charged with making and implementing rules and regulations within a specific area.

TABLE 11–2: Executive Departments

Department and Year Established	Principal Functions	Selected Subagencies
State (1789) (12,854 employees)	Negotiates treaties, develops foreign policy, protects citizens abroad.	Passport Services Office, Bureau of Diplomatic Security, Foreign Service, Bureau of Human Rights and Humanitarian Affairs, Bureau of Consular Affairs.
Treasury (1789) (104,100 employees)	Pays all federal bills, borrows money, collects federal taxes, mints coins and prints paper currency, supervises national banks.	Internal Revenue Service, U.S. Mint.
Interior (1849) (69,702 employees)	Supervises federally owned lands and parks, supervises Native American affairs.	U.S. Fish and Wildlife Service, National Park Service, Bureau of Indian Affairs, Bureau of Land Management.
Justice (1870)[a] (116,323 employees)	Furnishes legal advice to the president, enforces federal criminal laws, supervises federal prisons.	Federal Bureau of Investigation, Drug Enforcement Administration, Bureau of Prisons.
Agriculture (1889) (91,278 employees)	Provides assistance to farmers and ranchers, conducts agricultural research, works to protect forests.	Soil Conservation Service, Agricultural Research Service, Food Safety and Inspection Service, Federal Crop Insurance Corporation, Commodity Credit Corporation, Forest Service.
Commerce (1913)[b] (44,996 employees)	Grants patents and trademarks, conducts a national census, monitors the weather, protects the interests of businesses.	Bureau of the Census, Bureau of Economic Analysis, Patent and Trademark Office, National Oceanic and Atmospheric Administration.
Labor (1913)[b] (16,816 employees)	Administers federal labor laws, promotes the interests of workers.	Occupational Safety and Health Administration, Bureau of Labor Statistics, Employment Standards Administration, Employment and Training Administration.
Defense (1947)[c] (761,533 employees)	Manages the armed forces (army, navy, air force, and marines), operates military bases, is responsible for civil defense.	National Security Agency; Joint Chiefs of Staff; Departments of the Air Force, Navy, Army; Defense Advanced Research Projects Agency; Defense Intelligence Agency; the service academies.

[a]Formed from the Office of the Attorney General (created in 1789).
[b]Formed from the Department of Commerce and Labor (created in 1903).
[c]Formed from the Department of War (created in 1789) and the Department of the Navy (created in 1798).

form of government control over the rapidly growing business and industrial sector. This new form of organization, the independent regulatory agency, was supposed to make technical, nonpolitical decisions about rates, profits, and rules that would be for the benefit of all and that did not require congressional legislation. In the years that followed the creation of the ICC, other agencies were formed to regulate communication (the Federal Communications Commission) and nuclear power (the Nuclear Regulatory Commission). (The ICC was abolished in 1995.)

The Purpose and Nature of Regulatory Agencies. In practice, regulatory agencies are administered independently of all three branches of government. They were set up because Congress felt it was unable to handle the complexities and technicalities required

TABLE 11–2: Executive Departments (continued)

Department and Year Established	Principal Functions	Selected Subagencies
Housing and Urban Development (1965) (9,114 employees)	Deals with the nation's housing needs, develops and rehabilitates urban communities, oversees resale of mortgages.	Government National Mortgage Association, Office of Community Planning and Development, Office of Fair Housing and Equal Opportunity.
Transportation (1967) (57,042 employees)	Finances improvements in mass transit; develops and administers programs for highways, railroads, and aviation.	Federal Aviation Administration, Federal Highway Administration, National Highway Traffic Safety Administration, Federal Transit Administration.
Energy (1977) (15,715 employees)	Promotes the conservation of energy and resources, analyzes energy data, conducts research and development.	Federal Energy Regulatory Commission, National Nuclear Security Administration.
Health and Human Services (1979)[d] (86,532 employees)	Promotes public health, enforces pure food and drug laws, conducts and sponsors health-related research.	Food and Drug Administration, Public Health Service, Centers for Disease Control and Prevention, National Institutes of Health, Centers for Medicare and Medicaid Services.
Education (1979)[d] (4,294 employees)	Coordinates federal programs and policies for education, administers aid to education, promotes educational research.	Office of Special Education and Rehabilitation Service, Office of Elementary and Secondary Education, Office of Postsecondary Education, Office of Vocational and Adult Education, Office of Federal Student Aid.
Veterans Affairs (1988) (328,088 employees)	Promotes the welfare of veterans of the U.S. armed forces.	Veterans Health Administration, Veterans Benefits Administration, National Cemetery Systems.
Homeland Security (2003) (197,627 employees)	Attempts to prevent terrorist attacks within the United States, control America's borders, and minimize the damage from natural disasters.	U.S. Customs and Border Protection, U.S. Coast Guard, Secret Service, Federal Emergency Management Agency, U.S. Citizenship and Immigration Services, U.S. Immigration and Customs Enforcement.

[d]Formed from the Department of Health, Education, and Welfare (created in 1953).

to carry out specific laws in the public interest. Regulatory agencies and commissions actually combine some functions of all three branches of government—legislative, executive, and judicial. They are legislative in that they make rules that have the force of law. They are executive in that they provide for the enforcement of those rules. They are judicial in that they decide disputes involving the rules they have made.

Heads of regulatory agencies and members of agency boards or commissions are appointed by the president with the consent of the Senate, although they do not report to the president. When an agency is headed by a board rather than an individual, the members of the board cannot, by law, all be from the same political party. Presidents can influence regulatory agency behavior by appointing people of their own parties or individuals who share their political views when vacancies occur, in particular when the chair is vacant. Members may be removed by the president only for causes specified in the law creating the agency.

Agency Capture. Over the last several decades, some observers have concluded that regulatory agencies, although nominally independent, may in fact not always be so.

A mail clerk helps a customer in Fairfax, Virginia. The U.S. Postal Service, a government corporation, is currently taking a large loss on its operations. Still, the United States enjoys one of the lowest rates for domestic letter postage in the industrialized world—$0.46. The equivalent rate in U.S. dollars is $0.78 in Britain, $0.77 in France, and $0.80 in Japan. (Andrew Harrer/Bloomberg via Getty Images)

They contend that many agencies have been **captured** by the very industries and firms that they were supposed to regulate and therefore make decisions based on the interests of the industry, not the general public. The results have been less competition rather than more competition, higher prices rather than lower prices, and fewer choices rather than more choices for consumers.

Deregulation and Reregulation. During the presidency of Jimmy Carter (1977–1981), significant deregulation (the removal of regulatory restraints— the opposite of regulation) was initiated. For example, Carter appointed a chairperson of the Civil Aeronautics Board (CAB) who gradually eliminated regulation of airline fares and routes. Deregulation continued under President Ronald Reagan (1981– 1989). During the administration of George H. W. Bush (1989–1993), calls for reregulation of many businesses increased, and several new regulatory acts were passed.

Under President Bill Clinton (1993–2001), however, the Interstate Commerce Commission was eliminated, and the banking and telecommunications industries, along with many other sectors of the economy, were deregulated. At the same time, there was extensive regulation to protect the environment, a trend somewhat attenuated by the George W. Bush administration.

After the financial crisis of September 2008, many people saw inadequate regulation of the financial industry as a major cause of the nation's economic difficulties. During President Barack Obama's administration, therefore, reregulation of that industry became a major objective. After intense debate, Congress passed a comprehensive financial industry regulation plan in 2010.

Americans have had conflicting views about the amount of regulation that is appropriate for various industries ever since the government began to undertake serious regulatory activities. Many people find regulation to be contrary to the spirit of free enterprise and the American tradition of individualism. Yet in cases such as BP's Deepwater Horizon oil spill disaster in the Gulf of Mexico in April 2010, citizens of all political stripes were outraged to learn that the relevant regulatory agency at the time, the Minerals Management Service, had failed to do its job.

Capture
The act by which an industry being regulated by a government agency gains direct or indirect control over agency personnel and decision makers.

Government Corporation
An agency of government that administers a quasi-business enterprise. These corporations are used when government activities are primarily commercial.

Government Corporations

Another form of bureaucratic organization in the United States is the **government corporation.** Although the concept is borrowed from the world of business, there are important differences between public and private corporations.

A private corporation has shareholders (stockholders) who in principle elect a board of directors, who in turn choose the corporate officers, such as the CEO. When a private corporation makes a profit, it must pay taxes (unless it avoids them through various legal loopholes). It distributes the after-tax profits to shareholders as dividends or plows the profits back into the corporation to make new investments, or both.

A government corporation has a board of directors and managers, but it does not usually have any stockholders. The public cannot buy shares of stock in a typical government corporation, and if the entity makes a profit, it does not distribute the profit as dividends. Nor does it have to pay taxes on profits—the profits remain in the corporation. The largest and most famous such government corporation is the U.S. Postal Service, with 522,000 employees. Another well-known example is Amtrak, the passenger railway service, with a staff of more than 20,000.

Bankruptcy. The federal government can also take effective control of a private corporation in a number of different circumstances. One is bankruptcy. When a company files for bankruptcy, it asks a federal judge for relief from its creditors. The judge, operating under bankruptcy laws established by Congress (as specified in the Constitution), is ultimately responsible for the fate of the enterprise. When a bank fails, the government has a special interest in protecting customers who have deposited funds with the bank. For that reason, the failing institution is taken over by the Federal Deposit Insurance Corporation (FDIC), which ensures continuity of service to bank customers.

Government Ownership of Private Enterprises. The federal government can also obtain partial or complete ownership of a private corporation by purchasing its stock. Before 2008, such takeovers were rare, although they occasionally happened. When Continental Illinois, then the nation's seventh-largest bank, failed in 1984, the FDIC wound up in control of the institution for ten years before it could find a buyer. The FDIC pumped $4.5 billion of new capital—provided by the taxpayers—into the bank, ensuring its solvency.

The Bank Bailout. The Continental Illinois rescue provided a blueprint for the massive bank bailout initiated by Henry Paulson, President Bush's Treasury secretary, in October 2008. The Troubled Asset Relief Program (TARP) gave the Treasury the authority to spend up to $700 billion. Of this sum, about $400 billion was actually disbursed by Paulson and by Timothy Geithner, Obama's Treasury secretary. The government made investments in more than eight hundred businesses, including banks, automobile companies, and the giant insurance company AIG.

The bailout program was tremendously unpopular, but by 2011 most banks had paid back the government's investments.

⊕ **WWW**

Helpful Web Sites
Two publications are available online to help you learn more about the federal bureaucracy. The *Federal Register* is the official publication for executive branch documents. You can find it by searching on its name. The second is the *United States Government Manual*, which describes every federal department and agency. Type "gov manual" into a search engine.

Outside the front door of Fannie Mae headquarters, Washington D.C. When the Federal National Mortgage Association (Fannie Mae) started to fail, the federal government took over. Who ultimately paid for its losses? (Bill O'Leary/*The Washington Post*/Getty Images).

The auto companies and AIG had announced plans to do likewise. In October 2012, the Congressional Budget Office stated that TARP's final cost to the taxpayers was $24 billion.

The Government-Sponsored Enterprise. An additional type of corporation is the government-sponsored enterprise, a business created by the federal government itself, which then sells part or all of the corporation's stock to private investors. Until 2008, the leading examples of this kind of company were the Federal Home Loan Mortgage Corporation, known as Freddie Mac, and the Federal National Mortgage Association, commonly known as Fannie Mae. Both of these firms buy mortgages from banks and bundle them into securities that can be sold to investors. When the housing market collapsed, so—eventually—did Freddie Mac and Fannie Mae.

Investors had always assumed that the federal government backed the obligations of the two enterprises, even though the government had never issued an explicit guarantee. In September 2008, the implicit guarantee became real when Treasury secretary Paulson placed the two mortgage giants under a federal "conservatorship" and pumped billions in fresh capital—also provided by the taxpayers—into them through purchases of preferred and common stock. In contrast to the TARP investments, the sums invested in Freddie Mac and Fannie Mae have been paid back slowly. As of mid-2013, they still owed $51 billion of the $187 billion that the government had invested in them.

STAFFING THE BUREAUCRACY

There are two categories of bureaucrats: political appointees and civil servants. As noted earlier, the president can make political appointments to most of the top jobs in the federal bureaucracy. The president also can appoint ambassadors to foreign posts. All of the jobs that are considered "political plums" and that usually go to the politically well connected are listed in *Policy and Supporting Positions,* a book published by the Government Printing Office after each presidential election. Informally (and appropriately), this has been called the "Plum Book." The rest of the national government's employees belong to the civil service and obtain their jobs through a much more formal process.

LO3: Explain how government employees are hired and how they are administered.

Political Appointees

To fill the positions listed in the Plum Book, the president and the president's advisers solicit suggestions from politicians, businesspersons, and other prominent individuals. Appointments to these positions offer the president a way to pay off outstanding political debts. Presidents often use ambassadorships to reward individuals for their campaign contributions. But the president must also take into consideration such things as the candidate's work experience, intelligence, political affiliations, and personal characteristics.

The Aristocracy of the Federal Government. Political appointees are in some sense the aristocracy of the federal government. But their powers, although they appear formidable on paper, are often exaggerated. Like the president, a political appointee will occupy her or his position for a comparatively brief time. Political appointees often leave office before the president's term actually ends. In fact, the average term of service for political appointees is less than two years. As a result, most appointees have little background for their positions and may be mere figureheads. Often, they only respond to the paperwork that flows up from below. Additionally, the professional civil servants who make up the permanent civil service may not feel compelled to carry out their current chief's directives quickly, because they know that he or she will not be around for very long.

The Difficulty in Firing Civil Servants. This inertia is compounded by the fact that it is very difficult to discharge civil servants. In recent years, fewer than 0.1 percent of federal employees have been fired for incompetence. Because discharged employees may appeal their dismissals, many months or even years can pass before the issue is resolved conclusively. This occupational rigidity helps to ensure that most political appointees, no matter how competent or driven, will not be able to exert much meaningful influence over their subordinates, let alone implement dramatic changes in the bureaucracy itself.

History of the Federal Civil Service

When the federal government was formed in 1789, it had no career public servants but rather consisted of amateurs who were almost all Federalists. When Thomas Jefferson took over as president, few federal administrative jobs were held by members of his party, so he fired more than one hundred officials and replaced them with his own supporters. Then, for the next twenty-five years, a growing body of federal administrators gained experience and expertise, becoming in the process professional public servants. These administrators stayed in office regardless of who was elected president. The bureaucracy had become a self-maintaining, long-term element within government.

To the Victors Belong the Spoils. When Andrew Jackson took over the White House in 1828, he could not believe how many appointed officials (appointed before he became president, that is) were overtly hostile toward him and his Democratic Party. Because the bureaucracy was reluctant to carry out his programs, Jackson did the obvious: he fired federal officials—more than all his predecessors combined. The **spoils system**—an application of the principle that to the victors belong the spoils—became the standard method of filling federal positions. Whenever a new president was elected from a party different from the party of the previous president, there would be an almost complete turnover in the staffing of the federal government.

The Civil Service Reform Act of 1883. Jackson's spoils system survived for a number of years, but it became increasingly corrupt. In addition, the size of the bureaucracy increased by 300 percent between 1851 and 1881. As the bureaucracy grew larger, the cry for civil service reform became louder. Reformers began to look to the example of several European countries—in particular, Germany. That country had established a professional civil service that operated under a **merit system,** in which job appointments were based on competitive examinations.

In 1883, the **Pendleton Act—** or **Civil Service Reform Act**—was passed, placing the first limits on the spoils system. The act established the principle of employment on the basis of open, competitive examinations and created the **Civil Service Commission** to administer the personnel service. Only 10 percent of

Spoils System
The awarding of government jobs to political supporters and friends.

Merit System
The selection, retention, and promotion of government employees on the basis of competitive examinations.

Pendleton Act (Civil Service Reform Act)
An act that established the principle of federal government employment based on merit and created the Civil Service Commission to administer the personnel service.

Civil Service Commission
The initial central personnel agency of the national government; created in 1883.

President James A. Garfield was assassinated in 1881 by a disappointed office seeker, Charles J. Guiteau. The long-term effect of this event was to replace the spoils system with a permanent career civil service. This process began with the passage of the Pendleton Act in 1883, which established the Civil Service Commission. (Library of Congress)

federal employees were covered by the merit system initially. Later laws, amendments, and executive orders, however, increased the coverage to more than 90 percent of federal employees. The effects of these reforms were felt at all levels of government.

The Supreme Court strengthened the civil service system in 1976 and in 1980.[1] In those two cases, the Court used the First Amendment to forbid government officials from discharging or threatening to discharge public employees solely for not being supporters of the political party in power unless party affiliation is an appropriate requirement for the position. Additional enhancements to the civil service system were added in 1990.[2] The Court's ruling in that year effectively prevented the use of partisan political considerations as the basis for hiring, promoting, or transferring most public employees. An exception was permitted, however, for senior policymaking positions, which usually go to officials who will support the programs of the elected leaders.

The Civil Service Reform Act of 1978. In 1978, the Civil Service Reform Act abolished the Civil Service Commission and created two new federal agencies to perform its duties. To administer the civil service laws, rules, and regulations, the act created the Office of Personnel Management (OPM). The OPM is empowered to recruit, interview, and test potential government workers and determine who should be hired. The OPM makes recommendations to the individual agencies as to which persons meet the standards (typically, the top three applicants for a position), and the agencies then decide whom to hire. To oversee promotions, employees' rights, and other employment matters, the act created the Merit Systems Protection Board (MSPB). The MSPB evaluates charges of wrongdoing, hears employee appeals of agency decisions, and can order corrective action against agencies and employees.

Federal Employees and Political Campaigns. In 1933, when President Franklin D. Roosevelt set up his New Deal, an army of civil servants was hired to staff the many new agencies that were created. Because the individuals who worked in these agencies owed their jobs to the Democratic Party, it seemed natural for them to campaign for Democratic candidates. The Democrats who controlled Congress in the mid-1930s did not object. But in 1938, a coalition of conservative Democrats and Republicans took control of Congress and forced through the Hatch Act—or Political Activities Act—of 1939. The act prohibited federal employees from actively participating in the political management of campaigns. It also forbade the use of federal authority to influence nominations and elections, and it outlawed the use of bureaucratic rank to pressure federal employees to make political contributions.

The Hatch Act created a controversy that lasted for decades. Many contended that the act deprived federal employees of their First Amendment freedoms of speech and association. In 1972, a federal district court declared the act unconstitutional. The United States Supreme Court, however, reaffirmed the challenged portion of the act in 1973, stating that the government's interest in preserving a nonpartisan civil service was so great that the prohibitions should remain.[3] Twenty years later, Congress addressed the criticisms of the Hatch Act by passing the Federal Employees Political Activities Act of 1993. This act, which amended the Hatch Act, lessened the harshness of the 1939 act in several ways. Among other things, the 1993 act allowed federal employees to run for office in non-

---

1. *Elrod v. Burns,* 427 U.S. 347 (1976) and *Branti v. Finkel,* 445 U.S. 507 (1980).
2. *Rutan v. Republican Party of Illinois,* 497 U.S. 62 (1990).
3. *United States Civil Service Commission v. National Association of Letter Carriers,* 413 U.S. 548 (1973).

partisan elections, participate in voter-registration drives, make campaign contributions to political organizations, and campaign for candidates in partisan elections.

MODERN ATTEMPTS AT BUREAUCRATIC REFORM

As long as the federal bureaucracy exists, attempts to make it more open, efficient, and responsive to the needs of U.S. citizens will continue. The most important actual and proposed reforms in the last several decades include sunshine and sunset laws, privatization, incentives for efficiency and productivity, and more protection for so-called whistleblowers.

LO4: Evaluate different methods that have been put into place to reform bureaucracies and make them more efficient.

Sunshine Laws before and after 9/11

In 1976, Congress enacted the **Government in the Sunshine Act.** It required for the first time that all multiheaded federal agencies—agencies headed by a committee instead of an individual—hold their meetings regularly in public session. The bill defined *meeting* as almost any gathering, formal or informal, of agency members, including a conference telephone call. The only exceptions to this rule of openness are discussions of matters such as court proceedings or personnel problems, and these exceptions are specifically listed in the bill. Sunshine laws now exist at all levels of government.

Information Disclosure. In 1966, the federal government passed the Freedom of Information Act (FOIA), which required federal government agencies, with certain exceptions, to disclose to individuals information contained in government files. FOIA requests are helpful not just to individuals. Indeed, the major beneficiaries of the act have been news organizations, which have used it to uncover government waste, scandals, and incompetence.

For example, a Utah newspaper learned through FOIA requests that an air force acquisitions officer was engaging in corrupt actions that benefited Boeing Corporation. In 2012, FOIA requests revealed that Treasury Department officials had been disciplined for soliciting prostitutes and accepting gifts from corporate executives. Also in 2012, Fox News obtained documents showing that the General Services Administration (GSA) had wasted large sums in sponsoring lavish and pointless conferences for its employees.

Curbs on Information Disclosure. Since the terrorist attacks of September 11, 2001, the trend toward open government has been reversed at both the federal and the state levels. Within weeks after September 11, 2001, federal agencies removed hundreds, if not thousands, of documents from Internet sites, public libraries, and the reading rooms found in various federal government departments. Information contained in some of the documents included diagrams of power plants and pipelines, structural details on dams, and safety plans for chemical plants. The military also immediately began restricting information about its current and planned activities, as did the Federal Bureau of Investigation. These agencies were concerned that terrorists could make use of this information to plan attacks.

Sunset Laws

The size and scope of the federal bureaucracy can potentially be controlled through **sunset legislation,** which places government programs on a definite schedule for congressional consideration. Unless Congress specifically reauthorizes a particular federally operated program at the end of a designated period, the program will be terminated automatically—that is, its sun will set.

Government in the Sunshine Act A law that requires all committee-directed federal agencies to conduct their business regularly in public session.

Sunset Legislation Laws requiring that existing programs be reviewed regularly for their effectiveness and be terminated unless specifically extended as a result of these reviews.

"Who do I see to get big government off my back?"

The idea of sunset legislation was initially suggested by Franklin D. Roosevelt when he created the host of New Deal agencies in the 1930s. His adviser (and later Supreme Court justice), William O. Douglas, recommended that each agency's charter should include a provision allowing for its termination in ten years. Only an act of Congress could revitalize the agency. The proposal was never adopted. It was not until 1976 that a state legislature—Colorado's—adopted sunset legislation for state regulatory commissions, giving them a life of six years before their "suns set." Today, most states have some type of sunset law.

Privatization, or Contracting Out

Another approach to bureaucratic reform is **privatization,** which occurs when government services are replaced by services from the private sector. For example, the government has contracted with private firms to operate prisons. Supporters of privatization argue that some services can be provided more efficiently by the private sector. A similar scheme involves furnishing vouchers to government "clients" in lieu of services. Instead of supplying housing, the government could offer vouchers that recipients could use to "pay" for housing in privately owned buildings.

The privatization, or contracting-out, strategy has been most successful on the local level. Some municipalities have contracted with private companies for such services as trash collection. This approach is not a cure-all, however, because many functions, particularly on the national level, cannot be contracted out in any meaningful way. For example, the federal government could not contract out many of the Defense Department's functions to private firms.

The increase in the amount of government work being contracted out to the private sector has led to significant controversy in recent years. Some have criticized the lack of competitive bidding for many contracts that the government has awarded. Another concern is the perceived lack of federal government oversight over the work done by private contractors.

Incentives for Efficiency and Productivity

Privatization
The replacement of government services with services provided by private firms.

An increasing number of state governments are beginning to experiment with schemes to run their operations more efficiently and capably. These plans focus on maximizing the efficiency and productivity of government workers by providing incentives for improved performance. Some of the more promising measures have included permitting agencies that do not spend their entire budgets to keep some of the difference and reward employees with performance-based bonuses.

At the federal level, the Government Performance and Results Act of 1993 was designed to improve efficiency in the federal workforce. The act required all government agencies (except the Central Intelligence Agency) to describe their new goals and establish methods for determining whether those goals are being met. Goals may be broadly crafted (for example, reducing the time it takes to test a new drug before allowing it to be marketed) or narrowly crafted (for example, reducing the number of times a telephone rings before it is answered).

Helping Out the Whistleblowers

A **whistleblower** is someone who "blows the whistle" on gross governmental inefficiency or illegal action. Whistleblowers may be clerical workers, managers, or specialists, such as scientists.

Laws Protecting Whistleblowers. The 1978 Civil Service Reform Act prohibits reprisals against whistleblowers by their superiors, and it set up the Merit Systems Protection Board as part of this protection. Many federal agencies also have toll-free hotlines that employees can use anonymously to report bureaucratic waste and inappropriate behavior. About 35 percent of all calls result in agency action or follow-up.

Further protection for whistleblowers was provided in 1989, when Congress passed the Whistleblower Protection Act. That act established an independent agency, the Office of Special Counsel (OSC), to investigate complaints brought by government employees who have been demoted, fired, or otherwise sanctioned for reporting government fraud or waste.

Some state and federal laws encourage employees to blow the whistle on their employers' wrongful actions by providing monetary incentives to the whistleblowers. At the federal level, the False Claims Act of 1986 allows a whistleblower who has disclosed information about a fraud against the U.S. government to receive a monetary award. If the government chooses to prosecute the case and wins, the whistleblower receives between 15 and 25 percent of the proceeds. If the government declines to intervene, the whistleblower can bring a suit on behalf of the government and, if the suit is successful, will receive between 25 and 30 percent of the proceeds.

The Problem Continues. Despite these efforts to help whistleblowers, there is little evidence that they truly receive much protection. More than 41 percent of the employees who turned to the OSC for assistance in a recent three-year period stated that they were no longer employees of the government agencies on which they had blown the whistle. The government's difficulty in dismissing employees seems to magically disappear when the employee is a whistleblower.

Additionally, in 2006 the United States Supreme Court placed restrictions on lawsuits brought by public workers.[4] The

---

4. *Garcetti v. Ceballos,* 547 U.S. 410 (2006).

Whistleblower
In the context of government, someone who brings gross governmental inefficiency or an illegal action to the public's attention.

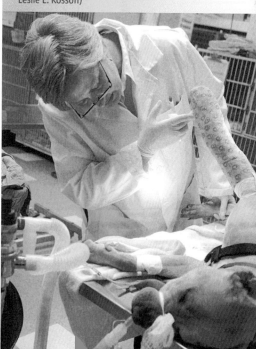

Dr. Victoria Hampshire, an oversight officer at the Food and Drug Administration, blew the whistle on a pet medicine that turned out to be harmful. Hampshire was removed from her position when the drug maker complained, but she was later cleared by an agency investigation. (AP Photo/ Leslie E. Kossoff)

Enabling Legislation
A statute enacted by Congress that authorizes the creation of an administrative agency and specifies the name, purpose, composition, functions, and powers of the agency being created.

case involved an assistant district attorney, Richard Ceballos, who wrote a memo asking if a county sheriff's deputy had lied in a search warrant affidavit. Ceballos claimed that he was subsequently demoted and denied a promotion. The outcome of the case turned on whether an employee has a First Amendment right to criticize an employment-related action. The Court deemed that when he wrote his memo, Ceballos was speaking as an employee, not a citizen, and was thus subject to his employer's disciplinary actions. The ruling will affect millions of governmental employees.

Protecting whistleblowers was one of Barack Obama's campaign promises in 2008. Yet many observers believe that in practice the Obama administration's record on whistleblowers has been one of the worst ever. Under Obama, eight persons have been charged with offenses under the Espionage Act, compared with none under President Bush. In some cases, those charged may in fact have compromised national security by their revelations. In others, however, the only apparent "damage" is embarrassment to the government.

BUREAUCRATS AS POLITICIANS AND POLICYMAKERS

Because Congress is unable to oversee the day-to-day administration of its programs, it must delegate certain powers to administrative agencies. Congress delegates power to agencies through **enabling legislation.** For example, the Federal Trade Commission was created by the Federal Trade Commission Act of 1914, the Equal Employment Opportunity Commission was created by the Civil Rights Act of 1964, and the Occupational Safety and Health Administration was created by the Occupational Safety and Health Act of 1970. The enabling legislation generally specifies the name, purpose, composition, functions, and powers of the agency.

LO5: Discuss how federal agencies make rules and what the role of Congress is in this process.

In theory, the agencies should put into effect laws passed by Congress. Laws are often drafted in such vague and general terms, however, that they provide limited guidance to agency administrators as to how they should be implemented. This means that the agencies themselves must decide how best to carry out the wishes of Congress.

The discretion given to administrative agencies is not accidental. Congress has long realized that it lacks the technical expertise and the resources to monitor the implementation of its laws. Hence, administrative agencies are created to fill the gaps. This gap-filling role requires an agency to formulate administrative rules (regulations) to put flesh on the bones of the law. But it also forces the agency itself to become an unelected policymaker.

The Rulemaking Environment

Rulemaking does not occur in a vacuum. Suppose that Congress passes a new air-pollution law. The Environmental Protection Agency (EPA) might decide to implement the new law through a technical regulation on power-plant emissions. This proposed regulation would be published in the *Federal Register,* a daily government publication, so that interested parties would have an opportunity to comment on it. Individuals and companies that opposed parts or all of the rule might then try to convince the EPA to revise or redraft the regulation. Some parties might try to persuade the agency to withdraw the proposed regulation altogether. In any event, the EPA would consider these comments in drafting the final version of the regulation.

Waiting Periods and Court Challenges. Once the final regulation has been published in the *Federal Register,* there is a sixty-day waiting period before the rule can be enforced. During that period, businesses, individuals, and state and local governments can ask Congress to overturn the regulation. After the sixty-day period has lapsed, the regulation can still be challenged in court by a party having a direct interest in the rule, such as a company that expects to incur significant costs in complying with it. The company could argue that the rule misinterprets the applicable law or goes beyond the agency's statutory purview. An allegation by the company that the EPA made a mistake in judgment probably would not be enough to convince the court to throw out the rule. The company instead would have to demonstrate that the rule itself was "arbitrary and capricious."

Controversies. How agencies implement, administer, and enforce legislation has resulted in controversy. For example, decisions made by agencies charged with administering the Endangered Species Act have led to protests from farmers, ranchers, and others whose economic interests have been harmed.

At times, a controversy may arise when an agency *refuses* to issue regulations to implement a particular law. When the EPA refused to issue regulations designed to curb the emission of carbon dioxide and other greenhouse gases, state and local governments, as well as a number of environmental groups, sued the agency. Those bringing the suit claimed that the EPA was not fulfilling its obligation to implement the provisions of the Clean Air Act. Ultimately, the Supreme Court held that the EPA had the authority to—and should—regulate such gases.[5]

Negotiated Rulemaking

Since the end of World War II in 1945, companies, environmentalists, and other special interest groups have challenged government regulations in court. In the 1980s, however, the sheer wastefulness of attempting to regulate through litigation became increasingly apparent. Today, a growing number of federal agencies encourage businesses and public-interest groups to become directly involved in drafting regulations. Agencies hope that such participation may help to prevent later courtroom battles over the regulations.

Congress formally approved such a process, which is called *negotiated rulemaking,* in the Negotiated Rulemaking Act of 1990. The act authorizes agencies to allow those who will be affected by a new rule to participate in the rule-drafting process. If an agency chooses to engage in negotiated rulemaking, it must publish in the *Federal Register* the subject and scope of the rule to be developed, the names of the parties that will be affected significantly by the rule, and other information. Representatives of the affected groups and other interested parties then may apply to be members of the negotiating committee. The agency is represented on the committee, but a neutral third party (not the agency) presides over the proceedings. Once the committee members have reached agreement on the terms of the proposed rule, a notice is published in the *Federal Register,* followed by a period for comments by any person or organization interested in the proposed rule. Negotiated rulemaking often is conducted under the condition that the participants promise not to challenge in court the outcome of any agreement to which they were a party.

Bureaucrats as Policymakers

Theories of public administration once assumed that bureaucrats do not make policy decisions but only implement the laws and policies promulgated by the president and legislative bodies. A more realistic view is that the agencies and departments of government play

---

5. *Massachusetts v. EPA,* 549 U.S. 497 (2007).

Iron Triangle
A three-way alliance among legislators in Congress, bureaucrats, and interest groups to make or preserve policies that benefit their respective interests.

important roles in policymaking. As we have seen, many government rules, regulations, and programs are in fact initiated by the bureaucracy, based on its expertise and scientific studies. How a law passed by Congress eventually is translated into action—from the forms to be filled out to decisions about who gets the benefits—usually is determined within each agency or department. Even the evaluation of whether a policy has achieved its purpose usually is based on studies that are commissioned and interpreted by the agency administering the program.

The bureaucracy's policymaking role often has been depicted as an *iron triangle*. Recently, many political scientists have come to see the concept of an *issue network* as a more accurate description of the typical policymaking process.

Iron Triangles. In the past, scholars often described the bureaucracy's role in the policymaking process by using the concept of an **iron triangle**—a three-way alliance among legislators in Congress, bureaucrats, and interest groups. Consider as an example the development of agricultural policy. Congress, as one component of the triangle, includes two major committees concerned with agricultural policy, the House Committee on Agriculture and the Senate Committee on Agriculture, Nutrition, and Forestry. The Department of Agriculture, the second component of the triangle, has almost 100,000 employees, plus thousands of contractors and consultants. Agricultural interest groups, the third component of the triangle, include many large and powerful associations, such as the American Farm Bureau Federation, the National Cattlemen's Beef Association, and the National Corn Growers Association. These three components of the iron triangle work together, formally or informally, to create policy.

For example, the various agricultural interest groups lobby Congress to develop policies that benefit their groups' economic welfare. Members of Congress cannot afford to ignore the wishes of interest groups because those groups are potential sources of voter support and campaign contributions. The legislators in Congress also work closely with the Department of Agriculture, which, in implementing a policy, can develop rules that benefit—or at least do not hurt—certain industries or groups. The Department of Agriculture, in turn, supports policies that enhance the department's budget and powers. In this way, according to theory, agricultural policy is created that benefits all three components of the iron triangle.

Issue Networks. With the growth in the complexity of government, policymaking also has become more complicated. The bureaucracy is larger, Congress has more committees and subcommittees, and interest groups are more powerful than

Two farmers walking together near their cows. What part do farmers play in agricultural policymaking at the federal level? (Gary Fandel/Bloomberg via Getty Images)

ever. Although iron triangles still exist, often they are inadequate as descriptions of how policy is made today. Frequently, different interest groups concerned about a certain area of policy have conflicting demands, which makes agency decision making difficult. Additionally, during periods of divided government, departments are pressured by the president to take one approach and by Congress to take another.

Many scholars now use the term *issue network* to describe the policymaking process. An **issue network** consists of individuals or organizations that support a particular policy position on the environment, taxation, consumer safety, or some other issue. Typically, an issue network includes legislators and/or their staff members, interest group leaders, bureaucrats, scholars and other experts, and representatives from the media. Members of a particular issue network work together to influence the president, members of Congress, administrative agencies, and the courts to affect public policy on a specific issue. Each policy issue may involve conflicting positions taken by two or more issue networks.

Issue Network
A group of individuals or organizations—which may consist of legislators and legislative staff members, interest group leaders, bureaucrats, scholars and other experts, and media representatives—that supports a particular policy position on a given issue.

Congressional Control of the Bureaucracy

Many political pundits doubt whether Congress can meaningfully control the federal bureaucracy. These commentators forget that Congress specifies in an agency's enabling legislation the powers of the agency and the parameters within which it can operate. Additionally, Congress has "the power of the purse" and theoretically could refuse to authorize or appropriate funds for a particular agency (see the discussion of the budgeting process in Chapter 9). Whether Congress would actually take such a drastic measure would depend on the circumstances. It is clear, however, that Congress does have the legal authority to decide whether or not to fund administrative agencies.

Congress also can exercise oversight over agencies. Congressional committees conduct investigations and hold hearings to oversee an agency's actions, reviewing them to ensure compliance with congressional intentions. The agency's officers and employees can be ordered to testify before a committee about the details of various actions. Through the questions and comments of members of the House or Senate during the hearings, Congress indicates its positions on specific programs and issues.

Congress can ask the Government Accountability Office (GAO) to investigate particular agency actions as well. The Congressional Budget Office (CBO) also conducts oversight studies. The results of a GAO or CBO study may encourage Congress to hold further hearings or make changes in the law. Even if a law is not changed explicitly by Congress, however, the views expressed in any investigations and hearings are taken seriously by agency officials, who often act on those views.

making a difference
WHAT THE GOVERNMENT KNOWS ABOUT YOU

The federal government collects billions of pieces of information on tens of millions of Americans each year. These data are stored in files and sometimes are exchanged among agencies. You are probably the subject of several federal records (for example, in the Social Security Administration, the Internal Revenue Service, and, if you are a male, the Selective Service).

Why Should You Care? Verifying the information that the government has about you can be important. On several occasions, the records of two people with similar names have become confused. Sometimes innocent persons have had the criminal records of other persons erroneously inserted into their files. Such disasters are not always caused by bureaucratic error. One of the most common crimes in today's world is "identity theft," in which one person makes use of another individual's personal identifiers (such as a Social Security number) to commit fraud. In some instances, identity thieves have been arrested or even jailed under someone else's name.

These students are accessing their personal records to see if they are accurate. (AP Photo/LG Patterson)

What Can You Do? The 1966 Freedom of Information Act (FOIA) requires that the federal government release, at your request, any identifiable information it has about you or about any other subject. Nine categories of material are exempted, however (classified material, confidential material on trade secrets, internal personnel rules, personal medical files, and the like). To request material, write directly to the Freedom of Information Act officer at the agency in question (say, the Department of Education). You must have a relatively specific idea about the document or information you want to obtain.

A second law, the Privacy Act of 1974, gives you access specifically to information the government may have collected about you. This law allows you to review records on file with federal agencies and to check those records for possible inaccuracies.

If you want to look at any records or find out if an agency has a record on you, write to the agency head or Privacy Act officer, and address your letter to the specific agency. State that "under the provisions of the Privacy Act of 1974, 5 U.S.C. 522a, I hereby request a copy of (or access to) _____." Then describe the record that you wish to investigate.

The General Services Administration (GSA) has published a citizen's guide, *Your Right to Federal Records,* that explains both the FOIA and the Privacy Act, and how to go about using them. You can locate this manual by entering its name into your favorite search engine.

key**terms**

bureaucracy 248
cabinet department 251
capture 256
Civil Service
    Commission 259
enabling legislation 264
government
    corporation 256

Government in the
    Sunshine Act 261
independent executive
    agency 251
independent regulatory
    agency 253
iron triangle 266

issue network 267
line organization 251
merit system 259
Pendleton Act (Civil
    Service Reform
    Act) 259

privatization 262
spoils system 259
sunset legislation 261
whistleblower 263

chapter**summary**

1 Bureaucracies are hierarchical organizations characterized by division of labor and extensive procedural rules. Bureaucracy is the primary form of organization of most major corporations and universities, as well as governments.

2 Since the founding of the United States, the federal bureaucracy has grown from a few employees to about 2.7 million (including the U.S. Postal Service but excluding the military). Federal, state, and local employees together make up about 16 percent of the nation's civilian labor force. Social Security, Medicare, Medicaid, and military defense are the largest components of federal spending.

3 The federal bureaucracy consists of fifteen cabinet departments, as well as a large number of independent executive agencies, independent regulatory agencies, and government corporations. These entities enjoy varying degrees of autonomy, visibility, and political support.

4 A federal bureaucracy of career civil servants was formed during Thomas Jefferson's presidency. Andrew Jackson implemented a spoils system through which he appointed his own political supporters. A civil service based on professionalism and merit was the goal of the Civil Service Reform Act of 1883. Concerns that the civil service be freed from the pressures of politics prompted the passage of the Hatch Act in 1939. The Civil Service Reform Act of 1978 made significant changes in the administration of the civil service.

5 There have been many attempts to make the federal bureaucracy more open, efficient, and responsive to the needs of U.S. citizens. The most important reforms have included sunshine and sunset laws, privatization, strategies to provide incentives for increased productivity and efficiency, and protection for whistleblowers.

6 Congress delegates much of its authority to federal agencies when it creates new laws. The bureaucrats who run these agencies may become important policymakers, because Congress has neither the time nor the technical expertise to oversee the administration of its laws. The agency rulemaking process begins when a proposed regulation is published. A comment period follows, during which interested parties may offer suggestions for changes. Because companies and other organizations have challenged many regulations in court, federal agencies now are authorized to allow parties that will be affected by new regulations to participate in the rule-drafting process.

7 Congress exerts ultimate control over all federal agencies, because it controls the federal government's purse strings. It also establishes the general guidelines by which regulatory agencies must abide. The appropriations process provides a way to send messages of approval or disapproval to particular agencies, as do congressional hearings and investigations of agency actions.

test**yourself**

LO1 *Discuss the nature of the federal bureaucracy, and identify the largest federal spending programs.*

In terms of federal dollars spent, the most important programs are:
    a. social programs, including Social Security and Medicare.
    b. the military and subsidies for corporations.
    c. foreign aid.

LO2 *Describe the various types of agencies and organizations that make up the federal executive branch.*

The heads of federal regulatory agencies and members of agency boards and commissions are appointed by:
    a. the president acting alone.
    b. the president with the consent of the Senate.
    c. the Supreme Court.

LO3 *Explain how government employees are hired and how they are administered.*

The first significant legislation aimed at making the federal civil service nonpartisan and independent was:
    a. The Civil Service Act of 1978.
    b. The Hatch Act.
    c. The Pendleton Act of 1883.

LO4 *Evaluate different methods that have been put into place to reform bureaucracies and make them more efficient.*

Privatization means that:
    a. the government must provide individuals with the information it has on them.
    b. private companies replace members of the civil service in providing a government service.
    c. bonuses are awarded for efficient work.

LO5 *Discuss how federal agencies make rules and what the role of Congress is in this process.*

An issue network consists of individuals or organizations that support a particular policy position. A typical issue network includes:
    a. Congress, the president's cabinet, and the Supreme Court.
    b. federal judges, congressional staff, and the heads of certain private corporations.
    c. legislators (or their staff), interest group leaders, bureaucrats, scholars and other experts, and the media.

Essay Question:

The U.S. attorney general, head of the Justice Department, is appointed by the president and is frequently the president's close political ally. Should the attorney general and other U.S. attorneys be appointed on a partisan basis? Why or why not?

Answers to multiple-choice questions: 1. a, 2. b, 3. c, 4. b, 5. c.

CourseMate

At the beginning of a Boston murder trial, the judge speaks with the assistant district attorney and the defense attorney. Our judicial system involves judges and juries at the local, state, and federal levels. (Pat Greenhouse/*The Boston Globe* via Getty Images)

The Judiciary

LEARNING OUTCOMES

The five **Learning Outcomes (LOs)** below are designed to help improve your understanding of this chapter. After reading this chapter, you should be able to:

■ **LO1** Explain the main sources of American law, including constitutions, statutes and regulations, and the common law tradition.

■ **LO2** Describe the structure of the federal court system and such basic judicial requirements as jurisdiction and standing to sue.

■ **LO3** Discuss the procedures used by the United States Supreme Court and the various types of opinions it hands down.

■ **LO4** Evaluate the manner in which federal judges are selected.

■ **LO5** Consider the ways in which the Supreme Court makes policy, and explain the forces that limit the activism of the courts.

Check your understanding of the material with the Test Yourself section at the end of the chapter.

As Alexis de Tocqueville, a French commentator on

American society in the 1800s, noted, "scarcely any political question arises in the United States that is not resolved, sooner or later, into a judicial question."[1] Our judiciary forms part of our political process. The instant that judges interpret the law, they become actors in the political arena—policymakers working within a political institution. The most

---

1. Alexis de Tocqueville, *Democracy in America* (New York: Harper & Row, 1966), p. 248.

Common Law
Judge-made law that originated in England from decisions shaped according to prevailing custom. Decisions were applied to similar situations and gradually became common to the nation.

Precedent
A court rule bearing on subsequent legal decisions in similar cases. Judges rely on precedents in deciding cases.

Stare Decisis
To stand on decided cases; the judicial policy of following precedents established by past decisions.

LO1: Explain the main sources of American law, including constitutions, statutes and regulations, and the common law tradition.

important political force within our judiciary is the United States Supreme Court. The justices of the Supreme Court are not elected but are appointed by the president and confirmed by the Senate, as are all other federal court judges.

How do courts make policy? Why do the federal courts play such an important role in American government? The answers to these questions lie, in part, in our colonial heritage. Most of American law is based on the English system, particularly the English *common law tradition*. In that tradition, the decisions made by judges constitute an important source of law. We open this chapter with an examination of this tradition and of the various other sources of American law. We then look at the federal court system—how it is organized, how its judges are selected, how these judges affect policy, and how they are restrained by our system of checks and balances.

SOURCES OF AMERICAN LAW

The body of American law includes the federal and state constitutions, statutes passed by legislative bodies, administrative law, and case law—the legal principles expressed in court decisions. Case law is based in part on the common law tradition, which dates to the earliest English settlements in North America.

The Common Law Tradition

In 1066, the Normans conquered England, and William the Conqueror and his successors began the process of unifying the country under their rule. One of the ways in which they did this was to establish king's courts. Before the conquest, disputes had been settled according to local custom. The king's courts sought to establish a common, or uniform, set of rules for the whole country. As the number of courts and cases increased, portions of the most important decisions of each year were gathered together and recorded in Year Books. Judges who were settling disputes similar to ones that had been decided before used the Year Books as the basis for their decisions. If a case was unique, judges had to create new rules, but they based their decisions on the general principles suggested by earlier cases. The body of judge-made law that developed under this system is still used today and is known as the **common law.**

The practice of deciding new cases with reference to former decisions—that is, according to **precedent**—became a cornerstone of the English and American judicial systems and is embodied in the doctrine of ***stare decisis*** (pronounced *ster*-ay dih-*si*-ses), a Latin phrase that means "to stand on decided cases." The doctrine of *stare decisis* obligates judges to follow the precedents set previously by their own courts or by higher courts that have authority over them.

For example, a lower state court in California would be obligated to follow a precedent set by the California Supreme Court. That lower court, however, would not be obligated to follow a precedent set by the supreme court of another state, because each state court system is independent. Of course, when the United States Supreme Court decides an issue, all of the nation's other courts are obligated to abide by the Court's decision, because the Supreme Court is the highest court in the land.

The doctrine of *stare decisis* provides a basis for judicial decision making in all countries that have common law systems. Today, the United States, Britain, and several dozen other countries have common law systems. Generally, those countries that were once colonies of Britain, including Australia, Canada, India, New Zealand, and others, have retained their English common law heritage.

Constitutions

The constitutions of the federal government and the states set forth the general organization, powers, and limits of government. The U.S. Constitution is the supreme law of the land. A law in violation of the Constitution, no matter what its source, may be declared unconstitutional and thereafter cannot be enforced. Similarly, the state constitutions are supreme within their respective borders (unless they conflict with the U.S. Constitution or federal laws and treaties made in accordance with it). The Constitution thus defines the political playing field on which state and federal powers are reconciled.

Case Law
Judicial interpretations of common law principles and doctrines, as well as interpretations of constitutional law, statutory law, and administrative law.

Statutes and Administrative Regulations

Although the English common law provides the basis for both our civil and our criminal legal systems, statutes (laws enacted by legislatures) have become increasingly important in defining the rights and obligations of individuals. Federal statutes may relate to any subject that is a concern of the federal government and may apply to areas ranging from hazardous waste to federal taxation. State statutes include criminal codes, commercial laws, and laws covering a variety of other matters. Cities, counties, and other local political bodies also pass statutes, which are called *ordinances*. These ordinances may be adopted to deal with such issues as real estate zoning proposals and public safety.

Rules and regulations issued by administrative agencies are another source of law. Today, much of the work of the courts consists of interpreting these laws and regulations and applying them to the specific circumstances of the cases that come before the courts.

Case Law

Because we have a common law tradition, in which the doctrine of *stare decisis* plays an important role, the decisions rendered by the courts also form an important body of law, collectively referred to as **case law.** Case law includes judicial interpretations of common law principles and doctrines, as well as interpretations of constitutional provisions, statutes, and administrative agency regulations. As you learned in previous chapters, it is up to the courts—and ultimately, if necessary, the Supreme Court—to decide what a constitutional provision or a statutory phrase means. In doing so, the courts, in effect, establish law.

The lawyer holding a microphone seeks a court ruling against the District of Columbia to stop the closing of fifteen public schools in 2013. Activists are concerned that the closures will hurt low-income and minority students. Why do the activists need an attorney? (Brendan Hoffman/Getty Images)

THE FEDERAL COURT SYSTEM

The United States has a dual court system, with state courts and federal courts. Each of the fifty

LO2: Describe the structure of the federal court system and such basic judicial requirements as jurisdiction and standing to sue.

Jurisdiction
The authority of a court to decide certain cases. Not all courts have the authority to decide all cases. Where a case arises and what its subject matter is are two jurisdictional issues.

Federal Question
A question that has to do with the U.S. Constitution, acts of Congress, or treaties. A federal question provides a basis for federal jurisdiction.

Diversity of Citizenship
The condition that exists when the parties to a lawsuit are from different states or when the suit involves a U.S. citizen and a government or citizen of a foreign country. Diversity of citizenship can provide a basis for federal jurisdiction.

Justiciable Controversy
A controversy that is real and substantial, as opposed to hypothetical or academic.

Litigate
To engage in a legal proceeding or seek relief in a court of law; to carry on a lawsuit.

***Amicus Curiae* Brief**
A brief (a document containing a legal argument supporting a desired outcome in a particular case) filed by a third party, or *amicus curiae* (Latin for "friend of the court"), who is not directly involved in the litigation but who has an interest in the outcome of the case.

Class-Action Suit
A lawsuit filed by an individual seeking damages for "all persons similarly situated."

states, as well as the District of Columbia, has its own independent system of courts. This means that there are fifty-two court systems in total. Here we focus on the federal courts.

Basic Judicial Requirements

In any court system, state or federal, certain requirements must be met before a case can be brought before a court. Two important requirements are *jurisdiction* and *standing to sue.*

Jurisdiction. A state court can exercise **jurisdiction** (the authority of the court to hear and decide a case) over the residents of a particular geographic area, such as a county or district. A state's highest court, or supreme court, has jurisdictional authority over all residents within the state.

Because the Constitution established a federal government with limited powers, federal jurisdiction is also limited. Article III, Section 1, of the U.S. Constitution limits the jurisdiction of the federal courts to cases that involve either a federal question or diversity of citizenship. A **federal question** arises when a case is based, at least in part, on the U.S. Constitution, a treaty, or a federal law. A person who claims that her or his rights under the Constitution, such as the right to free speech, have been violated could bring a case in a federal court. **Diversity of citizenship** exists when the parties to a lawsuit are from different states or (more rarely) when the suit involves a U.S. citizen and a government or citizen of a foreign country. The amount in controversy must be at least $75,000 before a federal court can take jurisdiction in a diversity case, however.

Given the significant limits on federal jurisdiction, most lawsuits and criminal cases are heard in state, rather than federal, courts. A defendant or a party to a dispute handled by a state court may file an appeal with a state appeals court, or even the state's supreme court. Appeals cannot be taken to a federal court, however, unless a federal question is involved.

Standing to Sue. Another basic judicial requirement is *standing to sue,* or a sufficient "stake" in a matter to justify bringing suit. The party bringing a lawsuit must have suffered a harm, or have been threatened by a harm, as a result of the action that led to the dispute in question. Standing to sue also requires that the controversy at issue be a justiciable (pronounced just-*tish*-a-bul) controversy. A **justiciable controversy** is a controversy that is real and substantial, as opposed to hypothetical or academic. In other words, a court will not give advisory opinions on hypothetical questions.

Parties to Lawsuits

In most lawsuits, the parties are the *plaintiff* (the person or organization that initiates the lawsuit) and the *defendant* (the person or organization against whom the lawsuit is brought). There may be a number of plaintiffs and defendants in a single lawsuit. In the last several decades, many lawsuits have been brought by interest groups (see Chapter 7). Interest groups play an important role in our judicial system, because they **litigate**—bring to trial—or assist in litigating most cases of racial or gender-based discrimination, virtually all civil liberties cases, and more than one-third of the cases involving business matters. Interest groups also file *amicus curiae* (pronounced ah-*mee*-kous *kur*-ee-eye) **briefs,** or "friend of the court" briefs, in more than 50 percent of these kinds of cases.

Sometimes, interest groups or other plaintiffs will bring a **class-action suit,** in which whatever the court decides will affect all members of a class similarly situated (such as users of a particular product manufactured by the defendant in the lawsuit). The strategy of class-action lawsuits was pioneered by such groups as the National Association for the Advancement of Colored People (NAACP), the Legal Defense Fund, and the Sierra Club, whose leaders believed that the courts would offer a more sympathetic forum for their views than would Congress.

Procedural Rules

Both the federal and the state courts have established procedural rules that shape the litigation process. These rules are designed to protect the rights and interests of the parties and to ensure that the litigation proceeds in a fair and orderly manner. The rules also serve to identify the issues that must be decided by the court—thus saving court time and expense. Court decisions may also apply to trial procedures. For example, the Supreme Court has held that the parties' attorneys cannot discriminate against prospective jurors on the basis of race or gender. Some lower courts have also held that people cannot be excluded from juries because of their sexual orientation or religion.

The parties must comply with procedural rules and with any orders given by the judge during the course of the litigation. When a party does not follow a court's order, the court can cite that person for contempt. A party who commits civil contempt (failing to comply with a court's order for the benefit of another party to the proceeding) can be taken into custody, fined, or both, until that party complies with the court's order. A party who commits *criminal* contempt (obstructing the administration of justice or disrespecting the rules of the court) also can be taken into custody and fined but cannot avoid punishment by complying with a previous order.

Types of Federal Courts

As you can see in Figure 12–1 below, the federal court system is basically a three-tiered model consisting of (1) U.S. district courts and various specialized courts of limited

Social Media in Politics

Unlike other branches of government, the courts often view social media as an annoyance. Judges don't want jurors to discuss or research their cases, but Twitter, Facebook, and similar tools make these rules hard to enforce. In San Francisco, a jury pool of six hundred people was dismissed because *all* of them had researched a high-profile case.

FIGURE 12–1: The Federal Court System

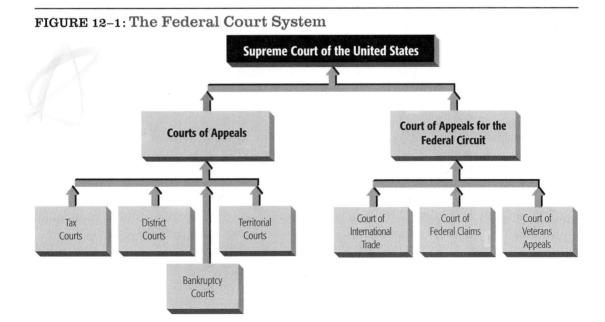

Trial Court
The court in which most cases begin.

General Jurisdiction
Exists when a court's authority to hear cases is not significantly restricted. A court of general jurisdiction normally can hear a broad range of cases.

Limited Jurisdiction
Exists when a court's authority to hear cases is restricted to certain types of claims, such as tax claims or bankruptcy petitions.

Appellate Court
A court having jurisdiction to review cases and issues that were originally tried in lower courts.

jurisdiction (not all of the latter are shown in the figure), (2) intermediate U.S. courts of appeals, and (3) the United States Supreme Court.

U.S. District Courts. The U.S. district courts are trial courts. A **trial court** is what the name implies—a court in which trials are held and testimony is taken. The U.S. district courts are courts of **general jurisdiction,** meaning that they can hear cases involving a broad array of issues. Federal cases involving most matters typically are heard in district courts. The other courts on the lower tier of the model shown in Figure 12–1 are courts of **limited jurisdiction,** meaning that they can try cases involving only certain types of claims, such as tax claims or bankruptcy petitions.

There is at least one federal district court in every state. The number of judicial districts can vary over time owing to population changes and corresponding caseloads. Today, there are ninety-four federal judicial districts. A party who is dissatisfied with the decision of a district court can appeal the case to the appropriate U.S. court of appeals, or federal **appellate court.** Figure 12–2 below shows the jurisdictional boundaries of the district courts (which are state boundaries, unless otherwise indicated by dotted lines within a state) and of the U.S. courts of appeals.

U.S. Courts of Appeals. There are thirteen U.S. courts of appeals—also referred to as U.S. circuit courts of appeals. Twelve of these courts, including the U.S. Court of Appeals,

FIGURE 12–2: Geographic Boundaries of Federal District Courts and Circuit Courts of Appeals

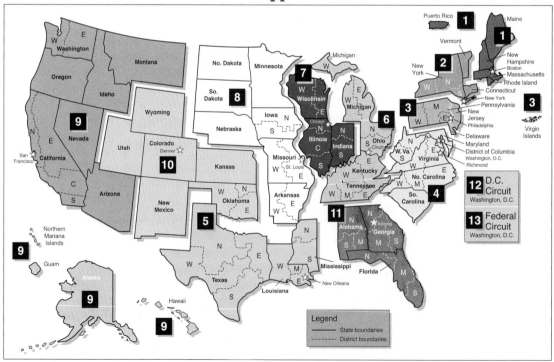

Source: Administrative Office of the United States Courts.

for the District of Columbia, hear appeals from the federal district courts located within their respective judicial circuits (geographic areas over which they exercise jurisdiction). The Court of Appeals for the Thirteenth Circuit, called the Federal Circuit, has national appellate jurisdiction over certain types of cases, such as cases involving patent law and those in which the U.S. government is a defendant.

Note that when an appellate court reviews a case decided in a district court, the appellate court does not conduct another trial. Rather, a panel of three or more judges reviews the record of the case on appeal, which includes a transcript of the trial proceedings, and determines whether the trial court committed an error. Usually, appellate courts look not at questions of *fact* (such as whether a party did commit a certain action, such as burning a flag) but at questions of *law* (such as whether the act of flag-burning is a form of speech protected by the First Amendment to the Constitution). An appellate court will challenge a trial court's finding of fact only when the finding is clearly contrary to the evidence presented at trial or when there is no evidence to support the finding.

A party can petition the United States Supreme Court to review an appellate court's decision. The likelihood that the Supreme Court will grant the petition is slim, however, because the Court reviews only a small percentage of the cases decided by the appellate courts. This means that decisions made by appellate courts usually are final.

The United States Supreme Court. The highest level of the three-tiered model of the federal court system is the United States Supreme Court. Although the Supreme Court can exercise original jurisdiction (that is, act as a trial court) in certain cases, such as those affecting foreign diplomats and those in which a state is a party, most of its work is as an appellate court. The Court hears appeals not only from the federal appellate courts, but also from the highest state courts. Note, though, that the United States Supreme Court can review a state supreme court decision only if a federal question is involved. Because of its importance in the federal court system, we look more closely at the Supreme Court later in this chapter.

Administrative Law Tribunals. In addition to the federal court system, federal administrative agencies and executive departments often employ administrative law judges, who resolve disputes arising under the rules governing their agencies. For example, the Social Security Administration might hold a hearing to determine whether an individual is entitled to collect a particular benefit. If all internal agency appeals processes have been exhausted, a party may have a right to take the case into the federal court system.

Federal Courts and the War on Terrorism

As noted, the federal court system includes a variety of trial courts of limited jurisdiction, dealing with matters such as tax claims or international trade. The government's attempts to combat terrorism have drawn attention to certain specialized courts that meet in secret. We look next at these courts, as well as at the role of the federal courts with respect to the detainees accused of terrorism.

The FISA Court. The federal government created the first secret court in 1978. In that year, Congress passed the Foreign Intelligence Surveillance Act (FISA), which established a court to hear requests for warrants for the surveillance of suspected spies. Officials can request a warrant without having to reveal to the suspect or to the public the information used to justify the warrant. The FISA court has approved almost all of the thousands of requests for warrants that officials have submitted. There is no public access to the court's proceedings or records.

"And don't go whining to some higher court."

(Al Ross/The New Yorker Collection/www.cartoonbank.com)

In the aftermath of the terrorist attacks on September 11, 2001, the Bush administration expanded the powers of the FISA court. Previously, the FISA had allowed secret domestic surveillance only if the purpose was to combat intelligence gathering by foreign powers. Amendments to the FISA enacted after 9/11 changed this wording to "a significant purpose"—meaning that warrants may now be requested to obtain evidence that can be used in criminal trials.

Alien "Removal Courts." In 1996, Congress passed the Anti-Terrorism and Effective Death Penalty Act. The new law was a response to the bombing of a federal building in 1995 in Oklahoma City, which killed 168 people. Even though the perpetrators of this crime were white U.S. citizens whose motives were entirely domestic, the new law focused on noncitizens. For example, the act created an alien "removal court" to hear evidence against suspected "alien terrorists." The judges in this court rule on whether there is probable cause for deportation. If so, a public deportation proceeding is held in a U.S. district court. The prosecution does not need to follow procedures that normally apply in criminal cases. In addition, the defendant cannot see the evidence that the prosecution used to secure the hearing.

The Federal Courts and Enemy Combatants. After the 9/11 attacks, the U.S. military took custody of hundreds of suspected terrorists seized in Afghanistan and elsewhere and held them at Guantánamo Bay, Cuba. The detainees were classified as *enemy combatants,* and, according to the Bush administration, they could be held indefinitely. The administration also claimed that because the detainees were not prisoners of war, they were not protected under international laws governing the treatment of such prisoners.

The handling of the prisoners at Guantánamo has been a source of ongoing controversy. The United States Supreme Court held, first in 2004 and then in 2006, that the Bush administration's treatment of these detainees violated the U.S. Constitution.[2]

In response to the Court's 2006 decision, Congress passed the Military Commissions Act of 2006. The act eliminated federal court jurisdiction over challenges by noncitizens held as enemy combatants based on *habeas corpus,* the right of a detained person to challenge the legality of his or her detention before a judge. In June 2008, in *Boumediene v. Bush,* the Court ruled that the provisions restricting the federal courts' jurisdictional author-

---

2. *Hamdi v. Rumsfeld,* 542 U.S. 507 (2004); *Hamdan v. Rumsfeld,* 548 U.S. 557 (2006).

ity over detainees' *habeas corpus* challenges were illegal.[3] The decision gave Guantánamo detainees the right to challenge their detention in federal civil courts.

In 2009, the Obama administration abolished the category of enemy combatant and promised to close the Guantánamo prison. (As of 2014, however, the prison remained open.) President Obama did not, however, move to try most of the detainees in U.S. civilian courts. Under the Military Commissions Act of 2009, a majority of the prisoners were to be tried in a revised system of military commissions. Further, in May 2009, Obama claimed the right to detain certain accused terrorists indefinitely without trial. In May 2010, a federal appeals court ruled that the administration had the right to detain prisoners indefinitely at Bagram Air Force Base in Afghanistan because the prison is located on foreign soil and within a war zone.[4]

THE SUPREME COURT AT WORK

The Supreme Court begins its regular annual term on the first Monday in October and usually adjourns in late June or early July of the next year. Special sessions may be held after the regular term ends, but only a few cases are decided in this way. More commonly, cases are carried over until the next regular session.

LO3: Discuss the procedures used by the United States Supreme Court and the various types of opinions it hands down.

Of the total number of cases that are decided each year in U.S. courts, those reviewed by the Supreme Court represent less than one in four thousand. Included in these, however, are decisions that profoundly affect our lives. In recent years, the United States Supreme Court has decided issues involving freedom of speech, the right to bear arms, health-care reform, campaign finance, capital punishment, the rights of criminal suspects, affirmative action programs, religious freedom, abortion, states' rights, and many other matters with significant consequences for the nation.

Because the Supreme Court exercises a great deal of discretion over the types of cases it hears, it can influence the nation's policies by issuing decisions in some types of cases and refusing to hear appeals in others, thereby allowing lower court decisions to stand. Indeed, the fact that George W. Bush assumed the presidency in 2001 instead of Al Gore, his Democratic opponent, was largely due to a Supreme Court decision to review a Florida court's ruling. In *Bush v. Gore,* the Supreme Court reversed the

Justice Clarence Thomas with his clerks. Where does the United States Supreme Court fit in terms of the hierarchy of the federal court system in this country? (David Hume Kennerly/Getty Images)

3. 553 U.S. 723 (2008).
4. *Maqaleh v. Gates,* 605 F.3d 84 (D.C.Cir. 2010).

Writ of *Certiorari*
An order issued by a higher court to a lower court to send up the record of a case for review.

Rule of Four
A United States Supreme Court procedure by which four justices must vote to grant a petition for review if a case is to come before the full court.

Oral Arguments
The arguments presented in person by attorneys to an appellate court. Each attorney presents reasons to the court why the court should rule in her or his client's favor.

Florida court's order to recount manually the votes in selected Florida counties—a decision that effectively handed the presidency to Bush.[5]

Which Cases Reach the Supreme Court?

Many people are surprised to learn that in a typical case, there is no absolute right of appeal to the United States Supreme Court. The Court's appellate jurisdiction is almost entirely discretionary—the Court chooses which cases it will decide. The justices never explain their reasons for hearing certain cases and not others, so it is difficult to predict which case or type of case the Court might select.

Factors That Bear on the Decision. A number of factors bear on the decision to accept a case. If a legal question has been decided differently by various lower courts, it may need resolution by the highest court. A ruling may be necessary if a lower court's decision conflicts with an existing Supreme Court ruling. In general, the Court considers whether the issue could have significance beyond the parties to the dispute. Another factor is whether the solicitor general is asking the Court to take a case. The solicitor general, a high-ranking presidential appointee within the Justice Department, represents the national government before the Supreme Court and promotes presidential policies in the federal courts. He or she decides what cases the government should request the Supreme Court to review and what position the government should take in cases before the Court.

Granting Petitions for Review. If the Court decides to grant a petition for review, it will issue a **writ of *certiorari*** (pronounced sur-shee-uh-*rah*-ree). The writ orders a lower court to send the Supreme Court a record of the case for review. The vast majority of the petitions for review are denied. A denial is not a decision on the merits of a case, nor does it indicate agreement with the lower court's opinion. (The judgment of the lower court remains in force, however.) Therefore, denial of the writ has no value as a precedent. The Court will not issue a writ unless at least four justices approve of it. This is called the **rule of four.**[6]

Court Procedures

Once the Supreme Court grants *certiorari* in a particular case, the justices do extensive research on the legal issues and facts involved in the case. (Of course, some preliminary research is necessary before deciding to grant the petition for review.) Each justice is entitled to four law clerks, who undertake much of the research and preliminary drafting necessary for the justice to form an opinion.

The Court normally does not hear any evidence, as is true with all appeals courts. The Court's consideration of a case is based on the abstracts, the record, and the briefs. The attorneys are permitted to present **oral arguments.** Unlike the practice in most courts, lawyers addressing the Supreme Court can be (and often are) questioned by the justices at any time during oral arguments. All statements and the justices' questions during oral arguments are recorded.

The justices meet to discuss and vote on cases in conferences held throughout the term. In these conferences, in addition to deciding cases already before the Court, the justices determine which new petitions for *certiorari* to grant. These conferences take place in the Court's oak-paneled chamber and are strictly private—no stenographers, audio recorders, or video cameras are allowed.

---

5. 531 U.S. 98 (2000).

6. The "rule of four" is modified when seven or fewer justices participate, which occurs from time to time. When that happens, as few as three justices can grant *certiorari*.

Decisions and Opinions

When the Court has reached a decision, its opinion is written. The **opinion** contains the Court's ruling on the issue or issues presented, the reasons for its decision, the rules of law that apply, and other information. In many cases, the decision of the lower court is **affirmed,** resulting in the enforcement of that court's judgment or decree. If the Supreme Court believes that the lower court made the wrong decision, however, the decision will be **reversed.** Sometimes, the case will be **remanded** (sent back to the court that originally heard the case) for a new trial or other proceeding. For example, a lower court might have held that a party was not entitled to bring a lawsuit under a particular law. If the Supreme Court holds to the contrary, it will remand (send back) the case to the trial court with instructions that the trial go forward.

The Court's written opinion sometimes is unsigned. This is called an opinion *per curiam* ("by the court"). Typically, the Court's opinion is signed by all the justices who agree with it. When in the majority, the chief justice decides who writes the opinion and may write it personally. When the chief justice is in the minority, the senior justice on the majority side assigns the opinion.

Types of Opinions. When all justices unanimously agree on an opinion, the opinion is written for the entire Court (all the justices) and can be deemed a **unanimous opinion.** When there is not a unanimous opinion, a **majority opinion** is written, outlining the views of the majority of the justices involved in the case. Often, one or more justices who feel strongly about making or emphasizing a particular point that is not made or emphasized in the majority written opinion will write a **concurring opinion.** That means the justice writing the concurring opinion agrees (concurs) with the conclusion given in the majority written opinion but wants to make or clarify a particular point or to voice disapproval of the grounds on which the decision was made. Finally, in other than unanimous opinions, one or more dissenting opinions are usually written by those justices who do not agree with the majority. The **dissenting opinion** is important because it often forms the basis of the arguments used years later if the Court reverses the previous decision and establishes a new precedent.

Publishing Opinions. Shortly after the opinion is written, the Supreme Court announces its decision from the bench. The clerk of the Court also releases the opinion for online publication. Ultimately, the opinion is published in the *United States Reports,* which is the official printed record of the Court's decisions.

The Court's Dwindling Caseload. Some have complained that the Court reviews too few cases each term, thus giving the lower courts insufficient guidance on important issues. Indeed, the number of signed opinions issued by the Court has dwindled notably since the 1980s. For example, in its 1982–1983 term, the Court issued signed opinions in 151 cases. By the early 2000s, this number had dropped to between 70 and 80 per term. In the term ending in June 2013, the number was 75.

THE SELECTION OF FEDERAL JUDGES

All federal judges are appointed. The Constitution, in Article II, Section 2, states that the president is to appoint the justices of the Supreme Court with the advice and consent of the Senate. Congress has established the same procedure for staffing other federal courts. This means that the Senate and the president jointly decide who shall fill every vacant judicial position, no matter what the level.

Opinion
A statement by a judge or a court of the decision reached in a case. An opinion sets forth the applicable law and details the reasoning on which the ruling was based.

Affirm
To declare that a court ruling is valid and must stand.

Reverse
To annul or make void a court ruling on account of some error or irregularity.

Remand
To send a case back to the court that originally heard it.

Unanimous Opinion
A court opinion or determination on which all judges agree.

Majority Opinion
A court opinion reflecting the views of the majority of the judges.

Concurring Opinion
A separate opinion prepared by a judge who supports the decision of the majority of the court but for different reasons.

Dissenting Opinion
A separate opinion in which a judge dissents from (disagrees with) the conclusion reached by the majority of the court and expounds his or her own views about the case.

LO4: Evaluate the manner in which federal judges are selected.

Senatorial Courtesy
In federal district court judgeship nominations, a tradition allowing a senator to veto a judicial appointment in her or his state.

There are currently 874 federal judicial posts at all levels, although at any given time many of these positions are vacant. Once appointed to a federal judgeship, a person holds that job for life. Judges serve until they resign, retire voluntarily, or die. Federal judges who engage in blatantly illegal conduct may be removed through impeachment, although such action is rare. In contrast to federal judges, many state judges—including the judges who sit on state supreme courts—are chosen by the voters in elections. Inevitably, judicial candidates must raise campaign funds. What arguments favor the election of judges? What problems can such a system create? We examine such questions in the *At Issue* feature on the facing page.

Judicial Appointments

Candidates for federal judgeships are suggested to the president by the Department of Justice, senators, other judges, the candidates themselves, and lawyers' associations and other interest groups. In selecting a candidate to nominate for a judgeship, the president considers not only the person's competence but also other factors, including the person's political philosophy (as will be discussed shortly), ethnicity, and gender.

The nomination process—no matter how the nominees are obtained—always works the same way. The president makes the actual nomination, submitting the name to the Senate. To reach a conclusion, the Senate Judiciary Committee (operating through subcommittees) invites testimony, both written and oral, at its various hearings. The Senate then either confirms or rejects the nomination.

Federal District Court Judgeship Nominations. Although the president officially nominates federal judges, in the past the nomination of federal district court judges actually originated with a senator or senators of the president's party from the state in which there was a vacancy (if such a senator existed). In effect, judicial appointments were a form of political patronage. President Jimmy Carter (1977–1981) ended this tradition by establishing independent commissions to oversee the initial nomination process. President Ronald Reagan (1981–1989) abolished Carter's nominating commissions and established complete presidential control of nominations.

A practice used in the Senate, called **senatorial courtesy,** is a constraint on the president's freedom to appoint federal district judges. Senatorial courtesy allows a senator of the president's political party to veto a judicial appointment in her or his state. During much of American history, senators from the "opposition" party (the party to which the president does not belong) have also enjoyed the right of senatorial courtesy, although their veto power has varied over time.

In 2000, Orrin Hatch, Republican chair of the Senate Judiciary Committee, announced that the opposition party (at that point, the Democrats) would no longer be allowed to invoke senatorial courtesy. When the Democrats took over the Senate following the elections of 2006, Senator Patrick J. Leahy (D., Vt.), chair of the Judiciary Committee, let it be known that the old bipartisan system of senatorial courtesy would return. Of course, the Republicans, who were now in the minority, were unlikely to object to a nomination submitted by Republican president George W. Bush, and the old practices did not become truly effective until Democratic president Barack Obama took office.

Federal Courts of Appeals Appointments. There are many fewer federal courts of appeals appointments than federal district court appointments, but they are more influential. Federal appellate judges handle more important matters, and therefore presidents take a keener interest in the nomination process for such judgeships. Also, the U.S. courts of appeals have become "stepping-stones" to the Supreme Court.

at issue

SHOULD STATE JUDGES BE ELECTED?

The nation's founders sought to insulate the courts from popular passions, and as a result, all of the judges and justices in the federal court system are appointed by the president and confirmed by the Senate. Federal judges and justices are appointed for life. In thirty-nine states, in contrast, some or all state judges must face election and reelection.

The question of whether state judges should be elected or whether they should be appointed has proved to be very divisive. Many in the legal community agreed with a former Oregon Supreme Court justice, Hans A. Linde, when he pointed out that "to the rest of the world, American adherence to judicial elections is as incomprehensible as our rejection of the metric system." Public opinion polls, however, regularly show strong public support for electing judges.

THE PEOPLE'S WILL SHOULD PREVAIL

Those who advocate the election of state judges see the issue as a simple matter of democracy. Judges cannot be insulated from politics. Governors who appoint judges are highly political creatures and are likely to appoint members of their own party. If politics is going to play a role, the people ought to have their say directly. In addition, researchers at the University of Chicago School of Law found that elected judges write more opinions than do appointed judges.

We let ordinary people participate in the legal process through the jury system, and they ought to be able to choose judges as well. That way, the people can be confident that judges will respond to popular concerns, such as the fear of crime. Without elections, judges living in safe, upscale neighborhoods may fail to appreciate what it is like to fear for your safety on an everyday basis.

ELECTING JUDGES LEADS TO CORRUPTION

Former United States Supreme Court justice Sandra Day O'Connor condemned the practice of electing judges: "No other nation in the world does that because they realize you are not going to get fair and impartial judges that way." Opponents of judicial elections observe that most voters do not have enough information to make sensible choices when they vote for judicial candidates. Therefore, campaign contributions wind up deciding judicial races.

Judicial candidates raise considerable funds from the lawyers who will appear before them if they win. Additional campaign funds are raised by special interest groups that want "their" candidate elected or reelected to the state court in question. People in favor of electing judges think that the candidates they vote for will, for example, be "tough on crime." Often, they are. But those who oppose judicial elections contend that elected judges will also tilt toward the wealthy groups that put them in office, and away from the interests of ordinary people.

FOR CRITICAL ANALYSIS

Why do you think that attorneys, as a group, contribute more to judicial campaigns than do members of other professions?

Supreme Court Appointments. As we have mentioned, the president nominates Supreme Court justices. As you can see in Table 12–1 on the following page, which summarizes the background of all Supreme Court justices to 2014, the most common occupational background of the justices at the time of their appointment has been private legal practice or state or federal judgeship. Those nine justices who were in federal executive posts at the time of their appointment held the high offices of secretary of State, comptroller of the Treasury, secretary of the Navy, postmaster general, secretary of the Interior, chairman of the Securities and Exchange Commission, and secretary of Labor. In the "Other" category under "Occupational Position before Appointment" in Table 12–1 are two justices who were professors of law (including William H. Taft, a former president) and one justice who was a North Carolina state employee with responsibility for organizing and revising the state's statutes.

TABLE 12-1: Background of Supreme Court Justices to 2014

	Number of Justices (112 = Total)		Number of Justices (112 = Total)
Occupational Position before Appointment		**Political Party Affiliation**	
Federal judgeship	31	Federalist (to 1835)	13
Private legal practice	25	Jeffersonian Republican (to 1828)	7
State judgeship	21	Whig (to 1861)	1
U.S. attorney general	7	Democrat	46
Deputy or assistant U.S. attorney general	2	Republican	44
U.S. solicitor general	3	Independent	1
U.S. senator	6	**Age on Appointment**	
U.S. representative	2	Under 40	5
State governor	3	41–50	33
Federal executive post	9	51–60	60
Other	3	61–70	14
Religious Background		**Gender**	
Protestant	83	Male	108
Roman Catholic	14	Female	4
Jewish	7	**Race**	
Unitarian	7	White (non-Hispanic)	109
No religious affiliation	1	African American	2
Educational Background		Hispanic	1
College graduate	96		
Not a college graduate	16		

Sources: Congressional Quarterly, *Congressional Quarterly's Guide to the U.S. Supreme Court* (Washington, D.C.: Congressional Quarterly Press, 1996); and authors' updates.

Partisanship and Judicial Appointments

In most circumstances, the president appoints judges or justices who belong to the president's own political party. Presidents see their federal judiciary appointments as the one sure way to institutionalize their political views long after they have left office. By 1993, for example, Presidents Ronald Reagan and George H. W. Bush together had appointed nearly three-quarters of all federal court judges. This preponderance of Republican-appointed federal judges strengthened the legal moorings of the conservative social agenda on a variety of issues, ranging from abortion to civil rights. President Bill Clinton, a Democrat, had the opportunity to appoint 371 federal district and appeals court judges, thereby shifting the ideological makeup of the federal judiciary. George W. Bush appointed 322 federal district and appeals court judges, again ensuring a majority of Republican-appointed judges in the federal courts.

Appointments by Bush. President George W. Bush also had the opportunity to fill two Supreme Court vacancies, those left by the death of Chief Justice William Rehnquist and by the retirement of Justice Sandra Day O'Connor. Bush appointed two conservatives to these positions—John G. Roberts, Jr., who became chief justice, and Samuel Alito, Jr., who replaced O'Connor. The appointment of Alito, in particular, strengthened the rightward movement of the Court that had begun years before with the appointment of Rehnquist as chief justice. This was because Alito was a reliable member of the Court's conservative wing, whereas O'Connor had been a "swing voter."

Appointments by Obama. President Barack Obama had two opportunities to fill Supreme Court vacancies in the first two years of his term. The vacancies resulted from the retirement of justices David Souter and John Paul Stevens. Both had been members of the Court's so-called liberal wing, so Obama's appointments did not change the ideological balance of the Court. Obama chose two women: Sonia Sotomayor, who had been an appeals court judge and is the Court's first Hispanic member, and Elena Kagan, who had been Obama's solicitor general.

The Senate's Role

Ideology also plays a large role in the Senate's confirmation hearings, and presidential nominees to the Supreme Court have not always been confirmed. In fact, almost 20 percent of presidential nominations to the Supreme Court have either been rejected or not been acted on by the Senate.

Confirming Supreme Court Appointments. The U.S. Senate had a long record of refusing to confirm the president's judicial nominations from the beginning of Andrew Jackson's presidency in 1829 to the end of Ulysses Grant's presidency in 1877. From 1894 until 1968, however, only three nominees were not confirmed. Then, from 1968 through 1987, four presidential nominees to the highest court were rejected.

Controversial Appointments. One of the most memorable of these rejections was the Senate's refusal to confirm Robert Bork—an unusually conservative nominee—in 1987. Many observers saw the Bork confirmation battle as a turning point after which confirmations became much more partisan. Another controversial appointment was that of Clarence Thomas, who underwent a volatile and acrimonious confirmation hearing in 1991, replete with charges against him of sexual harassment. He was ultimately confirmed by the Senate, nonetheless.

President Clinton had little trouble gaining approval for both of his nominees to the Supreme Court: Ruth Bader Ginsburg and Stephen G. Breyer. President George W. Bush's nominees faced hostile grilling in their confirmation hearings, however, and Bush was forced to withdraw the nomination of White House counsel Harriet Miers when it became clear she would not be confirmed.

Lower Court Appointments. Presidents have often had great trouble with appointments to district and appeals courts. For an extended period during the presidency of Bill Clinton, the Republican majority in Congress adopted a strategy of trying to block almost every action taken by the administration—including judicial appointments.

The modern understanding that sixty votes are required before the Senate will consider a major measure has given the minority party significant power as well. After 2000, the Democratic minority in the Senate was able to hold up many of George W. Bush's more controversial judicial appointments. Frustrated Republican senators threatened to use the "nuclear option," under which Senate rules would be revised to disallow filibusters against judicial nominees. In the end, a bipartisan group engineered a compromise to preserve the filibuster.

President Obama has also had considerable difficulty in getting his judicial candidates approved by the Senate. This was especially true after the 2010 elections, when a number of newly elected Republicans replaced Democratic senators.

POLICYMAKING AND THE COURTS

The partisan battles over judicial appointments reflect an important reality in today's American government: the importance of the judiciary in national politics. Because appointments to the federal bench are for life, the ideology of judicial appointees can affect national policy for years to come. Although the primary function of judges in our system of government is to interpret and apply the laws, inevitably judges make policy when carrying out this task. One of the major policymaking tools of the federal courts is their power of judicial review.

Judicial Review

The power of the courts to determine whether a law or action by the other branches of government is constitutional is known as the power of *judicial review*. This power enables the judicial branch to act as a check on the other two branches of government, in line with the system of checks and balances established by the U.S. Constitution.

The power of judicial review is not mentioned in the Constitution, however. Rather, it was established by the United States Supreme Court's decision in *Marbury v. Madison*.[7] In that case, in which the Court declared that a law passed by Congress violated the Constitution, the Court claimed such a power for the judiciary:

> *It is emphatically the province and duty of the Judicial Department to say what the law is. Those who apply the rule to a particular case must of necessity expound and interpret that rule. If two laws conflict with each other, the courts must decide on the operation of each.*

If a federal court declares that a federal or state law or policy is unconstitutional, the court's decision affects the application of the law or policy only within that court's jurisdiction. For this reason, the higher the level of the court, the greater the impact of the decision on society. Because of the Supreme Court's national jurisdiction, its decisions have the greatest impact. For example, when the Supreme Court held that an Arkansas state constitutional amendment limiting the terms of congresspersons was unconstitutional, laws establishing term limits in twenty-three other states also were invalidated.[8]

Judicial Activism and Judicial Restraint

Judicial scholars like to characterize judges and justices as being either "activist" or "restraintist."

Judicial Activism. The doctrine of **judicial activism** rests on the conviction that the federal judiciary should take an active role by using its powers to check the activities of Congress, state legislatures, and administrative agencies when those governmental bodies exceed their authority. One of the Supreme Court's most activist eras was the period from 1953 to 1969, when the Court was headed by Chief Justice Earl Warren. The Warren Court propelled the civil rights movement forward by holding, among other things, that laws permitting racial segregation violated the equal protection clause.

Judicial Activism
A doctrine holding that the federal judiciary should take an active role by using its powers to check the activities of governmental bodies when those bodies exceed their authority.

---

7. 5 U.S. 137 (1803).
8. *U.S. Term Limits v. Thornton*, 514 U.S. 779 (1995).

Judicial Restraint. In contrast, the doctrine of **judicial restraint** rests on the assumption that the courts should defer to the decisions made by the legislative and executive branches, because members of Congress and the president are elected by the people, whereas members of the federal judiciary are not. Because administrative agency personnel normally have more expertise than the courts do in the areas regulated by the agencies, the courts likewise should defer to agency rules and decisions. In other words, under the doctrine of judicial restraint, the courts should not thwart the implementation of legislative acts and agency rules unless they are clearly unconstitutional.

Political Implications. In the past, judicial activism was often linked with liberalism, and judicial restraint with conservatism. In fact, though, a conservative judge can be activist, just as a liberal judge can be restraintist. In the 1950s and 1960s, the Supreme Court was activist and liberal. Some observers believe that the Rehnquist Court, with its conservative majority, became increasingly activist over time.

After the election of Barack Obama as president in 2008, some observers suggested that the Court's conservative wing became still more activist in its approach to judicial interpretation. The *Citizens United v. Federal Election Commission* decision, in which the Court struck down long-standing campaign finance laws, lends credence to this view. Some believed that the Court was stepping back from conservative judicial activism when it upheld most of Obama's health-care reform legislation in June 2012. Others, however, note that the Court also blocked the attempt by Congress to force states to expand the Medicaid program. This step was an innovation in limiting the power of Congress.

John Roberts at his swearing-in ceremony at the White House. Because of his relative youth, he will remain chief justice for many years. How does someone become chief justice? (Joe Raedle/Getty Images)

Other terms that are often used to describe a justice's philosophy are *strict construction* and *broad construction*. Justices who believe in strict construction look to the "letter of the law" when they attempt to interpret the Constitution or a particular statute. Those who favor broad construction try to determine the context and purpose of the law.

Ideology and the Rehnquist Court

William H. Rehnquist, who died in 2005, became the sixteenth chief justice of the Supreme Court in 1986. He was known as a strong anchor of the Court's conservative wing. The Court's rightward movement, which began shortly after Rehnquist became chief justice, continued as other conservative appointments to the Court were made during the Reagan and George H. W. Bush administrations.

Interestingly, some previously conservative justices showed a tendency to migrate to a more liberal view of the law. Sandra Day O'Connor, the first female justice, gradually shifted to the left on a number of issues, including abortion. Generally, O'Connor and Justice Anthony Kennedy provided the "swing votes" on the Rehnquist Court.

Although the Court moved to the right during the Rehnquist era, it was closely divided in many cases. Consider the Court's rulings on states' rights. In 1995, the Court

www

Helpful Web Sites
Cornell University offers an easily searchable index of Supreme Court opinions, including some important historic decisions. Find it by typing "cornell supct" into your search engine.

Judicial Restraint
A doctrine holding that courts should defer to the decisions made by the elected representatives of the people in the legislative and executive branches.

held, for the first time in sixty years, that Congress had overreached its powers under the commerce clause when it attempted to regulate the possession of guns in school zones. According to the Court, the possession of guns in school zones had nothing to do with the commerce clause.[9] Yet in a 2005 case, the Court ruled that Congress's power to regulate commerce allowed it to ban marijuana use even when a state's law permitted such use and the growing and use of the drug were strictly local in nature.[10] What these two rulings had in common was that they supported policies generally considered to be conservative—the right to possess firearms on the one hand, and a strong line against marijuana on the other.

The Roberts Court

John Roberts became chief justice in 2005, following the death of Chief Justice Rehnquist. Replacing one conservative chief justice with another did not immediately change the Court's ideological balance. The real change came in January 2006, when Samuel Alito

---

9. *United States v. Lopez*, 514 U.S. 549 (1995).
10. *Gonzales v. Raich*, 545 U.S. 1 (2005).

Supreme Court justices (as of 2014). Sonia Sotomayor and Elena Kagan are the most recent additions to the United States Supreme Court. (Kagan—AP Photo/Alex Brandon; Sotomayor—AP Photo/Charles Dharapak; remaining photos—U.S. Supreme Court)

replaced Sandra Day O'Connor. Unlike O'Connor, Alito was firmly in the conservative camp. This fact had consequences. In a 2007 case, for example, the Court upheld a 2003 federal law banning partial birth abortion, by a close (five-to-four) vote.[11] The Supreme Court's conservative drift continued in the following years. In 2008, for example, the Court established the right of individuals to own guns for private use,[12] and it upheld lethal injection as an execution method.[13]

Judicial Implementation
The way in which court decisions are translated into action.

Although the Roberts Court is widely characterized as conservative, its philosophy is not identical to the conservatism of the Republicans in Congress or the broader conservative movement. True, justices such as Scalia and Thomas can rightly be characterized as in full agreement with the conservative movement. Justice Kennedy and even Chief Justice Roberts, however, clearly "march to their own drummer." As one example, the Court has shown a degree of sympathy for the rights of gay men and lesbians that cannot be found in the Republican Party platform. It was Justice Kennedy, after all, who in 2003 wrote the opinion in *Lawrence v. Texas* striking down laws that ban gay sex nationwide.[14] Chief Justice Roberts demonstrated his independence in 2012 by authoring the opinion that affirmed the constitutionality of Obamacare.[15]

The Court provided more examples of its brand of conservatism in 2013. The Court continued to take a favorable approach to gay rights, as described in chapters 3 and 5. It ruled that the federal government could not refuse to recognize same-sex marriages authorized by the states.[16] In contrast, to the satisfaction of conservatives, the Court struck down part of the Voting Rights Act of 1965.[17] Many observers thought that the Court would take the opportunity provided by a Texas case to strike down affirmative action programs in public colleges altogether. The Court avoided such a ruling, however, as described in the *Politics and Economics* feature on the following page.[18]

What Checks Our Courts?

Our judicial system is one of the most independent in the world. But the courts do not have absolute independence, for they are part of the political process. Political checks limit the extent to which courts can exercise judicial review and engage in an activist policy. These checks are exercised by the executive branch, the legislature, the public, and, finally, the judiciary itself.

Executive Checks. President Andrew Jackson was once supposed to have said, after Chief Justice John Marshall made an unpopular decision, "John Marshall has made his decision; now let him enforce it."[19] This purported remark goes to the heart of **judicial implementation**—the enforcement of judicial decisions in such a way that those decisions are translated into policy. The Supreme Court simply does not have any enforcement powers, and whether a decision will be implemented depends on the cooperation of the other two branches of government. Rarely, though, will a president refuse to enforce a Supreme Court decision, as President Jackson did. To take such an action could mean a

---

11. *Gonzales v. Carhart,* 550 U.S. 124 (2007).
12. *District of Columbia v. Heller,* 554 U.S. 570 (2008).
13. *Baze v. Rees,* 553 U.S. 35 (2008).
14. 539 U.S. 558 (2003).
15. *National Federation of Independent Business v. Sebelius,* 132 S.Ct. 2566 (2012).
16. *United States v. Windsor,* 570 U.S. ___ (2013).
17. *Shelby County v. Holder,* 570 U.S. ___ (2013).
18. *Fisher v. University of Texas,* 570 U.S. ___ (2013).
19. The decision that Jackson was referring to was *Cherokee Nation v. Georgia,* 30 U.S. 1 (1831).

politics and **economics**

GETTING AHEAD WITH
AND WITHOUT AFFIRMATIVE ACTION

The data prove what you might have guessed—if you graduate from college, you have a greater chance of earning a large lifetime income. The clear benefits of a college education persuade many young people to borrow dangerously large sums in order to get a college degree. The benefits also raise a question: Are racial and ethnic minorities adequately represented at our colleges and universities?

AFFIRMATIVE ACTION IN COLLEGE ADMISSIONS

Whether done formally or informally, affirmative action awards extra "points" to members of various racial or ethnic minorities when they seek admission to a college. This practice has faced many challenges over the years. Some states have outlawed it altogether through a popular vote. In 2003, in *Grutter v. Bollinger*, the United States Supreme Court allowed limited consideration of race in school admissions for purposes of diversity.[a]

FISHER V. UNIVERSITY OF TEXAS

The Supreme Court issued its most recent ruling on affirmative action in 2013. The case involved Abigail Fisher, who was rejected by the University of Texas (UT) at Austin in 2008.[b] UT admitted three-quarters of its students based on high school class rank. It admitted additional students based on academic and other factors. To promote diversity, these factors included race and Hispanic status. Fisher did not qualify by class rank, but her academic qualifications were better

than some of the minority group members who were admitted. (Indeed, by 2010 a majority of UT students were members of a racial or ethnic minority group—that is minority group members are a majority of the total population of Texas.)

In her lawsuit, Fisher argued that the university's admissions process violated the Fourteenth Amendment's equal protection clause. In its ruling, however, the Court did not completely ban the use of race as a factor in college admissions. Rather, it sent the case back to the appellate court and ordered that court to review the university's admissions practices more strictly.

PROBLEMS WITH AFFIRMATIVE ACTION

Some experts have argued that affirmative action can have negative effects. UCLA law professor Richard Sander and legal journalist Stuart Taylor argue that socioeconomic diversity is as important as racial diversity. Children of wealthy black and Latino professionals should not be favored over low-income white and Asian American students who are better qualified.

Sander and Taylor also argue that affirmative action can cause students to attend the wrong schools. Minority group members with low test scores who are admitted to elite schools may drop out more frequently than those who attend less prestigious institutions. Students can experience problems when they are not as well prepared as their classmates.

FOR CRITICAL ANALYSIS

Some argue that there should be no preferences for any group in college admissions—including athletes and children of alumni. Do you agree or disagree? Why?

a. 539 U.S. 306 (2003).
b. *Fisher v. University of Texas*, 570 U.S. ___ (2013).

significant loss of public support and could even lead to impeachment hearings in the House. More commonly, presidents exercise influence over the judiciary by appointing new judges and justices as federal judicial seats become vacant.

Executives at the state level may also refuse to implement court decisions with which they disagree. A notable example of such a refusal occurred in Arkansas after the Supreme Court ordered schools to desegregate "with all deliberate speed" in 1955.[20] Arkansas governor Orval Faubus refused to cooperate with the decision and used the state's National

20. *Brown v. Board of Education*, 349 U.S. 294 (1955)—referred to as the second *Brown* decision.

Guard to block the integration of Central High School in Little Rock. Ultimately, President Dwight Eisenhower had to federalize the Arkansas National Guard and send federal troops to Little Rock to quell the violence that had erupted.

Legislative Checks. Courts may make rulings, but often the legislatures at local, state, and federal levels are required to appropriate funds to carry out the courts' rulings. A court, for example, may decide that prison conditions must be improved, but it is up to the legislature to authorize the funds necessary to carry out the ruling. When such funds are not appropriated, the court that made the ruling, in effect, has been checked.

Courts' rulings can be overturned by constitutional amendments at both the federal and the state levels. For example, the Sixteenth Amendment to the U.S. Constitution, ratified in 1913, overturned a United States Supreme Court ruling that found the income tax to be unconstitutional. Proposed constitutional amendments to reverse court decisions on school prayer, abortion, and same-sex marriage have failed.

Finally, Congress or a state legislature can rewrite (amend) old laws or enact new ones to overturn a court's rulings if the legislature concludes that the court is interpreting laws or legislative intentions erroneously. For example, in 2009 Congress passed (and President Obama signed) the Lilly Ledbetter Fair Pay Act, which resets the statute of limitations for

When opinions are deeply divided about an issue, demonstrations often occur in front of the Supreme Court building in Washington, D.C. Here, protesters show their opposition to a tough new Arizona law targeting illegal immigrants.

filing an equal-pay lawsuit each time an employer issues a discriminatory paycheck. The law was a direct answer to *Ledbetter v. Goodyear,* in which the Supreme Court held that the statute of limitations begins at the date the pay was agreed upon, not at the date of the most recent paycheck.[21] The new legislation made it much easier for employees to win pay discrimination lawsuits.

Public Opinion. Public opinion plays a significant role in shaping government policy, and certainly the judiciary is not excepted from this rule. For one thing, persons affected by a Supreme Court decision that is contrary to their views may simply ignore it. Officially sponsored prayers were banned in public schools in 1962, yet it was widely known that the ban was (and still is) ignored in many southern and rural districts. What can the courts do in this situation? Unless someone complains about the prayers and initiates a lawsuit, the courts can do nothing.

Additionally, the courts themselves necessarily are influenced by public opinion to some extent. After all, judges are not "islands" in our society. Their attitudes are influenced by social trends, just as the attitudes and beliefs of all persons are.

Courts generally tend to avoid issuing decisions that they know will be noticeably at odds with public opinion. In part, this is because the judiciary, as a branch of the government, prefers to avoid creating divisiveness among members of the public. Also, a court—particularly the Supreme Court—may lose stature if it decides a case in a way that markedly diverges from public opinion.

Judicial Traditions and Doctrines. Supreme Court justices (and other federal judges) typically exercise self-restraint in fashioning their decisions. In part, this restraint stems from their knowledge that the other two branches of government and the public can exercise checks on the judiciary, as previously discussed. To a large degree, however, this restraint is mandated by various judicially established traditions and doctrines. For example, in exercising its discretion to hear appeals, the Supreme Court will not hear a meritless appeal just so it can rule on the issue. Also, when reviewing a case, the Supreme Court frequently narrows its focus to just one issue or one aspect of an issue involved in the case. The Court rarely makes broad, sweeping decisions on issues. Furthermore, the doctrine of *stare decisis* acts as a restraint because it obligates the courts, including the Supreme Court, to follow established precedents when deciding cases. Only rarely will courts overrule a precedent.

Hypothetical and Political Questions. Other judicial doctrines and practices also act as restraints. As already mentioned, the courts will hear

Bill Waller Jr., chief justice of the Mississippi Supreme Court, makes a campaign speech at the Neshoba County Fair. What are the consequences of holding judicial elections? (Kevin Dietsch/UPI/Landov)

21. 550 U.S. 618 (2007).

only what are called justiciable disputes—disputes that arise out of actual cases. In other words, a court will not hear a case that involves a merely hypothetical issue.

Additionally, if a political question is involved, the Supreme Court often will exercise judicial restraint and refuse to rule on the matter. A **political question** is one that the Supreme Court declares should be decided by the elected branches of government—the executive branch, the legislative branch, or those two branches acting together. For example, the Supreme Court has refused to rule on whether women in the military should be allowed to serve in combat units, preferring instead to defer to the executive branch's decisions on the matter. (In January 2013, the Department of Defense lifted the ban on women serving in combat units.) Generally, though, fewer questions are deemed political questions by the Supreme Court today than in the past.

Political Question
An issue that a court believes should be decided by the executive or legislative branch, or both.

The Impact of the Lower Courts. Higher courts can reverse the decisions of lower courts. Lower courts can act as a check on higher courts, too. Lower courts can ignore—and have ignored—Supreme Court decisions. Usually, they do so indirectly. A lower court might conclude, for example, that the precedent set by the Supreme Court does not apply to the exact circumstances in the case before the court. Alternatively, the lower court may decide that the Supreme Court's decision was ambiguous with respect to the issue before the lower court. The fact that the Supreme Court rarely makes broad and clear-cut statements on any issue makes it easier for lower courts to interpret the Supreme Court's decisions in different ways.

Should women in the military be in combat units? The United States Supreme Court refused to address this question. Why? (RAMZI HAIDAR/AFP/Getty Images)

making a difference
CHANGING THE LEGAL SYSTEM

The U.S. legal system may seem too complex to be influenced by one individual, but its power nonetheless depends on the support of individuals. The public has many ways of resisting, modifying, or overturning statutes and rulings of the courts.

Why Should You Care? You may find it worthwhile to attend one or more court sessions to see how the law works in practice. Legislative bodies may make laws and ordinances, but legislation is given its practical form by court rulings. Therefore, if you care about the effects of a particular law, pay attention to how the courts are interpreting it. For example, do you believe that sentences handed down for certain crimes are too lenient—or too strict? Legislative bodies can attempt to establish sentences for various offenses, but the courts inevitably retain considerable flexibility in determining what happens in any particular case.

What Can You Do? Public opinion can have an effect on judicial policies. There is probably an organization that pursues lawsuits to benefit whichever causes that you support. A prime example is the modern women's movement, which undertook long series of lawsuits to change the way women are treated in American life. The courts only rule on cases that are brought before them, and the women's movement changed American law by filing—and winning—case after case.

- In 1965, a federal circuit court opened a wide range of jobs for women by overturning laws that kept women out of work that was "too hard" for them.
- In 1971, the United States Supreme Court ruled that states could not prefer men when assigning the administrators of estates. (This case was brought by Ruth Bader Ginsburg, who was later to sit on the Court herself.)
- In 1974, the Court ruled that employers could not use the "going market rate" to justify lower wages for women.

A demonstrator outside of the Supreme Court as arguments are made in a 2013 case seeking to determine whether human genes can be patented. The Court invalidated the patent in question, which may result in cheaper treatments for breast and ovarian cancer. (Tom Williams/CQ Roll Call/Getty Images)

- In 1975, it ruled that women could not be excluded from juries.
- In 1978, an Oregon court became the first of many to find that a man could be prosecuted for raping his wife.
- In 1996, the Virginia Military Institute was forced to admit women as cadets.

Today, groups such as the National Organization for Women continue to support lawsuits to advance women's rights.

You can access an online site for information about the Supreme Court by entering "oyez" into your favorite search engine.

key terms

affirm 281	federal question 274	limited jurisdiction 276	rule of four 280
amicus curiae brief 274	general jurisdiction 276	litigate 274	senatorial courtesy 282
appellate court 276	judicial activism 286	majority opinion 281	*stare decisis* 272
case law 273	judicial	opinion 281	trial court 276
class-action suit 274	implementation 289	oral arguments 280	unanimous opinion 281
common law 272	judicial restraint 287	political question 293	writ of *certiorari* 280
concurring opinion 281	jurisdiction 273	precedent 272	
dissenting opinion 281	justiciable	remand 281	
diversity of	controversy 274	reverse 281	
citizenship 274			

chapter summary

1 American law is rooted in the common law tradition. The common law doctrine of *stare decisis* (which means "to stand on decided cases") obligates judges to follow precedents established previously by their own courts or by higher courts that have authority over them. Precedents established by the United States Supreme Court, the highest court in the land, are binding on all lower courts. Fundamental sources of American law include the U.S. Constitution and state constitutions, statutes enacted by legislative bodies, regulations issued by administrative agencies, and case law.

2 Article III, Section 1, of the U.S. Constitution limits the jurisdiction of the federal courts to cases involving (a) a federal question, which is a question based, at least in part, on the U.S. Constitution, a treaty, or a federal law, or (b) diversity of citizenship, which arises when parties to a lawsuit are from different states or when the lawsuit involves a foreign citizen or government. The federal court system is a three-tiered model consisting of (a) U.S. district (trial) courts and various lower courts of limited jurisdiction, (b) intermediate U.S. courts of appeals, and (c) the United States Supreme Court. Cases may be appealed from the district courts to the appellate courts. In most cases, the decisions of the federal appellate courts are final because the Supreme Court hears relatively few cases.

3 The Supreme Court's decision to review a case is influenced by many factors, including the significance of the issues involved and whether the solicitor general is asking the Court to take the case. After a case is accepted, the justices undertake research (with the help of their law clerks) on the

issues involved in the case, hear oral arguments from the parties, meet in conference to discuss and vote on the issues, and announce the opinion, which is then released for publication.

4 Federal judges are nominated by the president and confirmed by the Senate. Once appointed, they hold office for life, barring gross misconduct. The nomination and confirmation process, particularly for Supreme Court justices, is often extremely politicized. Democrats and Republicans alike realize that justices may occupy seats on the Court for decades and want to have persons appointed who share their views. Nearly 20 percent of all Supreme Court appointments have been either rejected or not been acted on by the Senate.

5 In interpreting and applying the law, judges inevitably become policymakers. The most important policymaking tool of the federal courts is the power of judicial review. This power was not mentioned specifically in the Constitution, but the Supreme Court claimed this power for the federal courts in its 1803 decision in *Marbury v. Madison.*

6 Judges who take an active role in checking the activities of the other branches of government sometimes are characterized as "activist" judges, and judges who defer to the decisions of the other branches sometimes are regarded as "restraintist" judges. The Warren Court of the 1950s and 1960s was activist in a liberal direction, whereas the Rehnquist and Roberts Courts have become increasingly activist in a conservative direction.

7 Checks on the powers of the federal courts include executive checks, legislative checks, public opinion, and judicial traditions and doctrines.

test**yourself**

LO1 *Explain the main sources of American law, including constitutions, statutes and regulations, and the common law tradition.*

One important source of American law is:
    a. the rights and duties of workers as expressed in employment agreements.
    b. case law based in part on the common law tradition.
    c. case law based in part on the federal tradition.

LO2 *Describe the structure of the federal court system and such basic judicial requirements as jurisdiction and standing to sue.*

The distinction between federal district courts and federal appellate courts can be summarized by the following statement:
    a. federal district courts are trial courts that hear evidence, but federal appellate courts do not hear evidence.
    b. federal district courts only hear appeals from federal appellate courts.
    c. federal appellate courts only accept cases involving state constitutions.

LO3 *Discuss the procedures used by the United States Supreme Court and the various types of opinions it hands down.*

"I'll take it all the way to the Supreme Court." A lawyer cannot truthfully promise this because:
    a. the Supreme Court may be too far away from the state in which the controversy occurred.

    b. the Supreme Court only hears a limited number of cases in which a federal question is involved.
    c. the Supreme Court is not in session for a full twelve months each year.

LO4 *Evaluate the manner in which federal judges are selected.*

The most common occupational position held by a Supreme Court justice before appointment has been:
    a. U.S. senator.
    b. state governor.
    c. federal judgeship.

LO5 *Consider the ways in which the Supreme Court makes policy, and explain the forces that limit the activism of the courts.*

When a federal court declares that a federal or state law or policy is unconstitutional, that court is engaging in:
    a. judicial review.
    b. congressional condemnation.
    c. administrative oversight.

Essay Question:
What are the benefits of having lifetime appointments to the United States Supreme Court? What problems might such appointments cause? What would be the likely result if Supreme Court justices faced term limits?

Answers to multiple-choice questions: 1. b, 2. a, 3. b, 4. c, 5. a.

CourseMate

Access CourseMate at www.cengagebrain.com for additional study tools: practice quizzes, key term flashcards and crossword puzzles, audio chapter summaries, simulations, animated learning modules, interactive timelines, videos, and American Government NewsWatch.

13

Domestic and Economic Policy

Los Angeles demonstrators call on President Obama to take strong action on climate change in February 2013. Are there steps the president can take to address this issue without relying on Congress? (David McNew/Getty Images)

LEARNING OUTCOMES

The five **Learning Outcomes (LOs)** below are designed to help improve your understanding of this chapter. After reading this chapter, you should be able to:

■ **LO1** Describe the five steps of the policymaking process, using the health-care reform legislation as an example.

■ **LO2** Explain why illegal immigration is seen as a problem, and cite some of the steps that have been taken in response to it.

■ **LO3** Evaluate how the nation has reacted to high oil prices and the controversy over global warming.

■ **LO4** Define *unemployment, inflation, fiscal policy, net public debt,* and *monetary policy.*

■ **LO5** Describe the various taxes that Americans pay, and discuss some of the controversies surrounding taxation.

Check your understanding of the material with the Test Yourself section at the end of the chapter.

Part of the public-policy debate in our nation involves domestic problems. **Domestic policy** can be defined as all laws, government planning, and government actions that concern internal issues of national importance. Consequently, the span of such policies is enormous. Domestic policies range from relatively simple issues, such as what the speed limit should be on interstate highways, to more complex ones, such as how best to protect our environment. Many of our domestic policies are formulated and implemented by the federal government, but a number of others are the result of the combined efforts of federal, state, and local governments.

We can define several types of domestic policy. *Regulatory policy* seeks to define what is and is not legal. Setting speed limits is obviously regulatory policy. *Redistributive*

Domestic Policy
All government laws, planning, and actions that concern internal issues of national importance, such as health care, the environment, and the economy.

297

298 PART FOUR • POLICYMAKING

policy transfers income from certain individuals or groups to others, often based on the belief that these transfers enhance fairness. Social Security is an example. *Promotional policy* seeks to foster or discourage various economic or social activities, typically through subsidies and tax breaks. A tax credit for buying a fuel-efficient car would qualify as promotional. Typically, whenever a policy decision is made, some groups will be better off and some groups will be hurt. All policymaking generally involves such a dilemma.

In this chapter, we look at domestic policy issues involving health care, immigration, and energy and the environment. We also examine national economic policies undertaken by the federal government—for example, the issue of the federal budget deficit. As we analyze the first of these issues, health care, we take a look at how public policy is made.

THE POLICYMAKING PROCESS: HEALTH CARE AS AN EXAMPLE

LO1: Describe the five steps of the policymaking process, using the health-care reform legislation as an example.

How does any issue get resolved? First, of course, the issue must be identified as a problem. Often, policymakers have only to open their local newspapers or letters from their constituents to discover that a problem is brewing. On rare occasions, a crisis—such as that brought about by the terrorist attacks of September 11, 2001—creates the need to formulate policy. Like most Americans, however, policymakers receive much of their information from the national media. Finally, various lobbying groups provide information to members of Congress.

No matter how simple or how complex the problem, those who make policy follow a number of steps. We can divide the process of policymaking into five steps: (1) agenda building, (2) policy formulation, (3) policy adoption, (4) policy implementation, and (5) policy evaluation.

The health-care legislation passed in 2010 can be used to illustrate this process. In March 2010, President Barack Obama signed into law the **Patient Protection and Affordable Care Act,** a massive overhaul of the nation's health-care funding system. A few days later, Obama signed the Health Care and Education Reconciliation Act, a series of adjustments to the main legislative package. These two measures constituted the most important legislative package in the United States between the 2008 and 2010 elections.

Health Care: Agenda Building

Patient Protection and Affordable Care Act
A law passed in 2010 that seeks, among other things, to provide health-care insurance to all American citizens. The act, nicknamed "Obamacare" by opponents and journalists, is supplemented by the Health Care and Education Reconciliation Act.

Gross Domestic Product (GDP)
The dollar value of all final goods and services produced in a one-year period.

First of all, an issue must get on the agenda. In other words, Congress must become aware that a problem requires congressional action. Agenda building may occur as the result of a crisis, a technological change, or a mass media campaign, as well as through the efforts of strong political personalities and effective lobbying groups. To understand how health care came to be an important issue, and how health-care reform became part of the national agenda, we need to examine the background of the issue.

Health Care's Role in the American Economy. Spending for health care is now estimated to account for 17.6 percent of the total U.S. economy. In 1965, about 6 percent of our national income was spent on health care, but that percentage has been increasing ever since. Per capita spending on health care is greater in the United States than almost anywhere else in the world. Measured by the percentage of the **gross domestic product (GDP)** devoted to health care, America spends almost twice as much as Britain or Japan. (The GDP is the dollar value of all final goods and services produced in a one-year period.)

As of 2010, before the reform legislation was implemented, government spending on health care constituted about 50 percent of total health-care spending. Private insurance accounted for more than 30 percent of payments for health care. The remainder—less than 20 percent—was paid directly by individuals or by charities. The government programs **Medicare** and **Medicaid** have been the main sources of hospital and other medical benefits for about 100 million Americans—one-third of the nation's population. Many of these people are elderly.

Medicare. The Medicare program, which was created in 1965 under President Lyndon Johnson, pays hospital and physician bills for U.S. residents over the age of sixty-five. Since 2006, Medicare has also paid for at least part of the prescription drug expenses of the elderly. In return for paying a tax on their earnings (currently set at 2.9 percent of wages and salaries) while in the workforce, retirees are assured that the majority of their hospital and physician bills will be paid for with public funds.

Medicaid. Within a few short years, the joint federal-state taxpayer-funded Medicaid program for the "working poor" has generated one of the biggest expansions of government entitlements ever. In 1990, federal Medicaid spending was about $41 billion. By 2013, spending on Medicaid, the Children's Health Insurance Program, and allied functions was $349 billion. At the end of the century, 34 million people were enrolled in the programs. Today, in the wake of the Great Recession, there are more than 60 million enrolled.

In recent years, the federal government has paid about 55 percent of Medicaid's total cost. The states pay the rest. Wealthy states must pick up a greater share of the tab than poor states. Medicaid costs have imposed major strains on the budgets of many states. As you will learn later in this section, the new health-care reform legislation adopted in 2010 will expand considerably the share of the population that is eligible for Medicaid. Much of the extra expense due to the new enrollees will be picked up by federal taxpayers.

The Problem of the Uninsured. In 2011, about 48 million Americans—more than 15 percent of the population—did not have health insurance. The uninsured population has been relatively young, in part due to Medicare, which covers almost everyone over the age of sixty-five. Also, younger workers are more likely to be employed in entry-level jobs without health-insurance benefits. The traditional system of health care in the United States was based on the assumption that employers would provide health insurance to working-age persons. Many small businesses, however, simply have not been

Medicare
A federal health-insurance program that covers U.S. residents over the age of sixty-five. The costs are met by a tax on wages and salaries.

Medicaid
A joint state-federal program that provides medical care to the poor (including indigent elderly persons in nursing homes). The program is funded out of general government revenues.

STONE SOUP © 2005 Jan Eliot. Reprinted by permission of Universal Uclick. All rights reserved.

able to afford to offer their workers health insurance. In 2011, employer-provided health insurance cost an average of $5,429 for single coverage and $15,073 for family coverage, according to the Kaiser Family Foundation.

The Problem of High Costs. High medical costs are a problem not only for individuals with inadequate or nonexistent insurance coverage. They are also a problem for the system as a whole. Over the last four decades, per capita spending on health care in the United States grew at an average rate of 4.9 percent per year, even when corrected for inflation. A main driver of the growth in health-care spending was new medical technologies and services.

In addition, people over the age of sixty-five run up health-care bills that are far larger than those incurred by the rest of the population. As a federal problem, therefore, health-care spending growth has been and will remain chiefly a Medicare issue, even after the passage of the new health-care measures. In 2011, the government's Medicare trustees reported that the Medicare trust fund was projected to run out of funds necessary to pay for all of its obligations in 2024. Such prospects explain why the issue of health-care cost containment was important during the 2009 election debates.

The International Experience. The Patient Protection and Affordable Care Act of 2010 attempts to provide universal health insurance for American citizens. The concept of universal health insurance is not new. Throughout the twentieth century, most economically advanced nations adopted such systems. American progressives considered it unacceptable that the United States could not do what these other nations had done—another argument for placing reform on the agenda.

Health Care: Policy Formulation

During the next step in the policymaking process, various policy proposals are discussed among government officials and the public. Such discussions may take place in the media and in the halls of Congress. Congress holds hearings, the president voices the administration's views, and the topic may even become a campaign issue.

For more than half a century, liberals have sought to establish a universal health-insurance system in this country. All attempts, however, went nowhere. After the 2008 elections, however, the Democrats were in complete control of Congress and the presidency. Universal health insurance now appeared to be politically possible.

Unlike previous proposals, the new universal health-insurance plans did not provide for a federal monopoly on basic health insurance. Instead, universal coverage would result from a mandate that all citizens must obtain health insurance from some source—an employer, Medicare or Medicaid, or a new plan sponsored by the federal government or a state government. Low-income families would receive a subsidy to help them pay their insurance premiums. Insurers could not reject applicants. A program of this nature was adopted by the state of Massachusetts in 2006 in response to a proposal by then Republican governor Mitt Romney.

Health Care: Policy Adoption

The third step in the policymaking process involves choosing a specific policy from among the proposals that have been discussed.

As president, Barack Obama largely delegated the drafting of a health-care plan to Congress. Obama's willingness to let Congress take the lead was a notable change. Recent presidents, such as George W. Bush and Bill Clinton, had sought to push presidential proposals through the legislative process without significant alteration. Obama's tactics eliminated much of the tug-of-war between Congress and the president that had been commonplace in past decades, but the political cost of letting Congress take the lead turned out to be high. Much of the political maneuvering required for passage was highly unpopular with the public.

Individual Mandate
In health-care reform, the requirement that all citizens obtain health-care insurance coverage from some source, public or private.

The Issue of Mandated Coverage. One key element of the proposed legislation was the *individual mandate*. Congressional Democrats adopted the **individual mandate** because without it, there was no way that the numbers would add up. Universal coverage was impossible unless everyone—healthy and sick alike—chipped in. Unfortunately for the Democrats, the individual mandate allowed the Republicans to accuse the Democrats of "forcing" people to do something, never a popular position in America.

New Taxes. Funding the legislation required additional taxes. Democrats in the House called for heavier taxes on the rich, while the Senate proposed taxes on drug and insurance companies. In the end, the two chambers compromised on some of each.

Public Reaction. Initially, popular support for health-care reform, as reported by opinion polls, was relatively high. Support eroded quickly, however, as Congress took up the actual legislation. The process of moving the reform through congressional channels gave the public a close look at how legislatures operate, and many citizens clearly were not happy with what they saw.

Passage. The House passed its bill in November 2009, and the Senate passed its version in December. Passing the reform legislation became more complicated in January 2010, after Republican Scott Brown won a Massachusetts special election to fill a vacant U.S. Senate seat. The election meant that the Senate Democrats lost their sixtieth vote, which was necessary to end filibusters. If the House and Senate versions of the bill were reconciled in a conference committee—the normal procedure—Senate Democrats would not be able to pass the resulting compromise, and the entire reform effort would collapse.

President Obama and then House Speaker Nancy Pelosi, however, patiently assembled enough Democratic support in the House to pass the Senate bill unaltered, thus eliminating the need for a conference committee. The House then immediately passed a reconciliation act, which was not subject to Senate filibuster.

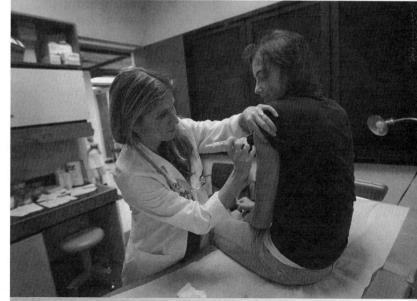

A Miami physician inoculates a thirteen-year-old patient with a vaccine. In 2013, Florida Republican governor Rick Scott reversed his position and supported an expansion of Medicaid under the federal Affordable Care Act. (Joe Raedle/Getty Images)

"Obamacare," as it was nicknamed, was the law of the land. Neither the Senate's bill nor the House's reconciliation measure received the vote of even a single Republican.

Details of the Legislation. Most of the major provisions of the new legislation did not go into effect until 2014. The long delay was established in part to allow systems such as state insurance pools to be set up more effectively, but the Democrats also wanted to keep costs down during the initial ten-year period. The lengthy implementation, however, presented political problems for the Democrats, who faced two national elections before most of the programs would be in effect. Voters in those elections would receive few of the promised benefits of the programs.

Some provisions took effect quickly, however. Young adults were allowed to stay on their parents' health plans until they turned twenty-six, and insurance companies could not drop people when they became sick.

In 2014, most of the program kicked in, including the following:

- A ban on excluding people with preexisting conditions from insurance plans.
- A requirement that most people obtain insurance or pay an income tax penalty.
- State health-insurance exchanges where individuals and small businesses can buy insurance.
- Subsidies to help persons with incomes up to four times the federal poverty level purchase coverage on the exchanges.
- Medicaid coverage for individuals with incomes up to 133 percent of the poverty level.

Significant taxes to pay for the new benefits were to be phased in from 2011 to 2018.

Health Care: Policy Implementation

The fourth step in the policymaking process involves the implementation of the policy alternative chosen by Congress. Government action must be implemented by bureaucrats, the courts, police, and individual citizens.

Congressional Opposition. Implementation would not occur, of course, if Obamacare could be abolished before it was fully effective. Republicans sought to accomplish exactly that. Complete repeal of the legislation, however, was difficult. Repeal would have to pass both chambers of Congress and survive a presidential veto. Republicans, in other words, needed a complete sweep in the 2012 elections, which they did not get.

Also, much of the reform package takes the form of an entitlement program, such as Medicare or Social Security. Funding for entitlement programs continues on a year-to-year basis unless it is explicitly altered or abolished. In other words, entitlements do not depend on annual budget votes in Congress for their continued survival. Therefore, even if Republicans in Congress were able to "defund" certain aspects of the reforms, most of the new policies would survive.

Opposition in the Courts. As you have learned in earlier chapters, many conservative state officials challenged the constitutionality of the Affordable Care Act in court. In 2012, however, the Supreme Court ruled that most of the act was constitutional. The one exception: the Court threw out the mechanism by which the federal government could force states to expand their Medicaid programs.

Opposition in the States. Medicaid expansion is fully funded by the federal government for the first six years and funded at 90 percent thereafter. Still, a large number of conservative state governments exercised their option to refuse expansion. As a result, several million low-income persons—many of them in southern states—were not covered when Obamacare was fully implemented in 2014. Many state governments also refused to participate in setting up health-insurance exchanges. The federal government, however, had the power to set up the exchanges in states where local officials refused to participate.

Health Care: Policy Evaluation

After a policy has been implemented, it is evaluated. When a policy has been in place for a given period of time, groups inside and outside the government conduct studies to determine how the program has actually worked. Based on this feedback and the perceived success or failure of the policy, a new round of policymaking initiatives may be undertaken to improve on the effort.

During 2013, many observers were concerned that the final rollout of the health-care reforms in 2014 would be chaotic. This was only a prediction, however. Of necessity, the reforms received very little real evaluation until they were fully in place.

IMMIGRATION

In recent years, immigration rates in the United States have been among the highest since their peak in the early twentieth century. Every year, more than 1 million people immigrate to this country legally, a figure that does not include the large number of unauthorized immigrants. Those who were born on foreign soil now constitute about 13 percent of the U.S. population—more than twice the percentage of thirty years ago.

LO2: Explain why illegal immigration is seen as a problem, and cite some of the steps that have been taken in response to it.

Since 1977, four out of five immigrants have come from Latin America or Asia. Hispanics have overtaken African Americans as the nation's largest minority. As you learned in Chapter 5, if current immigration rates continue, by 2050 minority groups collectively will constitute the majority of Americans. If such groups were to form coalitions, they could increase their political power dramatically. The "old guard" white majority would no longer dominate American politics.

The Issue of Unauthorized Immigration

Illegal immigration—or unauthorized immigration, to use the terminology of the Department of Homeland Security—has been a major national issue for many years. Latin Americans, especially

A member of Nuns on the Bus speaks at the end of the group's cross country trip to defend unauthorized immigrants. Why might some Catholics have a supportive attitude toward immigrants? (Justin Sullivan/Getty Images).

those migrating from Mexico, constitute the majority of individuals entering the United States without permission. In addition, many unauthorized immigrants enter the country legally, often as tourists or students, and then fail to return home when their visa status expires. Naturally, the unauthorized population is hard to count, but recent estimates have put the number of such persons at about 11 million.

A major complication in addressing the issue of unauthorized immigrants is that they frequently live in mixed households, in which one or more members of a family have lawful resident status, but others do not. A woman from Guatemala with permanent resident status, for example, might be married to a Guatemalan man who is in the country illegally. Often, the parents in a family are unauthorized, whereas the children, who were born in the United States, possess American citizenship. Mixed families mean that deporting the unauthorized immigrant will either break up a family or force one or more American citizens into exile.

Immigration Legislation

Some people regard the high rate of immigration as a plus for America because it offsets the low birthrate and aging population. Immigrants expand the workforce and help to support, through their taxes, government programs that benefit older Americans, such as Medicare and Social Security. Critics, though, fear that immigrants may take jobs away from American workers and alter the nature of American culture.

The split in the public's attitudes has been reflected in differences among the nation's leaders over how to handle the issue of illegal immigration. Most Republicans in Congress have favored a harder line toward illegal immigrants than have most Democrats. There have been exceptions. Republican president George W. Bush was a strong—if unsuccessful—advocate of immigration reform. By Obama's first term, however, Republicans in Congress were substantially united against reform.

State Immigration Laws. In April 2010, Arizona's governor signed the nation's toughest-ever bill on illegal immigration. The law criminalized the failure to carry immigration documents, and it required police to stop and question anyone suspected of being in the country illegally. Opponents contended that the act would lead to harassment of Latinos regardless of their citizenship status. Arizona had earlier passed the nation's toughest law penalizing employers who hired undocumented workers.

In June 2012, the United States Supreme Court ruled that Arizona could not make an immigrant's failure to register under federal law a state crime, could not make it a felony for illegal immigrants to work, and could not arrest people without warrants if they might be deportable under federal law. The Court did not block police from investigating the immigration status of anyone they might stop. It left the door open, however, to future challenges to this law based on equal protection principles.[1]

In 2011, Alabama adopted a new law aimed at illegal immigration that was in many respects even tougher than the Arizona legislation. Much of the law is currently blocked as a result of federal court rulings, however. Since 2010, Georgia, Indiana, South Carolina, and Utah have also passed laws similar to the ones in Arizona and Alabama.

Immigration and the Obama Administration. During his campaign, Barack Obama supported reforms that would give illegal immigrants a path toward citizenship. Reform was put off to allow Congress to concentrate on health-care issues, however. Obama

---

1. *Arizona v. United States,* 567 U.S. ___ (2012).

concentrated instead on border security and rounding up deportable persons. In fact, in Obama's first term, his administration deported 1.5 million illegal immigrants, an all-time record.

The resulting Latino dissatisfaction with the administration raised the question of whether Hispanics would turn out and vote for Democratic candidates in forthcoming elections. The 2012 Republican presidential candidates, however, took a hard line against illegal immigration. Also, in June 2012, Obama announced a new policy under which immigration authorities would suspend deportations of unauthorized immigrants who were brought into the country as children and who were not otherwise in trouble with the law. In the end, Latinos and Asian Americans turned out for the Democrats in large numbers during the 2012 elections.

The Republican Turn on Immigration. Clearly, the Republicans would be better off in the future if they could increase their support among immigrants, a growing share of the population. Indeed, following the elections, a substantial number of Republicans announced that they were adjusting their position on immigration and were now open to change. For the first time in years, immigration reform seemed possible. Proposals announced by a bipartisan group of senators would regularize the status of the 11 million unauthorized immigrants and open up a long-term path to citizenship. New possibilities for legal immigration would be available, especially for farmworkers and those with high-tech skills. The plans also called for even greater efforts to guarantee border security.

ENERGY AND THE ENVIRONMENT

A major part of President Obama's legislative agenda has been directed at energy and environmental issues. Energy policy addresses two major problems: (1) America's reliance on foreign oil, much of which is produced by unfriendly regimes, and (2) global warming purportedly caused by increased emissions of carbon dioxide (CO_2) and other greenhouse gases.

Energy Independence—A Strategic Issue

As of early 2013, America imported just under 40 percent of the petroleum it consumed. We relied on foreign oil much more heavily only a few years ago. In 2006, almost 60 percent of our oil came from abroad. More than one-third of U.S. imports come from two friendly neighbors, Canada and Mexico. Still, the world's largest oil exporters include nations that are not our friends. Russia is the world's second-largest oil exporter, after Saudi Arabia. Other major exporters include Venezuela and Iran, both openly hostile to the United States.

LO3: Evaluate how the nation has reacted to high oil prices and the controversy over global warming.

While the United States is far from attaining the goal of energy independence, the nation has taken significant steps in that direction. What changes were responsible for this turnaround?

High Prices and New Production. If the price of a commodity goes up, producers of that commodity have an incentive to produce more of it. The price of gasoline has certainly risen in recent years. In the summer of 2008, the price of gasoline exceeded $4 for the first time. The price has fluctuated since but remains high. Clearly, petroleum producers had an incentive to extract more crude oil, if possible. The question was, could they?

Some experts doubted that enough new oil could be extracted to keep prices from rising indefinitely. They underestimated the impact of increased applications of technology in the form of hydraulic fracturing, or **fracking.** This process involves injecting water, sand, and chemicals under high pressure into hydrocarbon-bearing rocks, releasing oil or natural gas. Expensive oil made fracking profitable.

Fracking has had an even greater impact on the supply of natural gas. A few years ago, it seemed likely that the United States would need to import natural gas. By 2012, however, so much natural gas was available domestically that the nation had run out of storage space. Low natural gas prices plus new air-pollution regulations made coal uncompetitive as a source of electricity. As a result, plans for 168 new coal-based power plants were abandoned, and about 100 existing plants were scheduled for retirement. Despite concerns that fracking might harm drinking-water supplies or otherwise damage the environment, use of the process continues to grow rapidly.

The Politics of Expensive Oil. The high price of gasoline is a political issue, and several 2012 presidential candidates claimed that, if elected, they would bring it down. Because crude oil prices are set worldwide, the ability of the federal government to affect these prices is very limited. Still, the government has taken some steps to encourage increased supplies of gasoline.

In 2009, President Obama issued higher fuel-efficiency standards for vehicles. By 2016, the new requirement will be 39 miles per gallon for cars and 30 miles per gallon for light trucks. Implemented in steps, the standards began to take effect with 2011 models.

The federal government also subsidizes the development of alternative fuels. Subsidies to encourage the production of ethanol from corn are controversial. Critics charge that ethanol production is an inefficient method of producing energy and makes food more expensive. Subsidies for renewable energy sources, such as windmills and solar power panels, have also attracted criticism. A problem with wind and especially solar power has been high costs. Prices have fallen rapidly, however, and use of these technologies has risen quickly. Still, they are a small fraction of the nation's power supply.

Disasters in the Energy Industry. For some years, opening new areas for oil and gas drilling has been a major plank in the Republican Party platform. Democrats have been more reluctant, but in March 2010 President Obama announced that major new offshore tracts in the Atlantic would be open to deep-sea drilling. Less than one month later, the BP *Deepwater Horizon* oil spill disaster in the Gulf of Mexico began. The spill, the largest in American history, resulted in a temporary moratorium on new offshore drilling.

A Texas worker unloads a mixture of oil, sediment, and water generated during hydraulic fracturing (fracking). Components of the mixture will be separated and either recycled or eliminated. Why is fracking controversial? (Jason Janik/Bloomberg via Getty Images)

Unlike many Democrats, Obama also favored building new energy plants that would use nuclear power. Electric utilities planned several new nuclear plants, but these plans were shelved almost immediately. The major problem was that nuclear power could not compete with the falling costs of natural gas. A second problem was safety. In March 2011, a giant tsunami struck northeast Japan and severely damaged four nuclear reactors located on the coast. The resulting radiation leaks convinced many people that new nuclear power plants would be dangerous.

Global Warming

In the 1990s, many scientists working on climate change began to conclude that average world temperatures would rise significantly in the twenty-first century. Gases released by human activity, principally carbon dioxide (CO_2), may be producing a "greenhouse effect," trapping the sun's heat and slowing its release into outer space.

The Global Warming Debate. Most scientists who perform research on the world's climate believe that global warming, or climate change, will be significant, but there is considerable disagreement as to how much warming will actually occur. It is generally accepted that world temperatures have already increased by about 0.74 degrees Celsius over the last century. The United Nations' Intergovernmental Panel on Climate Change predicts increases ranging from 1.0 to 4.8 degrees Celsius by 2100. This range of estimates is rather wide and reflects the uncertainties involved in predicting the world's climate.

Global warming has become a major political football to be kicked back and forth by conservatives and liberals. Former vice president Al Gore's Oscar-winning and widely viewed documentary on climate change, released in 2006, further fueled the debate. (Gore received the Nobel Peace Prize in 2007 for his work.) Titled *An Inconvenient Truth*, the film stressed that actions to mitigate global warming must be taken now if we are to avert a planet-threatening crisis. Environmental groups and others have been pressing the federal government to do just that.

Their efforts are complicated by the fact that a major share of the American electorate does not believe that global warming is happening or, if it is happening, that it is caused by human activities. Disbelief in global warming is a partisan phenomenon. According to one poll, skepticism about global warming among Republicans rose by 11 percentage points from 2008 to 2009, and a majority of Republicans now believe that global warming does not exist. The opinions of Democrats have not changed—about four-fifths of them accept that climate change is a problem. If there is no global warming, of course, there would be no reason to limit emissions of CO_2 and other greenhouse gases. By 2013, in the wake of super storms and droughts, skepticism about climate change among Republicans and independents had eased noticeably—but opposition to CO_2 restrictions remained strong.

Legislative Stalemate. The centerpiece of the Obama administration's legislative program on energy and the environment was a bill designed to limit greenhouse gas emissions. In June 2009, the House passed a bill, but in the Senate, the bill sank without a trace. The Republican takeover of the House in the 2010 elections meant that no action on greenhouse gas emissions was likely in the near future.

Despite the lack of government action, by 2011 CO_2 emissions in the United States were actually down from 2008. The most important cause was new power plants that used natural gas instead of coal. (Gas does release some CO_2, but less than half as much as coal.) More fuel-efficient cars also contributed to the reduction.

Recession
An economic downturn, usually characterized by a fall in the GDP and rising unemployment.

Unemployment
The inability of those who are in the labor force to find a job.

Inflation
A sustained rise in the general price level of goods and services.

LO4: Define *unemployment, inflation, fiscal policy, net public debt,* and *monetary policy.*

THE POLITICS OF ECONOMIC DECISION MAKING

Nowhere are the principles of public policymaking more obvious than in the economic decisions made by the federal government. The president and Congress (and to a growing extent, the judiciary) are constantly faced with questions of economic policy. Economic policy becomes especially important when the nation enters a recession.

Good Times, Bad Times

Like any economy that is fundamentally capitalist, the U.S. economy experiences ups and downs. Good times—booms—are followed by lean years. If a slowdown is severe enough, it is called a **recession.** Recessions are characterized by increased **unemployment,** the inability of those who are in the workforce to find a job. The government tries to moderate the effects of such downturns. In contrast, booms are historically associated with another economic problem that the government must address—rising prices, or **inflation.**

Measuring Unemployment. Estimates of the number of unemployed are prepared by the U.S. Department of Labor. The Bureau of the Census also generates estimates using survey research data. Critics of the published unemployment rate calculated by the federal government believe that it fails to reflect the true numbers of discouraged workers and "hidden unemployed." There is no exact way to measure discouraged workers, but the Department of Labor defines them as people who have dropped out of the labor force and are no longer looking for a job because they believe that the job market has little to offer them.

Job seekers wait in line at a job fair in Virginia in 2013. Why haven't high unemployment rates been more of an issue in recent years? (Andrew Harrer/Bloomberg via Getty Images)

Inflation. Rising prices, or inflation, can also be a serious economic and political problem. Inflation is a sustained upward movement in the average level of prices. Another way of defining inflation is as a decline in the purchasing power of money over time. The government measures inflation using the *consumer price index,* or CPI. The Bureau of Labor Statistics identifies a market basket of goods and services purchased by the typical consumer, and regularly checks the price of that basket. Over a period of many years, inflation can add up. For example, today's dollar is worth (very roughly) about a twentieth of what it was worth a century ago. In effect, today's dollar is a 1914 nickel.

The Business Cycle. Economists refer to the regular succession of economic expansions and contractions as the *business cycle.* An extremely severe recession is called a *depression,* as in the example of the Great Depression. By 1933, actual output was 35 percent below the nation's productive capacity. Unemployment reached 25 percent. Compared with this catastrophe, recessions since 1945 have usually been mild. Nevertheless, the United States has experienced recessions with some regularity. Recession years since 1960 have included 1970, 1974, 1980, 1982, 1990, 2001, and 2008.

To try to control the ups and downs of the national economy, the government has several policy options. One is to change the level of taxes or government spending. The other possibility involves influencing interest rates and the money side of the economy. We will examine taxing and spending, or fiscal policy, first.

Fiscal Policy

Fiscal policy is the domain of Congress. A fiscal policy approach to stabilizing the economy is often associated with the twentieth-century economist John Maynard Keynes (1883–1946). This British economist originated the school of thought that today is called **Keynesian economics,** which supports the use of government spending and taxing to help stabilize the economy. (*Keynesian* is pronounced *kayn-zee-*un.) Keynes believed that there was a need for government intervention in the economy, in part because after falling into a recession or depression, a modern economy may become trapped in an ongoing state of less-than-full employment.

Government Spending and Borrowing. Keynes developed his fiscal policy theories during the Great Depression of the 1930s. He believed that the forces of supply and demand operated too slowly on their own in such a serious recession. Unemployment meant people had less to spend, and because they could not buy things, more businesses failed, creating additional unemployment. It was a vicious cycle. Keynes's idea was simple: in such circumstances, the government should step in and engineer the spending that is needed to return the economy to a more normal state.[2]

The spending promoted by the government could take either of two forms. The government could increase its own spending, or it could cut taxes, allowing the taxpayer to undertake the spending instead. To have the effect Keynes wanted, however, it was essential that the spending be financed by borrowing. In other words, the government should run a **budget deficit**—it should spend more than it receives.

Discretionary Fiscal Policy. As mentioned, Keynes originally developed his fiscal theories as a way of lifting an economy out of a major disaster such as the Great Depression. Beginning with the presidency of John F. Kennedy (1961–1963), however, policymakers have attempted to use Keynesian methods to "fine-tune" the economy. This is discretionary fiscal policy—*discretionary* meaning left to the judgment, or discretion, of a policymaker.

The Timing Problem. Attempts to fine-tune the economy encounter a timing problem. It takes a while to collect and assimilate economic data. Months or a year may go by before an economic difficulty can be identified. After an economic problem is recognized, a solution must be formulated. There will be an action

2. Robert Skidelsky, *Keynes: The Return of the Master* (New York: PublicAffairs, 2010).

Fiscal Policy
The federal government's use of taxation and spending policies to affect overall business activity.

Keynesian Economics
A school of economic thought that tends to favor active federal government policymaking to stabilize economy-wide fluctuations, usually by implementing discretionary fiscal policy.

Budget Deficit
Government expenditures that exceed receipts.

WWW
Helpful Web Sites
Many consider Paul Krugman to be the dean of Keynesian economists today. Follow his *New York Times* blog and column by searching on "Krugman."

John Maynard Keynes (1883–1946) argued in favor of government intervention to smooth out economic booms and busts. (Walter Stoneman/Samuel Bourne/Getty Images)

Treasuries
U.S. Treasury securities—bills, notes, and bonds; debt issued by the federal government.

Public Debt, or National Debt
The total amount of debt carried by the federal government.

time lag between the recognition of a problem and the implementation of policy to solve it. Getting Congress to act can easily take a year or two. Finally, after fiscal policy is enacted, it takes time for it to have an effect on the economy. Because the fiscal policy time lags are long and variable, a policy designed to combat a recession may not produce results until the economy is already out of the recession.

Because of the timing problem, attempts by the government to employ fiscal policy in the last fifty years have typically taken the form of tax cuts or increases. Tax changes can take effect more quickly than government spending. In 2009, therefore, the Obama administration was employing an exceptional approach with its economic stimulus spending.

Criticisms of Keynes. Following World War II (1939–1945), Keynes's theories were integrated into the mainstream of economic thinking. There have always been economic schools of thought, however, that consider Keynesian economics to be fatally flawed. These schools argue either that fiscal policy has no effect or that it has negative side effects that outweigh any benefits. Some opponents of fiscal policy believe that the federal government should limit itself to monetary policy, which we will discuss shortly. Others believe that it is best for the government to do nothing at all.

2009–2013: The Eclipse of Fiscal Policy. It is worth noting that most voters have neither understood nor accepted Keynesian economics. Despite popular attitudes, politicians of both parties accepted Keynesian ideas for many years. Democratic president John F. Kennedy was perhaps the first Keynesian in the White House. Republican president Richard Nixon (1969–1974) is alleged to have said, "We are all Keynesians now." Even George W. Bush justified many of his policies using Keynesian language. During the first years of Obama's presidency, however, Keynesian thinking among Republicans in Congress vanished almost completely. Some members adopted the ideas of anti-Keynesian economists. The majority simply rejected countercyclical spending, reflecting the popular belief that during a recession the government should "tighten its belt."

It did not help the Keynesian cause that Obama's enormous stimulus package failed to end high rates of unemployment—Keynesian economists argued that the stimulus was less than half of what was needed to accomplish such a goal. When Obama, in his 2010 State of the Union address, employed the belt-tightening metaphor, Keynesians realized that they had lost control of the political discourse.

The unemployment rate remained close to 9 percent through 2011, a figure that traditionally would have ruled out short-term efforts to reduce the deficit. Still, Obama and the Republicans in the House issued competing budget plans that called for cuts in government spending. As you read in the *At Issue* feature in Chapter 11, one consequence was a series of crises resulting in spending cuts and tax increases. These changes in the direction of "austerity," together with slow-but-sure economic recovery, reduced the deficit by 2013. Keynesians blamed the austerity for the slow pace of economic recovery. Republicans argued that the slow pace was due to factors such as business uncertainty over the effects of Obamacare.

www
Helpful Web Sites
For economic policy arguments based on a rejection of Keynesianism, check out The Heritage Foundation by searching on "heritage issues economy."

Deficit Spending and the Public Debt

The government typically borrows by selling U.S. Treasury bills, notes, and bonds, known collectively as *Treasury securities* and informally as **treasuries.** The sale of these federal obligations to corporations, private individuals, pension plans, foreign governments, foreign businesses, and foreign individuals adds to this nation's **public debt, or national debt.** In the last few years, foreign governments, especially those of China and Japan, have come to own about 50 percent of the U.S. public debt. Thirty years ago, the share of the U.S. public debt held by foreigners was only 15 percent. Table 13–1 on the right shows the *net public debt* of the federal government since 1940.[3]

Table 13–1 does not take into account two very important variables: inflation and increases in population. A better way to examine the relative importance of the public debt is to compare it with the gross domestic product (GDP), as is done in Figure 13–1 on the next page. (As noted earlier in this chapter, the gross domestic product is the dollar value of all final goods and services produced in a one-year period.) In the figure, you see that the public debt reached its peak during World War II and fell until 1975. From about 1960 to 2008, the net public debt as a percentage of GDP ranged between 30 and 62 percent.

Deficit Spending. Can deficit spending go on forever? Certainly, it can go on for quite a long time for the U.S. government. After all, as long as individuals, businesses, and foreigners (especially foreign governments) are willing to purchase Treasury securities, the government can continue to engage in deficit spending. If deficit spending goes on long enough, however, the rest of the world—which owns about 50 percent of all treasuries—may lose faith in our government. Consequently, U.S. government borrowing might become more expensive. We, as taxpayers, are responsible for the interest that the federal government pays when it issues treasuries. A vicious cycle might occur—more deficit spending could lead to higher interest rate costs on the U.S. debt, leading in turn to even larger deficits.

So far, however, there has been little sign that such a problem is imminent. On the contrary, following the financial crisis that struck on September 15, 2008, panicked investors bought large amounts of treasuries in the belief that they were the safest instruments in existence. The interest that the U.S. government must pay on its borrowing is also very low. In May 2013, the average interest rate on four-week Treasury bills—the shortest term Treasury obligations—was 0.025 percent—for all practical purposes, an interest rate of zero. Correcting for inflation, anyone buying short-term treasuries was paying the U.S. government for the privilege of making loans to it. In 2011, the bond rating agency Standard & Poor's issued a warning about treasuries, but it had no effect on the market for the securities.

The Public Debt in Perspective. From 1960 until 1998, the federal government spent more than it received in all but two years. Some observers considered those ongoing budget deficits to be the negative result of Keynesian policies. Others argued that the deficits actually resulted from the abuse of Keynesianism. Politicians have been more than happy to run budget deficits in recessions, but they have often refused to implement the other side of Keynes's recommendations—to run a *budget surplus* during boom times.

In 1993, however, President Bill Clinton (1993–2001) obtained a tax increase as the nation emerged from a mild recession. Between the tax increase and the "dot-com boom," the United States had a budget

TABLE 13–1: Net Public Debt of the Federal Government

Year	Total (Billions of Current Dollars)
1940	$ 42.8
1945	235.2
1950	219.0
1960	236.8
1970	283.2
1980	711.9
1990	2,411.5
1995	3,604.3
1996	3,734.1
1997	3,772.3
1998	3,721.1
1999	3,632.4
2000	3,409.8
2001	3,319.6
2002	3,540.4
2003	3,913.4
2004	4,295.5
2005	4,592.2
2006	4,829.0
2007	5,035.1
2008	5,803.1
2009	7,544.7
2010	9,018.9
2011	10,128.0
2012	11,578.0*
2013	12,637.0*
2014	13,445.0*

End of year.

*Estimate.

Source: U.S. Office of Management and Budget.

---

3. Some sources use a much larger figure called the *gross public debt*. This statistic, however, includes sums that the federal government owes to itself.

FIGURE 13–1: Net Public Debt as a Percentage of the Gross Domestic Product

During World War II, the net public debt grew dramatically. It fell thereafter but rose again from 1975 to 1995. The percentage fell after 1995, only to rise dramatically after 2008.

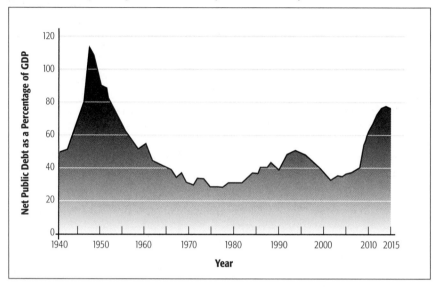

Sources: Bureau of Labor Statistics and Congressional Budget Office.

surplus each year from 1998 to 2002. Some commentators predicted that we would be running federal government surpluses for years to come.

Back to Deficit Spending. All of those projections went by the wayside because of several events. One event was the "dot-com bust," followed by the 2001–2002 recession, which lowered the rate of growth of not only the economy but also federal government tax receipts. Another event was a series of large tax cuts passed by Congress in 2001 and 2003 at the urging of President George W. Bush. A third event took place on September 11, 2001. As a result of the terrorist attacks, the federal government spent much more than it had planned to spend on security against terrorism. The government also had to pay for the war in Iraq in 2003 and the occupation of that country thereafter. Finally, Congress authorized major increases in spending on discretionary programs.

The Great Recession (2007–2009) dramatically increased the budget deficit and the level of public debt. Tax revenues collapsed, and spending on such items as unemployment compensation rose automatically. In addition, immediately upon taking office, President Obama obtained legislation from Congress that helped push the public debt to levels not seen since World War II. Such high levels of debt became a major political issue.

Monetary Policy
The use of changes in the amount of money in circulation to alter credit markets, employment, and the rate of inflation.

Federal Reserve System (the Fed)
The system created by Congress in 1913 to serve as the nation's central banking organization.

Monetary Policy

Controlling the rate of growth of the money supply is called **monetary policy.** This policy is the domain of the **Federal Reserve System,** also known simply as **the Fed.** The Fed is the most important regulatory agency in the U.S. monetary system.

The Fed performs a number of important functions. Perhaps the Fed's most important task is regulating the amount of money in circulation, which can be defined loosely as checking account balances and currency. The Fed also provides a system for transferring checks from one bank to another. In addition, it holds reserves deposited by most of the nation's banks, savings and loan associations, savings banks, and credit unions. Finally, it plays a role in supervising the banking industry.

Organization of the Federal Reserve System. A board of governors manages the Fed. This board consists of seven full-time members appointed by the president with the approval of the Senate. There are twelve Federal Reserve district banks. The most important unit within the Fed is the **Federal Open Market Committee.** This is the body that actually determines the future growth of the money supply and other important economy-wide financial variables. This committee is composed of the members of the Board of Governors, the president of the New York Federal Reserve Bank, and presidents of four other Federal Reserve banks, rotated periodically.

The Board of Governors of the Federal Reserve System is independent. The president can attempt to influence the board, and Congress can threaten to merge the Fed into the Treasury Department, but as long as the Fed retains its independence, its chairperson and governors can do what they please. Hence, any talk about "the president's monetary policy" or "Congress's monetary policy" is inaccurate. The Fed remains a relatively independent entity.

Loose and Tight Monetary Policies. The Federal Reserve System seeks to stabilize nationwide economic activity by controlling the amount of money in circulation. Changing the amount of money in circulation is a major aspect of monetary policy. You may have read a news report in which a business executive complained that money is "too tight." You may have run across a story about an economist who has warned that money is "too loose." In these instances, the terms *tight* and *loose* refer to the monetary policy of the Fed.

Credit, like any good or service, has a cost. The cost of borrowing—the interest rate—is similar to the cost of any other aspect of doing business. When the cost of borrowing falls, businesspersons can undertake more investment projects. When it rises, businesspersons undertake fewer projects. Consumers also react to interest rates when deciding whether to borrow funds to buy houses, cars, or other "big-ticket" items.

If the Fed implements a *loose monetary policy* (often called an "expansionary" policy), the supply of credit increases and its cost falls. If the Fed implements a *tight monetary policy* (often called a "contractionary" policy), the supply of credit falls (or fails to grow) and its cost increases. A loose money policy is often implemented as an attempt to encourage economic growth. You may be wondering why any nation would want a tight monetary policy. The answer is to control inflation. If money becomes too plentiful too quickly, prices on average increase, and the purchasing power of the dollar decreases.

Time Lags for Monetary Policy. You learned earlier that policymakers who implement fiscal policy—the manipulation of budget deficits and the tax system—experience problems with time lags. Similar problems face the Fed when it implements monetary policy.

Sometimes, accurate information about the economy is not available for months. Once the state of the economy is known, time may elapse before any policy can be put into effect. Still, the time lag in implementing monetary policy is usually much shorter than the lag in implementing fiscal policy. The Federal Open Market Committee meets eight times a year and can put a policy into effect relatively quickly. A change in the money supply may not have an effect for several months, however.

Federal Open Market Committee
The most important body within the Federal Reserve System. The Federal Open Market Committee decides how monetary policy should be carried out.

Benjamin S. Bernanke
was the chair of the Board of Governors of the Federal Reserve System through January 2014. Some commentators contend that the chair of the Fed is the most powerful person on earth, at least in terms of economics. Since the start of the Great Recession, the "Fed" has engaged in activities aimed at fighting recession that it has never engaged in before. (KEVIN DIETSCH/UPI/Newscom)

Monetary Policy during Recessions. A tight monetary policy is effective as a way of taming inflation. (Some would argue that it is the *only* way that inflation can be stopped.) If interest rates go high enough, people *will* stop borrowing. How effective, though, is a loose monetary policy at ending a recession? Under normal conditions, it is very effective. A loose monetary policy will spur an expansion in economic activity.

To combat the Great Recession, however, the Fed reduced its interest rate effectively to zero. It could not go any lower. Yet when consumers had credit, they were still reluctant to make major purchases. Many businesses found that they had little need to borrow to invest in new activities—and no need to hire new staff. Overall demand for goods and services was so low that companies could produce all they needed with their existing capacity and workforce. Monetary policy had run out of steam—using it was like "pushing on a string." The government has little power to force banks to lend, and it certainly has no power to make people borrow and spend. As a result, the Obama administration placed its bets on fiscal policy.

During 2008 and 2009, the Fed developed a new way to respond to the failure of banks to lend. Relying on its ability to create money, it began to make loans itself, without turning to Congress for appropriations. The Fed bought debt issued by corporations. It bought securities that were based on student loans and credit-card debt. By 2009, the Fed had loaned out close to $2 trillion in fresh credit. In 2010 and 2011, the Fed implemented yet another innovative policy, called *quantitative easing,* in an attempt to make monetary policy more effective. Quantitative easing essentially means buying quantities of long-term treasuries and mortgage-backed securities. In December 2012, the Fed announced that it would continue to hold interest rates down until the unemployment rate falls to 6.5 percent.

THE POLITICS OF TAXATION

Congress enacts tax laws at the federal level. The Internal Revenue Code, which is the federal tax code, encompasses thousands of pages, thousands of sections, and thousands of subsections—our tax system is not very simple.

LO5: Describe the various taxes that Americans pay, and discuss some of the controversies surrounding taxation.

Americans pay a variety of taxes. At the federal level, the income tax is levied on most sources of income. Social Security and Medicare taxes are assessed on wages and salaries. There is an income tax for corporations, which has an indirect effect on many individuals. The estate tax is collected from property left behind by those who have died. State and local governments also assess taxes on income, sales, and land. Altogether, the value of all taxes collected by the federal government and by state and local governments is about 27 percent of the gross domestic product. This is a substantial sum, but it is less than what many other countries collect.

Federal Income Tax Rates

Individuals and businesses pay income taxes based on tax rates. Not all of your income is taxed at the same rate. The first few dollars of income that you earn are not taxed at all. The highest rate is imposed on the "last" dollar of income that you make. This highest rate is the *marginal* tax rate. Table 13–2 on the next page shows the 2013 marginal tax rates for individuals and married couples. The higher the tax rate—the action on the part of the government—the greater the public's reaction to that tax rate. If the highest tax rate you pay on the income you make is 15 percent, then any method you can use to reduce your taxable income by one dollar saves you fifteen cents in tax liabilities that you owe the federal government. Individuals paying a 15 percent rate have a relatively small incentive to avoid paying taxes, but consider individuals who were faced with a tax rate of 94 percent in the 1940s during World War II. They had a tremendous incentive to find legal ways to reduce their taxable incomes. For every dollar of income that was somehow deemed non-taxable, these taxpayers would reduce tax liabilities by ninety-four cents.

Loopholes and Lowered Taxes

Individuals and corporations facing high tax rates will adjust their earning and spending behavior to reduce their taxes. They will also make concerted attempts to get Congress to add **loopholes** to the tax law that allow them to reduce their taxable incomes. When Congress imposed very high tax rates on high incomes, it also provided for more loopholes than it does today. For example, special provisions enabled investors in oil and gas wells to reduce their taxable incomes.

Progressive and Regressive Taxation. As Table 13–2 below shows, the greater your taxable income, the higher the marginal tax rate. Persons with large incomes pay a larger share of their income in income tax. A tax system in which rates go up with income is called a **progressive tax** system. The federal income tax is clearly progressive.

The income tax is not the only tax you must pay. For example, the federal Social Security tax is levied on all wage and salary income at a flat rate of 6.2 percent. (Employers pay another 6.2 percent, making the total effective rate 12.4 percent.) In 2013, however, there was no Social Security tax on wages and salaries in excess of $113,700. (This "cap" changes from year to year.) Persons with very high salaries, therefore, pay no Social Security tax on much of their wages.

In addition, the tax is currently not levied on investment income (including capital gains, rents, royalties, interest, dividends, or profits from a business). The wealthy receive a much greater share of their income from these sources than others do. As a result, the wealthy pay a much smaller portion of their income in Social Security taxes than do the working poor. The Social Security tax is therefore a **regressive tax.** To fund Medicare, a combined employer/employee 2.9 percent tax is also assessed on all wage income, with no upper limit.

During 2011 and 2012, Congress and the Obama administration agreed on a 2 percentage-point reduction in the Social Security payroll tax. The break, instituted as an economic stimulus measure, ended after the fiscal cliff negotiations in December 2012.

What Kind of Tax System Do We Have? The various taxes Americans pay pull in different directions. The Medicare tax, as applied to wages and salaries, is entirely flat—that is, neither progressive nor regressive. Because it is not levied on investment income, however, it is regressive overall. The federal estate tax is extremely progressive, because it is not imposed at all on

Loophole
A legal method by which individuals and businesses are allowed to reduce the tax liabilities they owe to the government.

Progressive Tax
A tax that rises in percentage terms as incomes rise.

Regressive Tax
A tax that falls in percentage terms as incomes rise.

TABLE 13–2: Marginal Tax Rates for Single Persons and Married Couples (2013)

Single Persons		Married Filing Jointly	
Marginal Tax Bracket	**Marginal Tax Rate**	**Marginal Tax Bracket**	**Marginal Tax Rate**
$0–$8,925	10%	$0–$17,850	10%
$8,926–$36,250	15%	$17,851–$72,500	15%
$36,251–$87,850	25%	$72,501–$146,400	25%
$87,851–$183,250	28%	$146,401–$223,050	28%
$183,251–$398,350	33%	$223,051–$398,350	33%
$398,351–$400,000	35%	$398,351–$450,000	35%
$400,001 and higher	39.6%	$450,001 and higher	39.6%

at issue

SHOULD THE RICH PAY EVEN MORE IN TAXES?

The rich have gotten richer during the last few decades—of that we are certain. In 1980, the top 1 percent of income earners made 9.3 percent of the nation's total income. Thirty years later, the top 1 percent of income earners made more than 20 percent of the nation's income.

WHY SHOULDN'T THE RICH PAY MORE TAXES?

Not only have the rich increased their share of the nation's income, they also have become wealthier. We are increasingly becoming a society divided by class. In the past ten years, the hourly pay of average workers, corrected for inflation, has not risen at all. During the same decade, the number of millionaires and billionaires skyrocketed.

In this context, it seems appropriate to raise taxes on the rich. After all, they are now paying much lower marginal tax rates than during much of the postwar history of the United States. There have been periods when marginal federal income tax rates on the very rich exceeded 90 percent. Today, the rate is 39.6 percent. In addition, the tax on capital gains, which make up a much larger share of the income of the rich than of other people, is only 15 percent (23.8 percent in the top tax bracket). Finally, state and local taxes favor the top 1 percent. They pay 8.4 percent of their income to state and local governments, as opposed to 12.4 percent of income paid by those in the bottom 20 percent.

Those who have benefited the most from America's economic system should pay more, particularly when the federal budget deficit is a major concern. Certainly, President Obama believes that the rich ought to do more. Of the tax increases in his 2013 proposed budget (which has no chance of being adopted), 86 percent would be borne by people making more than $200,000 per year. The rich argue that they are the "engines of economic growth" and should be encouraged to continue their hard work. Higher taxes, however, are not going to keep the wealthy from striving.

DON'T KILL THE GEESE THAT LAY THE GOLDEN EGGS

It is true that the top 1 percent of income earners now receive more of the national income than they did thirty years ago. Yet in those thirty years, the share of total income taxes paid by the top 1 percent of income earners increased from 18.3 percent to 38 percent. The top 1 percent of income-earning U.S. residents pay more than one-third of all federal income taxes in the United States.

The top-earning 5 percent of taxpayers pay more than the bottom 95 percent—58.7 percent of federal income taxes. The top 50 percent of earners account for 97.3 percent of all income tax paid. The number of those who pay nothing to support the federal government through the income tax continues to rise (although this lower-income group does pay Social Security and Medicare taxes).

An increasingly large number of Americans actually receive more through the federal income tax than they pay. As part of the Earned Income Tax Program, 25 million families and individuals with incomes of up to $48,000 receive payments that substantially reduce their Social Security and Medicare taxes.

If we use taxes to "soak the rich," we will tax the most productive individuals in the country. High marginal tax rates discourage effort. The higher the rate, the greater the discouragement, and this will reduce the rate of economic growth. More income will be redistributed, but is that the ultimate goal of our society? Indeed, Republicans in Congress believe that tax rates on top earners should go down, not up.

FOR CRITICAL ANALYSIS

Is it possible that higher taxes—and a lower after-tax income—could actually make some people work more?

smaller estates. Sales taxes are regressive, because the wealthy spend a relatively smaller portion of their income on items subject to the sales tax. Add everything up, and the tax system as a whole is slightly progressive. Should the system be more progressive, as President Obama has advocated? We discuss that issue in this chapter's *At Issue* feature above.

making a **difference**

LEARNING ABOUT ENTITLEMENT REFORM

Collectively, programs such as Medicare, Medicaid, Social Security, unemployment compensation, and several others are known as *entitlement programs*. They are called entitlements because if you meet certain qualifications—of age or income, for example—you are entitled to specified benefits. The federal government can estimate how much it will have to pay out in entitlements but cannot set an exact figure in advance. In this way, entitlement spending differs from other government spending. When Congress decides what it will give to the national park system, for example, it allocates an exact sum, and the park system cannot exceed that budget. Along with national defense, entitlements make up by far the greatest share of the federal budget. This fact led a Bush administration staff member to joke, "It helps to think of the government as an insurance company with an army."

Why Should You Care?

What happens to entitlements will affect your life in two major ways. Entitlement spending will largely determine how much you pay in taxes throughout your working lifetime. Entitlement policy will also determine how much support you receive from the federal government when you grow old. Because entitlements make up such a large share of the federal budget, it is not possible to address the issue of budget deficits without considering entitlement spending. Further, under current policies, spending on Medicare will rise in future years, placing ever-greater pressure on the federal budget. Sooner or later, entitlement reform will be impossible to avoid. However these programs are changed, you will feel the effects in your pocketbook throughout your life.

What Can You Do?

Should Medicare and Social Security benefits be high, with the understanding that taxes must therefore go up? Should these programs be cut back in the hope of avoiding deficits and tax increases? Do entitlements mean that the old are fleecing the young—or is that argument irrelevant because we will all grow old someday? Progressives and conservatives disagree strongly about these questions. You can develop your own opinions by learning more about entitlement reform. The following organizations take a conservative position on entitlements:

- National Center for Policy Analysis. Find its Web page on entitlement reform by entering "ncpa retirement" into your favorite Internet search engine.
- The Heritage Foundation. See what it has to say by searching on "heritage entitlements."

The following organizations take a liberal stand on entitlements:

- National Committee to Preserve Social Security and Medicare. You can locate the home page of this organization by typing in "ncpssm."
- AARP (formerly the American Association of Retired Persons). To learn this group's position on entitlements, enter "aarp work social."

key**terms**

budget deficit 309	fracking 306	loophole 315	progressive tax 315
domestic policy 297	gross domestic product (GDP) 298	Medicaid 299	public debt, or national debt 310
Federal Open Market Committee 313	individual mandate 301	Medicare 299	recession 308
Federal Reserve System (the Fed) 312	inflation 308	monetary policy 312	regressive tax 315
fiscal policy 309	Keynesian economics 309	Patient Protection and Affordable Care Act 298	treasuries 310
			unemployment 308

chaptersummary

1 Domestic policy consists of laws, government planning, and government actions that concern internal issues of national importance. Policies are created in response to public problems or public demand for government action.

2 The policymaking process is initiated when policymakers become aware—through the media or from their constituents—of a problem that needs to be addressed by the legislature and the president. The process of policymaking includes five steps: agenda building, policy formulation, policy adoption, policy implementation, and policy evaluation. Policy actions typically result in both costs and benefits for society.

3 Health-care spending accounts for almost 18 percent of the U.S. economy and is growing. Reasons for this growth include the increasing number of elderly persons and advancing technology. A major source of funding is Medicare, the federal program that pays health-care expenses of U.S. residents over the age of sixty-five. The federal government has tried to restrain the growth in Medicare spending.

4 More than 15 percent of the population does not have health insurance—a major political issue. Individual health-insurance policies (not obtained through an employer) are expensive and may be unobtainable at any price. In most wealthy countries, this problem is addressed by a universal health-insurance system under which the government provides basic coverage to all citizens. In 2010, Congress passed a health-care reform package that in time will provide near-universal coverage in the United States. It will require residents not already covered to purchase coverage, which will be subsidized for low-income persons.

5 Today, more than 1 million immigrants enter the United States each year, and foreign-born persons make up about 13 percent of the U.S. population. The status of illegal immigrants, who may number 11 million, is a major political issue. Some people wish to give such persons a legally recognized status and allow them someday to become citizens. Others call for tougher laws against illegal immigration and against hiring undocumented workers.

6 Issues concerning energy and the environment are on the nation's agenda today. One problem is our reliance on petroleum imports, given that many petroleum exporters are hostile to American interests. In recent years, however, production techniques such as fracking have increased the domestic supply of crude oil and especially of natural gas. Global warming, caused by the emission of CO_2 and other greenhouse gases, is a second major problem, although some dispute how serious it actually is.

7 Fiscal policy is the use of taxes and spending to affect the overall economy. Time lags in implementing fiscal policy can create serious difficulties. The federal government has run a deficit in most years since 1960. The deficit is met by U.S. Treasury borrowing. This adds to the public debt of the U.S. government. Although the budget was temporarily in surplus from 1998 to 2002, large deficits now seem likely for many years to come.

8 Monetary policy is controlled by the Federal Reserve System, or the Fed. Monetary policy consists of changing the rate of growth of the money supply in an attempt to either stimulate or cool the economy. A loose monetary policy, in which more money is created, encourages economic growth. A tight monetary policy, in which less money is created, may be the only effective way of ending an inflationary spiral.

9 U.S. taxes amount to about 27 percent of the gross domestic product. Individuals and corporations that pay taxes at the highest rates will try to pressure Congress into creating exemptions and tax loopholes. Loopholes allow high-income earners to reduce their taxable incomes.

test**yourself**

LO1 *Describe the five steps of the policymaking process, using the health-care reform legislation as an example.*

The policymaking process includes, but is not limited to:

    a. agenda building, policy formulation, and judicial approval.

    b. agenda building, policy formulation, and policy adoption.

    c. agenda building, policy formulation, and state referendums.

LO2 *Explain why illegal immigration is seen as a problem, and cite some of the steps that have been taken in response to it.*

Within U.S. borders, there are many illegal immigrants, numbering as many as:

    a. 3 million.

    b. 23 million.

    c. 11 million.

LO3 *Evaluate how the nation has reacted to high oil prices and the controversy over global warming.*

A major new source of increased energy supplies within the United States comes from:

    a. running existing wells at a faster pace.

    b. fracking (hydraulic fracturing).

    c. the new oil boom in Illinois.

LO4 *Define* unemployment, inflation, fiscal policy, net public debt, *and* monetary policy.

Fiscal policy involves:

    a. government spending and changes in the money supply in circulation.

    b. government taxation and the changes in the money supply in circulation.

    c. government taxing and spending policies.

LO5 *Describe the various taxes that Americans pay, and discuss some of the controversies surrounding taxation.*

The federal personal income tax system can be called:

    a. a progressive tax.

    b. a regressive tax.

    c. a degressive tax.

Essay Question:

Just how serious an offense should illegal immigration be? Construct arguments in favor of considering it a felony and arguments for viewing it as a mere civil infraction.

Answers to multiple-choice questions: 1. b, 2. c, 3. b, 4. c, 5. a.

Access CourseMate at **www.cengagebrain.com** for additional study tools: practice quizzes, key term flashcards and crossword puzzles, audio chapter summaries, simulations, animated learning modules, interactive timelines, videos, and American Government NewsWatch.

14

U.S. secretary of State John Kerry addresses a Friends of Syria meeting in the Arab nation of Qatar in 2013 after President Obama announced that the United States would supply Syrian rebels with U.S. arms. What problems could we face as a result of that decision? (Jacquelyn Martin/AFP/Getty Images)

Foreign Policy

LEARNING OUTCOMES

The five **Learning Outcomes (LOs)** below are designed to help improve your understanding of this chapter. After reading this chapter, you should be able to:

■ **LO1** Define *foreign policy*, and discuss moral idealism versus political realism in foreign policy.

■ **LO2** Describe recent foreign policy challenges that involve the use of force, including terrorism and the wars in Afghanistan and Iraq.

■ **LO3** Discuss the use of diplomacy in addressing such issues as nuclear proliferation, the rise of China, the confrontation between Israel and the Palestinians, and the economic crisis in Europe.

■ **LO4** Explain the roles of the president, executive agencies, and Congress in making U.S. foreign policy.

■ **LO5** Cite the main themes in the history of U.S. foreign policy.

Check your understanding of the material with the Test Yourself section at the end of the chapter.

On September 11, 2001, Americans were forced to change their view of national security and of their relations with the rest of the world—literally overnight. No longer could citizens of the United States believe that national security issues involved only threats overseas or that the American homeland could not be attacked.

Within a few days, it became known that the 9/11 attacks on the World Trade Center and on the Pentagon had been planned and carried out by a terrorist network named al Qaeda, which was directed by the radical Islamist leader Osama bin Laden. The network was closely linked to the Taliban government of Afghanistan, which had ruled that nation since 1996.

Americans were shocked by the success of the attacks. They wondered how our airport security systems could have failed so drastically. Shouldn't our intelligence community have known about, and defended against, this terrorist network? How could our foreign policy have been so blind to the anger of Islamist groups throughout the world?

In this chapter, we examine the tools of foreign policy and national security policy in the light of the many challenges facing the United States. One such challenge for U.S. foreign policymakers today is how best to respond to the threat of terrorism. We also review the history of American foreign policy.

FACING THE WORLD: FOREIGN AND DEFENSE POLICY

The United States is only one nation in a world with almost two hundred independent countries, many located in regions where armed conflict is ongoing. What tools does our nation have to deal with the many challenges to its peace and prosperity? One tool is **foreign policy.** By this term, we mean both the goals the government wants to achieve in the world and the techniques and strategies used to achieve them. These techniques and strategies include **diplomacy, economic aid, technical assistance,** and military intervention. Sometimes, foreign policies are restricted to statements of goals or ideas, such as the goal of helping to end world poverty, whereas at other times foreign policies involve comprehensive efforts to achieve particular objectives, such as preventing Iran from obtaining nuclear weapons.

As you will read later in this chapter, in the United States the **foreign policy process** usually originates with the president and those agencies that provide advice on foreign policy matters. Congressional action and national public debate often affect foreign policy formulation as well.

National Security and Defense Policies

As one aspect of overall foreign policy, **national security policy** is designed primarily to protect the independence and the political integrity of the United States. It concerns itself with the defense of the United States against actual or potential future enemies.

U.S. national security policy is based on determinations made by the Department of Defense, the Department of State, and a number of other federal agencies, including the National Security Council (NSC). The NSC acts as an advisory body to the president, and it has often been a rival to the State Department in influencing the foreign policy process.

Defense policy is a subset of national security policy. Generally, defense policy refers to the set of policies that direct the nature and activities of the U.S. armed forces. Defense policies are proposed by the leaders of the nation's military forces and the secretary of Defense, and are greatly influenced by congressional decision makers.

Diplomacy

Diplomacy is a major aspect of foreign policy. Diplomacy includes all of a nation's external relationships, from routine diplomatic communications to summit meetings among heads of state. More specifically, diplomacy refers to the settling of disputes and conflicts among nations by peaceful methods. Diplomacy is also the set of negotiating techniques by which a nation attempts to carry out its foreign policy. Of course, diplomacy can be successful only if the parties involved are willing to negotiate.

LO1: Define *foreign policy*, and discuss moral idealism versus political realism in foreign policy.

Foreign Policy
A nation's external goals and the techniques and strategies used to achieve them.

Diplomacy
The process by which states carry on political relations with each other; the process of settling conflicts among nations by peaceful means.

Economic Aid
Assistance to other nations in the form of grants, loans, or credits to buy the assisting nation's products.

Technical Assistance
The practice of sending experts in such areas as agriculture, engineering, and business to aid other nations.

Foreign Policy Process
The steps by which foreign policy goals are decided and acted on.

National Security Policy
Foreign and domestic policy designed to protect the nation's independence and political and economic integrity; policy that is concerned with the safety and defense of the nation.

Defense Policy
A subset of national security policy concerning the U.S. armed forces.

Idealism versus Realism in Foreign Policy

Moral Idealism
A philosophy that views nations as normally willing to cooperate and to agree on moral standards for conduct.

Political Realism
A philosophy that views each nation as acting principally in its own interest.

Since the earliest years of the republic, Americans have felt that their nation has a special destiny. The American experiment in political and economic liberty, it was thought, would provide the best possible life for its citizens and be a model for other nations. As the United States assumed greater status as a power in world politics, Americans came to believe that the nation's actions on the world stage should be guided by American political and moral principles.

Moral Idealism. This view of America's mission has led to the adoption of many foreign policy initiatives that are rooted in **moral idealism.** This philosophy views the world as fundamentally benign and assumes that most nations can be persuaded to take moral considerations into account when setting their policies.[1] In this perspective, nations should come together and agree to keep the peace, as President Woodrow Wilson (1913–1921) proposed for the League of Nations. Many foreign policy initiatives taken by the United States have been based on this idealistic view of the world.

One type of initiative is the distribution of economic aid, sometimes for the purpose of alleviating famine and at other times with the goal of promoting economic development. Humanitarian aid following natural disasters is another example. The United States provided substantial aid to the impoverished nation of Haiti following a disastrous 2010 earthquake. In 2011, an earthquake and tsunami devastated northeast Japan. While Japan is a developed nation and did not need economic help, the United States was still able to supply various kinds of specialized technical and medical assistance.

Political Realism. In opposition to the moral perspective is **political realism.** Realists see the world as a dangerous place in which each nation strives for its own survival and interests, regardless of moral considerations. The United States must therefore base its foreign policy decisions on cold calculations, without regard to morality. Realists believe that the United States must be prepared to defend itself militarily, because other nations are, by definition, dangerous. A strong defense will show the world that the United States is willing to protect its interests. The practice of political realism in foreign policy allows the United States to sell weapons to military dictators who will support its policies, to support American business around the globe, and to repel terrorism through the use of force.

American Foreign Policy—A Mixture of Both. It is important to note that the United States never has been guided by only one of these principles. Instead, both moral idealism and political realism affect foreign policymaking. At times, idealism and realism can pull in different directions, making it difficult to establish a coherent policy. The so-called Arab Spring serves as an example of such cross-currents in American foreign policy.

Acting on the basis of political realism, the United States built up long-standing relationships with various dictators in the Arab world. Examples included Hosni Mubarak of Egypt. Close relations with Mubarak helped guarantee the peace between Egypt and Israel. Given such alliances, the United States had to determine whether to support existing governments when they came under attack by popular rebellions.

President Obama and former Secretary of State Hillary Clinton had a different view of the situation, however. They did not believe that realism and idealism were necessarily in conflict—the United States could support democratic movements and remain true to its values. Such a course of action was realistic as well as idealistic, because in Egypt and Tunisia,

---

1. James M. McCormick, *American Foreign Policy and Process,* 6th ed. (Independence, Ky.: Cengage Learning, 2013).

initially at least, the rebels were winning. Championing popular movements increased the chances that we would be on good terms with the new governments in these countries.

Libya proved to be a special challenge, however. In that country, the rebels were immediately successful in taking power only in the eastern region. The United States and its European allies eventually intervened with air power to assist the rebels. By doing so, these nations were able to demonstrate that their support for Arab popular movements was serious and not just rhetorical.

Problems with Intervention. Most Libyans had a highly positive view of U.S. intervention, but that country also contains a number of radical Islamists. Some of these radicals launched a terrorist attack on the U.S. consulate in Benghazi, Libya, in 2012, killing four Americans. The incident touched off an ongoing political dispute, with Republicans claiming that the Obama administration had mishandled the affair.

The United States government has not always been willing to intervene abroad. In Syria, a rebellion against the dictatorship of Bashar al-Assad began in 2011, resulting in a civil war that by late-2013 had caused the deaths of more than 100,000 people. Not until August 2013 did the United States consider taking action in Syria.

Terrorism
A systematic attempt to inspire fear to gain political ends, typically involving the indiscriminate use of violence against noncombatants.

TERRORISM AND WARFARE

The foreign policy of the United States—whether idealist, realist, or both—must be formulated to deal with world conditions. Early in its history, the United States was a weak, new nation facing older nations well equipped for war. In the twenty-first century, the United States confronts different challenges. Now it must devise foreign and defense policies that will enhance its security in a world in which it is the global superpower. In some instances, these policies have involved the use of force.

LO2: Describe recent foreign policy challenges that involve the use of force, including terrorism and the wars in Afghanistan and Iraq.

The Emergence of Terrorism

Terrorism is a systematic attempt to inspire fear to gain political ends. Typically, terrorism involves the indiscriminate use of violence against noncombatants. In years past, terrorism was a strategy generally employed by radicals who wanted to change the status of a particular nation or province. For example, over many years the Irish Republican Army undertook terrorist attacks in the British province of Northern Ireland with the aim of driving out the British and uniting the province with the Republic of Ireland. In Spain, the ETA

A Syrian rebel loads his machine gun in 2013 during a battle with regime forces in the city of Aleppo. Why should the United States be concerned about the fighting in Syria? (Guillaume Briquet/AFP/Getty Images)

The late Osama bin Laden, leader of al Qaeda. On May 1, 2011, U.S. Navy SEALs raided bin Laden's hiding place in Abbottabad, Pakistan, and killed him. Why had it been so hard for the United States to track bin Laden down? (AP Photo)

organization has employed terrorism with the goal of creating an independent Basque state in Spain's Basque region. In the twenty-first century, however, the United States has confronted a new form of terrorism that is not associated with such clear-cut aims.

September 11. In 2001, terrorism came home to the United States in ways that few Americans could have imagined. In a well-coordinated attack, nineteen terrorists hijacked four airplanes and crashed three of them into buildings—two into the World Trade Center towers in New York City and one into the Pentagon in Washington, D.C. The fourth airplane crashed in a field in Pennsylvania, after the passengers fought the hijackers.

Why did the al Qaeda network plan and launch attacks on the United States? One reason was that the leaders of the network, including Osama bin Laden, were angered by the presence of U.S. troops on the soil of Saudi Arabia, which they regarded as sacred. They also saw the United States as the primary defender of Israel against the Palestinians. The attacks were intended to frighten and demoralize America so that it would withdraw its troops from the Middle East.

Al Qaeda's Aims. Al Qaeda's ultimate goals, however, were not limited to forcing the United States to withdraw from the Middle East. Al Qaeda envisioned worldwide revolutionary change, with all nations brought under the theocratic rule of an Islamist empire. Governments have successfully negotiated with terrorists who profess limited aims—today, radicals associated with the Irish Republican Army are part of a coalition government in Northern Ireland. There is no way to negotiate with an organization such as al Qaeda.

Domestic Terrorism in the United States. Al Qaeda, which by now has been weakened by American attacks, is not the only group ever to launch a terrorist attack on U.S. soil. Radicals opposed to the U.S. war in Vietnam set off bombs in the 1960s and 1970s. Right-wing terrorists were an issue in the 1990s—notably, a bomb set at a federal office building in Oklahoma City killed 168 people.

In more recent years, however, attacks by domestic Islamists have been the major concern. Such individuals are typically "self-radicalized" through the Internet and are not controlled by a foreign organization. As one example, in 2009 a Muslim U.S. Army psychiatrist fatally shot thirteen people at Fort Hood in Texas. The most recent outrage was the bombing at the Boston Marathon in 2013, which killed three people and cost fourteen victims at least one of their legs. The alleged perpetrators were two self-radicalized Muslim brothers, one of them a U.S. citizen.

The War on Terrorism

After 9/11, President George W. Bush implemented stronger security measures to help ensure homeland security and protect U.S. facilities and personnel abroad. The president sought and received congressional support for heightened airport security, new laws allowing greater domestic surveillance of potential terrorists, and increased funding for the military.

A New Kind of War. In September 2002, President Bush enunciated what became known as the "Bush Doctrine," or the doctrine of preemption. The concept of "preemptive war" as a defense strategy was a new element in U.S. foreign policy. The concept is based on the assumption that in the war on terrorism, self-defense must be *anticipatory*. President Bush stated in March 2003, just before launching the invasion of Iraq, "Responding to such enemies only after they have struck first is not self-defense, it is suicide."

Opposition to the Bush Doctrine. The Bush Doctrine had many critics. Some pointed out that preemptive wars against other nations have traditionally been waged by dictators and rogue states, not democratic nations. By employing such a strategy, the United States would seem to be contradicting its basic values. Others claimed that launching preemptive wars would make it difficult for the United States to pursue world peace in the future. By endorsing such a policy itself, the United States could hardly argue against the decisions of other nations to do likewise when they felt potentially threatened.

Wars in Iraq

In 1990, the Persian Gulf became the setting for a major challenge to the international system set up after World War II (1939–1945). President Saddam Hussein of Iraq sent troops into the neighboring oil sheikdom of Kuwait, occupying that country. This was the most clear-cut case of aggression against an independent nation in half a century. In January 1991, U.S.-led coalition forces launched a massive attack on Iraq. Iraqi troops retreated from Kuwait, and the First Gulf War ended.

As part of the cease-fire that ended the First Gulf War, Iraq agreed to allow UN weapons inspectors to oversee the destruction of its missiles and all chemical and nuclear weapons. In 1999, though, Iraq placed so many obstacles in the path of the UN inspectors that they withdrew from the country.

The Second Gulf War—The Iraq War. In 2002 and early 2003, President Bush began assembling an international coalition that might support further military action in Iraq. Bush was unable to convince the UN Security Council that military force was necessary in Iraq, so the United States took the initiative. In March 2003, U.S. and British forces invaded Iraq and within a month had toppled Hussein's dictatorship. The process of establishing order in Iraq turned out to be very difficult, however.

Occupied Iraq. The people of Iraq are divided into three principal ethnic groups. The Kurdish-speaking people of the north were overjoyed by the invasion. The Arabs adhering to the Shiite branch of Islam live principally in the south and constitute a majority of the population. They were deeply skeptical of U.S. intentions. The Arabs belonging to the Sunni branch of Islam live mainly to the west of Baghdad. Many Sunnis considered the occupation to be a disaster.

Social Media in Politics
The armed forces all have their own Facebook pages. For example, search on "us army." Although official, the page contains a vast array of posts and information.

The Insurgency. In short order, a Sunni guerrilla insurgency arose and launched attacks against the coalition forces. Iraq had begun to be a serious political problem for President Bush. A newly organized al Qaeda in Iraq sponsored suicide bombings and other attacks against coalition troops and the forces of the new Iraqi government. Al Qaeda also issued vitriolic denunciations of the Iraqi Shiites. Rhetoric was followed by violence. While Sunni and Shiite insurgents continued to launch attacks on coalition forces, the major bloodletting in the country now took place between Sunnis and Shiites. By late 2006, polls indicated that about two-thirds of Americans wanted to see an end to the Iraq War—a sentiment expressed in the 2006 elections.

A U.S. Army soldier embraces a member of the Afghan National Army (ANA) at the end of a training program in May 2013. The participating Afghan soldiers received certificates in disabling explosives, a highly sophisticated activity. U.S.-led coalition forces are winding down their operations before withdrawing the bulk of their troops at the end of 2014, and they are racing to prepare Afghan forces to take over. (Dibyangshu Sarkar/AFP/Getty Images)

Iraqi Endgame. In January 2007, President Bush announced a major increase, or "surge," in U.S. troop strength. Skeptics doubted that the new troop levels would have much effect on the outcome. In April 2007, however, Sunni tribal leaders rose up against al Qaeda and called in U.S. troops to help them. Al Qaeda, it seems, had badly overplayed its hand by terrorizing the Sunni population.

During subsequent months, the Iraqi government gained substantial control over its own territory. Still, American attitudes toward the war remained negative. In 2008, President Bush and Iraqi prime minister Nouri al-Maliki negotiated a deadline for withdrawing U.S. troops. In fact, U.S. combat forces left Iraq in August 2010. The rest of the American troops were out by the end of 2011.

Afghanistan

The Iraq War was not the only military effort launched by the Bush administration as part of the war on terrorism. The first military effort was directed against al Qaeda camps in Afghanistan and the Taliban regime, which had ruled most of Afghanistan since 1996. In late 2001, after building a coalition of international allies and anti-Taliban rebels within Afghanistan, the United States began an air campaign against the Taliban regime. The anti-Taliban rebels, known as the Northern Alliance, were able to take Kabul, the capital, and oust the Taliban from power.

The Return of the Taliban. The Taliban were defeated, but not destroyed. U.S. forces were unable to locate Osama bin Laden and other top al Qaeda leaders. The Taliban and al Qaeda both retreated to the rugged mountains between Afghanistan and Pakistan, where they were able to establish bases on the Pakistani side of the border. In 2003, the Taliban began to launch attacks against Afghan soldiers, foreign aid workers, and American troops. Through 2008 and 2009, the Taliban were able to take over a number of Pakistani districts, even as the United States began attacking suspected Taliban and al Qaeda targets in Pakistan using small unmanned aircraft.

Obama and Afghanistan. In February 2009, President Obama dispatched seventeen thousand additional soldiers to Afghanistan. In December 2009, Obama announced that he would send an additional thirty thousand troops to Afghanistan but would begin troop withdrawals in July 2011.

The Death of bin Laden. The CIA and other U.S. intelligence forces were unable to develop information on Osama bin Laden's whereabouts until 2010. In that year and in 2011, the intelligence agencies obtained evidence that bin Laden might be living in a highly secure residential compound in Abbottabad, Pakistan. Pakistan's military academy is located in Abbottabad, which led many observers to surmise that bin Laden was living under the protection of members of Pakistan's military.

On May 1, 2011, U.S. Navy SEALs launched a helicopter raid on the compound. In a brief firefight, the SEALs killed bin Laden and four others. Americans responded to President Obama's announcement of the operation with relief and satisfaction. Reactions in Pakistan itself were mostly negative—the raid was generally seen as a violation of Pakistan's sovereignty.

Cold War
The ideological, political, and economic confrontation between the United States and the Soviet Union following World War II.

U.S. DIPLOMATIC EFFORTS

The United States has dealt with many international problems through diplomacy, rather than the use of armed force. Some of these issues include the proliferation of nuclear weapons, the growing power of China, the confrontation between Israel and the Palestinians, and the ongoing economic crisis in Europe.

Nuclear Weapons

In 1945, the United States was the only nation to possess nuclear weapons. Several nations quickly joined the "nuclear club," however, including the Soviet Union in 1949, Britain in 1952, France in 1960, and China in 1964. Few nations have made public their nuclear weapons programs since China's successful test of nuclear weapons in 1964. India and Pakistan were among the most recent nations to do so, detonating nuclear devices within a few weeks of each other in 1998. North Korea conducted an underground nuclear explosive test in October 2006. Several other nations are suspected of possessing nuclear weapons or the capability to produce them in a short time.

LO3: Discuss the use of diplomacy in addressing such issues as nuclear proliferation, the rise of China, the confrontation between Israel and the Palestinians, and the economic crisis in Europe.

With nuclear weapons, materials, and technology available worldwide, it is conceivable that terrorists could obtain a nuclear device and use it in a terrorist act. In fact, a U.S. federal indictment filed in 1998 charged Osama bin Laden and his associates with trying to buy nuclear bomb–making components "at various times" since 1992.

Nuclear Stockpiles. More than twenty-two thousand nuclear warheads are known to be stocked worldwide, though the exact number is uncertain. Although the United States and Russia have dismantled some of their nuclear weapons systems since the end of the **Cold War** and the dissolution of the Soviet Union in 1991 (discussed later in this chapter), both still retain sizable nuclear arsenals. More alarming is the fact that since the dissolution of the Soviet Union, the security of its nuclear arsenal has declined. There have been reported thefts, smugglings, and illicit sales of nuclear material from the former Soviet Union.

Nuclear Proliferation: Iran. For years, the United States, the European Union, and the UN have tried to prevent Iran from becoming a nuclear power. In spite of these efforts, many observers believe that Iran is now in the process of developing nuclear weapons—although Iran maintains that it is interested in developing nuclear power only for peaceful purposes. Continued diplomatic attempts to at least slow down Iran's quest for a nuclear bomb have so far proved ineffectual. Upon taking office, President Obama attempted to participate in talks with Iran that included Britain, China, France, Germany, and Russia. By this time, the

North Korean leader Kim Jong-un and former NBA star Dennis Rodman watch North Korean and U.S. players in an exhibition basketball game in North Korea. Rodman was heavily criticized in the United States for this appearance. Why might he have drawn such a reaction? (AP Photo/VICE Media, Jason Mojica)

UN Security Council had already voted three rounds of sanctions against Iran in reaction to its nuclear program.

By 2012, it was clear that sanctions against Iran were beginning to damage that country's economy. Of special importance was the U.S. campaign to persuade other nations to stop importing Iranian oil, which enjoyed increasing success. In 2012, it was disclosed that the United States had successfully destroyed many of Iran's nuclear enrichment centrifuges by deploying a specially designed computer virus. Threats that Israel or the United States might bomb Iran's nuclear sites added to the pressure. Is the use of armed force necessary to stop Iran from developing nuclear weapons? We discuss that topic in the *At Issue* feature on the facing page.

Nuclear Proliferation: North Korea. North Korea tested a nuclear device in 2006. An agreement reached in February 2007 provided that North Korea would start disabling its nuclear facilities and allow UN inspectors into the country. In July 2007, North Korea dismantled one of its nuclear reactors and admitted UN inspectors.

By 2009, however, North Korea was pulling back from its treaty obligations. In April, the country tested a long-range missile capable of delivering a nuclear warhead. After the UN Security Council issued a statement condemning the test, North Korea ordered UN inspectors out of the country, broke off negotiations, and conducted a second nuclear test. The United States and other parties have sought to persuade China to take the lead in bringing North Korea back to the negotiating table—China is the one nation that has significant economic leverage over North Korea.

Tensions increased in March 2013 after North Korea's government, under its new dictator, Kim Jong-un, issued a series of provocative statements and gestures. These included a threat to launch a preemptive nuclear strike against the United States, cutting off the telephone "hot line" with South Korea, and declaring a "state of war" with South Korea. Experts were uncertain as to the meaning of these provocations.

The New Power: China

Normal Trade Relations (NTR) Status A status granted through an international treaty by which each member nation must treat other members as well as it treats the country that receives its most favorable treatment. This status was formerly known as *most-favored-nation status.*

American policy has been to engage the Chinese in diplomatic and economic relationships in the hope of turning the nation in a more pro-Western direction. An important factor in U.S.-Chinese relations has been the large and growing trade ties between the two countries. In 1980, China was granted most-favored-nation status for tariffs and trade policy on a year-to-year basis. To prevent confusion, in 1998 the status was renamed **normal trade relations (NTR) status.** In 2000, Congress approved a permanent grant of NTR status to China.

at issue

SHOULD AMERICA—OR ISRAEL—ATTACK IRAN'S NUCLEAR SITES?

Since at least 2002, Western intelligence services have contended that Iran is attempting to develop nuclear weapons. Iran denies this claim. Its supreme leader, Ayatollah Ali Khamenei, has even issued a fatwa (an Islamic legal ruling) stating that the production and use of nuclear weapons are forbidden under Islam. The Iranian government claims that its uranium enrichment program is aimed only at developing nuclear power. Yet Iran appears to be enriching uranium well past the level needed to fuel a nuclear reactor—its enrichment program is close to producing weapons-grade material.

For several years, Israel has stated that it is prepared to bomb Iranian nuclear sites rather than let that nation obtain nuclear weapons. Some politicians in the United States have argued that we should support Israel in launching a preemptive strike at Iran's uranium enrichment facilities. Bear in mind that, more than any other nation, Israel may be at risk from a nuclear-equipped Iran. In 2005, Iranian president Mahmoud Ahmadinejad made a statement that was widely translated as "Israel should be wiped off the map." A more accurate translation was "The government of Israel should vanish from the pages of time," a sentiment only marginally less alarming.

THE TIME IS NOW— DESTROY IRAN'S ENRICHMENT SITES

The position of the hawks on this issue is clear: The longer we wait, the harder it will be to destroy Iran's numerous, well-protected, and widely dispersed uranium enrichment facilities. Israel is clearly ready to take the lead but needs U.S. support. The hawks do not

believe that Iran can retaliate by launching a Middle Eastern war. They point out that the United States has at least two aircraft carriers in the region that would go into action immediately if Iranian aircraft threatened Israel with conventional weapons. The fact is, the world cannot allow a nuclear-armed Iran because that country's leaders will attempt to annihilate Israel. Those leaders may also be willing to sell their technology to terrorists.

IRAN IS NOT FOOLISH ENOUGH TO USE A NUCLEAR BOMB

The doves on this issue contend that air strikes would only slow down Iran's nuclear development, not stop it altogether. Doves also do not believe that Iranian leaders would commit national suicide by using nuclear bombs against Israel. Historically, nations have become more risk averse once they have acquired nuclear weapons. If Israel, with the support of the United States, were to engage in air strikes against Iran, that nation would respond furiously. Oil shipping in the region would come to a halt. The people of Iran would rally around their leaders—and Iran would now have an even greater motivation to develop nuclear weapons. The majority of Israelis do not want their government to bomb Iran. Why should we?

FOR CRITICAL ANALYSIS

Under what conditions would it be appropriate to launch an air strike against Iran's nuclear facilities? What results might follow from such a strike?

While officially Communist, China today permits a striking degree of free enterprise. China has become substantially integrated into the world economic system, and it exports considerably more goods and services to the United States than it imports. As a result, its central bank has built up a huge reserve of U.S. federal government treasuries and other American obligations. Ultimately, the books must balance, but instead of importing U.S. goods and services, the Chinese have imported U.S. securities. The resulting economic imbalances are good for Chinese exporters, but create financial problems in both countries. The United States has repeatedly asked China to address these imbalances by allowing its currency to rise in value relative to the American dollar. Recently, Chinese authorities have allowed some movement.

WWW
Helpful Web Sites
The United Nations Web site contains a treasure trove of international statistics. To access this site, enter "un en" into an Internet search engine.

Chinese president Xi Jinping and his wife Peng Liyuan visit Mexico in June 2013. China's top leaders—invariably male—often avoid appearing in public with their wives. Peng Liyuan, however, is a People's Liberation Army folksinger who holds a civilian rank equivalent to major general. She was nationally famous years before her husband became China's leader. (Elizabeth Ruiz/AFP/Getty Images)

China's Explosive Economic Growth. The growth of the Chinese economy during the last thirty-five years is one of the most important developments in world history. For the past several decades, the Chinese economy has grown at a rate of about 10 percent annually, a long-term growth rate previously unknown in human history. Never have so many escaped poverty so quickly.

China now produces more steel than America and Japan combined. It generates more than 40 percent of the world's output of cement. Skyscrapers fill the skyline of every major Chinese city.

In 2007, for the first time, China manufactured more passenger automobiles than did the United States. China is building a limited-access highway system that, when complete, will be longer than the U.S. interstate highway system. Chinese demand for raw materials, notably petroleum, has led at times to dramatic increases in the price of oil and other commodities. By 2030, if not before, the economy of China is expected to be larger than that of the United States. China, in short, will become the world's second superpower.

The Issue of Taiwan. Inevitably, economic power translates into military potential. Is this a problem? It could be if China had territorial ambitions. At this time, China does not appear to have an appetite for non-Chinese territory. But China has always considered the island of Taiwan to be Chinese territory. In principle, Taiwan agrees. Taiwan calls itself the "Republic of China" and officially considers its government to be the legitimate ruler of the entire country—both Taiwan and mainland China. This diplomatic fiction has remained in effect since 1949, when the Chinese Communist Party won a civil war and drove the anti-Communist forces off the mainland.

China's position is that sooner or later, Taiwan must rejoin the rest of China. The position of the United States is that this reunification must not come about by force. Is peaceful reunification possible? China holds up Hong Kong as an example. Hong Kong came under Chinese sovereignty peacefully in 1997. The people of Taiwan, however, are far from considering Hong Kong to be an acceptable precedent.

Chinese Nationalism. Growing expressions of Chinese nationalism have raised concern in some of China's neighbors. China has recently engaged in disputes with Japan, the Philippines, Vietnam, and other Asian nations over the ownership of uninhabited islands in the East China and South China seas. In 2011, President Obama visited Australia and promised to establish a new U.S. force at Darwin, on Australia's north coast. This development was widely perceived as an attempt to reassure nations in the area that were concerned about potential Chinese pressure. In one arena—cyberspace—Chinese-American relations were already quite heated. In 2013, the United States accused the Chinese military of sponsoring cyberattacks on U.S. computer networks.

Israel and the Palestinians

As a longtime supporter of the state of Israel, the United States has undertaken to persuade the Israelis to negotiate with the Palestinian Arabs who live in the territories occupied by Israel. The conflict between Israel and the Palestinians, which began in 1948, has been extremely hard to resolve. The internationally recognized solution is for Israel to yield the West Bank and the Gaza Strip to the Palestinians in return for effective security commitments and abandonment by the Palestinians of any right of return to Israel proper. The Palestinians, however, have been unwilling to stop terrorist attacks on Israel, and Israel has been unwilling to dismantle its settlements in the occupied territories. Further, the two parties have been unable to come to an agreement on how much of the West Bank should go to the Palestinians and what compensation (if any) the Palestinians should receive for abandoning all claims to settlement in Israel proper.

Talks with the PLO. In 1991, under pressure from the United States, the Israelis opened talks with the Palestine Liberation Organization (PLO). In 1993, the PLO and Israel agreed to set up Palestinian self-government in the West Bank and the Gaza Strip. In the months that followed, Israeli troops withdrew from much of the occupied territories, and the new Palestinian Authority assumed police duties.

The Collapse of the Israeli-Palestinian Peace Process. Although negotiations between the Israelis and the Palestinians resulted in more agreements, the agreements were rejected by Palestinian radicals, who began a campaign of suicide bombings in Israeli cities. In 2002, the Israeli government moved tanks and troops into Palestinian towns to kill or capture the terrorists. One result of the Israeli reoccupation was an almost complete—if temporary—collapse of the Palestinian Authority. Groups such as Hamas (the Islamic Resistance Movement), which did not accept peace with Israel even in principle, moved into the power vacuum.

In February 2004, Israeli prime minister Ariel Sharon announced a plan under which Israel would withdraw from the Gaza Strip, regardless of whether a deal could be reached with the Palestinians. Sharon's plan met with strong opposition, but ultimately the withdrawal took place.

The Rise of Hamas. In January 2006, the militant group Hamas won a majority of the seats in the Palestinian legislature. American and European politicians refused to talk to Hamas until it agreed to rescind its avowed desire to destroy Israel. In June 2007, the uneasy balance between the Hamas-dominated Palestinian legislature and the PLO president broke down. After open fighting between the two parties, Hamas wound up in complete control of the Gaza Strip, and the PLO retained exclusive power in the West Bank.

Israel sought to pressure the Hamas regime in the Gaza Strip to relinquish power through an economic blockade. Hamas retaliated by firing a series of rockets into Israel. In January 2009, Israel temporarily re-occupied the Gaza Strip.

In February 2009, Israelis elected a new, more conservative government under Prime Minister Benjamin Netanyahu. The tough positions advocated by the new government threatened to create a fresh obstacle to the peace process. In particular, the new government accelerated the growth of Israeli settlements on the West Bank, even though the Obama administration opposed such settlements.

The Blockade of Gaza. The Israeli blockade of Gaza was thrust into prominence in May 2010, when Turkish activists attempted to breach the blockade with six ships carrying

President Obama and Israeli's Prime Minister Netanyahu are shown outside the Oval Office of the White House. Obama has attempted to push Netanyahu to accept a diplomatic solution to the Palestinian problem. Why would a U.S. president seek to influence the head of the Israeli government? (Amos Moshe Milner/GPO via Getty Images)

humanitarian aid and construction materials. Israeli commandos seized the ships, resulting in the death of nine activists. Widespread condemnation of the commando raid and the blockade itself followed.

The blockade was officially justified as a way of keeping weapons out of the hands of Hamas. The materials barred from Gaza, however, were not limited to arms or even construction materials, but included such small luxuries as spices and pastries. In the weeks following the flotilla incident, Israel substantially reduced the list of prohibited imports.

UN Recognition. In September 2011, the Palestinian Authority appealed to the United Nations to recognize the West Bank and Gaza as an independent Palestinian state. The plan was vehemently opposed by Israel, and the United States promised to veto any recognition in the UN Security Council. Indeed, Obama opposed the measure with some of the strongest pro-Israeli rhetoric in years. Clearly, Obama was no longer attempting to restart Israeli-Palestinian negotiations—rather, he was running for reelection.

The Economic Crisis in Europe

U.S. foreign relations are not just a matter of waging wars or trying to prevent them. International economic coordination is another major field of action. One such issue—discussed in a previous section—is our trade relations with China. In 2010, 2011, and 2013, however, an even greater threat was posed by some of our closest international friends, the nations of Europe.

The Debt Crisis. The seventeen nations that share a common currency—the euro—were hit hard by the worldwide financial panic of 2008. In Greece and, to a lesser extent, Portugal, governments had borrowed irresponsibly. In Ireland and Spain, many real estate loans went sour, threatening the survival of the banks that had made the loans. Ireland and Spain found themselves in danger when their governments assumed the debts of the threatened banks.

These nations of the so-called euro periphery began running out of funds to service their debts, and they faced ruinous interest rates if they attempted to borrow in the financial markets. If a nation such as Britain, Japan, or the United States faced such a crisis, it could rely on its central bank—in America, the Fed—to serve as *lender of last resort* and simply "print" the necessary money. But the periphery nations did not control their own money supplies, and the European Central Bank (ECB) was barred from acting as lender of last resort. Investors began pulling funds out of the troubled nations, reducing their money supplies further. The panic threatened to spread to Italy.

Would the euro periphery countries eventually be forced to leave the euro so that they could reflate their economies? That was the question. Eurozone nations did come up with bailout plans for Greece, Ireland, Portugal, and eventually Spain, but the adequacy of these supports was widely questioned.

The German Question. A major response of the ECB to the crisis was to demand that periphery governments follow policies of fiscal austerity, in which they would meet their debts by major reductions in spending and increases in taxes. Such a policy directly contradicted the advice of Keynesian economics. Keynesians argued that austerity would push the periphery further into recession, thus making the debt crisis even harder to resolve. Leaders of key nations such as Germany, however, were profoundly hostile to Keynesianism.

An alternative would be to strengthen European institutions. Eurozone banks could be backed by a euro-wide support facility, as in the United States. The eurozone could issue joint eurobonds to support troubled governments. Such measures, however, were blocked by Germany and several of its smaller allies within the eurozone. The German government, under Angela Merkel, believed that such measures would force the German taxpayer to bail out the rest of Europe.

President Obama was among a number of world leaders calling for a German change of course. Obama's calculation was that a European austerity policy would plunge the continent back into recession, thus damaging the U.S. economy and slowing its recovery. In 2013, advocates of expansionary policies received support from an unexpected source. The new government of Japan, under Prime Minister Shinzō Abe, introduced a series of expansionary monetary and fiscal policies that were meant to boost Japan out of a long period of economic stagnation.

WHO MAKES FOREIGN POLICY?

Given the vast array of challenges in the world, developing a comprehensive U.S. foreign policy is a demanding task. Does this responsibility fall to the president, to Congress, or to both acting jointly? There is no easy answer to this question because, as constitutional authority Edwin S. Corwin once observed, the U.S. Constitution created between the president and Congress an "invitation to struggle" for control over the foreign policy process. Let us look first at the powers given to the president by the Constitution.

LO4: Explain the roles of the president, executive agencies, and Congress in making U.S. foreign policy.

Constitutional Powers of the President

The Constitution confers on the president broad powers that are either explicit or implied in key constitutional provisions. Article II vests the executive power of the government in the president. The presidential oath of office, given in Article II, Section 1, requires that the president "solemnly swear" to "preserve, protect and defend the Constitution of the United States."

War Powers. In addition, and perhaps more important, Article II, Section 2, designates the president as "Commander in Chief of the Army and Navy of the United States." Starting with Abraham Lincoln, all presidents have interpreted this authority broadly. Indeed, since George Washington's administration, the United States has been involved in at least 125 undeclared wars that were conducted under presidential authority. For example, in 1950 Harry Truman ordered U.S. armed forces in the Pacific to counter North Korea's invasion of South Korea. Bill Clinton sent troops to Haiti and Bosnia. George W. Bush initiated wars in Afghanistan and Iraq, and Barack Obama undertook air strikes to support rebels in Libya.

Treaties and Executive Agreements. Article II, Section 2, of the Constitution also gives the president the power to make treaties, provided that the Senate concurs. Presidents usually have been successful in getting treaties through the Senate. In addition to this formal treaty-making power, the president makes use of executive agreements (discussed in Chapter 10). Since World War II (1939–1945), executive agreements have accounted for almost 95 percent of the understandings reached between the United States and other nations.

Executive agreements have a long and important history. During World War II, Franklin D. Roosevelt reached several agreements with Britain, the Soviet Union, and other countries. In other important agreements, Presidents Eisenhower, Kennedy, and Johnson all promised support to the government of South Vietnam. In total, since 1946 more than eight thousand executive agreements with foreign countries have been made. There is no way to obtain an accurate count, because perhaps as many as several hundred of these agreements have been made secretly.

Other Constitutional Powers. An additional power conferred on the president in Article II, Section 2, is the right to appoint ambassadors, other public ministers, and consuls. In Section 3 of that article, the president is given the power to recognize foreign governments by receiving their ambassadors.

The Executive Branch and Foreign Policymaking

There are at least four foreign policymaking sources within the executive branch, in addition to the president. These are the (1) Department of State, (2) National Security Council, (3) intelligence community, and (4) Department of Defense.

The Department of State. In principle, the State Department is the executive agency that has primary authority over foreign affairs. It supervises U.S. relations with the nearly two hundred independent nations around the world and with the United Nations and other multinational groups, such as the Organization of American States. It staffs embassies and consulates throughout the world. It does this with one of the smallest budgets of the cabinet departments.

Newly elected presidents usually tell the American public that the new secretary of State is the nation's chief foreign policy adviser. In the Obama administration, this statement was a true description of the role of secretaries of State Hillary Clinton and John Kerry. Under most presidents since World War II, however, the preeminence of the State Department in foreign policy has been limited. The State Department's image within the White House Executive Office and Congress (and even with foreign governments) has been poor—it has often been seen as a slow, plodding, bureaucratic maze of inefficient, indecisive individuals.

It is not surprising that the State Department has often been overshadowed in foreign policy. It has no natural domestic constituency as does, for example, the Department of Defense, which can call on defense contractors for support. Instead, the State Department has what might be called *negative constituents*—U.S. citizens who openly oppose the government's policies.

The National Security Council. The job of the National Security Council (NSC), created by the National Security Act of 1947 and managed by the national security adviser, is to advise the president on the integration of "domestic, foreign, and military policies relating to the national security." As it has turned out, the NSC—consisting of the president, the vice president, the secretaries of State and Defense, and often the chairperson of the

Joint Chiefs of Staff and the director of the Central Intelligence Agency (CIA)—is used in just about any way the president wants to use it.

The role of national security adviser to the president seems to adjust to fit the player. Some advisers have come into conflict with heads of the State Department. Henry A. Kissinger, President Richard Nixon's flamboyant and aggressive national security adviser, rapidly gained ascendancy over William Rogers, the secretary of State. More recently, Condoleezza Rice played an important role as national security adviser during George W. Bush's first term. Like Kissinger, Rice eventually became secretary of State.

Under President Obama, however, the national security adviser has ceased to be the most important foreign policy adviser. Obama's national security advisers have been minor figures, and in contrast to previous administrations, they have not been part of the president's cabinet.

The Intelligence Community. No discussion of foreign policy would be complete without some mention of the **intelligence community.** This consists of the forty or more government agencies and bureaus that are involved in intelligence activities. The CIA, created as part of the National Security Act of 1947, is the key official member of the intelligence community.

President George W. Bush is shown with his National Security Council (NSC) the day after the terrorist attacks on September 11, 2001. At that time, the NSC consisted of the director of the Central Intelligence Agency, the secretary of Defense, the secretary of State, the vice president, the chairman of the Joint Chiefs of Staff, and, of course, the national security adviser. How important is the NSC's role in determining U.S. foreign policy? (AP Photo/Doug Mills)

Intelligence activities consist mostly of overt information gathering, but covert actions also are undertaken. Covert actions, as the name implies, are carried out in secret, and the American public rarely finds out about them. The CIA covertly aided in the overthrow of the Mossadegh regime in Iran in 1953 and was instrumental in destabilizing the Allende government in Chile from 1970 to 1973.

During the mid-1970s, the "dark side" of the CIA was partly uncovered when the Senate undertook an investigation of its activities. One of the major findings of the Senate Select Committee on Intelligence was that the CIA had routinely spied on American citizens domestically—supposedly a prohibited activity. Consequently, the CIA came under the scrutiny of oversight committees within Congress.

Intelligence Community
The government agencies that gather information about the capabilities and intentions of foreign governments or that engage in covert actions.

The Pentagon takes its name from its unusual shape. When the media refer to "The Pentagon," they are making reference to the Department of Defense. (Hisham Ibrahim/Photodisc/Getty Images)

By 2001, the agency had come under fire again. Problems included the discovery that one of its agents was spying on behalf of a foreign power, the inability of the agency to detect the nuclear arsenals of India and Pakistan, and, above all, its failure to obtain advance knowledge about the 9/11 terrorist attacks.

The Intelligence Community and the War on Terrorism. With the rise of terrorism as a threat, the intelligence agencies have received more funding and enhanced surveillance powers, but these moves have also provoked fears of civil liberties violations. Legislation enacted in 2004 established the Office of the Director of National Intelligence to oversee the intelligence community.

A simmering controversy that came to a head in 2009 concerned the CIA's use of a technique called *waterboarding* while interrogating several prisoners in the years immediately following 9/11. Before 9/11, the government had defined waterboarding as a form of torture, but former vice president Dick Cheney, a public advocate of the practice, denied that it was. One concern was whether Bush administration officials would face legal action as a result of the practice. In May 2009, President Obama, even as he denounced waterboarding, assured CIA employees that no member of the agency would be penalized for following Justice Department rulings that had legitimized harsh interrogation methods.

The Department of Defense. The Department of Defense (DOD) was created in 1947 to bring all of the various activities of the American military establishment under the jurisdiction of a single department headed by a civilian secretary of Defense. At the same time, the Joint Chiefs of Staff, consisting of the commanders of the various military branches and a chairperson, was created to formulate a unified military strategy. In 2013, however, the department's funds were cut again.

Although the Department of Defense is larger than any other federal department, it declined in size after the fall of the Soviet Union in 1991. In the subsequent ten years, the total number of civilian employees was reduced by about 400,000, to approximately 665,000. Military personnel were also reduced in number. The defense budget remained relatively flat for several years, but with the advent of the war on terrorism and the use of military forces in Afghanistan and Iraq, funding was again increased, and with it, the size of the civilian staff.

Congress Balances the Presidency

A new interest in the balance of power between Congress and the president on foreign policy questions developed during the Vietnam War (1965–1975). Sensitive to public frustration over the long and costly war and angry at Richard Nixon for some of his other actions as president, Congress attempted to establish limits on the power of the president in setting foreign and defense policy.

The War Powers Resolution. In 1973, Congress passed the War Powers Resolution over President Nixon's veto. The act limited the president's use of troops in military action without congressional approval. Most presidents, however, have not interpreted the "consultation" provisions of the act as meaning that Congress should be consulted before military action is taken. Instead, Presidents Ford, Carter, Reagan, George H. W. Bush, and Clinton ordered troop movements and then informed congressional leaders.

The War Powers Resolution was in the news again in 2011, when President Obama failed to seek congressional support for air strikes to support the rebels in Libya. The House passed a resolution rebuking the president, but the Senate refused to consider it.

The Power of the Purse. One of Congress's most significant constitutional powers is the so-called power of the purse. The president may order that a certain action be taken, but that order cannot be executed unless Congress funds it. When the Democrats took control of Congress in January 2007, many asked whether the new Congress would use its power of the purse to bring an end to the Iraq War, in view of strong public opposition to the war. Congress's decision was to add conditions to an emergency war-funding request submitted by the president. The conditions required the president to establish a series of timelines for the removal of American troops from Iraq. President George W. Bush immediately threatened to veto any bill that imposed such conditions on the funding. His threat carried the day.

In this circumstance, the power of Congress was limited by political considerations. Congress did not even consider the option of refusing to fund the war altogether. For one thing, there was not enough support in Congress for such an approach. For another, the Democrats did not want to be accused of placing the troops in Iraq in danger. Additionally, the threat of a presidential veto significantly limited Congress's power. The Democrats simply did not have a large enough majority to override a veto.

THE MAJOR FOREIGN POLICY THEMES

Although some observers might suggest that U.S. foreign policy is inconsistent and changes with the current occupant of the White House, the long view of American diplomatic ventures reveals some major themes underlying foreign policy. In the early years of the nation, presidents and the people generally agreed that the United States should avoid foreign entanglements and concentrate instead on its own development. From the beginning of the twentieth century until the present, however, a major theme has been increasing global involvement. The theme of the post–World War II years was the containment of communism. A theme for at least the first part of the twenty-first century is containing terrorism.

LO5: Cite the main themes in the history of U.S. foreign policy.

The Formative Years: Avoiding Entanglements

The founders of the United States had a basic mistrust of European governments. This was a logical position at a time when the United States was so weak militarily that it could not influence European developments directly. Moreover, being protected by oceans that took weeks to cross certainly allowed the nation to avoid entangling alliances. During the 1800s, therefore, the United States generally stayed out of European conflicts and politics. In the Western Hemisphere, however, the United States pursued

Monroe Doctrine
A policy statement made by President James Monroe in 1823, which set out three principles: (1) European nations should not establish new colonies in the Western Hemisphere, (2) European nations should not intervene in the affairs of independent nations of the Western Hemisphere, and (3) the United States would not interfere in the affairs of European nations.

Isolationist Foreign Policy
A policy of abstaining from an active role in international affairs or alliances, which characterized U.S. foreign policy toward Europe during most of the 1800s.

Soviet Bloc
The Soviet Union and the Eastern European countries that installed Communist regimes after World War II and that were dominated by the Soviet Union.

an active expansionist policy. The nation purchased Louisiana in 1803, annexed Texas in 1845, gained substantial territory from Mexico in 1848, purchased Alaska in 1867, and annexed Hawaii in 1898.

The Monroe Doctrine. President James Monroe, in his message to Congress on December 2, 1823, stated that this country would not accept foreign intervention in the Western Hemisphere. In return, the United States would not meddle in European affairs. The **Monroe Doctrine** was the underpinning of the U.S. **isolationist foreign policy** toward Europe, which continued throughout the 1800s.

The Spanish-American War and World War I. The end of the isolationist policy started with the Spanish-American War in 1898. Winning the war gave the United States possession of Guam, Puerto Rico, and the Philippines (which gained independence in 1946). On the heels of that war came World War I (1914–1918). The United States declared war on Germany in 1917 because that country refused to give up its campaign of sinking all ships headed for Britain, including passenger ships from America. (Large passenger ships of that time commonly held more than a thousand people, so the sinking of such a ship was a disaster comparable to the attack on the World Trade Center.)

In the 1920s, the United States went "back to normalcy," as President Warren G. Harding urged it to do. U.S. military forces were largely disbanded, defense spending dropped to about 1 percent of the total annual national income, and the nation returned to a period of isolationism.

The Era of Internationalism

Isolationism was permanently shattered by the bombing of the U.S. naval base at Pearl Harbor, Hawaii, on December 7, 1941. The surprise attack by the Japanese caused the deaths of 2,403 American servicemen and wounded 1,143 others. Eighteen warships were sunk or seriously damaged, and 188 planes were destroyed at the airfields. President Franklin Roosevelt asked Congress to declare war on Japan immediately, and the United States entered World War II.

At the conclusion of the war, the United States was the only major participating country to emerge with its economy intact, and even strengthened. The United States was also the only country to have control over operational nuclear weapons. President Harry Truman had made the decision to use two atomic bombs in August 1945, to end the war with Japan. (Historians still argue over the necessity of this action, which ultimately killed more than 100,000 Japanese and left an equal number permanently injured.) The United States truly had become the world's superpower.

The Cold War. The United States had become an uncomfortable ally of the Soviet Union after Adolf Hitler's invasion of that country. Soon after World War II ended, relations between the Soviet Union and the West deteriorated. The Soviet Union wanted a weakened Germany, and to achieve this, it insisted that Germany be divided in two, with East Germany becoming a buffer against the West. Little by little, the Soviet Union helped to install Communist governments in Eastern European countries, which were soon referred to collectively as the **Soviet bloc.** In response, the United States encouraged the rearming of Western Europe. The Cold War had begun.[2]

---

2. See John Lewis Gaddis, *The United Nations and the Origins of the Cold War* (New York: Columbia University Press, 1972).

Containment Policy. In 1947, a remarkable article was published in *Foreign Affairs* magazine, signed by "X." The actual author was George F. Kennan, chief of the policy-planning staff for the State Department. The doctrine of **containment** set forth in the article became—according to many—the bible of Western foreign policy. "X" argued that whenever and wherever the Soviet Union could successfully challenge the West, it would do so. He recommended that our policy toward the Soviet Union be "firm and vigilant containment of Russian expansive tendencies." [3]

The containment theory was expressed clearly in the **Truman Doctrine,** which was enunciated by President Harry Truman in 1947. Truman held that the United States must help countries in which a Communist takeover seemed likely. Later that year, he backed the Marshall Plan, an economic assistance plan for Europe that was intended to prevent the expansion of Communist influence there. In 1949, the United States, along with several European nations, entered into a military alliance called the North Atlantic Treaty Organization, or NATO, to offer a credible response to any Soviet military attack.

President Truman
ordered two atomic bomb attacks in Japan in 1945. Was his decision justified? (Photo Courtesy of U.S. Air Force)

Superpower Relations

During the Cold War, there was never any direct military conflict between the United States and the Soviet Union. Only on occasion did the United States enter a conflict with any Communist country in a significant way. Two such occasions were in Korea and in Vietnam.

After the end of World War II, northern Korea was occupied by the Soviet Union, and southern Korea was occupied by the United States. The result was two rival Korean governments. In 1950, North Korea invaded South Korea. Under UN authority, the United States entered the war, which prevented an almost certain South Korean defeat. When U.S. forces were on the brink of conquering North Korea, however, China joined the war on the side of the North, resulting in a stalemate. An armistice signed in 1953 led to the two Koreas that exist today. U.S. forces have remained in South Korea since that time.

The Vietnam War (1965–1975) also involved the United States in a civil war between a Communist north and pro-Western south. When the French army in Indochina was defeated by the Communist forces of Ho Chi Minh in 1954 and the two Vietnams were created, the United States assumed the role of supporting the South Vietnamese government against North Vietnam. President John F. Kennedy sent sixteen thousand "advisers" to help South Vietnam, and after Kennedy's death in 1963, President Lyndon Johnson greatly increased the scope of that support. American forces in Vietnam at the height of the U.S. involvement totaled more than 500,000 troops. In excess of 58,000 Americans were killed and 300,000 were wounded in the conflict. A peace agreement in 1973 allowed U.S. troops to leave the country, and in 1975, North Vietnam easily occupied Saigon (the South Vietnamese capital) and unified the nation.

Over the course of the Vietnam War, the debate concerning U.S. involvement became extremely heated and, as mentioned previously, spurred congressional efforts to limit the ability of the president to commit forces to armed combat. The military draft was also a major source of contention during the Vietnam War.

The Cuban Missile Crisis. Perhaps the closest the two superpowers came to a nuclear confrontation was the Cuban missile crisis in 1962. The Soviets placed missiles in Cuba,

Containment
A U.S. diplomatic policy adopted by the Truman administration to contain Communist power within its existing boundaries.

Truman Doctrine
The policy adopted by President Harry Truman in 1947 to halt Communist expansion in southeastern Europe.

3. X, "The Sources of Soviet Conduct," *Foreign Affairs,* July 1947, p. 575.

In a famous meeting in Yalta in February 1945, British prime minister Winston Churchill (left), U.S. president Franklin Roosevelt (center), and Soviet leader Joseph Stalin (right) decided the fate of several nations in Europe, including Germany. What happened to Germany immediately after World War II? (Library of Congress)

ninety miles off the U.S. coast, in response to Cuban fears of an American invasion and to try to balance an American nuclear advantage. President Kennedy and his advisers rejected the option of invading Cuba, setting up a naval blockade around the island instead. When Soviet vessels appeared near Cuban waters, the tension reached its height. After intense negotiations between Washington and Moscow, the Soviet ships turned around on October 25, and on October 28 the Soviet Union announced the withdrawal of its missile operations from Cuba. In exchange, the United States agreed not to invade Cuba in the future. It also agreed to remove some of its own missiles that were located near the Soviet border in Turkey.

A Period of Détente. The French word **détente** means a relaxation of tensions. By the end of the 1960s, it was clear that some efforts had to be made to reduce the threat of nuclear war between the United States and the Soviet Union. The Soviet Union had gradually begun to catch up in the building of strategic nuclear delivery vehicles in the form of bombers and missiles, thus balancing the nuclear scales between the two countries. Each nation had acquired the military capacity to destroy the other with nuclear weapons.

As the result of lengthy negotiations under Secretary of State Henry Kissinger and President Nixon, the United States and the Soviet Union signed the **Strategic Arms Limitation Treaty (SALT I)** in May 1972. That treaty limited the number of offensive missiles each country could deploy.

The policy of détente was not limited to the U.S. relationship with the Soviet Union. Seeing an opportunity to capitalize on increasing friction between the Soviet Union and the People's Republic of China, Kissinger secretly began negotiations to establish a new relationship with China. President Nixon eventually visited that nation in 1972. The visit set the stage for the formal diplomatic recognition of that country, which occurred during the Carter administration (1977–1981).

Nuclear Arms Agreements with the Soviet Union. President Ronald Reagan (1981–1989) initially took a hard line against the Soviet Union. In 1987, however, after several years of negotiations, the United States and the Soviet Union signed the

Détente
A French word meaning a relaxation of tensions. The term characterized U.S.-Soviet relations as they developed under President Richard Nixon and Secretary of State Henry Kissinger.

Strategic Arms Limitation Treaty (SALT I)
A treaty between the United States and the Soviet Union to stabilize the nuclear arms competition between the two countries. SALT I talks began in 1969, and the treaty was signed in 1972.

Intermediate-Range Nuclear Forces Treaty. The result was the dismantling of four thousand intermediate-range missiles.

In 1991, President George H. W. Bush and the Soviet Union signed the Strategic Arms Reduction Treaty (START). Implementation was complicated by the collapse of the Soviet Union in December 1991. In 1992, however, the treaty was re-signed by Russia and other former Soviet republics.

The Dissolution of the Soviet Union. After the fall of the Berlin Wall in 1989, it was clear that the Soviet Union had relinquished much of its political and military control over the states of Eastern Europe that formerly had been part of the Soviet bloc. No one expected the Soviet Union to dissolve into separate states as quickly as it did, however. Although Gorbachev tried to adjust the Soviet constitution and political system to allow greater autonomy for the republics within the union, demands for political, ethnic, and religious autonomy grew. On the day after Christmas in 1991, the Soviet Union was officially dissolved.

Russia after the Soviet Union. In 2000, Boris Yeltsin, president of the newly independent and democratic Russian Federation, resigned because of poor health. He named Vladimir Putin, architect of the Russian military effort against an independence movement in the province of Chechnya, as acting president. A few months later, Putin won the presidency in a national election. Putin chipped away at Russia's democratic institutions, slowly turning the country into what was, in essence, an elected autocracy. When Putin's second term as president came to an end in 2008, he could not immediately run for reelection. He therefore engineered the election of one of his supporters, Dmitry Medvedev, as president. Medvedev promptly appointed Putin as prime minister. It was clear that Putin retained real power in Russia, and in 2012 Putin again took the presidency.

In recent years, the United States has become concerned over Russia's aggressive attitude toward its neighbors. In 2008, Russian troops entered Georgia to prevent that nation from retaking an autonomous region that was under Russian protection. On several occasions since 2005, Russia has cut off the transmission of natural gas to Europe as a result of disputes. Russia also reacted angrily to U.S. plans for antimissile defenses in Eastern Europe, aimed at protecting Europe from a possible future Iranian attack. Russia appeared to believe that the defenses were directed against it instead. Still, the United States needed Russian assistance in matters such as curbing Iran's nuclear program. The 1992 START agreement expired in December 2009. In April 2010, President Obama and Russian president Medvedev signed New START, a follow-on treaty. New START reduced the number of permitted warheads to 1,550 for each side, a drop of about 30 percent from previous agreements. After some delays, the Senate ratified the treaty in December 2010.

Russia's Future. Even as Russia reasserts itself as a great power, its future is in doubt. Its population is dropping and may fall as low as 132 million by 2050, down from 150 million. Russia has not only a low birthrate but also a very high death rate—Russian life expectancy for men is below that of India, despite the widespread poverty in that country. If Russia's population continues to fall, its ability to project power will decline as well.

Russian president Vladimir Putin has gradually chipped away at the freedoms of his people. Recent targets of his wrath have included gays and foreigners who adopt Russian orphans. (Mark III Photonics/Shutterstock.com)

making a difference
WORKING FOR HUMAN RIGHTS

In many countries throughout the world, human rights are not protected. In some nations, people are imprisoned, tortured, or killed because they oppose the current regime. In other nations, certain ethnic or racial groups are oppressed by the majority population.

Why Should You Care? The defense of human rights is unlikely to put a single dollar in your pocket, so why get involved? The strongest reason for involving yourself with human rights issues in other countries is simple moral altruism—unselfish regard for the welfare of others.

A broader consideration, however, is that human rights abuses are often associated with the kind of dictatorial regimes that are likely to provoke wars. To the extent that the people of the world can create a climate in which human rights abuses are unacceptable, they may also create an atmosphere in which national leaders believe that they must display peaceful conduct generally. This, in turn, might reduce the frequency of wars, some of which could involve the United States. And wars always have costs—in the form of dollars, and in the form of American lives.

What Can You Do? How can you work for the improvement of human rights in other nations? One way is to join an organization that attempts to keep watch over human rights violations. (Two such organizations are listed at the end of this feature.) By publicizing human rights violations, such groups try to pressure nations into changing their practices. Sometimes, these organizations are able to apply enough pressure and cause enough embarrassment that victims may be freed from prison or allowed to emigrate.

Another way to work for human rights is to keep informed about the state of affairs in other nations and to write personally to governments that violate human rights or to their embassies, asking them to cease these violations.

These Amnesty International activists are protesting alleged human rights abuses. What do you think they want President Barack Obama to do? (Win McNamee/Getty Images)

If you want to receive general information about the position of the United States on human rights violations, you can contact the State Department:

> Department's Bureau of Democracy,
> Human Rights, and Labor

To find the bureau's page online, enter "state human rights" into a search engine.

Amnesty International U.S.A. and the American Friends Service Committee (AFSC) are well known for their watchdog efforts in countries that violate human rights for political reasons. To find Amnesty International, you can search on "amnestyusa." For the AFSC, type "afsc" into a search engine.

key**terms**

Cold War 327	foreign policy	moral idealism 322	Strategic Arms
containment 339	process 321	national security	Limitation Treaty
defense policy 321	intelligence	policy 321	(SALT I) 340
détente 340	community 335	normal trade relations	technical assistance 321
diplomacy 321	isolationist foreign	(NTR) status 328	terrorism 323
economic aid 321	policy 338	political realism 322	Truman Doctrine 339
foreign policy 321	Monroe Doctrine 338	Soviet bloc 338	

chapter**summary**

1 Foreign policy includes the nation's external goals and the techniques and strategies used to achieve them. National security policy, which is one aspect of foreign policy, is designed to protect the independence and the political and economic integrity of the United States. Diplomacy involves the nation's external relationships and is an attempt to resolve conflict without resort to arms. U.S. foreign policy is based both on moral idealism and on political realism.

2 Terrorism is the attempt to create fear to gain political ends, usually by violence against noncombatants. It has become a major challenge facing the United States and other nations. The United States waged war on terrorism after the attacks of September 11, 2001.

3 In 1991 and again in 2003, the United States sent combat troops to Iraq. The second war in Iraq, begun in 2003, succeeded in toppling the decades-long dictatorship of Saddam Hussein, but led to a long, grinding conflict with insurgent forces. The United States also went to war in Afghanistan to track down al Qaeda, which was responsible for the 9/11 attacks, and to expel the Taliban government that had supported the terrorists.

4 Recent diplomatic efforts by the United States include containing the nuclear ambitions of Iran and North Korea. The rise of China as a superpower introduces a series of issues the United States must address. American efforts to promote the peace process between Israel and the Palestinians have had limited success. World economic issues, such as trade with China and the European debt crisis, demand U.S. attention.

5 The formal power of the president to make foreign policy derives from the U.S. Constitution, which designates the president as commander in chief of the army and navy. Presidents have interpreted this authority broadly. They also have the power to make treaties and executive agreements. In principle, the State Department is the executive agency with primary authority over foreign affairs. The National Security Council also plays a major role. The intelligence community consists of government agencies engaged in information gathering and covert operations. To establish some limits on the power of the president to intervene abroad, Congress passed the War Powers Resolution in 1973.

6 During the 1800s, the United States stayed out of European conflicts and politics, so these years have been called the period of isolationism. The end of the policy of isolationism toward Europe started with the Spanish-American War of 1898. U.S. involvement in European politics became more extensive when the United States entered World War I in 1917. World War II marked a lasting change in American foreign policy. The United States was the only major country to emerge from the war with its economy intact and the only country with operating nuclear weapons.

7 Soon after World War II, the Cold War began. A policy of containment, which assumed an expansionist Soviet Union, was enunciated in the Truman Doctrine. Following the apparent arms equality of the United States and the Soviet Union, both states adopted a policy of détente.

8 The United States signed arms control agreements with the Soviet Union under Presidents Nixon, Reagan, and George H. W. Bush. After the fall of the Soviet Union, Russia emerged as a less threatening state. Under President Vladimir Putin, however, Russia has moved away from democracy and in part returned to its old autocratic traditions.

test**yourself**

LO1 *Define* foreign policy, *and discuss moral idealism versus political realism in foreign policy.*

As part of foreign policy, national security policy is designed to:
   a. ensure that the fifty states respect each other's borders.
   b. ensure that all other countries respect each other's borders.
   c. protect the independence and political integrity of the United States.

LO2 *Describe recent foreign policy challenges that involve the use of force, including terrorism and the wars in Afghanistan and Iraq.*

Acts of terrorism are:
   a. the result of small-country governments' attempts to gain new territory.
   b. systematic attempts to inspire fear to gain political ends.
   c. due to large-country governments that failed in diplomacy.

LO3 *Discuss the use of diplomacy in addressing such issues as nuclear proliferation, the rise of China, the confrontation between Israel and the Palestinians, and the economic crisis in Europe.*

The two countries that today represent the most serious problems with nuclear proliferation are:
   a. Iran and North Korea.
   b. Japan and Germany.
   c. China and Brazil.

LO4 *Explain the roles of the president, executive agencies, and Congress in making U.S. foreign policy.*

The intelligence community is involved in foreign policy and consists of:
   a. the CIA and the Department of Defense.
   b. more than forty government agencies and bureaus involved in intelligence activities.
   c. the CIA and the National Security Council (NSC).

LO5 *Cite the main themes in the history of U.S. foreign policy.*

The Cold War refers to a period during which:
   a. the Soviet Union and the United States faced off throughout the world.
   b. the United States reverted back to isolationist policies.
   c. the United States engaged in economic conflict with many Asian countries.

Essay Question:

Some people believe that if no U.S. military personnel were stationed abroad, terrorists would have less desire to harm Americans or the United States. Do you agree? Why or why not?

Answers to multiple-choice questions: 1. c, 2. b, 3. a, 4. b, 5. a.

CourseMate

Access CourseMate at www.cengagebrain.com for additional study tools: practice quizzes, key term flashcards and crossword puzzles, audio chapter summaries, simulations, animated learning modules, interactive timelines, videos, and American Government NewsWatch.

Appendix A

The Declaration of Independence

In Congress, July 4, 1776

A Declaration by the Representatives of the United States of America, in General Congress assembled. When in the Course of human Events, it becomes necessary for one People to dissolve the Political Bands which have connected them with another, and to assume among the Powers of the Earth, the separate and equal Station to which the Laws of Nature and of Nature's God entitle them, a decent Respect to the Opinions of Mankind requires that they should declare the causes which impel them to the Separation.

We hold these Truths to be self-evident, that all Men are created equal, that they are endowed by their Creator with certain unalienable Rights, that among these are Life, Liberty, and the Pursuit of Happiness— That to secure these Rights, Governments are instituted among Men, deriving their just Powers from the Consent of the Governed, that whenever any Form of Government becomes destructive of these Ends, it is the Right of the People to alter or to abolish it, and to institute new Government, laying its Foundation on such Principles, and organizing its Powers in such Forms, as to them shall seem most likely to effect their Safety and Happiness. Prudence, indeed, will dictate that Governments long established should not be changed for light and transient Causes; and accordingly all Experience hath shewn, that Mankind are more disposed to suffer, while Evils are sufferable, than to right themselves by abolishing the Forms to which they are accustomed. But when a long Train of Abuses and Usurpations, pursuing invariably the same Object, evinces a Design to reduce them under absolute Despotism, it is their Right, it is their Duty, to throw off such Government, and to provide new Guards for their future Security. Such has been the patient Sufferance of these Colonies; and such is now the Necessity which constrains them to alter their former Systems of Government. The History of the present King of Great-Britain is a History of repeated Injuries and Usurpations, all having in direct Object the Establishment of an absolute Tyranny over these States. To prove this, let Facts be submitted to a candid World.

He has refused his Assent to Laws, the most wholesome and necessary for the public Good.

He has forbidden his Governors to pass Laws of immediate and pressing Importance, unless suspended in their Operation till his Assent should be obtained; and when so suspended, he has utterly neglected to attend to them.

He has refused to pass other Laws for the Accommodation of large Districts of People, unless those People would relinquish the Right of Representation in the Legislature, a Right inestimable to them, and formidable to Tyrants only.

He has called together Legislative Bodies at Places unusual, uncomfortable, and distant from the Depository of their Public Records, for the sole Purpose of fatiguing them into Compliance with his Measures.

He has dissolved Representative Houses repeatedly, for opposing with manly Firmness his Invasions on the Rights of the People.

He has refused for a long Time, after such Dissolutions, to cause others to be elected; whereby the Legislative Powers, incapable of Annihilation, have returned to the People at large for their exercise; the State remaining in the mean time exposed to all the Dangers of Invasion from without, and Convulsions within.

He has endeavoured to prevent the Population of these States; for that Purpose obstructing the Laws for Naturalization of Foreigners; refusing to pass others to encourage their Migrations hither, and raising the Conditions of new Appropriations of Lands.

He has obstructed the Administration of Justice, by refusing his Assent to Laws for establishing Judiciary Powers.

He has made Judges dependent on his Will alone, for the Tenure of their offices, and the Amount and payment of their Salaries.

He has erected a Multitude of new Offices, and sent hither Swarms of Officers to harrass our People, and eat out their Substance.

He has kept among us, in Times of Peace, Standing Armies, without the consent of our Legislatures.

He has affected to render the Military independent of, and superior to the Civil Power.

He has combined with others to subject us to a Jurisdiction foreign to our Constitution, and unacknowledged by our Laws; giving his Assent to their Acts of pretended Legislation:

For quartering large Bodies of Armed Troops among us:

For protecting them, by a mock Trial, from Punishment for any Murders which they should commit on the Inhabitants of these States:

For cutting off our Trade with all Parts of the World:

For imposing Taxes on us without our Consent:

For depriving us, in many cases, of the Benefits of Trial by Jury:

For transporting us beyond Seas to be tried for pretended Offences:

For abolishing the free System of English Laws in a neighbouring Province, establishing therein an arbitrary Government, and enlarging its Boundaries, so as to render it at once an Example and fit Instrument for introducing the same absolute Rule into these Colonies:

For taking away our Charters, abolishing our most valuable Laws, and altering fundamentally the Forms of our Governments:

For suspending our own Legislatures, and declaring themselves invested with Power to legislate for us in all Cases whatsoever.

He has abdicated Government here, by declaring us out of his Protection and waging War against us.

He has plundered our Seas, ravaged our Coasts, burnt our towns, and destroyed the Lives of our People.

He is, at this Time, transporting large Armies of foreign Mercenaries to compleat the works of Death, Desolation, and Tyranny, already begun with circumstances of Cruelty and Perfidy, scarcely parallelled in the most barbarous Ages, and totally unworthy the Head of a civilized Nation.

He has constrained our fellow Citizens taken Captive on the high Seas to bear Arms against their Country, to become the Executioners of their Friends and Brethren, or to fall themselves by their Hands.

He has excited domestic Insurrections amongst us, and has endeavoured to bring on the Inhabitants of our Frontiers, the merciless Indian Savages, whose known Rule of Warfare, is an undistinguished Destruction, of all Ages, Sexes and Conditions.

In every state of these Oppressions we have Petitioned for Redress in the most humble Terms: Our repeated Petitions have been answered only by repeated Injury. A Prince, whose Character is thus marked by every act which may define a Tyrant, is unfit to be the Ruler of a free People.

Nor have we been wanting in Attentions to our British Brethren. We have warned them from Time to Time of Attempts by their Legislature to extend an unwarrantable Jurisdiction over us. We have reminded them of the Circumstances of our Emigration and Settlement here. We have appealed to their native Justice and Magnanimity, and we have conjured them by the Ties of our common Kindred to disavow these Usurpations, which, would inevitably interrupt our Connections and Correspondence. They too have been deaf to the Voice of Justice and of Consanguinity. We must, therefore, acquiesce in the Necessity, which denounces our Separation, and hold them, as we hold the rest of Mankind, Enemies in War, in Peace, Friends.

We, therefore, the Representatives of the UNITED STATES OF AMERICA, in General Congress Assembled, appealing to the Supreme Judge of the World for the Rectitude of our Intentions, do, in the Name, and by the Authority of the good People of these Colonies, solemnly Publish and Declare, That these United Colonies are, and of Right ought to be, Free and Independent States; that they are absolved from all Allegiance to the British Crown, and that all political Connection between them and the State of Great-Britain, is and ought to be totally dissolved; and that as Free and Independent States, they have full Power to levy War, conclude Peace, contract Alliances, establish Commerce, and to do all other Acts and Things which Independent States may of right do. And for the support of this declaration, with a firm Reliance on the Protection of divine Providence, we mutually pledge to each other our lives, our Fortunes, and our sacred Honor.

Appendix B

The Constitution of the United States*

The Preamble

We the People of the United States, in Order to form a more perfect Union, establish Justice, insure domestic Tranquility, provide for the common defence, promote the general Welfare, and secure the Blessings of Liberty to ourselves and our Posterity, do ordain and establish this Constitution for the United States of America.

The Preamble declares that "We the People" are the authority for the Constitution (unlike the Articles of Confederation, which derived their authority from the states). The Preamble also sets out the purposes of the Constitution.

Article I. (Legislative Branch)

The first part of the Constitution, Article 1, deals with the organization and powers of the lawmaking branch of the national government, the Congress.

Section 1. Legislative Powers

All legislative Powers herein granted shall be vested in a Congress of the United States, which shall consist of a Senate and House of Representatives.

Section 2. House of Representatives

Clause 1: Composition and Election of Members. The House of Representatives shall be composed of Members chosen every second Year by the People of the several States, and the Electors in each State shall have the Qualifications requisite for Electors of the most numerous Branch of the State Legislature.

Each state has the power to decide who may vote for members of Congress. Within each state, those who may vote for state legislators may also vote for members of the House of Representatives (and, under the Seventeenth Amendment, for U.S. senators). When the Constitution was written, nearly all states limited voting rights to white male property owners or taxpayers at least twenty-one years old. Subsequent amendments granted voting power to African American men, all women, and eighteen-year-olds.

---

* The spelling, capitalization, and punctuation of the original have been retained here. Brackets indicate passages that have been altered by amendments to the Constitution. We have added article titles (in parentheses), section titles, and clause designations. We have also inserted annotations in blue italic type.

Clause 2: Qualifications. No Person shall be a Representative who shall not have attained to the Age of twenty five Years, and been seven Years a Citizen of the United States, and who shall not, when elected, be an Inhabitant of that State in which he shall be chosen.

Each member of the House must be at least twenty-five years old, a citizen of the United States for at least seven years, and a resident of the state in which she or he is elected.

Clause 3: Apportionment of Representatives and Direct Taxes. Representatives [and direct Taxes][1] shall be apportioned among the several States which may be included within this Union, according to their respective Numbers [which shall be determined by adding to the whole Number of free Persons, including those bound to Service for a Term of Years, and excluding Indians not taxed, three fifths of all other Persons].[2] The actual Enumeration shall be made within three Years after the first Meeting of the Congress of the United States, and within every subsequent Term of ten Years, in such Manner as they shall by Law direct. The Number of Representatives shall not exceed one for every thirty Thousand, but each State shall have at Least one Representative; and until such enumeration shall be made, the State of New Hampshire shall be entitled to chuse three, Massachusetts eight, Rhode Island and Providence Plantations one, Connecticut five, New York six, New Jersey four, Pennsylvania eight, Delaware one, Maryland six, Virginia ten, North Carolina five, South Carolina five, and Georgia three.

A state's representation in the House is based on the size of its population. Population is counted in each decade's census, after which Congress reapportions House seats. Since early in the twentieth century, the number of seats has been limited to 435.

Clause 4: Vacancies. When vacancies happen in the Representation from any State, the Executive Authority thereof shall issue Writs of Election to fill such Vacancies.

The "Executive Authority" is the state's governor. When a vacancy occurs in the House, the governor calls a special election to fill it.

---

1. Modified by the Sixteenth Amendment.
2. Modified by the Fourteenth Amendment.

Clause 5: Officers and Impeachment. The House of Representatives shall chuse their Speaker and other Officers; and shall have the sole Power of Impeachment.

The power to impeach is the power to accuse. In this case, it is the power to accuse members of the executive or judicial branch of wrongdoing or abuse of power. Once a bill of impeachment is issued, the Senate holds the trial.

Section 3. The Senate

Clause 1: Term and Number of Members. The Senate of the United States shall be composed of two Senators from each State [chosen by the Legislature thereof],[3] for six Years; and each Senator shall have one Vote.

Every state has two senators, each of whom serves for six years and has one vote in the upper chamber. Since the Seventeenth Amendment in 1913, all senators have been elected directly by voters of the state during the regular election.

Clause 2: Classification of Senators. Immediately after they shall be assembled in Consequence of the first Election, they shall be divided as equally as may be into three Classes. The Seats of the Senators of the first Class shall be vacated at the Expiration of the second Year, of the second Class at the Expiration of the fourth Year, and of the third Class at the Expiration of the sixth Year, so that one third may be chosen every second Year; [and if Vacancies happen by Resignation, or otherwise, during the Recess of the Legislature of any State, the Executive thereof may make temporary Appointments until the next Meeting of the Legislature, which shall then fill such Vacancies].[4]

One-third of the Senate's seats are open to election every two years (in contrast, all members of the House are elected simultaneously).

Clause 3: Qualifications. No Person shall be a Senator who shall not have attained to the Age of thirty Years, and been nine Years a Citizen of the United States, and who shall not, when elected, be an Inhabitant of that State for which he shall be chosen.

Every senator must be at least thirty years old, a citizen of the United States for a minimum of nine years, and a resident of the state in which he or she is elected.

Clause 4: The Role of the Vice President. The Vice President of the United States shall be President of the Senate, but shall have no Vote, unless they be equally divided.

The vice president presides over meetings of the Senate but cannot vote unless there is a tie. The Constitution gives no other official duties to the vice president.

Clause 5: Other Officers. The Senate shall chuse their other Officers, and also a President pro tempore, in the Absence of the Vice President, or when he shall exercise the Office of President of the United States.

The Senate votes for one of its members to preside when the vice president is absent. This person is usually called the president pro tempore because of the temporary nature of the position.

Clause 6: Impeachment Trials. The Senate shall have the sole Power to try all Impeachments. When sitting for that Purpose, they shall be on Oath or Affirmation. When the President of the United States is tried, the Chief Justice shall preside: And no Person shall be convicted without the Concurrence of two thirds of the Members present.

The Senate conducts trials of officials that the House impeaches. The Senate sits as a jury, with the vice president presiding if the president is not on trial.

Clause 7: Penalties for Conviction. Judgment in Cases of Impeachment shall not extend further than to removal from Office, and disqualification to hold and enjoy any Office of honor, Trust, or Profit under the United States: but the Party convicted shall nevertheless be liable and subject to Indictment, Trial, Judgment, and Punishment, according to Law.

On conviction of impeachment charges, the Senate can only force an official to leave office and prevent him or her from holding another office in the federal government. The individual, however, can still be tried in a regular court.

Section 4. Congressional Elections: Times, Manner, and Places

Clause 1: Elections. The Times, Places and Manner of holding Elections for Senators and Representatives, shall be prescribed in each State by the Legislature thereof; but the Congress may at any time by Law make or alter such Regulations, except as to the Places of chusing Senators.

Congress set the Tuesday after the first Monday in November in even-numbered years as the date for congressional elections. In states with more than one seat in the House, Congress requires that representatives be elected from districts within each state. Under the Seventeenth Amendment, senators are elected at the same places as other officials.

Clause 2: Sessions of Congress. [The Congress shall assemble at least once in every Year, and such Meeting shall be on the first Monday in December, unless they shall by Law appoint a different Day.][5]

Congress has to meet every year at least once. The regular session now begins at noon on January 3 of each year, subsequent to the Twentieth Amendment, unless Congress passes a law to fix a different date. Congress stays in session until its members vote to adjourn. Additionally, the president may call a special session.

Section 5. Powers and Duties of the Houses

Clause 1: Admitting Members and Quorum. Each House shall be the Judge of the Elections, Returns, and

---

3. Repealed by the Seventeenth Amendment.
4. Modified by the Seventeenth Amendment.

5. Changed by the Twentieth Amendment.

Qualifications of its own Members, and a Majority of each shall constitute a Quorum to do Business; but a smaller Number may adjourn from day to day, and may be authorized to compel the Attendance of absent Members, in such Manner, and under such Penalties as each House may provide.

Each chamber may exclude or refuse to seat a member-elect.

The quorum rule requires that 218 members of the House and 51 members of the Senate be present to conduct business. This rule normally is not enforced in the handling of routine matters.

Clause 2: Rules and Discipline of Members. Each House may determine the Rules of its Proceedings, punish its Members for disorderly Behaviour, and, with the Concurrence of two thirds, expel a Member.

The House and the Senate may adopt their own rules to guide their proceedings. Each may also discipline its members for conduct that is deemed unacceptable. No member may be expelled without a two-thirds majority vote in favor of expulsion.

Clause 3: Keeping a Record. Each House shall keep a Journal of its Proceedings, and from time to time publish the same, excepting such Parts as may in their Judgment require Secrecy; and the Yeas and Nays of the Members of either House on any question shall, at the Desire of one fifth of those Present, be entered on the Journal.

The journals of the two chambers are published at the end of each session of Congress.

Clause 4: Adjournment. Neither House, during the Session of Congress, shall, without the Consent of the other, adjourn for more than three days, nor to any other Place than that in which the two Houses shall be sitting.

Congress has the power to determine when and where to meet, provided, however, that both chambers meet in the same city. Neither chamber may recess for more than three days without the consent of the other.

Section 6. Rights of Members

Clause 1: Compensation and Privileges. The Senators and Representatives shall receive a Compensation for their services, to be ascertained by Law, and paid out of the Treasury of the United States. They shall in all Cases, except Treason, Felony and Breach of the Peace, be privileged from Arrest during their Attendance at the Session of their respective Houses, and in going to and returning from the same; and for any Speech or Debate in either House, they shall not be questioned in any other Place.

Congressional salaries are to be paid by the U.S. Treasury rather than by the members' respective states. The original salaries were $6 per day; in 1857 they were $3,000 per year. Both representatives and senators were paid $165,200 in 2007.

Treason is defined in Article III, Section 3. A felony is any serious crime. A breach of the peace is any indictable offense less than treason or a felony. Members cannot be

arrested for things they say during speeches and debates in Congress. This immunity applies to the Capitol Building itself and not to their private lives.

Clause 2: Restrictions. No Senator or Representative shall, during the Time for which he was elected, be appointed to any civil Office under the Authority of the United States, which shall have been created, or the Emoluments whereof shall have been increased during such time; and no Person holding any Office under the United States, shall be a Member of either House during his Continuance in Office.

During the term for which a member was elected, he or she cannot concurrently accept another federal government position.

Section 7. Legislative Powers: Bills and Resolutions

Clause 1: Revenue Bills. All Bills for raising Revenue shall originate in the House of Representatives; but the Senate may propose or concur with Amendments as on other Bills.

All tax and appropriation bills for raising money have to originate in the House of Representatives. The Senate, though, often amends such bills and may even substitute an entirely different bill.

Clause 2: The Presidential Veto. Every Bill which shall have passed the House of Representatives and the Senate, shall, before it becomes a Law, be presented to the President of the United States; If he approve he shall sign it, but if not he shall return it, with his Objections to the House in which it shall have originated, who shall enter the Objections at large on their Journal, and proceed to reconsider it. If after such Reconsideration two thirds of that House shall agree to pass the Bill, it shall be sent together with the Objections, to the other House, by which it shall likewise be reconsidered, and if approved by two thirds of that House, it shall become a Law. But in all such Cases the Votes of both Houses shall be determined by Yeas and Nays, and the Names of the Persons voting for and against the Bill shall be entered on the Journal of each House respectively. If any Bill shall not be returned by the President within ten Days (Sundays excepted) after it shall have been presented to him, the Same shall be a Law, in like Manner as if he had signed it, unless the Congress by their Adjournment prevent its Return in which Case it shall not be a Law.

When Congress sends the president a bill, he or she can sign it (in which case it becomes law) or send it back to the chamber in which it originated. If it is sent back, a two-thirds majority of each chamber must pass it again for it to become law. If the president neither signs it nor sends it back within ten days, it becomes law anyway, unless Congress adjourns in the meantime.

Clause 3: Actions on Other Matters. Every Order, Resolution, or Vote to which the Concurrence of the Senate and House of Representatives may be necessary (except on a question of Adjournment) shall be presented to the President of the United States; and before the Same shall take Effect, shall be approved by him, or being disapproved by him, shall be repassed by two thirds of the Senate and House of Representatives, according to the Rules and Limitations prescribed in the Case of a Bill.

The president must have the opportunity to either sign or veto everything that Congress passes, except votes to adjourn and resolutions not having the force of law.

Section 8. The Powers of Congress

Clause 1: Taxing. The Congress shall have Power To lay and collect Taxes, Duties, Imposts and Excises, to pay the Debts and provide for the common Defence and general Welfare of the United States; but all Duties, Imposts and Excises shall be uniform throughout the United States;

Duties are taxes on imports and exports. Impost is a generic term for tax. Excises are taxes on the manufacture, sale, or use of goods.

Clause 2: Borrowing. To borrow Money on the credit of the United States;

Congress has the power to borrow money, which is normally carried out through the sale of U.S. treasury bonds on which interest is paid. Note that the Constitution places no limit on the amount of government borrowing.

Clause 3: Regulation of Commerce. To regulate Commerce with foreign Nations, and among the several States, and with the Indian Tribes;

This is the commerce clause, which gives to Congress the power to regulate interstate and foreign trade. Much of the activity of Congress is based on this clause.

Clause 4: Naturalization and Bankruptcy. To establish an uniform Rule of Naturalization, and uniform Laws on the subject of Bankruptcies throughout the United States;

Only Congress may determine how aliens can become citizens of the United States. Congress may make laws with respect to bankruptcy.

Clause 5: Money and Standards. To coin Money, regulate the Value thereof, and of foreign Coin, and fix the Standard of Weights and Measures;

Congress mints coins and prints and circulates paper money. Congress can establish uniform measures of time, distance, weight, and so on. In 1838, Congress adopted the English system of weights and measurements as our national standard.

Clause 6: Punishing Counterfeiters. To provide for the Punishment of counterfeiting the Securities and current Coin of the United States;

Congress has the power to punish those who copy American money and pass it off as real. Currently, the punishment is a fine up to $5,000 and/or imprisonment for up to fifteen years.

Clause 7: Roads and Post Offices. To establish Post Offices and post Roads;

Post roads include all routes over which mail is carried—highways, railways, waterways, and airways.

Clause 8: Patents and Copyrights. To promote the Progress of Science and useful Arts, by securing for limited Times to Authors and Inventors the exclusive Right to their respective Writings and Discoveries;

Authors' and composers' works are protected by copyrights established by copyright law, which currently is the Copyright Act of 1976, as amended. Copyrights are valid for the life of the author or composer plus seventy years. Inventors' works are protected by patents, which vary in length of protection from fourteen to twenty years. A patent gives a person the exclusive right to control the manufacture or sale of her or his invention.

Clause 9: Lower Courts. To constitute Tribunals inferior to the supreme Court;

Congress has the authority to set up all federal courts, except the Supreme Court, and to decide what cases those courts will hear.

Clause 10: Punishment for Piracy. To define and punish Piracies and Felonies committed on the high Seas, and Offences against the Law of Nations;

Congress has the authority to prohibit the commission of certain acts outside U.S. territory and to punish certain violations of international law.

Clause 11: Declaration of War. To declare War, grant Letters of Marque and Reprisal, and make Rules concerning Captures on Land and Water;

Only Congress can declare war, although the president, as commander in chief, can make war without Congress's formal declaration. Letters of marque and reprisal authorized private parties to capture and destroy enemy ships in wartime. Since the middle of the nineteenth century, international law has prohibited letters of marque and reprisal, and the United States has honored the ban.

Clause 12: The Army. To raise and support Armies, but no Appropriation of Money to that Use shall be for a longer Term than two Years;

Congress has the power to create an army; the money used to pay for it must be appropriated for no more than two-year intervals. This latter restriction gives ultimate control of the army to civilians.

Clause 13: Creation of a Navy. To provide and maintain a Navy;

This clause allows for the maintenance of a navy. In 1947, Congress created the U.S. Air Force.

Clause 14: Regulation of the Armed Forces. To make Rules for the Government and Regulation of the land and naval Forces;

Congress sets the rules for the military mainly by way of the Uniform Code of Military Justice, which was enacted in 1950 by Congress.

Clause 15: The Militia. To provide for calling forth the Militia to execute the Laws of the Union, suppress Insurrections and repel Invasions;

The militia is known today as the National Guard. Both Congress and the president have the authority to call the National Guard into federal service.

Clause 16: How the Militia Is Organized. To provide for organizing, arming, and disciplining the Militia, and for governing such Part of them as may be employed in the Service of the United States, reserving to the States respectively, the Appointment of the Officers, and the Authority of training the Militia according to the discipline prescribed by Congress;

This clause gives Congress the power to "federalize" state militia (National Guard). When called into such service, the National Guard is subject to the same rules that Congress has set forth for the regular armed services.

Clause 17: Creation of the District of Columbia. To exercise exclusive Legislation in all Cases whatsoever, over such District (not exceeding ten Miles square) as may, by Cession of particular States, and the Acceptance of Congress, become the Seat of the Government of the United States, and to exercise like Authority over all Places purchased by the Consent of the Legislature of the State in which the Same shall be, for the Erection of Forts, Magazines, Arsenals, dock-Yards, and other needful Buildings;—And

Congress established the District of Columbia as the national capital in 1791. Virginia and Maryland had granted land for the District, but Virginia's grant was returned because it was believed it would not be needed. Today, the District covers sixty-nine square miles.

Clause 18: The Elastic Clause. To make all Laws which shall be necessary and proper for carrying into Execution the foregoing Powers, and all other Powers vested by this Constitution in the Government of the United States, or in any Department or Officer thereof.

This clause—the necessary and proper clause, or the elastic clause—grants no specific powers, and thus it can be stretched to fit different circumstances. It has allowed Congress to adapt the government to changing needs and times.

Section 9. The Powers Denied to Congress

Clause 1: Question of Slavery. The Migration or Importation of such Persons as any of the States now existing shall think proper to admit, shall not be prohibited by the Congress prior to the Year one thousand eight hundred and eight, but a Tax or duty may be imposed on such Importation, not exceeding ten dollars for each Person.

"Persons" referred to slaves. Congress outlawed the slave trade in 1808.

Clause 2: Habeas Corpus. The privilege of the Writ of Habeas Corpus shall not be suspended, unless when in Cases of Rebellion or Invasion the public Safety may require it.

A writ of habeas corpus is a court order directing a sheriff or other public officer who is detaining another person to "produce the body" of the detainee so the court can assess the legality of the detention.

Clause 3: Special Bills. No Bill of Attainder or ex post facto Law shall be passed.

A bill of attainder is a law that inflicts punishment without a trial. An ex post facto law is a law that inflicts punishment for an act that was not illegal when it was committed.

Clause 4: Direct Taxes. [No Capitation, or other direct, Tax shall be laid, unless in Proportion to the Census or Enumeration herein before directed to be taken.][6]

A capitation is a tax on a person. A direct tax is a tax paid directly to the government, such as a property tax. This clause was intended to prevent Congress from levying a tax on slaves per person and thereby taxing slavery out of existence.

Clause 5: Export Taxes. No Tax or Duty shall be laid on Articles exported from any State.

Congress may not tax any goods sold from one state to another or from one state to a foreign country. (Congress does have the power to tax goods that are bought from other countries, however.)

Clause 6: Interstate Commerce. No Preference shall be given by any Regulation of Commerce or Revenue to the Ports of one State over those of another: nor shall Vessels bound to, or from, one State, be obliged to enter, clear, or pay Duties in another.

Congress may not treat different ports within the United States differently in terms of taxing and commerce powers. Congress may not give one state's port a legal advantage over the ports of another state.

Clause 7: Treasury Withdrawals. No Money shall be drawn from the Treasury, but in Consequence of Appropriations made by Law; and a regular Statement and Account of the Receipts and Expenditures of all public Money shall be published from time to time.

Federal funds can be spent only as Congress authorizes. This is a significant check on the president's power.

Clause 8: Titles of Nobility. No Title of Nobility shall be granted by the United States: And no Person holding any Office of Profit or Trust under them, shall, without the Consent of the Congress, accept of any present, Emolument, Office, or Title, of any kind whatever, from any King, Prince, or foreign State.

No person in the United States may hold a title of nobility, such as duke or duchess. This clause also discourages bribery of American officials by foreign governments.

Section 10. Those Powers Denied to the States

Clause 1: Treaties and Coinage. No State shall enter into any Treaty, Alliance, or Confederation; grant Letters of

---

6. Modified by the Sixteenth Amendment.

Marque and Reprisal; coin Money; emit Bills of Credit; make any Thing but gold and silver Coin a Tender in Payment of Debts; pass any Bill of Attainder, ex post facto Law, or Law impairing the Obligation of Contracts, or grant any Title of Nobility.

Prohibiting state laws "impairing the Obligation of Contracts" was intended to protect creditors. (Shays' Rebellion—an attempt to prevent courts from giving effect to creditors' legal actions against debtors—occurred only one year before the Constitution was written.)

Clause 2: Duties and Imposts. No State shall, without the Consent of the Congress, lay any Imports or Duties on Imports or Exports, except what may be absolutely necessary for executing its inspection Laws; and the net Produce of all Duties and Imposts, laid by any State on Imports or Exports, shall be for the Use of the Treasury of the United States; and all such Laws shall be subject to the Revision and Controul of the Congress.

Only Congress can tax imports. Further, the states cannot tax exports.

Clause 3: War. No State shall, without the Consent of Congress, lay any Duty of Tonnage, keep Troops, or Ships of War in time of Peace, enter into any Agreement or Compact with another State, or with a foreign Power or engage in War, unless actually invaded, or in such imminent Danger as will not admit of delay.

A duty of tonnage is a tax on ships according to their cargo capacity. No states may tax ships according to their cargo unless Congress agrees. Additionally, this clause forbids any state to keep troops or warships during peacetime or to make a compact with another state or foreign nation unless Congress so agrees. A state, in contrast, can maintain a militia, but its use has to be limited to disorders that occur within the state—unless, of course, the militia is called into federal service.

Article II. (Executive Branch)

Section 1. The Nature and Scope of Presidential Power

Clause 1: Four-Year Term. The executive Power shall be vested in a President of the United States of America. He shall hold his Office during the Term of four Years, and, together with the Vice President, chosen for the same Term, be elected, as follows.

The president has the power to carry out laws made by Congress, called the executive power. He or she serves in office for a four-year term after election. The Twenty-second Amendment limits the number of times a person may be elected president.

Clause 2: Choosing Electors from Each State. Each State shall appoint, in such Manner as the Legislature thereof may direct, a Number of Electors, equal to the whole Number of Senators and Representatives to which the State may be entitled in the Congress; but no Senator or Representative, or Person holding an Office of Trust

or Profit under the United States, shall be appointed an Elector.

The "Electors" are known more commonly as the "electoral college." The president is elected by electors—that is, representatives chosen by the people—rather than by the people directly.

Clause 3: The Former System of Elections. [The Electors shall meet in their respective States, and vote by Ballot for two Persons, of whom one at least shall not be an Inhabitant of the same State with themselves. And they shall make a List of all the Persons voted for, and of the Number of Votes for each; which List they shall sign and certify, and transmit sealed to the Seat of the Government of the United States, directed to the President of the Senate. The President of the Senate shall, in the Presence of the Senate and House of Representatives, open all the Certificates, and the Votes shall then be counted. The Person having the greatest Number of Votes shall be the President, if such Number be a Majority of the whole Number of Electors appointed; and if there be more than one who have such Majority, and have an equal Number of Votes, then the House of Representatives shall immediately chuse by Ballot one of them for President; and if no Person have a Majority, then from the five highest on the List the said House shall in like Manner chuse the President. But in chusing the President, the Votes shall be taken by States, the Representation from each State having one Vote; A quorum for this Purpose shall consist of a Member or Members from two thirds of the States, and a Majority of all the States shall be necessary to a Choice. In every Case, after the Choice of the President, the Person having the greater Number of Votes of the Electors shall be the Vice President. But if there should remain two or more who have equal Votes, the Senate shall chuse from them by Ballot the Vice President.][7]

The original method of selecting the president and vice president was replaced by the Twelfth Amendment. Apparently, the framers did not anticipate the rise of political parties and the development of primaries and conventions.

Clause 4: The Time of Elections. The Congress may determine the Time of chusing the Electors, and the Day on which they shall give their Votes; which Day shall be the same throughout the United States.

Congress set the Tuesday after the first Monday in November every fourth year as the date for choosing electors. The electors cast their votes on the Monday after the second Wednesday in December of that year.

Clause 5: Qualifications for President. No person except a natural born Citizen, or a Citizen of the United States, at the time of the Adoption of this Constitution, shall be eligible to the Office of President; neither shall any Person be eligible to that Office who shall not have attained to the Age of thirty five Years, and been fourteen Years a Resident within the United States.

---

7. Changed by the Twelfth Amendment.

The president must be a natural-born citizen, be at least thirty-five years of age when taking office, and have been a resident within the United States for at least fourteen years.

Clause 6: Succession of the Vice President. [In Case of the Removal of the President from Office, or of his Death, Resignation or Inability to discharge the Powers and Duties of the said Office, the same shall devolve on the Vice President, and the Congress may by Law provide for the Case of Removal, Death, Resignation or Inability, both of the President and Vice President, declaring what Officer shall then act as President, and such Officer shall act accordingly, until the Disability be removed, or a President shall be elected.][8]

This section provided for the method by which the vice president was to succeed to the presidency, but its wording is ambiguous. It was replaced by the Twenty-fifth Amendment.

Clause 7: The President's Salary. The President shall, at stated Times, receive for his Services, a Compensation, which shall neither be encreased nor diminished during the Period for which he shall have been elected, and he shall not receive within that Period any other Emolument from the United States, or any of them.

The president maintains the same salary during each four-year term. Moreover, she or he may not receive additional cash payments from the government. Originally set at $25,000 per year, the salary is currently $400,000 a year plus a $50,000 nontaxable expense account.

Clause 8: The Oath of Office. Before he enter on the Execution of his Office, he shall take the following Oath or Affirmation: "I do solemnly swear (or affirm) that I will faithfully execute the Office of President of the United States, and will to the best of my Ability, preserve, protect and defend the Constitution of the United States."

The president is "sworn in" prior to beginning the duties of the office. Currently, the taking of the oath of office occurs on January 20, following the November election. The ceremony is called the inauguration. The oath of office is administered by the chief justice of the United States Supreme Court.

Section 2. Powers of the President
Clause 1: Commander in Chief. The President shall be Commander in Chief of the Army and Navy of the United States, and of the Militia of the several States, when called into the actual Service of the United States; he may require the Opinion, in writing, of the principal Officer in each of the executive Departments, upon any Subject relating to the Duties of their respective Offices, and he shall have Power to grant Reprieves and Pardons for Offences against the United States, except in Cases of Impeachment.

The armed forces are placed under civilian control because the president is a civilian but still commander in chief of

the military. The president may ask for the help of the head of each of the executive departments (thereby creating the cabinet). The cabinet members are chosen by the president with the consent of the Senate, but they can be removed without Senate approval.

The president's clemency powers extend only to federal cases. In those cases, he or she may grant a full or conditional pardon, or reduce a prison term or fine.

Clause 2: Treaties and Appointment. He shall have Power, by and with the Advice and Consent of the Senate, to make Treaties, provided two thirds of the Senators present concur; and he shall nominate, and by and with the Advice and Consent of the Senate, shall appoint Ambassadors, other public Ministers and Consuls, Judges of the supreme Court, and all other Officers of the United States, whose Appointments are not herein otherwise provided for, and which shall be established by Law; but the Congress may by Law vest the Appointment of such inferior Officers, as they think proper, in the President alone, in the Courts of Law, or in the Heads of Departments.

Many of the major powers of the president are identified in this clause, including the power to make treaties with foreign governments (with the approval of the Senate by a two-thirds vote) and the power to appoint ambassadors, Supreme Court justices, and other government officials. Most such appointments require Senate approval.

Clause 3: Vacancies. The President shall have Power to fill up all Vacancies that may happen during the Recess of the Senate, by granting Commissions which shall expire at the end of their next Session.

The president has the power to appoint temporary officials to fill vacant federal offices without Senate approval if the Congress is not in session. Such appointments expire automatically at the end of Congress's next term.

Section 3. Duties of the President
He shall from time to time give to the Congress Information of the State of the Union, and recommend to their Consideration such Measures as he shall judge necessary and expedient; he may, on extraordinary Occasions, convene both Houses, or either of them, and in Case of Disagreement between them, with Respect to the Time of Adjournment, he may adjourn them to such Time as he shall think proper; he shall receive Ambassadors and other public Ministers; he shall take Care that the Laws be faithfully executed, and shall Commission all the Officers of the United States.

Annually, the president reports on the state of the union to Congress, recommends legislative measures, and proposes a federal budget. The State of the Union speech is a statement not only to Congress but also to the American people. After it is given, the president proposes a federal budget and presents an economic report. At any time, the president may send special messages to Congress while it is in session. The president has the power to call special sessions,

---

8. Modified by the Twenty-fifth Amendment.

to adjourn Congress when its two chambers do not agree on when to adjourn, to receive diplomatic representatives of other governments, and to ensure the proper execution of all federal laws. The president further has the ability to empower federal officers to hold their positions and to perform their duties.

Section 4. Impeachment

The President, Vice President and all civil Officers of the United States, shall be removed from Office on Impeachment for, and Conviction of, Treason, Bribery, or other high Crimes and Misdemeanors.

Treason denotes giving aid to the nation's enemies. The definition of high crimes and misdemeanors is usually given as serious abuses of political power. In either case, the president or vice president may be accused by the House (called an impeachment) and then removed from office if convicted by the Senate. (Note that impeachment does not mean removal but rather refers to an accusation of treason or high crimes and misdemeanors.)

Article III. (Judicial Branch)

Section 1. Judicial Powers, Courts, and Judges

The judicial Power of the United States, shall be vested in one supreme Court, and in such inferior Courts as the Congress may from time to time ordain and establish. The Judges, both of the supreme and inferior Courts, shall hold their Offices during good Behaviour, and shall, at stated Times, receive for their Services a Compensation, which shall not be diminished during their Continuance in Office.

The Supreme Court is vested with judicial power, as are the lower federal courts that Congress creates. Federal judges serve in their offices for life unless they are impeached and convicted by Congress. The payment of federal judges may not be reduced during their time in office.

Section 2. Jurisdiction

Clause 1: Cases under Federal Jurisdiction. The judicial Power shall extend to all Cases, in Law and Equity, arising under this Constitution, the Laws of the United States, and Treaties made, or which shall be made, under their Authority;—to all Cases affecting Ambassadors, other public Ministers and Consuls;—to all Cases of admiralty and maritime Jurisdiction;—to Controversies to which the United States shall be a Party;—to Controversies between two or more States; [—between a State and Citizens of another State;—][9] between Citizens of different States;—between Citizens of the same State claiming Lands under Grants of different States, [and between a State, or the Citizens thereof, and foreign States, Citizens or Subjects.][10]

The federal courts take on cases that concern the meaning of the U.S. Constitution, all federal laws, and treaties. They

also can take on cases involving citizens of different states and citizens of foreign nations.

Clause 2: Cases for the Supreme Court. In all Cases affecting Ambassadors, other public Ministers and Consuls, and those in which a State shall be a Party, the supreme Court shall have original Jurisdiction. In all the other Cases before mentioned, the supreme Court shall have appellate Jurisdiction, both as to Law and Fact, with such Exceptions, and under such Regulations as the Congress shall make.

In a limited number of situations, the Supreme Court acts as a trial court and has original jurisdiction. These cases involve a representative from another country or involve a state. In all other situations, the cases must first be tried in the lower courts and then can be appealed to the Supreme Court. Congress may, however, make exceptions. Today, the Supreme Court acts as a trial court of first instance on rare occasions.

Clause 3: The Conduct of Trials. The Trial of all Crimes, except in Cases of Impeachment, shall be by Jury; and such Trial shall be held in the State where the said Crimes shall have been committed; but when not committed within any State, the Trial shall be at such Place or Places as the Congress may by Law have directed.

Any person accused of a federal crime is granted the right to a trial by jury in a federal court in that state in which the crime was committed. Trials of impeachment are an exception.

Section 3. Treason

Clause 1: The Definition of Treason. Treason against the United States, shall consist only in levying War against them, or, in adhering to their Enemies, giving them Aid and Comfort. No Person shall be convicted of Treason unless on the Testimony of two Witnesses to the same overt Act, or on Confession in open Court.

Treason is the making of war against the United States or giving aid to its enemies.

Clause 2: Punishment. The Congress shall have Power to declare the Punishment of Treason, but no Attainder of Treason shall work Corruption of Blood, or Forfeiture except during the Life of the Person attainted.

Congress has provided that the punishment for treason ranges from a minimum of five years in prison and/or a $10,000 fine to a maximum of death. "No Attainder of Treason shall work Corruption of Blood" prohibits punishment of the traitor's heirs.

Article IV. (Relations among the States)

Section 1. Full Faith and Credit

Full Faith and Credit shall be given in each State to the public Acts, Records, and judicial Proceedings of every other State. And the Congress may by general Laws prescribe the Manner in which such Acts, Records and Proceedings shall be proved, and the Effect thereof.

---

9. Modified by the Eleventh Amendment.
10. Modified by the Eleventh Amendment.

All states are required to respect one another's laws, records, and lawful decisions. There are exceptions, however. A state does not have to enforce another state's criminal code. Nor does it have to recognize another state's grant of a divorce if the person obtaining the divorce did not establish legal residence in the state in which it was given.

Section 2. Treatment of Citizens

Clause 1: Privileges and Immunities. The Citizens of each State shall be entitled to all Privileges and Immunities of Citizens in the several States.

A citizen of a state has the same rights and privileges as the citizens of another state in which he or she happens to be.

Clause 2: Extradition. A Person charged in any State with Treason, Felony, or other Crime, who shall flee from Justice, and be found in another State, shall on Demand of the executive Authority of the State from which he fled, be delivered up, to be removed to the State having Jurisdiction of the Crime.

Any person accused of a crime who flees to another state must be returned to the state in which the crime occurred.

Clause 3: Fugitive Slaves. [No Person held to Service or Labour in one State, under the Laws thereof, escaping into another, shall, in Consequence of any Law or Regulation therein, be discharged from such Service or Labour, but shall be delivered up on Claim of the Party to whom such Service or Labour may be due.][11]

This clause was struck down by the Thirteenth Amendment, which abolished slavery in 1865.

Section 3. Admission of States

Clause 1: The Process. New States may be admitted by the Congress into this Union; but no new State shall be formed or erected within the Jurisdiction of any other State; nor any State be formed by the Junction of two or more States, or Parts of States, without the Consent of the Legislatures of the States concerned as well as of the Congress.

Only Congress has the power to admit new states to the union. No state may be created by taking territory from an existing state unless the state's legislature so consents.

Clause 2: Public Land. The Congress shall have Power to dispose of and make all needful Rules and Regulations respecting the Territory or other Property belonging to the United States; and nothing in this Constitution shall be so construed as to Prejudice any Claims of the United States, or of any particular State.

The federal government has the exclusive right to administer federal government public lands.

Section 4. Republican Form of Government

The United States shall guarantee to every State in this Union a Republican Form of Government, and shall protect each of them against Invasion; and on Application of the Legislature, or of the Executive (when the Legislature cannot be convened) against domestic Violence.

Each state is promised a republican form of government— that is, one in which the people elect their representatives. The federal government is bound to protect states against any attack by foreigners or during times of trouble within a state.

Article V. (Methods of Amendment)

The Congress, whenever two thirds of both Houses shall deem it necessary, shall propose Amendments to this Constitution, or on the Application of the Legislatures of two thirds of the several States, shall call a Convention for proposing Amendments, which, in either Case, shall be valid to all Intents and Purposes, as Part of this Constitution, when ratified by the Legislatures of three fourths of the several States, or by Conventions in three fourths thereof, as the one or the other Mode of Ratification may be proposed by the Congress; Provided that no Amendment which may be made prior to the Year One thousand eight hundred and eight shall in any Manner affect the first and fourth Clauses in the Ninth Section of the First Article; and that no State, without its Consent, shall be deprived of its equal Suffrage in the Senate.

Amendments may be proposed in either of two ways: a two-thirds vote of each chamber (Congress) or at the request of two-thirds of the states. Ratification of amendments may be carried out in two ways: by the legislatures of three-fourths of the states or by the voters in three-fourths of the states. No state may be denied equal representation in the Senate.

Article VI. (National Supremacy)

Clause 1: Existing Obligations. All Debts contracted and Engagements entered into, before the Adoption of this Constitution shall be as valid against the United States under this Constitution, as under the Confederation.

During the Revolutionary War and the years of the Confederation, Congress borrowed large sums. This clause pledged that the new federal government would assume those financial obligations.

Clause 2: Supreme Law of the Land. This Constitution, and the Laws of the United States which shall be made in Pursuance thereof; and all Treaties made, or which shall be made, under the Authority of the United States, shall be the supreme Law of the Land; and the Judges in every State shall be bound thereby, any Thing in the Constitution or Laws of any State to the Contrary notwithstanding.

This is typically called the supremacy clause; it declares that federal law takes precedence over all forms of state law. No government at the local or state level may make or enforce any law that conflicts with any provision of the Constitution, acts of Congress, treaties, or other rules and regulations issued by the president and his or her subordinates in the executive branch of the federal government.

---

11. Repealed by the Thirteenth Amendment.

Clause 3: Oath of Office. The Senators and Representatives before mentioned, and the Members of the several State Legislatures, and all executive and judicial Officers, both of the United States and of the several States, shall be bound by Oath or Affirmation, to support this Constitution; but no religious Test shall ever be required as a Qualification to any Office or public Trust under the United States.

Every federal and state official must take an oath of office promising to support the U.S. Constitution. Religion may not be used as a qualification to serve in any federal office.

Article VII. (Ratification)

The Ratification of the Conventions of nine States shall be sufficient for the Establishment of this Constitution between the States so ratifying the Same.

Nine states were required to ratify the Constitution. Delaware was the first and New Hampshire the ninth.

Done in Convention by the Unanimous Consent of the States present the Seventeenth Day of September in the Year of our Lord one thousand seven hundred and Eighty seven and of the Independence of the United States of America the Twelfth. In witness whereof we have hereunto subscribed our Names,

Attest William Jackson Secretary

DELAWARE	Geo. Read Gunning Bedford jun John Dickinson Richard Bassett Jaco. Broom
MARYLAND	James McHenry Dan of St. Thos. Jenifer Danl. Carroll
VIRGINIA	John Blair James Madison Jr.
NORTH CAROLINA	Wm. Blount Richd. Dobbs Spaight Hu. Williamson
SOUTH CAROLINA	J. Rutledge Charles Cotesworth Pinckney Charles Pinckney Pierce Butler
GEORGIA	William Few Abr. Baldwin

Go. WASHINGTON
Presid't. and deputy from Virginia

NEW HAMPSHIRE	John Langdon Nicholas Gilman
MASSACHUSETTS	Nathaniel Gorham Rufus King
CONNECTICUT	Wm. Saml. Johnson Roger Sherman
NEW YORK	Alexander Hamilton
NEW JERSEY	Wh. Livingston David Brearley Wm. Paterson Jona. Dayton
PENNSYLVANIA	B. Franklin Thomas Mifflin Robt. Morris Geo. Clymer Thos. FitzSimons Jared Ingersoll James Wilson Gouv. Morris

Articles in addition to, and amendment of, the Constitution of the United States of America, proposed by Congress and ratified by the Legislatures of the several states, pursuant to the Fifth Article of the original Constitution.

Amendments to the Constitution of the United States

(The Bill of Rights)[12]

Amendment I.
(Religion, Speech, Assembly, and Petition)

Congress shall make no law respecting an establishment of religion, or prohibiting the free exercise thereof; or abridging the freedom of speech, or of the press; or the right of the people peaceably to assemble, and to petition the Government for a redress of grievances.

Congress may not create an official church or enact laws limiting the freedom of religion, speech, the press, assembly, and petition. These guarantees, like the others in the Bill of Rights (the first ten amendments), are not absolute—each may be exercised only with regard to the rights of other persons.

Amendment II.
(Militia and the Right to Bear Arms)

A well regulated Militia, being necessary to the security of a free State, the right of the people to keep and bear Arms, shall not be infringed.

To protect itself, each state has the right to maintain a volunteer armed force. States and the federal government regulate the possession and use of firearms by individuals.

Amendment III.
(The Quartering of Soldiers)

No Soldier shall, in time of peace be quartered in any house, without the consent of the Owner, nor in time of war, but in a manner to be prescribed by law.

Before the Revolutionary War, it had been common British practice to quarter soldiers in colonists' homes. Military troops do not have the power to take over private houses during peacetime.

Amendment IV.
(Searches and Seizures)

The right of the people to be secure in their persons, houses, papers, and effects, against unreasonable searches and seizures, shall not be violated, and no Warrants shall

---

12. On September 25, 1789, Congress transmitted to the state legislatures twelve proposed amendments, two of which, having to do with congressional representation and congressional pay, were not adopted. The remaining ten amendments became the Bill of Rights. In 1992, the amendment concerning congressional pay was adopted as the Twenty-seventh Amendment.

issue, but upon probable cause, supported by Oath or affirmation, and particularly describing the place to be searched, and the persons or things to be seized.

Here the word warrant means "justification" and refers to a document issued by a magistrate or judge indicating the name, address, and possible offense committed. Anyone asking for the warrant, such as a police officer, must be able to convince the magistrate or judge that an offense probably has been committed.

Amendment V.
(Grand Juries, Self-Incrimination, Double Jeopardy, Due Process, and Eminent Domain)

No person shall be held to answer for a capital, or otherwise infamous crime, unless on a presentment or indictment of a Grand Jury, except in cases arising in the land or naval forces, or in the Militia, when in actual service in time of War or public danger; nor shall any person be subject for the same offence to be twice put in jeopardy of life or limb; nor shall be compelled in any criminal case to be a witness against himself, nor be deprived of life, liberty, or property, without due process of law; nor shall private property be taken for public use, without just compensation.

There are two types of juries. A grand jury considers physical evidence and the testimony of witnesses and decides whether there is sufficient reason to bring a case to trial. A petit jury hears the case at trial and decides it. "For the same offence to be twice put in jeopardy of life or limb" means to be tried twice for the same crime. A person may not be tried for the same crime twice or forced to give evidence against herself or himself. No person's right to life, liberty, or property may be taken away except by lawful means, called the due process of law. Private property taken for use in public purposes must be paid for by the government.

Amendment VI.
(Criminal Court Procedures)

In all criminal prosecutions, the accused shall enjoy the right to a speedy and public trial, by an impartial jury of the State and district wherein the crime shall have been committed, which district shall have been previously ascertained by law, and to be informed of the nature and cause of the accusation; to be confronted with the witnesses against him; to have compulsory process for obtaining witnesses in his favor, and to have the Assistance of Counsel for his defence.

Any person accused of a crime has the right to a fair and public trial by a jury in the state in which the crime took place. The charges against that person must be indicated. Any accused person has the right to a lawyer to defend him or her and to question those who testify against him or her, as well as the right to call people to speak in his or her favor at trial.

Amendment VII.
(Trial by Jury in Civil Cases)

In Suits at common law, where the value in controversy shall exceed twenty dollars, the right of trial by jury shall be preserved, and no fact tried by jury, shall be otherwise re-examined in any Court of the United States, than according to the rules of the common law.

A jury trial may be requested by either party in a dispute in any case involving more than $20. If both parties agree to a trial by a judge without a jury, the right to a jury trial may be put aside.

Amendment VIII.
(Bail, Cruel and Unusual Punishment)

Excessive bail shall not be required, nor excessive fines imposed, nor cruel and unusual punishments inflicted.

Bail is that amount of money that a person accused of a crime may be required to deposit with the court as a guarantee that she or he will appear in court when requested. The amount of bail required or the fine imposed as punishment for a crime must be reasonable compared with the seriousness of the crime involved. Any punishment judged to be too harsh or too severe for a crime shall be prohibited.

Amendment IX.
(The Rights Retained by the People)

The enumeration in the Constitution, of certain rights, shall not be construed to deny or disparage others retained by the people.

Many civil rights that are not explicitly enumerated in the Constitution are still held by the people.

Amendment X.
(Reserved Powers of the States)

The powers not delegated to the United States by the Constitution, nor prohibited by it to the States, are reserved to the States respectively, or to the people.

Those powers not delegated by the Constitution to the federal government or expressly denied to the states belong to the states and to the people. This amendment in essence allows the states to pass laws under their "police powers."

Amendment XI.
(Ratified on February 7, 1795— Suits against States)

The Judicial power of the United States shall not be construed to extend to any suit in law or equity, commenced or prosecuted against one of the United States by Citizens of another State, or by Citizens or Subjects of any Foreign State.

This amendment has been interpreted to mean that a state cannot be sued in federal court by one of its own citizens, by a citizen of another state, or by a foreign country.

Amendment XII.
(Ratified on June 15, 1804— Election of the President)

The Electors shall meet in their respective states, and vote by ballot for President and Vice-President, one of whom, at least, shall not be an inhabitant of the same State with themselves; they shall name in their ballots the person voted for as President, and in distinct ballots the person voted for as Vice-President, and they shall make distinct lists of all persons voted for as President, and of all persons voted for as Vice-President, and of the number of votes for each, which lists they shall sign and certify, and transmit sealed to the seat of the government of the United States, directed to the President of the Senate;—The President of the Senate shall, in the presence of the Senate and House of Representatives, open all the certificates and the votes shall then be counted;— The person having the greatest number of votes for President, shall be the President, if such number be a majority of the whole number of Electors appointed; and if no person have such majority, then from the persons having the highest numbers not exceeding three on the list of those voted for as President, the House of Representatives shall choose immediately, by ballot, the President. But in choosing the President, the votes shall be taken by States, the representation from each State having one vote; a quorum for this purpose shall consist of a member or members from two-thirds of the States, and a majority of all States shall be necessary to a choice. [And if the House of Representatives shall not choose a President whenever the right of choice shall devolve upon them, before the fourth day of March next following, then the Vice-President shall act as President, as in the case of the death or other constitutional disability of the President.][13]—The person having the greatest number of votes as Vice-President, shall be the Vice-President, if such number be a majority of the whole number of Electors appointed, and if no person have a majority, then from the two highest numbers on the list, the Senate shall choose the Vice-President; a quorum for the purpose shall consist of two-thirds of the whole number of Senators, and a majority of the whole number shall be necessary to a choice. But no person constitutionally ineligible to the office of President shall be eligible to that of Vice-President of the United States.

The original procedure set out for the election of president and vice president in Article II, Section 1, resulted in a tie in 1800 between Thomas Jefferson and Aaron Burr. It was not until the next year that the House of Representatives chose Jefferson to be president. This amendment changed the procedure by providing for separate ballots for president and vice president.

---

13. Changed by the Twentieth Amendment.

Amendment XIII.
(Ratified on December 6, 1865— Prohibition of Slavery)

Section 1.

Neither slavery nor involuntary servitude, except as a punishment for crime whereof the party shall have been duly convicted, shall exist within the United States, or any place subject to their jurisdiction.

Some slaves had been freed during the Civil War. This amendment freed the others and abolished slavery.

Section 2.

Congress shall have power to enforce this article by appropriate legislation.

Amendment XIV.
(Ratified on July 9, 1868— Citizenship, Due Process, and Equal Protection of the Laws)

Section 1.

All persons born or naturalized in the United States, and subject to the jurisdiction thereof, are citizens of the United States and of the State wherein they reside. No State shall make or enforce any law which shall abridge the privileges or immunities of citizens of the United States; nor shall any State deprive any person of life, liberty, or property, without due process of law; nor deny to any person within its jurisdiction the equal protection of the laws.

Under this provision, states cannot make or enforce laws that take away rights given to all citizens by the federal government. States cannot act unfairly or arbitrarily toward, or discriminate against, any person.

Section 2.

Representatives shall be apportioned among the several States according to their respective numbers, counting the whole number of persons in each State, excluding Indians not taxed. But when the right to vote at any election for the choice of electors for President and Vice President of the United States, Representatives in Congress, the Executive and Judicial officers of a State, or the members of the Legislature thereof, is denied to any of the male inhabitants of such State, being [twenty-one][14] years of age, and citizens of the United States, or in any way abridged, except for participation in rebellion, or other crime, the basis of representation therein shall be reduced in the proportion which the number of such male citizens shall bear to the whole number of male citizens twenty-one years of age in such State.

Section 3.

No person shall be a Senator or Representative in Congress, or elector of President and Vice President, or hold any office, civil or military, under the United States, or under any State, who having previously taken an oath, as a member of Congress, or as an officer of the United States, or as a member of any State legislature, or as an executive or judicial officer of any State, to support the Constitution of the United States, shall have engaged in insurrection or rebellion against the same, or given aid or comfort to the enemies thereof. But Congress may by a vote of two-thirds of each House, remove such disability.

This provision forbade former state or federal government officials who had acted in support of the Confederacy during the Civil War to hold office again. It limited the president's power to pardon those persons. Congress removed this "disability" in 1898.

Section 4.

The validity of the public debt of the United States, authorized by law, including debts incurred for payment of pensions and bounties for services in suppressing insurrection or rebellion, shall not be questioned. But neither the United States nor any State shall assume or pay any debt or obligation incurred in aid of insurrection or rebellion against the United States, or any claim for the loss or emancipation of any slave, but all such debts, obligations and claims shall be held illegal and void.

Section 5.

The Congress shall have power to enforce, by appropriate legislation, the provisions of this article.

Amendment XV.
(Ratified on February 3, 1870— The Right to Vote)

Section 1.

The right of citizens of the United States to vote shall not be denied or abridged by the United States or by any State on account of race, color, or previous condition of servitude.

No citizen can be refused the right to vote simply because of race or color or because that person was once a slave.

Section 2.

The Congress shall have power to enforce this article by appropriate legislation.

Amendment XVI.
(Ratified on February 3, 1913— Income Taxes)

The Congress shall have power to lay and collect taxes on incomes, from whatever source derived, without apportionment among the several States, and without regard to any census or enumeration.

This amendment allows Congress to tax income without sharing the revenue so obtained with the states according to their population.

---

14. Changed by the Twenty-sixth Amendment.

Amendment XVII.
(Ratified on April 8, 1913—
The Popular Election of Senators)

Section 1.

The Senate of the United States shall be composed of two Senators from each State, elected by the people thereof, for six years; and each Senator shall have one vote. The electors in each State shall have the qualifications requisite for electors of the most numerous branch of the State legislatures.

Section 2.

When vacancies happen in the representation of any State in the Senate, the executive authority of such State shall issue writs of election to fill such vacancies: Provided, That the legislature of any State may empower the executive thereof to make temporary appointments until the people fill the vacancies by election as the legislature may direct.

Section 3.

This amendment shall not be so construed as to affect the election or term of any Senator chosen before it becomes valid as part of the Constitution.

This amendment modified portions of Article I, Section 3, that related to election of senators. Senators are now elected by the voters in each state directly. When a vacancy occurs, either the state may fill the vacancy by a special election, or the governor of the state involved may appoint someone to fill the seat until the next election.

Amendment XVIII.
(Ratified on January 16, 1919—
Prohibition)

Section 1.

After one year from the ratification of this article the manufacture, sale, or transportation of intoxicating liquors within, the importation thereof into, or the exportation thereof from the United States and all territory subject to the jurisdiction thereof for beverage purposes is hereby prohibited.

Section 2.

The Congress and the several States shall have concurrent power to enforce this article by appropriate legislation.

Section 3.

This article shall be inoperative unless it shall have been ratified as an amendment to the Constitution by the legislatures of the several States, as provided in the Constitution, within seven years from the date of the submission hereof to the States by the Congress.[15]

This amendment made it illegal to manufacture, sell, and transport alcoholic beverages in the United States.

---

15. The Eighteenth Amendment was repealed by the Twenty-first Amendment.

Amendment XIX.
(Ratified on August 18, 1920—
Women's Right to Vote)

Section 1.

The right of citizens of the United States to vote shall not be denied or abridged by the United States or by any State on account of sex.

Section 2.

Congress shall have power to enforce this article by appropriate legislation.

Women were given the right to vote by this amendment, and Congress was given the power to enforce this right.

Amendment XX.
(Ratified on January 23, 1933—
The Lame Duck Amendment)

Section 1.

The terms of the President and Vice President shall end at noon on the 20th day of January, and the terms of Senators and Representatives at noon on the 3d day of January, of the years in which such terms would have ended if this article had not been ratified; and the terms of their successors shall then begin.

This amendment modified Article I, Section 4, Clause 2, and other provisions relating to the president in the Twelfth Amendment. The taking of the oath of office was moved from March 4 to January 20.

Section 2.

The Congress shall assemble at least once in every year, and such meeting shall begin at noon on the 3d day of January, unless they shall by law appoint a different day.

Congress changed the beginning of its term to January 3. The reason the Twentieth Amendment is called the Lame Duck Amendment is because it shortens the time between when a member of Congress is defeated for reelection and when he or she leaves office.

Section 3.

If, at the time fixed for the beginning of the term of the President, the President elect shall have died, the Vice President elect shall become President. If a President shall not have been chosen before the time fixed for the beginning of his term, or if the President elect shall have failed to qualify, then the Vice President elect shall act as President until a President shall have qualified; and the Congress may by law provide for the case wherein neither a President elect nor a Vice President elect shall have qualified, declaring who shall then act as President, or the manner in which one who is to act shall be selected, and such person shall act accordingly until a President or Vice President shall have qualified.

This part of the amendment deals with problem areas left ambiguous by Article II and the Twelfth Amendment. If the president dies before January 20 or fails to qualify for office, the presidency is to be filled as described in this section.

Section 4.

The Congress may by law provide for the case of the death of any of the persons from whom the House of Representatives may choose a President whenever the rights of choice shall have devolved upon them, and for the case of the death of any of the persons from whom the Senate may choose a Vice President whenever the right of choice shall have devolved upon them.

Congress has never created legislation pursuant to this section.

Section 5.

Sections 1 and 2 shall take effect on the 15th day of October following the ratification of this article.

Section 6.

This article shall be inoperative unless it shall have been ratified as an amendment to the Constitution by the legislatures of three-fourths of the several States within seven years from the date of its submission.

Amendment XXI.
(Ratified on December 5, 1933—
The Repeal of Prohibition)

Section 1.

The eighteenth article of amendment to the Constitution of the United States is hereby repealed.

Section 2.

The transportation or importation into any State, Territory, or possession of the United States for delivery or use therein of intoxicating liquors, in violation of the laws thereof, is hereby prohibited.

Section 3.

This article shall be inoperative unless it shall have been ratified as an amendment to the Constitution by conventions in the several States, as provided in the Constitution, within seven years from the date of the submission hereof to the States by the Congress.

The amendment repealed the Eighteenth Amendment but did not make alcoholic beverages legal everywhere. Rather, they remained illegal in any state that so designated them. Many such "dry" states existed for a number of years after 1933. Today, there are still "dry" counties within the United States, in which the sale of alcoholic beverages is illegal.

Amendment XXII.
(Ratified on February 27, 1951—
Limitation of Presidential Terms)

Section 1.

No person shall be elected to the office of the President more than twice, and no person who has held the office of President, or acted as President, for more than two years of a term to which some other person was elected President shall be elected to the office of President more than once. But this Article shall not apply to any person

holding the office of President when this Article was proposed by the Congress, and shall not prevent any person who may be holding the office of President, or acting as President, during the term within which this Article becomes operative from holding the office of President or acting as President during the remainder of such term.

Section 2.

This article shall be inoperative unless it shall have been ratified as an amendment to the Constitution by the legislatures of three-fourths of the several States within seven years from the date of its submission to the States by the Congress.

No president may serve more than two elected terms. If, however, a president has succeeded to the office after the halfway point of a term in which another president was originally elected, then that president may serve for more than eight years, but not to exceed ten years.

Amendment XXIII.
(Ratified on March 29, 1961—
Presidential Electors for
the District of Columbia)

Section 1.

The District constituting the seat of Government of the United States shall appoint in such manner as the Congress may direct:

A number of electors of President and Vice President equal to the whole number of Senators and Representatives in Congress to which the District would be entitled if it were a State, but in no event more than the least populous State; they shall be in addition to those appointed by the States, but they shall be considered, for the purposes of the election of President and Vice President, to be electors appointed by a State; and they shall meet in the District and perform such duties as provided by the twelfth article of amendment.

Section 2.

The Congress shall have power to enforce this article by appropriate legislation.

Citizens living in the District of Columbia have the right to vote in elections for president and vice president. The District of Columbia has three presidential electors, whereas before this amendment it had none.

Amendment XXIV.
(Ratified on January 23, 1964—
The Anti–Poll Tax Amendment)

Section 1.

The right of citizens of the United States to vote in any primary or other election for President or Vice President, for electors for President or Vice President, or for Senator or Representative in Congress, shall not be denied or abridged by the United States, or any State by reason of failure to pay any poll tax or other tax.

Section 2.

The Congress shall have power to enforce this article by appropriate legislation.

No government shall require a person to pay a poll tax to vote in any federal election.

Amendment XXV.
(Ratified on February 10, 1967—
Presidential Disability and
Vice Presidential Vacancies)

Section 1.

In case of the removal of the President from office or of his death or resignation, the Vice President shall become President.

Whenever a president dies or resigns from office, the vice president becomes president.

Section 2.

Whenever there is a vacancy in the office of the Vice President, the President shall nominate a Vice President who shall take office upon confirmation by a majority vote of both Houses of Congress.

Whenever the office of the vice presidency becomes vacant, the president may appoint someone to fill this office, provided Congress consents.

Section 3.

Whenever the President transmits to the President pro tempore of the Senate and the Speaker of the House of Representatives his written declaration that he is unable to discharge the powers and duties of his office, and until he transmits to them a written declaration to the contrary, such powers and duties shall be discharged by the Vice President as Acting President.

Whenever the president believes she or he is unable to carry out the duties of the office, she or he shall so indicate to Congress in writing. The vice president then acts as president until the president declares that she or he is again able to carry out the duties of the office.

Section 4.

Whenever the Vice President and a majority of either the principal officers of the executive departments or of such other body as Congress may by law provide, transmit to the President pro tempore of the Senate and the Speaker of the House of Representatives their written declaration that the President is unable to discharge the powers and duties of his office, the Vice President shall immediately assume the powers and duties of the office as Acting President.

Thereafter, when the President transmits to the President pro tempore of the Senate and the Speaker of the House of Representatives his written declaration that no inability exists, he shall resume the powers and duties of his office unless the Vice President and a majority of either the principal officers of the executive department or of such other body as Congress may by law provide, transmit within four days to the President pro tempore of the Senate and the Speaker of the House of Representatives their written declaration that the President is unable to discharge the powers and duties of his office. Thereupon Congress shall decide the issue, assembling within forty-eight hours for that purpose if not in session. If the Congress, within twenty-one days after receipt of the latter written declaration, or, if Congress is not in session, within twenty-one days after Congress is required to assemble, determines by two-thirds vote of both Houses that the President is unable to discharge the powers and duties of his office, the Vice President shall continue to discharge the same as Acting President; otherwise, the President shall resume the powers and duties of his office.

Whenever the vice president and a majority of the members of the cabinet believe that the president cannot carry out her or his duties, they shall so indicate in writing to Congress. The vice president shall then act as president. When the president believes that she or he is able to carry out her or his duties again, she or he shall so indicate to the Congress. However, if the vice president and a majority of the cabinet do not agree, Congress must decide by a two-thirds vote within three weeks who shall act as president.

Amendment XXVI.
(Ratified on July 1, 1971—
Voting Rights for Eighteen-Year-Olds)

Section 1.

The right of citizens of the United States, who are eighteen years of age or older, to vote shall not be denied or abridged by the United States or by any State on account of age.

No one eighteen years of age or older can be denied the right to vote in federal or state elections by virtue of age.

Section 2.

The Congress shall have power to enforce this article by appropriate legislation.

Amendment XXVII.
(Ratified on May 7, 1992—
Congressional Pay)

No law, varying the compensation for the services of the Senators and Representatives, shall take effect, until an election of representatives shall have intervened.

This amendment allows the voters to have some control over increases in salaries for congressional members. Originally submitted to the states for ratification in 1789, it was not ratified until 203 years later, in 1992.

Appendix C
Federalist Papers No. 10 and No. 51

In 1787, after the newly drafted U.S. Constitution was submitted to the thirteen states for ratification, a major political debate ensued between the Federalists (who favored ratification) and the Anti-Federalists (who opposed ratification). Anti-Federalists in New York were particularly critical of the Constitution, and in response to their objections, Federalists Alexander Hamilton, James Madison, and John Jay wrote a series of eighty-five essays in defense of the Constitution. The essays were published in New York newspapers and reprinted in other newspapers throughout the country.

For students of American government, the essays, collectively known as the Federalist Papers, are particularly important because they provide a glimpse of the founders' political philosophy and intentions in designing the Constitution—and, consequently, in shaping the American philosophy of government.

We have included in this appendix two of these essays: Federalist Papers No. 10 and No. 51. Each essay has been annotated by the authors to indicate its importance in American political thought and to clarify the meaning of particular passages.

Federalist Paper No. 10

Federalist Paper No. 10, penned by James Madison, has often been singled out as a key document in American political thought. In this essay, Madison attacks the Anti-Federalists' fear that a republican form of government will inevitably give rise to "factions"—small political parties or groups united by a common interest—that will control the government. Factions will be harmful to the country because they will implement policies beneficial to their own interests but adverse to other people's rights and to the public good. In this essay, Madison attempts to lay to rest this fear by explaining how, in a large republic such as the United States, there will be so many different factions, held together by regional or local interests, that no single one of them will dominate national politics.

Madison opens his essay with a paragraph discussing how important it is to devise a plan of government that can control the "instability, injustice, and confusion" brought about by factions.

Among the numerous advantages promised by a well-constructed Union, none deserves to be more accurately developed than its tendency to break and control the violence of faction. The friend of popular governments never finds himself so much alarmed for their character and fate as when he contemplates their propensity to this dangerous vice. He will not fail, therefore, to set a due value on any plan which, without violating the principles to which he is attached, provides a proper cure for it. The instability, injustice, and confusion introduced into the public councils have, in truth, been the mortal diseases under which popular governments have everywhere perished, as they continue to be the favorite and fruitful topics from which the adversaries to liberty derive their most specious declamations. The valuable improvements made by the American constitutions on the popular models, both ancient and modern, cannot certainly be too much admired; but it would be an unwarrantable partiality to contend that they have as effectually obviated the danger on this side, as was wished and expected. Complaints are everywhere heard from our most considerate and virtuous citizens, equally the friends of public and private faith and of public and personal liberty, that our governments are too unstable, that the public good is disregarded in the conflicts of rival parties, and that measures are too often decided, not according to the rules of justice and the rights of the minor party, but by the superior force of an interested and overbearing majority. However anxiously we may wish that these complaints had no foundation, the evidence of known facts will not permit us to deny that they are in some degree true. It will be found, indeed, on a candid review of our situation, that some of the distresses under which we labor have been erroneously charged on the operation of our governments; but it will be found, at the same time, that other causes will not alone account for many of our heaviest misfortunes; and, particularly, for that prevailing and increasing distrust of public engagements and alarm for private rights which are echoed from one end of the continent to the other. These must be chiefly, if not wholly, effects of the unsteadiness and injustice with which a factious spirit has tainted our public administration.

Madison now defines what he means by the term faction.

By a faction I understand a number of citizens, whether amounting to a majority or minority of the whole, who are united and actuated by some common

363

impulse of passion, or of interest, adverse to the rights of other citizens, or the permanent and aggregate interests of the community.

Madison next contends that there are two methods by which the "mischiefs of faction" can be cured: by removing the causes of faction or by controlling their effects. In the following paragraphs, Madison explains how liberty itself nourishes factions. Therefore, to abolish factions would involve abolishing liberty—a cure "worse than the disease."

There are two methods of curing the mischiefs of faction: the one, by removing its causes; the other, by controlling its effects.

There are again two methods of removing the causes of faction: the one, by destroying the liberty which is essential to its existence; the other, by giving to every citizen the same opinions, the same passions, and the same interests.

It could never be more truly said than of the first remedy that it was worse than the disease. Liberty is to faction what air is to fire, an aliment without which it instantly expires. But it could not be a less folly to abolish liberty, which is essential to political life, because it nourishes faction than it would be to wish the annihilation of air, which is essential to animal life, because it imparts to fire its destructive agency.

The second expedient is as impracticable as the first would be unwise. As long as the reason of man continues fallible, and he is at liberty to exercise it, different opinions will be formed. As long as the connection subsists between his reason and his self-love, his opinions and his passions will have a reciprocal influence on each other; and the former will be objects to which the latter will attach themselves. The diversity in the faculties of men, from which the rights of property originate, is not less an insuperable obstacle to a uniformity of interests. The protection of these faculties is the first object of government. From the protection of different and unequal faculties of acquiring property, the possession of different degrees and kinds of property immediately results; and from the influence of these on the sentiments and views of the respective proprietors ensues a division of the society into different interests and parties.

The latent causes of faction are thus sown in the nature of man; and we see them everywhere brought into different degrees of activity, according to the different circumstances of civil society. A zeal for different opinions concerning religion, concerning government, and many other points, as well of speculation as of practice; an attachment to different leaders ambitiously contending for pre-eminence and power; or to persons of other descriptions whose fortunes have been interesting to the human passions, have, in turn, divided mankind into parties, inflamed them with mutual animosity, and rendered them much more disposed to vex and oppress each other than to co-operate for their common good. So strong is this propensity of mankind to fall into mutual animosities that where no substantial occasion presents

itself the most frivolous and fanciful distinctions have been sufficient to kindle their unfriendly passions and excite their most violent conflicts. But the most common and durable source of factions has been the various and unequal distribution of property. Those who hold and those who are without property have ever formed distinct interests in society. Those who are creditors, and those who are debtors, fall under a like discrimination. A landed interest, a manufacturing interest, a mercantile interest, a moneyed interest, with many lesser interests, grow up of necessity in civilized nations, and divide them into different classes, actuated by different sentiments and views. The regulation of these various and interfering interests forms the principal task of modern legislation and involves the spirit of party and faction in the necessary and ordinary operations of government.

No man is allowed to be a judge in his own cause, because his interest would certainly bias his judgment, and, not improbably, corrupt his integrity. With equal, nay with greater reason, a body of men are unfit to be both judges and parties at the same time; yet what are many of the most important acts of legislation but so many judicial determinations, not indeed concerning the rights of single persons, but concerning the rights of large bodies of citizens? And what are the different classes of legislators but advocates and parties to the causes which they determine? Is a law proposed concerning private debts? It is a question to which the creditors are parties on one side and the debtors on the other. Justice ought to hold the balance between them. Yet the parties are, and must be, themselves the judges; and the most numerous party, or in other words, the most powerful faction must be expected to prevail. Shall domestic manufacturers be encouraged, and in what degree, by restrictions on foreign manufacturers? [These] are questions which would be differently decided by the landed and the manufacturing classes, and probably by neither with a sole regard to justice and the public good. The apportionment of taxes on the various descriptions of property is an act which seems to require the most exact impartiality; yet there is, perhaps, no legislative act in which greater opportunity and temptation are given to a predominant party to trample on the rules of justice. Every shilling with which they overburden the inferior number is a shilling saved to their own pockets.

It is in vain to say that enlightened statesmen will be able to adjust these clashing interests and render them all subservient to the public good. Enlightened statesmen will not always be at the helm. Nor, in many cases, can such an adjustment be made at all without taking into view indirect and remote considerations, which will rarely prevail over the immediate interest which one party may find in disregarding the rights of another or the good of the whole.

The inference to which we are brought is that the causes of faction cannot be removed and that relief is only to be sought in the means of controlling its *effects*.

Having concluded that "the causes of faction cannot be removed," Madison now looks in some detail at the other method by which factions can be cured—by controlling their effects. This is the heart of his essay. He begins by positing a significant question: How can you have self-government without risking the possibility that a ruling faction, particularly a majority faction, might tyrannize over the rights of others?

If a faction consists of less than a majority, relief is supplied by the republican principle, which enables the majority to defeat its sinister views by regular vote. It may clog the administration, it may convulse the society; but it will be unable to execute and mask its violence under the forms of the Constitution. When a majority is included in a faction, the form of popular government, on the other hand, enables it to sacrifice to its ruling passion or interest both the public good and the rights of other citizens. To secure the public good and private rights against the danger of such a faction, and at the same time to preserve the spirit and the form of popular government, is then the great object to which our inquiries are directed. Let me add that it is the great desideratum by which alone this form of government can be rescued from the opprobrium under which it has so long labored and be recommended to the esteem and adoption of mankind.

Madison now sets forth the idea that one way to control the effects of factions is to ensure that the majority is rendered incapable of acting in concert in order to "carry into effect schemes of oppression." He goes on to state that in a democracy, in which all citizens participate personally in government decision making, there is no way to prevent the majority from communicating with one another and, as a result, acting in concert.

By what means is this object attainable? Evidently by one of two only. Either the existence of the same passion or interest in a majority at the same time must be prevented, or the majority, having such coexistent passion or interest, must be rendered, by their number and local situation, unable to concert and carry into effect schemes of oppression. If the impulse and the opportunity be suffered to coincide, we well know that neither moral nor religious motives can be relied on as an adequate control. They are not found to be such on the injustice and violence of individuals, and lose their efficacy in proportion to the number combined together, that is, in proportion as their efficacy becomes needful.

From this view of the subject it may be concluded that a pure democracy, by which I mean a society consisting of a small number of citizens, who assemble and administer the government in person, can admit of no cure for the mischiefs of faction. A common passion or interest will, in almost every case, be felt by a majority of the whole; a communication and concert results from the form of government itself; and there is nothing to check the inducements to sacrifice the weaker party or an obnoxious individual. Hence it is that such democracies have

ever been spectacles of turbulence and contention; have ever been found incompatible with personal security or the rights of property; and have in general been as short in their lives as they have been violent in their deaths. Theoretic politicians, who have patronized this species of government, have erroneously supposed that by reducing mankind to a perfect equality in their political rights, they would at the same time be perfectly equalized and assimilated in their possessions, their opinions, and their passions.

Madison now moves on to discuss the benefits of a republic with respect to controlling the effects of factions. He begins by defining a republic and then pointing out the "two great points of difference" between a republic and a democracy: a republic is governed by a small body of elected representatives, not by the people directly; and a republic can extend over a much larger territory and embrace more citizens than a democracy can.

A republic, by which I mean a government in which the scheme of representation takes place, opens a different prospect and promises the cure for which we are seeking. Let us examine the points in which it varies from pure democracy, and we shall comprehend both the nature of the cure and the efficacy which it must derive from the Union.

The two great points of difference between a democracy and a republic are: first, the delegation of the government, in the latter, to a small number of citizens elected by the rest; secondly, the greater number of citizens and greater sphere of country over which the latter may be extended.

In the following four paragraphs, Madison explains how in a republic, particularly a large republic, the delegation of authority to elected representatives will increase the likelihood that those who govern will be "fit" for their positions and that a proper balance will be achieved between local (factional) interests and national interests. Note how he stresses that the new federal Constitution, by dividing powers between state governments and the national government, provides a "happy combination in this respect."

The effect of the first difference is, on the one hand, to refine and enlarge the public views by passing them through the medium of a chosen body of citizens, whose wisdom may best discern the true interest of their country and whose patriotism and love of justice will be least likely to sacrifice it to temporary or partial considerations. Under such a regulation it may well happen that the public voice, pronounced by the representatives of the people, will be more consonant to the public good than if pronounced by the people themselves, convened for the purpose. On the other hand, the effect may be inverted. Men of factious tempers, of local prejudices, or of sinister designs, may, by intrigue, by corruption, or by other means, first obtain the suffrages, and then betray the interests of the people. The question resulting is, whether small or extensive republics are most favorable to the election of proper guardians of the public weal; and it is clearly decided in favor of the latter by two obvious considerations.

In the first place it is to be remarked that however small the republic may be the representatives must be raised to a certain number in order to guard against the cabals of a few; and that however large it may be they must be limited to a certain number in order to guard against the confusion of a multitude. Hence, the number of representatives in the two cases not being in proportion to that of the constituents, and being proportionally greatest in the small republic, it follows that if the proportion of fit characters be not less in the large than in the small republic, the former will present a greater option, and consequently a greater probability of a fit choice.

In the next place, as each representative will be chosen by a greater number of citizens in the large than in the small republic, it will be more difficult for unworthy candidates to practice with success the vicious arts by which elections are too often carried; and the suffrages of the people being more free, will be more likely to center on men who possess the most attractive merit and the most diffusive and established characters.

It must be confessed that in this, as in most other cases, there is a mean, on both sides of which inconveniencies will be found to lie. By enlarging too much the number of electors, you render the representative too little acquainted with all their local circumstances and lesser interests; as by reducing it too much, you render him unduly attached to these, and too little fit to comprehend and pursue great and national objects. The federal Constitution forms a happy combination in this respect; the great and aggregate interests being referred to the national, the local and particular to the State legislatures.

Madison now looks more closely at the other difference between a republic and a democracy—namely, that a republic can encompass a larger territory and more citizens than a democracy can. In the remaining paragraphs of his essay, Madison concludes that in a large republic, it will be difficult for factions to act in concert. Although a factious group—religious, political, economic, or otherwise—may control a local or regional government, it will have little chance of gathering a national following. This is because in a large republic, there will be numerous factions whose work will offset the work of any one particular faction ("sect"). As Madison phrases it, these numerous factions will "secure the national councils against any danger from that source."

The other point of difference is the greater number of citizens and extent of territory which may be brought within the compass of republican than of democratic government; and it is this circumstance principally which renders factious combinations less to be dreaded in the former than in the latter. The smaller the society, the fewer probably will be the distinct parties and interests composing it; the fewer the distinct parties and interests, the more frequently will a majority be found of the same party; and the smaller the number of individuals composing a majority, and the smaller the compass within which they are placed, the more easily will they concert and execute their plans of oppression. Extend the sphere and you take in a greater variety of parties and interests; you make it less probable that a majority of the whole will have a common motive to invade the rights of other citizens; or if such a common motive exists, it will be more difficult for all who feel it to discover their own strength and to act in unison with each other. Besides other impediments, it may be remarked that, where there is a consciousness of unjust or dishonorable purposes, communication is always checked by distrust in proportion to the number whose concurrence is necessary.

Hence, it clearly appears that the same advantage which a republic has over a democracy in controlling the effects of faction is enjoyed by a large over a small republic—is enjoyed by the Union over the States composing it. Does this advantage consist in the substitution of representatives whose enlightened views and virtuous sentiments render them superior to local prejudices and to schemes of injustice? It will not be denied that the representation of the Union will be most likely to possess these requisite endowments. Does it consist in the greater security afforded by a greater variety of parties, against the event of any one party being able to outnumber and oppress the rest? In an equal degree does the increased variety of parties comprised within the Union increase this security. Does it, in fine, consist in the greater obstacles opposed to the concert and accomplishment of the secret wishes of an unjust and interested majority? Here again the extent of the Union gives it the most palpable advantage.

The influence of factious leaders may kindle a flame within their particular States but will be unable to spread a general conflagration through the other States. A religious sect may degenerate into a political faction in a part of the Confederacy; but the variety of sects dispersed over the entire face of it must secure the national councils against any danger from that source. A rage for paper money, for an abolition of debts, for an equal division of property, or for any other improper or wicked project, will be less apt to pervade the whole body of the Union than a particular member of it, in the same proportion as such a malady is more likely to taint a particular county or district than an entire State.

In the extent and proper structure of the Union, therefore, we behold a republican remedy for the diseases most incident to republican government. And according to the degree of pleasure and pride we feel in being republicans ought to be our zeal in cherishing the spirit and supporting the character of federalists.

Publius
(James Madison)

Federalist Paper No. 51

Federalist Paper *No. 51, also authored by James Madison, is another classic in American political theory. Although the Federalists wanted a strong national government, they had not abandoned the traditional American view, particularly notable during the revolutionary era, that those holding powerful government positions could not be trusted to put national interests and the common good above their own personal interests. In this essay, Madison explains why the separation of the national government's powers into three branches—executive, legislative, and judicial—and a federal structure of government offer the best protection against tyranny.*

To what expedient, then, shall we finally resort, for maintaining in practice the necessary partition of power among the several departments as laid down in the Constitution? The only answer that can be given is that as all these exterior provisions are found to be inadequate the defect must be supplied, by so contriving the interior structure of the government as that its several constituent parts may, by their mutual relations, be the means of keeping each other in their proper places. Without presuming to undertake a full development of this important idea I will hazard a few general observations which may perhaps place it in a clearer light, and enable us to form a more correct judgment of the principles and structure of the government planned by the convention.

In the next two paragraphs, Madison stresses that for the powers of the different branches (departments) of government to be truly separated, the personnel in one branch should not be dependent on another branch for their appointment or for the "emoluments" (compensation) attached to their offices.

In order to lay a due foundation for that separate and distinct exercise of the different powers of government, which to a certain extent is admitted on all hands to be essential to the preservation of liberty, it is evident that each department should have a will of its own; and consequently should be so constituted that the members of each should have as little agency as possible in the appointment of the members of the others. Were this principle rigorously adhered to, it would require that all the appointments for the supreme executive, legislative, and judiciary magistracies should be drawn from the same fountain of authority, the people, through channels having no communication whatever with one another. Perhaps such a plan of constructing the several departments would be less difficult in practice than it may in contemplation appear. Some difficulties, however, and some additional expense would attend the execution of it. Some deviations, therefore, from the principle must be admitted. In the constitution of the judiciary department in particular, it might be inexpedient to insist rigorously on the principle: first, because peculiar qualifications

being essential in the members, the primary consideration ought to be to select that mode of choice which best secures these qualifications; second, because the permanent tenure by which the appointments are held in that department must soon destroy all sense of dependence on the authority conferring them.

It is equally evident that the members of each department should be as little dependent as possible on those of the others for the emoluments annexed to their offices. Were the executive magistrate, or the judges, not independent of the legislature in this particular, their independence in every other would be merely nominal.

In the following passages, which are among the most widely quoted of Madison's writings, he explains how the separation of the powers of government into three branches helps to counter the effects of personal ambition on government. The separation of powers allows personal motives to be linked to the constitutional rights of a branch of government. In effect, competing personal interests in each branch will help to keep the powers of the three government branches separate and, in so doing, will help to guard the public interest.

But the great security against a gradual concentration of the several powers in the same department consists in giving to those who administer each department the necessary constitutional means and personal motives to resist encroachments of the others. The provision for defense must in this, as in all other cases, be made commensurate to the danger of attack. Ambition must be made to counteract ambition. The interest of the man must be connected with the constitutional rights of the place. It may be a reflection on human nature that such devices should be necessary to control the abuses of government. But what is government itself but the greatest of all reflections on human nature? If men were angels, no government would be necessary. If angels were to govern men, neither external nor internal controls on government would be necessary. In framing a government which is to be administered by men over men, the great difficulty lies in this: you must first enable the government to control the governed; and in the next place oblige it to control itself. A dependence on the people is, no doubt, the primary control on the government; but experience has taught mankind the necessity of auxiliary precautions.

This policy of supplying, by opposite and rival interests, the defect of better motives, might be traced through the whole system of human affairs, private as well as public. We see it particularly displayed in all the subordinate distributions of power, where the constant aim is to divide and arrange the several offices in such a manner as that each may be a check on the other—that the private interest of every individual may be a sentinel over the public rights. These inventions of prudence cannot be less requisite in the distribution of the supreme powers of the State.

Madison now addresses the issue of equality among the branches of government. The legislature will necessarily predominate, but if the executive is given an "absolute negative" (absolute veto power) over legislative actions, this also could lead to an abuse of power. Madison concludes that the division of the legislature into two "branches" (parts, or chambers) will act as a check on the legislature's powers.

But it is not possible to give to each department an equal power of self-defense. In republican government, the legislative authority necessarily predominates. The remedy for this inconveniency is to divide the legislature into different branches; and to render them, by different modes of election and different principles of action, as little connected with each other as the nature of their common functions and their common dependence on the society will admit. It may even be necessary to guard against dangerous encroachments by still further precautions. As the weight of the legislative authority requires that it should be thus divided, the weakness of the executive may require, on the other hand, that it should be fortified. An absolute negative on the legislature appears, at first view, to be the natural defense with which the executive magistrate should be armed. But perhaps it would be neither altogether safe nor alone sufficient. On ordinary occasions it might not be exerted with the requisite firmness, and on extraordinary occasions it might be perfidiously abused. May not this defect of an absolute negative be supplied by some qualified connection between this weaker department and the weaker branch of the stronger department, by which the latter may be led to support the constitutional rights of the former, without being too much detached from the rights of its own department?

If the principles on which these observations are founded be just, as I persuade myself they are, and they be applied as a criterion to the several State constitutions, and to the federal Constitution, it will be found that if the latter does not perfectly correspond with them, the former are infinitely less able to bear such a test.

In the remainder of the essay, Madison discusses how a federal system of government, in which powers are divided between the states and the national government, offers "double security" against tyranny.

There are, moreover, two considerations particularly applicable to the federal system of America, which place that system in a very interesting point of view.

First. In a single republic, all the power surrendered by the people is submitted to the administration of a single government; and the usurpations are guarded against by a division of the government into distinct and separate departments. In the compound republic of America, the power surrendered by the people is first divided between two distinct governments, and then the portion allotted to each subdivided among distinct and separate departments. Hence a double security arises to the rights of the people. The different governments will control each other, at the same time that each will be controlled by itself.

Second. It is of great importance in a republic not only to guard the society against the oppression of its rulers, but to guard one part of the society against the injustice of the other part. Different interests necessarily exist in different classes of citizens. If a majority be united by a common interest, the rights of the minority will be insecure. There are but two methods of providing against this evil: the one by creating a will in the community independent of the majority—that is, of the society itself; the other, by comprehending in the society so many separate descriptions of citizens as will render an unjust combination of a majority of the whole very improbable, if not impracticable. The first method prevails in all governments possessing an hereditary or self-appointed authority. This, at best, is but a precarious security; because a power independent of the society may as well espouse the unjust views of the major as the rightful interests of the minor party, and may possibly be turned against both parties. The second method will be exemplified in the federal republic of the United States. Whilst all authority in it will be derived from and dependent on the society, the society itself will be broken into so many parts, interests and classes of citizens, that the rights of individuals, or of the minority, will be in little danger from interested combinations of the majority. In a free government the security for civil rights must be the same as that for religious rights. It consists in the one case in the multiplicity of interests, and in the other in the multiplicity of sects. The degree of security in both cases will depend on the number of interests and sects; and this may be presumed to depend on the extent of country and number of people comprehended under the same government. This view of the subject must particularly recommend a proper federal system to all the sincere and considerate friends of republican government, since it shows that in exact proportion as the territory of the Union may be formed into more circumscribed Confederacies, or States, oppressive combinations of a majority will be facilitated; the best security, under the republican forms, for the rights of every class of citizen, will be diminished; and consequently the stability and independence of some member of the government, the only other security, must be proportionally increased. Justice is the end of government. It is the end of civil society. It ever has been and ever will be pursued until it be obtained, or until liberty be lost in the pursuit. In a society under the forms of which the stronger faction can readily unite and oppress the weaker, anarchy may as truly be said to reign as in a state of nature, where the weaker individual is not secured against the violence of the stronger; and as, in the latter state, even the stronger individuals are prompted, by the uncertainty of their condition, to submit to a government which may protect the weak as well as themselves; so, in the former state, will the more powerful factions or parties be gradually induced, by a like motive, to wish for a government which will protect all parties, the weaker as well as the more powerful. It can be little doubted that if the State of Rhode Island was separated from the Confederacy and left to itself, the insecurity of rights under the popular form of government within such narrow limits would be displayed by such reiterated oppressions of factious majorities that some power altogether independent of the people would soon be called for by the voice of the very factions whose misrule had proved the necessity of it. In the extended republic of the United States, and among the great variety of interests, parties, and sects which it embraces, a coalition of a majority of the whole society could seldom take place on any other principles than those of justice and the general good; whilst there being thus less danger to a minor from the will of a major party, there must be less pretext, also, to provide for the security of the former, by introducing into the government a will not dependent on the latter, or, in other words, a will independent of the society itself. It is no less certain than it is important, notwithstanding the contrary opinions which have been entertained, that the larger the society, provided it lie within a practicable sphere, the more duly capable it will be of self-government. And happily for the republican cause, the practicable sphere may be carried to a very great extent by a judicious modification and mixture of the *federal principle*.

Publius
(James Madison)

Glossary

A

Actual Malice Either knowledge of a defamatory statement's falsity or a reckless disregard for the truth.

Advice and Consent Terms in the Constitution describing the U.S. Senate's power to review and approve treaties and presidential appointments.

Affirm To declare that a court ruling is valid and must stand.

Affirmative Action A policy in educational admissions or job hiring that gives special attention or compensatory treatment to traditionally disadvantaged groups in an effort to overcome present effects of past discrimination.

Agenda Setting Determining which public-policy questions will be debated or considered.

***Amicus Curiae* Brief** A brief (a document containing a legal argument supporting a desired outcome in a particular case) filed by a third party, or *amicus curiae* (Latin for "friend of the court"), who is not directly involved in the litigation but who has an interest in the outcome of the case.

Anti-Federalist An individual who opposed the ratification of the new Constitution in 1787. The Anti-Federalists were opposed to a strong central government.

Appellate Court A court having jurisdiction to review cases and issues that were originally tried in lower courts.

Appointment Power The authority vested in the president to fill a government office or position.

Appropriation The passage, by Congress, of a spending bill specifying the amount of authorized funds that actually will be allocated for an agency's use.

Arraignment The first act in a criminal proceeding, in which the defendant is brought before a court to hear the charges against him or her and enter a plea of guilty or not guilty.

Australian Ballot A secret ballot prepared, distributed, and tabulated by government officials at public expense. Since 1888, all states have used the Australian ballot rather than an open, public ballot.

Authoritarianism A type of regime in which only the government itself is fully controlled by the ruler. Social and economic institutions exist that are not under the government's control.

Authority The right and power of a government or other entity to enforce its decisions and compel obedience.

Authorization A formal declaration by a legislative committee that a certain amount of funding may be available to an agency. Some authorizations terminate in a year; others are renewable automatically without further congressional action.

B

Bias An inclination or a preference that interferes with impartial judgment.

Bicameral Legislature A legislature made up of two parts, called chambers. The U.S. Congress, composed of the House of Representatives and the Senate, is a bicameral legislature.

Bicameralism The division of a legislature into two separate assemblies.

Bill of Rights The first ten amendments to the U.S. Constitution.

Block Grant A federal grant that provides funds to a state or local government for a general functional area, such as criminal justice or mental-health programs.

Budget Deficit Government expenditures that exceed receipts.

Bureaucracy A large organization that is structured hierarchically to carry out specific functions.

C

Cabinet An advisory group selected by the president to aid in making decisions. The cabinet includes the heads of fifteen executive departments and others named by the president.

Cabinet Department One of the fifteen major departments of the executive branch.

Capitalism An economic system characterized by the private ownership of wealth-creating assets, free markets, and freedom of contract.

Capture The act by which an industry being regulated by a government agency gains direct or indirect control over agency personnel and decision makers.

Case Law Judicial interpretations of common law principles and doctrines, as well as interpretations of constitutional law, statutory law, and administrative law.

Casework Personal work for constituents by members of Congress.

Categorical Grant A federal grant to a state or local government for a specific program or project.

Caucus System A meeting of party members to select candidates and propose policies.

Checks and Balances A major principle of the American system of government whereby each branch of the government can check the actions of the others.

Chief Diplomat The role of the president in recognizing foreign governments, making treaties, and effecting executive agreements.

Chief Executive The role of the president as head of the executive branch of the government.

Chief Legislator The role of the president in influencing the making of laws.

Chief of Staff The person who is named to direct the White House Office and advise the president.

Civil Disobedience A nonviolent, public refusal to obey allegedly unjust laws.

Civil Liberties Those personal freedoms, including freedom of religion and of speech, that are protected for all individuals in a society.

Civil Rights Generally, all rights rooted in the Fourteenth Amendment's guarantee of equal protection under the law.

Civil Service A collective term for the body of employees working for the government. Generally, civil service is understood to apply to all those who gain government employment through a merit system.

Civil Service Commission The initial central personnel agency of the national government; created in 1883.

Class-Action Suit A lawsuit filed by an individual seeking damages for "all persons similarly situated."

Closed Primary A type of primary in which the voter is limited to choosing candidates of the party of which he or she is a member.

Coattail Effect The influence of a popular candidate on the electoral success of other candidates on the same party ticket. The effect is increased by the party-column ballot, which encourages straight-ticket voting.

Cold War The ideological, political, and economic confrontation between the United States and the Soviet Union following World War II.

Commander in Chief The role of the president as supreme commander of the military forces of the United States and of the state National Guard units when they are called into federal service.

Commerce Clause The section of the Constitution in which Congress is given the power to regulate trade among the states and with foreign countries.

Commercial Speech Advertising statements, which increasingly have been given First Amendment protection.

Common Law Judge-made law that originated in England from decisions shaped according to prevailing custom. Decisions were applied to similar situations and gradually became common to the nation.

Concurrent Powers Powers held jointly by the national and state governments.

Concurring Opinion A separate opinion prepared by a judge who supports the decision of the majority of the court but for different reasons.

Confederal System A system consisting of a league of independent states, in which the central government created by the league has only limited powers over the states.

Confederation A political system in which states or regional governments retain ultimate authority except for those powers they expressly delegate to a central government.

Conference Committee A special joint committee appointed to reconcile differences when bills pass the two chambers of Congress in different forms.

Consensus General agreement among the citizenry on an issue.

Conservatism A set of beliefs that includes advocacy of a limited role for the national government in helping individuals, support for traditional values and lifestyles, and a cautious response to change.

Conservative Movement An American movement launched in the 1950s that provides a comprehensive ideological framework for conservative politics.

Constituent One of the persons represented by a legislator or other elected or appointed official.

Constitutional Power A power vested in the president by Article II of the Constitution.

Containment A U.S. diplomatic policy adopted by the Truman administration to contain Communist power within its existing boundaries.

Continuing Resolution A temporary funding law that Congress passes when an appropriations bill has not been passed by the beginning of the new fiscal year on October 1.

Cooperative Federalism A model of federalism in which the states and the national government cooperate in solving problems.

Credentials Committee A committee used by political parties at their national conventions to determine which delegates may participate. The committee inspects the claim of each prospective delegate to be seated as a legitimate representative of his or her state.

D

De Facto Segregation Racial segregation that occurs because of patterns of racial residence and similar social conditions.

Defamation of Character Wrongfully hurting a person's good reputation.

Defense Policy A subset of national security policy concerning the U.S. armed forces.

De Jure Segregation Racial segregation that occurs because of laws or administrative decisions by public agencies.

Democracy A system of government in which political authority is vested in the people.

Democratic Party One of the two major American political parties evolving out of the Republican Party of Thomas Jefferson.

Democratic Republic A republic in which representatives elected by the people make and enforce laws and policies.

Détente A French word meaning a relaxation of tensions. The term characterized U.S.-Soviet relations as they developed under President Richard Nixon and Secretary of State Henry Kissinger.

Devolution The transfer of powers from a national or central government to a state or local government.

Diplomacy The process by which states carry on political relations with each other; the process of settling conflicts among nations by peaceful means.

Diplomatic Recognition The formal acknowledgment of a foreign government as legitimate.

Direct Democracy A system of government in which political decisions are made by the people directly, rather than by their elected representatives.

Direct Primary A primary election in which voters decide party nominations by voting directly for candidates.

Direct Technique An interest group technique that uses direct interaction with government officials to further the group's goals.

Discharge Petition A procedure by which a bill in the House of Representatives may be forced (discharged) out of a committee that has refused to report it for consideration by the House.

Dissenting Opinion A separate opinion in which a judge dissents from (disagrees with) the conclusion reached by the majority of the court and expounds his or her own views about the case.

Diversity of Citizenship The condition that exists when the parties to a lawsuit are from different states or when the suit involves a U.S. citizen and a government or citizen of a foreign country. Diversity of citizenship can provide a basis for federal jurisdiction.

Divided Government A situation in which one major political party controls the presidency and the other controls Congress or in which one party controls a state governorship and the other controls the state legislature.

Divided Opinion Public opinion that is polarized between two quite different positions.

Domestic Policy All government laws, planning, and actions that concern internal issues of national importance, such as health care, the environment, and the economy.

Dual Federalism A model of federalism that looks on national and state governments as co-equal sovereign powers. Neither the state government nor the national government should interfere in the other's sphere.

E

Earmarks Special provisions in legislation to set aside funds for projects that have not passed an impartial evaluation by agencies of the executive branch. Also known as *pork*.

Economic Aid Assistance to other nations in the form of grants, loans, or credits to buy the assisting nation's products.

Elastic Clause, or Necessary and Proper Clause The clause in Article I, Section 8, that grants Congress the power to do whatever is necessary to execute its specifically delegated powers.

Electoral College A group of persons, called electors, who are selected by the voters in each state. This group officially elects the president and the vice president of the United States.

Elector A member of the electoral college, which selects the president and vice president. Each state's electors are chosen in each presidential election year according to state laws.

Elite Theory The argument that society is ruled by a small number of people who exercise power to further their self-interests.

Emergency Power An inherent power exercised by the president during a period of national crisis.

Enabling Legislation A statute enacted by Congress that authorizes the creation of an administrative agency and specifies the name, purpose, composition, functions, and powers of the agency being created.

Enumerated Powers Powers specifically granted to the national government by the Constitution. The first seventeen clauses of Article I, Section 8, specify most of the enumerated powers of Congress.

Equality As a political value, the idea that all people are of equal worth.

Establishment Clause The part of the First Amendment prohibiting the establishment of a church officially supported by the national government.

Exclusionary Rule A judicial policy prohibiting the admission at trial of illegally seized evidence.

Executive Agreement An international agreement made by the president, without senatorial ratification, with the head of a foreign state.

Executive Budget The budget prepared and submitted by the president to Congress.

Executive Office of the President (EOP) An organization established by President Franklin D. Roosevelt to assist the president in carrying out major duties.

Executive Order A rule or regulation issued by the president that has the effect of law.

Executive Privilege The right of executive officials to withhold information from, or to refuse to appear before, a legislative committee or a court.

Expressed Power A power of the president that is expressly written into the Constitution or into statutory law.

F

Fall Review The annual process in which the OMB, after receiving formal federal agency requests for funding for the next fiscal year, reviews the requests, makes changes, and submits its recommendations to the president.

Federal Election Commission (FEC) The federal regulatory agency with the task of enforcing federal campaign laws. As a practical matter, the FEC's role is largely limited to collecting data on campaign contributions.

Federalist An individual who was in favor of the adoption of the U.S. Constitution and the creation of a federal union with a strong central government.

Federal Mandate A requirement in federal legislation that forces states and municipalities to comply with certain rules.

Federal Open Market Committee The most important body within the Federal Reserve System. The Federal Open Market Committee decides how monetary policy should be carried out.

Federal Question A question that has to do with the U.S. Constitution, acts of Congress, or treaties. A federal question provides a basis for federal jurisdiction.

Federal Register A publication of the U.S. government that prints executive orders, rules, and regulations.

Federal Reserve System (the Fed) The system created by Congress in 1913 to serve as the nation's central banking organization.

Feminism The movement that supports political, economic, and social equality for women.

Filibuster The use of the Senate's tradition of unlimited debate as a delaying tactic to block a bill.

First Budget Resolution A resolution passed by Congress in May that sets overall revenue goals and spending targets for the following fiscal year.

Fiscal Having to do with government revenues and expenditures.

Fiscal Federalism A process by which funds raised through taxation or borrowing by one level of government (usually the national government) are spent by another level (typically, state or local governments).

Fiscal Policy The federal government's use of taxation and spending policies to affect overall business activity.

Fiscal Year (FY) A twelve-month period that is used for bookkeeping, or accounting, purposes. Usually, the fiscal year does not coincide with the calendar year. For example, the federal government's fiscal year runs from October 1 through September 30.

Focus Group A small group of individuals who are led in discussion by a professional consultant to gather opinions on, and responses to, candidates and issues.

Foreign Policy A nation's external goals and the techniques and strategies used to achieve them.

Foreign Policy Process The steps by which foreign policy goals are decided and acted on.

Fracking Also called hydraulic fracturing, the injection of a high-pressure solution of water, sand, and chemicals into hydrocarbon-bearing rocks, releasing oil or natural gas.

Franchise The right to vote.

Franking A policy that enables members of Congress to send material through the mail by substituting their facsimile signature (frank) for postage.

Free Exercise Clause The provision of the First Amendment guaranteeing the free exercise of religion.

Free-Rider Problem The difficulty that interest groups face in recruiting members when the benefits they achieve can be gained without joining the group.

Front-Loading The practice of moving presidential primary elections to the early part of the campaign to maximize the impact of these primaries on the nomination.

Front-Runner The presidential candidate who appears to be ahead at a given time in the primary season.

G

Gag Order An order issued by a judge restricting the publication of news about a trial or a pretrial hearing to protect the accused's right to a fair trial.

Gender Discrimination Any practice, policy, or procedure that denies equality of treatment to an individual or to a group because of gender.

Gender Gap The difference between the percentage of women who vote for a particular candidate and the percentage of men who vote for the candidate.

General Election An election, normally held on the first Tuesday in November, that determines who will fill various elected positions.

General Jurisdiction Exists when a court's authority to hear cases is not significantly restricted. A court of general jurisdiction normally can hear a broad range of cases.

Generational Effect A long-lasting effect of the events of a particular time on the political opinions of those who came of political age at that time.

Gerrymandering The drawing of legislative district boundary lines for the purpose of obtaining partisan advantage. A district is said to be gerrymandered when its shape is altered substantially to determine which party will win it.

GOP A nickname for the Republican Party, which stands for "grand old party."

Government The preeminent institution within a society. Government has the ultimate authority to decide how conflicts will be resolved and how benefits and privileges will be allocated.

Government Corporation An agency of government that administers a quasi-business enterprise. These corporations are used when government activities are primarily commercial.

Government in the Sunshine Act A law that requires all committee-directed federal agencies to conduct their business regularly in public session.

Grandfather Clause A device used by southern states to disenfranchise African Americans. It restricted voting to those whose grandfathers had voted before 1867.

Great Compromise The compromise between the New Jersey and Virginia plans that created one chamber of the Congress based on population and one chamber representing each state equally; also called the Connecticut Compromise.

Gross Domestic Product (GDP) The dollar value of all final goods and services produced in a one-year period.

H

Hatch Act An act passed in 1939 that restricted the political activities of government employees. It also prohibited a political group from spending more than $3 million in any campaign and limited individual contributions to a campaign committee to $5,000.

Head of State The role of the president as ceremonial head of the government.

Hispanic Someone who can claim a heritage from a Spanish-speaking country. Hispanics may be of any race.

House Effect In public opinion polling, an effect in which one polling organization's results consistently differ from those reported by other poll takers.

I

Imminent Lawless Action Test The current standard established by the Supreme Court for evaluating the legality of advocacy speech. Such speech can be forbidden only when it is "directed to inciting . . . imminent lawless actions."

Impeachment An action by the House of Representatives to accuse the president, vice president, or other civil officers of the United States of committing "Treason, Bribery, or other high Crimes and Misdemeanors."

Incorporation Theory The view that most of the protections of the Bill of Rights apply to state governments through the Fourteenth Amendment's due process clause.

Independent A voter or candidate who does not identify with a political party.

Independent Executive Agency A federal agency that is not part of a cabinet department but reports directly to the president.

Independent Expenditures Unregulated political expenditures by PACs, organizations, and individuals that are not coordinated with candidate campaigns or political parties.

Independent Regulatory Agency An agency outside the major executive departments charged with making and implementing rules and regulations within a specific area.

Indirect Primary A primary election in which voters choose convention delegates, and the delegates determine the party's candidate in the general election.

Indirect Technique An interest group technique that uses third parties to influence government officials.

Individual Mandate In health-care reform, the requirement that all citizens obtain health-care insurance coverage from some source, public or private.

Inflation A sustained rise in the general price level of goods and services.

Inherent Power A power of the president derived from the statements in the Constitution that "the executive Power shall be vested in a President" and that the president should "take Care that the Laws be faithfully executed."

Initiative A procedure by which voters can propose a law or a constitutional amendment.

Institution An ongoing organization that performs certain functions for society.

Instructed Delegate A legislator who is an agent of the voters who elected him or her and who votes according to the views of constituents, regardless of personal beliefs.

Intelligence Community The government agencies that gather information about the capabilities and intentions of foreign governments or that engage in covert actions.

Interest Group An organized group of individuals sharing common objectives who actively attempt to influence policymakers.

Iron Triangle A three-way alliance among legislators in Congress, bureaucrats, and interest groups to make or preserve policies that benefit their respective interests.

Isolationist Foreign Policy A policy of abstaining from an active role in international affairs or alliances, which characterized U.S. foreign policy toward Europe during most of the 1800s.

Issue Advocacy Advertising Advertising paid for by interest groups that support or oppose a candidate or a candidate's position on an issue without mentioning the candidate, voting, or elections.

Issue Network A group of individuals or organizations—which may consist of legislators and legislative staff members, interest group leaders, bureaucrats, scholars and other experts, and media representatives—that supports a particular policy position on a given issue.

J

Joint Committee A legislative committee composed of members from both chambers of Congress.

Judicial Activism A doctrine holding that the federal judiciary should take an active role by using its powers to check the activities of governmental bodies when those bodies exceed their authority.

Judicial Implementation The way in which court decisions are translated into action.

Judicial Restraint A doctrine holding that courts should defer to the decisions made by the elected representatives of the people in the legislative and executive branches.

Judicial Review The power of the Supreme Court or any court to examine and possibly declare unconstitutional federal or state laws and other acts of government.

Jurisdiction The authority of a court to decide certain cases. Not all courts have the authority to decide all cases. Where a case arises and what its subject matter is are two jurisdictional issues.

Justiciable Controversy A controversy that is real and substantial, as opposed to hypothetical or academic.

K

Keynesian Economics A school of economic thought that tends to favor active federal government policymaking to stabilize economy-wide fluctuations, usually by implementing discretionary fiscal policy.

Kitchen Cabinet The informal advisers to the president.

L

Labor Movement The economic and political expression of working class interests.

Latino An alternative to the term *Hispanic* that is preferred by many.

Lawmaking The process of establishing the legal rules that govern society.

Legislature A governmental body primarily responsible for the making of laws.

Legitimacy Popular acceptance of the right and power of a government or other entity to exercise authority.

Libel A written defamation of a person's character, reputation, business, or property rights. The defamatory statement must be observed by a third party.

Liberalism A set of beliefs that includes advocacy of positive government action to improve the welfare of individuals, support for civil rights, and tolerance for political and social change.

Libertarianism A political ideology based on skepticism or opposition toward most government activities.

Liberty The greatest freedom of the individual that is consistent with the freedom of other individuals in the society.

Limited Government A government with powers that are limited either through a written document or through widely shared beliefs.

Limited Jurisdiction Exists when a court's authority to hear cases is restricted to certain types of claims, such as tax claims or bankruptcy petitions.

Line-Item Veto The power of an executive to veto individual lines or items within a piece of legislation without vetoing the entire bill.

Line Organization In the federal government, an administrative unit that is directly accountable to the president.

Literacy Test A test administered as a precondition for voting, often used to prevent African Americans from exercising their right to vote.

Litigate To engage in a legal proceeding or seek relief in a court of law; to carry on a lawsuit.

Lobbyist An organization or individual who attempts to influence the passage, defeat, or content of legislation and the government's administrative decisions.

Loophole A legal method by which individuals and businesses are allowed to reduce the tax liabilities they owe to the government.

M

Madisonian Model A structure of government proposed by James Madison, in which the powers of the government are separated into three branches: executive, legislative, and judicial.

Majoritarianism A political theory holding that in a democracy, the government ought to do what the majority of the people want.

Majority Leader of the House Elected by members of the majority party to foster cohesion and to act as a spokesperson for the majority party.

Majority Opinion A court opinion reflecting the views of the majority of the judges.

Majority Rule A basic principle of democracy asserting that the greatest number of citizens in any political unit should select officials and determine policies.

Media The channels of mass communication.

Medicaid A joint state-federal program that provides medical care to the poor (including indigent elderly persons in nursing homes). The program is funded out of general government revenues.

Medicare A federal health-insurance program that covers U.S. residents over the age of sixty-five. The costs are met by a tax on wages and salaries.

Merit System The selection, retention, and promotion of government employees on the basis of competitive examinations.

Midterm Elections National elections in which candidates for president are not on the ballot. In midterm elections, voters choose all members of the U.S. House of Representatives and one-third of the members of the U.S. Senate.

Minority Leader of the House The party leader elected by members of the minority party in the House.

Monetary Policy The use of changes in the amount of money in circulation to alter credit markets, employment, and the rate of inflation.

Monroe Doctrine A policy statement made by President James Monroe in 1823, which set out three principles: (1) European nations should not establish new colonies in the Western Hemisphere, (2) European nations should not intervene in the affairs of independent nations of the Western Hemisphere, and (3) the United States would not interfere in the affairs of European nations.

Moral Idealism A philosophy that views nations as normally willing to cooperate and to agree on moral standards for conduct.

N

National Committee A standing committee of a national political party established to direct and coordinate party activities between national party conventions.

National Convention The meeting held every four years by each major party to select presidential and vice-presidential candidates, write a platform, choose a national committee, and conduct party business.

National Security Council (NSC) An agency in the Executive Office of the President that advises the president on national security.

National Security Policy Foreign and domestic policy designed to protect the nation's independence and political and economic integrity; policy that is concerned with the safety and defense of the nation.

Natural Rights Rights held to be inherent in natural law, not dependent on governments. John Locke stated that natural law, being superior to human law, specifies certain rights of "life, liberty, and property." These rights, altered to become "life, liberty, and the pursuit of happiness," are asserted in the Declaration of Independence.

Normal Trade Relations (NTR) Status A status granted through an international treaty by which each member nation must treat other members as well as it treats the country that receives its most favorable treatment. This status was formerly known as *most-favored-nation status.*

O

Obscenity Sexually offensive material. Obscenity can be illegal if it is found to violate a four-part test established by the United States Supreme Court.

Office-Block, or Massachusetts, Ballot A form of general election ballot in which candidates for elective office are grouped together under the title of each office. It emphasizes voting for the office and the individual candidate, rather than for the party.

Office of Management and Budget (OMB) A division of the Executive Office of the President. The OMB assists the president in preparing the annual budget, clearing and coordinating departmental agency budgets, and supervising the administration of the federal budget.

Ombudsperson A person who hears and investigates complaints by private individuals against public officials or agencies (from the Swedish word *ombudsman,* meaning "representative").

Open Primary A primary in which any voter can vote in either party primary (but must vote for candidates of only one party).

Opinion A statement by a judge or a court of the decision reached in a case. An opinion sets forth the applicable law and details the reasoning on which the ruling was based.

Opinion Leader One who is able to influence the opinions of others because of position, expertise, or personality.

Opinion Poll A method of systematically questioning a small, selected sample of respondents who are deemed representative of the total population.

Oral Arguments The arguments presented in person by attorneys to an appellate court. Each attorney presents reasons to the court why the court should rule in her or his client's favor.

Order A state of peace and security. Maintaining order by protecting members of society from violence and criminal activity is the oldest purpose of government.

Oversight The process by which Congress follows up on laws it has enacted to ensure that they are being enforced and administered in the way Congress intended.

P

Pardon A release from the punishment for, or legal consequences of, a crime. A pardon can be granted by the president before or after a conviction.

Party-Column, or Indiana, Ballot A form of general election ballot in which all of a party's candidates for elective office are arranged in one column under the party's label and symbol. It emphasizes voting for the party, rather than for the office or individual.

Party Identification Linking oneself to a particular political party.

Party Organization The formal structure and leadership of a political party, including election committees; local, state, and national executives; and paid professional staff.

Party Platform A document drawn up at each national convention, outlining the policies, positions, and principles of the party.

Patient Protection and Affordable Care Act A law passed in 2010 that seeks, among other things, to provide health-care insurance to all American citizens. The act, nicknamed "Obamacare" by opponents and journalists, is supplemented by the Health Care and Education Reconciliation Act.

Patronage The practice of rewarding faithful party workers and followers with government employment and contracts.

Peer Group A group consisting of members who share common social characteristics. Such groups play an important part in the socialization process, helping to shape attitudes and beliefs.

Pendleton Act (Civil Service Reform Act) An act that established the principle of federal government employment based on merit and created the Civil Service Commission to administer the personnel service.

Pluralism A theory that views politics as a conflict among interest groups. Political decision making is characterized by bargaining and compromise.

Plurality A number of votes cast for a candidate that is greater than the number of votes for any other candidate but not necessarily a majority.

Pocket Veto A special veto exercised by the chief executive after a legislative body has adjourned. Bills not signed by the chief executive die after a specified period of time.

Police Power The authority to legislate for the protection of the health, morals, safety, and welfare of the people. In the United States, most police power is reserved to the states.

Political Action Committee (PAC) A committee set up by and representing a corporation, labor union, or special interest group. PACs raise campaign donations.

Political Consultant A paid professional hired to devise a campaign strategy and manage a campaign.

Political Culture The patterned set of ideas, values, and ways of thinking about government and politics that characterizes a people.

Political Ideology A comprehensive set of beliefs about the nature of people and the role of government.

Political Party A group of political activists who organize to win elections, operate the government, and determine public policy.

Political Question An issue that a court believes should be decided by the executive or legislative branch, or both.

Political Realism A philosophy that views each nation as acting principally in its own interest.

Political Socialization The process by which people acquire political beliefs and values.

Political Trust The degree to which individuals express trust in the government and political institutions, usually measured through a specific series of survey questions.

Politics The struggle over power or influence within organizations or informal groups that can grant or withhold benefits or privileges.

Poll Tax A special tax that had to be paid as a qualification for voting. The Twenty-fourth Amendment to the Constitution outlawed the poll tax in national elections, and in 1966, the Supreme Court declared it unconstitutional in state elections as well.

Popular Sovereignty The concept that ultimate political authority is based on the will of the people.

Precedent A court rule bearing on subsequent legal decisions in similar cases. Judges rely on precedents in deciding cases.

Presidential Primary A statewide primary election of delegates to a political party's national convention, held to determine a party's presidential nominee.

President Pro Tempore The senator who presides over the Senate in the absence of the vice president.

Primary Election An election in which political parties choose their candidates for the general election.

Prior Restraint Restraining an activity before it has actually occurred. When expression is involved, this means censorship.

Privatization The replacement of government services with services provided by private firms.

Progressive Tax A tax that rises in percentage terms as incomes rise.

Property Anything that is or may be subject to ownership. As conceived by the political philosopher John Locke, the right to property is a natural right superior to human law (laws made by government).

Public Agenda Issues that are perceived by the political community as meriting public attention and governmental action.

Public Debt, or National Debt The total amount of debt carried by the federal government.

Public Figure A public official, movie star, or other person known to the public because of his or her positions or activities.

Public Interest The best interests of the overall community; the national good, rather than the narrow interests of a particular group.

Public Opinion The aggregate of individual attitudes or beliefs shared by some portion of the adult population.

R

Ratification Formal approval.

Realignment A large-scale, lasting change in the types of voters who support each of the major political parties.

Reapportionment The allocation of seats in the House of Representatives to each state after a census.

Recall A procedure allowing the people to vote to dismiss an elected official from office before his or her term has expired.

Recession An economic downturn, usually characterized by a fall in the GDP and rising unemployment.

Reconciliation A special rule that can be applied to budget bills sent from the House of Representatives to the Senate. Reconciliation measures cannot be filibustered.

Redistricting The redrawing of the boundaries of the congressional districts within each state.

Referendum An electoral device whereby legislative or constitutional measures are referred by the legislature to the voters for approval or disapproval.

Registration The entry of a person's name onto the list of registered voters for elections. To register, a person must meet certain legal requirements of age, citizenship, and residency.

Regressive Tax A tax that falls in percentage terms as incomes rise.

Remand To send a case back to the court that originally heard it.

Representation The function of members of Congress as elected officials representing the views of their constituents as well as larger national interests.

Representative Assembly A legislature composed of individuals who represent the population.

Representative Democracy A form of government in which representatives elected by the people make and enforce laws and policies, but in which the monarchy may be retained in a ceremonial role.

Reprieve A formal postponement of the execution of a sentence imposed by a court of law.

Republic A form of government in which sovereign power rests with the people, rather than with a king or a monarch.

Republican Party One of the two major American political parties. It emerged in the 1850s as an antislavery party and consisted of former northern Whigs and antislavery Democrats.

Reverse To annul or make void a court ruling on account of some error or irregularity.

Reverse Discrimination Discrimination against individuals who are not members of a minority group.

Rule of Four A United States Supreme Court procedure by which four justices must vote to grant a petition for review if a case is to come before the full court.

Rules Committee A standing committee of the House of Representatives that provides special rules under which specific bills can be debated, amended, and considered by the House.

S

Sampling Error The difference between a sample result and the true result if the entire population had been interviewed.

Second Budget Resolution A resolution passed by Congress in September that sets binding limits on taxes and spending for the following fiscal year.

Select Committee A temporary legislative committee established for a limited time period and for a special purpose.

Senate Majority Leader The chief spokesperson of the majority party in the Senate, who directs the legislative program and party strategy.

Senate Minority Leader The party officer in the Senate who commands the minority party's opposition to the policies of the majority party and directs the legislative program and strategy of his or her party.

Senatorial Courtesy In federal district court judgeship nominations, a tradition allowing a senator to veto a judicial appointment in her or his state.

Seniority System A custom followed in both chambers of Congress specifying that the member of the majority party with the longest term of continuous service will be given preference when a committee chairperson (or a holder of some other significant post) is selected.

Separate-but-Equal Doctrine The doctrine holding that separate-but-equal facilities do not violate the equal protection clause of the Fourteenth Amendment to the U.S. Constitution.

Separation of Powers The principle of dividing governmental powers among different branches of government.

Service Sector The sector of the economy that provides services—such as health care, banking, and education—in contrast to the sector that produces goods.

Sexual Harassment Unwanted physical or verbal conduct or abuse of a sexual nature that interferes with a recipient's job performance, creates a hostile work environment, or carries with it an implicit or explicit threat of adverse employment consequences.

Signing Statement A written declaration that the president may make when signing a bill into law. It may contain instructions to the bureaucracy on how to administer the law or point to sections of the law that the president considers unconstitutional or contrary to national security interests.

Slander The public uttering of a false statement that harms the good reputation of another. The statement must be made to, or within the hearing of, someone other than the defamed party.

Social Contract A voluntary agreement among individuals to secure their rights and welfare by creating a government and abiding by its rules.

Social Movement A movement that represents the demands of a large segment of the public for political, economic, or social change.

Socialism A political ideology based on strong support for economic and social equality. Socialists traditionally envisioned a society in which major businesses were taken over by the government or by employee cooperatives.

Socioeconomic Status The value assigned to a person due to occupation or income. A professional person with a substantial income, for example, has high socioeconomic status.

Soft Money Campaign contributions unregulated by federal or state law, usually given to parties and party committees to help fund general party activities.

Sound Bite A brief, memorable comment that can easily be fit into news broadcasts.

Soviet Bloc The Soviet Union and the Eastern European countries that installed Communist regimes after World War II and that were dominated by the Soviet Union.

Speaker of the House The presiding officer in the House of Representatives. The Speaker is chosen by the majority party and is the most powerful and influential member of the House.

Spin An interpretation of political events that is favorable to a candidate or officeholder.

Spin Doctor A political adviser who tries to convince journalists of the truth of a particular interpretation of events.

Splinter Party A new party formed by a dissident faction within a major political party. Often, splinter parties have emerged when a particular personality was at odds with the major party.

Spoils System The awarding of government jobs to political supporters and friends.

Spring Review The annual process in which the Office of Management and Budget (OMB) requires federal agencies to review their programs, activities, and goals, and submit their requests for funding for the next fiscal year.

Standing Committee A permanent committee in the House or Senate that considers bills within a certain subject area.

Stare Decisis To stand on decided cases; the judicial policy of following precedents established by past decisions.

State A group of people occupying a specific area and organized under one government. It may be either a nation or a subunit of a nation.

State Central Committee The principal organized structure of each political party within each state. This committee is responsible for carrying out policy decisions of the party's state convention.

State of the Union Message An annual message to Congress in which the president proposes a legislative program. The message is addressed not only to Congress but also to the American people and to the world.

Statutory Power A power created for the president through laws enacted by Congress.

Straight-Ticket Voting Voting exclusively for the candidates of one party.

Strategic Arms Limitation Treaty (SALT I) A treaty between the United States and the Soviet Union to stabilize the nuclear arms competition between the two countries. SALT I talks began in 1969, and the treaty was signed in 1972.

Strict Scrutiny A judicial standard for assessing the constitutionality of a law or government action when the law or action threatens to interfere with a fundamental right or potentially discriminates on the basis of race.

Suffrage The right to vote. A vote given in favor of a proposed measure, candidate, or the like.

Sunset Legislation Laws requiring that existing programs be reviewed regularly for their effectiveness and be terminated unless specifically extended as a result of these reviews.

Superdelegate A party leader or elected official who is given the right to vote at the party's national convention. Superdelegates are not elected at the state level.

Super PAC A political organization that aggregates unlimited contributions by individuals and organizations to be spent independently of candidate committees.

Supremacy Clause The constitutional provision that makes the Constitution and federal laws superior to all conflicting state and local laws.

Supremacy Doctrine A doctrine that asserts the priority of national law over state laws. This principle is stated in Article VI of the Constitution.

Symbolic Speech Expression made through articles of clothing, gestures, movements, and other forms of nonverbal communication.

T

Technical Assistance The practice of sending experts in such areas as agriculture, engineering, and business to aid other nations.

Terrorism A systematic attempt to inspire fear to gain political ends, typically involving the indiscriminate use of violence against noncombatants.

Third Party A political party other than the two major political parties (Republican and Democratic).

Ticket Splitting Voting for candidates of two or more parties for different offices. For example, a voter splits her ticket if she votes for a Republican presidential candidate and for a Democratic congressional candidate.

Totalitarian Regime A form of government that controls all aspects of the political, social, and economic life of a nation.

Tracking Poll A poll that is taken continuously—sometimes every day—to determine how support for an issue or candidate changes over time.

Treasuries U.S. Treasury securities—bills, notes, and bonds; debt issued by the federal government.

Trial Court The court in which most cases begin.

Truman Doctrine The policy adopted by President Harry Truman in 1947 to halt Communist expansion in southeastern Europe.

Trustee A legislator who acts according to her or his conscience and the broad interests of the entire society.

Twelfth Amendment An amendment to the Constitution, adopted in 1804, that specifies the separate election of the president and the vice president by the Electoral College.

Twenty-fifth Amendment A 1967 amendment to the Constitution that establishes procedures for filling presidential and vice-presidential vacancies and makes provisions for presidential incapacity.

Two-Party System A political system in which only two parties have a reasonable chance of winning.

U

Unanimous Opinion A court opinion or determination on which all judges agree.

Unemployment The inability of those who are in the labor force to find a job.

Unicameral Legislature A legislature with only one legislative chamber, as opposed to a bicameral (two-chamber) legislature, such as the U.S. Congress. Today, Nebraska is the only state in the Union with a unicameral legislature.

Unitary System A centralized governmental system in which ultimate governmental authority rests in the hands of the national, or central, government.

Unit Rule A rule by which all of a state's electoral votes are cast for the presidential candidate who receives a plurality of the votes in that state.

Universal Suffrage The right of all adults to vote for their representatives.

V

Veto Message The president's formal explanation of a veto, which accompanies the vetoed legislation when it is returned to Congress.

Vote-Eligible Population The number of people who, at a given time, enjoy the right to vote in national elections.

Voter Turnout The percentage of citizens taking part in the election process; the number of eligible voters who actually "turn out" on Election Day to cast their ballots.

Voting-Age Population The number of people of voting age living in the country at a given time, regardless of whether they have the right to vote.

W

War Powers Resolution A law passed in 1973 spelling out the conditions under which the president can commit troops without congressional approval.

Whig Party A major party in the United States during the first half of the nineteenth century, formally established in 1836. The Whig Party was anti-Jackson and advocated spending on infrastructure.

Whip A member of Congress who aids the majority or minority leader of the House or the Senate.

Whistleblower In the context of government, someone who brings gross governmental inefficiency or an illegal action to the public's attention.

White House Office The personal office of the president, which tends to presidential political needs and manages the media.

White Primary A state primary election that restricted voting to whites only. Outlawed by the Supreme Court in 1944.

Writ of *Certiorari* An order issued by a higher court to a lower court to send up the record of a case for review.

Writ of *Habeas Corpus* *Habeas corpus* means, literally, "you have the body." A writ of *habeas corpus* is an order that requires jailers to bring a prisoner before a court or judge and explain why the person is being held.

Index

A

AARP (formerly American Association of Retired Persons), 317
accomplishments of, 150–151
Abe, Shinzo, 333
Abortion
partial-birth, 83, 289
privacy rights and, 9, 81–83
special interest groups and, 150
Absentee ballots, 186
Accuracy in Media, 140
Accused, rights of
basic rights, 84–85
exclusionary rule, 85–86
gag orders and, 80
Miranda warning, 85
Actual malice, 79
Adams, John, 24, 158
Adams, John Quincy, 22, 158, 185, 226
Adams, Samuel, 37
Adarand Constructors, Inc. v. Peña, 108–109
Adelson, Sheldon, 178, 179
Administrative agency, as source of American law, 273
Administrative law tribunals, 277
Administrative Procedure Act, 236
Advertising
campaigns ads by special interest groups, 178
"daisy girl," 135–136
First Amendment protection and, 75
issue advocacy, 177
media's profit-making function and, 133
negative, 135–136
political, 135–136
Advice and consent, 229
Affirmation of judgment, 281
Affirmative action, 107–109
college admission and, 290
defined, 107

end of, 109
limits on, 108–109
Affordable Care Act, 62
Afghanistan
al Qaeda and, 327–328
American invasion of, 228
federalization of National Guard, 53
Northern Alliance, 326
Taliban government in, 320, 326
AFL (American Federation of Labor), 146
AFL-CIO, 146
African Americans
civil rights and, 93–100, 145
consequences of slavery and, 94–97
equality and, 9
extralegal methods of enforcing white supremacy, 95–96
fertility rate of, 105
importance of religion, 192
Jim Crow laws, 95
lynching and, 95–96
percentage change in U.S. ethnic distribution, 105
political participation by, 99–100
as public officials, 172
school integration and, 96
separate-but-equal doctrine, 95, 96
support of Democratic Party, 160
voter behavior, 99–100, 123
voting rights of, 94, 95, 99, 190, 191
Agenda building, health care and, 298–300
Agenda setting
by Congress, 199
defined, 119
by media, 119
Agriculture Department
functions of, 254
subagencies of, 254
Agriculture interest groups, 146
Ahmadinejad, Mahmoud, 329

AIG, 257–258
al-Assad, Bashar, 2, 323
Alien "removal" courts, 278
Alito, Samuel, 41, 284–285, 288, 289
Allende, Salvador, 335
al-Maliki, Nouri, 326
al Qaeda
in Afghanistan, 327–328
in Pakistan, 326
reasons for attack, 324
September 11, 2001 terrorist attacks and, 320
American Automobile Association (AAA), 145
American Bar Association (ABA), 147
American Civil Liberties Union (ACLU), 113
American Crossroads, 179
American Dairy Association, 145
American Farm Bureau Federation, 146
American Federation of Labor (AFL), 146
American Federation of Teachers, 147
American Friends Service Committee, 342
American Indians
assimilation, 107
demographic collapse of, 106–107
gambling casinos, 107
American Israel Public Affairs Committee, 150
American Journalism Review, 140
American Medical Association (AMA), 148
American Revolution, 5, 23–28
Americans for Democratic Action, 150
Americans for Tax Reform, 150
American Woman Suffrage Association, 101
Amicus curiae brief, 274
Amnesty International, 342

AMTRAK, 257
Anthony, Susan B., 100
Anti-Federalists, 36–37, 157–158
Anti-Ku Klux Klan Act (Civil
Rights Act of 1872), 94
Antiterrorism and Effective
Death Penalty Act, 87–88, 278
Appellate court, 276–277, 282
Appointment power, 227
Appropriation, 218
Arab Spring, 322–323
Aristocracy, 4
Armitage, David, 27
Arraignment, 84
Arthur, Chester, 242
Articles of Confederation, 46, 53
drafting, 28
government under, 28–29
weaknesses of, 29–30
Asian Americans
percentage change in U.S.
ethnic distribution, 105
political participation by, 100
voting behavior, 123
Assembly, freedom of, 68
Association of General
Contractors of America, 147
Astroturf lobbying, 153
Aurora Colorado shooting, 70
Australia, federal system of
government in, 47
Australian ballot, 186
Authoritarianism, 4
Authority, 3
Authorization, 218
Auto industry
Great Recession and bailout, 11
higher fuel efficiency standards,
306
Ayotte, Kelly, 198

B

Bad tendency rule, 75–76
Bagram Air Force Base, 279
Ballots
absentee, 186
Australian, 186
Indiana, 186
Massachusetts, 186
office-block, 186
party-column, 186
Banking industry
bank bailout, 257–258

banking crisis of 2008, 257–258
government ownership of, 257
Great Recession and bailout, 11
national bank, 54
Bankruptcy, government control
of private corporations and,
257
Benghazi consulate attack, 323
Benton v. Maryland, 68
Bernanke, Ben, 313
Bias, in media, 138–139
Bicameralism, 197
Bicameral legislature, 31, 197
Biden, Joe, 240, 241, 242
Big government, 11–12
Great Recession and, 11
health care reform and, 161
Iraq War and, 11
liberals and, 15
mid-term elections of 2010 and,
161
Obamacare and, 11
Bill, becomes a law, 215–216
Bill of Rights. *See also individual
amendments*
adoption of, 38
defined, 9
extending to state government,
67
freedom of expression (*See*
Press, freedom of; Speech,
freedom of)
incorporating Fourteenth
Amendment into, 68–69
incorporation theory, 68–69
ratification, 38
rights of noncitizens, 105
Bin Laden, Osama, 320, 324
death of, 233, 240, 327
Bipartisan Campaign Reform Act,
177
Blackmun, Harry A., 75
Blanket primary, 182
Block grants, 60
Blue states, 161
Boehner, John, 13, 162, 213, 219
Boeing Corporation, 261
Bork, Robert, 285
Bosnia, 333
American troops sent to, 228
Boston Globe, 134
Boston Marathon bombing, 324
Boston Tea Party, 23

Boumediene v. Bush (2008),
292–293
Bowers v. Hardwick, 110
BP Deepwater Horizon oil spill,
256, 306
Bradford, William, 21
Branch Ministries, Inc., 73
Brandeis, Louis, 48
Brandenburg v. Ohio, 76
Brazil, federal system of
government in, 47
Brewer, Jan, 62
Breyer, Stephen, 41, 285, 288
Broad construction, 287
Brown, John, 55
Brown, Linda Carol, 96
Brown, Oliver, 96
Brown, Scott, 301
*Brown v. Board of Education of
Topeka,* 96
Bryan, Williams Jennings, 159,
161
Buckley v. Valeo, 176
Budget. *See* Federal budget
Budget and Impoundment
Control Act, 217
Budget deficit
deficit spending and, 311
defined, 309
Keynes and, 309
public debt and, 311–312
Budget surplus, 311–312
Bull Moose Progressive Party, 166
Bureaucracy, 247–268
congressional control of, 267
defined, 248
efficiency and productivity
incentives for, 262–263
history of civil service, 259–261
iron triangles, 266
issue network, 266–267
merit system, 259
nature of, 248–250
organization of federal,
250–258
cabinet departments, 251
chart of, 252
government corporations,
256–258
independent executive
agencies, 251–252
independent regulatory
agencies, 253–256

policymaking and, 264–267
political appointees, 258–259
private, 248–249
privatization and, 262
public, 248–249
reform, modern attempts at, 261–264
size of, 249–250
spoils system, 259
staffing, 258–261
sunset legislation, 261–262
sunshine laws and, 261
whistleblowers and, 263–264
Bureaucrats, as policymakers and politicians, 264–267
Bureau of the Budget, 241
Burger, Warren, 76
Burma, 3
Burr, Aaron, 226
Bush, George H. W., 230
   appointments by, 103
   approval rating of, 130
   armed forces ordered by
      into combat without congressional approval, 337
      into Middle East, 228
      into Panama, 228
   election of 1992, 166
   First Gulf War and, 325
   Flag Protection Act, 74
   foreign policy and, 341
   judicial appointment and, 284
   plan to end governmental inefficiency, 248
   reregulation and, 256
   Soviet Union and, 341
Bush, George W., 236
   approval rating of, 130
   armed forces ordered by
      invasion of Afghanistan, 228
      invasion of Iraq, 228
      in Iraq, 325–326, 333
   bank bailout, 257–258
   Cheney as vice president, 242
   election of 2000, 161
      demographics and, 122
      electoral college, 185, 226
      Latino vote, 124
      Muslim American support for, 124
      Supreme Court decision and, 279–280

without majority of vote, 226
   election of 2004, 161
      demographics and, 122
   enemy combatant detainees, 278
   federal government's reach expanded by, 58
   federalization of National Guard, 53
   financial crisis of 2008 and deregulation, 256
   as fund-raiser, 233
   immigration reform, 304
   Iraq war and, 228, 230, 325–326, 337
   Iraq War and, 11
   judicial appointment, 284, 285
   Keynesian economics, 310
   lobbying reform, 154
   No Child Left Behind Act, 58
   partial-birth abortions, 83
   plan to end governmental inefficiency, 248
   public approval of, 233
   signing statements and, 237
   tax cuts, 312
   war on terrorism, 235, 278, 324–325
   warrantless wiretaps, 87
   waterboarding and, 336
Bush Doctrine, 325
Bush v. Gore (2000), 292–293
Business cycle, 309
Business interest groups, 146
Busing, 97

C

Cabinet
   defined, 238
   kitchen, 239
   members of, 238–239
   presidential use of, 239
Cabinet departments
   defined, 251
   listed, 254–255
   president and, 251
Campaign financing, 175–180
   Bipartisan Campaign Reform Act, 177
   Buckley v. Valeo, 176
   Citizens decision, 177, 178, 287
   current environment of, 177–180

evolution of, 176–177
   Federal Election Campaign Act (FECA), 176
   501(c)4 organizations, 179–180
   527 organizations, 178
   independent expenditures, 177–178
   interest groups and, 176–180
   Internet and, 138
   issue advocacy advertising, 177
   political action committees (PACs), 176–177
   president as fund-raiser, 232–233
   presidential candidate committees, 180
   public financing for primaries, 180
   regulating, 176–177
   soft money, 177
   super PACs, 178, 179
Campaigns
   advertising, 135–136
   candidate-centered, 174
   candidate visibility and appeal, 175
   changes in, from those earlier, 174–175
   coattail effect and, 205
   federal employees and, 260–261
   financing (*See* Campaign financing)
   focus groups and, 175
   interest groups and assistance with, 152
   Internet and, 138
   managing news coverage, 137
   media and, 135–139
   negative advertising, 135–136
   opinion polls and, 175
   political consultants and, 174–175
   power of incumbency, 205, 206
   presidential debates, 137
   professional, 174–175
   twenty-first century, 172–175
   winning strategy of, 175
Canada
   federal system of government in, 47
   lobbying by, 151
   U.S. oil imports from, 305

Candidate(s), 172–173
African Americans as, 172
candidate-centered campaigns,
174
coattail effect and, 186, 205
for congressional elections, 205
front-runner, 183
perception of, and voting
behavior, 192
power of incumbency, 205, 206
professionals as, 173
recruiting, by political parties,
154–155
visibility and appeal of, 175
women as, 173
Cantwell v. Connecticut, 68
Capitalism
defined, 10
laissez-faire capitalism, 15
Capture, 255–256
Caribbean, lobbying by, 151
Carter, Jimmy
armed forces ordered by
into combat without
congressional approval,
337
China and, 340
deregulation, 256
election of 1980, 128
judicial appointment and, 282
Mondale and, 242
People's Republic of China
recognized by, 229
plan to end governmental
inefficiency, 248
Carville, James, 174
Case law, 273
Casework, 199
Categorical grants, 59–60
Catholics
Democratic Party and, 159
voting behavior, 122, 123
Caucus, 181, 183
Ceballos, Richard, 264
Census Bureau, measuring
unemployment, 308
Central Intelligence Agency (CIA)
creation of, 335
criticism of, 336
failure to detect nuclear
arsenals of India and
Pakistan, 336
Certiorari, writ of, 280

Chamber of Commerce, U.S., 146
Change to Win Coalition, 146
Checks and balances, 34, 35
judicial review and, 286
Cheney, Dick, 236, 242, 336
Chicago Tribune, 134
Chief diplomat, 229–230
Chief executive, 227–228
Chief legislator, 230–231
Chief of staff, 240
Child Online Protection Act
(COPA), 77
Children
political socialization of, 118–119
pornography and, 76–77
Children's Internet Protection Act
(CIPA), 77
China
aid provided to North Korea by,
339
Communist Party of, 3
economic growth of, 330
foreign policy and, 328–331
formal diplomatic recognition
of, 340
nationalism, 330–331
normal trade relations (NTR)
status and, 328
nuclear weapons and, 327
ownership of U.S. public debt,
310
President Carter's recognition
of, 229
relationship with North Korea,
328
Taiwan and, 330
CHIP (Children's Health
Insurance Program), 250
Christianity, nation's founders
and, 24
Chrysler, 11
CIO (Congress of Industrial
Organizations), 146
Circuit courts of appeals, U.S.,
276–277
Citizens United v. Federal
Election Commission, 42,
177, 178, 287
City political machines, 156
Civil Aeronautic Board, 256
Civil contempt, 275
Civil disobedience, 97
Civil liberties, 66–89

Bill of Rights and, 67–69
versus civil rights, 92
defined, 8
freedom of expression, 73–81
freedom of religion, 69–73
freedom of speech, 73–79
freedom of the press, 79–81
of immigrants, and national
security, 87–88
privacy rights, 81–84
rights of accused vs. rights of
society, 84–86
search and seizure, 89
vs. security issues, 86–88
suspended during Civil War,
235
Civil right(s), 92–113
African Americans and
consequences of slavery,
93–97
American Indians and, 105–107
versus civil liberties, 92
civil rights movement, 97–100
defined, 92
extending equal protection,
107–109
of gay males and lesbians,
110–112
immigration and, 104–105
King's philosophy of
nonviolence, 97
Latinos and, 104–105
March on Washington, 98
modern legislation regarding,
98–100
women and, 100–104
Civil Rights Act
of 1866, 94
of 1872 (Anti-Ku Klux Klan Act),
94
of 1875 (Second Civil Rights
Act), 94
of 1964, 98–99, 107, 264
Title VII, 99, 103
of 1968, 99
ineffectiveness of early civil
rights laws, 94–96
Civil Rights Cases, 94
Civil rights movement, 97–100,
145, 160
Civil service
defined, 227
difficulty in firing, 259

history of, 259–261
merit system, 259
political campaigns and,
260–261
whistleblowers and, 263–264
Civil Service Commission,
259–260
Civil Service Reform Act
of 1883, 259–260
of 1978, 260, 263
Civil unions, 112
Civil War
civil liberties suspended during,
235
national government's growth
and, 56
political parties during, 158
slavery and, 55–56
states' rights and, 55–56
Class-action suits, 274–275
Clinton, Bill, 73, 184
appointments by, 103
approval rating of, 130
armed forces ordered by
to bomb Serbia, 228
to Bosnia, 228, 333
into combat without
congressional approval,
337
to Haiti, 228, 333
budget surplus during,
311–312
deregulation, 256
"don't ask, don't tell" policy, 111
election of
of 1992, 166
of 1996, 122
without majority of vote, 185,
226
as fund-raiser, 233
impeachment of, 238
judicial appointment and, 284,
285
line-item veto, 232
national health-insurance
system, 300–301
plan to end governmental
inefficiency, 248
welfare reform, 58
Clinton, Hillary Rodham, 10, 103,
173, 240
Arab Spring and, 322–323
as Secretary of State, 334

Closed primary, 182
Cloture, 201–202
Coattail effect, 186
Coercive Acts, 23
Cohort effect, 121
Colbert, Stephen, 132, 139
Cold War
defined, 327
superpower relations during, 338
Colleges
affirmative action and
admission, 290
campus speech and behavior
codes, 79
segregation, 96
student activity fees, 78–79
Colonial America
British taxation of, 23
Continental Congresses, 23
Declaration of Independence,
26–28
establishment of, 21–22
Mayflower compact, 21–22
rise of Republicanism, 27–28
Comedy Central, 132
Commander in chief, 228–229
Commerce
defined, 55
interstate, 55
intrastate, 55
Commerce clause, 40, 288
defined, 54
Gibbons v. Ogden, 54–55
limiting national government's
authority under, 61
Commerce Department
functions of, 254
subagencies of, 254
Commercial speech, 75
Committee of Concerned
Journalists, 140
Common Cause, 149–150
Common law
defined, 272
tradition of, 272
Common Sense (Paine), 24–25
Communication Decency Act
(CDA), 77
Concurrent powers, 51
Concurring opinions, 281
Confederal system
defined, 46
flow of power in, 47

Confederation, 26, 28
Conference committee, 211–212
Conflict resolution, Congress
and, 199
Congress, 196–219. *See also*
House of Representatives, of
the United States; Senate, of
the United States
apportionment and, 205–209
bicameralism of, 197
budget and, 215–219
bureaucracy and control of by,
267
checks and balances, 34, 35
checks on courts and, 291–292
committees of
members of, selection of, 212
power of, 210
structure of, 209–212
types of, 210–212
contacting representative, 220
Democratic control of, 12,
160–161, 300
earmarks and, 198
elections for, 197, 204–209
voter turnout and, 188, 189
foreign policy and balancing
president, 336–337
formal leadership in, 212–215
functions of, 197–199
conflict-resolution, 199
lawmaking, 197–198
oversight, 199
public-education, 199
representation function, 198
service to constituents, 199
incumbency and power of, 205,
206
iron triangles, 266
lawmaking, 197–198
bill becomes a law, 215–216
president as chief legislator
and, 230–232
logrolling, 198
members of
age of, 202, 204
compared to citizenry, 202–204
income and wealth of, 202, 204
minorities, 204
perks of, 202–203
privileges and immunities of,
203–204
professional staff, 203

religion of, 204
requirements for office, 172
salary of, 202
term of, 197
women as, 102–103, 173, 204
opposition to Obamacare, 302
powers of
constitutional amendments, 200–201
to declare war, 40, 228
enumerated, 49, 200
inherent, 50
necessary and proper clause, 49–50, 201
to override presidential veto, 232
of the purse, 337
regulate foreign and interstate commerce, 40
president as chief legislator, 230–231
public opinion regarding, 196
Republican control of, 11, 161, 162
seniority system, 212
separation of powers, 34
Congressional Budget Office, 61, 267
Congressional elections, 204–209
candidates for, 205
coattail effect, 205
direct primaries and, 205
midterm gains and losses by party of president, 205
power of incumbency, 205, 206
requirements for, 204
Congressional Union, 101
Congress of Confederation, 28–29
Congress of Industrial Organizations (CIO), 146
Connecticut Compromise, 32, 197
Consensus, 117, 118
Consent of the people, 5
Conservative movement, 14
Conservatives/conservatism
Cuban Americans, 124
defined, 13
economic status and, 121–123
favoring state government, 59
four-cornered ideological grid, 16, 121
global warming and, 307
judicial restraint and, 286

modern, 14
Muslim Americans, 124
Republican Party and, 13
on traditional political spectrum, 15
values of, 14
Constituent governments, 47
Constituents
defined, 197
as lobbyists, 153
of president, 233
service to, by members of Congress, 199
Constitutional Convention, 30–36, 47
Constitutional democracy, 6
Constitutional powers, 235
Constitution of United States, 20–42. *See also* Bill of Rights
altering, 38–41
formal amendment process of, 38–39
informal means to, 39–41
Amendments to
First (*See* First Amendment)
Second, 42
Third, 68, 81
Fourth, 40, 68, 81, 84, 86
Fifth, 68, 81, 84, 85
Sixth, 68, 80, 84, 85
Eighth, 68, 84, 85
Ninth, 68, 81
Tenth, 45
Twelfth, 200, 226
Thirteenth, 93
Fourteenth (*See* Fourteenth Amendment)
Fifteenth, 93, 94, 95, 190
Sixteenth, 200, 291
Seventeenth, 197
Nineteenth, 101, 190
Twentieth, 201
Twenty-third, 185
Twenty-fourth, 95
Twenty-fifth, 201, 242
Twenty-sixth, 190
to check courts, 291
listed, 39
Article I of, 197, 237
Section 4 of, 204
Section 6 of, 203
Section 8 of, 39–40, 49, 54, 200, 201

Section 9 of, 88
Article II of, 40, 237
Section 1, 185, 225, 242, 333
Section 2, 227, 281, 333
Section 3, 231
Article III of, Section 1, 40, 274
Article IV of, Section 2, 53
Article V of, 38
Article VI of
Clause 2 of, 51
Section 1, 53
Christianity and, 24
commerce clause, 54
drafting, 30–38
checks and balances, 34, 35
Constitutional Convention, 30–36, 47
electoral college and, 34
Great Compromise, 32
Madisonian model, 34
New Jersey Plan, 31–32
separation of powers, 34
slavery and, 32–33
Supremacy doctrine, 32
three-fifths compromise, 32–33
Virginia Plan, 31
equal protection clause, 95, 96, 102
necessary and proper clause, 49–50, 54
powers under
of Congress, 39–40
of president, 40, 235
Preamble to, 20
ratification, 35–38
rights of noncitizens, 105
slavery under, 93
as source of American law, 273
supremacy clause of, 51, 53
Consumer movement, 149
Consumer price index, 308
Consumer Reports, 149
Consumers Union, 149
Containment policy, 339
Contempt of court, 275
Continental Illinois, 257
Continuing resolution, 219
Contracting-out strategy, 262
Contractionary monetary policy, 313
Convention delegates, 155–156

Cooperative federalism
  defined, 58
  methods of implementing,
    59–61
  New Deal and, 57–58
Cornwallis, Charles, 27–28
Corwin, Edwin S., 333
Cott, Nancy, 100
Council of Economic Advisers,
  239
Council on Environmental
  Quality, 239
Court of Appeals for the
  Thirteenth Circuit, 277
Courts, 271–294
  appellate courts, 276–277
  common law tradition and, 272
  contempt of court, 275
  executive checks, 289–291
  federal (*See* Federal court
    system)
  impact of lower courts, 293
  judicial activism, 286
  judicial restraint, 287
  judicial traditions and doctrine,
    292
  legislative checks, 291–292
  parties to lawsuits, 274–275
  policymaking function,
    286–293
  political question, 293
  procedural rules, 275
  requirements to bring case
    before, 274
  sources of American law and,
    272–273
  Supreme Court (*See* Supreme
    Court of United States)
  trial courts, 276
Courts of appeal, U.S., 276–277,
  282
Cracking, in redistricting, 207
Crawford, William H., 226
Credentials committee, 184
Criminal contempt, 275
Cross burning, 74
Crossley, Archibald, 126
*Cruzan v. Director, Missouri
  Department of Health,* 83
Cuba, Cuban Missile Crisis,
  339–340
Cuban Americans, 104
  voting behavior, 124

Cuban missile crisis, 339–340
Culture
  dominant, 8
  political, 8

D

"Daisy Girl" ad, 135–136
Daley, Richard J., 156
Davis v. Bandemer, 206–207
Death with dignity law, 61
Debt ceiling, 219
Declaration of Independence
  natural rights and social
    contracts, 26–27
  significance of, 27
  universal truths, 26
Declaration of Sentiments, 100
De facto segregation, 97
Defamation of character, 77
Defendants, 274
  pretrial rights, 84
Defense Department, 321
  creation of, 336
  foreign policymaking and, 336
  functions of, 254
  size of, 336
  subagencies of, 254
Defense of Marriage Act, 52,
  111–112
Defense policy, defined, 321
Defense spending, amount of
  federal budget, 250, 251
Deficit spending
  Obama and stimulus package,
    310
  public debt and, 310–312
De Jonge v. Oregon, 68
De jure segregation, 97
Delegates
  caucus system for choosing, 183
  convention activities, 184
  to national convention, 181
  seating, 184
  selecting, 155–156
  superdelegates, 181
Democracy
  constitutional, 6
  defined, 4
  direct, 4–5
  elite theory and, 7
  for groups, 8
  majoritarianism and, 7
  pluralism and, 8

  principles of, 6
  in United States, 6–8
Democratic Party
  blue states and, 161
  Congress controlled by,
    160–161, 300
  convention delegates, 155–156,
    168
  debt ceiling crisis, 219
  economic status, 121–123
  education and, 123
  fiscal cliff and sequester, 219
  formation of, 158
  gender gap and, 125
  geographic region and, 125
  health care reform, 300
  history of, 158–162
  immigration issue and,
    304–305
  liberalism and, 14
  midterm elections of 2010 and,
    161
  National Convention of, in 1968,
    181
  Obama and young voters, 121
  party identification and,
    166–167
  populism and, 159
  in post-Civil War period, 159
  race and ethnicity, 123–125
  regaining control of
    presidential primary,
    183–184
  today, 161–162
  voters who grew up in Great
    Depression, 121
Democratic republic
  compared to representative
    democracy, 6
  defined, 6
Democratic-Republicans, 158
Depression, 309. *See also* Great
  Depression
Deregulation, 256
Desegregation, 96
Détente, 340
Devolution, 58–59
Dictator, 4
Dictators, 3
Diplomacy
  as aspect of foreign policy, 321
  defined, 321
Diplomatic recognition, 229

Direct democracy
  dangers of, 5
  defined, 4
Direct primary, 181, 205
Direct techniques of interest
    groups, 151–152
Discharge petition, 210
Discouraged workers, 308
Discretionary fiscal policy, 309
Discrimination
  affirmative action and, 107–109
  dealing with, 113
  employment, 99
  gender and, 100–101
  housing, 99
  against potential jurors, 275
  race and, 93–100, 104–107
  reverse, 108
  sexual orientation and, 110–112
  wage, 104
Dissenting opinion, 281
District courts, United States,
    276
Diversity of citizenship, 274
Divided government, 157, 160–
    161
Divided opinion, 117, 118
Dole, Robert, 122
Domestic policy, 298–307
  defined, 297
  energy and environment,
    305–307
  health care and, 298–303
  immigration, 303–305
  promotional policy, 298
  redistributive policy, 297–298
  regulatory policy, 297
Domestic Policy Council, 240
Dominant culture, 8
Double jeopardy, 68, 85
Douglas, William O., 81, 262
Dred Scott v. Sandford, 93
Dual federalism, 57
Due process, limits on rights of,
    and deportees, 87–88
Due process clause, 94

E

Earmarked expenditures, 154
  Congress evading ban on, 218
  defined, 198
Earned Income Tax Program, 316
Earth Day, 149

East Germany, 338
Economic aid, 321
Economic equality, 10
Economic interest groups,
    146–149
Economic policy, 308–315
  deficit spending and public
    debt, 310–312
  fiscal policy, 309–310
  monetary policy, 312–314
  politics of taxation, 314–315
*Economic Report of the
    President,* 218
Economic status
  liberalism and conservatism,
    121–123
  voting behavior and, 121–123
Economy
  health care's role in, 298–299
  presidential elections and, 234
Education
  affirmative action and college
    admission, 290
  aid to church-related schools,
    69–70
  busing, 97
  forbidding teaching of
    evolution, 72
  No Child Left Behind Act, 58
  political socialization and, 119
  school integration and, 96,
    290–291
  school prayer and, 71–72
  school vouchers, 70–71
  separate-but-equal doctrine, 96
  voting behavior and, 123
Education Department
  functions of, 255
  subagencies of, 255
Egalitarianism, 10
Egypt
  Arab Spring, 322
  dictatorial rule in, 3
  unitary system of government
    in, 46
Eighth Amendment, 68, 84, 85
Eisenhower, Dwight, 160, 227,
    228
  cabinet of, 239
  pact with vice president
    regarding incapacity of,
    242
  school integration and, 96, 291

South Vietnam supported by, 334
Elastic clause, 49–50
Elections. *See also* Presidential
    elections; Primary elections
  economic issues influence on,
    161
  general, 173
  organization and running of, by
    political parties, 154
  primary, 173
  types of ballots, 186
Electoral college
  choosing president, 225–226
  criticism of, 185–186
  defined, 34, 164
  drafting Constitution and, 34
  election of 2000, 161, 226
  election of 2012, 163
  electors, 185
  unit rule, 164
  winner-take-all system, 164
Electors, 164
  choosing, 185
  defined, 185
  faithless, 185
Elite theory, 7
Emancipation Proclamation and,
    93
Emergency powers, 235
Employment discrimination
  Civil Rights Act and, 99
  gender-based, 103–104
Enabling legislation, 264
Endangered Species Act, 265
Enemy combatant detainees,
    278–279
Energy Department
  functions of, 255
  subagencies of, 255
Energy policy, 305–307
  America's reliance on foreign
    oil, 305
  disasters in energy industry,
    306–307
  fracking, 306
  higher fuel efficiency standards
    for vehicles, 306
  legislation to limit greenhouse
    gas emissions, 307
  new U.S. production, 305–306
  politics of expensive oil, 306
  subsidies for alternative fuels,
    306

Enforcement Act of 1870, 94
Engel v. Vitale, 71
Entitlement programs
 controversy over value of, 12
 defined, 12
 reform of, 317
Enumerated powers, 49, 200
Environmental Defense Fund, 149
Environmental interest groups, 149
Environmental policy, 305–307
 America's reliance on foreign oil, 305
 global warming, 307
 legislation to limit greenhouse emission, 307
Equal Employment Opportunity Commission (EEOC), 99, 113, 264
 affirmative action and, 108
Equality
 African Americans and, 9
 defined, 9
 economic, 10
 liberty versus, 9–10
Equal Pay Act, 104
Equal protection clause, 38, 95, 96, 205
 affirmative action and, 107–108
 gender discrimination and, 102
Equal Rights Amendment, 100, 150
Eras
 of divided government, 160–161
 of good feelings, 158
 New Deal, 160
Espionage Act, 75
Establishment clause, 69
Estate tax, 314, 315
Ethanol, 306
Ethnicity, voting behavior and, 123–125
European Central Bank (ECB), 332
European Union (EU)
 as confederal system of government, 46
 debt crisis, 332–333
 lobbying by, 151
Everson v. Board of Education, 68
Evidence, exclusionary rule, 85–86
Evolution, teaching of, 72

Exclusionary rule, 68, 85–86
 good faith exception, 86
 plain view doctrine, 86
Executive agreements, 40, 230, 334
Executive branch
 checks and balances, 34, 35
 electoral college, 34
 separation of powers, 34
 structure of, 250–258
Executive budget, 215, 217
Executive Office of the President, 239–241
 agencies within, 239
 defined, 239
 National Security Council, 241
 Office of Management and Budget, 241
 White House Office, 239, 240
Executive orders, 236
Executive privilege, 236–237
Expansionary monetary policy, 313
Export taxes, 33
Ex post facto laws, limits on rights of, and deportees, 88
Expressed powers, 49, 235
Expression, freedom of. *See* Press, freedom of; Speech, freedom of

F

Facebook, impact on public opinion, 120
Factions, among delegates to Constitutional Convention, 30–31
Fairness and Accuracy in Reporting, 140
Fairness Doctrine, 120
Fair Pay Restoration Act, 104
Faithless electors, 185
Fall review, 217
False Claims Act, 263
Family, political socialization and, 118–119
Fannie Mae, 258
Farm Bureau, 146
Faubus, Orval, 96, 290–291
Fed. *See* Federal Reserve System (Fed)
Federal budget, 215–219
 budget deficit and Keynes, 309

budget resolutions and crisis, 218–219
budget sequestration, 137
categories of spending, 250, 251
Congress and, 218
continuing resolution, 219
debt ceiling and, 219
defense spending, 250, 251
election-year budgets, 218
executive budget, 215, 217
fiscal cliff and sequester, 219
preparing budget, 217–218
size of, 250
social spending of, 250, 251
Federal budget deficit
 debate over size of, 253
 Great Recession and increase in, 250
 percent of GDP, 253
Federal Circuit, 277
Federal Communications Commission (FCC), Fairness Doctrine, 120
Federal court system, 273–279
 alien "removal" courts, 278
 basic judicial requirements for cases, 274
 constitutional authority for, 274
 enemy combatants and, 278–279
 executive checks, 289–291
 FISA court, 277–278
 impact of lower courts on, 293
 judicial activism, 286
 judicial appointment, 281–287
 judicial restraint, 287
 judicial traditions and doctrine, 292
 jurisdiction, 274
 legislative checks, 291–292
 parties to lawsuits, 274–275
 policymaking function of, 286–293
 procedural rules, 275
 Supreme Court (*See* Supreme Court of United States)
 types of courts
  administrative law tribunals, 277
  courts of appeals, 276–277
  district courts, 276
  Supreme Court, 277

as three-tiered system, 275–276
war on terrorism and, 277–279
Federal Deposit Insurance Corporation (FDIC), 257
Federal Election Campaign Act (FECA), 176
Federal Election Commission (FEC), 165
  creation of, 176
  501(c)4 organizations, 179–180
Federal Employees Political Activities Act, 260
Federal government. *See* National government
Federal grants
  block, 60
  categorical, 59–60
  conditions attached to, 60–61
Federal Home Loan Mortgage Corporation, 258
Federalism, 45–63
  arguments against, 49
  arguments for, 47–48
  benefit of, for United States, 48
  characteristics of, 47
  constitutional basis for, 49–53
  cooperative, 57–58
  devolution, 58–59
  dispute over division of power, 53–61
  dual, 57
  fiscal federalism, 60
  politics of, 58–59
  same-sex marriage recognition and, 52
  Supreme Court and
    early years, 53–56
    today, 61–62
Federalist Papers, 34, 36, 49, 144, 203
Federalists, 157–158
  ratification of Constitution, 36–37
Federal mandates, 61
Federal National Mortgage Association, 258
Federal Open Market Committee, 313
Federal question, 274, 277
Federal Register, 236, 264, 265
Federal Regulation of Lobbying Act, 153

Federal Reserve System (Fed)
  Board of Governors of, 313
  defined, 312
  functions of, 312–313
  organization of, 313
Federal system, 47. *See also* Federalism
Federal Trade Commission (FTC), 264
Federal Trade Commission Act, 264
Feminine Mystique, The (Friedan), 100
Feminism, 100
Ferraro, Geraldine, 103
Fertility rate, 104–105
Fifteenth Amendment, 56, 93, 94, 95, 190
Fifth Amendment, 68, 81, 84, 85
Filibuster, 201, 202
  advantages and disadvantages of, 203
  constitutionality of, 203
  increased use of, 202
  reconciliation, 202
Films. *See* Movies
First Amendment, 42
  clear and present danger, 75
  commercial speech, 75
  cross burning, 74
  establishment clause, 69
  federal employees and, 260
  flag burning, 74
  freedom of press (*See* Press, freedom of)
  freedom of religion (*See* Religion, freedom of)
  freedom of speech (*See* Speech, freedom of)
  free exercise clause, 73
  hate speech, 67
  imminent lawless action test, 76
  incorporation theory, 68
  interest groups and, 144
  privacy rights and, 81
  symbolic speech, 74
First Bank of the United States, 54
First budget resolution, 218
First Continental Congress, 23
First Gulf War, 325
FISA court, 277–278
Fiscal cliff, 117, 219

Fiscal federalism, 60
Fiscal policy, 309–310
  criticism of Keynes, 310
  defined, 60, 309
  discretionary fiscal policy, 309
  government spending and borrowing, 309
Fiscal year cycle, 217
Fisher, Abigail, 109
Fisher v. University of Texas, 109, 290
501(c)4 organizations, 179–180
527 organizations, 178
Flag Protection Act, 74
Focus group, 175
Food stamps, 250
Ford, Gerald, armed forces ordered by into combat without congressional approval, 337
Foreign Affairs, 339
Foreign governments, lobbying by, 151
Foreign Intelligence Surveillance Act (FISA), 277
Foreign policy, 320–342
  Afghanistan and, 326–327
  American, 322–323
  Arab Spring, 322–323
  China and, 328–331
  Congressional powers and, 336–337
  containment policy, 339
  defense policy, 321
  defined, 321
  diplomacy, 321
  economic crisis in Europe, 332–333
  human rights and, 342
  intelligence community and, 335–336
  Iraq, wars in, 325–326
  isolationist, 338
  Israel and Palestinians, 331–332
  moral idealism and, 322–323
  National Security Council and, 334–335
  national security policy and, 321
  nuclear weapons, 327–328
  political realism and, 322–323
  presidential powers and, 333–334

process of, 321
September 11, 2001 and
changed view of, 320–321
State Department and, 334
techniques and strategies of,
321
terrorism and, 323–327
themes in, 337–341
formative years, 337–338
internationalism, 338–339
superpower relations, 339–
341
Truman Doctrine, 339
Fort Hood shooting, 324
Fourteenth Amendment, 42, 56,
87, 93–94
affirmative action and, 107–108
due process clause of, 94
equal protection clause, 38, 95,
205
gender discrimination and,
102
incorporating Bill of Rights
into, 68–69
incorporation theory, 68–69
rights of deportees and, 87
Fourth Amendment, 68, 81, 84,
86
Fox News, 120, 139, 261
Fracking, 306
France
nuclear weapons and, 327
unitary system of government,
46
Franchise, 190
Franking, 202–203
Franklin, Benjamin, 30
Freddie Mac, 258
Freedom
of press (*See* Press, freedom of)
of religion (*See* Religion,
freedom of)
of speech (*See* Speech,
freedom of)
Freedom House, 2
Freedom of Access to Clinic
Entrances Act, 82
Freedom of Information Act
(FOIA), 261, 268
Free exercise clause, 73
Free-rider problem, 145
French and Indian War, 23
French Revolution, 5

Friedan, Betty, 100
Front-loading, 183–184
Front-runner, 183
Fulton, Robert, 54
Fundamental Orders of
Connecticut, 23

G

Gag orders, 80
Gallup, George, 126
Gallup poll, 126
Garfield, James, 242
Gates, Robert, 240
Gay Activist Alliance, 110
Gay Liberation Front, 110
Gay men and lesbians
civil unions, 112
"don't ask, don't tell," 111
growth in rights movement of,
110
in military, 111
privacy rights and, 9
rights and status of, 110–112,
289
same-sex marriage, 10, 52,
111–112, 289
state and local laws targeting,
110–111
Geithner, Timothy, 257
Gender discrimination, 100–101
Gender gap, 125
General election, 173
General jurisdiction, 276
General Motors, 11
General Services Administration
(GSA), 261, 268
Generational effect, 121
Geographic region, public
opinion and, 125
George III, English king, 23, 27
Germany
at close of World War II, 338
East, 338
EU debt crisis and, 333
federal system of government
in, 47
West, 338
Gerry, Elbridge, 206
Gerrymandering, 206–208
Ghana, unitary system of
government in, 46
Gibbons, Thomas, 54
Gibbons v. Ogden, 54–55

Gideon v. Wainwright, 68, 85
Gillibrand, Kirsten, 160
Gingrich, Newt, 178, 179, 182,
212
Ginsburg, Ruth Bader, 103, 285,
288
Gitlow v. New York, 68, 75–76
Global warming
debate over, 307
interest groups and, 149
Goldwater, Barry, 14, 135
Good faith exception, 86
Google, 134
GOP (grand old party), 159
Gorbachev, Mikhail, 341
Gore, Al
election of 2000, 161, 166
demographics and, 122
electoral college, 226
Supreme Court decision and,
279–280
global warming and, 307
Government
authority and legitimacy of, 3
based on consent of the people,
5
big government, 11–12
confederal system, 46
defined, 2
divided, 157
limited, 6
limiting power of, 2–3
need for, 2
as preeminent institution, 2
public opinion about, 129–131
security and order, 2
size and scope of, 11–12
types of, 4
unitary system of, 46
Government Accountability
Office, 267
Government corporations,
256–258
bankruptcy and government
control of private
corporation, 257
defined, 256
government ownership of
private enterprise, 257
Government in the Sunshine Act,
261
Government Performance and
Results Act, 263

Government regulation. *See also*
   Regulation
   deregulation, 256
   reregulation, 256
Governors, popular election of, 164
Graber, Doris A., 120
Grandfather clause, 95
Grant, Ulysses, 285
Grants
   block, 60
   categorical, 59–60
Great Britain
   colonization of America and, 21–23
   health care spending and, 298
   nuclear weapons and, 327
   representative democracy, 6
   unitary system of government in, 46
Great Compromise, 32
Great Depression
   cooperative federalism, 57–58
   generational effect and, 121
   Keynes and budget deficit, 309
   New Deal and, 160
   unemployment during, 309
Great Recession
   auto industry and bailout, 11
   bank bailout, 11, 257–258
   big government and, 11
   budget deficit during, 314
   deregulation and, 256
   election of 2008 and, 161
   housing crisis, 258
   impact on state budgets, 60
   monetary policy and interest rate during, 314
   spending and growth in federal deficit, 250
   stimulus package and, 11, 250
   unemployment during, 309
Greece, dept crisis, 332–333
Green, Steven K., 24
Greenhouse gas emission, 307
Green Party, 166
Grenada, American invasion of, 228
Griswold v. Connecticut, 68, 81
Gross domestic product (GDP)
   defined, 298
   health care spending and, 298
   public debt as percentage of, 311

Grutter v. Bollinger, 109, 290
Guam, 338
Guantánamo Bay, Cuba, detainees held at, 278–279
Gun control issue, 288, 289
   ban on assault-type weapons, 70
Gun-Free School Zone Act, 61

H

Habeas corpus, writ of, 84, 278–279
Hagel, Chuck, 210
Haiti, 322, 333
   American troops sent to, 228
Hamas, 331
Hamilton, Alexander, 203
   Constitutional Convention and, 30
   elite theory and, 7
   Federalist Papers and, 36
Harding, Warren G., 338
Harrison, Benjamin, 185
Harrison, William Henry, 242
Hatch, Orrin, 177, 282
Hatch Act, 176, 260–261
Hate speech, 67
Hayes, Rutherford B., 185
Head of state, 226–227
Health and Human Services, Department of
   functions of, 255
   subagencies of, 255
Health care, 298–303
   agenda building, 298–300
   high costs and, 300
   individual mandate, 301
   international experience, 300
   Medicare and Medicaid costs, 299
   new taxes to fund, 301
   opposition to implementation of Obamacare, 302–303
   per capita spending on, 298–299
   policy adoption, 300–302
   policy evaluation, 303
   policy formation, 300
   policy implementation, 302–303
   reform of
      individual mandate, 62
      lawsuits against, 62, 289
      mid-term elections of 2010, 161

role in American economy, 298–299
   uninsured and problem of, 299–300
   universal coverage and, 300
Health Care and Education Reconciliation Act, 298
Hearst Television, 135
Henry, Patrick, 37
Hibbs, Douglas, 234
Hidden unemployment, 308
Highway construction, federal grants and, 60
Hiroshima, 228
Hispanics
   defined, 104
   fertility rate of, 105
   immigration issue and Republican Party, 124–125, 305
   vs. Latino, 104
   percentage change in U.S. ethnic distribution, 105
   political participation by, 100
   presidential election of 2012, 162
   Republican Party and, 162
   voting behavior, 124–125
Hitler, Adolf, 338
Ho Chi Minh, 339
Holmes, Oliver Wendell, 75
Homeland Security, Department of, 251
   functions of, 255
   subagencies of, 255
Honest Leadership and Open Government Act, 154
Hong Kong, 330
Hoover, Herbert, 160
Hostile-environment harassment, 103–104
House effect, 128
House of Representatives, of the United States. *See also* Congress
   budget and, 215–219
   committees of, 209–212
   contacting representative, 220
   debate in, 201–202
   differences between Senate and, 201
   gerrymandering, 206–208

incumbency and power of, 205, 206
leadership in, 212–214
lobbying rules, 153–154
majority leader of, 213
members of
    age of, 202, 204
    election of, 197
    income and wealth of, 202, 204
    minorities, 204
    perks of, 202–203
    privileges and immunities of, 203–204
    professional staff, 203
    religion of, 204
    term of, 197
    women as, 204
minority leader of, 213–214
minority-majority districts, 208–209
reapportionment, 205–209
redistricting, 205–206
Republican control of, 161–162
requirements for office, 172
Rules Committee of, 212
rules of, 201
seniority system, 212
size of, 201
speaker of, 213
whips in, 214
winning seat in, cost of, 205
House Rules Committee, 212
Housing
    discrimination and, 99
    housing assistance and federal grants, 60
Housing and Urban Development, Department of
    functions of, 255
    subagencies of, 255
Human rights, 342
Hussein, Saddam
    First Gulf War and, 325
    Iraq War and, 325

I

Illegal immigrants
    constitutional rights of, 105
    path to citizenship for, 106
Immigrants/immigration, 303–305
    Arizona immigration controversy, 304

attempts at reform, 304–305
change in U.S. ethnic distribution, 104–105
civil rights of, 104–105
constitutional rights of noncitizens, 105
domestic policy, 303–305
due process and deportees, 87–88
ex post facto laws and deportees, 88
freedom of speech and deportees, 88
Hispanic vs. Latino, 104
limiting state government authority over, 62
mixed families, 304
national security and civil liberties of, 87–88
path to citizenship for unauthorized, 106
political socialization and media, 133
rates of, 303
Republican Party and Hispanic voters, 124–125
state immigration laws, 304
unauthorized immigration issue, 303–304
Imminent lawless action test, 76
Impeachment, 237–238
Implied power, 54
Income tax
    congressional power to impose, 200
    imposed during Civil War, 56
    as progressive tax, 315
    rates of, 314, 315
    rich paying more taxes, 316
An Inconvenient Truth (film), 307
Incorporation theory, 68–69
Independent executive agencies, 251–252
Independent expenditures, 177–178
Independent regulatory agencies, 253–256
    agency capture, 255–256
    deregulation and reregulation, 256
    purpose and nature of, 254–255

Independents
    defined, 154
    midterm elections of 2010 and, 161
    rise of, 166–167, 174
India
    federal system of government in, 47
    nuclear weapons and, 327, 336
Indiana ballot, 186
Indirect primary, 181
Indirect techniques of interest groups, 151, 152–153
Individual mandate, 62, 301
Inflation
    defined, 308
    measuring, 308
    monetary policy and, 313
Information disclosure, 261
Information government knows about private citizens, 268
Inherent powers, 235
    of national government, 50
Initiatives, defined, 4
In re Oliver, 68
In re Quinlan, 83
Institute of Electrical and Electronic Engineers, 147
Institutions, 2
Instructed delegate, 198
Intelligence community
    defined, 335
    foreign policymaking and, 335–336
    war on terrorism and, 336
Intelligent design, 72
Interest groups, 143–154
    campaign assistance by, 152
    campaign financing and, 176–180
    compared to political parties, 144
    constituents as lobbyists, 153
    defined, 143
    direct techniques, 151–152
    economic, 146–149
    527 organizations, 178
    free-rider problem, 145
    indirect techniques, 151, 152–153
    iron triangles, 266
    issue advocacy advertising, 177

issue network, 266–267
lawsuits brought by, 274–275
lobbying techniques, 151–152
poor Americans and, 148–149
public-interest, 149–150
public pressure generated by, 153
ratings game, 152
reasons to join, 145
social movements and, 145
strategies of, 151–154
types of, 146–151
Intergovernmental Panel on Climate Change, 307
Interior Department
functions of, 254
subagencies of, 254
Intermediate-Range Nuclear Force (INF) Treaty, 341
Internal Revenue Code, 314
Internet
campaigns and, 138
as news source, 131, 134
pornography on, 77
Interstate commerce, 40, 55
Interstate Commerce Commission (ICC), 253–254, 256
Interstate compacts, 53
Interstate relations, 53
Intolerable Acts, 23
Intrastate commerce, 55
Iran
nuclear weapons and, 327–328
as oil exporter, 305
as theocracy, 4
Iraq. *See also* Iraq War (Second Gulf War)
American invasion of, in 2003, 228, 325
Bush Doctrine, 325
end game for war, 326
federalization of National Guard, 53
First Gulf War, 325
insurgency, 325
invasion of Kuwait, 325
Kurdish community in, 325
more troops sent to, by Obama, 228
occupation of, 325
Second Gulf War, 325
Shiite community in, 325
Sunni community in, 325

three principal ethnic/religious groups in, 325
UN weapons inspection, 325
Iraq War (Second Gulf War)
big government and, 11
Bush Doctrine, 325
Congress and power of the purse, 337
cost of and deficit spending, 312
end game for, 326
insurgency, 325
international support for, 230
occupation, 325
withdrawal of American troops, 326
Ireland, IRA and, 323, 324
dept crisis, 332
Irish Republican Army, 323
Iron triangles, 266
Isolationist foreign policy, 338
Israel
attacking Iran's nuclear sites, 329
conflict with Palestinians and, 331–332
unitary system of government in, 46
United States as primary defender of, against Palestinians, 324
Issue advocacy advertising, 177
Issue network, 266–267

J

Jackson, Andrew, 226, 285, 289
kitchen cabinet, 239
spoils system, 259
Jamestown, colony at, 21
Japan
attack on Pearl Harbor, 338
expansionary monetary policy, 333
health care spending and, 298
lobbying by, 151
ownership of U.S. public debt, 310
unitary system of government in, 46
Jay, John, 24, 36
Jefferson, Thomas, 24, 185, 259
Declaration of Independence, 26–27
electoral college and, 226

establishment clause, 69
Republican Party of, 158
Jews, voting behavior, 122, 123
Jim Crow laws, 95
Johnson, Andrew, 237
Johnson, Gary, 165
Johnson, Lyndon B., 14
affirmative action, 108
as chief legislator, 231
"daisy girl" ad, 135–136
election of 1964, 135–136
Medicare, creation of, 299
pact with president regarding incapacity of, 242
plan to end governmental inefficiency, 248
South Vietnam supported by, 334
Vietnam War and, 228, 339
Joint committee, 211
Judges. *See also* Supreme Court justices
election of state judges, 283
federal, 281–287
judicial traditions and doctrine, 292
Judicial activism, 286
Judicial implementation, 289
Judicial powers
checks and balances, 34, 35
separation of powers, 34
Judicial restraint, 287
Judicial review
checks and balances and, 34, 286
defined, 40
Federalist Papers and, 36
informal constitutional change and, 40
Judiciary. *See* Courts
Judiciary Committee, 282
Jurisdiction
defined, 274
of federal court system, 274
general, 276
limited, 276
Jury
prospective members of, discrimination against, 275
right to impartial, 68
Justice Department, 249
functions of, 254

solicitor general and, 280
subagencies of, 254
Justiciable controversy, 274
Justiciable question, 205

K

Kagan, Elena, 41, 103, 285, 288
Kennan, George F., 339
Kennedy, Anthony, 41, 288, 289
Kennedy, John F., 225
  Cuban missile crisis, 339–340
  debate with Nixon, 137
  discretionary fiscal policy, 309
  election of, without majority of
    vote, 185, 226
  federal forces sent to
    Mississippi by, 96
  Keynesian economics, 310
  pact with vice president
    regarding incapacity of,
    242
  South Vietnam supported by,
    334
  Vietnam War and, 228, 339
Kerry, John F.
  election of 2004, demographics
    and, 122
  as Secretary of State, 334
Keynes, John Maynard, 309
  criticism of, 310
Keynesian economics, 309–311
  European debt crisis and, 333
Khamenei, Ayatollah Ali, 329
Kim Jong-un, 2, 328
King, Martin Luther, Jr., 97–98
Kissinger, Henry A., 335, 340
Kitchen cabinet, 239
Klein, Ezra, 134
Klopfer v. North Carolina, 68
Korean War, 235, 339
Krugman, Paul, 253
Ku Klux Klan, 76
Kurds in Iraq, 325
Kuwait, Iraq's invasion of, 325

L

Labor Department
  functions of, 254
  measuring unemployment, 308
  subagencies of, 254
Labor interest groups, 146
Labor movement, 146
Laissez-faire capitalism, 15

Landon, Alfred, 125
Lasswell, Harold, 2
Latino. *See also* Hispanics
  defined, 104
  vs. Hispanic, 104
Lawmaking
  bureaucracy and policymaking,
    264–267
  defined, 197
  as function of Congress, 197–198
  negotiated rulemaking, 265
  president as chief legislator
    and, 230–232
  president's veto power, 231–232
  waiting periods and court
    challenges, 264–265
Lawrence v. Texas, 110, 289
Laws
  bill becomes a law process,
    215–216
  case, 273
  common law, 272
  Jim Crow, 95
  oversight, 199
  rewriting, as check on courts,
    291–292
  sodomy, 110
  sources of American law,
    272–273
  sunset, 261–262
  sunshine, 261
Lawsuits
  basic requirements to bring,
    274
  class-action, 274–275
  diversity of citizenship, 274
  interest groups and, 274–275
  parties to, 274–275
  standing to sue, 274
League of Nations, 322
League of Women Voters, 150
Leahy, Patrick, 202, 282
Lebanon, American troops sent
  to, 228
Ledbetter, Lilly, 104
Ledbetter v. Goodyear, 292
Legal Defense Fund, 275
Legislation
  enabling, 264
  negotiated rulemaking, 265
  sunset, 261–262
Legislative Reorganization Act,
  153

Legislature
  bicameral, 31
  checks and balances, 34, 35
  defined, 4
  president and passing, 230–232
  president's veto power, 231–232
  separation of powers, 34
  unicameral, 28
Legitimacy, defined, 3
Lemon test, 70
Lemon v. Kurtzman, 69–70
Lesbians. *See* Gay men and
  lesbians
Lewinsky, Monica, 238
Libel, 77
  actual malice, 79
  defined, 79
  public figures and, 79
Liberals/liberalism
  big government and, 15
  defined, 13
  Democratic Party and, 14
  economic status and, 121–123
  four-cornered ideological grid,
    16, 121
  judicial activism and, 286
  modern, 13
  on traditional political
    spectrum, 15
  values of, 13
Libertarianism
  defined, 15
  economic status and, 121
  four-cornered ideological grid,
    16
  on traditional political
    spectrum, 15
Libertarian Party, 166
Liberty. *See also* Civil liberties
  defined, 3
  equality versus, 9–10
  order versus, 8–9
Libya, 228
  air strikes, 333
  Arab Spring, 322–323
  dictatorial rule in, 3
Lilly Ledbetter Fair Pay Act, 104,
  291
Limbaugh, Rush, 80
Limited government, 6
Limited jurisdiction, 276
Lincoln, Abraham, 27, 333
  cabinet of, 239

election of, without majority of vote, 185, 226
Emancipation Proclamation and, 93
emergency power use, 235
Republican Party of, 158
Line-item veto, 232
Line Item Veto Act, 232
Line organization, 251
Literacy tests, 95
Literary Digest, 125
Litigate, 274
Livingston, Robert, 54
Living wills, 83
Lobbying
Astroturf, 153
by foreign governments, 151
origin of term, 151
techniques used in, 151–152
Lobbying Disclosure Act (LDA), 153
Lobbyists
activities of, 152
constituents as, 153
defined, 143, 153
regulating, 153–154
Local government, voter turnout for, 188
Local legislative bodies, 17
Local party machinery, 156
Locke, John, 26–27
Logrolling, 198
Loopholes, 315
Loose monetary policy, 313
Louisiana Purchase, 50
Lower courts, 293
Lynching, 95–96

M

Madison, James, 132, 144–145, 157
Bill of Rights, 38
Constitutional Convention and, 30–31
Federalist Papers and, 36, 49
Madisonian model and, 34
on problems of pure democracy, 5
slavery and drafting Constitution, 33
Madisonian model, 34
Mail, voting by, 186
Majoritarianism, 7
Majority, 6

Majority leader of the House, 213
Majority opinion, 281
Majority rule, 6
Malloy v. Hogan, 68
Mapp v. Ohio, 68, 86
Marbury v. Madison, 40, 286
March on Washington, 98
Marginal tax rate, 314
Marijuana, medical, 61
Marriage, same-sex, 52, 111–112
Marshall, John, 53–54, 56, 61, 289
Marshall, Thurgood, 86
Marshall Plan, 339
Martinez, Susana, 162
Massachusetts ballot, 186
Massachusetts Bay Colony, 22
Massachusetts Body of Liberties, 23
Matalin, Mary, 174
Material incentives for joining interest groups, 145
Mayflower compact, 21–22
McCain, John, election of 2008
demographics and, 122
Palin as running mate, 241
McCain-Feingold Act, 177
McConnell, Mitch, 214
McCulloch, James William, 54
McCulloch v. Maryland, 50, 53, 54
McDonald v. Chicago, 68
McGovern-Fraser Commission, 181
Means, Russell, 107
Media, 131–139
agenda setting by, 119–120
bias in, 138–139
continuing influence of television, 135
defined, 119
entertainment function, 132
functions of, 132–134
identifying public problems, 132–133
impact of new media, 120
impact on, public opinion, 119–120
information disclosure and, 261
new patterns of media consumption, 134–135
news reporting function, 132
political campaigns and, 135–139

popularity of, 119–120
profit function of, 133
providing political forum, 133
socializing new generations, 133
social networking, 120
spin, 137
spin doctors, 137
talk radio, 120
Medicaid
creation of, 150
defined, 299
described, 299
expansion of, by Obamacare, 302–303
federal budget spent on, 250, 251
federal grants and, 60
government spending on, 299
health-care reform and, 62
Medicare
creation of, 150, 299
defined, 299
described, 299
entitlement reform, 317
federal budget spent on, 250, 251
government spending on, 299
prescription drug coverage, 299
spending growth problem, 300
taxes for, 314, 315
Medvedev, Dmitry, 230, 341
Megan's Law, 133
Meredith, James, 96
Merit system, 259
Merit Systems Protection Board (MSPB), 260
Merkel, Angela, 333
Mexican Americans, 104
Mexico
federal system of government in, 47
illegal immigrants from, 304
U.S. oil imports from, 305
Mid-term elections
of 2006, 161
of 2010, 161
midterm gains and losses by party of president, 205
voter turnout and, 188
Miers, Harriet, 285

Military
  Articles of Confederation and, 29–30
  federal budget spent on, 250, 251
  gay men and lesbians in, 111
  president as commander in chief, 228–229
  women and military combat, 102
Military Commissions Act, 278, 279
Miller v. California, 76
Minerals Management Service, 256
Minority leader of the house, 213–214
Minority-majority districts, 208–209
Minor parties
  ideological third parties, 165–166
  impact of, 166
  role in U.S. politics, 165–166
  splinter parties, 166
  state and federal laws favoring two parties, 164–165
Miranda, Ernesto, 85
Miranda v. Arizona, 85
Mondale, Walter, 242
Monetary policy, 312–314
  defined, 312
  loose (expansionary), 313
  organization of Federal Reserve System, 313
  quantitative easing, 314
  during recession, 314
  tight (contractionary), 313
  time lags for, 313
Monroe, James, 158, 338
Monroe Doctrine, 338
Montesquieu, Baron de, 37
Moral idealism, 322–323
Mossadegh, Mohammad, 335
Motor voter bill, 190
Mott, Lucretia, 100
Movies, prior restraint, 80
Mubarak, Hosni, 322
Muir, John, 149
Muslim Americans, voting behavior, 124
Myanmar, 3

N

NAACP (National Association for the Advancement of Colored People), 96, 145, 150, 275

Nader, Ralph, 149, 166
Nagasaki, 228
NARAL Pro-Choice America, 150
National American Woman Suffrage Association, 101
National Association for the Advancement of Colored People (NAACP), 96, 145, 150, 275
National Association of Manufacturers, 146
National Audubon Society, 149
National Center for Policy Analysis, 317
National committee, 156
National Committee to Preserve Social Security and Medicare, 317
National convention
  convention activities, 155, 184
  defined, 155
  delegates to, 155–156, 168, 183
  as meeting of party elites, 181
  party platform, 155
  reform of, 181
  seating delegates, 184
  superdelegates to, 181
National debt, 253, 312. *See also* Federal budget deficit
National Economic Council, 240
National Education Association (NEA), 147
National government
  aristocracy of, 258
  budget, 215–219
  bureaucracy of
    congressional control of, 267
    organization of, 250–258
    policymaking and, 264–267
    reform of, modern attempts at, 261–264
    size of, 249–250
    staffing, 258–261
  cooperative federalism, 57–58
  devolution, 58–59
  dual federalism, 57
  health care spending, 299–300
  powers of, 49–50
    Civil War and, 55–56
    commerce clause, 55, 61
    concurrent, 51

    division of, between state government and, continuing dispute over, 56–61
    enumerated powers, 49
    implied, 54
    inherent powers, 50
    to levy taxes, 51
    necessary and proper clause, 49–50, 54
    prohibited, 51
    supremacy clause and, 51–53
    same-sex marriage and, 62
National Guard, federalization of, and deployment to Afghanistan/Iraq, 53
National Organization for Women (NOW), 100, 145, 150
National Public Radio, 133
National Review, 140
National Rifle Association, 150
National Right to Life Committee, 150
National security
  civil rights of immigrants and, 87–88
  privacy rights versus, 9, 86–87
National Security Act, 334
National Security Adviser, 234, 240
National Security Agency (NSA)
  surveillance by, 87
  warrantless wiretaps, 87
National Security Council (NSC), 241, 321
  creation and purpose of, 335
  foreign policymaking and, 334–335
National security policy, 321
National Security Staff, 239
National Wildlife Federation, 149
National Woman Suffrage Association, 100–101
NATO. *See* North Atlantic Treaty Organization (NATO)
Natural rights, 26
Navy SEALS, 327
Near v. Minnesota, 68
Nebraska Press Association v. Stuart, 80
Necessary and proper clause, 49–50, 54, 201
Negative advertising, 135–136
Negative constituents, 334

Negotiated rulemaking, 265
Negotiated Rulemaking Act, 265
Netanyahu, Benjamin, 331, 332
Net public debt, 311
New Deal, 57–58, 160, 238, 260, 262
New England town meetings, 4
New Jersey Plan, 31–32
New Republic, 140
News
  being critical consumer of, 140
  bias in, 138–139
  political campaigns and
    managing, 137
  reporting of, as function of
    media, 132
Newspapers
  bias in, 138–139
  falling revenues and financial
    difficulty, 134
  as news source, 131
  online, 134
New START Treaty, 230, 341
New York Times, 134
New York Times Co. v. Sullivan, 79
New York Times v. United States, 74
Nineteenth Amendment, 101, 190
Ninth Amendment, 68, 81
Nixon, Richard, 241
  Cambodia invasion and, 228
  China and, 340
  debate with Kennedy, 137
  devolution, 58
  election of, without majority of
    vote, 185, 226
  impeachment and, 237–238
  Keynesian economics, 310
  pact with president regarding
    incapacity of, 242
  plan to end governmental
    inefficiency, 248
  Strategic Arms Limitation
    Treaty (SALT I), 340
  veto of War Powers Resolution,
    228–229
  Vietnam War and, 228, 337
  War Powers Resolution vetoed
    by, 337
  Watergate break-in and,
    236–237
No Child Left Behind Act, 58
Nonviolent public disobedience, 97

Normal trade relations (NTR)
  status, 328
Norquist, Grover, 150
North Atlantic Treaty
  Organization (NATO), 339
Northern Alliance, 326
Northern Ireland, 323, 324
North Korea
  dictatorial rule in, 2
  Kim Jong-un's leadership of, 2
  Korean war and, 339
  nuclear weapons and, 327, 328
  South Korea invaded by, 339
Northwest Ordinance, 29
Nuclear energy, 307
Nuclear option, 285
Nuclear Regulatory Commission,
  254
Nuclear weapons, 228, 230,
  327–328, 340–341
  attacking Iran's nuclear sites,
    329

O

Obama, Barack, 1, 10, 173, 224, 240
  appointments
    federal district court judges,
      285
    to Supreme Court, 103
  Arab Spring and, 322
  armed forces ordered by
    air strike in Libya, 228
    air strikes in Libya, 228
    more troops to Afghanistan,
      228
  bank bailout, 11
  Biden as vice president, 241
  birth certificate controversy,
    225
  budget sequestration, 137
  cabinet of, 238–239
  California air pollution
    regulations and, 59
  deficit spending and, 312
  "don't ask, don't tell" policy, 111
  election of 2008, 100
    African American support for,
      123
    demographics and, 122
    economic issue and, 161
    Hispanic vote, 124
    public financing and, 180

  election of 2012, 162, 163
    debates, 138
    demographics and, 122
    economy and, 234
    gender gap, 125
    geographic region and, 125
    Hispanic vote, 124
    national convention, 184
  enemy combatants, 279
  federalization of National
    Guard, 53
  as fund-raiser, 233
  health care reform, 11, 62,
    298–303
  higher fuel efficiency standards,
    306
  immigration reform, 304–305
  Israeli-Palestinian negotiations,
    331, 332
  judicial appointment, 285
  Keynesian economics, 310
  Libya air strikes, 333
  limit greenhouse gas emissions,
    307
  monetary policy and, 314
  national security advisor, 335
  negotiations to curb nuclear
    proliferation, 327
  nuclear weapon reduction
    treaty, 230
  plan to end governmental
    inefficiency, 248
  public opinion and, 116, 233
  reregulation, 256
  Russia and, 341
  signing statements and, 237
  stimulus plan, 60, 250, 310
  waterboarding and, 336
  White House Office, 240
  young voter to Democratic
    Party, 121
Obamacare, 289
  big government and, 11
  opposition to implementation of,
    302–303
  policymaking process,
    298–303
Obscenity, 76–77
  definitional problem, 76
  pornography on Internet, 77
  protecting children, 76–77
Occupational Safety and Health
  Act, 264

Occupational Safety and Health Administration, 264
Occupy Wall Street movement, elite theory and, 7
O'Connor, Sandra Day, 103, 284, 285, 287, 289
Office-block ballot, 186
Office of Administration, 239
Office of Management and Budget (OMB), 217–218, 239, 241
Office of National Drug Control Policy, 239
Office of Personnel Management (OPM), 260
Office of Science and Technology Policy, 239
Office of Special Counsel (OSC), 263
Office of the Attorney General, 249
Office of the Vice President, 239
Office of United States Trade Representative, 239
Ogden, Aaron, 54
Oil industry
    BP Deepwater Horizon oil spill, 256
    disasters in energy industry, 306–307
    fracking, 306
    new U.S. production and, 305–306
    politics of expensive oil, 306
    U.S. dependency on foreign oil, 305
Oklahoma City bombing, 278, 324
Oligarchy, 4
Ombudsperson, 199
Open primaries, 182
Opinion leaders, influence of, 119
Opinion polls
    campaigns and use of, 175
    defined, 125
    history of, 125–126
    house effect, 128
    problems with, 127–129
    questions asked in, 128
    sampling errors, 127
    sampling techniques, 126–127
    unscientific and fraudulent, 128–129
    weighting sample, 127

Opinions
    concurring, 281
    defined, 281
    dissenting, 281
    majority, 281
    per curiam, 281
    publishing, 281
    of Supreme Court of United States, 281
    unanimous, 281
Oral arguments, 280
Order
    defined, 2
    liberty versus, 8–9
Ordinances, 273
Oversight, 199

P

Packing, in redistricting, 207
Paine, Thomas, 24–25
Pakistan
    al Qaeda and Taliban in, 326
    nuclear weapons and, 327, 336
    Osama bin Laden and, 327
Palestinian Authority, 331
Palestinian Liberation Organization (PLO), 331
Palestinians
    conflict with Israel and, 331–332
    United States as primary defender of Israel against, 324
Palin, Sarah, 103, 241
Panama, American troops sent to, 228
Pardon, 227
Paris, Treaty of, 28
Parker v. Gladden, 68
Parks, Rosa, 97
Partial-birth abortions, 83, 289
Party-column ballot, 186
Party identification
    defined, 166
    independent voters and, 166–167
Party identifiers, 205
Party organization, 155–157
    defined, 155
    local party machinery, 156
    national, 155
    national chairperson, 155
    national committee, 156
    party-in-government, 156–157

patronage, 156
    state, 156
Party platform, 155
Paterson, William, 31
Patient Protection and Affordable Care Act, 11, 289
    details of, 302
    passage of, 301–302
    policymaking process, 298–303
    reconciliation used for, 202
Patronage, 156, 232, 282
Paul, Alice, 101
Paul, Ron, 182
Paulson, Henry, 257, 258
Pearl Harbor, 9, 338
Peer group, political socialization and, 119
Pelosi, Nancy, 102, 213, 301
Pendleton Act, 259
Pennsylvania Charter of Privileges, 23
Pennsylvania Frame of Government, 23
Pentagon Papers case, 74
People's Republic of China. *See* China
Per curiam, opinion, 281
Perot, Ross, 166
Personal Responsibility and Work Opportunity Reconciliation Act, 60
Petition, right to, 68
Philippines
    Spanish-American War and, 338
    unitary system of government in, 46
Physician-assisted suicide, 83–84
Pinckney, Charles, 32
Plaintiff, 274
Plain view doctrine, 86
Plessy, Homer, 94–95
Plessy v. Ferguson, 94–95, 96
Plum Book, 258
Pluralism, 8
Plurality, 164
Pocket veto, 232
Police
    limits on conduct of, 84
    searches and interacting with, 89
Police power
    defined, 50
    search and seizure, 89

states and, 50, 57

Policy adoption, health care and, 300–302

Policy and Supporting Positions, 258

Policy evaluation, health care, 303

Policy formation, health care and, 300

Policy implementation, health care, 302–303

Policymaking. *See also* Domestic policy; Economic policy
courts and, 286–293
process of, 298–303

Political action committees (PACs), 175
campaign financing and, 176–177
defined, 176
number of, 176
soft money, 177
spending by, 176
super PACs, 178, 179

Political Activities Act, 176, 260

Political appointees, 258–259

Political consultant, 174–175

Political culture
defined, 8
public opinion and, 129–130

Political ideologies, 13–16
conservatism, 13–14
defined, 13
four-cornered ideological grid, 15
liberalism, 14
traditional political spectrum, 15

Political parties, 157–167
compared to interest groups, 144
defined, 143
functions of, 154–155
history of, in U.S., 157–162
major, influence of minor party on, 165–166
minor, role of, in U.S. politics, 165–166
national chairperson of, 155
national committee, 156
national party organization, 155
organization of, 155–157

party-in-government, 156–157
party platform, 155
patronage, 156
platform of, 155
in power, opposition to, 156–157
president as chief of, 232–234
splinter parties, 166
state party organizations, 156
today, 161–162
voter behavior and, 191

Political question, 293

Political realism, 322–323

Political socialization, 8, 117–125
defined, 117–118
education and, 119
family and, 118–119
new generations and media, 133
opinion leaders and, 119
peers and peer groups, 119
second chance at, 119
two-party system and, 163

Political trust, 129–130

Politics, 2

Poll taxes, 95

Popular Front for the Liberation of Palestine (PFLP), 88

Popular sovereignty, 5

Populist, on four-cornerd ideological grid, 16

Populists, 159

Postal Service, U. S., 257

Powell, Colin, 100

Powell, Lewis, 108

Powell v. Alabama, 68

Powers
concurrent, 51
enumerated, 49
expressed, 49
implied, 54
inherent, 50
limiting government power, 2–3
of national government, 49–50
prohibited, 51
of state government, 50–51

Prayer, in schools, 71–72, 292

Precedent, 272

Preemptive war, 325

President, 224–244
becoming
age of, 225
birth controversies, 225
constitutional requirements for, 225

process of, 225–226
cabinet, 238–239
cabinet departments and, 251
checks and balances, 34, 35
checks on courts and, 289–291
as commander in chief, 40
communicating with, 244
constituencies of, 233
creating congressional agenda, 231
death or incapacitation of, 201
electoral college, 34
executive agreements and, 40
executive organization, 238–241
foreign policy made by, 333–334
going public, 234
impeachment and, 237–238
powers of
appointment, 227, 258–259, 281–283
constitutional, 235, 333–334
diplomatic recognition, 229
emergency, 235
executive agreement, 230, 334
executive orders, 236
executive privilege, 236–237
expressed, 235
to grant reprieves and pardons, 227–228
inherent, 235
patronage, 232
proposal and ratification of treaties, 229–230
removal, 227
signing statements, 237
statutory, 235
treaties, 334
veto, 231–232
war powers, 333
wartime, 235
public approval of, 233–234
requirements for office, 172
roles of
chief diplomat, 229–230
chief executive, 227–228
chief legislator, 230–231
chief of party, 232–234
commander in chief, 228–229
head of state, 226–227
wartime powers, 228–229
salary of, 225

separation of powers, 34
State of the Union address and, 231
succession to, 242–243
Presidential elections
    of 1800, 158
    of 1824, 158
    of 1828, 158
    of 1896, 161
    of 1912, 159, 166
    of 1932, 160
    of 1936, opinion polls predicting, 125–126
    of 1964, 135–136
    of 1980, opinion polls, 128
    of 1992, 166
    of 1996, demographics and, 122
    of 2000, 161
        demographics and, 122
        electoral college, 161, 226
        impact of minor party on, 166
        Supreme Court decision and, 279–280
    of 2004, 161
        demographics and, 122
    of 2008
        demographics and, 122
        economic issue and, 161
        political parties and, 161
    of 2012, 162, 163
        campaign spending on, 175, 179
        debates, 137–138
        demographics and, 122
        as longest campaign, 180
    campaign financing, 175
    candidate committees and financing, 180
    candidates who run for, 172–173
    coattail effect, 205
    debates and, 137–138
    economic report of, 218
    economy and, 234
    electoral college, 185–186, 225–226
    executive budget, 215, 217
    gender gap and, 125
    national conventions, 184
    by other than direct popular vote, 225–226
    popular election of, 164
    primaries, 181–184
    voter turnout, 188–190

winner-take-all system, 164
Presidential primaries, 172–173
    as beauty contest, 181
    front-loading, 183–184
    historical perspective on, 181
    reforming, 181
    types of, 181–183
Press, freedom of, 68, 79–81
    clear and present danger, 75
    gag orders, 80
    libel, 79
    prior restraint, 73–74, 80
Price, Betsy, 17
Primary elections (primaries)
    blanket, 182
    closed, 182
    defined, 173
    direct, 181, 205
    early, and consequences of, 183
    historical perspective on, 181
    indirect, 181
    open, 182
    presidential (See Presidential primaries)
    proportional and winner-take-all, 181–182
    public financing for, 180
    run-off, 182
    top-two, 182–183
Prior restraint, 73–74, 80
Prisons, privatization of, 262
Privacy Act of 1974, 268
Privacy rights, 68, 81–84
    abortion and, 9, 81–83
    constitution and, 81
    national security versus, 9, 86–87
    right to die and, 83–84
    roving wiretaps, 86–87
    USA Patriot Act, 86
    warrantless wiretaps, 87
Privatization, 262
Probable cause
    arrest and, 84
    for search warrants, 86, 89
Professionals, interest groups of, 147–148
Profits, making, as media function, 133
Progressives, term of, 16
Progressive tax, 315
Progressivism, 159–160
Prohibition, 38

Promotional policy, 298
Property
    defined, 10
    right to, and capitalism, 10
Proportional primary, 181–182
Proportional representation, 164
Proposition 8, 73, 112
Prosecutors, limits on conduct of, 84
Protestants
    Republican Party and, 159
    voting behavior, 122, 123
Prurient interest, 76
Public agenda
    defined, 132
    setting by media, 132–133
Public debt
    deficit spending and, 311
    defined, 312
    historical perspective on, 311–312
    net, 311
    as percentage of gross domestic product, 311
    perspectives on, 311–312
Public employee unions, 147
Public figure, libel and, 79
Public interest, 149–150
Public-interest groups, 149–150
Public Interest Research Groups (PIRGs), 149
Public opinion, 116–131
    about government, 129–131
    check on courts and, 292
    consensus, 117
    defined, 117
    demographic factors and, 121–125
    divided, 117, 118
    economic status and, 121–123
    education and, 123
    formation of, 117–125
    gender gap and, 125
    generational effect, 121
    geographic region and, 125
    going public, 234
    measuring, 125–129
    media and, 119–120
    policymaking and, 130–131
    political culture and, 129–130
    political process and, 129–131
    political socialization and, 117–125
    of president, 233–234

race and ethnicity, 123–125
religious influence on, 123
Supreme Court and, 292
trend in most important problem, 131
Public policy, media and investigative function, 133
Public pressure, 153
Public problems
identifying by media, 132–133
trends in most important, 131
Puerto Ricans, 104
Puerto Rico, 338
Punishment, cruel and unusual, 68, 85
Purposive incentives for joining interest groups, 145
Putin, Vladimir, 341

Q
Qaddafi, Muammar, 3
Quantitative easing, 314
Questions, in opinion polls, 128
Quinlan, Karen Ann, 83

R
Race
affirmative action programs and, 107–109
redistricting based on, 208–209
voting behavior and, 123–125
Race riots, 160
Radio
bias in, 138–139
as entertainment source, 132
Fairness Doctrine, 120
First Amendment freedoms and, 80–81
talk radio, 120
Randolph, A. Philip, 98
Randolph, Edmund, 31
Randomness, principle of, 126
Ranking committee member, 212
Ratification
Bill of Rights, 37–38
defined, 35
of United States Constitution, 35–38
Ratings game, 152
Reagan, Ronald, 225
appointments, to Supreme Court, 103

approval rating of, 130
armed forces ordered by
into combat without congressional approval, 337
to invade Grenada, 228
into Lebanon, 228
deregulation, 256
devolution, 58
economic prosperity under, 121
election of 1980, 128
on federalism, 49
foreign policy and, 340–341
gender gap, 125
government employment under, 249–250
judicial appointment and, 282, 284
line-item veto and, 232
plan to end governmental inefficiency, 248
Soviet Union and, 340–341
unemployment rate and reelection of, 234
Realignment
of 1896, 159
of 1932, 160
defined, 159
Recall, 4
Recession
defined, 308
monetary policy and, 314
monetary policy during, 314
unemployment and, 308
Reconciliation, 202
Redistributive policy, 297–298
Redistricting
after 2010 census, 208
defined, 205
gerrymandering, 206–208
minority-majority districts, 208–209
packing and cracking, 207
race-based, 208–209
Red states, 161
Referendum, 4
Reform Party, 166
Regents of the University of California v. Bakke, 108
Regressive tax, 315
Regulation
campaign financing, 176–177
of lobbyists, 153–154

negotiated rulemaking, 265
waiting periods and court challenges, 264–265
Regulatory agencies, 253–256
agency capture, 255–256
deregulation and reregulation, 256
purpose and nature of, 254–255
Regulatory policy, 297
Rehnquist, William, 284–285
Rehnquist Court, 287–288
Reid, Harry, 214
Reinhart, Carmen, 253
Religion
aid to church-related schools, 69–70
endorsement of candidate by religious organizations, 73
establishment clause, 69
forbidding teaching of evolution, 72
freedom of, 69–73
free exercise clause, 73
importance of, to African Americans, 192
nation's founders and, 24
political attitudes and, 123
religious displays on public property, 72–73
separation of church and state, 69–73
Remandment of court case, 281
Removal power, 227
Representation
defined, 198
instructed-delegate view of, 198
by members of Congress, 198
trustee-view of, 198
Representative assembly, 21
Representative democracy
compared to democratic republic, 6
defined, 6
principles of, 6
Reprieve, 227
Republic, 5
Republicanism, rise of, 27–28
Republican Party
of Abraham Lincoln, 158
anti-Keynesian economics, 310
budget sequestration, 137
Congress controlled by, 161
conservatism and, 13

convention delegates, 155–156, 168

debt ceiling crisis, 219

devolution, 58

economic status and, 121–123

education and, 123

fiscal cliff and sequester, 219

formation of, 158

geographic region and, 125

global warming disbelief, 307

GOP nickname, 159

Hispanic vote and immigration issue, 124–125, 162

history of, 158–162

immigration issue and, 305

midterm elections of 2010 and, 161

opposition to Obamacare, 302

party identification and, 166–167

in post-Civil War period, 159

race and ethnicity, 123–125

red states and, 161

regaining control of presidential primary, 183–184

Tea Party movement and, 162

of Thomas Jefferson (Democratic Republicans), 158

today, 161–162

Reregulation, 256

Reserved powers, 50

Resolution of Independence, 26

Reversal of judgment, 281

Reverse discrimination, 108

Rice, Condoleezza, 100, 103, 335

Rights. *See also* Bill of Rights natural, 26

Right to die, 83–84

Right-to-work laws, 147, 148

Roberts, John G. Jr., 41, 62, 284, 287, 288–289

Roberts Court, 287, 288–289

Robinson v. California, 68

Robocalls, 127

Roe v. Wade, 81

Rogoff, Kenneth, 253

Romney, George, 225

Romney, Mitt, 1, 173, 182, 300

election of 2012, 162, 234

campaign spending on, 179

debates, 137–138

demographics and, 122, 125

ministers endorsement of, 73

national convention, 184

religion and voters for, 123

Ryan as running mate, 242

Roosevelt, Franklin D., 13

Bureau of the Budget and, 241

as chief legislator, 231

conservatives' view of, 13

election of 1936, opinion polls predicting, 125–126

emergency power use, 235

establishment of Executive Office of the President, 239

generational effect and, 121

Great Depression and, 160

inherent powers and internment camps, 235

New Deal and, 57, 123, 160, 238, 260, 262

Soviet Union recognized by, 229

use of emergency powers by, 235

World War II and, 334, 338

Roosevelt, Theodore

election of 1912, 159, 166

as progressive, 159, 166

Roper, Elmo, 126

Roper poll, 126

Rove, Karl, 177

Roving wiretaps, 86–87

Rulemaking

environment of, 264–265

negotiated, 265

Rule of four, 280

Rules Committee, 201

Run-off primary, 182

Russia

dissolution of Soviet Union and, 341

New START agreement, 341

nuclear weapon reduction treaty and, 230

nuclear weapons and, 327, 341

as oil exporter, 305

Strategic Arms Reduction Treaty (START), 341

Rustin, Bayard, 98

Ryan, Paul, 212, 242

S

Safe seats, 212

Sales tax, 316

Same-sex marriage, 10, 62, 73, 289

Defense of Marriage Act, 111–112

state recognition of, 51, 52, 111–112

Sampling error, 127

Sampling techniques for opinion polls, 126–127

Sandy Hook shooting, 70

Santorum, Rick, 182

Saudi Arabia

American troops stationed in, 324

First Gulf War and, 325

as oil exporter, 305

Scalia, Antonin, 41, 288, 289

Schiavo, Terry, 83

Schools

affirmative action and college admission, 290

busing, 97

church-related, government aid to, 69–70

forbidding teaching of evolution, 72

freedom of speech and students, 78–79

political socialization and, 119

prayer in, 71–72

school integration and, 96, 290–291

student activity fees, 78–79

vouchers and, 70–71

School vouchers, 70–71

Schumer, Charles, 187

Scott, Tim, 100

Search and seizure, unreasonable constitutional prohibition of, 40, 84, 86

exclusionary rule, 85–86

interacting with police, 89

probable cause, 86, 89

Search warrants, probable cause and, 86

Second Amendment, ban on assault-type weapons, 70

Second Bank of the United States, 54

Second budget resolution, 218

Second Civil Rights Act (Civil Rights Act of 1875), 94

Second Continental Congress, 24–25, 28

Second Gulf War. *See* Iraq War (Second Gulf War)

Security
vs. civil liberties, 86–88
national security policy, 321

Segregation
buses, 97
de facto, 97
de jure, 97
school integration and, 96
separate-but-equal doctrine, 95, 96

Select committee, 211

Senate, of the United States. *See also* Congress
budget and, 215–219
checks and balances, 34, 35
cloture, 201–202
committees of, 209–212
contacting representative, 220
debate in, 201–202
differences between House of Representatives and, 201
elections for, 204–209
filibustering in, 201, 202
incumbency and power of, 205, 206
judicial appointment and, 281–287
leadership in, 214–215
lobbying rules, 153–154
majority leader of, 215
members of
age of, 202, 204
election of, 197
income and wealth of, 202, 204
minorities, 204
perks of, 202–203
privileges and immunities of, 203–204
professional staff, 203
religion of, 204
term of, 197
women as, 102–103, 204
minority leader of, 215
nuclear option, 285
powers of, 200
president pro tempore of, 214
ratification of treaties and, 229–230
reconciliation, 202
requirements for office, 172

rules of, 201
senatorial courtesy, 282
seniority system, 212
separation of powers, 34
size of, 201
vice president as president of, 214, 241
whips in, 215
winning seat in, cost of, 205
Senate majority leader, 215
Senate minority leader, 215
Senatorial courtesy, 282
Seniority system, 212
Separate-but-equal doctrine, 40, 95
Separation of church and state, 69–73
Separation of powers, 34
Separatists, 21
September 11, 2001 terrorist attacks, 324
al Qaeda and, 320
big government and, 11
changed view of security and foreign policy afterwards, 320–321
CIA failure to obtain advance knowledge of, 336
enemy combatants detainees, 278–279
powers of FISA court expanded after, 278
reasons for attack, 324
rights of noncitizens, 105
security vs. privacy rights after, 9
spending on security afterwards, 312
sunshine laws after, 261
Taliban government in Afghanistan, 320
Sequester, 219, 253
Serbia, American bombing of, 228
Service sector, 146
Seventeenth amendment, 197
Sexual harassment, 103–104
Sharon, Ariel, 331
Shays, Daniel, 30
Shays' Rebellion, 30
Sherman, Roger, 32
Shiites in Iraq, 325
Sierra Club, 149, 275
Signing statements, 237

Silver, Nate, 234
Sixteenth Amendment, 200, 291
Sixth Amendment, 68, 80, 84, 85
Slander, 77–78
Slavery/slaves
Civil War and, 55–56, 158
Connecticut Compromise, 32
consequences of, for African Americans, 94–97
drafting Constitution and, 32–33
Emancipation Proclamation and, 93
end of, 93
three-fifths compromise, 32–33
Whig Party and, 158
SNAP (Supplementary Nutrition Assistance Program), 250
Social contract, 27
Socialism
defined, 15
on traditional political spectrum, 15
Social movements
civil rights movement, 145, 160
consumer, 149
defined, 145
labor movement, 146
Social networking, impact on public opinion, 120
Social Security
as entitlement program, 12
entitlement reform, 317
federal budget spent on, 250, 251
income caps and, 315
taxes for, 314, 315
Socioeconomic status
defined, 192
voter behavior and, 121–125
Sodomy laws, 110
Soft money
defined, 177
restricted by Bipartisan Campaign Reform Act, 177
Solar energy, 306
Solicitor general, 280
Solidary incentives for joining interest groups, 145
Somalia, absence of central government in, 2
Sotomayor, Sonia, 41, 103, 285, 288
Sound bite, 135

Souter, David, 285
Southern Christian Leadership Conference (SCLC), 97, 145
South Korea
  invaded by North Korea, 339
  Korean war and, 339
  lobbying by, 151
Soviet Bloc, 338
Soviet Union
  beginning of Korean War, 339
  Cold War and, 338
  Cuban missile crisis, 339–340
  détente and, 340
  dissolution of, 341
  Intermediate-Range Nuclear Force (INF) Treaty, 341
  nuclear weapons and, 327
  Roosevelt's recognition of, 229
  Russia after, 341
  Strategic Arms Limitation Treaty (SALT I), 340
  Strategic Arms Reduction Treaty (START), 341
  superpower relations with United States and, 339–341
Spain
  dept crisis, 332–333
  ETA organization and terrorism, 323–324
Spanish-American War, 338
Speaker of the House, 213
Speech, freedom of, 8–9, 68
  clear and present danger, 75
  commercial speech, 75
  imminent lawless action test, 76
  limits on rights of, and deportees, 88
  obscenity, 76–77
  prior restraint, 73–74
  slander, 77–78
  student speech, 78–79
  symbolic speech, 74
Speech, hate, 67
Spin, 137
Spin doctor, 137
Splinter party, 166
Spoiler effect, 166
Spoils system, 259
Spring review, 217
Stamp Act, 23
Standing committees, 210–211

Standing to sue, 274
Stanton, Elizabeth Cady, 100
Stare decisis, 272, 292
State Bureau of Democracy, U.S. Department of, 342
State central committee, 156
State courts
  basic judicial requirements for cases, 274
  election of judges, 283
  procedural rules, 275
State Department, 249, 321
  foreign policymaking and, 334
  functions of, 254
  subagencies of, 254
State government
  cooperative federalism, 57–58
  devolution, 58–59
  dual federalism, 57
  extending Bill of Rights to, 67
  fiscal federalism, 60
  Great Recession and budgets of, 60
  immigration laws, 304
  interstate compacts, 53
  interstate relations, 53
  legislature, requirements of members of, 172
  Medicaid spending and, 299
  powers of, 38, 50–51
    Civil War and, 55–56
    concurrent, 51
    division of, between national government and, continuing dispute over, 56–61
    to levy taxes, 51
    police, 50, 57
    prohibited, 51
    reserved, 50
    supremacy clause and, 51, 53
  prohibited from entering into treaty and, 51
  same-sex marriage recognized by, 51, 52, 62, 112
  states' rights
    recent Supreme Court trend toward, 61
    shift back to, before Civil War, 56
State of the Union address, 231
State party organization, 156

States
  constitutions of, 21, 26, 28, 273
  defined, 26, 28
  red and blue states, 161
  statutes, 273
Statutes, as source of American law, 273
Statutory powers, 235
Stevens, John Paul, 285
Stewart, Jon, 132
Stewart, Potter, 76
Stimulus package, 60
  big government and, 11
  deficit spending and fiscal policy, 310
  unemployment rate and, 310
Stone, Lucy, 101
Stonewall Inn, 110
Straight-ticket voting, 166–167, 186
Strategic Arms Limitation Treaty (SALT I), 340
Strategic Arms Reduction Treaty (START), 341
Strict construction, 287
Strict scrutiny, 108–109
Succession Act, 243
Suffrage
  defined, 100
  universal, 6
  women's, 100–101
Sugar Act, 23
Suicide, physician-assisted, 83–84
Sunlight Foundation, 179
Sunnis in Iraq, 325
Sunset legislation, 261–262
Sunshine laws, 261
Superdelegates, 181
Super PACs, 178, 179
Super Tuesday, 183
Supplemental Nutrition Assistance Program (SNAP), as entitlement program, 12
Supremacy clause, 51–53
Supremacy doctrine, 32
Supreme Court justices
  appointments, 33, 281–285
  partisanship and, 284–285
  Senate's role in confirmation, 285
  background of, 283, 284

photo of, 288
strict or broad construction, 287
Supreme Court of United States, 277
after Civil War, 57
campaign ads, 178
caseload of, 281
cases that reach, 280
checks and balances, 34, 35
decisions of, 281
dual federalism and, 57
executive checks, 289–291
executive checks over, 289–291
federalism and, 53–55, 61–62
as highest court in land, 274, 277
impact of lower courts on, 293
judicial activism, 286
judicial restraint, 287
judicial review and, 40
judicial traditions and doctrine, 292–293
legislative checks, 291–292
legislative checks over, 291–292
Marshall Court, 53–54
opinions of, 281
political question, 293
procedures of, 280
public opinion, 292
Rehnquist Court, 287–288
Roberts Court, 287, 288–289
rule of four, 280
rulings of
abortion, 81–83
affirmative action, 108
apportionment, 206–207
candidates' financing of campaign, 176
civil rights, 94–97
civil service system, 260
commercial speech, 75
death with dignity law, 61
emergency power, 235
enemy combatant detainees, 278–279
establishment clause, 69
evolution, teaching of, 72
executive privilege, 237
free legal counsel, 85
gun free zone, 61
health-care reform, 62, 302
immigration, 62

incorporation theory, 68–69
Line Item Veto Act, 232
medical marijuana, 61
Miranda rule, exceptions to, 85
obscenity, 76–77
physician-assisted suicide, 83–84
prior restraint, 73–74
same-sex marriage, 62, 112
school prayer, 71–72
school vouchers, 71
separate-but-equal doctrine, 95, 96
sodomy laws, 110
symbolic speech, 74
voting rights, 62
whistleblowers, 263–264
solicitor general and, 280
states' rights, trend toward, 61
at work, 279–281
Sweden, unitary system of government in, 46
Symbolic speech, 74
Syria, 323
al-Assad's leadership of, 2
dictatorial rule in, 2

T

Taft, William Howard, 166, 226, 283
Taiwan, 330
Taliban
in Afghanistan, 320, 326
in Pakistan, 325, 326
Talk radio, 120
Taxes, 314–315
estate, 315
export, 33
to fund Obamacare, 301
income (See Income tax)
loopholes and, 315
marginal tax rate, 314
Medicare, 314, 315
progressive, 315
regressive, 315
rich paying more, 316
sales, 316
Social Security, 314, 315
types of, 314–315
Tea Party movement, 150, 162
elite theory and, 7
opposition to Obamacare, 302

Technical assistance, 321
Television
bias in, 138–139
as entertainment source, 132
First Amendment freedoms and, 80–81
influence on political process, 135
as news source, 131
Temporary Assistance for Needy Families (TANF), 250
Ten Commandments, 73
Tenth Amendment, 45, 50–51
Terrorism. *See also* al Qaeda; War on terrorism
death of bin Laden, 327
domestic, 324
emergence of, 323–324
September 11, 2001, 324
Theocracy, 4
Third Amendment, 68, 81
Third Parties
defined, 165
ideological, 165–166
impact of, 166
splinter parties, 166
state and federal laws favoring two parties, 164–165
Thirteenth Amendment, 56, 93
Thomas, Clarence, 41, 74, 285, 288, 289
Three-fifths compromise, 32–33
Ticket splitting, 157
Tight monetary policy, 313
Tinker v. Des Moines School District, 74
Tocqueville, Alexis de, 144, 271
Top-two primary, 182–183
Totalitarianism, 4
Totalitarian regime, 4
Town meetings, 4
Tracking polls, 127, 175
Transportation, Department of
functions of, 255
subagencies of, 255
Treasuries, 310
Treasury, Department of, 241, 249
functions of, 254
subagencies of, 254
Treasury Department, 261
Treaties
proposed by president, 229–230, 334

ratification of, 229–230
recent efforts, 230
Trial
  rights and, 85
  right to speedy, 68, 85
Trial courts, 276
Troubled Asset Relief Program
    (TARP), 257–258
Truman, Harry, 227, 228
  decision to use atomic bomb
      against Japan and, 228,
      338
  election of, without majority of
      vote, 185, 226
  election of 1948, 126, 128
  emergency power use, 235
  troops sent to Korea, 228, 333
  Truman Doctrine and, 339
Truman Doctrine, 339
Trustee, 198
Tunisia, 322
  dictatorial rule in, 3
Twelfth Amendment, 200, 226
Twentieth Amendment, 201
Twenty-fifth Amendment, 201,
    242
Twenty-fourth Amendment, 95
Twenty-sixth Amendment, 190
Two-party system
  defined, 157
  endurance of, reasons for,
      162–165
  historical foundations of, 162–163
  state and federal laws favoring,
      164–165
Two Treatises on Government
    (Locke), 26
Tyler, John, 242

U

UN. *See* United Nations (UN)
Unanimous opinion, 281
Unemployment
  defined, 308
  discouraged workers, 308
  during Great Recession, 309
  hidden, 308
  measuring, 308
  rate of, and presidential
      elections, 234
  stimulus package and, 310
Unemployment benefits, federal
    grants, 60

Unfunded Mandates Reform Act,
    61
Unicameral legislature, 28
Unions
  affirmative action, 108
  membership in, declining, 146,
      147
  political environment today, 147
  public employees, 147
  right-to-work laws, 147, 148
Unitary system
  defined, 46
  flow of power in, 47
United Nations (UN)
  Intergovernmental Panel on
      Climate Change, 307
  weapons inspection in Iraq, 325
United States
  benefits of federalism for, 48
  democracy in, kind of, 6–8
  fertility rate of, 104–105
  health care spending in, 298–299
United States Constitution. *See*
    Constitution of United States
United States Reports, 281
*United States v. Curtiss-Wright
    Export Corp.,* 235
United States v. Nixon, 237
Unit rule, 164
Universal health insurance, 300
Universal suffrage, 6
University. *See* Colleges
Urban League, 145
USA Patriot Act, 86
U.S. Treasury securities, 310

V

Venezuela, as oil exporter, 305
Ventura, Jesse, 166
Versailles Treaty, 230
Veterans Affairs, Department of
  functions of, 255
  subagencies of, 255
Veto
  line-item, 232
  override of, 232
  pocket, 232
  president's power of, 231–232
  veto message, 231
Veto message, 231
Vice president, 241–243
  death or incapacity of, 243
  job of, 241–242

presidential succession and,
    242–243
  as president of the Senate, 214
Vietnamese Americans, voting
    behavior, 123
Vietnam War, 74, 160, 228
  American involvement in, 339
  generational effect and, 121
Virginia Company of London, 21
Virginia Plan, 31
Vote-eligible population, 189
Voter turnout
  calculating, 189–190
  for congressional elections,
      188, 189
  defined, 188
  impact of restrictive voting laws
      on, 188
  low, and effect of, 188–189
  for presidential elections,
      188–190
  voter identification and, 188
Voting. *See also* Voting behavior
  African Americans and,
      99–100
  ballots for, 186
  fraud in, 186–187
  legal restrictions on, 190–191
  by mail, 186
  registration for, 99, 190
    age requirements, 193
    motor voter bill, 190
    property requirements, 190
    requirements for, current
        eligibility and, 190
    residency requirements, 193
    time limits, 193
  straight-ticket, 186
  voter identification, 187–188
Voting-age population, 189
Voting behavior
  demographic influences,
      121–125
  economic status and, 121–123
  education and, 123
  gender and, 125
  geographic regions and, 125
  by groups for presidential
      elections 1996-2012, 123
  issue preference, 192
  party identification, 191
  perception of candidate and,
      192

race and ethnicity, 123–125
religion and, 123
straight-ticket voting, 166–167
women, 125
Voting fraud, 186–187
Voting rights
African Americans, 94, 95, 99, 190, 191
age and, 190, 193
grandfather clause, 95
literacy tests, 95
poll taxes, 95
white primary, 95
women and, 100–101, 190
Voting Rights Act, 99, 191, 208
preclearance for voting procedure changes, 62

W

Wage discrimination, 104
War Department, 249
War on terrorism, 324–325
alien "removal courts," 278
Bush Doctrine, 325
cooperation from allies sought for, 230
enemy combatants and courts, 278–279
enemy combatants detainees, 278–279
federal courts and, 277–279
FISA court, 277–278
intelligence community and, 336
opposition to Bush Doctrine, 325
preemptive war, 325
War Powers Resolution, 228–229, 337
Warren, Earl, 85, 96, 286
Warren, Elizabeth, 200
Warren, Rick, 120
Wartime powers of president, 228–229

Washington, George, 157
Constitutional Convention and, 30, 31
slavery and drafting Constitution, 33
Washington community, 233
Watergate break-in, 121, 236–237
Wave elections, 161
Wealthy/wealthy, paying more taxes, 316
Welfare programs, federal grants for, 60
Welfare reform, 48
block grants and, 60
control transferred to states, 58
West Germany, 338
Whig Party, 158
Whips, 214, 215
Whistle-Blower Protection Act, 263
White House, communicating with, 244
White House Military Office, 240
White House Office, 239, 240
White primary, 95
White supremacy, 95–96
Whitman, Meg, 103
William the Conqueror, 272
Wilson, James, 30
Wilson, Woodrow, 13, 40, 230, 238
election of, without majority of vote, 185, 226
election of 1912, 159–160, 166
League of Nations and, 322
Wind energy, 306
Winner-take-all electoral system, 164
Winner-take-all primary, 181–182
Wiretaps
roving, 86–87
warrantless, 87
Wolf v. Colorado, 68

Women
as candidates, 173
civil rights of, 100–104
in Congress, 204
discrimination in workplace, 103–104
Equal Rights Amendment and, 101
gender-based discrimination and, 102, 103–104
gender gap and, 125
in politics, 102–103
sexual harassment, 103–104
voting behavior, 125
voting right, 99–100, 190
wage discrimination, 104
women's movement, 100–102, 145
Workplace discrimination. *See* Employment discrimination
World War I, isolationist foreign policy and, 338
World War II, 239, 334
atomic bombs dropped on Japan and, 338
emergency power and fall of France, 235
Japanese attack on Pearl Harbor, 338
Yalta Conference and, 338
Writ
of *certiorari,* 280
of *habeas corpus,* 84

Y

Yalta Conference, 338
Year Books, 272
Yeltsin, Boris, 341
Your Right to Federal Records, 268
YouTube, 132, 134